Information Technology and Moral Philosophy

Information technology is an integral part of the practices and institutions of postindustrial society. It is also a source of hard moral questions and thus is both a probing and a relevant area for moral theory. In this volume, an international team of philosophers sheds light on many of the ethical issues arising from information technology, including informational privacy, the digital divide and equal access, e-trust, and teledemocracy. Collectively, these essays demonstrate how accounts of equality and justice and property and privacy benefit from taking into account how information technology has shaped our social and epistemic practices and our moral experiences. Information technology changes the way we look at the world and deal with one another. It calls, therefore, for a re-examination of notions such as friendship, care, commitment, and trust.

Jeroen van den Hoven is professor of moral philosophy at Delft University of Technology. He is editor-in-chief of *Ethics and Information Technology*, a member of the IST Advisory Group of the European Community in Brussels, scientific director of the 3TU Centre for Ethics and Technology in The Netherlands, and coauthor, with Dean Cocking, of *Evil Online*.

John Weckert is a Professorial Fellow at the Centre for Applied Philosophy and Public Ethics at Charles Sturt University in Australia. He is editor-in-chief of *NanoEthics: Ethics for Technologies that Converge at the Nanoscale* and has published widely in the field of computer ethics.

Information Technology and Moral Philosophy

Edited by

JEROEN VAN DEN HOVEN

Delft University of Technology, The Netherlands

JOHN WECKERT

Charles Sturt University, Australia

CAMBRIDGE
UNIVERSITY PRESS

CAMBRIDGE UNIVERSITY PRESS
Cambridge, New York, Melbourne, Madrid, Cape Town, Singapore,
São Paulo, Delhi, Dubai, Tokyo, Mexico City

Cambridge University Press
32 Avenue of the Americas, New York, NY 10013-2473, USA

www.cambridge.org
Information on this title: www.cambridge.org/9780521671613

First published 2008
Reprinted 2009 (twice)
First paperback edition 2010

A catalog record for this publication is available from the British Library.

Library of Congress Cataloging in Publication Data
Information technology and moral philosophy / [edited by] Jeroen van
den Hoven, John Weckert.
p. cm.
Includes bibliographical references and index.
ISBN-13: 978-0-521-85549-5 (hardback)
1. Information technology – Moral and ethical aspects. I. Hoven,
Jeroen van den. II. Weckert, John.
T58.5I53745   2007
303.48'33–dc22   2007016850

ISBN 978-0-521-85549-5 Hardback
ISBN 978-0-521-67161-3 Paperback

Contents

List of Contributors

James Bohman is Danforth Professor of Philosophy at Saint Louis University in the United States. He is the author of *Public Deliberation: Pluralism, Complexity and Democracy* (1996) and *New Philosophy of Social Science: Problems of Indeterminacy* (1991). He has recently coedited *Deliberative Democracy* (with William Rehg) and *Perpetual Peace: Essays on Kant's Cosmopolitan Ideal* (with Matthias Lutz-Bachmann) and has published articles on topics related to cosmopolitan democracy and the European Union. His most recent book is *Democracy across Borders* (2007).

Geoffrey Brennan is professor in the Social and Political Theory Group, Research School of Social Sciences, the Australian National University, Canberra, Australia; professor of political science, Duke University; and professor of philosophy at University of North Carolina–Chapel Hill in the United States. Among his most recent publications is *The Economy of Esteem*, with Philip Pettit (2004).

Terrell Ward Bynum is professor of philosophy and director, Research Center on Computing and Society, Southern Connecticut State University, New Haven. He was a cofounder of the ETHICOMP series of international computer ethics conferences and has chaired the Committee on Philosophy and Computing for the American Philosophical Association and the Committee on Professional Ethics for the Association for Computing Machinery. He is coeditor of the textbook *Computer Ethics and Professional Responsibility* (2004). In June 2005, he delivered the Georg Henrik von Wright Keynote Lecture on Ethics at the European Computing and Philosophy Conference in Sweden.

Dean Cocking is Senior Research Fellow/lecturer at the Centre for Applied Philosophy and Public Ethics, Charles Sturt University, Canberra, Australia. He is currently working on a book titled *Intending Evil and Using People* and with Jeroen van den Hoven, a book on *Evil Online* (forthcoming).

Dag Elgesem is professor, Department of Information Science and Media Studies, University of Bergen, Norway. Among his recent publications is his contribution to *Trust Management* (2006), titled "Normative Structures in Trust Management."

Charles Ess is professor of philosophy and religion and Distinguished Professor of Interdisciplinary Studies, Drury University in Springfield, Missouri, and Professor II, Programme for Applied Ethics, Norwegian University of Science and Technology, Trondheim. Ess has received awards for teaching excellence and scholarship and has published extensively in comparative (East–West) philosophy, applied ethics, discourse ethics, history of philosophy, feminist biblical studies, and computer-mediated communication. With Fay Sudweeks, he cochairs the biennial Cultural Attitudes towards Technology and Communication (CATaC) conferences. He has served as a visiting professor at IT-University, Copenhagen (2003) and as a Fulbright Senior Scholar at University of Trier (2004).

Mary Flanagan is associate professor and director of the Tiltfactor Laboratory, in the Department of Film and Media Studies at Hunter College, New York City. The laboratory researches and develops computer games and software systems to teach science, mathematics, and applied programming skills to young people, especially girls and minorities. Flanagan, who has extensive experience in software design, has developed methods of engaging girls and women in science and technology. She has garnered more than twenty international awards for this work. Flanagan created *The Adventures of Josie True* (www.josietrue.com), the award-winning science and mathematics environment for middle-school girls and is now collaborating on integrating human values in the design of software. She is the coeditor of *re:skin* (2006) and has recently received an artwork commission from HTTP Gallery in London.

Luciano Floridi (www.wolfson.ox.ac.uk/~floridi) is Fellow of St Cross College, University of Oxford, United Kingdom, where, with Jeff Sanders, he coordinates the Information Ethics Research Group, and professor of logic and epistemology, Università degli Studi di Bari, Italy. His area of research is the philosophy of information. His works include more than fifty articles and several books on epistemology and the philosophy of computing and information. He is the editor of *The Blackwell Guide to the Philosophy of Computing and Information*. He is currently working on a series of articles that will form the basis of a new book on the philosophy of information. He is vice-president of the International Association for Philosophy and Computing (www.iacap.org).

Alvin I. Goldman is Board of Governors Professor of Philosophy and Cognitive Science at Rutgers University, New Jersey. He is best known for his work in epistemology, especially social epistemology, and interdisciplinary philosophy of mind. His three most recent books are *Knowledge in a Social World* (1999), *Pathways to Knowledge* (2002), and *Simulating Minds: The Philosophy, Psychology, and Neuroscience of Mindreading* (2006). A Fellow of the American Academy of Arts and Science, he has served as president of the American Philosophical Association (Pacific Division) and of the Society for Philosophy and Psychology.

Wendy J. Gordon is professor of law and Paul J. Liacos Scholar in Law, Boston University School of Law, Boston, Massachusetts. Professor Gordon has served as a visiting Senior Research Fellow at St John's College, Oxford, and as a Fulbright scholar. She is the author of numerous articles, including "Render Copyright unto Caesar: On Taking Incentives Seriously," *University of Chicago Law Review, 71* (2004) and "A Property Right in Self-Expression: Equality and Individualism in the Natural Law of Intellectual Property," *Yale Law Journal, 102* (1993); she is coeditor of two books, including, with Lisa Takeyama and Ruth Towse, *Developments in the Economics of Copyright: Research and Analysis* (2005).

Daniel C. Howe is on the staff of the Media Research Laboratory at New York University.

Deborah G. Johnson is Anne Shirley Carter Olsson Professor of Applied Ethics and chair of the Department of Science, Technology, and Society at the University of Virginia. Johnson is the author/editor of six books, including *Computer Ethics*, which is now in its third edition. Her work focuses on the ethical and social implications of technology, especially information technology. Johnson received the John Barwise Prize from the American Philosophical Association in 2004, the Sterling Olmsted Award from the Liberal Education Division of the American Society for Engineering Education in 2001, and the ACM SIGCAS Making a Difference Award in 2000.

Steve Matthews teaches philosophy at School of Humanities and Social Sciences and is a Senior Research Fellow at the Centre for Applied Philosophy and Public Ethics (an ARC-funded special research centre) at Charles Sturt University, New South Wales, Australia. He is a visiting Fellow at University of Melbourne and Australian National University. Relevant areas of interest include ethical issues raised by computer-mediated communication and ethical questions of identity and agency, especially as raised in legal and psychiatric contexts. Recent articles include "Establishing Personal Identity in Cases of DID," *Philosophy, Psychiatry, and Psychology, 10* (2003) and "Failed Agency and the Insanity Defence," *International Journal of Law and Psychiatry, 27* (2004).

Seumas Miller is professor of philosophy at Charles Sturt University and at Australian National University and director of the Centre for Applied Philosophy and Public Ethics (an Australian Research Council–funded

special research centre). He is the author of more than 100 academic articles and ten books, including *Social Action* (Cambridge University Press,
2001), *Ethical Issues in Policing*, with John Blackler (2005), *Terrorism and
Counter-Terrorism* (forthcoming), and *Institutional Corruption* (Cambridge
University Press, forthcoming).

James H. Moor is a professor of philosophy at Dartmouth College, New Hamp-
shire, and is an adjunct professor with the Centre for Applied Philosophy
and Public Ethics at the Australian National University, Canberra, Australia.
His publications include work on computer ethics, nanoethics, philosophy
of artificial intelligence, philosophy of mind, philosophy of science, and
logic. He is editor-in-chief of the journal *Minds and Machines* and is associate
editor of the journal *NanoEthics*. He is the president of the International
Society for Ethics and Information Technology (INSEIT) and has received
the American Computing Machinery SIGCAS Making a Difference Award
and the American Philosophical Association Barwise Prize. His most recent
article is "The Nature, Importance, and Difficulty of Machine Ethics," in
IEEE Intelligent Systems, July/August, 2006.

Helen Nissenbaum is associate professor in the Department of Culture and
Communication, New York University and Senior Fellow, Information Law
Institute, New York University School of Law. She is coeditor of the journal
Ethics and Information Technology and has recently edited, with Monroe Price,
Academy & the Internet (2004).

Philip Pettit is L. S. Rockefeller University Professor of Politics and Human
Values, Princeton University, New Jersey. Among recent books, he has published, with Geoffrey Brennan, *The Economy of Esteem* (2004) and, with Frank
Jackson and Michael Smith, *Mind, Morality and Explanation: Selected Collaborations* (2004).

Thomas M. Powers is assistant professor of philosophy at the University
of Delaware and was a National Science Foundation Research Fellow at
the University of Virginia. His main research interests are ethical theory,
Kant, computer ethics, and philosophy of technology. He has edited, with
P. Kamolnick, *From Kant to Weber: Freedom and Culture in Classical German Social
Theory* (1999). He has also published chapters in a number of collections
and articles in the journal *Ethics and Information Technology*.

Emma Rooksby is a Research Fellow at the Centre for Applied Philosophy
and Public Ethics at Australian National University. Her research interests include computer ethics, philosophy, and literature. Her publications
include *Ethics and the Digital Divide* (2007). She was recently awarded a postdoctoral research fellowship at University of Western Australia.

Cass R. Sunstein is Karl N. Llewellyn Professor of Jurisprudence, Law School
and Department of Political Science, University of Chicago. Among his
recent publications is *Infotopia: How Many Minds Produce Knowledge* (2006).

Jeroen van den Hoven is professor of moral philosophy at the Department of Philosophy of the Faculty of Technology, Policy, and Management at Delft University of Technology and is a Professorial Fellow at the Centre for Applied Philosophy and Public Ethics at Australian National University. He is editor-in-chief of *Ethics and Information Technology*. He was a Research Fellow at the Netherlands Institute for Advanced Study (NIAS), Royal Dutch Academy of Arts and Sciences in 1994 and received research fellowships from University of Virginia (1996) and Dartmouth College (1998).

John Weckert is a Professorial Fellow at the Centre for Applied Philosophy and Public Ethics and professor of information technology, both at Charles Sturt University. He has published widely on the ethics of information and communication technology and is the founding editor-in-chief of the journal *NanoEthics: Ethics for Technologies That Converge at the Nanoscale*.

Introduction

All successful technologies change our lives. Up until the last fifteen years, cars had changed things more than computers had. Mainframe computers by then had changed administration and management, production in corporations, and scientific research, but they had a minimal effect on everyday life. It was really only with the advent of the World Wide Web and the incorporation of computer chips in many common appliances that the lives of most people were changed by computer technology. One of the most important features of information technology (IT) today is its ubiquity. This ubiquity is a result of what James Moor calls *the logical malleability* of computers. Computers can be programmed to do a large variety of different things; route information packets on the Internet, simulate hurricanes, make music, and instruct robots. They can be adapted to many different devices and put to many different uses. They allow us to work online, shop online, relax by playing computer games interactively with people from all over the world, get our news, study for our degrees, and find most of the information that we require.

The technology has not only changed what we do, but also how we do it. E-mail, chat rooms, blogs, and other forms of computer-mediated communication have altered how we communicate, and with whom we communicate and interact. It has changed how we relate to each other and how we experience our relations with others.

Information technology has also prompted us to revisit some important concepts and questions in moral philosophy, a number of which are discussed in this volume. As long ago as 1978, the impact of computers on philosophy in general was discussed by Aaron Sloman (1978), and more recently by Bynum and Moor (1998). The emphasis in this volume is not on philosophical concepts in general but rather on key concepts of moral philosophy: justice and equality, privacy, property, agency, collective action, democracy, public sphere, trust, esteem. The notions of property and theft, for example, particularly in the guises of intellectual property and copying,

1

arise in ways that they have not before with the ease of making multiple copies identical with the original at zero cost and the ease of transmitting those copies to large numbers of people. The notions of sharing and fair use even seem to be less clear in peer-to-peer contexts. For example, where sharing with friends might once have involved lending a book to three or four people, sharing now involves sending a file to hundreds or thousands of acquaintances in a file-sharing network. With whom does the responsibility lie when illegal or unjustifiable copying does take place?

Aspects of democracy are being examined afresh because of the influence of the Internet. Does the Internet give rise to a new public sphere that is not bound by geography? Does the freedom to select information lead to a situation where individuals forego opportunities to expose themselves to multiple and critical points of view? Is information gained from the blogosphere reliable compared to information and opinions gained from the traditional media? Because all of these issues bear on democracy in new ways, a reassessment of the conditions for democracy seems required.

The online world also poses problems, for example, concerning personal identity, personal relationships, friendship, privacy, trust, and esteem, that have not arisen previously. Who or what does it mean to be 'a person online,' or to have a real friendship online, and, can there be trust and esteem in this ephemeral electronic environment? Cocking, Matthews, Pettit, and Brennan examine these issues. Before the advent of the Internet, such discussions would not have been possible, except perhaps as thought experiments.

The Internet may also give a boost to the quest for a global ethics. Are conflicts between different cultures and value systems worldwide brought to the fore because of connectedness among the peoples of the world, or, does the technological link establish a platform for common practices that increases chances of finding interesting modes of conviviality?

Computers too have had an impact on discussions of moral responsibility. Can machines, in the form of computers, be morally responsible? How does computer use affect the moral responsibility of the humans using them? The vast increase in information, and its easy access by many via the Internet, has changed the landscape somewhat with respect to applications of theories of distributive justice. The advent of ubiquitous IT has not only led to a reexamination of various ethical notions, it has brought about discussions that suggest that new approaches to ethics are necessary.

The previous discussion demonstrates the impact that information technology has had on moral philosophy, but the impact can and should go the other way as well, that is, moral philosophy should also have an impact on the design and development of IT. A careful analysis of key concepts, for example, privacy, can lead to more careful, adequate, and responsible design of computer systems, particularly if we believe that moral values should play a part at the design stage. At a more general level, these philosophical analyses inform the types of systems that are designed and developed, and even perhaps influence the kind of research that is undertaken that enables particular systems to be developed at all.

Chapter 1 is by Terry Bynum, who first brought the importance of Norbert Wiener to the attention of those interested in the ethics of information technology. He shows how, as early as the 1940s, Wiener recognised the power and potential of automation and potential ethical and social problems. These ethical and social impacts were explored by Wiener against the background of his conceptions of human purpose and the good life, and, more specifically, with reference to his principles of freedom, equality, and benevolence. Bynum goes on to describe the metaphysics underlying Wiener's views and considers how they are similar to, in some respects, the positions of both Moor and Floridi, who describe their views in the chapters that follow.

In Chapter 2, Moor argues that with the rapid developments in technology, particularly in genetics, neuroscience, and nanotechnology, a new approach to ethics is required. He argues that the 'logical malleability' of computers led to so-called policy vacuums that require careful ethical analysis to fill, and extends this idea to the malleability of life (genetic technology), of material (nanotechnology), and of mind (neurotechnology). This, in turn, leads to policy vacuums in these new areas, which, Moor argues, require a new approach to ethics. The tripartite approach that he outlines involves first, seeing ethics as ongoing and dynamic and not just something to be done after the technology has been developed; second, as requiring much more collaboration between ethicists, scientists, and others; and third, as requiring a more sophisticated ethical analysis.

Information ethics, or as it is commonly called, computer ethics, has normally been seen, Floridi argues, as a microethics. He believes that this is a mistake and too restrictive. In Chapter 3, he develops information ethics as a macroethics, a form of environmental ethics that extends current environmental ethics from applying to living things to all informational objects, that is, to everything. All informational objects have at least minimal, and overridable, ethical value, and, hence, can be ethical patients. Nonhumans, including animals and computer systems, can also be ethical agents once the notion of moral responsibility is divorced from that of moral agency. Floridi's four fundamental principles of information ethics are: (1) entropy ought not to be caused in the infosphere; (2) entropy ought to be prevented in the infosphere; (3) entropy ought to be removed from the infosphere; and (4) the flourishing of informational entities, as well as the whole infosphere, ought to be promoted by preserving, cultivating, and enriching their properties.

Chapters 4–11 are all in some way related to the Internet, and Chapters 4–6 of these are concerned with democracy. Chapter 4, by Bohman, examines the idea that the Internet can be, or is, a facilitator of democracy, including transnational democracy. His aim in the chapter is to defend the view that democratising publics can form on the Internet, a technology that has features relevantly different from previous technologies, such as many-to-many communication. He begins by analysing new forms of political authority and public spheres, moves on to institutionalised authority, and, finally, develops the contribution made by transnational public spheres to the democratisation of international society. Sunstein (Chapter 5) is also interested in the Internet and democracy, but from a different point of view. His concern is the ability that the Internet gives to people to determine in advance what they view, what sort of information they can get, and with whom they interact. Although this has beneficial aspects, in increasing choice, for example, it also restricts a person's variety of information, thereby limiting exposure to contrary points of view, and it limits the number of common experiences that citizens have. Sunstein demonstrates the importance of both of these for a well-functioning democracy. Chapter 6 again concerns democracy and the Internet, but this time in relation to the reliability of the knowledge or information gained from blogs, as opposed to the conventional media. Goldman is interested primarily in epistemic conceptions of democracy, where democracy is seen as the best system for 'tracking the truth'. The central question that Goldman examines is whether the Internet is a more or less reliable source of information than the conventional media, for purposes of public political knowledge.

Chapters 7–10 are Internet-related chapters that are all concerned with online relationships. In Chapter 7, Cocking's primary interest is the extent to which people can have rich relationships and true friendships through computer-mediated communication only. His argument that this is probably not possible is based on an examination of normal offline communication and relationships, particularly with regard to how we present ourselves to others. Online we have much greater control of our self-presentation, at least in text-only communication, and this restricts in significant ways our relationships and interactions with each other. In Chapter 8, Matthews is also interested in relationships and how these are, or might be, affected by information technology. His focus however is on personal identity. Identity, in the sense of character, is a result partly of our relationships with others, especially close relationships, and he explores how two applications of information technology, computer-mediated communication and cyborgs, can affect those relationships and, thereby, our identities. He emphasises normative aspects of identity and suggests ways that these should influence information technology design.

Trust is an important aspect of relationships and also, more generally, for society. In Chapter 9, Pettit argues that trust, as opposed to mere reliance, is not possible between real people whose only contact is through the Internet, given the Internet as it currently exists. He distinguishes two types of trust: *primary trust*, based on loyalty, virtue and so on, and *secondary trust*, which is based on the fact that humans savour esteem. The Internet is not an environment in which enough information can be provided to justify a belief in someone's loyalty and so on, and it cannot show that someone is being held in esteem by being trusted. On the Internet, we all wear the Ring of Gyges. Chapter 10 considers further the idea of esteem on the Internet. Brennan and Pettit assume, reasonably, that people in general have a desire for the esteem of others and a related desire for a good reputation. They argue that, even though people may have different e-identities online, it does not follow that a good e-reputation is not desired and is not possible. Their case involves a careful examination of pseudonyms and anonymity, and they argue that people can and do really care about their virtual reputations.

In Chapter 11, Charles Ess explores the possibility of a global ethics for this global network. Two pitfalls that must be avoided are the extremes of ethical dogmatism on the one hand and ethical relativism on the other. Those who maintain that there are universal ethical values are in danger of the first extreme, and those who resist that view must be wary of the second extreme. Ess argues for ethical pluralism, the view that while there are relevant moral differences between cultures, when seen in a broader context can be seen to be different interpretations of fairly generally held values that could form the basis of a global ethics. He illustrates his argument with examples from different Eastern and Western traditions, which, at least superficially, appear to have very different moral values.

Responsibility has long been a central topic in ethics and IT, where the focus is on the responsibilities of computing professionals and on who can or should be held responsible for computer malfunctions. In Chapter 12, Miller examines a different aspect, the notion of collective responsibility in relation to knowledge acquisition and dissemination by means of information and communication technology. He argues that the storage, communication, and retrieval of knowledge by means of information and communication technology (ICT) can be considered a joint action in this context. This allows him to apply his account of collective moral responsibility to the ICT case. The relevant human players, systems designers, and software engineers, for example, and not the computers, have collective moral responsibility for any epistemic outcomes. Given that there is now discussion of whether or not computers can be morally responsible, this is a nontrivial result. Moral responsibility, which bears on this last point, also arises in Chapter 13, but in a very different way. Johnson and Powers are concerned with the moral agency of computer systems, and compare such systems with human surrogate agents, arguing that, while there are differences, the similarities are substantial. Their argument is that these systems can be considered moral agents, but the question of whether or not they, that is, the computer systems, could also have moral responsibility is left open.

Chapters 14 and 15 cover topics that have always been central to computer ethics – intellectual property and privacy. In Chapter 14, Wendy Gordon gives a detailed analysis of intellectual property concerns from both con-sequentialist and deontological perspectives, using a recent court decision in the United States as a case study. The central issue in this case was the extent to which a provider of technology should be held responsible for the uses to which that technology should be put, in this case, the infringement of copyright. An important feature of the argument of this chapter is the analysis of the ways in which information and communication technologies bear on the legal and ethical issues of property and copying. The thrust of the argument is that unauthorized copying the work of others in the dig-ital context is not necessarily wrong, from either consequentialist or from deontological (in this case, Lockean) perspectives.

The issue of privacy is commonly raised in the context of the use of various technologies. In Chapter 15, van den Hoven construes the privacy debates as discussions about different moral grounds used to protect personal data. The strongest and most important grounds, prevention of harm, fairness, and nondiscrimination, can be shared among advocates of a liberal concep-tion of the self and its identity and individual rights as well as opponents of such a view. Only if we make this distinction will be able to overcome the privacy problems in the context of concrete policy and technology decisions.

Chapter 16, by Flanagan, Howe, and Nissenbaum, however, explores tak-ing these and other values into account in the design and development stages of the software – a more proactive approach. Technology is not neu-tral, on their account, and values can be embodied within it. They develop their argument around a case study, a computer game designed to teach girls computer programming skills. Their conclusion is not only that val-ues can be designed into software (their study suggests ways of achieving this), but that designers have a duty to take moral values into account when designing computer programs.

In Chapter 17, Elgesem consider the question of whether, and under what circumstance, it might be legitimate to proscribe research, using research in information technology as an example. He argues that such proscription is justifiable only in cases where there is harm to identifiable individuals. Although he concedes that there is no sharp distinction between pure and applied research, there is, nevertheless, a useful distinction and that, in the latter case, it is more likely that identifiable individuals might be harmed. Therefore, it will be easier to justify proscription of applied research than pure research, which should rarely or never be stopped by governments.

Since the expansion of the Internet and especially the World Wide Web, there has been much discussion of the so-called digital divide; the divide between those with access and those without. In Chapter 18, van den Hoven and Rooksby develop a normative analysis of informational inequalities, and argue that information is a Rawlsian primary good. This Rawlsian framework enables them both to spell out criteria for the just distribution of access to information and to give a theoretical basis to the claim that the digital divide ought to be bridged.

In conclusion, information technology, as it has developed over the past couple of decades, has considerably altered our lives and experiences. This is especially true since the advent of the Internet and home computers. However, apart from changing lives, it has also has provided food for thought for moral philosophy and for philosophy more generally. Old philosophical and conceptual categories and concepts require review and old problems arise in novel ways. Some of the challenges facing philosophers are addressed in this book.

References

Bynum, W. T. and Moor, J. H. (Eds.) 1998. *The digital phoenix: How computers are changing chilosophy*. Oxford: Blackwell.

Sloman, A. 1978. *The computer revolution in philosophy*. Atlantic Highlands, NJ: Humanities Press.

Norbert Wiener and the Rise of Information Ethics

Terrell Ward Bynum

> To live effectively is to live with adequate information. Thus, communication and control belong to the essence of man's inner life, even as they belong to his life in society.
>
> *Norbert Wiener*

SCIENCE, TECHNOLOGY, AND ETHICS

Major scientific and technological innovations often have profound social and ethical effects. For example, in Europe during the sixteenth and seventeenth centuries, Copernicus, Newton, and other scientists developed a powerful new model of the universe. This stunning scientific achievement led to increased respect for science and for the power of human reasoning. During that same era, recently invented printing-press technology made it possible to spread knowledge far and wide across Europe, instead of leaving it, as before, in the hands of a privileged minority of scholars. Inspired by these scientific and technological achievements, philosophers, such as Hobbes, Locke, and Rousseau, re-examined human nature and the idea of a good society. They viewed human beings as *rational agents* capable of thinking for themselves and acquiring knowledge through science and books. In addition, they interpreted society as a creation of informed, rational citizens working together through *social contracts*. These philosophical developments laid foundations for ethical theories such as those of Bentham and Kant, and for political changes such as the American Revolution and the French Revolution.[1]

Today, after far-reaching scientific achievements in physics, biology, and cybernetics – and after recent technological advances in digital computing

---

[1] The social, political, scientific, and technological developments mentioned here were much more complex than this brief paragraph indicates. There is no intention here to defend any form of technological determinism. For a helpful, relevant discussion, see Gorniak-Kocikowska (1996).

and information networks – philosophers are again rethinking the nature of human beings and of society. A pioneer in these philosophical developments was Norbert Wiener (1894–1964), who founded information ethics as a field of academic research in the 1940s. Wiener was a child prodigy who graduated from high school at age eleven and earned an undergraduate degree in mathematics at age fifteen (Tufts 1909). His graduate studies were in biology at Harvard (1909–1910), in philosophy at Cornell (1910–1911), and at Harvard (1911–1914), where he studied philosophy of science with Josiah Royce. At age eighteen, Wiener received a Harvard PhD in mathematical logic and then went to Cambridge University in England for postdoctoral studies with philosopher Bertrand Russell.

THE BIRTH OF INFORMATION ETHICS

Wiener's creation of the field of information ethics was an unexpected by-product of a weapons-development effort in World War II. In the early 1940s, while he was a mathematics faculty member at MIT, Wiener joined with other scientists and engineers to design a new kind of antiaircraft cannon. Warplanes had become so fast and agile that the human eye and hand were much less effective at shooting them down. Wiener and his colleagues decided that an appropriate cannon should be able to 'perceive' a plane, calculate its likely trajectory, and then decide where to aim the gun and when to fire the shell. These decisions were to be carried out by the cannon itself, and part of the cannon had to 'talk' with another part without human intervention. The new gun, therefore, would be able to

1. Gather information about the external world,
2. Derive logical conclusions from that information,
3. Decide what to do, and then
4. Carry out the decision.

To create such a machine, Wiener and his colleagues developed a new branch of science which Wiener named *cybernetics*, from the Greek word for the steersman or pilot of a ship. He defined cybernetics as the science of information feedback systems and the statistical study of communications. In the midst of these wartime efforts, he realized that cybernetics, when combined with the new digital computers that he had just helped to invent, would have enormous social and ethical implications:

It has long been clear to me that the modern ultra-rapid computing machine was in principle an ideal central nervous system to an apparatus for automatic control; and that its input and output need not be in the form of numbers or diagrams but might very well be, respectively, the readings of artificial sense organs, such as photoelectric cells or thermometers, and the performance of motors or solenoids. . . . Long before Nagasaki and the public awareness of the atomic bomb, it had occurred to me that we were here in the presence of another social potentiality of unheard-of importance for good and for evil. (Wiener 1948, p. 36)

During the War, Wiener met often with computing engineers and theorists, such as Claude Shannon and John von Neumann. He collaborated regularly with physiologist Arturo Rosenblueth and logician Walter Pitts, who had been a student of philosopher Rudolph Carnap. Near the end of the War, and immediately afterwards, this circle of thinkers was joined by psychologists, sociologists, anthropologists, economists, and a philosopher of science. Wiener and his collaborators had come to believe 'that a better understanding of man and society ... is offered by this new field' (Wiener 1948, p. 39).

Shortly after the War, in 1948, Wiener published *Cybernetics: or Control and Communication in the Animal and the Machine.* In that book, he explained some key ideas about cybernetics and computing machines, and he explored the implications for physiology, medicine, psychology, and social theory. A few passages included comments on ethics, such as the above-quoted remark about 'good and evil' – comments that aroused the interest of many readers. Wiener was encouraged to write a follow-up book focusing primarily upon ethics, and so in 1950 he published *The Human Use of Human Beings: Cybernetics and Society* (revised and reprinted in 1954), in which he said this:

That we shall have to change many details of our mode of life in the face of the new machines is certain; but these machines are secondary in all matters of value ... to the proper evaluation of human beings for their own sake. . . . (Wiener 1950, p. 2)

Wiener devoted his book to the task of educating people about possible harms and future benefits that might result from computing and communications technologies.

In the book, *The Human Use of Human Beings*, Wiener laid philosophical foundations for the scholarly field that today is variously called 'computer ethics' or 'ICT ethics' or 'information ethics'. In this chapter, the term 'information ethics' has been selected, because Wiener's analyses can be applied to many different means of storing, processing, and transmitting information, including, for example, animal perception and memory, human thinking, telephones, telegraph, radio, television, photography, computers, information networks, and so on. (The field of 'computer ethics' is viewed here as a subfield of information ethics.)

CYBERNETICS AND HUMAN NATURE

According to Wiener, 'we must know as scientists what man's nature is and what his built-in purposes are' (Wiener 1954, p. 182). In *The Human Use of Human Beings*, he provided a cybernetic account of human nature that is, in many ways, reminiscent of Aristotle (see Bynum 1986). For example, he viewed all animals, including human beings, as information processors that

1. Take in information from the outside world by means of their perceptions,
2. Process that information in ways that depend upon their physiologies, and
3. Use that processed information to interact with their environments.

Many animals, and especially humans, can store information within their bodies and use it to adjust future activities on the basis of past experiences. Like Aristotle, Wiener viewed humans as the most sophisticated information processors of the entire animal kingdom. The definitive information-processing activities within a human being, according to Aristotle, are 'theoretical and practical reasoning'; and according to Wiener, theoretical and practical reasoning are made possible by human physiology:

I wish to show that the human individual, capable of vast learning and study, which may occupy about half of his life, is physically equipped...for this capacity. Variety and possibility are inherent in the human sensorium – and indeed are the key to man's most noble flights – because variety and possibility belong to the very structure of the human organism. (Wiener 1954, pp. 51–52)

Cybernetics takes the view that the structure of... the organism is an index of the performance that may be expected from it. The fact that...the mechanical fluidity of the human being provides for his almost indefinite intellectual expansion is highly relevant to the point of view of this book. (Wiener 1954, p. 57, italics in the original)

Wiener considered *flourishing as a person* to be the overall *purpose* of a human life – flourishing in the sense of realizing one's full human potential in variety and possibility of choice and action. To achieve this purpose, a person must engage in a diversity of information-processing activities, such as perceiving, organizing, remembering, inferring, deciding, planning, and acting. Human flourishing, therefore, is utterly dependent upon information processing:

Information is a name for the content of what is exchanged with the outer world as we adjust to it, and make our adjustment felt upon it. The process of receiving and of using information is the process of our adjusting to the contingencies of the outer environment, and of our living effectively within that environment. The needs and the complexity of modern life make greater demands on this process of information than ever before.... To live effectively is to live with adequate information. Thus, communication and control belong to the essence of man's inner life, even as they belong to his life in society. (Wiener 1954, pp. 17–18)

Besides thinking and reasoning, there are other types of information processing that must go on within the body of a person if he or she is to flourish. Human beings, as biological organisms, need exquisitely organized bodies with all the parts integrated and working together as a whole. If the parts become disconnected or do not communicate with each other in an appropriate way, the person will die or be seriously disabled. Different body parts (sense organs, limbs, and brain, for example) must communicate with each other in a way that integrates the organism, enabling activities like hand–eye coordination, legs moving to carry out a decision to walk, and so forth. Such inner-body communication includes 'feedback loops' for kinesthetic signals to coordinate limb positions, motions, and balance.

Biological processes within a person's body, such as breathing, eating, drinking, perspiring, and excreting, cause the atoms and molecules that make up the body of that person to be exchanged for external ones from the surrounding environment. In this way, essentially all the matter and energy of the body get replaced approximately every eight years. In spite of this change of *substance*, the complex organization or *form* of the body must be maintained to preserve life, functionality, and personal identity. As long as the *form* or *pattern* is preserved, by various 'homeostatic' biological processes, the person remains in existence, even if all the matter-energy has been replaced. As Wiener poetically said:

We are but whirlpools in a river of ever-flowing water. We are not stuff that abides, but patterns that perpetuate themselves. (Wiener 1954, p. 96)

The individuality of the body is that of a flame . . . of a form rather than of a bit of substance. (Wiener 1954, p. 102)

Wiener's cybernetic account of human nature, therefore, is that a person consists of a complex pattern of information embodied in matter and energy. Although the *substance* changes, the *form* must persist if the person is to flourish or even to exist. Thus, a human being is an 'information object', a dynamic form, or pattern persisting in an ever-changing flow of matter and energy. This cybernetic understanding of human nature has significant social and ethical implications, as illustrated in the next section.

CYBERNETICS AND SOCIETY

According to Wiener, just as human individuals can be viewed as dynamic, cybernetic entities, so communities and societies can be analyzed in a similar way:

It is certainly true that the social system is an organization like the individual; that it is bound together by a system of communication; and that it has a dynamics, in which circular processes of a feedback nature play an important part. (Wiener 1948, p. 33)

Wiener pointed out, in chapter VIII of *Cybernetics*, that societies and groups can be viewed as *second-order* cybernetic systems because their constituent parts are themselves cybernetic systems. This is true not only of human communities, but also, for example, of beehives, ant colonies, and certain herds of mammals. According to Wiener's cybernetic understanding of society, the processing and flow of information are crucial to the nature and the functioning of the community. Communication, he said, is 'the central phenomenon of society' (Wiener 1950, p. 229).

Wiener's analyses included discussions of telecommunication networks and their social importance. During his later life, there already existed on Earth a diversity of telephone, telegraph, teletype, and radio facilities that comprised a crude global 'net'. Thus, although he died in 1964, several years before the creation of the Internet, Wiener had already explored, in the 1950s and early 1960s, a number of social and ethical issues that are commonly associated today with the Internet. One of Wiener's topics was the possibility of working on the job from a distance using telecommunication facilities. Today, we would call this 'teleworking' or 'telecommuting'. Wiener illustrated this possibility by imagining an architect in Europe who manages the construction of a building in America without ever leaving Europe. The architect uses telephones, telegraphs, and an early form of faxing called 'Ultrafax' to send and receive blueprints, photographs, and instructions. Today's issues of teleworking and possible 'outsourcing' of jobs to other countries, therefore, were already briefly explored by Wiener in the early 1950s (Wiener 1950, pp. 104–105; 1954, p. 98).

Another telecommunications topic that Wiener examined was the possibility of 'virtual communities' (as *we* would call them). Already in 1948, he noted that 'Properly speaking, the community extends only so far as there extends an effectual transmission of information' (Wiener 1948, p. 184). And, in 1954, he said this:

Where a man's word goes, and where his power of perception goes, to that point his control and in a sense his physical existence is extended. To see and to give commands to the whole world is almost the same as being everywhere.... Even now the transportation of messages serves to forward an extension of man's senses and his capabilities of action from one end of the world to another. (Wiener 1954, pp. 97–98)

It was clear to Wiener that long-distance telecommunication facilities, especially when they become more robust, will open up many possibilities for people to cooperate together 'virtually' (as we would say today), either on the job, or as members of groups and organizations, or even as citizens participating in government. (See Wiener's discussion of a possible world government in the *Human Use of Human Beings*, 1954, p. 92.)

SOCIETY AND 'INTELLIGENT' MACHINES

Before 1950, Wiener's social analyses dealt with communities consisting primarily of humans or other animals. From 1950 onward, however, beginning with the publication of *The Human Use of Human Beings*, Wiener assumed that *machines will join humans as active participants in society*. For example, some machines will participate along with humans in the vital activity of creating, sending, and receiving messages that constitute the 'cement' that binds society together:

It is the thesis of this book that society can only be understood through a study of the messages and the communication facilities which belong to it; and that in the future development of these messages and communication facilities, messages between man and machines, between machines and man, and between machine and machine, are destined to play an ever-increasing part. (Wiener 1950, p. 9)

Wiener predicted, as well, that certain machines, namely digital computers with robotic appendages, will participate in the workplace, replacing thousands of human factory workers, both blue-collar and white-collar. He also foresaw artificial limbs – cybernetic 'prostheses' – that will merge with human bodies to help persons with disabilities, or even to endow able-bodied persons with unprecedented powers. 'What we now need,' he said, 'is an independent study of systems involving both human and mechanical elements' (Wiener 1964, p. 77). Today, we would say that Wiener envisioned societies in which 'cyborgs' would play a significant role and would have ethical policies to govern their behavior.

A special concern that Wiener often expressed involved machines that learn and make decisions. He worried that some people, blundering like sorcerers' apprentices, might create agents that they are unable to control – agents that could act on the basis of values that all humans do not share. It is risky, he noted, to replace human judgment with machine decisions, and he cautioned that a prudent man

will not leap in where angels fear to tread, unless he is prepared to accept the punishment of the fallen angels. Neither will he calmly transfer to the machine made in his own image the responsibility for his choice of good and evil, without continuing to accept a full responsibility for that choice. (Wiener 1950, pp. 211–212)

the machine . . . which can learn and can make decisions on the basis of its learning, will in no way be obliged to make such decisions as we should have made, or will be acceptable to us. For the man who is not aware of this, to throw the problem of his responsibility on the machine, whether it can learn or not, is to cast his responsibility to the winds, and to find it coming back seated on the whirlwind. (Wiener 1950, p. 212)

Wiener noted that, to prevent this kind of disaster, the world will need ethical rules for artificial agents, as well as new technology to instill those rules effectively into the agents.

In summary, then, Wiener foresaw future societies living in what he called the 'Machine Age' or the 'Automatic Age'. In such a society, machines would be integrated into the social fabric, as well as the physical environment. They would create, send, and receive messages; gather information from the external world; make decisions; take actions; reproduce themselves;

and be merged with human bodies to create beings with vast new powers. Wiener's predictions were not mere speculations, because he himself had already designed or witnessed early versions of devices, such as game-playing machines (checkers, chess, war, business), artificial hands with motors controlled by the person's brain, and self-reproducing machines like nonlinear transducers. (See, especially, Wiener 1964.)

Wiener's descriptions of future societies and their machines elicited, from others, various questions about the machines that Wiener envisioned: Will they have minds and be conscious? Will they be 'alive'? Wiener considered such questions to be vague semantic quibbles, rather than genuine scientific issues. He thought of machines and human beings alike as physical entities with capacities that are explained by the interaction of their parts and the outside world. The working parts of machines are 'lumps' of metal, plastic, silicon, and other materials; while the working parts of humans are exquisitely small atoms and molecules.

Now that certain analogies of behavior are being observed between machine and the living organism, the problem as to whether the machine is alive or not is, for our purposes, semantic and we are at liberty to answer it one way or the other as best suits our convenience. (Wiener 1954, p. 32)

Answers to questions about machine consciousness, thinking, or purpose are similarly semantic choices, according to Wiener; although he did believe that questions about the 'intellectual capacities' of machines, when appropriately stated, could be genuine scientific questions:

Cybernetics takes the view that the structure of... the organism is an index of the performance that may be expected from it.... Theoretically, if we could build a machine whose mechanical structure duplicated human physiology, then we could have a machine whose intellectual capacities would duplicate those of human beings. (Wiener 1954, p. 57; italics in the original)

In his 1964 book, *God and Golem, Inc.*, Wiener expressed skepticism that machines would ever duplicate the complex structure of a human brain because electronic components were too large and impossible to cram together like the neurons packed into a human brain. (One wonders what his view would be today, given recent developments in microcircuitry.)

A GOOD HUMAN LIFE AND THE PRINCIPLES OF JUSTICE

In the first chapter of the first edition of *The Human Use of Human Beings*, Wiener explained to his readers that the book examines possible harms and benefits from the introduction of cybernetic machines and devices into society. After identifying specific risks or possible benefits, he explored actions that might be taken or policies that might be adopted to avoid harm or to secure a benefit. He often discussed 'human values' and explored ways to defend or advance them. Some of the values that he considered include *life, health, security, knowledge, opportunity, ability, democracy, happiness, peace,* and most of all, *freedom.*

As I have explained, Wiener considered the *overall purpose* of a human life to be *flourishing as a person* in the sense of realizing one's full human potential in variety and possibility of choice and action. To flourish, then, requires reasoning, thinking, and learning – essentially, internal information-processing activities which, at their best, lead to flexible, creative adaptation to the environment and many alternatives for human choice and action. Different individuals, however, are endowed with different talents and desires, and they are presented with a wide range of opportunities and challenges, so there are many different ways to flourish as a human being.

Like Aristotle, Wiener considered people to be *fundamentally social,* and so he believed that they must live together in organized communities if they are to have a good life. But society can be very oppressive and stifle human flourishing, rather than encourage it or support it. Society, therefore, must have ethical policies – *principles of justice* – to protect individuals from oppression and maximize freedom and opportunities. In *The Human Use of Human Beings* (1950), Wiener stated such policies and referred to them as 'great principles of justice'. He did not give names to them, but for the sake of clarity and ease of reference, let us assign names here. Using Wiener's own words as definitions yields the following list (Wiener 1950, pp. 112–113):

1. *The Principle of Freedom* – Justice requires 'the liberty of each human being to develop in his freedom the full measure of the human possibilities embodied in him'.
2. *The Principle of Equality* – Justice requires 'the equality by which what is just for A and B remains just when the positions of A and B are interchanged'.
3. *The Principle of Benevolence* – Justice requires 'a good will between man and man that knows no limits short of those of humanity itself'.

To minimize social oppression and to maximize opportunities and choice, Wiener stated a fourth principle that we can call 'The Principle of Minimum Infringement of Freedom':

The Principle of Minimum Infringement of Freedom – 'What compulsion the very existence of the community and the state may demand must be exercised in such a way as to produce no unnecessary infringement of freedom'. (Wiener 1950, p. 113)

In summary, the above-described conceptions of human purpose and a good life are the tools with which Wiener explored the social and ethical impacts of information and communication technology. He dealt with a wide diversity of issues, including many topics that are considered important in computer ethics today. (See Bynum 2000, 2004, 2005.) Some of those topics are discussed briefly in the next section; but before proceeding, we need to consider some underlying metaphysical ideas in Wiener's social and ethical writings – ideas that shed light on his information ethics legacy and provide insight into computer ethics developments which have occurred since his death.

ENTROPY AND THE METAPHYSICS OF INFORMATION ETHICS

As a scientist and engineer, Wiener made frequent use of the laws of thermodynamics. Although originally discovered through efforts to build better heat engines, these laws of nature apply to every physical process in the universe. According to the first law, matter-energy can be changed from one form to another, but can neither be created nor destroyed. According to the second law, a certain amount of order or structure – and therefore a certain amount of *information* – is lost whenever any physical change takes place in a closed physical system. According to the third law, the universe *is* such a closed system. It follows from the laws of thermodynamics, then, that every physical change destroys some of the information encoded in matter-energy. *Entropy* is a measure of this lost information.

The laws of thermodynamics and the associated notion of entropy lend themselves to a metaphysical theory of the nature of the universe that Wiener presupposed in his information ethics writings. According to this metaphysical view, everything in the universe is the result of the interaction of two fundamental 'stuffs' – information and matter-energy. Neither of these can exist on its own; each requires the other. Every physical process is both a creative 'coming-to-be' and a destructive 'fading away'. So-called physical objects are really slowly changing patterns – information objects – that persist for a while in the ever-changing flow of matter-energy. Metaphorically expressed: the two creative 'stuffs' of our universe – matter-energy and information – mix and swirl in a 'cosmic dance', giving birth to all that ever was and all that ever will be, till the end of time.

The second law of thermodynamics, with its associated loss of information, determines that time can flow only in one direction and cannot be reversed. On this view, increasing entropy is 'the great destroyer' that eventually dismantles all patterns and structures. This will be the ultimate fate of every physical entity – even great literary works, priceless sculptures, wonderful music, magnificent buildings, mountain ranges, living organisms, ecosystems, political empires, Earth, moon, and stars. In this sense, increasing entropy can be viewed as a 'natural evil' that threatens everything that humans hold dear.

This theory is reminiscent of important metaphysical ideas in a variety of the world's great cultures. For example, matter-energy and information are much like Aristotle's 'matter' and 'form' – all objects consist of both, and neither can occur without the other; so when all form is lost, no individual object can remain. Similarly, the ongoing creative flow of matter-energy and information in the universe is much like the Taoist 'flow' with the mixing

and mingling of yin and yang. And the 'cosmic dance' of information with
matter-energy reminds one of the creative–destructive dance of the Hindu
god Shiva Nataraj.

In his information ethics writings, Wiener did not dwell at length upon
his metaphysical assumptions, but he did call upon them from time to time.
In chapter II of *The Human Use of Human Beings* (1954), for example, he
spoke of entropy as 'the Devil', a powerful 'arch enemy' of all order and
structure in the universe – the ultimate 'evil' that works against all purpose
and meaning. In chapter V of that same book, he described human beings
as 'whirlpools in a river of ever-flowing water . . . not stuff that abides, but
patterns that perpetuate themselves'. He also said that 'The individuality of
the body is that of a flame . . . of a form rather than of a bit of substance'.
And he was very clear that information is not the same sort of 'stuff' as
matter-energy. The brain, he said,

does not secrete thought 'as the liver does bile', as the earlier materialists claimed,
nor does it put it out in the form of energy, as the muscle puts out its activity.
Information is information, not matter or energy. (Wiener 1948, p. 155)

This metaphysical 'theory of everything', which underlies Wiener's information ethics, apparently anticipated some recent developments in contemporary theoretical physics, especially the so-called holographic theory of the
universe. Consider the following remarks regarding the work of theoretical
physicist Lee Smolin (2001):

What is the fundamental theory like? The chain of reasoning involving holography
suggests to some, notably Lee Smolin . . . that such a final theory must be concerned
not with fields, not even with spacetime, but rather with information exchange
among physical processes. If so, the vision of information as the stuff the world
is made of will have found a worthy embodiment. (Bekenstein 2003)

The fourth principle is that 'the universe is made of processes, not things'. Thus reality consists of an evolving network of relationships, each part of which is defined only
in reference to other parts. . . . The *weak holographic principle* goes further in asserting that there are no things, only processes, and that these processes are merely the
exchange of data. . . . According to this theory, the three-dimensional world *is* the flow
of information. Making sense of this idea certainly poses a challenge, but as Smolin
points out, making sense of seemingly wild and crazy ideas is exactly how physics
progresses to the next level of understanding. (Renteln 2002; italics in the original)

THE EXPLANATORY POWER OF WIENER'S METAPHYSICAL IDEAS

In Wiener's metaphysics, the flow of matter-energy and the flow of information are the two creative powers of the universe. If we assume that Wiener's
metaphysical theory is correct, we gain a useful perspective not only on the
current 'Information Revolution', but also on the earlier Industrial Revolution of the eighteenth and nineteenth centuries. That prior Revolution

used heat engines and electricity to harness the flow of matter-energy for human purposes[2]; and, as a result, it became one of history's most powerful sources of change, with vast social and ethical repercussions.

Similarly the so-called 'Information Revolution', which Wiener referred to as 'the Second Industrial Revolution', is occurring right now because human beings have begun to use computers and related devices – information technology (IT) – *to harness the other creative power of the universe: the flow of information.*[3] This tremendous human achievement, in which Wiener played such an important role, will surely transform the world even more than the original Industrial Revolution did in its own time. As a result, perhaps no other technology will ever come close to the social and ethical significance of IT. This provides an answer to people who have raised provocative questions about the need for a separate area of study called 'computer ethics'. Such thinkers have asked questions like these:

Given the fact that other machines besides computers have had a big impact upon society, why is there no 'automobile ethics'? – no 'railroad ethics'? – no 'sewing machine ethics'? Why do computers need an 'ethics' of their own? (See Gotterbarn 1991 and Maner 1996.)

Automobiles, railroads, and sewing machines were part of the Industrial Revolution, and they helped (along with hundreds of other kinds of machines) to harness the flow of matter-energy. However, computer technology is bringing about a social and ethical revolution of its own by harnessing, according to Wiener's metaphysics, the other creative power of the universe. So Wiener's metaphysics explains why computing technology merits a separate area of ethical study.

It is a remarkable fact about the history of computer ethics that, until recently, Wiener's foundation for the field was essentially ignored – even unknown – by later computer ethics scholars. This unhappy circumstance was due in part to Wiener himself, who did not fully and explicitly present his theory in a systematic way. Instead he introduced parts of it from time to time as the need arose in his writings. During the last quarter of the twentieth century, therefore, the field of computer ethics developed without the benefit of Wiener's foundation. In spite of this, his metaphysics provides a helpful perspective on recent computer ethics developments. Consider, for example, the influential theories of Moor and Floridi.

---

[2] The Industrial Revolution, with its various engines, motors, and machines, took a giant step forward in harnessing changes in matter-energy. Prior important steps in harnessing this 'flow' included the discovery and control of fire, the invention of tools, and the development of farming.

[3] The Information Revolution, with its digital computers and various communications technologies, took a giant step forward in harnessing the 'flow' of information. Prior important steps in harnessing this 'flow' included the development of language, the invention of writing, and the invention of the printing press.

Moor's Computer Ethics Theory

Moor's insightful and very practical account of the nature of computer ethics makes sense of many aspects of computer ethics and provides conceptual tools to analyze a wide diversity of cases. Moor's account of computer ethics (see, especially, Moor 1985, 1996) has been the most influential one, to date. His view is that computer technology is 'logically malleable' in the sense that hardware can be constructed and software can be adjusted, syntactically and semantically, to create devices that will carry out almost any task. As a result, computing technology empowers people to do a growing number of things that could never be done before. Moor notes, however, that just because we *can* do something new, this does not mean that we *ought* to do it, or that it would be *ethical* to do it. Indeed, there may be no 'policies' in place – no laws, rules, or standards of good practice – to govern the new activity. When this happens, we face what Moor calls an ethical 'policy vacuum', which needs to be filled by adjusting or extending already existing policies, or by creating new ones. The new or revised policies, however, should be ethically justified before they can be adopted.

Even when computing is 'merely' doing old tasks in different ways, says Moor, something new and important may nevertheless be happening. In particular, the old tasks may become 'informationalized' in the sense that 'the processing of information becomes a crucial ingredient in performing and understanding the activities themselves' (Moor 1996). Such 'informational enrichment' can sometimes change the meanings of old terms, creating 'conceptual muddles' that have to be clarified before new policies can be formulated.

Moor did not base his views upon Wiener, but his key concepts and procedures are supported and reinforced by Wiener's theory. Thus, if computing technology actually does harness one of the fundamental creative forces in the universe, as Wiener's metaphysics assumes, then we certainly would expect it to generate brand new possibilities for which we do not yet have policies – that is, Moor's 'policy vacuums'. In addition, Moor's term 'informational enrichment' is used to describe processes that harness the flow of information to empower human beings – the very hallmark of the Information Revolution from Wiener's point of view. (Wiener's metaphysical ideas also shed light on other key aspects of Moor's theory, but space does not permit a full discussion of them here.[4])

Floridi's Foundation for Computer Ethics

Another influential computer ethics theory – certainly the most metaphysical one – is Floridi's 'information ethics'[5], which he developed as a

---

[4] See my paper, 'The Copernican Revolution in Ethics', based upon my keynote address at E-CAP2005, Vasteros, Sweden, June 2005 (Bynum, 2007).

[5] Floridi uses the term 'information ethics' in a technical sense of his own, and not in the broad sense in which it is used here.

'foundation' for computer ethics. (See, for example, Floridi 1999 and Floridi and Sanders 2004.) Like Moor's theory, Floridi's was not derived from Wiener, but nevertheless can be supported and reinforced through Wiener's metaphysics. Both Wiener and Floridi, for example, consider *entropy* to be a 'natural evil' that can harm or destroy anything that anyone might value. For both thinkers, therefore, needlessly increasing entropy would be an action that unjustifiably generates evil. Because entropy is a measure of lost information (in the physicist's sense of this term), anything that preserves or increases such information could be construed as good because it is the opposite of entropy, and therefore it is the opposite of evil.

This conclusion leads Floridi to attribute at least minimal ethical worth to any object or structure that preserves or increases information. For example, 'informational entities' in cyberspace, like databases, hypertexts, Web sites, Web bots, blogs, and so on, have at least minimal ethical value, because they encode or increase information and thus resist, or even decrease entropy (i.e., evil). Because of this minimal worth of 'informational entities', says Floridi, 'a process or action may be morally good or bad irrespective of its [pleasure and pain] consequences, motives, universality, or virtuous nature'. (See Floridi and Sanders 2004, p. 93; bracketed phrase added for clarity.) Because his information ethics (IE) theory identifies a kind of moral worth not covered by utilitarianism, deontologism, contractualism, or virtue ethics, Floridi considers IE to be a new 'macroethics' on a par with these more traditional ethical theories.

Another aspect of Floridi's theory that is reinforced by Wiener's metaphysics is the need for ethical rules to govern 'artificial agents' such as softbots and robots. Wiener argued in chapter X of *The Human Use of Human Beings* (1954) that the world soon would need ethical rules covering the activities of decision-making machines such as robots. Similarly, Floridi's IE includes the idea of 'artificial evil' generated by artificial agents – and the need for ethical principles to minimize such evil. (Wiener's metaphysical ideas also shed light on several other key aspects of Floridi's theory, but space does not permit a full discussion of them here.[6])

WIENER'S METHODOLOGICAL CONTRIBUTIONS TO COMPUTER ETHICS

Besides providing a powerful metaphysical underpinning for information ethics, Wiener employed several important methodological strategies. However, he did not normally 'step back' from what he was doing and offer his readers some metaphilosophical explanations about his methods or procedures. Consequently, to uncover his methodology, we must observe his

[6] Again, see my paper, 'The Copernican Revolution in Ethics', based upon my keynote address at E-CAP2005, Vasteros, Sweden, June 2005 (Bynum, 2007).

practices. Doing so reveals at least *three useful strategies* or procedures that he employed.

Information Ethics and Human Values

One of Wiener's strategies was to explore or envision the impacts of information and communication technologies upon human values with an eye toward advancing and defending those values. As noted, some of the values that Wiener addressed included *life, health, security, knowledge, opportunity, ability, freedom, democracy, happiness,* and *peace.* For example, in *The Human Use of Human Beings* (1954), Wiener explored,

1. risks to *peace* and *security* that could result if governments were to base military strategies or decisions upon computers playing 'war games' (chapter X);
2. risks to workers' *opportunities* and *happiness* if computerized 'automatic factories' were introduced too quickly, or too callously, by the business community (chapter IX); and
3. possible increases in *ability* and *opportunity* for persons with disabilities who use computerized prostheses (chapter X).

Other computer ethics thinkers who came after Wiener have taken a similar 'human values' approach, developing strategies of their own with various names, such as 'Value Sensitive Design' and 'Disclosive computer ethics'. (See, for example, Bynum 1993; Friedman and Nissenbaum 1996; Friedman 1997; Johnson 1997; Brey 2000; and Introna and Nissenbaum 2000.)

Identifying and Dealing with Information Ethics Problems or Opportunities

A second methodology that Wiener employed is best described with the aid of Moor's later classical account of computer ethics. Some of Wiener's analyses can be seen to involve the following five steps, which are very much like the ones Moor recommends:

Step One: *Identify an ethical problem or positive opportunity* regarding the integration of information technology into society. If a problem or opportunity can be foreseen before it occurs, we should develop ways to solve the problem or benefit from the opportunity before being surprised by – and therefore unprepared for – its appearance.

Step Two: If possible, *apply existing 'policies'* (as Moor would call principles, laws, rules, and practices), using *precedent and traditional interpretations* to resolve the problem or to benefit from the opportunity.

Step Three: If existing policies or relevant concepts appear to be ambiguous or vague when applied to the new problem or opportunity, *clarify ambiguities and vagueness.* (In Moor's language: identify and eliminate 'conceptual muddles'.)

Step Four: If precedent and existing interpretations, including the new clarifications, are insufficient to resolve the problem or to benefit from the opportunity, one should *revise the old policies or create new, ethically justified ones.* (In Moor's language, one should identify 'policy vacuums' and then formulate and ethically justify new policies to fill the vacuums.)

Step Five: *Apply the new or revised policies* to resolve the problem or to benefit from the opportunity.

A good example of this strategy in Wiener's writings can be found in the many discussions in books, articles and news interviews (e.g., chapter IX of *The Human Use of Human Beings,* 1954), in which he analyzed possible 'automatic factories' that would use computers to eliminate or drastically decrease blue-collar and white-collar jobs. He identified risks that would result from such computerized factories, including massive unemployment and economic harm. In addition, he pointed out that the very meaning of the term 'factory worker' would change as factory jobs were radically altered. He noted that existing labor practices, work rules, labor regulations, and labor laws would be insufficient to handle the resulting social and economic crisis; and he recommended that new policies be developed before such a crisis even occurs. He met with labor leaders, business executives, and public policy makers to offer advice on developing new policies.

Proactively Improving the World

In keeping with his 'Principle of Benevolence', Wiener actively sought ways to improve the lives of his fellow human beings using information technology. For example, he worked with others to design an artificial hand with finger-control motors activated by the person's brain (Wiener 1964, p. 78). He also worked on a 'hearing glove' to help deaf persons understand speech by means of special vibrations in a 'cybernetic glove' (Wiener 1954, pp. 167–174). In addition, at Wiener's suggestion, two simple machines were built – the 'moth' and the 'bedbug' – which confirmed Wiener's cybernetic analyses of the medical problems of 'intentional tremor' and 'Parkinsonian tremor' (Wiener 1954, pp. 163–167).

WIENER'S INFORMATION ETHICS LEGACY

Norbert Wiener was a child prodigy, a prize-winning mathematician, a celebrated scientist, and a communications engineer. He played a leading role (with others like von Neumann, Shannon, and Turing) in the creation of the very technology and science that launched the Information Revolution.

He also was a philosopher who could see the enormous ethical and social implications of his own work and that of his colleagues. As a result, Wiener created information ethics as an academic subject and provided it with a metaphysical foundation, a new theory of human nature and society, a new understanding of human purpose, a new perspective on social justice, several methodological strategies, and a treasure trove of computer ethics comments, examples, and analyses (see Bynum 2000, 2004, 2005). The issues that he analyzed, or at least touched upon, decades ago include topics that are still considered 'contemporary' today: agent ethics, artificial intelligence, machine psychology, virtual communities, teleworking, computers and unemployment, computers and security, computers and religion, computers and learning, computers for persons with disabilities, the merging of human bodies and machines, the responsibilities of computer professionals, and many other topics as well. His contributions to information ethics scholarship and practice will remain important for decades to come.

References

Bekenstein, J. D. 2003. Information in the holographic universe. *Scientific American*, August. Retrieved January 7, 2005, http://sufizmveinsan.com/fizik/holographic.html.

Brey, P. 2000. Disclosive computer ethics. *Computers and Society, 30*, 4, 10–16.

Bynum, T. W. 1986. *Aristotle's theory of human action*. University Microfilms. Doctoral dissertation, Graduate Center of the City University of New York.

Bynum, T. W. 1993. Computer ethics in the computer science curriculum, in T. W. Bynum, W. Maner, and J. L. Fodor (Eds.), *Teaching computer ethics*. New Haven, CT: Research Center on Computing and Society (also at http://www.computerethics.org).

Bynum, T. W. 2000. The foundation of computer ethics. *Computers and Society, 30*, 2, 6–13.

Bynum, T. W. 2004. Ethical challenges to citizens of 'The Automatic Age': Norbert Wiener on the information society'. *Journal of Information, Communication and Ethics in Society, 2*, 2, 65–74.

Bynum, T. W. 2005. The impact of the 'Automatic Age' on our moral lives in R. Cavalier (Ed.), *The impact of the Internet on our moral lives*. New York: State University of New York Press, pp. 11–25.

Bynum, T. W. 2007. The Copernican revolution in ethics, in G. Dodig Crnkovic and S. Stuart (Eds), *Computation, information, cognition: the nexus and the liminal*. Newcastle upon Tyne: Cambridge Scholars Publishing, 2007.

Floridi, L. 1999. Information ethics: on the theoretical foundations of computer ethics, *Ethics and Information Technology, 1*, 1, 37–56.

Floridi, L., and Sanders, J. W. 2004. The foundationalist debate in computer ethics, in R. A. Spinello and H. T. Tavani (Eds.), *Readings in cyberethics* (2nd ed.). Sudbury, MA: Jones and Bartlett, pp. 81–95.

Friedman, B. (Ed.). 1997. *Human values and the design of computer technology*. Cambridge, UK: Cambridge University Press.

Friedman, B., and Nissenbaum, H. 1996. Bias in computer systems, *ACM Transactions on Information Systems, 14*, 3, 330–347.

Gorniak-Kocikowska, K. 1996. The computer revolution and the problem of global ethics, in T. W. Bynum and S. Rogerson (Eds.), *Global information ethics,* a special issue of *Science and Engineering Ethics, 2,* 2, 177–190.

Gotterbarn, D. 1991. Computer ethics: Responsibility regained. *National Forum: The Phi Beta Kappa Journal, 71,* 26–31.

Introna, L. D. and Nissenbaum, H. 2000. Shaping the Web: Why the politics of search engines matters, *The Information Society, 16,* 3, 1–17.

Johnson, D. G. 1997. Is the global information infrastructure a democratic technology? *Computers and Society, 27,* 3, 20–26.

Maner, W. 1996. Unique ethical problems in information technology, in T. W. Bynum and S. Rogerson (Eds.), *Global information ethics,* A special issue of *Science and Engineering Ethics, 2,* 2, 137–154.

Moor, J. H. 1985. What is computer ethics?, in T. W. Bynum (Ed.), *Computers and ethics,* Oxford, UK: Blackwell, pp. 263–275. Also published as the October 1985 special issue of *Metaphilosophy.*

Moor, J. H. 1996. Reason, relativity and responsibility in computer ethics', a keynote address at ETHICOMP96 in Madrid, Spain. Later published in *Computers and Society, 28,* 1.

Renteln, P. 2002. Review of L. Smolin, *Three roads to quantum gravity. American Scientist, 90,* 1.

Smolin, L. 2001. *Three roads to quantum gravity.* New York, NY: Basic Books.

Wiener, N. 1948. *Cybernetics: or Control and communication in the animal and the machine.* Cambridge, MA: Technology Press.

Wiener, N. 1950–1954. *The Human use of human beings: Cybernetics and society.* New York: Houghton Mifflin, 1950. (2nd ed. rev., Doubleday Anchor, 1954.)

Wiener, N. 1964. *God & Golem, Inc.: A comment on certain points where cybernetics impinges on religion.* Cambridge, MA: MIT Press.

Why We Need Better Ethics for Emerging Technologies[1]

James H. Moor

INTRODUCTION

New technological products are emerging. We learn about them regularly in the news. Information technology continually spawns new and popular applications and accessories. Indeed, much of the news itself is produced and transmitted through ever newer and more diverse information technology. But it is not only growth in information technology that is salient; other technologies are expanding rapidly. Genetic technology is a growth industry with wide applications in foods and medicine. Other technologies, such as nanotechnology and neurotechnology, are less well-established but have produced striking developments that suggest the possibility of considerable social and ethical impact in the not too distant future.

The emergence of these potentially powerful technologies raises the question about what our technological future will be like. Will the quality of our lives improve with increased technology or not? I believe the outcome of technological development is not inevitable. We, at least collectively, can affect our futures by choosing which technologies to have and which not to have and by choosing how technologies that we pursue will be used. The question really is: How well will we choose? The emergence of a wide variety of new technologies should give us a sense of urgency in thinking about the ethical (including social) implications of new technologies. Opportunities for new technology are continually arriving at our doorstep. Which kinds should we develop and keep? And, how should we use those that we do keep?

The main argument of this paper is to establish that we are living in a period of technology that promises dramatic changes and in a period of time in which it is not satisfactory to do ethics as usual. Major technological upheavals are coming. Better ethical thinking in terms of being better

[1] This chapter was originally published in 2005 in *Ethics and Information Technology*, 7, 3, 111–119.

informed and better ethical action in terms of being more proactive are required.

TECHNOLOGICAL REVOLUTIONS

'Technology' is ambiguous. When speaking of a particular kind of technology, such as airplane technology, we sometimes refer to its paradigm and sometimes to its devices and sometimes to both. A *technological paradigm* is a set of concepts, theories, and methods that characterize a kind of technology. The technological paradigm for airplanes includes the concept of a machine that flies, the theory of aerodynamics, and the method of using surfaces to achieve and control flight. A *technological device* is a specific piece of technology. The Wright brothers' airplane and commercial jetliners are examples of technological devices. Technological devices are *instances* or *implementations* of the technological paradigm. *Technological development* occurs when either the technological paradigm is elaborated in terms of improved concepts, theories, and methods, or the instances of the paradigm are improved in terms of efficiency, effectiveness, safety, and so forth. Of course, technological development has occurred in numerous technologies over thousands of years.

But in some cases, technological development has an enormous social impact. When that happens, a *technological revolution* occurs.[2] Technological revolutions do not arrive fully mature. They take time and their futures, like the futures of small children, are difficult to predict. We do have an idea of how children typically develop, and, likewise, I believe we have an idea of how revolutions typically develop. I will try to articulate that conception in terms of a plausible model of what happens during a typical technological revolution.

We can understand a technological revolution as proceeding through three stages: (1) the introduction stage, (2) the permeation stage (Moor 1985), and (3) the power stage (Moor 2001). Of course, there are not sharp lines dividing the stages any more than there are sharp lines dividing children, adolescents, and adults. In the first stage, the *introduction stage*, the earliest implementations of the technology are esoteric, often regarded as intellectual curiosities or even as playthings more than as useful tools. Initially, only a few people are aware of the technology, but some are fascinated by it and explore its capabilities. Gradually, the devices improve and operate effectively enough to accomplish limited goals. Assuming that the technology is novel and complex, the cost in money, time, and resources to

---

[2] The term 'revolutionary technology' is used colloquially sometimes to describe new and improved technological devices. A new mousetrap might be said to be 'revolutionary' if it catches many more mice than earlier models. I will use 'revolutionary technology' in a much stronger sense requiring that the technology have significant social impact.

use the technology will typically be high. Because of these limitations, the technology's integration into society will be minor, and its impact on society will be marginal.

In the second stage, the *permeation stage*, the technological devices are standardized. The devices are more conventional in design and operation. The number of users grows. Special training classes may be given to educate more people in the use of the technology. The cost of application drops, and the development of the technology begins to increase as the demand for its use increases. The integration into society will be moderate, and its overall impact on society becomes noticeable as the technological devices are adopted more widely.

Finally, in the third stage, the *power stage*, the technology is firmly established. The technology is readily available and can be leveraged by building upon existing technological structures. Most people in the culture are affected directly or indirectly by it. Many understand how to use it or can benefit from it by relying on people who do understand and use it. Economy of scale drives down the price, and wide application provides pressure and incentive for improvements. The integration into society will be major, and its impact on society, if it is truly a revolutionary technology, will be significant. The impact of the technology on society is what marks it essentially as revolutionary. Toasters have undergone technological development, but toaster technology has not had a significant level of impact on our society. As wonderful and improved as toasters are, there is no toaster revolution; whereas there has been a technological revolution due to developments of the automobile and electricity. Take toasters out of society and not much is changed. Remove automobiles or electricity and our contemporary society would have to make massive adjustments.

This tripartite model for an open technological revolution is summarized by the following table:

Stages of an Open Technological Revolution

	Introduction	Permeation	Power
Devices	Esoteric	Standardized	Leveraged
Users/beneficiaries	Few	Select	Many
Understanding	Elite	Trained	Common
Cost per use	High	Medium	Low
Usefulness	Limited	Moderate	High
Integration into society	Minor	Moderate	Major
Social impact	Marginal	Noticeable	Significant

Social impact inevitably reflects the other factors mentioned in the table and in addition includes the effect that the technology has on the behavior and practices of the society. A technological revolution has a large-scale transforming effect on the manner in which a society functions.

In giving this description of technological revolutions, I have been making some assumptions that need to be made more explicit. This is a model of *open* technological revolutions in the sense that the revolution occurs in an open society and the technology is accessible directly or indirectly by the general public as a good or service over time. I have been assuming a liberal democratic state in which market forces, even if regulated, play an important role. These are the conditions under which technological revolutions can flourish. The automobile revolution and electrification revolution are examples of reasonably open technological revolutions. In closed revolutions, the access to the technology remains severely restricted by social, political, or economic forces. For example, a ruling elite or a military may maintain control by limiting access to and use of particular technologies. The development of nuclear weapons would be an example of a closed technological revolution. Closed technological revolutions, by definition, will control the dispersal of the technology so that they are unlikely to proceed through all of the aspects of the permeation and power stages in this model. Here, we will be considering open technological revolutions granting, of course, that the openness of a revolution may be a matter of degree and may vary across societies and time.[3]

Revolutions do not come from nowhere or vanish suddenly into nothing. A prerevolutionary period exists in which basic concepts and understanding develop that make the introduction stage possible. A postrevolutionary period exists in which the technology is well-established. Development may still be made, but the significance of the technology will not increase proportionally and eventually may decline or disappear if the technology is replaced with even better technology.

---

[3] The model presented here has similarities to but should not be confused with Schumpeter's well-known and controversial model for capitalistic economics (Schumpeter 1952). Joseph Schumpeter (1883–1950) was a respected economist who analyzed the evolution and cyclic nature of capitalism. Schumpeter developed a rich concept of entrepreneurship. According to Schumpeter, entrepreneurs are essential drivers of capitalism. They innovate not only by improving technological inventions but also by introducing new products, identifying new sources of supply, finding new markets, and developing new forms of organization. With regard to technological development, his theory can be described in terms of cycles of invention, innovation, and diffusion. Schumpeter believed that these cycles of capitalism would lead to growth and improved living standards. But, he also believed that, regrettably, capitalism was likely to destroy itself by attacking freedoms and private property that made capitalism possible. The model presented in this paper is not aimed at explaining the nature and fate of capitalism. The model here focuses on the nature of open technological revolutions in which a free market is one of the enabling conditions. Schumpeter's model does not distinguish between technological development and technological revolution (toasters vs. computers), which is a central distinction of the model in this paper. Distinguishing the power stage from the permeation stage is crucial in identifying those technologies that have a significant level of social impact and consequently will have the most serious ethical impact.

As an example of this model of a technological revolution, consider the computer/information revolution. In the prerevolutionary stage, many concepts and devices were developed that laid the groundwork for the revolution. Concepts from mathematics used by Alan Turing in his theoretical analysis of computing were crucial preparation for the development of computing technology. Early computational devices from the abacus to Gottfried Leibniz's calculating machine to Charles Babbage's difference engine were precursors illustrating that machines could be used for calculation. But the computer revolution, as we think of it in modern terms, began around World War II. The early machines were certainly esoteric. In Britain, the Colossus computer, the first large-scale electronic digital computer, was specialized to break codes. In the United States, ENIAC (Electronic Numerical Integrator and Computer) was used in some calculations for the Manhattan Project as well as for calculations of ballistic trajectories.

After World War II, computers were developed in an open environment for more general purposes and the introduction stage into society really began. Throughout the 1950s and 1960s, large mainframe computers were used by elite institutions, such as banks, large companies, universities, and governments that could afford them. Improvements in their usability and capability were gradually made, but those computers were far from user friendly in today's sense. Input was often done by stacks of punched cards, and output was mostly text or even punched tape with limited control over the format. These behemoth machines made some specific jobs easier, but, in general, they were not useful for most activities in the workplace, school, or home. Early projections, even by some who were quite knowledgeable about computers, claimed that only a relatively small number of computers would be necessary for society in the long run.

The permeation stage began with the introduction of personal computers in the late 1970s and early 1980s. Early in this period, most homes did not have personal computers, although they were found in some schools and offices. Training classes were given to ensure that people were computer literate. They were useful for select projects but not particularly useful for many activities even in a well-equipped office. The cost of computing dropped compared to the earlier expensive mainframes, and the impact computing had in the office was noticeable in that it changed procedures for performing routine activities in schools and workplaces on a broader scale.

By 2000, the shift was being made into the power stage. Most people and homes had computers. A business did not have to be concerned about its customers being computer literate or knowing how to use the Web; it could assume this. This basic common knowledge of the Web and use of computers could then be leveraged to advertise and sell ordinary products. The cost of computing dropped even more so that many people now own more than one computer and have wide access to computers in public and workplaces.

E-mail is an assumed form of communication. Online commerce and banking is soaring. The Web is now *a*, if not *the*, standard reference source for information for most people. Computer chips used for medical applications are implanted in us and computer chips for a large variety of purposes are embedded in our environment. The computer in its many manifestations is thoroughly integrated into advanced society. Thus, the computer revolution provides a nice example of the model of how an open technological revolution unfolds.

To identify a technological revolution, one must consider the technological paradigm, the technological devices that instantiate the paradigm, and the social impact of these devices. The paradigm will evolve and be articulated in new ways over time but will be identifiable as alterations of the original version of the paradigm. In the example of the computer revolution, the concept of computation is an essential feature of the basic paradigm. Over time, this paradigm has evolved to include parallel processing, genetic algorithms, and new architectures, but these are regarded as different ways of doing computation. To determine what paradigm stage is occurring, all of the devices that instantiate the paradigm for a society at that time need to be considered. Although some devices that implement the paradigm will be more developed than others, the overall status of these various devices needs to be assessed in terms of the items in the table of factors of an open technological revolution. The social impact of the devices instantiating the paradigm is most indicative of the stage of development. Without a significant social impact from the overall set of these devices, the revolution has not yet occurred. Of course, a technological paradigm or device may be said to be revolutionary when it initially appears, but such a remark should be understood as an anticipatory projection into the future. It is an assertion that in the future there will be devices that instantiate the paradigm that meet the conditions of the power stage of a technological revolution.

A technological revolution will have many technological developments within it. Some, perhaps many, of these developments will not be revolutionary under the criteria in the table. They will never reach the power stage. But, some of these embedded technological developments may satisfy the criteria for a technological revolution sufficiently to qualify as subrevolutions within the more general revolution. A *subrevolution* is a technological revolution that is embedded in another. The subrevolution will have a more specific paradigm that is a restricted version of the general paradigm and will have devices that instantiate its more specific paradigm that will be special cases of the more general revolution. The subrevolution will move through the stages of a technological revolution though possibly not at the same times or at the some rate as the more general revolution in which the subrevolution is embedded.

Consider mobile cell phone technology as an example of a subrevolution within the computer revolution. In 1973, Martin Cooper made the first call

on a portable cell phone the size of a brick that was jokingly called 'the brick.'
Few had one or wanted one. Mobile phones gradually became smaller and
were installed as car phones. This had moderate usefulness at least for those
who drove cars and needed to communicate. Today, mobile phones are
small, portable, and highly functional. They are used to take photographs,
text message, play games, and, of course, send and receive phone calls.
Mobile phones outsell landline phones in some nations. Many people in
advanced societies can and do use them. They are thoroughly integrated
into society and are having significant social impact.

The World Wide Web is another example of a subrevolution within the
computer revolution. The concept of the Web was established as a paradigm
of linked and searchable documents with domains of access on the Internet.
But its initial impact on society was marginal. For example, one esoteric,
but not too exciting, early use of the Web in the 1990s was to watch the
level of a coffee pot in a remote location. The World Wide Web was in
the introduction stage. Over the years, as devices, such as browsers and
Web languages improved, the Web became more useful and was recognized
as a place to display and share information. In this permeation stage of
the revolution, courses were established to train people and companies in
setting up their own Web pages. A select number found the Web useful,
but a majority did not. Today, of course, the Web provides a much used
method of exchanging information and conducting business. The Web has
reached the power stage. The devices instantiating the Web paradigm today
support everything from banking to blogging. Having access to the Web and
knowing how to use it are commonplace. The Web is integrated into our
lives, useful for most people, and has significant social impact.

TECHNOLOGICAL REVOLUTIONS AND ETHICS

Technology, particularly revolutionary technology, generates many ethical
problems. Sometimes the problems can be treated easily under extant ethical policies. All things being equal, using a new technology to cheat on
one's taxes is unethical. The fact that new technology is involved does not
alter that. But, because new technology allows us to perform activities in
new ways, situations may arise in which we do not have adequate policies
in place to guide us. We are confronted with *policy vacuums*. We need to
formulate and justify new policies (laws, rules, and customs) for acting in
these new kinds of situations. Sometimes we can anticipate that the use of
the technology will have consequences that are clearly undesirable. As much
as possible, we need to anticipate these consequences and establish policies
that will minimize the deleterious effects of the new technology. At other
times, the subtlety of the situation may escape us at least initially, and we will
find ourselves in a situation of assessing the matter as consequences unfold.
Formulating and justifying new policies is made more complex by the fact

that the concepts that we bring to a situation involving policy vacuums may not provide a unique understanding of the situation. The situation may have analogies with different and competing traditional situations. We find ourselves in a *conceptual muddle* about which way to understand the matter in order to formulate and justify a policy.

An example from information technology will be helpful. Today wireless computing is commonplace. Wi-Fi zones allowing public use are popular, and some have proposed making entire cities Wi-Fi areas. We can sit outside in the sun and use a Wi-Fi arrangement to make connections with a network. This is something we couldn't do before. One might at first believe that it is no different from being hardwired to a network. But is it? If one can sit outside in the sun and connect to the network wirelessly, others, assuming there are no security barriers, can as well. Having others so easily connect was not possible when a wire connection was required. A kind of sport developed called 'wardriving' in which people drive around attempting to connect wirelessly to other people's networks especially if they are not public networks. Is wardriving ethical? A policy vacuum exists at least in cases of private Wi-Fi connections.

As we consider possible policies on wardriving, we begin to realize there is a lack of conceptual clarity about the issue. Wardriving might be regarded as trespassing. After all, apparently the wardriver is invading someone's computer system that is in a private location. Conceptually, this would seem to be a case of trespass. But the wardriver may understand it differently. The electronic transmission is in a public street and the wardriver remains on the public street. He is not entering the dwelling where the computer system is located. Indeed, he may be nowhere nearby.[4] In searching for a new policy, we discover we have a conceptual muddle. We find ourselves torn among different conceptualizations, each of which has some plausibility.

The relationship between resolving conceptual muddles and filling policy vacuums is complex. In some cases, sufficient analogies can be drawn with related concepts and situations so that conceptual confusion is resolved first. In the case of Wi-Fi one might consider various kinds of trespass to determine how similar or dissimilar they are to what occurs in Wi-Fi situations. But resolution through analogies may not be decisive or convincing. Another approach is to consider the consequences of various policies that could fill the vacuum. Some better policies may emerge. In that case, selecting that policy would not only fill the vacuum but also would likely have an effect on clarifying the conceptual muddle. For example, if one could show that allowing people to employ Wi-Fi connections to use other people's unsecured computer systems caused little harm, then tolerance toward wardriving

[4] The distance can be quite large. The Guinness world record for Wi-Fi connections is 310 kilometers or about 192 miles. See http://www.wired.com/news/culture/0,1284,64440,00 .html.

might be adopted as the correct policy, and, conceptually, wardriving would not be considered trespassing. The point is that sometimes a conceptual muddle is resolved first, through analogies or other reasoning, which in turn will influence the selection of a policy. And sometimes the policy is selected first based on analysis of consequences or other justificatory methods, and the conceptual muddle is thereby resolved in reference to the new policy.

Let me summarize my position thus far. I have proposed a tripartite model for understanding open, technological revolutions. What makes the technological change truly revolutionary is its impact on society. The computer/information revolution nicely illustrates this model. Ethical problems can be generated by a technology at any of the three stages, but the number of ethical problems will be greater as the revolution progresses. According to this model more people will be involved, more technology will be used, and, hence, more policy vacuums and conceptual muddles will arise as the revolution advances. Thus, the greater our ethical challenge will be during the last stage of the revolution.

This argument is forceful for computing, in part, because we can see the dramatic effects computing has had and the ethical problems it has raised. But what of the emerging technologies? How do we know they will follow the model, be revolutionary, and create an increasing number of ethical problems?

THREE RAPIDLY DEVELOPING TECHNOLOGIES

Genetic technology, nanotechnology, and neurotechnology are three rapidly developing technological movements. Each of these has been progressing for awhile. None of the three has progressed as far as computer technology in terms of its integration and impact on society. Of the three, genetic technology is perhaps furthest along. Genetic testing of patients is common. In vitro fertilization is widely used. Many foods are engineered and more and more animals are being cloned. Techniques for using DNA to establish the guilt of criminals or to free the falsely imprisoned or to identify natural disaster victims are used routinely. Stem cell research is ongoing and promises inroads against heretofore devastating medical conditions. Genetic technology has permeated our culture, but it falls short of the power stage.

Nanotechnology produces materials through manipulation and self-assembly of components at the nanometer scale. Progress has been made in terms of the production of items such as nanotubes, protective films, and biosensors. Some of these products currently have practical benefits, and others still being developed are not far from having practical applications. Some researchers expect that in the future some medical testing will be done through ingested nanobiosensors that can detect items such as blood type, bacteria, viruses, antibodies, DNA, drugs, or pesticides. The fulfillment of the overall promise of nanotechnology in terms of new products is a considerable distance from the power stage.

Similarly, neurotechnology has been evolving with the developments of various brain scanning devices and pharmaceutical treatment techniques. We know much about brain functioning. Although brain surgery has been common for a long time, neurotechnology still remains somewhat far from the power stage of a technological revolution.

Although these technologies are not fully developed, it is not unreasonable to expect that they will continue along a revolutionary path and bring with them an increasing cluster of new ethical issues. First, all of the technologies possess an essential feature of revolutionary technology, namely they are propelled in vision and in practice by an important generic capability – all of these technologies have potential malleability over a large domain. Consider computing technology again as an example. Computing has this generic capability in terms of logic malleability. Computers are logically malleable machines in that they can be shaped to do any task that one can design, train, or evolve them to do. Syntactically, computers are logically malleable in terms of the number and variety of logical states and operations. Semantically, computers are logically malleable in that the states and operations of a computer can be taken to represent anything we wish. Because computers given this logical malleability are universal tools, it should not be surprising that they are widely used, highly integrated into society, and have had an enormous impact.

Each of the developing technologies mentioned has a similar generic capability. Each offers some important form of malleability. Genetic technology has the feature of life malleability. Genetics provides the basis for generating life forms on our planet. If this potential can be mastered, then genetic diseases can be cured, and resistance to nongenetic diseases can be enhanced. Both the quantity and quality of our lives can be improved. Clearly a significant impact on society would take place. Indeed, life malleability offers the possibility of enhancements of current forms of life, the creation of extinct forms, and the creation of forms that have never existed.

Nanotechnology has the generic capability of material malleability. The historical vision of nanotechnology has been that in principle material structures of any sort can be created through the manipulation of atomic and molecular parts, as long the laws of nature are not disobeyed. If we are clever and arrange the ingredients to self-assemble, we can create them in large quantities. Some researchers suggest that nanostructures could assemble other nanostructures or could self-replicate. How possible all of this is remains an open empirical question. But if the pursuit comes to fruition, then machines that produced many of the objects we desire, but which are difficult to obtain, might be a possibility. In this event, nanotechnology would have a truly significant impact on society.

Neurotechnology has the potential generic capability of mind malleability. If minds are brains and neurotechnology develops far enough to construct and manipulate brains, neurotechnology could be the most revolutionary of all of the technologies. Minds could be altered, improved, and extended in ways that would be difficult for our minds to comprehend.

All of these technologies are grounded in visions of enormous general capacities to manipulate reality as summarized by the following table:

Information technology	Logic malleability
Genetic technology	Life malleability
Nanotechnology	Material malleability
Neurotechnology	Mind malleability

All of these technologies are conducted under paradigms suggesting that they hold great power over and control of the natural world. Each could bring about worlds unlike those we have ever experienced.

The second reason, in addition to malleability, that these areas are good candidates for being revolutionary technology, is that these technologies tend to converge. The technologies reinforce and support each other. Each of them is an enabling technology. There are at least three ways that these technologies converge. In one kind of convergence, a technology serves us a *tool* to assist another technology. An excellent example of this is illustrated by the human genome project. The purpose of the project was to discover the sequences of the three billion chemical base pairs that make up human DNA and identify the 20,000–25,000 genes in human DNA. All of this was accomplished ahead of schedule because of enabling tools – computers that analyzed the data and robots that manipulated the samples. Because the human genome is now known along with other genomes, genetic technology has been catapulted ahead. Some believe that genetic technology in turn can be used as an enabling tool in nanotechnology. Because DNA serves as a way to order the arrangement of molecules in nature, its sequencing capability might be adapted by nanotechnologists to organize and orient the construction of nanostructures out of molecules attached to the DNA.

Convergence of technology may also occur with one technology serving as a *component* of another. When computer chips are implanted in brains to assist paralyzed patients to act, or to relieve tremors, or to restore vision, the convergence of technologies produces miraculous outcomes through the interaction of neurology and computing. Finally, convergence may occur by taking aspects of another technology as a *model*. Thus, some computing technology employs connectionist architecture that models network activity on neural connectivity, and other computing technology employs genetic algorithms that simulate evolutionary processes to produce results that are more fit for doing particular jobs.

Thus, convergence may involve one technology enabling another technology as a tool, as a component, or as a model. The malleability and convergence of these developing technologies make revolutionary outcomes likely. Revolutionary outcomes make ethical considerations ever more important.

BETTER ETHICS

The number of ethical issues that arise tracks the development of a technological revolution. In the introduction stage, there are few users and limited uses of the technology. This is not to suggest that no ethical problems occur, only that they are fewer in number. One of the important ethical issues during the introduction stage of the computer revolution was whether a central government database for all U.S. citizens should be created. It would have made government more efficient in distributing services, but it would have made individual privacy more vulnerable. The decision was made not to create it. During the permeation stage of a technological revolution, the number of users and uses grows. The technology is more integrated into society. More ethical issues should be expected. In the computer revolution, an increasing number of personal computers and computer applications were purchased. Indeed, because more people owned computers and could share files, ethical issues involving property and privacy were more numerous and acute. During the power stage, many people use the technology. The technology has a significant social impact that leads to an increased number of ethical issues. During the power stage of the computer revolution, the number of ethical issues has increased over the number in the permeation stage. Almost every day, papers report on new ethical problems or dilemmas created by computer technology. For example, identity theft by computer is more easily accomplished in today's highly networked world than it was in the days of freestanding personal computers let alone in the days of isolated large mainframes. Or, as another example, in these days of the easily accessible and powerful Web, the solicitation of children by child molesters has increased. In light of this conjecture about the relationship between the stages of a technological revolution and the increase of ethical problems, I will propose the following hypothesis:

Moor's Law: As technological revolutions increase their social impact, ethical problems increase.

This phenomenon happens not simply because an increasing number of people are affected by the technology but because inevitably revolutionary technology will provide numerous novel opportunities for action for which well thought out ethical policies will not have been developed.

From the computer/information revolution alone we can expect an increase in ethical problems. But other major technologies are afoot that have the promise to be revolutionary on the model of an open revolution. Although genetic technology, nanotechnology, and neurotechnology are not yet fully developed in this regard, they have two features that suggest that such development is likely. First, each is driven by a conception of a general capability of the field: a malleability. Just as computing is based on logic malleability, genetic technology is based on life malleability, nanotechnology is based on material malleability, and neurotechnology is based on mental malleability. They offer us the capabilites of building new bodies, new environments, and even new minds. Such fundamental capabilities are very likely to be funded, to be developed, and to have significant social impact. Second, the emerging technologies are converging. They enable each other as tools, as components, and as models. This convergence will move all these technologies forward in a revolutionary path. Thus, we can expect an increase in ethical issues in the future as the technologies mature.

The ethical issues that we will confront will not only come in increasing numbers but will come packaged in terms of complex technology. Such ethical issues will require a considerable effort to be understood as well as a considerable effort to formulate and justify good ethical policies. This will not be ethics as usual. People who both understand the technologies and are knowledgeable about ethics are in short supply just as the need is expanding.

Consider too that many of the emerging technologies not only affect the social world but affect us as functioning individuals. We normally think of technology as providing a set of tools for doing things in the world. But with these potentially revolutionary technologies, we ourselves will be changed. Computer chips and nanostructures implanted in us, along with genetic and neurological alterations, will make us different creatures – creatures that may understand the world in new ways and perhaps analyze ethical issues differently.

Assuming that emerging technologies are destined to be revolutionary technologies and assuming that the ethical ramifications of this will be significant, what improvements could we make in our approach to ethics that would help us? Let me suggest three ways that would improve our ethical approach to technology. First, we need realistically to take into account that ethics is an ongoing and dynamic enterprise. When new technologies appear, there is a commendable concern to do all of the ethics first, or, as sometimes suggested, place a moratorium on technological development until ethics catches up (Joy 2000). Such proposals are better than saving ethics until the end after the damage is done. But the ethics first approach, with or without a moratorium, has limitations. We can foresee only so far into the future, even if we were to cease technological development. We cannot anticipate every ethical issue that will arise from the developing technology. Because of the limitations of human cognitive systems, our ethical understanding of developing technology will never be complete. Nevertheless, we can do much to unpack the potential consequences of new technology. We have to do as much as we can while realizing applied ethics is a dynamic enterprise that continually requires reassessment of the situation (Moor and Weckert 2004). Like advice given to a driver in a foreign land, constant vigilance is the only sensible approach.

The second improvement that would make ethics better would be establishing better collaborations among ethicists, scientists, social scientists, and technologists. We need a multidisciplinary approach.[5] Ethicists need to be informed about the nature of the technology and to press for an empirical basis for what is and what is not a likely consequence of its development and use. Scientists and technologists need to confront considerations raised by ethicists and social scientists, considerations that may affect aspects of the next grant application or risky technological development.

The third improvement that would make ethics better would be to develop more sophisticated ethical analyses. Ethical theories themselves are often simplistic and do not give much guidance to particular situations. Often the alternative is to do technological assessment in terms of cost–benefit analysis. This approach too easily invites evaluation in terms of money while ignoring or discounting moral values that are difficult to represent or translate into monetary terms.

At the very least we need to do more to be more proactive and less reactive in doing ethics. We need to learn about the technology as it is developing and to project and assess possible consequences of its various applications. Only if we see the potential revolutions coming, will we be motivated and prepared to decide which technologies to adopt and how to use them. Otherwise, we leave ourselves vulnerable to a tsunami of technological change.[6]

References

Brey, P. 2000. Method in Computer Ethics: Towards a Multi-Level Interdisciplinary Approach. *Ethics and Information Technology,* 2, 2, 125–129.

Joy, P. 2000. Why the Future Doesn't Need Us. *Wired 8,*4. Retrieved July 15 2007 from: http://www.wired.com/wired/archive/8.04/joy.html.

Moor, J. H. 2001. The Future of Computer Ethics: You Ain't Seen Nothin' Yet! *Ethics and Information Technology,* 3, 2, 89–91.

Moor, J. H. 1985. What Is Computer Ethics? *Metaphilosophy, 16,* 4, 266–275.

Moor, J. H. and Weckert, J. 2004. Nanoethics: Assessing the Nanoscale from an Ethical Point of View, in D. Baird, A. Nordmann, and J. Schummer (Eds.), *Discovering the Nanoscale.* Amsterdam: IOS Press, pp. 301–310.

Schumpeter, J. A. 1952. *Capitalism, Socialism, and Democracy* (4th ed.). London: George Allen & Unwin Ltd.

[5] Nicely elaborated in Brey (2000).

[6] A version of this chapter was given as the International Society of Ethics and Information Technology (INSEIT) presidential address at the 2005 Computer Ethics: Philosophical Enquiry (CEPE) Conference at University of Twente. I am indebted to many for helpful comments and particularly to Philip Brey, Luciano Floridi, Herman Tavani, and John Weckert.

3

Information Ethics: Its Nature and Scope

Luciano Floridi

The world of the future will be an ever more demanding struggle against the limitations of our intelligence, not a comfortable hammock in which we can lie down to be waited upon by our robot slaves.

(Wiener 1964, p. 69)

1. A UNIFIED APPROACH TO INFORMATION ETHICS

In recent years, information ethics (IE) has come to mean different things to different researchers working in a variety of disciplines, including computer ethics, business ethics, medical ethics, computer science, the philosophy of information, social epistemology, and library and information science. Perhaps this Babel was always going to be inevitable, given the novelty of the field and the multifarious nature of the concept of information itself.[1] It is certainly unfortunate, for it has generated some confusion about the specific *nature* and *scope* of IE. The problem, however, is not irremediable, for a unified approach can help to explain and relate the main senses in which IE has been discussed in the literature. The approach is best introduced schematically and by focusing our attention on a moral agent *A*.

Suppose *A* is interested in pursuing whatever she considers her best course of action, given her predicament. We shall assume that *A*'s evaluations and actions have *some* moral value, but no specific value needs to be introduced. Intuitively, *A* can use some information (information as a *resource*) to generate some other information (information as a *product*) and in so doing affect her informational environment (information as *target*). Now, since the appearance of the first works in the 1980s,[2] information ethics has been claimed to be the study of moral issues arising from one or another of these three distinct 'information arrows' (see Figure 3.1). This, in

[1] On the various senses in which 'information' may be understood, see Floridi (2004).
[2] An early review is provided by Smith (1996).

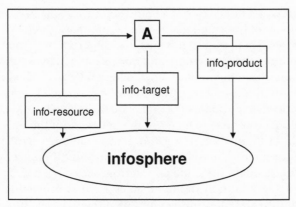

FIGURE 3.1. The 'External' R(esource) P(roduct) T(arget) Model.

turn, has paved the way to a fruitless compartmentalization and false dilemmas, with researchers either ignoring the wider scope of IE, or arguing as if only one 'arrow' and its corresponding microethics (that is a practical, field-dependent, applied, and professional ethics) provided *the* right approach to IE. The limits of such narrowly constructed interpretations of IE become evident once we look at each 'informational arrow' more closely.

1.1. Information-as-a-Resource Ethics

Consider first the crucial role played by information as a *resource* for *A*'s moral evaluations and actions. Moral evaluations and actions have an epistemic component, because *A* may be expected to proceed 'to the best of her information', that is, *A* may be expected to avail herself of whatever information she can muster, in order to reach (better) conclusions about what can and ought to be done in some given circumstances.

Socrates already argued that a moral agent is naturally interested in gaining as much valuable information as the circumstances require, and that a well-informed agent is more likely to do the right thing. The ensuing 'ethical intellectualism' analyses evil and morally wrong behaviour as the outcome of deficient information. Conversely, *A*'s *moral responsibility* tends to be directly proportional to *A*'s degree of information: any decrease in the latter usually corresponds to a decrease in the former. This is the sense in which information occurs in the guise of judicial evidence. It is also the sense in which one speaks of *A*'s informed decision, informed consent, or well-informed participation. In Christian ethics, even the worst sins can be forgiven in the light of the sinner's insufficient information, as a counterfactual evaluation is possible: had *A* been properly informed, *A* would have acted differently and, hence, would not have sinned (Luke 23:44). In a secular context, Oedipus and Macbeth remind us how the (inadvertent) mismanagement of informational resources may have tragic consequences.

From a *resource* perspective, it seems that the machine of moral thinking and behaviour needs information, and quite a lot of it, to function properly. However, even within the limited scope adopted by an analysis based solely on information as a resource, care should be exercised lest all ethical discourse is reduced to the nuances of higher quantity, quality, and intelligibility of informational resources. The more the better is not the only, nor always the best rule of thumb. For the withdrawal (sometimes explicit and conscious) of information can often make a significant difference. *A* may need to lack (or intentionally preclude herself from accessing) some information in order to achieve morally desirable goals, such as protecting anonymity, enhancing fair treatment or implementing unbiased evaluation. Famously, Rawls' 'veil of ignorance' exploits precisely this aspect of information-as-a-resource ethics, in order to develop an impartial approach to justice (Rawls 1999). Being informed is not always a blessing and might even be morally wrong or dangerous.

Whether the presence (quantitative and qualitative) or the absence (total) of information-as-a-resource is in question, it is obvious that there is a perfectly reasonable sense[3] in which information ethics may be described as the study of the moral issues arising from 'the triple A': *availability, accessibility*, and *accuracy* of informational resources, independently of their format, kind and physical support. Rawls' position has been already mentioned. Other examples of issues in IE, understood as an information-as-resource ethics, are the so-called *digital divide*, the problem of *infoglut* and the analysis of the *reliability* and *trustworthiness* of information sources (Floridi 1995).

1.2. Information-as-a-Product Ethics

A second but closely related sense in which information plays an important moral role is as a *product* of *A*'s moral evaluations and actions. *A* is not only an information consumer but also an information producer, who may be subject to constraints while being able to take advantage of opportunities. Both constraints and opportunities call for an ethical analysis. Thus, IE, understood as information-as-a-product ethics, may cover moral issues arising, for example, in the context of *accountability, liability, libel legislation, testimony, plagiarism, advertising, propaganda, misinformation*, and, more generally,

[3] One may recognise in this approach to information ethics a position broadly defended by van den Hoven (1995) and more recently by Mathiesen (2004), who criticises Floridi (1999a) and is in turn criticised by Mather (2004). Whereas van den Hoven purports to present his approach to IE as an enriching perspective contributing to the debate, Mathiesen means to present her view, restricted to the informational needs and states of the moral agent, as the only correct interpretation of IE. Her position is thus undermined by the problems affecting any microethical interpretation of IE, as Mather well argues.

of *pragmatic rules of communication* à la Grice. Kant's analysis of the immorality of *lying* is one of the best-known case studies in the philosophical literature concerning this kind of information ethics. The boy crying wolf, Iago misleading Othello, or Cassandra and Laocoon pointlessly warning the Trojans against the Greeks' wooden horse, remind us how the ineffective management of informational products may have tragic consequences.

1.3. Information-as-a-Target Ethics

Independently of *A*'s information input (information resource) and output (information product), there is a third sense in which information may be subject to ethical analysis, namely when *A*'s moral evaluations and actions affect the informational environment. Think, for example, of *A*'s respect for, or breach of, someone's information *privacy* or *confidentiality*. *Hacking*, understood as the unauthorised access to an information system (usually computerised) is another good example. It is not uncommon to mistake it for a problem to be discussed within the conceptual frame of an ethics of information resources. This misclassification allows the hacker to defend his position by arguing that no use of, let alone misuse of, the accessed information has been made. Yet, hacking, properly understood, is a form of breach of privacy. What is in question is not what *A* does with the information, which has been accessed without authorisation, but what it means for an informational environment to be accessed by *A* without authorisation. So the analysis of hacking belongs to an information-as-target ethics. Other issues here include *security, vandalism* (from the burning of libraries and books to the dissemination of viruses), *piracy, intellectual property, open source, freedom of expression, censorship, filtering,* and *contents control.* Mill's analysis 'Of the Liberty of Thought and Discussion' is a classic of IE interpreted as information-as-target ethics. Juliet, simulating her death, and Hamlet, re-enacting his father's homicide, show how the risky management of one's informational environment may have tragic consequences.

1.4. The Limits of Any Microethical Approach to Information Ethics

At the end of this overview, it seems that the Resource Product Target (RPT) model, summarised in Figure 3.1, may help one to get some initial orientation in the multiplicity of issues belonging to different interpretations of information ethics. The model is also useful to explain why any technology that radically modifies the 'life of information' is going to have profound implications for any moral agent. Information and communication technologies (ICT), by transforming, in a profound way, the informational context in which moral issues arise, not only add interesting new dimensions to old problems, but lead us to rethink, methodologically, the very grounds on which our ethical positions are based.

At the same time, the model rectifies the excessive emphasis placed on specific technologies (this happens most notably in *computer ethics*), by concentrating on the more fundamental phenomenon of information in all its variety and long tradition. This was Wiener's position,[4] and I have argued (Floridi 1999a; Floridi and Sanders 2002) that the various difficulties encountered in the philosophical foundations of computer ethics are connected to the fact that computer ethics have not yet been recognised as primarily environmental ethics whose main concern is (or should be) the ecological management and well-being of the *infosphere*. Despite these advantages, however, the RPT model can still be criticised for being inadequate, in two respects:

1. On the one hand, the model is still too simplistic. Arguably, several important issues belong *mainly but not only* to the analysis of just one 'informational arrow'. A few examples well illustrate the problem: someone's testimony (e.g., Iago's) is someone else's trustworthy information (i.e., Othello's); A's responsibility may be determined by the information A holds ('apostle' means 'messenger' in Greek), but it may also concern the information A issues (e.g., Judas' kiss); censorship affects A, both as a user and as a producer of information; misinformation (i.e., the deliberate production and distribution of misleading information) is an ethical problem that concerns all three 'informational arrows'; freedom of speech also affects the availability of offensive content (e.g., child pornography, violent content and socially, politically, or religiously disrespectful statements) that might be morally questionable and should not circulate.
2. On the other hand, the model is insufficiently inclusive. There are many important issues that cannot easily be placed on the map at all, for they really emerge from, or supervene on, the interactions among the 'informational arrows'. Two significant examples may suffice: the 'panopticon' or 'big brother', that is, the problem of *monitoring and controlling* anything that might concern A; and the debate about information *ownership* (including copyright and patents legislation), which affects both users and producers while shaping their informational environment.

So the criticism is fair. The RPT model is indeed inadequate. Yet, *why* it is inadequate is a different matter. The tripartite analysis just provided is unsatisfactory, despite its partial usefulness, precisely because any interpretation of information ethics based on only one of the 'informational arrows' is bound to be too reductive. As the examples I have mentioned emphasize, supporters of narrowly constructed interpretations of information ethics as

---

[4] The classic reference here is to Wiener (1950, 1954). Bynum (2001) has convincingly argued that Wiener should be considered the 'father' of information ethics.

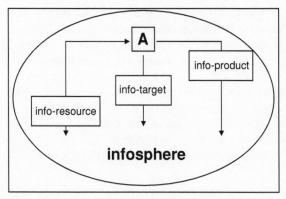

FIGURE 3.2. The 'Internal' R(esource) P(roduct) T(arget) Model.

a *microethics* are faced by the problem of being unable to cope with a wide variety of relevant issues, which remain either uncovered or inexplicable. In other words, the model shows that idiosyncratic versions of IE, which privilege only some limited aspects of the information cycle, are unsatisfactory. We should not use the model to attempt to pigeonhole problems neatly, which is impossible. We should rather exploit it as a useful scheme to be superseded, in view of a more encompassing approach to IE as a *macroethics*, that is, a theoretical, field-independent, applicable ethics. Philosophers will recognise here a Wittgensteinian ladder.

In order to climb up on, and then throw away, any narrowly constructed conception of information ethics, a more encompassing approach to IE needs to

1. bring together the three 'informational arrows';
2. consider the whole information cycle (including creation, elaboration, distribution, storage, protection, usage and possible destruction); and
3. analyse informationally all entities involved (including the moral agent *A*) and their changes, actions and interactions, by treating them not apart from, but as part of the informational environment, or *infosphere*, to which they belong as informational systems themselves (see Figure 3.2).

Whereas steps (i) and (ii) do not pose particular problems and may be shared by other approaches to IE, step (iii) is crucial but involves a shift in the conception of 'information' at stake. Instead of limiting the analysis to (veridical) semantic contents – as any narrower interpretation of IE as a microethics inevitably does – an ecological approach to information ethics looks at information from an object-oriented perspective and treats it as entity. In other words, we move from a (broadly constructed) epistemological conception of information ethics to one which is typically ontological.

A simple analogy may help to introduce this new perspective.[5] Imagine looking at the whole universe from a chemical *level of abstraction* (I shall return to this in the next section). Every entity and process will satisfy a certain chemical description. An agent *A*, for example, will be 70 percent water and 30 percent something else. Now consider an informational level of abstraction. The same entities will be described as clusters of data (i.e., as informational objects). More precisely, *A* (like any other entity) will be a discrete, self-contained, encapsulated package containing

1. the appropriate data structures, which constitute the nature of the entity in question (i.e., the state of the object, its unique identity and its attributes); and
2. a collection of operations, functions, or procedures, which are activated by various interactions or stimuli (i.e., messages received from other objects or changes within itself) and correspondingly define how the object behaves or reacts to them.

At this level of abstraction, informational systems as such, rather than just living systems in general, are raised to the role of agents and patients of any action, with environmental processes, changes and interactions equally described informationally.

Understanding the *nature* of IE ontologically, rather than epistemologically, modifies the interpretation of the *scope* of IE. Not only can an ecological IE gain a global view of the whole life-cycle of information, thus overcoming the limits of other microethical approaches, but it can also claim a role as a macroethics, that is, as an ethics that concerns the whole realm of reality. This is what we shall see in the next section.

2. INFORMATION ETHICS AS MACROETHICS

This section provides a quick and accessible overview of information ethics understood as a macroethics (henceforth, simply *information ethics*). For reasons of space, I will neither attempt to summarise the specific arguments, relevant evidence, and detailed analyses required to flesh out the ecological approach to IE, nor try to unfold its many philosophical implications. The goal is rather to provide a general flavour of the theory.

The section is divided into two parts. The first consists of six questions and answers that introduce IE. The second consists of six objections and replies that I hope will dispel some common misunderstandings concerning IE.

---

[5] For a detailed analysis and defence of an object-oriented modelling of informational entities, see Floridi (1999a, 2003) and Floridi and Sanders (2004b).

2.1. What is IE?

IE is an *ontocentric, patient-oriented, ecological* macroethics (Floridi 1999a). An intuitive way to unpack this answer is by comparing IE to other environmental approaches.

Biocentric ethics usually grounds its analysis of the moral standing of bioentities and ecosystems on the intrinsic worthiness of *life* and the intrinsically negative value of *suffering*. It seeks to develop a patient-oriented ethics in which the 'patient' may be not only a human being, but also any form of life. Indeed, land ethics extends the concept of patient to any component of the environment, thus coming close to the approach defended by information ethics.[6] Any form of life is deemed to enjoy some essential proprieties or moral interests that deserve and demand to be respected, at least minimally if not absolutely, that is, in a possibly overridable sense, when contrasted with other interests. So biocentric ethics argues that the nature and well-being of the patient of any action constitute (at least partly) its moral standing and that this makes important claims on the interacting agent, claims that, in principle, ought to contribute to the guidance of the agent's ethical decisions and the constraint of the agent's moral behaviour. The 'receiver' of the action is placed at the core of the ethical discourse, as a centre of moral concern, while the 'transmitter' of any moral action is moved to its periphery.

Substitute now 'life' with 'existence', and it should become clear what IE amounts to. IE is an ecological ethics that replaces *biocentrism* with *ontocentrism*. IE suggests that there is something even more elemental than life, namely *being* – that is, the existence and flourishing of all entities and their global environment – and something more fundamental than suffering, namely *entropy*. Entropy is most emphatically *not* the physicists' concept of thermodynamic entropy. Entropy here refers to any kind of *destruction* or *corruption* of informational objects (mind, not of information), that is, any form of impoverishment of *being*, including *nothingness*, to phrase it more metaphysically.[7]

---

[6] Rowlands (2000), for example, has recently proposed an interesting approach to environmental ethics in terms of naturalization of *semantic* information. According to Rowlands: 'There is value in the environment. This value consists in a certain sort of information, information that exists in the relation between affordances of the environment and their indices. This information exists independently of . . . sentient creatures. . . . The information is *there*. It is in the world. What makes this information value, however, is the fact that it is valued by valuing creatures [because of evolutionary reasons], or that it would be valued by valuing creatures if there were any around' (p. 153).

[7] *Destruction* is to be understood as the complete annihilation of the object in question, which ceases to exist; compare this to the process of 'erasing' an entity irrevocably. *Corruption* is to be understood as a form of pollution or depletion of some of the properties of the object, which ceases to exist as that object and begins to exist as a different object minus the properties that have been corrupted or eliminated. This may be compared to a process degrading the integrity of the object in question.

IE then provides a common vocabulary to understand the whole realm of *being* through an informational *level of abstraction* (see Section 2.2). IE holds that *being/information* has an intrinsic worthiness. It substantiates this position by recognising that any informational entity has a *Spinozian* right to persist in its own status, and a *Constructionist* right to flourish, that is, a right to improve and enrich its existence and essence. As a consequence of such 'rights', IE evaluates the duty of any moral agent in terms of contribution to the growth of the *infosphere* (see Sections 2.5 and 2.6) and any process, action, or event that negatively affects the whole infosphere – not just an informational entity – as an increase in its level of entropy and hence an instance of evil (Floridi and Sanders 1999, 2001; Floridi 2003).

In IE, the ethical discourse concerns any entity, understood informationally, that is, not only all persons, their cultivation, well-being, and social interactions, not only animals, plants, and their proper natural life, but also anything that exists, from paintings and books to stars and stones – anything that may or will exist, such as future generations – and anything that was but is no more, such as our ancestors or old civilizations. Indeed, according to IE, even ideal, intangible, or intellectual objects can have a minimal degree of moral value, no matter how humble, and so be entitled to some respect. UNESCO, for example, recognises this in its protection of 'masterpieces of the oral and intangible heritage of humanity' (http://www.unesco.org/culture/heritage/intangible/) by attributing them an intrinsic worth.

IE is impartial and universal because it brings to ultimate completion the process of enlargement of the concept of what may count as a centre of a (no matter how minimal) moral claim, which now includes every instance of *being* understood informationally (see Section 2.4), no matter whether it is physically implemented or not. In this respect, IE holds that every entity, as an expression of *being*, has a dignity, constituted by its mode of existence and essence (the collection of all the elementary proprieties that constitute it for what it is), which deserve to be respected (at least in a minimal and overridable sense) and, hence, place moral claims on the interacting agent and ought to contribute to the constraint and guidance of his ethical decisions and behaviour. This ontological equality principle means that any form of reality (any instance of *information/being*), simply for the fact of *being* what it is, enjoys a minimal, initial, overridable, equal right to exist and develop in a way that is appropriate to its nature. In the history of philosophy, this view can already be found advocated by Stoic and Neoplatonic philosophers.

The conscious recognition of the ontological equality principle presupposes a disinterested judgment of the moral situation from an objective perspective, that is, a perspective as nonanthropocentric as possible. Moral behaviour is less likely without this epistemic virtue. The application of the ontological equality principle is achieved, whenever actions are impartial, universal, and caring.

The crucial importance of the radical change in ontological perspective cannot be overestimated. Bioethics and environmental ethics fail to achieve a level of complete impartiality, because they are still biased against what is inanimate, lifeless, intangible, or abstract. (Even land ethics is biased against technology and artefacts, for example.) From their perspective, only what is intuitively alive deserves to be considered as a proper centre of moral claims, no matter how minimal, so a whole universe escapes their attention. Now, this is precisely the fundamental limit overcome by IE, which further lowers the minimal condition that needs to be satisfied, in order to qualify as a centre of moral concern, to the common factor shared by any entity, namely its informational state. And, because any form of *being* is in any case also a coherent body of information, to say that IE is infocentric is tantamount to interpreting it, correctly, as an ontocentric theory.

2.2. What is a Level of Abstraction?

The *method of abstraction* has been formalised in Floridi and Sanders (2004a, 2004c). The terminology has been influenced by an area of computer science, called *formal methods*, in which discrete mathematics is used to specify and analyse the behaviour of information systems. Despite that heritage, the idea is not at all technical and, for the purposes of this paper, no mathematics is required, for only the basic idea will be outlined.

Let us begin with an everyday example. Suppose we join Anne (A), Ben (B), and Carole (C) in the middle of a conversation. Anne is a collector and potential buyer; Ben tinkers in his spare time; and Carole is an economist. We do not know the object of their conversation, but we are able to hear this much:

A. Anne observes that it (whatever 'it' is) has an antitheft device installed, is kept garaged when not in use, and has had only a single owner;
B. Ben observes that its engine is not the original one, that its body has been recently repainted, but that all leather parts are very worn;
C. Carole observes that the old engine consumed too much, that it has a stable market value, but that its spare parts are expensive.

The participants view the object under discussion according to their own interests, which constitute their conceptual interfaces or, more precisely, their own *levels of abstraction* (LoA). They may be talking about a car, or a motorcycle or even a plane, because any of these three systems would satisfy descriptions A, B, and C. Whatever the reference is, it provides the source of information and is called the *system*. Each LoA (imagine a computer interface) an analysis of the system possible, the result of which is called a *model* of the system (see Figure 3.3). For example, one might say that Anne's LoA matches that of an owner, Ben's that of a mechanic, and Carole's that

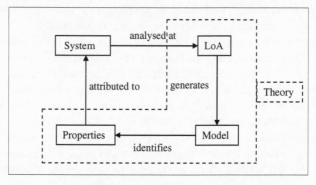

FIGURE 3.3. The scheme of a theory.

of an insurer. Evidently a system may be described at a range of LoAs and so can have a range of models.

A LoA can now be defined as a finite but nonempty set of *observables*, which are expected to be the building blocks in a theory characterised by their very choice. Because the systems investigated may be entirely abstract or fictional, the term 'observable' should not be confused here with 'empirically perceivable'. An *observable* is just an *interpreted typed variable*, that is, a typed variable together with a statement of feature of the system under consideration that it stands for. An interface (called a *gradient of abstractions*) consists of a collection of LoAs. An interface is used in analysing some system from varying points of view or at varying LoAs. In the example, Anne's LoA might consist of *observables* for security, method of storage, and owner history; Ben's might consist of observables for engine condition, external body condition, and internal condition; and Carole's might consist of observables for running cost, market value, and maintenance cost. The *gradient of abstraction* might consist, for the purposes of the discussion, of the set of all three LoAs.

The method of abstraction allows the analysis of systems by means of models developed at specific gradients of abstractions. In the example, the LoAs happen to be disjoint but in general they need not be. A particularly important case is that in which one LoA includes another. Suppose, for example, that Delia (D) joins the discussion and analyses the system using a LoA that includes those of Anne and Carole plus some other observables. Let's say that Delia's LoA matches that of a buyer. Then Delia's LoA is said to be more concrete, or finely grained or lower, than Anne's and Carole's, which are said to be more abstract, or more coarsely grained or higher; for Anne's or Carole's LoA abstract some observables which are still 'visible' at Delia's LoA. Basically, not only has Delia all the information about the system that Anne and Carole might have, she also has a certain amount of information that is unavailable to either of them.

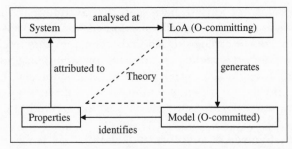

FIGURE 3.4. The SLMS scheme with ontological commitment.

It is important to stress that LoAs can be nested, disjoined, or overlapping and need not be hierarchically related, or ordered in some scale of priority, or support some syntactic compositionality (the molecular is made by more atomic components).

We can now use the method of abstraction and the concept of LoA to make explicit the ontological commitment of a theory, in the following way.

A theory comprises at least a LoA and a model. The LoA allows the theory to analyse the system under analysis and to elaborate a model that identifies some properties of the system at the given LoA (see Figure 3.3). The ontological commitment of a theory can be clearly understood by distinguishing between a *committing* and a *committed* component, within the scheme.

A theory commits itself ontologically by opting for a specific LoA. Compare this to the case in which one has chosen a specific kind of car (say a Volkswagen Polo) but has not bought one yet. However, a theory is ontologically committed in full by its model, which is therefore the bearer of the specific commitment. The analogy here is with the specific car one has actually bought (that red, four-wheeled, etc. specific object in the car park that one owns). To summarise, by adopting a LoA a theory commits itself to the existence of certain types of objects, the types constituting the LoA (by deciding to buy a Volkswagen Polo one shows one's commitment to the existence of that kind of car), while by adopting the ensuing models the theory commits itself to the corresponding tokens (by buying that particular vehicle, which is a physical token of the type Volkswagen Polo, one commits oneself to that token, for example, one has to insure it). Figure 3.4 summarizes this distinction. By making explicit the ontological commitment of a theory, it is clear that the method of abstraction plays an absolutely crucial role in ethics. For example, different theories may adopt androcentric, anthropocentric, biocentric, or ontocentric LoAs, even if this is often left implicit. IE is committed to a LoA that interprets reality – that is, any system – informationally. The resulting model consists of informational objects and processes.

In the previous section, we have seen that an informational LoA has many advantages over a biological one, adopted by other forms of environmental ethics. Here it can be stressed that, when any other level of analysis becomes irrelevant, IE's higher LoA can still provide the agent with some minimal normative guidance. That is, when, for example, even land ethics fails to take into account the moral value of 'what there is', IE still has the conceptual resources to assess the moral situation and indicate a course of action.

A further advantage of an informational-ontic LoA is that it allows the adoption of a unified model for the analysis of the three arrows and their environment in the RPT model. In particular, this means gaining a more precise and accurate understanding of what can count as a moral agent and as a moral patient, as we shall see in the next two sections.

2.3. What Counts As a Moral Agent, According to IE?

A moral agent is an *interactive, autonomous*, and *adaptable transition system* that can perform *morally qualifiable actions* (Floridi and Sanders 2004b). As usual, the definition requires some explanations.

First, we need to understand what a *transition system* is. Let us agree that a system is characterised, at a given LoA, by the properties it satisfies at that LoA. We are interested in systems that change, which means that some of those properties change value. A changing system has its evolution captured, at a given LoA and any instant, by the values of its attributes. Thus, an entity can be thought of as having states, determined by the value of the properties that hold at any instant of its evolution. For then, any change in the entity corresponds to a state change and vice versa. This conceptual approach allows us to view any entity as having states. The lower the LoA, the more detailed the observed changes and the greater the number of state components required to capture the change. Each change corresponds to a transition from one state to another. Note that a transition may be nondeterministic. Indeed, it will typically be the case that the LoA under consideration abstracts the observables required to make the transition deterministic. As a result, the transition might lead from a given initial state to one of several possible subsequent states. According to this view, the entity becomes a transition system. For example, the system being discussed by Anne in the previous section might be imbued with state components for location, depending on whether it is in use, whether it is turned on, whether the antitheft device is engaged, and is dependent upon the history of its owners, and its energy consumption. The operation of garaging the object might take as input a driver and have the effect of placing the object in the garage with the engine off and the antitheft device engaged, leaving the history of owners unchanged and outputting a certain amount of energy. The 'in-use' state component could nondeterministically take either value, depending on the particular instantiation of the transition (perhaps the object is not in use; it is being garaged for the night; or perhaps the driver is listening to the cricket game on its radio in the solitude of the garage). The precise definition depends on the LoA. With the explicit assumption that the system under consideration forms a transition system, we are now ready to apply the method of abstraction to the analysis of agenthood.

A transition system is *interactive* when the system and its environment (can) act upon each other. Typical examples include input or output of a value, or simultaneous engagement of an action by both agent and patient – for example gravitational force between bodies.

A transition system is *autonomous* when the system is able to change state without direct response to interaction, that is, it can perform internal transitions to change its state. So an agent must have at least two states. This property imbues an agent with a certain degree of complexity and independence from its environment.

Finally, a transition system is *adaptable* when the system's interactions (can) change the transition rules by which it changes state. This property ensures that an agent might be viewed, at the given LoA, as learning its own mode of operation in a way that depends critically on its experience.

All we need to understand now is the meaning of 'morally qualifiable action'. Very simply, an action qualifies as moral if it can cause moral good or evil. Note that this interpretation is neither consequentialist nor intentionalist in nature. We are neither affirming nor denying that the specific evaluation of the morality of the agent might depend on the specific outcome of the agent's actions or on the agent's original intentions or principles.

With all the definitions in place, it becomes possible to understand why, according to IE, *artificial agents* (not just digital agents but also social agents such as companies, parties, or hybrid systems formed by humans and machines or technologically augmented humans) count as moral agents that are morally *accountable* for their actions. (More on the distinction between responsibility and accountability presently.)

The enlargement of the class of moral agents by IE brings several advantages. Normally, an entity is considered a moral agent only if

(i) it is an *individual* agent and
(ii) it is *human-based*, in the sense that it is either human or at least reducible to an identifiable aggregation of human beings, who remain the only morally responsible sources of action, like ghosts in the legal machine.

Regarding (i), limiting the ethical discourse to *individual agents* hinders the development of a satisfactory investigation of *distributed morality*, a macroscopic and growing phenomenon of global moral actions and collective responsibilities, resulting from the 'invisible hand' of systemic interactions among several agents at a local level.

And as far as (ii) is concerned, insisting on the necessarily *human-based nature* of the agent means undermining the possibility of understanding another major transformation in the ethical field, the appearance of artificial agents that are sufficiently informed, 'smart', autonomous and able to perform morally relevant actions independently of the humans who created them, causing 'artificial good' and 'artificial evil' (Floridi and Sanders 1999, 2001).

Of course, accepting that artificial agents may be moral agents is not devoid of problems. We have seen that morality is usually predicated upon *responsibility* (see Section 1). So it is often argued that artificial agents cannot be considered moral agents because they are not morally responsible for their actions because holding them responsible would be a conceptual mistake (see Floridi and Sanders 2004b for a more detailed discussion of the following arguments). The point raised by the objection is that agents are moral agents only if they are *responsible* in the sense of being prescriptively assessable in principle. An agent x is a moral agent only if x can in principle be put on trial.

The immediate impression is that the 'lack of responsibility' objection is merely confusing the *identification* of x as a moral agent with the *evaluation* of x as a morally responsible agent. Surely, the counterargument goes, there is a difference between being able to say who or what is the moral source or cause of (and hence it is accountable for) the moral action in question, and being able to evaluate, prescriptively, whether and how far the moral source so identified is also morally responsible for that action, and hence deserves to be praised or blamed, and in case rewarded or punished accordingly.

Well, that immediate impression is indeed wrong. There is no confusion. Equating identification and evaluation is actually a shortcut. The objection is saying that identity (as a moral agent) without responsibility (as a moral agent) is empty, so we may as well save ourselves the bother of all these distinctions and speak only of morally responsible agents and moral agents as co-referential descriptions. But here lies the real mistake. For we can now see that the objection has finally shown its fundamental presupposition, namely, that we should reduce all prescriptive discourse to responsibility analysis. But this is an unacceptable assumption, a juridical fallacy. There is plenty of room for prescriptive discourse that is independent of responsibility-assignment and, hence, requires a clear identification of moral agents.

Consider the following example. There is nothing wrong with identifying a dog as the source of a morally good action, hence, as an agent playing a crucial role in a moral situation and, therefore, as a moral agent. Search-and-rescue dogs are trained to track missing people. They often help save lives, for which they receive much praise and rewards from both their owners and the people they have located. Yet, this is not the point. Emotionally, people may be very grateful to the animals, but for the dogs it is a game and they cannot be considered morally *responsible* for their actions. The point is that the dogs are involved in a moral game as main players and, hence, that we can rightly identify them as moral agents *accountable* for the good or evil they can cause.

All this should ring a bell. Trying to equate identification and evaluation is really just another way of shifting the ethical analysis from considering x as the moral agent/source of a first-order moral action y to considering x as a possible moral patient of a second-order moral action z, which is the moral evaluation of x as being morally responsible for y. This is a typical Kantian move, with roots in Christian theology. However, there is clearly more to moral evaluation than just responsibility because x is capable of moral action even if x cannot be (or is not yet) a morally responsible agent.

By distinguishing between *moral responsibility*, which requires intentions, consciousness, and other mental attitudes, and *moral accountability*, we can now avoid anthropocentric and anthropomorphic attitudes towards agent-hood. Instead, we can rely on an ethical outlook not necessarily based on punishment and reward (responsibility-oriented ethics) but on moral agent-hood, accountability, and censure. We are less likely to assign responsibility at any cost, forced by the necessity to identify individual, human agent(s). We can stop the regress of looking for the *responsible* individual when something evil happens, because we are now ready to acknowledge that sometimes the moral source of evil or good can be different from an individual or group of humans (note that this was a reasonable view in Greek philosophy). As a result, we are able to escape the dichotomy:

(i) [(responsibility → moral agency) → prescriptive action], versus
(ii) [(no responsibility → no moral agency) → no prescriptive action].

There can be moral agency in the absence of moral responsibility. Promoting normative action is perfectly reasonable even when there is no responsibility, but only moral accountability and the capacity, for moral action.

Being able to treat nonhuman agents as moral agents facilitates the discussion of the morality of agents not only in cyberspace but also in the biosphere – where animals can be considered moral agents without their having to display free will, emotions, or mental states – and in contexts of 'distributed morality', where social and legal agents can now qualify as moral agents. The great advantage is a better grasp of the moral discourse in nonhuman contexts.

All this does not mean that the concept of 'responsibility' is redundant. On the contrary, the previous analysis makes clear the need for further analysis of the concept of responsibility itself, especially when the latter refers to the ontological commitments of creators of new agents and environments. This point is further discussed in Section 2.5. The only 'cost' of a 'mind-less morality' approach is the extension of the class of agents and moral agents to embrace artificial agents. It is a cost that is increasingly worth paying the more we move towards an advanced information society.

2.4. What Counts As a Moral Patient, According to IE?

All entities, *qua* informational objects, have an intrinsic moral value, although possibly quite minimal and overridable, and, hence, they can count as moral patients, subject to some equally minimal degree of moral respect understood as *disinterested, appreciative,* and *careful attention* (Hepburn 1984).

Deflationist theories of intrinsic worth have tried to identify, in various ways, the minimal conditions of possibility of the lowest possible degree of intrinsic worth, without which an entity becomes intrinsically worthless, and hence deserves no moral respect. Investigations have led researchers to move from more restricted to more inclusive, anthropocentric conditions and then further on towards biocentric conditions. As the most recent stage in this dialectical development, IE maintains that even biocentric analyses are still biased and too restricted in scope.

If ordinary human beings are not the only entities enjoying some form of moral respect, what else qualifies? Only sentient beings? Only biological systems? What justifies including some entities and excluding others? Suppose we replace an anthropocentric approach with a biocentric one. Why biocentrism and not ontocentrism? Why can biological *life* and its *preservation* be considered morally relevant phenomena in themselves, independently of human interests, but not *being* and its *flourishing*? In many contexts, it is perfectly reasonable to exercise moral respect towards inanimate entities *per se*, independently of any human interest; could it not be just a matter of ethical sensibility, indeed of an ethical sensibility that we might have had (at least in some Greek philosophy such as the Stoics' and the Neoplatonists'), but have then lost? It seems that any attempt to exclude nonliving entities is based on some specific, low LoA and its corresponding observables, but that this is an arbitrary choice. In the scale of beings, there may be no good reasons to stop anywhere but at the bottom. As Naess (1973) has maintained, 'all things in the biosphere have an equal right to live and blossom'. There seems to be no good reason not to adopt a higher and more inclusive, ontocentric LoA. Not only inanimate but also ideal, intangible, or intellectual objects can have a minimal degree of moral value, no matter how humble, and so be entitled to some respect.

Deep ecologists have already argued that inanimate things too can have some intrinsic value. In a famous article, White (1967) asked 'Do people have ethical obligations toward rocks?' and answered that 'To almost all Americans, still saturated with ideas historically dominant in Christianity . . . the question makes no sense at all. If the time comes when to any considerable group of us such a question is no longer ridiculous, we may be on the verge of a change of value structures that will make possible measures to cope with the growing ecologic crisis. One hopes that there is enough time left'. According to IE, this is the right ecological perspective *and* it makes perfect sense for *any* religious tradition (including, but not only, the Judeo-Christian one) for which the whole universe is God's creation, is inhabited by the divine, and is a gift to humanity, of which the latter needs to take care (see Section 3.6). IE translates all this into informational terms. If something can be a moral patient, then its nature can be taken into consideration by a moral agent *A*, and contribute to shaping *A*'s action, no matter how minimally. According to IE, the minimal criterion for qualifying as an object that, as a moral patient, may rightly claim some degree of respect, is more general than any biocentric reference to the object's attributes as a biological or living entity; it is informational. This means that the informational nature of an entity, that may, in principle, act as a patient of a moral action, is the lowest threshold that constitutes its minimal intrinsic worth, which in turn may deserve to be respected by the agent. Alternatively, and to put it more concisely, being an informational object *qua* informational object is the minimal condition of possibility of moral worth and, hence, of normative respect. In more metaphysical terms, IE argues that all aspects and instances of *being* are worth some initial, perhaps minimal and overridable, form of moral respect.

Enlarging the conception of what can count as a centre of moral respect has the advantage of enabling one to make sense of the innovative nature of ICT, as providing a new and powerful conceptual frame. It also enables one to deal more satisfactorily with the original character of some of its moral issues, by approaching them from a theoretically strong perspective. Throughout time, ethics has steadily moved from a narrow to a more inclusive concept of what can count as a centre of moral worth, from the citizen to the biosphere (Nash 1989). The emergence of cyberspace, as a new environment in which human beings spend much of their lives, explains the need to enlarge further the conception of what can qualify as a moral patient. IE represents the most recent development in this ecumenical trend, a Platonist and ecological approach without a biocentric bias, as it were.

IE is ontologically committed to an informational modelling of *being* as the whole infosphere. The result is that no aspect of reality is extraneous to IE and the whole environment is taken into consideration. For whatever is in the infosphere is informational (better, is accessed and modeled informationally) and whatever is not in the infosphere is something that cannot be.

More than 50 years ago, Leopold defined land ethics as something that 'changes the role of *Homo sapiens* from conqueror of the land-community to plain member and citizen of it. It implies respect for his fellow-members, and also respect for the community as such. The land ethic simply enlarges the boundaries of the community to include soils, waters, plants, and animals, or collectively: the land' (Leopold 1949, p. 403). IE translates environmental ethics into terms of infosphere and informational objects, for the land we inhabit is not just the earth.

2.5. What Are Our Responsibilities As Moral Agents, According to IE?

Like demiurges, we have 'ecopoietic' responsibilities towards the whole infosphere. Information ethics is an ethics addressed not just to 'users' of the world but also to producers who are 'divinely' responsible for its creation and well-being. It is an ethics of *creative stewardship* (Floridi 2002, 2003; Floridi and Sanders 2005).

The term 'ecopoiesis' refers to the morally-informed construction of the environment, based on an ecologically-oriented perspective. In terms of a philosophical anthropology, the ecopoietic approach, supported by IE, is embodied by what I have termed *homo poieticus* (Floridi 1999b). *Homo poieticus* is to be distinguished from *homo faber*, user and 'exploitator' of natural resources, from *homo oeconomicus*, producer, distributor, and consumer of wealth, and from *homo ludens* (Huizinga 1970), who embodies a leisurely playfulness devoid of the ethical care and responsibility characterising the constructionist attitude. *Homo poieticus* is a demiurge who takes care of reality to protect it and make it flourish.

The ontic powers of *homo poieticus* have been steadily increasing. Today, *homo poieticus* can variously exercise them (in terms of control, creation, or modelling) over himself (e.g., genetically, physiologically, neurologically, and narratively), over his society (e.g., culturally, politically, socially, and economically) and over his natural or artificial environments (e.g., physically and informationally). The more powerful *homo poieticus* becomes as an agent, the greater his duties and responsibilities become, as a *moral agent*, to oversee not only the development of his own character and habits but also the well-being and flourishing of each of his ever expanding spheres of influence, to include the whole infosphere.

To move from individual virtues to global values, an *ecopoietic* approach is needed that recognises our *responsibilities* towards the environment (including present and future inhabitants) as its enlightened creators, stewards, or supervisors, not just as its virtuous users and consumers.

2.6. What Are the Fundamental Principles of IE?

IE determines what is morally right or wrong, what ought to be done, what the duties, the 'oughts' and the 'ought nots' of a moral agent are, by means of four basic moral laws. They are formulated here in an informational vocabulary and in a patient-oriented version, but an agent-oriented one is easily achievable in more metaphysical terms of 'dos' and 'don'ts' (compare this list to the similar ones available in medical ethics, where 'pain' replaces 'entropy'):

  0. entropy ought not to be caused in the infosphere (null law);
  1. entropy ought to be prevented in the infosphere;
  2. entropy ought to be removed from the infosphere; and

3. the flourishing of informational entities as well as of the whole infosphere ought to be promoted by preserving, cultivating and enriching their properties.

What is good for informational entities and for the infosphere in general? This is the basic moral question asked by IE. We have seen that the answer is provided by a minimalist theory: any informational entity is recognised to be the centre of some basic ethical claims, which deserve recognition and should help to regulate the implementation of any informational process involving it. It follows that approval or disapproval of *A*'s decisions and actions should also be based on how these affect the well-being of the infosphere, that is, on how successful or unsuccessful they are in respecting the ethical claims attributable to the informational entities involved, and, hence, in improving or impoverishing the infosphere. The duty of any moral agent should be evaluated in terms of contribution to the sustainable blooming of the infosphere, and any process, action, or event that negatively affects the whole infosphere – not just an informational object – should be seen as an increase in its level of entropy and hence an instance of evil.

The four laws clarify, in very broad terms, what it means to live as a responsible and caring agent in the infosphere. On the one hand, a process is increasingly deprecable, and its agent-source is increasingly blameworthy, the lower is the number-index of the specific law that it fails to satisfy. Moral mistakes may occur and entropy may increase if one wrongly evaluates the impact of one's actions because projects conflict or compete, even if those projects aim to satisfy IE moral laws. This is especially the case when 'local goodness', that is, the improvement of a region of the infosphere, is favoured to the overall disadvantage of the whole environment. More simply, entropy may increase because of the wicked nature of the agent (this possibility is granted by IE's negative anthropology). On the other hand, a process is already commendable, and its agent-source praiseworthy, if it satisfies the *conjunction* of the null law with at least one other law, not the *sum* of the resulting effects. Note that, according to this definition,

(a) an action is unconditionally commendable only if it never generates any entropy in the course of its implementation; and
(b) the best moral action is the action that succeeds in satisfying all four laws at the same time.

Most of the actions that we judge morally good do not satisfy such strict criteria, for they achieve only a balanced positive moral value, that is, although their performance causes a certain quantity of entropy, we acknowledge that the infosphere is in a better state on the whole after their occurrence. (Compare this to the utilitarianist appreciation of an action that causes more benefits than damages for the overall welfare of the agents and patients.) Finally, a process that satisfies only the null law – the level of entropy in the infosphere remains unchanged after its occurrence – either has no moral value (that is, it is morally irrelevant or insignificant), or it is equally deprecable and commendable, though in different respects.

3. SIX RECURRENT MISUNDERSTANDINGS

Since the early 1990s,[8] when IE was first introduced as an environmental macroethics and a foundationalist approach to computer ethics, some standard objections have circulated that seem to be based on a few basic misunderstandings.[9] The point of this final section is not convincing the reader that no reasonable disagreement is possible about the value of IE. Rather, the goal here is to remove some ambiguities and possible confusions that might prevent the correct evaluation of IE, so that disagreement can become more constructive.

3.1. Informational Objects, Not News

By defending the intrinsic moral worth of *informational objects*, IE does not refer to the moral value of any other piece of well-formed and meaningful data such as an email, the *Britannica*, or Newton's *Principia*. What IE suggests is that we adopt an informational LoA to approach the analysis of *being* in terms of a minimal common ontology, whereby human beings as well as animals, plants, artefacts, and so forth are interpreted as informational entities. IE is not an ethics of the BBC news.

3.2. Minimalism Not Reductionism

IE does not reduce people to mere numbers, nor does it treat human beings as if they were no more important than animals, trees, stones, or files. The minimalism advocated by IE is methodological. It means to support the view that entities can be analysed by focusing on their lowest common denominator, represented by an informational ontology. Other levels of abstraction can then be evoked in order to deal with other, more human-centred values.

3.3. Applicable Not Applied

Given its ontological nature and wide scope, one may object that IE works at a level of metaphysical abstraction too philosophical to make it of any direct utility for immediate needs and applications. Yet, this is the inevitable price

---

[8] Fourth International Conference on Ethical Issues of Information Technology (Department of Philosophy, Erasmus University, The Netherlands, 25–27 March, 1998, published as Floridi (1999a).

[9] For a good example of the sort of confusions that may arise concerning information ethics, see Himma (2005).

to be paid for any foundationalist project. One must polarise theory and practice to strengthen both. IE is not immediately useful to solve specific ethical problems (including computer ethics problems), but it provides the conceptual grounds that then guide problem-solving procedures. Thus, IE has already been fruitfully applied to deal with the 'tragedy of the digital commons' (Greco and Floridi 2004), the digital divide (Floridi 2002), the problem of telepresence (Floridi 2005b), game cheating (Sicart 2005), the problem of privacy (Floridi 2005a) and environmental issues (York 2005).

3.4. Implementable Not Inapplicable

A related objection is that IE, by promoting the moral value of any entity, is inapplicable because it is too demanding or supererogatory. In this case, it is important to stress that IE supports a *minimal* and *overridable* sense of ontic moral value. Environmental ethics accepts culling as a moral practice and does not indicate as one's duty the provision of a vegetarian diet to wild carnivores. IE is equally reasonable: fighting the decaying of *being* (information entropy) is the general approach to be followed, not an impossible and ridiculous struggle against thermodynamics, or the ultimate benchmark for any moral evaluation, as if human beings had to be treated as mere numbers. 'Respect and take care of all entities for their own sake, if you can', this is the injunction. We need to adopt an ethics of stewardship towards the infosphere; is this really too demanding or unwise? Perhaps we should think twice: is it actually easier to accept the idea that all nonbiological entities have no intrinsic value whatsoever? Perhaps, we should consider that the ethical game may be more opaque, subtle, and difficult to play than humanity has so far wished to acknowledge. Perhaps, we could be less pessimistic: human sensitivity has already improved quite radically in the past, and may improve further. Perhaps, we should just be cautious: given how fallible we are, it may be better to be too inclusive than discriminative. In each of these answers, one needs to remember that IE is meant to be a macroethics for creators not just users of their surrounding 'nature', and this new situation brings with it demiurgic responsibilities that may require a special theoretical effort.

3.5. Preservation and Cultivation Not Conservation

IE does not support a morally conservationist or laissez faire attitude, according to which *homo poieticus* would be required not to modify, improve, or interfere in any way with the natural course of things. On the contrary, IE is fundamentally proactive, in a way similar to *restorationist* or *interventionist ecology*. The unavoidable challenge lies precisely in understanding how reality can be better shaped. A gardener transforms the environment for the better, that's why he needs to be very knowledgeable. IE may be, but has no bias in principle, against abortion, eugenics, GM food, human cloning, animal experiments and other highly controversial, yet technically and scientifically possible ways of transforming or 'enhancing' reality. But it is definitely opposed to any associated ignorance of the consequences of such radical transformations.

3.6. A Secular, Not a Spiritual or Religious Approach

IE is compatible with, and may be associated with religious beliefs, including a Buddhist (Herold 2005) or a Judeo-Christian view of the world. In the latter case, the reference to Genesis 2:15 readily comes to one's mind. *Homo poieticus* is supposed 'to tend (*'abad*) and exercise care and protection over (*shamar*)' God's creation. Stewardship is a much better way of rendering this stance towards reality than dominion. Nevertheless, IE is based on a secular philosophy. *Homo poieticus* has a vocation for responsible stewardship in the world. Unless some other form of intelligence is discovered in the universe, he cannot presume to share this burden with any other being. *Homo poieticus* should certainly not entrust his responsibility for the flourishing of *being* to some transcendent power. As the Enlightenment has taught us, the religion of reason can be immanent. If the full responsibility of humanity is then consistent with a religious view, this can only be a welcome conclusion, not a premise.

4. CONCLUSION

There is a famous passage in one of Einstein's letters that well summarises the perspective advocated by IE. Some five years prior to his death, Albert Einstein received a letter from a 19-year-old girl grieving over the loss of her younger sister. The young woman wished to know what the famous scientist might say to comfort her. On March 4, 1950, Einstein wrote to this young person:

A human being is part of the whole, called by us 'universe', a part limited in time and space. He experiences himself, his thoughts and feelings, as something separated from the rest, a kind of optical delusion of his consciousness. This delusion is a kind of prison for us, restricting us to our personal desires and to affection for a few persons close to us. Our task must be to free ourselves from our prison by widening our circle of compassion to embrace all humanity and the whole of nature in its beauty. Nobody is capable of achieving this completely, but the striving for such achievement is in itself a part of the liberation and a foundation for inner security (Einstein 1954).

Does the informational LoA of IE provide an additional perspective that can further expand the ethical discourse, so as to include the world of morally significant phenomena involving informational objects? Or does it represent a threshold beyond which nothing of moral significance really happens? Does looking at reality through the highly philosophical lens of an informational analysis improve our ethical understanding, or is it an ethically pointless (when not misleading) exercise? IE argues that the agent-related *behaviour* and the patient-related *status* of informational objects *qua* informational objects can be morally significant, over and above the instrumental function that may be attributed to them by other ethical approaches, and hence that they can contribute to determining, normatively, ethical duties and legally enforceable rights. IE's position, like that of any other macroethics, is not devoid of problems. But it can interact with other macroethical theories and contribute an important new perspective: a process or action may be morally good or bad, irrespective of its consequences, motives, universality, or virtuous nature, but depending on how it affects the infosphere. An ontocentric ethics provides an insightful perspective. Without IE's contribution, our understanding of moral facts in general, not just of ICT-related problems in particular, would be less complete.

ACKNOWLEDGEMENTS

I would like to thank Alison Adam, Jeroen van den Hoven, and John Weckert for their editorial feedback on a previous version of this chapter, Ken Herold and Karen Mather for their useful comments, and Paul Oldfield for his careful copyediting.

References

Bynum, T. 2001. Computer ethics: Basic concepts and historical overview, in *The Stanford encyclopedia of philosophy*. Retrieved 28 May 2006 from http://plato.stanford.edu/entries/ethics-computer/.

Einstein, A. 1954. *Ideas and opinions*. New York: Crown Publishers.

Floridi, L. 1995. Internet: Which future for organized knowledge, Frankenstein or Pygmalion? *International Journal of Human-Computer Studies, 43*, 261–274.

Floridi, L. 1999a. Information ethics: On the theoretical foundations of computer ethics, *Ethics and Information Technology, 1*, 1, 37–56. Reprinted in 2004, with some modifications, in *Ethicomp Journal, 1*, 1.

Floridi, L. 1999b. *Philosophy and computing: An introduction*. London and New York: Routledge.

Floridi, L. 2002. Information ethics: An environmental approach to the digital divide, *Philosophy in the Contemporary World, 9*, 1, 39–45. Text of the keynote speech delivered at the UNESCO World Commission on the Ethics of Scientific Knowledge and Technology (COMEST), First Meeting of the Sub-Commission on the Ethics of the Information Society (UNESCO, Paris, June 18–19, 2001).

Floridi, L. 2003. On the intrinsic value of information objects and the infosphere, *Ethics and Information Technology, 4*, 4, 287–304.

Floridi, L. 2004. Information, in L Floridi (Ed.), *The Blackwell guide to the philosophy of computing and information*. Oxford: Blackwell, pp. 40–61.

Floridi, L. 2005a. An interpretation of informational privacy and of its moral value, in *Proceedings of CEPE 2005–6th Computer Ethics: Philosophical Enquiries conference, Ethics of New Information Technologies*. The Netherlands: University of Twente, Enschede.

Floridi, L. 2005b. The philosophy of presence: From epistemic failure to successful observation, *Presence: Teleoperators and Virtual Environments, 14*, 6, 656–667.

Floridi, L., and Sanders, J. W. 1999. Entropy as evil in information ethics, *Etica & Politica, special issue on Computer Ethics, 1*, 2.

Floridi, L., and Sanders, J. W. 2001. Artificial evil and the foundation of computer ethics, *Ethics and Information Technology, 3*, 1, 55–66.

Floridi, L., and Sanders, J. W. 2002. Computer ethics: Mapping the foundationalist debate, *Ethics and Information Technology, 4*, 1, 1–9.

Floridi, L., and Sanders, J. W. 2004a. The method of abstraction, in M. Negrotti (Ed.), *Yearbook of the Artificial. Nature, Culture, and Technology. Models in Contemporary Sciences*. Bern: Peter Lang, pp. 177–220.

Floridi, L., and Sanders, J. W. 2004b. On the morality of artificial agents. *Minds and Machines, 14*, 3, 349–379.

Floridi, L., and Sanders, J. W. 2004c. Levellism and the method of abstraction. The final draft of this paper is available as IEG – Research Report 22.11.04. Retrieved 28 May 2006 from http://www.wolfson.ox.ac.uk/~floridi/pdf/latmoa.pdf.

Floridi, L., and Sanders, J. W. 2005. Internet ethics: The constructionist values of homo poieticus, in R. Cavalier (Ed.), *The Impact of the Internet on Our Moral Lives*. New York: SUNY.

Greco, G. M., and Floridi, L. 2004. The tragedy of the digital commons, *Ethics and Information Technology, 6*, 2, 73–82.

Hepburn, R. 1984. *Wonder and other essays*. Edinburgh: Edinburgh University Press.

Herold, K. 2005. A Buddhist model for the informational person, in *Proceedings of the Second Asia Pacific Computing and Philosophy Conference, January 7–9*, Bangkok, Thailand. Retrieved 28 May 2006 from http://library1.hamilton.edu/eresrs/AP-CAP2005-Herold.pdf.

Himma, K. E. 2005. There's something about Mary: The moral value of things *qua* information objects, *Ethics and Information Technology, 6*, 3, 145–159.

Huizinga, J. 1970. *Homo ludens: a study of the play element in culture*. London: Paladin. First published in 1938.

Leopold, A. 1949. *The Sand County almanac*. New York: Oxford University Press.

Mather, K. 2004. Object oriented goodness: A response to Mathiesen's What is information ethics? *Computers and Society, 34*, 3.

Mathiesen, K. 2004. What is information ethics? *Computers and Society, 34*, 1.

Naess, A. 1973. The shallow and the deep, long-range ecology movement, *Inquiry, 16*, 95–100.

Nash, R. F. 1989. *The rights of nature*. Madison, WI: University of Wisconsin Press.

Rawls, J. 1999. *A theory of justice* (rev. ed.). Oxford: Oxford University Press.

Rowlands, M. 2000. *The environmental crisis: Understanding the value of nature*. Basingstoke: Macmillan.

Sicart, M. 2005. On the foundations of evil in computer game cheating, in *Proceedings of the Digital Games Research Association's 2nd International Conference – Changing Views: Worlds in Play, June 16–20*, Vancouver, British Columbia.

Smith, M. M. 1996. Information ethics: An hermeneutical analysis of an emerging area in applied ethics, PhD thesis, University of North Carolina at Chapel Hill, NC.

van den Hoven, J. 1995. Equal access and social justice: Information as a primary good, in *ETHICOMP95: An international conference on the ethical issues of using information technology*. Leicester, UK: De Montfort University.

White, L. J. 1967. The historical roots of our ecological crisis, *Science, 155*, 1203–1207.

Wiener, N. 1950. *The human use of human beings: Cybernetics and society*. Boston, MA: Houghton Mifflin.

Wiener, N. 1954. *The human use of human beings: Cybernetics and society* (rev. ed.). Boston, MA: Houghton Mifflin.

Wiener, N. 1964. *God and Golem, Inc.: A comment on certain points where cybernetics impinges on religion.* Cambridge, MA: MIT Press.

York, P. F. 2005. Respect for the world: Universal ethics and the morality of terraforming. PhD Thesis, University of Queensland.

4

The Transformation of the Public Sphere

Political Authority, Communicative Freedom, and Internet Publics

James Bohman

Two relatively uncontroversial social conditions that have long been widely identified across many different modern theories of democracy: namely, the need for a rich associative life of civil society, and for the technological, institutional, and communicative infrastructure that permits the expression and diffusion of public opinion. Historically, the public sphere as a sphere of public opinion and communication has developed in interaction with a relatively unified structure of political authority: the state and its monopoly powers. Indeed, citizens of modern polities came to regard themselves as members or participants in various publics primarily through the attempts of states to censor and restrict public communication. Along with many other complex factors, the emergence of rights of communication and the democratization of state authority have emerged hand-in-hand. With the advent of new forms of political authority that directly impact the structure of communication across borders, new forms of publicity have also emerged and with them new public spheres.

If new forms of communication and structures of publicity do indeed exist across borders, this would give special salience to deliberation as an important basis for democratization, as well as for transnational institutional design. Given the differences between democratic arrangements that presuppose a singular *demos* and decentered ones that organize *demoi*, we should not expect that all democracies have exactly the same communicative infrastructure. This means that transnational civil society and public spheres face different difficulties with regard to independently constituted political authority from those faced by 'strong,' or state, public spheres. In the case of the state, publics provide access to influence over the sovereign power of the state, by mediating public opinion through the collective deliberation of the *demos*. In transnational polities, the democratizing effect of publics consists in the creation of communicative networks that are as dispersed and distributed as the authority with which they interact. The issue to be explored here is, as John Dewey put it, how to elaborate 'those conditions under which the inchoate public may function democratically' (Dewey 1988, p. 327).

In the case of transnational politics, the inchoate publics under consideration are plural, and that makes a great deal of difference as to how we are to conceive of their emergence and contribution to global democratization. Such an account is decentered, insofar as it takes a whole array of transnational publics as necessary in order to enable such freedom, and in that these publics need not collect themselves into a single 'global' public sphere in the way that citizens as national publics that aimed at restricting the centralized authority of the early modern state as it infringed upon their communicative freedom through censorship needed to.

My aim here is to show that democratizing publics can form on the Internet through a similar process of gaining communicative freedom through conflict with new forms of political authority. First, I begin with an analysis of new forms of political authority and new public spheres, precisely because they provide a useful structural analogue that could help in solving the difficult problems of the structural transformation of the conditions of democracy. Whether in institutions or in publics, the transformation is from a unitary to a disaggregated or distributive form. In the case of authority, the unitary state form has already been disaggregated into a multiplicity of principal/agent relations. In the case of the public sphere, the transformation is from a unitary forum to a 'distributive' public, of the type best exemplified in computer-mediated network forms of communication. If this analysis is successful, such a transformation of the public sphere might provide a model or structural analogue for the kind of empirical and conceptual changes necessary to develop any theory of genuinely transnational democracy. Second, I describe the sort of institutionalized authority in light of which such publics were formed and with which they interact and attempt to influence. It is important here to understand the exact nature of global political authority and the ways in which publics form by resisting the influence of such authority in the communicative domain. The third step is to develop the particular contribution that transnational public spheres make to the democratization of international society. The development of such public spaces for the exercise of communicative freedom is an essential requirement of nondomination. When communicatively free participants in the public sphere interact with empowered institutions, they acquire and extend their normative powers, the powers to secure and transform their own normative statuses as citizens affected by such institutions.

This argument is concerned primarily with the following two questions: what sort of public spheres are appropriate for realizing communicative freedom under these new conditions of political authority? How can emerging transnational publics interact with the forms of political authority typical of powerful international institutions? Before taking up the issues related to Internet publics. I turn first to political authority, the transformation of which constitutes a new problematic situation analogous to the effects of state power on newly emerging publics in the early modern period.

PUBLICS, PRINCIPALS, AND AGENTS: THE TRANSFORMATION OF POLITICAL AUTHORITY

What makes contestation so salient in the context of current international institutions? Contestation has typically emerged in periods of large-scale institutional shifts in the distribution of political authority, as was historically the case, for example, with the rise of the mercantilist state, and now recurs with the emergence of powerful international institutions. More often than not, these shifts in political authority beyond the state have been pursued as a matter of policy by states themselves, mostly through 'denationalization' and, thus, by the delegation of authority to international bodies and institutions that act as agents through which they may achieve their own interests. These policies have especially been pursued with regard to economic integration and the protection of markets from financial volatility, with some groups more than others bearing the costs of such policies (Dryzek 1996, p. 79ff). Even apart from the emergence of fully supranational polities such as the European Union, such institutional strategies disperse political authority widely and at a variety of levels.

By comparison, state-oriented public spheres have had significantly different features. Even when citizens do not influence decisions directly, they are able to exercise certain normative powers. In participating in free and fair elections and in casting their votes, citizens have the normative power to change representatives and office holders and to express their consent to being governed. Given this channel for influence, citizens may be said to at least have 'electoral sovereignty.' This normative power of the collective will of the citizenry is dependent on the role of citizens within an institutional framework or distributed system of normative powers. In the event that political authority strays outside of the available means to exert democratic influence, citizens can also exercise accountability through the 'contestatory sovereignty' of the *demos*, as when the voice of the people becomes salient in periods of constitutional crisis or reform.[1] In a democracy, then, the location of sovereignty becomes an issue when the 'people' find their institutions and those who exercise authority through them unresponsive. Often authority is unresponsive not because citizens as a collective body are disempowered, but because these democratic institutions were constructed for a public that is different from the one that currently exists. Similarly, in the international arena, many powerful institutions, such as the International

---

[1] Pettit (2000, pp. 105–146) makes the useful distinction between the authorial and the editorial dimensions of 'the people' with regard to the content of laws.

Monetary Fund or World Bank, lack any mechanism of creating public influence over their agendas.

Viewed in terms of opportunities for public influence, international institutions introduce a further problem for their interaction with the public. To the extent that they are organized into a plurality of levels, international institutions amplify the heterogeneous polyarchy of political authority that is already characteristic of contemporary democracies. In so doing, they may sometimes extend the antidemocratic tensions within the modern administrative state, particularly those based on the modern phenomenon of 'agency,' a form of authority that is meant to solve the problem of social control for central and hierarchical authority. These new types of hierarchical relationships have been pervasive in modern economies organized around the firm as the unit of production (Arrow 1985, p. 37). They are hierarchical because they are based on asymmetrical information: the principal delegates the authority to the agent to act in his or her interest precisely because the principal does not possess the resources, information, or expertise necessary to perform the relevant tasks. Given that the principals may not be in a position to monitor their agents, even when given the opportunity, the division of epistemic labor creates pervasive asymmetries of competence and access to information.

These asymmetries are accentuated when they operate in highly uneven and asymmetrical social relations created by globalization and its indefinite social activity. One might object that the presence of economic actors such as corporations makes the term 'exploitation' descriptively more accurate. However, exploitation does not identify the distinctly normative character of these forms of authority. As large-scale organizations, often with vast resources, corporations operate more as nascent political authorities, in that they are quite successful in imposing statuses and duties in the terms of cooperation, even upon states. While not employing simple coercion, such organizations act as dominators by devaluing citizenship and being able to change important statuses and powers that are necessary for democracy.

Such pervasive asymmetries are also more pervasive insofar as they have filtered into many situations of ordinary life, from stepping on an elevator to taking prescription drugs. The problem is not only in access to information, but also in the ability to interpret it, since most of us, for example, are 'unable to render medical diagnoses, to test the purity of food and drugs before ingesting them, to conduct structural tests of skyscrapers before entering them, or to make safety checks of elevators, automobiles, or airplanes before embarking on them' (Shapiro 1987, p. 627). To this list, we can now add 'unable to assess the myriad of global financial markets and instruments.' Such relationships of epistemic dependence and asymmetrical information define the specific relations of *agency*: in which one person (the *agent*) is dealing with others (third parties) on behalf of another or others (the *principals*). This epistemic asymmetry is a practical challenge to democracy.[2] As Karl Llewellyn already pointed out, the very idea of self-government is eroded by agency relationships to the degree that principals find that 'it is repeatedly necessary to give agents powers wider than those they are normally expected to use' (Llewellyn 1930, p. 483). What interests me here is not the full economic theory that motivates this analysis, but the incompletely defined normative powers that are entailed in the principal/agent relationship. The demand for self-government is not the solution, since it would attempt to assert the form of political authority that necessitated agency relations in the first place: that of a singular, self-legislating *demos*. The issue, as I see it, is rather to constitute a democratic form of dispersed authority rather than recreate a form of legitimation that cannot solve the problem of new forms of domination.

How can such reversal be avoided and authority democratized? Civil society remains too disaggregated to provide any political solution, however much the bottom-up strategy seems appealing and inherently democratic. Practices of empowerment by nongovernment organizations (NGOs) may have paradoxes built into them, when less well-off civil society organizations become accountable to better-off organizations in exchange for resources and assistance (see Ewig 1997, p. 97). Similarly, powerful institutions may co-opt and capture the NGOs that monitor them, especially if they have a say in the composition of the consultative bodies and thus exercise control over the public that influences them. New groups aggregated so as to function as the *demos* of all those affected creates a new and higher level *demos* as, at best, a heterogeneous aggregate. Absent in this picture of democratization is the distinctive infrastructure of communicative power that may act to reshape such social relations and their hierarchies. One task that reflects the distinctive kind of communication that goes on in the public sphere is its ability to raise topics or express concerns that cut across social spheres: this not only circulates information about the state and the economy, but it also establishes a forum for criticism in which the boundaries of these spheres can be crossed and challenged, primarily in response to citizens' demands for accountability and influence.

Putting the public sphere back into the political structure leads to a very different understanding of deliberative political activity, one that does not automatically consider the entitlements of participants in terms of a relationship of those who govern to those who are governed. The public sphere is not only necessary as a theoretical term in order to explain why these structures are so interconnected in democratic societies; it also suggests that democratic politics has the structural role of mediating interaction among civil society, markets, and formal political institutions. This form of mediation suggests why neither top-down nor bottom-up strategies for global politics can stand on their own. Such strategies fail because they ignore

---

[2] On this issue, see Bohman (1996).

conditions for the success of both democracy and empowerment, found in the proper relations among responsive institutions, a vibrant civil society, and robust communication across public spheres. John Dewey seems to have come closest to developing the proper transnational alternative strategy of democratization when he responded to Walter Lippmann's criticism of the 'phantom' public in modern, complex societies; instead of regarding them as separate spheres, he argued for the ongoing interaction between institutions and the publics that constitute them (Dewey 1988, p. 255 and 314). The capabilities of citizens may sometimes outstrip the institutions that constitute their normative powers, as when the public for whom they were created no longer exists (as was the case for the rural and agrarian public of early American democracy). Given complex and overlapping interdependence, many citizens now see the need for new institutions that are more transparent, inclusive, responsive, and cosmopolitan (see Soysal 1994).

Even when authority is disaggregated, citizens still may exercise certain powers through the public sphere, simply in defining themselves as a public and interacting with institutions accordingly. In the first instance, a public sphere institutionalizes a particular kind of relationship between persons. As members of a public, persons can regard each other as having, at the very least, the capacity and standing to address and to be addressed by each other's acts of communication. Call this the 'communicative freedom' of publics, a form of freedom that may take on a constructive role by which members grant each other rights and duties in their roles of participants in the public sphere. This freedom emerges from the interaction between the communicative power of participants in the public sphere and those more limited normative powers that they may have in their roles within various institutions. By acquiring such communicative freedom beyond the control of even a disaggregated authority, membership in a public uses the creative and constructive powers of communication and public opinion to reshape the operations of authority that were freed by delegation to an agent from the obligations of office holders to citizens. One way that such a public can effect a reversal of control is to see its emergence as recapturing the constituent power of the people, now in a dispersed form, when their constitutive power as citizens has failed.

This gap between public spheres and institutions creates the open question for citizens as to whether the authority of their institutions has been legitimately exercised. The beginnings of popular control, and thus the preconditions for democratization, are not to be found in the moment of original authorization by either the sovereign and the unified *demos*, but in something that is more spatially, temporally, and institutionally dispersed. In the next section, I want to develop an alternative, normative conception of the power of publics and citizens and of the role of communicatively generated power in the achievement of nondomination and legitimate political authority. This account will help us to see what the transnational public sphere contributes to nondomination, where freedom from domination is manifested in the exercise of distinctly normative powers. Democratization, I argue, is best thought of as the creative interaction between communicative freedom and the exercise of normative powers, between the powers that one and the same group of people may have in their roles as citizens and participants of public spheres.

Before I turn to the public sphere as a location for the emergence and exercise of communicative freedom, let me address an issue that is in some sense prior and fundamental to the difficulty of obtaining a foothold for democratization. What sort of public sphere is appropriate to challenging and reconstructing relations of political authority, especially ones that lie outside the boundaries of nation state? Such transnational public spheres cannot be the same as the ones that emerged to help democratize the state. They will not be unified, but 'distributed' public spheres. This will allow us to ask the question of popular control or the will of the people in a different way, so that it is not a phantom public but something more akin to the generalized other in Mead's sense. Or, as Aristotle put it: "'all' can be said in a variety of ways,' in the corporate sense or in the distributive sense of each and every one (*Politics*, 1261b). In order to become political again, the public sphere is undergoing a transformation from one to the other. With this change, the possibilities for popular control are now disaggregated into the constituent power of dispersed publics to initiate democratization. Transnational polities have to look for ways in which to distribute the processes of popular control and influence across institutional structures and levels.

PUBLICS AND THE PUBLIC SPHERE: SOME CONCEPTUAL ISSUES

In order to adopt this transformationalist approach, it is first necessary to set aside some misleading assumptions that guide most conceptions of the public sphere and complicate any discussion of transnational democratization.[3] These assumptions are normatively significant, precisely because they directly establish the connection between the public sphere and the democratic ideal of deliberation among free and equal citizens. They can be misleading when the suggested connection between them is overly specific, and leave out two essential conditions for the existence of a public sphere in large and highly differentiated modern societies that are crucial to understanding what sort of public sphere transnational polities might require. The first is the necessity in modern societies of a technological mediation of public communication, so that a realizable public sphere can no longer be thought of as a forum for face-to-face communication. There are other ways to realize the public forum and its multiple forms of dialogical exchange

---

[3] This discussion in this section builds my earlier discussion of the Internet as a public sphere (Bohman 2004).

that are also more appropriate to modern forms of popular control and democratic public influence. The second feature is historical: technologically mediated public spheres have emerged through challenging political authority, specifically the state's authority to censor communication. In this respect sustaining a sphere of free communication has been crucial to the expansion of emerging normative powers and freedoms of citizens.

Once the concept is seen in a properly historical way, the public sphere (or *Öffentlichkeit* in the broad sense of communication having the property of publicness) is not a univocal normative ideal. Nevertheless, it does still have necessary conditions. First, a public sphere that has democratic significance must be a forum, that is, a social space in which speakers may express their views to others who, in turn, respond to them and raise their own opinions and concerns. Second, a democratic public sphere must manifest commitments to freedom and equality in the communicative interaction. Such interaction takes the specific form of a conversation or dialogue, in which speakers and hearers treat each other with equal respect and freely exchange speaker and hearer roles in their responses to each other. This leads to a third necessary feature for any public sphere that corrects for the limits of face-to-face interaction: communication must address an indefinite audience. In this sense, any social exclusion undermines the existence of a public sphere. Expansive dialogue must be indefinite in just this sense, and, with the responses of a wider audience, new reasons and forms of communication may emerge. Communication is then 'public' if it is directed at an indefinite audience with the expectation of a response. In this way, a public sphere depends upon repeated and open-ended interaction, and, as such, requires technologies and institutions to secure its continued existence and regularize opportunities and access to it.

If this account of the necessary features of public communication is correct, then the very existence of the public sphere is always dependent on some form of communications technology, to the extent that it requires the expansion of dialogue beyond face-to-face encounters. Historically, writing first served to open up this sort of indefinite social space of possibilities with the spatial extension of the audience and the temporal extension of possible responses. Taking the potential of writing further, the printed word produced a new form of communication based on a one-to-many form of interaction. Television and radio did not essentially alter this one-to-many extension of communicative interaction, even as they eased entry requirements of literacy for hearers and raised the costs of adopting the speaker role to a mass audience.

Perhaps more controversially, computer-mediated communication (especially on the Internet) also extends the public forum, by providing a new unbounded space for communicative interaction. But its innovative potential lies not just in its speed and scale, but also in its new form of address or interaction. As a *many-to-many* mode of communication, it has radically lowered the costs of interaction with an indefinite and potentially large audience, especially with regard to adopting the speaker role without the costs of the mass media. Moreover, such many-to-many communication holds out the promise of capturing the features of dialogue and communication more robustly than the print medium. This network-based extension of dialogue suggests the possibility of re-embedding the public sphere in a new and potentially larger set of institutions. At present, there is a lack of congruity between existing political institutions and these expanded forms of public communicative interaction. Hence, the nature of the public or publics is changing along with the nature of the authority with which it interacts.

Before leaping from innovative possibilities to an unwarranted optimism about the Internet's contribution to global democracy, it is first necessary to look more closely at the requirements of publicity and how the Internet might fulfill them. The sheer potential of the Internet to become a public sphere is insufficient to establish democracy at this scale for two reasons. First, this mediated many-to-many communication may increase interactivity without preserving the essential features of dialogue, such as responsive uptake. And second, the Internet may be embedded in institutions that do not help in transforming its communicative space into a public sphere. Even if it is a free and open space, the Internet could simply be a marketplace or a commons, as Lessig and others have argued (Lessig 1999, p. 141). Even if this were so, however, actors could still transform such communicative resources and embed them within institutions that seek to extend dialogue and sustain deliberation. What would make it a 'public sphere'?

Consider first the normative features of communicative public interaction. Publicity at the level of social action is most basic, in the sense that all other forms of publicity presuppose it. Social acts are public only if they meet two basic requirements. First, they are not only directed to an indefinite audience, but also offered with some expectation of a response, especially with regard to interpretability and justifiability. The description of the second general feature of publicity is dominated by spatial metaphors; public actions constitute a common and open 'space' for interaction with indefinite others – or, as Habermas puts it, publicity in this broadest sense is simply 'the social space generated by communicative action' (Habermas 1996, p. 360). This is where agency and creativity of participants becomes significant, to the extent that such normative expectations and social space can be created by participants' attitudes towards each other and their communicative activities. How did the public sphere historically extend beyond concern with public opinion and the publicity of communication, to acquire political functions?

In his *Structural Transformation of the Public Sphere*, Habermas tells an historical story of the creation of distinctly modern public sphere that depends upon just such a free exercise of the creative powers of communication. In contrast to the representative public of the aristocracy for whom nonparticipants are regarded as spectators, participation in a democratic public is fundamentally open. 'The issues discussed became 'general,' not merely in their significance but also in their accessibility: everyone had to be able to participate' (Habermas 1989, p. 38). Even when the public was in fact a group of people discussing in a salon or newspaper, it also was interested in its own adherence to norms of publicity and regarded itself as a public within a larger public. Because the public sphere of this sort required such universal access, participants in the public sphere resisted any restrictions and censorship imposed by state interests. These restrictions (at least in England) were placed precisely on information related to transnational trade, thought to violate state interests in maintaining control over the colonies. This conflict with authority was so great that, at least in England, the development of the public sphere was marked by the continual confrontation of the authority of the Crown and Parliament with the press, particularly with regard to their attempt to assert authority over the public sphere itself (Habermas 1989, p. 60). For participants in the public sphere, such censorship threatened to undermine the openness and freedom of communication in the public sphere and thus the status of being a member of the public. This status was one of fundamental equality, of being able to address others and be addressed by them in turn – an equality that authority and status could not alter.

This specifically egalitarian expansion of the public sphere requires a more elaborate institutional structure to support it (such as that achieved by the modern democratic state but not identical with it), as the social contexts of communication are enlarged with the number of relevant speakers and audience. In public spheres, there is a demand for the inclusion of all those who participate and recognize each other as participants; this inclusion is not merely a matter of literal size or scope but of mutually granted equal standing. Contrary to misleading analogies to the national public sphere, such a development hardly demands that the public sphere be 'integrated with media systems of matching scale that occupy the same social space as that over which economic and political decisions will have an impact' (Garnham 1995). But, if the only effective way to create a public sphere across a differentiated social space is through multiple communicative networks rather than an encompassing mass media, then the global public sphere should not be expected to mirror the cultural unity and spatial congruence of the national public sphere; as a public of publics, it permits a decentered public sphere with many different levels. Disaggregated networks must always be embedded in some other set of social institutions rather than an assumed unified national public sphere. Once we examine the potential ways in which the Internet can expand the features of communicative interaction using such distributive and network forms, the issue of whether or not the Internet can support public spheres changes in character. Whether the Internet is a public sphere depends on the political agency of those concerned with its public character.

The main lesson to be drawn from these preliminaries is that discussions of the democratic potential of any form of communication (such as the Internet) cannot be satisfied with listing its positive or intrinsic features, as for example its speed, its scale, its 'anarchic' nature, its ability to facilitate resistance to centralized control as a network of networks, and so on. The same is true for its negative effects or consequences, such as its well-known disaggregative character or its anonymity. Taken together, both these considerations tell against regarding the Internet as a variation of existing print and national public spheres. Rather, the space opened up by computer-mediated communication supports a new sort of 'distributive' rather than unified public sphere with new forms of interaction. By 'distributive,' I mean a form of communication that 'decenters' the public sphere; it is a public of publics rather than a distinctively unified and encompassing public sphere in which all communicators participate. Here there is also clear analogy to current thinking on human cognition. The conception of rationality employed in most traditional theories tends to favor hierarchical structures, where reason is a higher-order executive function. One might argue that this is the only real possibility, given that collective reasoning can only be organized hierarchically, in a process in which authority resides at only one highest level. There is no empirical evidence that human reasoning occurs only in this way, however. As Susan Hurley points out, much of cognitive science has rejected such a view of a central cognitive process and its 'vertical modularity' and has replaced it with one of 'leaky boundaries' and 'horizontal modularity' in which 'each layer or horizontal module is dynamic' and extends 'from input through output and back to input in various feedback loops' (Hurley 1999, p. 274).[4] By analogy (and by analogy only), this kind of recursive structure is best organized in social settings through dynamically overlapping and interacting units, rather than distinct units related to a central unit of deliberation exercising executive control. In complex operations, such as guiding a large vessel into harbor, no one person possesses sufficient knowledge to fulfill the task. Errors can only be determined post hoc. Given that most polities do not exhibit such a unitary structure, the escalation of power in attempts to assert central control not only has antidemocratic consequences but also serves to undermine gains in rationality.

Rather than simply offering a new version of the existing print-mediated public sphere, the Internet becomes a public sphere only through agents

---

[4] Here, and earlier in her *Natural Reasons* (1989), Susan Hurley argues that borders can be more or less democratic, in terms of promoting epistemic values of inquiry and the moral value of autonomy as constitutive of democracy. For examples of this form of cognition in social settings, see Hutchings (1995).

who engage in reflexive and democratic activity. In other words, for the Internet to create a new form of publicity beyond the mere aggregate of all its users, it must first be constituted as a public sphere by those people whose interactions exhibit the features of dialogue and are concerned with its publicity. In order to support a public sphere and technologically mediate the appropriate norms, the network form must become a viable means for the expansion of the possibilities of dialogue and of the deliberative, second-order features of communicative interaction. These features are indeed not the same as manifested in previous political public spheres (such as the bourgeois public sphere of private persons), but can nonetheless give rise to such higher-order and reflexive forms of publicity.

In the next section, I argue that it is precisely such a distributive public sphere that can respond to the new, post–Westphalian world of politics that is in very significant ways located beyond the state. With the emergence of new distributive publics, dispersed and denationalized authority of agents could once again become the subject of public debate, even if the consequences of such authority are not uniformly felt. The most obvious example is the exercise of corporate power over the Internet and the attempt to control universal access so as to create the functional equivalent of censorship without centralized public authority. Such a concern with publicity also creates attitudes of common public concern, as illustrated below by the role of dispersed publics who sought to revere the reversal of agency in the disputes about the Multinational Agreement on Investment. This shows the potential democratizing power of new distributive publics in their relation to predominant forms of global political authority. It is no accident that this authority is exercised precisely within a structurally similar, new historical setting with the potential to undermine the public sphere. This provides a possibility of freedom from domination that is not only a matter of being a 'citizen in a free state,' but also depends on the capability of becoming a free participant in a public sphere embedded in other public spheres.

COMMUNICATIVE FREEDOM AND THE DISTRIBUTIVE PUBLIC SPHERE: THE ROLE OF AGENCY

As I have discussed thus far, communicative freedom operates in a generic modern public sphere, that is, one that combines both face-to-face and mediated communication. The typical forms of such mediation now seem inadequate to a public sphere writ large enough to obtain on the global level. Even if this were possible, it would hardly create the conditions for communicative freedom necessary for democracy. Two problems are now emerging: the first concerns the issue of a feasible form of mediation and the possibilities for communicative freedom within it; and the second takes up the possibility of new formal and institutional forms that could interact and mediate such preconditions transnationally and have the potential for interaction between the normative powers of institutional roles, such as citizen and office holder, and the communicative freedom of members of publics created by interacting publics. The first issue concerns informal network forms of communication such as the Internet; the second concerns new forms of highly dispersed deliberation, such as those emerging in certain practices and institutions of the European Union, primarily at the level of policy formation. Both permit the exercise of new forms of political agency, while at the same time demanding the agency of those who might otherwise suffer the reversal of agency, both as users and as principals.

If the Internet communication has no intrinsic features, it is because, like writing, it holds out many different possibilities for transforming the public sphere. At the same time, the Internet does have certain structural features that are relevant to issues of agency and control. Here it is useful to distinguish between hardware and software. As hardware, the World Wide Web is a network of networks with technical properties that enable the conveyance of information over great distances with near simultaneity. This hardware can be used for different purposes, as embodied in software that configures participants as 'users.' Indeed, as Lessig notes, 'an extraordinary amount of control can be built in the environment that people know in cyberspace,' perhaps even without their knowledge (Lessig 1999, p. 217). Such computer programs depend on software in a much broader sense. Software not only includes the variety of programs available, but also shapes the ways in which people improvise and collaborate to create new possibilities for interaction. Software, in the latter sense, includes both the modes of social organization mediated through the network and the institutions in which such communication is embedded. For example, the indeterminacy of the addressees of an anonymous message can be settled by reconfiguring the Internet into an intranet, creating a private space that excludes others and defines the audience. This is indeed how most corporations use the Web today, creating inaccessible and commercial spaces within networks by the use of firewalls and other devices that protect commercial and monetary interactions among corporations and anonymous consumers. The Web thus enables political and social power to be distributed in civil society, but it also permits such power to be manifested less in the capacity to interfere with others than in the capacity to exclude them from interaction and constrain the freedom and openness of the Internet as a public space. This same power may alter other mediated public spheres, as when the *New York Times* offers to deliver a 'personalized' paper that is not identical with the one that other citizens in the political public sphere are reading.

The fact that social power is manifested in technological mediation reveals the importance of institutions in preserving and maintaining public space, and the Internet is no exception. Saskia Sassen has shown how the Internet has historically reflected the institutions in which it as been embedded and configured. Its 'anarchist' phase reflected the ways in which it was created in universities and for scientific purposes. While the Web still bears the marks of this phase as possibilities of distributed power, it is arguably entering a different phase, in which corporations increasingly privatize this common space as a kind of *terra nullia* for their specific purposes, such as financial transactions. 'We are at a particular historical moment in the history of electronic space when powerful corporate actors and high performance networks are strengthening the role of private electronic space and altering the structure of public electronic space' (Sassen 1998, p. 191). At the same time, it is also clear that civil society groups, especially transnational groups, are using the Web for their own political and public purposes, where freedom and interconnectivity are what is valued. We are now in a period of the development of the software and hardware of the Internet in which the very nature of the Web is at issue. More specifically, its 'political' structure and distribution of authority over hardware and software as such is at issue, with similar processes of political decentralization and social contestation taking place in both domains. Those concerned with the publicity, freedom and openness of the Internet as a public space may see those features of the Internet that extend dialogical interaction threatened by the annexation of the Internet by the resources of large-scale economic enterprises. Addressing such a concern requires that civil society actors not only contest the alterations of public space, but that these actors place themselves between the corporations, software makers, access providers, and other powerful agents. 'Users' can reflexively configure themselves as agents and intermediaries, and, thus, as a public.

This parallel between the Internet and the early modern print media suggests a particular analysis of the threats to public space. It is now commonplace to say that the Internet rids communication of intermediaries, that is, those various professional communicators whose mass-mediated communication is the focus of much public debate and discussion. Dewey lauded such a division of labor to the extent that it can improve deliberation, not merely by creating a common public sphere but also by evolving 'the subtle, delicate, vivid and responsive art of communication.' This latter task is, at least in part, best fulfilled by professional communicators who disseminate the best available information and technologies to large audiences of citizens. Even with this dependence on intermediating techniques of communication, the public need not simply be the object of techniques of persuasion. Rather than merely a 'mass' of cultural dopes, mediated communication makes a 'rational public' possible, in the sense that 'the public as a whole can generally form policy preferences that reflect the best available information' (Page 1995, p. 194). If we focus upon the totality of political information available and this surprising empirical tendency (as noted by Benjamin Page and others) for the public to correct media biases and distortions over time, it is possible to see how mediated communication can enhance the interaction among various participants in the communication presupposed in public deliberation. In complex, large-scale and pluralistic societies, mediated communication is unavoidable if there are to be channels of communication broad enough to address the highly heterogeneous audiences of all of their members and to treat issues that vary with regard to the epistemic demands on speakers in diverse locales.

Given their attachments to various institutions and technologies, some proponents of deliberation often claim that publics suffer a net normative loss in the shift to networked communication, further amplified given 'the control revolution' by which various corporations and providers act as agents for individuals and give them the capacity to control who addresses them and to whom they may respond (Shapiro 1999, p. 23). Or, to put the critics' point in the terms that I have been using here, the mass public sphere is not replaced by any public sphere at all; rather, communicative mediation is replaced by forms of control that make dialogue and the expansion of the deliberative features of communication impossible. In the terms of economic theory, agents whose purpose it is to facilitate individual control over the communicative environment replace intermediaries. Such a relation once again shifts the direction of control from principals to the agents whom they delegate. It is simply false to say that individuals possess immediate control; they have control only through assenting to an asymmetrical relationship to various agents who structure the choices in the communicative environment of cyberspace.

There is more than a grain of truth in this pessimistic diagnosis of the control revolution. But this leaves out part of the story concerning how the public exercises some control over intermediaries, at least over those concerned with publicity. As with the relation of agent and principal, the problem here is to develop democratic modes of interaction between expert communicators and their audiences in the public sphere. Citizens must now resist the 'mediaization of politics' on a par with the agency relations implicit in its technization by experts. The challenge is twofold. First of all, the public must challenge the credibility of expert communicators especially in their capacities to set agendas and frames for discussing issues. And, second, as in the case of cooperating with experts, the public must challenge the reception of their own public communication by the media themselves, especially insofar as they must also report, represent, and even construct the 'public opinion' of citizens who are distant strangers. This self-referential aspect of public communication can only be fulfilled by interactions between the media and the public, who challenge ways in which publics are both addressed and represented.

Such problems of expertise and mediaization are exacerbated as the mediated interaction between principals and agents becomes predominant in modern political and public spheres, thereby creating new forms of social interaction and political relationships that reorder in space and time and become structured in ways less and less like mutually responsive, face-to-face dialogue (Thompson 1995, p. 85). Analogous considerations of agency and asymmetries of access to the norms that shape communicative interaction are relevant to the Internet. It is clear that corporations can, and do, function among the main institutional actors in developing electronic space and in exerting an influence that often restricts communication in ways even more impervious to corporate media and political parties. Just as the technological mediation of features of communicative interaction opens such a space for agency, the formation of public spheres requires counter-intermediaries and counter-public spaces of some kind or other to maintain their publicness. In other words, the sustainability of such spaces over time depends precisely upon the agency of those who are concerned with the character of public opinion and, thus, with influencing the construction of the public space by whatever technical means of communication are available. The Internet and its governance now lack the means to institutionalize the public sphere, especially since there are no functional equivalents to the roles played by journalists, judges, and other intermediaries who regulate and protect the publicity of political communication in the mass media.

Who occupies these roles, which were once the technology of mediation changes? The Internet has not yet achieved a settled form in which intermediaries have been established and professionalized. As in the emerging public spheres of early modernity, the potential intermediary roles must emerge from those who organize themselves in cyberspace as a public sphere. This role falls to those organizations in civil society that have become concerned with the publicity of electronic space and seek to create, institutionalize, expand and protect it. Such organizations can achieve their goals only if they act self-referentially and insist that they have a right to exercise communicative freedom in shaping and appropriating electronic public space. Thus, contrary to Shapiro and Sunstein, it is not that the Internet gets rid of intermediaries as such; rather it operates in a public space in which the particular *democratic* intermediaries have lost their influence. Thus, this is not a necessary structural consequence of its form of communication.

With the development of the Internet as a public sphere, we may expect its 'reintermediarization,' that is, the emergence of new intermediaries who counter its privatization and individualization brought about by access and content providers for commercial purposes and who construct the user as a private person rather than as a member of the public. Actors can play the role of 'counterintermediaries' when they attempt to bypass these narrow social roles on the Internet; that is, when they seek to avoid the role of a 'user' in relation to a 'provider' who sets the terms of how the Internet may be employed. The first area in which this has already occurred is in Internet self-governance organizations that express their interest in countering trends to annexation and privatization. Here institutions, such as Internet-standard-setting bodies, have attempted to institute public deliberation on the legal and technological standards that govern the Internet (Froomkin 2003).

This and other examples of a deliberative process through multiple inter-mediaries might be termed 'reintermediarization.'

Given that what is needed in order to secure various public spaces are alternatives to the current set of intermediaries rather than the absence of them, civil society organizations have distinctive advantages in taking on such a responsibility for publicity in cyberspace. They have organiza-tional identities so that they are no longer anonymous; they also take over the responsibility for responsiveness that remains indeterminate in many-to-many communication. Most of all, they employ the Internet, but not as 'users'; they create their own spaces, promote interactions, conduct deliber-ation, make information available, and so on. As I mentioned above, a variety of organizations created a forum for debate on the Multilateral Agreement on Investment (MAI), an issue that hardly registered in the national media. Not only did these organizations make the MAI widely available, they also held detailed online discussions of the merits of its various provisions (Smith and Smythe 2001, p. 183). As a tool for various forms of activism, the Internet promotes a vibrant civil society; it extends the public sphere of civil society, but does not necessarily transform it. The point is not simply to create a Web site or to convey information. The Internet becomes something more only when sites are made to be public spaces in which free, open and responsive dialogical interaction takes place. This sort of project is not uncommon and includes experiments among neighborhood groups, NGOs, and others. The civil society organization acts as an intermediary in a different and public-regarding way – not as an expert communicator, but rather as the creator and facilitator of institutional 'software' that socializes the commons and makes it a public space. Such software creates a cosmopolitan political space, a normed communicative commons of indefinite interaction.

As long as there are actors who will create and maintain transnational communication, this sort of serial and distributed public sphere is poten-tially global in scope. Its unity is to be found in the general conditions for the formation of publics themselves, and in the actions of those who see themselves as constituting a public against this background. Membership in these shifting publics is to be found in civil society, in formal and infor-mal organizations that emerge to discuss and deliberate on the issues of the day. The creation of publics is a matter of communicators becoming concerned with and acting to create the general conditions that make such a process possible; once such agents are present, it is a matter for formal institutionalization, just as sustaining the conditions for the national public sphere is a central concern of the citizens of democratic nation states. In the case of such shifting and potentially transnational publics, the institutions that sustain publicity and become the focus of the self-referential activity of civil society must also be innovative if they are to have their commu-nicative basis in dispersed and decentered forms of publicity. At the same time, these institutions must be deliberative and democratic. Because they become the location for second-order reflexive political deliberation and activity, these institutions are part of the public sphere as a higher-order and self-governing form of publicity that transforms the Internet from a commons to an institutionally organized and embedded democratic space in which citizens exercise normative powers.

In the next section, I make use of the structural analogue between conditions of publics and democratic institutions by turning to the potential constructive role of distributive publics, that is, to the sort of institutional designs with which such publics could interact so as to expand communicative freedom. Once institutionalized, these commitments to the freedom of participants could secure necessary conditions for nondomination with respect to dispersed authority.

FROM PUBLICS TO PUBLIC SPHERE: THE INSTITUTIONAL FORM OF TRANSNATIONAL DEMOCRACY

I have argued that the reflexive agency of actors in new publics could establish positive and enabling conditions for democratic deliberation. The public must itself be embedded in an institutional context, not only if it is to secure the conditions of publicity, but also in order to promote the interaction among publics that is required for deliberative democracy. Thus, both network forms of communication and the publics formed in them must be embedded in a larger institutional and political context if they are to be transformed into public spheres in which citizens can make claims and expect an appropriate response. In much the same way that they have responded to censorship, publics interact with institutions in order to shape them and to secure their own communicative freedom. In so doing, they expand their normative powers of citizens – powers to shape the conditions of communication rather than simply demand immunity from interference.

There are several reasons to think that current democratic institutions are insufficient for this task. For one thing, states have promoted the privatization of various media spaces for communication, including not only the Internet but also broadcast frequencies. Even if the Internet is not intrinsically anarchistic, and even if states were willing to do more in the way of protecting the public character of cyberspace, it remains an open question whether this form of communication can escape the way in which state sovereignty monopolizes power over political space and time, including public space and the temporality of deliberation. It is precisely the Internet's potentially 'aterritorial' character that makes it difficult to square with centralized forms of authority over a delimited territory. This sort of process of deterritorialization, however, does not require convergence, especially since Internet use may reflect inequalities in the access to rule-making institutions as well as older patterns of subordination at the international level. It is also true that people do not as yet have patterns of communication sufficient to identify with each other on cosmopolitan terms. Nonetheless, new possibilities that the Internet affords for deliberation and access to influence in its distributive and network forms do not require such strong preconditions in order to open up new forms of democratization.

It is certainly not the case that states have been entirely ineffective in sustaining these conditions, nor is it true that national public spheres are so culturally limited that they serve no democratic purpose. Rather, what is at stake is whether such public spheres will cease to be as politically important. If the Internet escapes territoriality, then there will be no analogue at the institutional level for the particular connections and feedback relations between the national public sphere and the democratic state. Whatever the institutions that are able to promote and protect such a dispersed and disaggregated public sphere, they will represent a novel political possibility as long as they do not 'merely replicate on a larger scale the typical modern political form' (Ruggie 1996, p. 195). This access to political influence through mediated communication will not be attained once and for all, as it was in the unified public sphere of nation states in which citizens gain influence through the complex of parliamentary or representative institutions. Currently, Internet publics are 'weak' publics, who exert such influence over decision-making institutions through public opinion generally. But they may become 'strong' publics when they are able to exercise influence through institutionalized decision procedures with regularized opportunities for input. Transnational institutions are adequately democratic if they permit such access to influence distributively across various domains and levels, rather than merely aggregatively in the summative public sphere of all citizens. Because there is no single institution to which strong publics are connected, the contrast between weak and strong publics is much more fluid than the current usage presupposes.

Before turning to the question of how public spheres may be institutionalized transnationally, let me consider an objection put forth by Will Kymlicka, if only to show the specific difference that transnational publics make as preconditions for democratization. Because the political institutions of democracy must be territorially congruent with the available forms of publicity, the difficulties posed by the disunity of a global public sphere cut much deeper for the idea of deliberative democracy. As Kymlicka has pointed out, territoriality continues to survive by other means, particularly since 'language is increasingly important in defining the boundaries of political communities and the identities of the actors' (Kymlicka 1999, p. 120). For this reason, Kymlicka argues, national communities 'remain the primary forum for participatory democratic debates.' Whereas international forums are dominated by elites, national public spheres are more likely to be spaces for egalitarian, mass participation in the vernacular language and are thus the only forums that guarantee 'genuine' democratic participation and influence. Moreover, Kymlicka argues that, since deliberation depends on common cultural frameworks, such as shared newspapers and political parties, the scope of a deliberative community must be limited to those who share a political culture. Transnational democracy cannot be either participatory and deliberative, and perhaps not even 'genuinely' democratic at all (Dahl 1999, p. 19ff). This argument is particularly challenging to the view defended here, since it employs the same idea of a dialogical public sphere within a democracy oriented to deliberation in order to reach the *opposite* conclusion. Can mediated communication and the extension of dialogue go beyond a territorial, self-governing linguistic community?

Without a single location of public power, the unified public sphere that Kymlicka makes a necessary condition of democracy becomes an impediment, rather than an enabling condition for mass participation in decisions at a single location of authority. The minimal criterion of adequacy is that, even with the diffusion of authority, participants in the public sphere would have to be sufficiently empowered to create opportunities and access to influence over transnational decision-making. Currently such publics are weak, in the sense that they exert influence only through general public opinion. Or, as in the case of NGOs with respect to human rights, publics may rely heavily on supranational judicial institutions, adjudication boards, and other already constituted and authoritative bodies. In order that publics use their communicative freedom to transform normative powers, they need not ever become strong publics in the national sense of being connected to a particular set of parliamentary or representative institutions.[5] However, even strong publics do not rule. That is because strong publics can be regularized through the entrenched connection between the public opinion formed in them to a particular sort of legislatively empowered collective will. Although this mechanism is inadequate for situations of the dispersed institutional distribution of processes that form a popular will, transnational institutions would still have to permit agents to influence deliberation and decisions through the exercise of their communicative freedom across various domains and levels.

Rather than look for a single axis on which to connect emerging publics to decision-making processes in international and transnational institutions, it will be more useful to consider a variety of possible forms of communication, given the various ways in which connections can be made between communicative freedom and normative powers in the public sphere. Although the Internet provides a paradigm case of a distributive public sphere, the European Union provides the fullest and most exemplary case. I will consider only one aspect of the debate about the E.U.'s 'democratic deficit'

---

[5] On the distinction between strong and weak publics, see Nancy Fraser (1989). Habermas (1996, chapter 7) appropriates this distinction in his 'two-track model of democracy.' The requirements of a strong public sphere for both are closely tied to access to influence over legislation that produces coercive law.

here: proposals that are suggestive of how a polycentric form of publicity might permit rather different forms of democratic deliberative influence than the national public formed around parliamentary debate.

While the full range of possible forms of institutionalization cannot be considered fully here, the European Union is a transnational political entity and, as such, obviously lacks the unitary and linguistic features of previous public spheres. I will consider only one aspect of the interaction between transnational publics and political institutions: practices of decision making that are suggestive of how a polycentric form of publicity would permit a more, rather than less, directly deliberative form of governance, once we abandon the assumption that there must be a unified public sphere connected to a single set of state-like authority structures that impose uniform policies over its entire territory. As Charles Sabel has argued, a 'directly deliberative' design in many ways incorporates epistemic innovations and increased capabilities of economic organizations, in the same way as the regulatory institutions of the New Deal followed the innovative patterns of industrial organization in the centralized mass production they attempted to administer and regulate (Dorf and Sabel 1996, p. 292). Roughly, such a form of organization uses nested and collaborative forms of decision-making based on highly dispersed collaborative processes of jointly defining problems and setting goals already typical in many large firms with dispersed sites of production. One such process is found in the use of the Open Method of Coordination (OMC) for many different policies (such as unemployment or poverty reduction) within the E.U., best described as 'a decentralized specification of standards, disciplined by systematic comparison' (Sabel and Cohen 1998).[6] In this process, citizens in France, Greece, and elsewhere deliberate as publics about policies simultaneously with E.U. citizens at different locations and compare and evaluate the results.

As a deliberative process, the OMC requires a design that promotes a great deal of interaction both within E.U. organizations and across sites and locations. Within the normative framework established by initial goals and benchmarks, the process of their application requires deliberation at various levels of scale. At all levels, citizens can introduce concerns and issues based on local knowledge of problems, even as they are informed by the diverse solutions and outcomes of other planning and design bodies. Local solutions can also be corrected and tested by the problem solving of other groups. Thus, although these publics are highly dispersed and distributed, various levels of deliberation permit public testing and correction, even if they do not hierarchically override decisions at lower levels. Such a collaborative process of setting goals and defining problems produces a shared body of knowledge and common goals, even if the solutions need not be uniform

---

[6] For a more direct application to the E.U., see Cohen and Sabel (2003). My description of the OMC as a deliberative procedure owes much to their account.

across or within various organizations and locations. Sabel calls this 'learning by monitoring' and proposes ways in which administrative agencies could employ such distributive processes even while evaluating performance at lower levels by systematic comparisons across sites. Furthermore, innovative solutions are not handed down from the top, since collective learning does not assume that the higher levels are epistemically superior.

From this brief description, it is possible to see why the OMC provides a space for ongoing reflection on agendas and problems, as well as promotes an interest in inclusiveness and diversity of perspectives. These enabling conditions for democracy can take advantage of the intensified interaction across borders that are byproducts of processes of the thickening of the communicative infrastructure across state borders. This sort of federalism provides for modes of accountability in this process itself, even while allowing for local variations that go beyond the assumption of the uniformity of policy over a single bounded territory typical of nation state regulation. Sabel and Cohen argue that the European Union already has features of a directly deliberative polyarchy in the implementation of the OMC in its economic, industrial, and educational standards. The advantage of such deliberative methods is that the interaction at different levels of decision-making promotes robust accountability; accountability operates upward and downward and, in this way, cuts across the typical distinction of vertical and horizontal accountability (O'Donnell 1994, p. 61). Thus, directly deliberative polyarchy describes a method of decision making in institutions across various levels and with plural authority structures.

The question still remains: who is the public at large at the level of democratic experimentation and implementation in directly deliberative processes? Sabel and Cohen provide no clear answer to this question, asserting only that the process must be open to the public (Cohen and Sabel 2003, p. 368). The problem for institutional design of directly deliberative democracy is to create precisely the appropriate feedback relations between disaggregated publics and such a polycentric decision-making process. As my discussion of the Internet shows, there is a technology through which this form of publicity is produced and which expands and maintains the deliberative potential of dialogue. Thus, at least in some of its decision-making processes, the E.U. could seek to marry directly deliberative decision making to computer-assisted, mediated, and distributive forms of publicity. Most of all, implementing this design would require experimentation in reconciling the dispersed form of many-to-many communication with the demands of the forum. Rather than providing an institutional blueprint, such direct and vigorous interaction among dispersed publics at various levels of decision making creates new forums and publics around locations at which various sort of decisions are debated and discussed. This sort of Internet counterpublic sphere is potentially transnational, as is the case in the public that formed around the Agreement on Investment. Appropriately designed decision-making processes, such as those in the E.U., combined with the existence of a suitable form of publicity, at least show how dialogue could be technologically and institutionally extended and democratically empowered in a transnational context.

NGOs and other actors in international civil society are often able to gain influence through consultation and contestation, sometimes involving public processes of deliberation. In most international organizations, this influence is primarily due not only to internal norms of transparency and accountability, but also via the mechanisms of various adjudicative and judicial institutions that empower individual citizens with rights of appeal. This sort of institutional architecture promotes deliberation through accountability and monitoring, and works particularly well with regard to national authorities and their normative commitments. Such adjudicative bodies also expand the possibilities of contestatory influence in the international context in the same way that civil rights law in the United States or antidiscrimination laws of various sorts in many different countries produce compliance. This sort of judicial influence may also work, as Andrew Moravcsik has suggested, as moral pressure without the backing of real sanctions: 'The decisive casual links lie in civil society: international pressure works when it can work through free and influential public opinion and an independent judiciary' (Moravcsik, 1995, p. 158). As the E.U. case shows, these uses of communicative freedom, and the normative powers created from recognition of the status of free and equal members of a public, need not then be understood as only applying to adjudicative institutions. Thus, although highly dispersed and distributed, various levels of deliberation permit testing and correction across a variety of mutually informative criteria. This method, with its diverse institutional structure, takes advantage of the enabling conditions of the public sphere that have produced the thickening of the communicative infrastructure needed for deliberation across state borders.

These examples of transnational public spheres (including the Internet public sphere of the debates about the MAI and the use of the OMC in the E.U.) bear out the significance of an interactive approach to the democratization of new social conditions that Dewey suggested in *The Public and Its Problems*. In response to Lippmann's insistence that the influence of experts replaces that of the public, Dewey conceded that 'existing political practice, with its complete ignoring of occupational groups and the organized knowledge and purposes that are involved in the existence of such groups, manifests a dependence upon a summation of individuals quantitatively' (Dewey 1991, pp. 50–51). In response to Lippmann's elitist view of majority rule, Dewey held on to the possibility and feasibility of democratic participation by the well-informed citizen, but only if democracy creatively reshapes its institutions to fit 'a scattered, mobile and manifold public' and interdependent communities that have yet to recognize themselves as a publics and form their own distinct common interests. Thus, the solution is a transformation both of what it is to be a public and of the institutions with which the public interacts. Such an interaction will provide the basis for determining how the functions of the new form of political organization will be limited and expanded, the scope of which is 'something to be critically and experimentally determined' (Dewey 1988, p. 281) in democracy as a mode of practical inquiry (such as that exemplified in the OMC method of problem solving). Thus, it is Dewey's conception of the interaction of public and institutions that is responsible not only for their democratic character but also for the mechanism of their structural transformation.

This approach to the transformation of the role of the public in a democracy has three implications for the problem of democratizing international society. First, neither bottom-up nor top-down strategies are sufficient to take advantage of communicative power; nor are contestation and consultation alone sufficient for nondomination. Rather, as my argument for the democratic minimum suggests, the capacity to initiate deliberation is essential. Beyond the minimum, the full potential for transnational democracy requires a constant interaction among institutions and publics, indeed one that is fully reciprocal and co-constitutive; publics must not only be shaped by institutions and their normative powers, but also must shape them. Second, as the E.U. examples show, democracy and nondomination at this level of aggregation are more likely to be promoted by a highly differentiated institutional structure with multiple levels and domains as well as multiple communities and publics rather than just through consultation in a single institutionalized decision-making process. Communicative freedom in a public sphere remains a minimal requirement of nondominating institutions, since the existence of many domains and levels permits citizens to address others, and be addressed by them, in multiple ways and to employ the resources of multiple jurisdictions and overlapping memberships against structures of domination and exploitative hierarchies. Third, such freedom will require a structure that has both interrelated local and cosmopolitan dimensions, each with their own normative powers. This interactive, polyarchic, and multilevel strategy is followed here in order to develop a transnational form of democracy and constitutionalism consistent with nondomination. When publics shape institutions and, in turn, are shaped by them, democracy emerges as the fruitful interaction between the openness of communicative freedom and the institutional recognition of normative statuses and powers.

In no role or location other than as citizens in democratic institutions do members of modern societies exercise their normative powers of imposing obligations and changing statuses – and resisting those who would dominate others by usurping these powers. Certainly, other forms of authority exist in modern societies that also make it possible for these statuses and obligations to change without popular influence or the discursive control of citizens. Democracy itself is then the joint exercise of these powers and capacities, so that they are not under the control of any given individual or group of citizens, as well as their possibility of the joint, creative redefinition in circumstances in which they have become the source of domination. The central precondition for such nondomination is the existence of the public sphere, a space for the exercise of communicative freedom. This space must now be transnational and, thus, a new kind of public sphere with new forms of technological and institutional mediation. Without this open structure of publics, the overlapping and crosscutting dimensions of interactions across various political communities could not secure the freedom that is a necessary condition for nondomination. Publics provide a social location for the power to initiate communication and deliberation that is essential to any minimally democratic order.

CONCLUSION

My argument here has been two-sided. On the one hand, I have developed an account of the potential of the new distributive form of the public sphere for creating certain preconditions for democracy, specifically, the conditions necessary for communicative freedom that emerges in the mutual recognition of participants in the public sphere and in their struggles to maintain the public sphere against censorship and other arbitrary forms of dominating political authority. On the other hand, I have argued that such freedoms can be secured only through the development of innovative institutions, in which a minimum of democratic equality becomes entrenched in various basic rights granted to citizens. In each case, new circumstances suggest rethinking both democracy and the public sphere outside the limits of their previous historical forms. Rethinking publicity allows us to see that some critical diagnoses of the problems of new forms of communication and publics for democracy are short-circuited by a failure to think beyond what is politically familiar. If my argument is correct that distributive publics are able to preserve and extend the dialogical character of the public sphere in a potentially cosmopolitan form, then a deliberative transnational democracy can be considered a 'realistic utopia' in Rawls' sense; these new public spheres extend the range of political possibilities for a deliberative democracy across borders.

If these obligation-constituting elements of dialogue are preserved and extended within the new form of a deliberative public sphere, then a further essential democratic element is also possible: that the public sphere can serve as a source of agency and social criticism. In either adopting the role of the critic or in taking up such criticism in the public sphere, speakers adopt the standpoint of the 'generalized other,' the relevant critical perspective that opens up a potential standpoint of a free and more inclusive community. As Mead put it: 'The question whether we belong to a larger community is answered in terms of whether our own actions call out a response in this wider community, and whether its response is reflected back into our own conduct' (Mead 1934, pp. 270–271). This sort of mutual responsiveness and interdependence is possible only in a democratic form of communication that accommodates multiple perspectives. To the question of the applicability of such norms and institutions internationally, Mead is quite optimistic: 'Could a conversation be conducted internationally? The question is a question of social organization.' Organization requires agency, and the democratic reorganization of technological mediation begins with the interventions of democratic agents and intermediaries, both of which require publics. In the early modern period, publics have formed as spaces for communicative freedom in opposition to the attempts by states to exert political authority over them in censorship. Similarly, today publics can become aware of themselves as publics in challenging those dispersed forms of political, legal, and economic authority that seek to control and restrict the Internet as a space for communicative freedom across borders.

References

Arrow, K. 1985. The economics of agency, in J. Pratt and R. Zeckhauser (Eds.), *Principals and agents*. Cambridge, MA: Harvard Business School Press.

Bohman, J. 1996. Democracy as inquiry, inquiry as democratic. *American Journal of Political Science, 43*, 590–607.

Bohman, J. 2004. Expanding dialogue: The public sphere, the Internet, and transnational democracy, in J. Roberts and N. Crossley (Eds.), *After Habermas: Perspectives on the public sphere*. London: Blackwell, pp. 131–155.

Cohen, J., and Sabel, C. 2003. Sovereignty and solidarity: EU and US, in J. Zeitlin and D. Trubek (Eds.), *Governing work and welfare in the new economy: European and American experiments*. Oxford: Oxford University Press.

Dahl, R. 1999. Can international organizations be democratic? A skeptic's view, in I. Shapiro and C. Hacker-Cordón (Eds.), *Democracy's edges*. New York: Cambridge University Press.

Dewey, J. 1988. The public and its problems, in *John Dewey: The later works, 1925–1927* (Vol. 2). Carbondale, IL: Southern Illinois University Press.

Dewey, J. 1991. Liberalism and social action, in *John Dewey: The later works, 1925–1927* (Vol. 11). Carbondale, IL: Southern Illinois University Press.

Dorf, M., and Sabel, C. 1996. The constitution of democratic experimentalism. *Columbia Law Review, 98*, 2, 267–473.

Dryzek, J. 1996. *Democracy in capitalist times*. Oxford: Oxford University Press.

Ewig, C. 1999. Strengths and limits of the NGO Women's Movement Model, *Latin American Research Review, 34*, 3, 75–102.

Fraser, N. 1989. Rethinking the public sphere, in C. Calhoun (Ed.), *Habermas and the public sphere*. Cambridge, MA: MIT Press, pp. 109–142.

Froomkin, M. 2003. Habermas@discourse.net: Towards a critical theory of Cyberspace. *Harvard Law Review, 116*, 3, 751–873.

Garnham, N. 1995. The mass media, cultural identity, and the public sphere in the modern world. *Public Culture, 5*, 243–271.

Habermas, J. 1989. *The structural transformation of the public sphere.* Cambridge, MA: MIT Press.

Habermas, J. 1996. *Between facts and norms.* Cambridge, MA: MIT Press.

Hurley, S. 1989. *Natural reasons.* New York: Oxford University Press.

Hurley, S. 1999. Rationality, democracy, and leaky boundaries, in I. Shapiro and C. Hacker-Cordón (Eds.), *Democracy's edges.* New York: Cambridge University Press.

Hutchings, E. 1995. *Cognition in the wild.* Cambridge, MA: MIT Press.

Kymlicka, W. 1999. Citizenship in an era of globalization, in I. Shapiro and C. Hacker-Cordón (Eds.), *Democracy's edges.* New York: Cambridge University Press.

Lessig, L. 1999. *Code and other laws of cyberspace.* New York: Basic Books.

Llewellyn, K. 1930. Agency, in *Encyclopedia of the Social Sciences,* Volume I. New York: MacMillan.

Mead, G. H. 1934. *Mind, self, and society.* Chicago: University of Chicago Press.

Moravcsik, A. 1995. Explaining international human rights regimes: Liberal theory and Western Europe. *European Journal of International Relations, 1,* 2, 157–189.

O'Donnell, G. 1994. Delegative democracy. *Journal of Democracy, 5,* 55–69.

Page, B. 1995. *Who deliberates?* Chicago: University of Chicago Press.

Pettit, P. 2000. Democracy, electoral and contestatory, in I. Shapiro and S. Macedo (Eds), *Designing democratic institutions.* New York: New York University Press.

Ruggie, G. 1996. *Constructing the world polity.* London: Routledge.

Sabel, C., and Cohen, J. 1998. Directly-deliberative polyarchy, in *Private governance, democratic constitutionalism, and supranationalism.* Florence: European Commission, pp. 3–30.

Sassen, S. 1998. *Globalization and its discontents.* New York: New Press.

Shapiro, A. 1999. *The control revolution.* New York: New Century Books.

Shapiro, S. 1987. The social control of impersonal trust. *American Journal of Sociology, 93,* 3, 623–658.

Smith, J., and Smythe, E. 2001. Globalization, citizenship and technology: The Multilateral Agreement on Investment meets the Internet, in F. Webster (Ed.), *Culture and politics in the age of information.* London: Routledge.

Soysal, Y. 1994. *Limits of citizenship: Migrants and postnational membership in Europe.* Chicago: University of Chicago Press.

Thompson, J. 1995. *Media and modernity.* Palo Alto, CA: Stanford University Press.

5

Democracy and the Internet[1]

Cass R. Sunstein

Is the Internet a wonderful development for democracy? In many ways it certainly is. As a result of the Internet, people can learn far more than they could before, and they can learn it much faster. If you are interested in issues that relate to public policy – air quality, wages over time, motor vehicle safety, climate change – you can find what you need to know in a matter of seconds. If you are suspicious of the mass media and want to discuss issues with like-minded people, you can do that, transcending the limitations of geography in ways that could barely be imagined even a decade ago. And if you want to get information to a wide range of people, you can do that, via email, blogs, or Web sites; this is another sense in which the Internet is a great boon for democracy.

But in the midst of the celebration, I want to raise a note of caution. I do so by emphasizing one of the most striking powers provided by emerging technologies: the growing power of consumers to 'filter' what they see. As a result of the Internet and other technological developments, many people are increasingly engaged in the process of 'personalization', which limits their exposure to topics and points of view of their own choosing. They filter in and they also filter out, with unprecedented powers of precision. Relevant Web sites and blogs are being created every week. Consider just a few representative examples from recent years:

1. Broadcast.com has 'compiled hundreds of thousands of programs so you can find the one that suits your fancy . . . For example, if you want to see all the latest fashions from France twenty-four hours of the day you can get them. If you're from Baltimore living in Dallas and you want to listen to WBAL, your hometown station, you can hear it' (Sikes and Pearlman 2000, pp. 204, 211).

[1] This chapter borrows from Sunstein (2001) and Sunstein (2007). The excerpts used here are reprinted by permission.

2. Sonicnet.com allows you to create your own musical universe, consisting of what it calls 'Me Music'. Me Music is 'A place where you can listen to the music you love on the radio station YOU create ... A place where you can watch videos of your favorite artists and new artists. ...'

3. Zatso.com allows users to produce 'a personal newscast'. Its intention is to create a place 'where you decide what's news'. Your task is to tell 'what TV news stories you're interested in', and Zatso.com turns that information into a specifically designed newscast. From the main 'This is the News I Want' menu, you can choose stories with particular words and phrases, or you can select topics, such as sports, weather, crime, health, government/politics, and much more.

4. Info Xtra offers 'news and entertainment that's important to you', and it allows you to find this 'without hunting through newspapers, radio and websites'. Personalized news, local weather, and even your daily horoscope will be delivered to you once you specify what you want and when you want it.

5. TiVo, a television recording system, is designed, in the words of its Web site, to give 'you the ultimate control over your TV viewing'. It does this by putting 'you at the center of your own TV network, so you'll always have access to whatever you want, whenever you want'. TiVo 'will automatically find and digitally record your favorite programs every time they air' and will help you create 'your personal TV line-up'. It will also learn your tastes, so that it can 'suggest other shows that you may want to record and watch based on your preferences'.

6. Intertainer, Inc. provides 'home entertainment services on demand', not limited to television but also including music, movies, and shopping. Intertainer is intended for people who want 'total control' and 'personalized experiences'. It is 'a new way to get whatever movies, music and television you want anytime you want on your PC or TV'.

7. George Bell, the Chief Executive Officer of the search engine Excite, exclaims, 'We are looking for ways to be able to lift chunks of content off other areas of our service and paste them onto your personal page so you can constantly refresh and update that 'newspaper of me'. About 43 percent of our entire user data base has personalized their experience on Excite' (Sikes and Pearlman 2000, p. 25).

Of course these developments make life much more convenient and, in some ways, much better; we all seek to reduce our exposure to uninvited noise. But from the standpoint of democracy, filtering is a mixed blessing. An understanding of the mix will permit us to obtain a better sense of what makes for a well-functioning system of free expression. Above all, I urge that, in a heterogeneous society, such a system requires something other than free, or publicly unrestricted, individual choices. On the contrary, it imposes two distinctive requirements. First, people should be exposed to materials that they would not have chosen in advance. *Unanticipated encounters*, involving topics and points of view that people have not sought out and perhaps find quite irritating, are central to democracy and even to freedom itself. Second, many or most citizens should have a range of *common experiences*. Without shared experiences, a heterogeneous society will have a much more difficult time addressing social problems; people may even find it hard to understand one another.

A THOUGHT EXPERIMENT

To see the issue, let us engage in a thought experiment – an apparently utopian dream, one of complete individuation, in which consumers can entirely personalize (or 'customize') their own communications universe.

Imagine a system of communications in which each person has unlimited power of individual design. If people want to watch news all the time, they would be entirely free to do exactly that. If they dislike news, and want to watch basketball in the morning and situation comedies at night, that would be fine too. If people care only about America and want to avoid international issues entirely, that would be very simple indeed; so too if they care only about New York, or Chicago, or California. If people want to restrict themselves to certain points of view, by limiting themselves to conservatives, moderates, liberals, socialists, vegetarians, or Nazis, that would be entirely feasible with a simple 'point and click'. If people want to isolate themselves and speak only with like-minded others, that is feasible too.

A number of newspapers are now allowing readers to create filtered versions, containing exactly what they want, and no more. If you are interested in getting help with the design of an entirely individual paper, you can consult a number of sites, including individual.com and crayon.net. To be sure, the Internet greatly increases people's ability to expand their horizons, as millions of people are now doing; but many people are using it to produce narrowness, not breadth. MIT professor Nicholas Negroponte thus refers to the emergence of what he called 'the Daily Me' – a communications package that is personally designed, with components fully chosen in advance.

Of course this is not entirely different from what has come before. People who read newspapers do not all read the same newspaper; some people do not read any newspaper at all. People make choices among magazines based on their tastes and their points of view. But in the emerging situation, there is a difference of degree, if not of kind. What *is* different is a dramatic increase in individual control over content and a corresponding decrease in the power of general interest intermediaries, including newspapers, magazines, and broadcasters. For all of their problems and their unmistakable limitations and biases, these intermediaries have performed some important democratic functions.

People who rely on such intermediaries have a range of chance encounters, involving shared experience with diverse others and also exposure to material that they did not specifically choose. You might, for example, read the city newspaper and, in the process, come across a range of stories that you would not have selected if you had the power to control what you see. Your eyes may come across a story about Berlin, crime in Los Angeles, or innovative business practices in Tokyo, and you may read those stories, although you would not place them in your 'Daily Me'. You might watch a particular television channel and, when your favorite program ends, you might see the beginning of another show – one that you would not have chosen in advance. Reading *Time* magazine, you might come across a discussion of endangered species in Madagascar and this discussion might interest you and even affect your behavior, although you would not have sought it out in the first instance. A system in which individuals lack control over the particular content that they see has a great deal in common with a public street, where you might encounter not only friends, but a heterogeneous variety of people engaged in a wide array of activities (including perhaps political protests and begging).

In fact a risk with a system of perfect individual control is that it can reduce the importance of the 'public sphere' and of common spaces in general. One of the important features of such spaces is that they tend to ensure that people will encounter materials on important issues, whether or not they have specifically chosen the encounter. And when people see materials that they have not chosen, their interests, and even their views, might change as a result. At the very least, they will know a bit more about what their fellow citizens are thinking. As it happens, this point is closely connected with an important, and somewhat exotic, constitutional principle to which I now turn.

PUBLIC (AND PRIVATE) FORUMS

In the popular understanding, the free speech principle forbids government from 'censoring' speech it disapproves of. In the standard cases, the government attempts to impose penalties, either civil or criminal, on political dissent, and on speech that it considers dangerous, libelous, or sexually explicit. The question is whether the government has a legitimate, and sufficiently weighty, basis for restricting the speech that it seeks to control.

But a central part of free speech law, with important implications for thinking about the Internet, takes a quite different form. In the United States, the Supreme Court has also held that streets and parks must be kept open to the public for expressive activity.[2] Hence, governments are obliged

---

[2] *Hague v. CIO*, 307 US 496 (1939).

to allow speech to occur freely on public streets and in public parks, even if many citizens would prefer to have peace and quiet and even if it seems irritating to come across protesters and dissidents whom one would like to avoid. To be sure, the government is allowed to impose restrictions on the 'time, place, and manner' of speech in public places. No one has a right to use fireworks and loudspeakers on the public streets at midnight to complain about the size of the defense budget. However, time, place, and manner restrictions must be both reasonable and limited, and government is essentially obliged to allow speakers, whatever their views, to use public property to convey messages of their choosing.

The public forum doctrine promotes three important functions.[3] First, it ensures that speakers can have access to a wide array of people. If you want to claim that taxes are too high or that police brutality against African-Americans is common, you can press this argument on many people who might otherwise fail to hear the message. Those who use the streets and parks are likely to learn something about the substance of the argument urged by speakers; they might also learn the nature and intensity of views held by their fellow citizens. Perhaps their views will be changed; perhaps they will become curious enough to investigate the question on their own.

Second, the public forum doctrine allows speakers not only to have access to heterogeneous people but also to the specific people and the specific institutions with which they have a complaint. Suppose, for example, that you believe that the state legislature has behaved irresponsibly with respect to crime or health care for children. The public forum ensures that you can make your views heard by legislators, simply by protesting in front of the state legislature itself.

Third, the public forum doctrine increases the likelihood that people generally will be exposed to a wide variety of people and views. When you go to work, or visit a park, it is possible that you will have a range of unexpected encounters, however fleeting or seemingly inconsequential. You cannot easily wall yourself off from contentions or conditions that you would not have sought out in advance, or that you would have chosen to avoid if you could. Here, too, the public forum doctrine tends to ensure a range of experiences that are widely shared – streets and parks are public property – and also a set of exposures to diverse circumstances. In a pluralistic democracy, an important shared experience is, in fact, the very experience of society's diversity. A central idea here must be that these exposures help promote understanding and perhaps, in that sense, freedom. And all of these points are closely connected to democratic ideals.

Of course there is a limit to how much can be done on streets and in parks. Even in the largest cities, streets and parks are insistently *local.*

[3] I draw here on the excellent treatment in Zatz (1998).

But many of the social functions of streets and parks, as public forums, are performed by other institutions too. In fact society's general interest intermediaries – newspapers, magazines, television broadcasters – can be understood as public forums of an especially important sort, perhaps, above all, because they expose people to new, unanticipated topics and points of view.

When you read a city newspaper or a national magazine, your eyes will come across a number of articles that you might not have selected in advance and, if you are like most people, you will read some of those articles. Perhaps you did not know that you might have an interest in minimum wage legislation, or Somalia, or the latest developments in Jerusalem; but a story might catch your attention. What is true for topics is also true for points of view. You might think that you have nothing to learn from someone whose view you abhor, but once you come across the editorial pages, you might well read what they have to say, and you might well benefit from the experience. Perhaps you will be persuaded on one point or another. At the same time, the front page headline, or the cover story in *Newsweek*, is likely to have a high degree of salience for a wide range of people.

Television broadcasters have similar functions in what has, perhaps above all, become an institution – the evening news. If you tune into the evening news, you will learn about a number of topics that you would not have chosen in advance. Because of its speech and immediacy, television broadcasters perform these public forum-type functions still more than general interest intermediaries in the print media. The lead story on the networks is likely to have a great deal of public salience, helping to define central issues, and creating a kind of shared focus of attention, for many millions of people. And what happens after the lead story – dealing with a menu of topics both domestically and internationally – creates something like a speakers' corner beyond anything imagined in Hyde Park. As a result, people's interest is sometimes piqued, and they might well become curious and follow up, perhaps changing their perspective in the process.

None of these claims depends on a judgment that general interest inter-mediaries are unbiased, or always do an excellent job, or deserve a monopoly over the world of communications. The Internet is a boon partly because it breaks that monopoly; so too for the proliferation of television and radio shows, and even channels, that have some specialized identity. (Consider the rise, within the United States, of Fox News, appealing to a more conserva-tive audience.) All that I am claiming is that general interest intermediaries expose people to a wide range of topics and views at the same time that they provide shared experiences for a heterogeneous public. Indeed, gen-eral interest intermediaries of this sort have large advantages over streets and parks precisely because most tend to be so much less local and so much more national, even international. Typically, they expose people to questions and problems in other areas, even other nations.

SPECIALIZATION − AND FRAGMENTATION

In a system with public forums and general interest intermediaries, people will frequently come across materials that they would not have chosen in advance − and for diverse citizens, this provides something like a common framework for social experience. A fragmented communications market will change things significantly.

Not surprisingly, many people tend to choose like-minded sites and like-minded discussion groups. Many of those with committed views on one or another topic − gun control, abortion, affirmative action − speak mostly with each other. It is exceedingly rare for a site with an identifiable point of view to provide links to sites with opposing views; but it is very common for such a site to provide links to like-minded sites.

With a dramatic increase in options, and a greater power to customize, comes an increase in the range of actual choices. Those choices are likely, in many cases, to mean that people will try to find material that makes them feel comfortable, or that is created by and for people like themselves. This is what the 'Daily Me' is all about. Of course many people also seek out new topics and ideas. And to the extent that people do not, the increase in options is hardly bad on balance; among other things, it will greatly increase variety, the aggregate amount of information, and the entertainment value of actual choices. But there are serious risks as well. If diverse groups are seeing and hearing quite different points of view, or focusing on quite different topics, mutual understanding might be difficult, and it might turn out to be hard for people to get together to try to solve problems that a society faces. If millions of people are mostly listening to political conservatives and learning about issues and speaking with one another via identifiably conservative outlets, problems will arise if millions of other people are mostly or only listening to people and stations with an altogether different point of view.

We can sharpen our understanding of this problem if we attend to the phenomenon of *group polarization*. The idea is that *after deliberating with one another, people are likely to move toward a more extreme point in the direction to which they were previously inclined, as indicated by the median of their predeliberation judgments.* With respect to the Internet, the implication is that groups of people, especially if they are like-minded, will end up thinking the same thing that they thought before − but in more extreme form.

Consider some examples of the basic phenomenon, which has been found in more than a dozen nations.[4]

1. After discussion, citizens of France become more critical of the United States and its intentions with respect to economic aid.
2. After discussion, whites predisposed to show racial prejudice offer more negative responses to the question whether racism on the part

[4] For citations and general discussion, see Sunstein (2003).

of whites is responsible for conditions faced by African-Americans in American cities.
3. After discussion, whites predisposed not to show racial prejudice offer more positive responses to the same question.
4. A group of moderately profeminist women will become more strongly profeminist after discussion.

It follows that, for example, after discussion with one another, according to the predeliberation judgment paradigm, those inclined to think that President Clinton was a crook will be quite convinced of this point; those inclined to favor more aggressive affirmative action programs will become quite extreme on the issue if they talk among one another; and those who believe that tax rates are too high will, after talking together, come to think that large, immediate tax reductions are an extremely good idea.

The phenomenon of group polarization has conspicuous importance to the current communications market, where groups with distinctive identities increasingly engage in within-group discussion. If the public is balkanized, and if different groups design their own preferred communications packages, the consequence will be further balkanization, as group members move one another toward more extreme points in line with their initial tendencies. At the same time, different deliberating groups, each consisting of like-minded people, will be driven increasingly far apart, simply because most of their discussions are with one another. Extremist groups will often become more extreme.

Why does group polarization occur? There have been two main explanations, both of which have been extensively investigated. Massive support has been found on behalf of both explanations.[5]

The first explanation emphasizes the role of persuasive arguments, and of what is, and is not, heard within a group of like-minded people. It is based on a common sense intuition: any individual's position on any issue is (fortunately!) a function, at least in part, of which arguments seem convincing. If your position is going to move as a result of group discussion, it is likely to move in the direction of the most persuasive position defended within the group, taken as a collective. Of course – and this is the key point – a group whose members are already inclined in a certain direction will offer a disproportionately large number of arguments supporting that same direction, and a disproportionately small number of arguments going the other way. The result of discussion will, therefore, be to move the group, taken as a collective, further in the direction of their initial inclinations. To be sure, individuals with the most extreme views will sometimes move toward a more moderate position. But the group, as a whole, moves as a statistical

---

[5] See Sunstein (2003) for details.

regularity to a more extreme position consistent with its predeliberation leanings.

The second mechanism, involving social comparison, begins with the claim that people want to be perceived favorably by other group members and also to perceive themselves favorably. Once they hear what others believe, they adjust their positions in the direction of the dominant position. People may wish, for example, not to seem too enthusiastic, or too restrained, in their enthusiasm for affirmative action, feminism, or an increase in national defense; hence their views may shift when they see what other people and, in particular, what other group members think.

Group polarization is a human regularity; but social context can decrease, increase, or even eliminate it. For present purposes, the most important point is that group polarization will significantly increase if people think of themselves, antecedently or otherwise, as part of a group having a shared identity and a degree of solidarity. If, for example, a group of people in an Internet discussion group think of themselves as opponents of high taxes, or advocates of animal rights, their discussions are likely to move them in quite extreme discussions. If they think of themselves in this way, group polarization is both more likely and more extreme. Therefore, significant changes, in point of view and perhaps eventually behavior, should be expected for those who listen to a radio show known to be conservative, or a television program dedicated to traditional religious values or to exposing white racism.

This should not be surprising. If ordinary findings of group polarization are a product of limited argument pools and social influences, it stands to reason that, when group members think of one another as similar along a salient dimension, or if some external factor (politics, geography, race, sex) unites them, group polarization will be heightened.

Group polarization is occurring every day on the Internet. Indeed, it is clear that the Internet is serving, for many, as a breeding ground for extremism, precisely because like-minded people are deliberating with one another, without hearing contrary views. Hate groups are the most obvious example. Consider one extremist group, the so-called Unorganized Militia, the armed wing of the Patriot movement, 'which believes that the federal government is becoming increasingly dictatorial with its regulatory power over taxes, guns and land use' (Zook 1996). A crucial factor behind the growth of the Unorganized Militia 'has been the use of computer networks', allowing members 'to make contact quickly and easily with like-minded individuals to trade information, discuss current conspiracy theories, and organize events' (Zook 1996). The Unorganized Militia has a large number of Web sites, and those sites frequently offer links to related sites. It is clear that Web sites are being used to recruit new members and to allow like-minded people to speak with one another and to reinforce or strengthen existing convictions. It is also clear that the Internet is playing a crucial role in permitting people who would otherwise feel isolated, or move on to something else, to band together, to spread rumors, many of them paranoid and hateful.

There are numerous other examples along similar lines. A group naming itself the White Racial Loyalists calls on all 'White Racial Loyalists to go to chat rooms and debate and recruit with NEW people, post our URL everywhere, as soon as possible'. Another site announces that 'Our multi-ethnic United States is run by Jews, a 2% minority, who were run out of every country in Europe.... Jews control the U.S. media, they hold top positions in the Clinton administration ... and now these Jews are in control – they used lies spread by the media they run and committed genocide in our name'. To the extent that people are drawn together because they think of each other as like-minded, and as having a shared identity, group polarization is all the more likely.

Of course we cannot say, from the mere fact of polarization, that there has been a movement in the *wrong* direction. Perhaps the more extreme tendency is better; indeed, group polarization is likely to have fueled many movements of great value, including, and for example, the movement for civil rights, the antislavery movement, the movement for equality on the basis of gender. All of these movements were extreme in their time, and within-group discussion bred greater extremism; but extremism need not be a word of opprobrium. If greater communications choices produce greater extremism, society may, in many cases, be better off as a result.

But when group discussion tends to lead people to more strongly held versions of the same view with which they began, and if social influences and limited argument pools are responsible, there is legitimate reason for concern. Consider discussions among hate groups on the Internet and else-where. If the underlying views are unreasonable, it makes sense to fear that these discussions may fuel increasing hatred and a socially corrosive form of extremism. This does not mean that the discussions can or should be regulated in a system dedicated to freedom of speech. But it does raise questions about the idea that 'more speech' is necessarily an adequate remedy – especially if people are increasingly able to wall themselves off from competing views.

The basic issue here is whether something like a *public sphere*, with a wide range of voices, might not have significant advantages over a system in which isolated consumer choices produce a highly fragmented speech market. The most reasonable conclusion is that it is extremely important to ensure that people are exposed to views other than those with which they currently agree, in order to protect against the harmful effects of group polarization on individual thinking and on social cohesion. This does not mean that the government should jail or fine people who refuse to listen to others. Nor is what I have said inconsistent with approval of deliberating enclaves, on the Internet or elsewhere, designed to ensure that positions that would otherwise be silenced or squelched have a chance to develop. Readers will be able to think of their own preferred illustrations; consider, perhaps, the views of people with disabilities. The great benefit of such enclaves is that positions may emerge that otherwise would not and that deserve to play a large role in the heterogeneous public. Properly understood, the case of *enclaves*, or more simply discussion groups of like-minded people, is that they will improve social deliberation, democratic and otherwise. For these improvements to occur, members must not insulate themselves from competing positions, or at least any such attempts at insulation must not be a prolonged affair.

Consider in this light the ideal of *consumer sovereignty*, which underlies much of contemporary enthusiasm for the Internet. Consumer sovereignty means that people can choose to purchase, or to obtain, whatever they want. For many purposes this is a worthy ideal. But the adverse effects of group polarization show that with respect to communications, consumer sovereignty is likely to produce serious problems for individuals and society at large – and these problems will occur by a kind of iron logic of social interactions.

SOCIAL CASCADES

The phenomenon of group polarization is closely related to the widespread phenomenon of *social cascades*. Cascade effects are common on the Internet, and we cannot understand the relationship between democracy and the Internet without having a sense of how cascades work.

It is obvious that many social groups, both large and small, seem to move both rapidly and dramatically in the direction of one or another set of beliefs or actions.[6] These sorts of cascades often involve the spread of information; in fact that they are driven by information. A key point here is that if you lack a great deal of private information, you may well rely on information provided by the statements or actions of others. Here is a stylized example: If Joan is unaware whether abandoned toxic waste dumps are in fact hazardous, she may be moved in the direction of fear if Mary seems to think that fear is justified. If Joan and Mary both believe that fear is justified, then Carl may end up thinking that too, if he lacks reliable independent information to the contrary. If Joan, Mary, and Carl believe that abandoned hazardous waste dumps are hazardous, Don will have to have a good deal of confidence to reject their shared conclusion.

This example shows how information travels and often becomes quite entrenched, even if it is entirely wrong. The view, widespread in many African-American communities, that white doctors are responsible for the spread of AIDS among African-Americans is a recent illustration. Often

[6] See, for example, Bikhchandani, Hirshleifer & Welch (1998), p. 151.

cascades of this kind are quite local and take different form in different communities. Hence, one group may end up believing something and another group the exact opposite, and the reason is the rapid transmission of one piece of information within one group and a different piece of information in the other. In a balkanized speech market, this danger takes a particular form: Different groups may be led to quite different perspectives, as local cascades lead people in dramatically different directions. The Internet dramatically increases the likelihood of rapid cascades based on false information. Of course low-cost Internet communication also makes it possible for truth, and corrections, to spread quickly as well. But sometimes this happens much too late. In that event, balkanization is extremely likely. As a result of the Internet, cascade effects are more common than they have ever been before.

As an especially troublesome example, consider widespread doubts in South Africa, where about 20 percent of the adult population is infected by the AIDS virus, about the connection between HIV and AIDS. South African President Mbeki is a well-known Internet surfer, and he learned the views of the 'denialists' after stumbling across one of their Web sites. The views of the denialists are not scientifically respectable – but to a nonspecialist, many of the claims on their (many) sites seem quite plausible. At least for a period, President Mbeki both fell victim to a cybercascade and, through his public statements, helped to accelerate one, to the point where many South Africans at serious risk are not convinced by an association between HIV and AIDS. It seems clear that this cascade effect has turned out to be literally deadly.

I hope that I have shown enough to demonstrate that for citizens of a heterogeneous democracy, a fragmented communications market creates considerable dangers. There are dangers for each of us as individuals; constant exposure to one set of views is likely to lead to errors and confusions, or to unthinking conformity (emphasized by John Stuart Mill). And to the extent that the process makes people less able to work cooperatively on shared problems, by turning collections of people into noncommunicating confessional groups, there are dangers for society as a whole.

COMMON EXPERIENCES

In a heterogeneous society, it is extremely important for diverse people to have a set of common experiences. Many of our practices reflect a judgment to this effect. National holidays, for example, help constitute a nation, by encouraging citizens to think, all at once, about events of shared importance. And they do much more than this. They enable people, in all their diversity, to have certain memories and attitudes. At least this is true in nations where national holidays have a vivid and concrete meaning. In the United States, many national holidays have become mere days-off from work, and the precipitating occasion – President's Day, Memorial Day, Labor Day – has come to be nearly invisible. This is a serious loss. With the possible exception of Independence Day, Martin Luther King Day is probably the closest thing to a genuinely substantive national holiday, largely because that celebration involves something that can be treated as a concrete and meaningful celebration. In other words, it is *about* something.

Communications and the media are, of course, exceptionally important here. Sometimes millions of people follow the presidential election, or the Super Bowl, or the coronation of a new monarch; and many of them do so because of the simultaneous actions of others. The point very much bears on the historic role of both public forums and general interest intermediaries. Public parks are, of course, places where diverse people can congregate and see one another. General interest intermediaries, if they are operating properly, give a simultaneous sense of problems and tasks.

Why are these shared experiences so desirable? There are three principal reasons:

1. Simple enjoyment is probably the least of it, but it is far from irrelevant. People like many experiences more, simply because they are being shared. Consider a popular movie, the Super Bowl, or a presidential debate. For many of us, these are goods that are worth less, and possibly worthless, if many others are not enjoying or purchasing them too. Hence a presidential debate may be worthy of individual attention, for many people, simply because so many other people consider it worthy of individual attention.

2. Sometimes shared experiences ease social interactions, permitting people to speak with one another, and to congregate around a common issue, task, or concern, whether or not they have much in common with one another. In this sense they provide a form of social glue. They help make it possible for diverse people to believe that they live in the same culture. Indeed they help constitute that shared culture, simply by creating common memories and experiences and a sense of common tasks.

3. A fortunate consequence of shared experiences – many of them produced by the media – is that people who would otherwise see one another as quite unfamiliar, can come instead to regard one another as fellow citizens with shared hopes, goals, and concerns. This is a subjective good for those directly involved. But it can be objective good as well, especially if it leads to cooperative projects of various kinds. When people learn about a disaster faced by fellow citizens, for example, they may respond with financial and other help. The point applies internationally, as well as domestically; massive relief efforts are often made possible by virtue of the fact that millions of people learn, all at once, about the relevant need.

How does this bear on the Internet? The basic point is that an increasingly fragmented communications universe will reduce the level of shared experiences having salience to diverse people. This is a simple matter of numbers. When there were three television networks, much of what appeared would have the quality of a genuinely common experience. The lead story on the evening news, for example, would provide a common reference point for many millions of people. To the extent that choices proliferate, it is inevitable that diverse individuals and diverse groups will have fewer shared experiences and fewer common reference points. It is possible, for example, that some events, which are highly salient to some people, will barely register with others. And it is possible that some views and perspectives that will seem obvious for many people will, for others, seem barely intelligible.

This is hardly a suggestion that everyone should be required to watch the same thing. A degree of plurality, with respect to both topics and points of view, is highly desirable. Moreover, talk about *requirements* misses the point. My only claim is that a common set of frameworks and experiences is valuable for a heterogeneous society, and that a system with limitless options, making for diverse choices, will compromise the underlying values.

PROPOSALS

My goal here has been to understand what makes for a well-functioning system of free expression, and to show how consumer sovereignty, in a world of limitless options, is likely to undermine that system. The essential point is that a well-functioning system includes a kind of public sphere, one that fosters common experiences, in which people hear messages that challenge their prior convictions and in which citizens can present their views to a broad audience. I do not intend to offer a comprehensive set of policy reforms or any kind of blueprint for the future. In fact, this may be a domain in which a problem exists for which there is no useful cure. The genie might simply be out of the bottle. But it will be useful to offer a few ideas, if only by way of introduction to questions, which are likely to engage public attention in the first decades of the twenty-first century.

In thinking about reforms, it is important to have a sense of the problems we aim to address, and some possible ways of addressing them. If the discussion thus far is correct, there are three fundamental concerns from the democratic point of view. These include:

1. the need to promote exposure to materials, topics, and positions that people would not have chosen in advance, or at least enough exposure to produce a degree of understanding and curiosity;
2. the value of a range of common experiences; and
3. the need for exposure to substantive questions of policy and principle, combined with a range of positions on such questions.

Of course, it would be ideal if citizens were demanding, and private information providers were creating, a range of initiatives designed to alleviate the underlying concerns. Perhaps they will; there is some evidence to this effect. In fact, new technology creates growing opportunities for exposure to diverse points of view and growing opportunities for shared experiences. Private choices may create far more in the way of exposure to new topics and points of view and a larger range of shared experiences. But, to the extent that they fail to do so, it is worthwhile to consider both private and public initiatives designed to pick up the slack.

Drawing on recent developments in regulation, in general, we can see the potential appeal of five simple alternatives. Of course different proposals would work better for some communications outlets than others. I will speak here of both private and public responses, but the former should be favored: They are less intrusive, and, in general, they are likely to be more effective as well.

Disclosure

Producers of communications might disclose important information on their own, about the extent to which they are promoting democratic goals. To the extent that they do not, they might be subject, not to regulation, but to disclosure requirements. In the environmental area, this strategy has produced excellent results. The mere fact that polluters have been asked to disclose toxic releases has produced voluntary, low-cost reductions. Apparently fearful of public opprobrium, companies have been spurred to reduce toxic emissions on their own. The same strategy has been used in the context of both movies and television, with ratings systems designed partly to increase parental control over what children see. On the Internet, many sites disclose that their site is inappropriate for children. Disclosure could be used far more broadly. Television broadcasters might, for example, be asked to disclose their public interest activities. On a quarterly basis, they might say whether, and to what extent, they have provided educational programming for children, free air time for political candidates, and closed captioning for the hearing impaired. They might also be asked whether they have covered issues of concern to the local community and allowed opposing views a chance to speak. In the United States, the Federal Communications Commission has already taken steps in this direction; it could do in a lot more. Of course disclosure is unlikely to be a full solution to the problems that I have discussed here. But modest steps in this direction are likely to do little harm and at least some good.

Self regulation

Producers of communications might engage in *voluntary self-regulation*. Some of the difficulties in the current speech market stem from relentless competition for viewers and listeners, competition that leads to a situation that many journalists abhor, and from which society does not benefit. The competition might be reduced via a code of appropriate conduct, agreed upon by various companies, and encouraged but not imposed by government. In the United States, the National Association of Broadcasters maintained such a code for several decades, and there is growing interest in voluntary self-regulation for both television and the Internet. The case for this approach is that it avoids government regulation and, at the same time, reduces some of the harmful effects of market pressures. Any such code could, for example, call for an opportunity for opposing views to speak, or for avoiding unnecessary sensationalism, or for offering arguments rather than quick 'sound-bites' whenever feasible. On television, as distinct from the Internet, the idea seems quite feasible. But perhaps some bloggers and Internet sites could also enter into informal, voluntary arrangements, agreeing to create links, an idea to which I will shortly turn.

Subsidy

The government might subsidize speech, as, for example, through publicly subsidized programming or publicly subsidized Web sites. This is, of course, the idea that motivates the notion of a Public Broadcasting System (PBS). But it is reasonable to ask whether the PBS model is not outmoded in the current communications environment. Other approaches, similarly designed to promote educational, cultural, and democratic goals, might well be ventured. Perhaps government could subsidize a 'Public.Net' designed to promote debate on public issues among diverse citizens – and to create a right of access to speakers of various sorts (Shapiro 1999).

Links

Web sites might use links and hyperlinks to ensure that viewers learn about sites containing opposing views. A liberal magazine's Web site might, for example, provide a link to a conservative magazine's Web site, and the conservative magazine might do the same to a liberal magazine's Web site. The idea would be to decrease the likelihood that people will simply hear echoes of their own voices. Of course many people would not click on the icons of sites whose views seem objectionable; but some people would, and in that sense the system would not operate so differently from general interest intermediaries and public forums. Here, too, the ideal situation would be voluntary action, not government mandates.

Public sidewalk

If the problem consists in the failure to attend to public issues, the most popular Web sites in any given period might offer links and hyperlinks, designed to ensure more exposure to substantive questions.[7] Under such a system, viewers of especially popular sites would see an icon for sites that deal with substantive issues in a serious way. It is well established that whenever there is a link to a particular place from a major site, such as MSNBC, the traffic is huge. Nothing here imposes any requirements on viewers. People would not be required to click on links and hyperlinks. But it is reasonable to expect that many viewers would do so, if only to satisfy their curiosity. The result would be to create a kind of Internet 'sidewalk', promoting some of the purposes of the public forum doctrine. Ideally those who create Web sites might move in this direction on their own. To those who believe that this step would do no good, it is worth recalling that advertisers are willing to spend a great deal of money to obtain brief access to people's eyeballs. This strategy might be used to create something like a public sphere as well.

These are brief thoughts on some complex subjects. My goal has not been to evaluate any proposal in detail, but to give a flavor of some possibilities for those concerned to promote democratic goals in a dramatically changed environment (Sunstein 2001, 2006). The basic question is whether it might be possible to create spaces that have some of the functions of public forums and general interest intermediaries in the age of the Internet. It seems clear that government's power to regulate effectively is diminished as the number of options expands. I am not sure that any response would be worthwhile, all things considered. But I am sure that if new technologies diminish the number of common spaces and reduce, for many, the number of unanticipated, unchosen exposures, something important will have been lost. The most important point is to have a sense of what a well-functioning democratic order requires.

ANTICENSORSHIP, BUT WELL-BEYOND ANTICENSORSHIP

My principal claim here has been that a well-functioning democracy depends on far more than restraints on official censorship of controversial ideas and opinions. It also depends on some kind of public sphere, in which a wide range of speakers have access to a diverse public – and also to particular institutions and practices, against which they seek to launch objections.

Emerging technologies, including the Internet, are hardly an enemy here. They hold out far more promise than risk, especially because they allow people to widen their horizons. But to the extent that they weaken the power of general interest intermediaries and increase people's ability to wall themselves off from topics and opinions that they would prefer to avoid, they create serious dangers. And, if we believe that a system of free expression calls for unrestricted choices by individual consumers, we will not even

[7] For discussion, see Chin (1997).

understand the dangers as such. Whether such dangers will materialize will ultimately depend on the aspirations, for freedom and democracy alike, by whose light we evaluate our practices. What I have sought to establish here is that, in a free republic, citizens aspire to a system that provides a wide range of experiences – with people, topics, and ideas – that would not have been selected in advance.

References

Bikhchandani, S., Hirshleifer, D., and Welch, I. 1998. Learning from the behavior of others: Conformity, fads, and informational cascades. *Journal of Economic Perspectives, 12*, 3, 151–170.

Chin, A. 1997. Making the World Wide Web safe for democracy. *Hastings Communications and Entertainment Law Journal, 19*, 309.

Shapiro, A. 1999. *The control revolution.* New York: Basic Books.

Sikes, A. C., and Pearlman, E. 2000. *Fast forward: America's leading experts reveal how the Internet is changing your life.* New York: HarperTrade.

Sunstein, C. R. 2007. *Republic.com 2.0.* Princeton: Princeton University Press.

Sunstein, C. R. 2006. *Infotopia: How many minds produce knowledge.* New York: Oxford University Press.

Sunstein, C. R. 2003. *Why societies need dissent.* Cambridge, MA: Harvard University Press.

Sunstein, C. R. 2001. *Republic.com.* Princeton: Princeton University Press.

Zatz, N. D. 1998. Sidewalks in cyberspace: Making space for public forums in the electronic environment. *Harvard Journal of Law and Technology, 12*, 149.

Zook, M. 1996. The unorganized militia network: Conspiracies, computers, and community. *Berkeley Planning Journal, 11.* Retrieved June 5, 2006 from http://www.zook.info/Militia_paper.html.

6

The Social Epistemology of Blogging

Alvin I. Goldman

DEMOCRACY AND THE EPISTEMIC PROPERTIES OF INTERNET-BASED COMMUNICATION

The impact of the Internet on democracy is a widely discussed subject. Many writers view the Internet, potentially at least, as a boon to democracy and democratic practices. According to one popular theme, both e-mail and Web pages give ordinary people powers of communication that have hitherto been the preserve of the relatively wealthy (Graham 1999, p. 79). So the Internet can be expected to close the influence gap between wealthy citizens and ordinary citizens, a weakness of many procedural democracies.

I want to focus here on another factor important to democracy, a factor that is emphasized by so-called epistemic approaches to democracy. According to epistemic democrats, democracy exceeds other systems in its ability to 'track the truth'. According to Rousseau, for example, the people under a democracy can track truths about the 'general will' and the 'common good' (Rousseau 1762, book 4). Recent proponents of epistemic democracy include Estlund (1990, 1993), Grofman and Feld (1988), and List and Goodin (2001). Their idea is that, assuming certain political outcomes are 'right' or 'correct', democracy is better than competing systems at choosing these outcomes.

Elsewhere, I have proposed a variant on the epistemic approach to democracy (Goldman 1999, chapter 10). Epistemic theorists of democracy usually assume that, on a given issue or option, the same option or candidate is right, or correct, for all voters. A system's competence with respect to that issue is its probability of selecting the correct option. Under the variant I propose, different citizen-specific options may be right for different citizens.[1] In a given election, for example, candidate X may be the best, or right, choice *for you* (i.e., relative to your desiderata) and candidate Y may be the best,

[1] Thanks to Christian List (personal communication) for suggesting this formulation of how my approach differs from standard approaches to epistemic democracy.

or right, choice *for me* (i.e., relative to my desiderata). Even if we make this assumption, however, we can still say what an overall good result would be from a democratic point of view. Democratically speaking, it would be good if as many citizens as possible get an outcome that is right *for them.* Now in the electoral situation, it might seem as if this is precisely what majority voting automatically brings about, at least in two-candidate races. If every voter votes for the candidate who is best for them, then the candidate who is best for a majority of voters will be elected, and a majority of voters will get the outcome that is right for them.[2]

But what guarantees that a voter will vote for the candidate who really is best for them? This isn't guaranteed by a procedure like majority rule. Even if candidate X is *in fact* best for you – in terms of the results the two candidates would respectively produce, if elected – you may not *know* that X is best for you. On the contrary, you may be mistakenly persuaded that Y is best for you. The difficulty of knowing, or truly believing,[3] which one would be best derives in part from the fact that each candidate for office tries to convince as many voters as possible that he or she is the best candidate for those voters, whether or not this is actually so. With each candidate's campaign aimed at persuading you of his or her superiority, it may not be trivial to determine (truly) who would be best according to your desiderata. Hence, it is a crucial part of a democratic framework, or system, that there be institutions, structures, or mechanisms that assist citizens in acquiring and possessing politically relevant information, where by 'information possession' I mean true belief and by 'politically relevant' information I mean information that is relevant to their political choices.

Which factors determine how well citizens acquit themselves in getting relevant information or knowledge on political matters (where 'knowledge', like 'information', entails truth)? This partly depends on citizens themselves, in ways we shall explore in the next section. But it also depends partly on the institutional structures used in the communication or transmission of information and misinformation. This is why the media play a critical role in a democracy. It is a commonplace that democracy requires a free press. Why? Because only a free press can ferret out crucial political truths and communicate them to the public. It is the responsibility of reporters and editors to seek and publish the truth about matters of state because, as I have argued, knowing the truth is crucial to citizens making correct decisions (correct as judged by their own desiderata). The foregoing theme expresses traditional thinking on this topic.

[2] See Goldman (1999, chapter 10) for a detailed defense of this claim.

[3] Here, and in Goldman (1999), I understand 'knowledge' in the sense of 'true belief', which I consider to be a *weak* sense of 'knowledge'. The notion that there is such a weak sense of knowledge (in addition to a strong sense of knowledge, more commonly explored by epistemologists) is briefly defended in Goldman (1999). I expect to offer additional defense of this thesis in future writing.

For the acquisition of knowledge to occur, it isn't sufficient that there be a free press that publishes or broadcasts the relevant truths. It is equally critical that members of the public receive and believe those truths. If truths are published but not read, or published and read but not believed, the public won't *possess* the information (or knowledge) that is important for making correct decisions. In recent years, however, there has been a waning of influence by the conventional news media – newspapers and network television news – in the United States. The daily readership of newspapers dropped from 52.6 percent of adults in 1990 to 37.5 percent in 2000, and the drop was steeper in the 20-to-49-year-old cohort. This cohort is and will probably remain, as it ages, more comfortable with electronic media in general and the Web in particular (Posner 2005). Is the waning impact of the conventional media, staffed by professional journalists, a bad sign for the epistemic prospects of the voting public? Will the public's propensity to form accurate political beliefs be impaired as compared with the past, or compared with what would hold if the conventional media retained the public's trust and allegiance? This raises the question of whether the Web, or the Internet, is better or worse in epistemic terms than the conventional media, in terms of public political knowledge generated by the respective communication structures. This is the central question of this chapter.

EPISTEMIC COMPARISONS OF THE CONVENTIONAL MEDIA AND THE BLOGOSPHERE

There are many ways in which the Web, or the Internet, is used in communicating information. The Internet is a platform with multiple applications. We are not concerned here with all applications of the Internet, only with one of the more recent and influential ones, namely, blogging and its associated realm, the blogosphere. Richard Posner (2005) argues that blogging is gradually displacing conventional journalism as a source of news and the dissection of news. Moreover, Posner argues – though with some qualifications and murkiness in his message – that this is not inimical to the public's epistemic good. The argument seems to be that blogging, as a medium of political communication and deliberation, is no worse from the standpoint of public knowledge than conventional journalism. Posner highlights this point in the matter of error detection.

[T]he blogosphere as a whole has a better error-correction machinery than the conventional media do. The rapidity with which vast masses of information are pooled and sifted leaves the conventional media in the dust. Not only are there millions of blogs, and thousands of bloggers who specialize, but, what is more, readers post comments that augment the blogs, and the information in those comments, as in the blogs themselves, zips around blogland at the speed of electronic transmission.

This means that corrections in blogs are also disseminated virtually instantaneously, whereas when a member of the mainstream media catches a mistake, it may take weeks to communicate a retraction to the public . . .

The charge by mainstream journalists that blogging lacks checks and balances is obtuse. The blogosphere has *more* checks and balances than the conventional media, only they are different. The model is Friedrich Hayek's classic analysis of how the economic market pools enormous quantities of information efficiently despite its decentralized character, its lack of a master coordinator or regulator, and the very limited knowledge possessed by each of its participants.

In effect, the blogosphere is a collective enterprise – not 12 million separate enterprises, but one enterprise with 12 million reporters, feature writers and editorialists, yet almost no costs. It's as if the Associated Press or Reuters had millions of reporters, many of them experts, all working with no salary for free newspapers that carried no advertising. (Posner 2005, pp. 10–11)

In these passages, Posner seems to be saying that the blogosphere is more accurate, and, hence, it is a better instrument of knowledge, than the conventional media. But elsewhere he introduces an important qualification, namely, that the bloggers are parasitical on the conventional media.

They [bloggers] copy the news and opinion generated by the conventional media, without picking up any of the tab. The degree of parasitism is striking in the case of those blogs that provide their readers with links to newspaper articles. The links enable the audience to read the articles without buying the newspaper. The legitimate gripes of the conventional media is not that bloggers undermine the overall accuracy of news reporting, but that they are free riders who may in the long run undermine the ability of the conventional media to finance the very reporting on which bloggers depend. (Posner 2005, p. 11)

As I would express it, the point to be learned is that we cannot compare the blogosphere and the conventional news outlets as two wholly independent and alternative communication media, because the blogosphere (in its current incarnation, at least) isn't independent of the conventional media; it piggybacks, or freerides, on them. Whatever credit is due to the blogs for error correction shouldn't go to them alone, because their error-checking ability is derivative from the conventional media.

It would also be a mistake to confuse the aforementioned theme of Posner's article with the whole of his message, or perhaps even its principal point. Posner's principal point is to explain the decline of the conventional media in economic terms. Increase in competition in the news market, he says, has brought about more polarization, more sensationalism, more healthy skepticism, and, in summary, 'a better matching of supply to demand' (2005, p. 11). Most people do not demand, that is, do not seek, better quality news coverage; they seek entertainment, confirmation (of their prior views), reinforcement, and emotional satisfaction. Providers of news have been forced to give consumers what they want. This is a familiar theme from economics-minded theorists.

What this implies, however, is that Posner's analysis is only tangentially addressed to our distinctively epistemic question: Is the public better off or worse off, in terms of knowledge or true belief (on political subjects), with the current news market? Granted, that the *public at large* isn't interested – at least not exclusively interested – in accurate political knowledge, that doesn't mean that *we* shouldn't take an interest in this subject. It is perfectly appropriate for theorists of democracy and public ethics to take an interest in this question, especially in light of the connection presented between successful democracy and the citizenry's political knowledge. So let us set aside Posner's larger message and focus on the two mass-communication mechanisms he identifies to see how they fare in *social epistemological* terms, that is, in terms of their respective contributions to true versus false beliefs.[4]

To Filter or Not to Filter

Stay a moment longer, however, with Posner. Posner points to the familiar criticism that 'unfiltered' media like blogs have bad consequences. Critics complain that blogs exacerbate social tensions by handing a powerful communication platform to extremists. Bad people find one another in cyberspace and gain confidence in their crazy ideas. The virtue of the conventional media is that they filter out extreme views. Expressing a similar idea in terms of truth-relatedness, the conventional media may be said to filter out *false* views, and thereby do not tempt their readership into accepting these false views, as blogs are liable to do.

Posner rejects this argument for filtering. First, he says that the argument for filtering is an argument for censorship, a first count against it. Moreover, there is little harm and some good in unfiltered media. The goods he proceeds to discuss, however, aren't linked to true belief. One good is that twelve million people write rather than stare passively at a screen. Another good is that people are allowed to blow off steam. Still another good is that it enables the authorities to keep tabs on potential troublemakers. Conceding that these may be goods, they obviously have little or nothing to do with the kind of epistemic good that interests us. The question remains open whether communication systems that filter or those that don't have superior epistemic properties, specifically, are better at promoting true belief and/or avoiding error.

What exactly is meant by *filtering*? Perhaps the standard conception of filtering involves a designated channel of communication and a system of

---

4 More precisely, this is the conception of social epistemology that I commend in Goldman (1999). I call this conception *veritistic social epistemology*. For discussions of alternative approaches to social epistemology, see Goldman (2002, 2004, 2007).

people with three kinds of roles. First, there are prospective senders, people who would *like* to send a message. Second, there are prospective receivers, people who might receive messages that are sent. Third, there is a filterer, or gatekeeper, an individual or group with the power to select which of the proffered messages are sent via the designated channel and which are not. When a gatekeeper disallows a proffered message, this is filtering. Although some might call any form of filtering 'censorship', this term is not generally applied to all forms of filtering. Nor is filtering universally regarded as an 'infringement' of speech, as censorship perhaps is.

Let me provide some examples to support these claims. Consider conventional scientific journals as examples of communication channels. Scientific journals obviously engage in filtering. Not all articles submitted for publication in a given journal are published. The function of the peer-review process is precisely to select those submissions that will be published and those that won't. Nobody considers the process of peer review to be 'censorship'. Nor does anyone, to my knowledge, consider it an 'infringement' of speech.

Another example is the (common-law) system of trial procedure. In this system, the prospective speakers, or communicators, are the parties to the dispute, or their legal counsel, and witnesses called before the court. The principal receiver is the 'trier of fact,' often a set of jurors. The gatekeeper is the judge, who oversees the communications that occur in court. The judge applies rules of procedure and rules of evidence to decide which speakers may speak and which messages will be allowed during the trial. Only witnesses that pass certain tests are allowed to testify; only items of evidence meeting certain criteria are admitted into court; and only certain lines of argument and rebuttal, only certain lines of questioning of witnesses, are permitted. This is a massive amount of filtering, but nobody describes such filtering as 'censorship,' and such filtering is generally not called an 'infringement' of speech.

Furthermore, these filtering practices are commonly rationalized in terms of (something like) helping the relevant audience to determine the truth. Of course, philosophers of science debate the ultimate aims of science. At a minimum, however, geological studies are undertaken to determine the truth about the geological past, and experimental studies of various sorts are aimed at ascertaining truths about causal relationships among variables. Similarly, the overarching (though not exclusive) aim of trial procedures is to enable triers of fact to judge the truth about substantive matters of fact before the court.[5] To the extent that filtering is part and parcel of those trial procedures, filtering is evidently thought to be conducive to the aim of

[5] For extended defenses of this truth-oriented, or veritistic, account of the rationale for trial procedures, see Goldman (1999, chapter 9) and Goldman (2005). In partial support of this interpretation, consider the following statement of the *Federal Rules of Evidence*, as a fundamental basis for the rules that follow: 'These rules [evidence] shall be construed to

promoting knowledge and avoiding error. Even if the current filtering system for legal evidence isn't ideal (some evidentiary exclusions aimed at truth enhancement don't really help), most theorists would probably agree that some kind of filtering has salutary effects in terms of truth determination.

The conventional news media also employ filtering techniques. Newspapers employ fact checkers to vet a reporter's article before it is published. They often require more than a single source before publishing an article, and limit reporters' reliance on anonymous sources. These practices seem likely to raise the veritistic quality of the reports newspapers publish and hence the veritistic quality of their readers' resultant beliefs. At a minimum, they reduce the number of errors that might otherwise be reported and believed. Thus, from a veritistic point of view, filtering looks promising indeed. Isn't that an argument for the superiority of the conventional news media over blogging, so long as knowledge and error avoidance are the ends being considered?

Let us reflect on this argument by reflecting on the nature of filtering. In order for people to believe truths and avoid believing falsehoods, some selections must be made at one or more stages in the processes that ultimately produce belief (or doxastic states generally). But at what stage of a process is selection – that is, filtering – necessary and helpful? If we are dealing with a process that includes reporting (in philosophy, usually referred to as 'testimony'), three different stages of the process may be distinguished: the *reporting* stage, the *reception* stage, and the *acceptance* (believing) stage. Filtering normally refers to the reporting stage. Some messages that prospective speakers would like to send are winnowed out by a gatekeeper, so they don't actually get transmitted over the designated channel. But we can also think of filtering as occurring at either the reception or the acceptance stage. Consider a system in which every message anybody wants to send over a designated channel is actually sent. This doesn't mean that no filtering occurs in the process as a whole. On the contrary, potential receivers can choose which messages they wish to receive, that is, read, and digest. They do this by first selecting which channels to tune in to and then selecting which messages aired or displayed on those channels to 'consume' (read or listen to). This too is a kind of filtering. Finally, having read a certain number of messages on a given topic – messages with possibly inconsistent contents – readers must decide which of these messages to believe. The ones they reject can be called 'filtered out' messages.

In earlier technological eras, before the Internet, public speech was usually limited, at least over the channels with large capacities. A person could stand on his soapbox and deliver his chosen message, but it wouldn't reach many hearers. A person could send a letter to anyone he wished, but only

secure . . . promotion of growth and development of the law of evidence to the end that the truth may be ascertained and proceedings justly determined' (Rule 102).

one receiver would get it. Channels reaching larger audiences – for example, newspapers, radio, and television – were typically limited in the quantity of messages they could convey, so some filtering had to occur at the reporting stage. The Internet has changed all this, so the question arises whether filtering really needs to be done at the reporting stage. Why not eliminate filtering at this stage, as blogging and other Internet applications easily allow? As we have seen, this doesn't mean eliminating all filtering. But why not let the necessary filtering occur at the reception and acceptance stages rather than the reporting stage?

One problem lies with the reliability of the filtering. If receivers are poor at estimating the reliability of the channels over which messages are sent, they won't do a very good filtering job at the reception stage. They may regularly tune in channels with low reliability. If receivers are poor at estimating the accuracy of the specific messages they receive and read, they also won't do a very good filtering job at the acceptance stage. For receivers of this kind, it might be desirable to have filtering performed at the reporting stage – as long as this filtering would be sufficiently reliable. Presumably, the advantage of having news delivered by dedicated, well-trained professionals embedded in a rigorous journalistic enterprise is that the filtering performed before dissemination generates a high level of reliability among stories actually reported. Of course, 'high' reliability doesn't mean perfect reliability. If the American public has recently become disenchanted with the press and network news because of well-publicized errors, that disenchantment may itself be an unfortunate mistake. Receivers might not have better, more reliable, sources to which to turn.

Posner is not so worried about people being excessively credulous about communications found in blogs. He is optimistic that they make accurate assessments of the reliability of such unfiltered media:

[Most] people are sensible enough to distrust communications in an unfiltered medium. They know that anyone can create a blog at essentially zero cost, that most bloggers are uncredentialed amateurs, that bloggers don't employ fact checkers and don't have editors and that a blogger can hide behind a pseudonym. They know, in short, that until a blogger's assertions are validated (as when the mainstream media acknowledge an error discovered by a blogger), there is no reason to repose confidence in what he says. (Posner 2005, p. 11)

This is unrealistically sanguine. People may vaguely know these things about blogs in general, but they may not be good as applying these precepts to the specific blogs that most appeal to them. Precisely because what these blogs assert often confirms their own prior views or prejudices, they may repose excessive trust in them. Moreover, it is noteworthy that Posner concedes the need to 'validate' a blogger's assertions. But how is an assertion to be 'validated' except by recourse to a different, and more reliable, source? Posner's example of such a validation is an error concession by a mainstream medium.

But this points precisely to the necessity of using a mainstream medium, a filtered medium! If we are trying to compare the veritistic credentials of a *pure* blogosphere with a *pure* set of mainstream media, this hardly vindicates the pure blogosphere because without the mainstream media to appeal to for validation, Posner implicitly concedes, the reader can't know whom to trust.

BLOGGING AS AN ADVERSARIAL PROCESS

Of course, the reliability of the blogosphere shouldn't be identified with the reliability of a single blog. The presumptive virtue of the blogosphere is that it's a system of blogs with checks and balances that are collectively stronger than the filtering mechanisms of the conventional media. Posner draws an analogy to the way the economic market pools enormous quantities of information without a master regulator. Another analogy worth examining is the adversarial system of the common-law trial procedure. Many blogs are aptly characterized as forums for the zealous advocacy of a particular political position. News is interpreted through the lens of their advocacy position, which involves lots of bias. But this doesn't mean that the blogosphere as a whole is similarly biased. There are blogs for every point of view. Maybe it's a good global system that allows these different advocates to argue for their respective points of view and lets the reader decide. Maybe this is good even in terms of truth determination. Isn't that, after all, a primary rationale for the adversary process in the British-American trial system? Each contending party in a legal dispute is represented by an attorney who is expected to be a zealous advocate for the party he or she represents. This means arguing factual issues in a way favorable to his or her party. This sort of structure is thought by many to be a very good method of truth-determination. Many essays and quips from historical theorists (e.g., John Milton, John Stuart Mill, Oliver Wendell Holmes[6]) have bolstered the idea of a 'free market for ideas' in which contending parties engage in argumentative battle from which truth is supposed to emerge.

However, a little reflection on the adversarial system in the law reveals some nontrivial differences between the system as instantiated there and in the blogosphere. First, the adversarial system in legal proceedings involves oversight by a judge who requires the advocates to abide by rules of evidence and other procedural canons. Nothing like this holds in the blogosphere. Second, the adversaries in a trial address their arguments to a neutral trier of fact, which is chosen (at least in theory) by its ability to be neutral. Advocates are permitted to disqualify potential jurors ('for cause') if they

---

[6] Milton wrote: 'Let [Truth] and Falsehood grapple; who ever knew Truth put to the worse, in a free and open encounter' (1959, p. 561). Holmes wrote: '[The] best test of truth is the power of the thought to get itself accepted in the competition of the market' (1919, p. 630).

have characteristics likely to tilt them in favor of one party rather than the other. In the case of blog readers, however, there is no presumption of neutrality. Readers may be as partial or 'interested' as the most extreme of bloggers. Under this scenario, is it reasonable to expect readers to be led to the truth by an adversarial proceeding? Third, a crucial difference between jurors and blog readers is that jurors are required to listen to the entire legal proceeding, including all arguments from each side. Because the litigants are systematically offered opportunities to rebut their opponents' arguments, jurors will at least be exposed to a roughly equal quantity of arguments on each side. The analogue is dramatically untrue in the case of blog users. Quite the opposite. For one thing, the number of blogs in the blogosphere is so large that readers couldn't possibly read them all even if they wanted to. Moreover, as many commentators indicate, there is a strong tendency for people with partisan positions to seek out blogs that confirm their own prior prejudices and ignore the rest. Nothing constrains them to give equal time to opposing positions. This is an important disanalogy with the trial format, and renders very dubious the truth-determining properties of the adversarial system exemplified by the blogosphere.

SOCIAL MECHANISMS AND USERS' PSYCHOLOGICAL STATES

A major ambition of social epistemology (in the guise I have presented it) is to compare the knowledge consequences of alternative social practices, institutions, or mechanisms. In the theory of legal adjudication, for example, it might compare the knowledge consequences of having trial procedures accord with the adversarial (common-law) system or the so-called inquisitorial (civil-law) system. In the civil-law system, typical on the Continent, the entire inquiry is conducted by judges, who gather evidence, call witnesses, interrogate the witnesses, and make final judgments. Attorneys are assigned a very secondary role. There is no battle between legal teams, as there frequently is in the common-law tradition. Social epistemology would consider each system and inquire into the accuracy rate of its verdicts. Accuracy rates, of course, are not easy to ascertain, for obvious reasons. But if accuracy is the preeminent aim of an adjudication system, we should do the best we can to gauge the accuracy propensity of each system, so as to adopt the better one (or, if large-scale institutional transformation isn't feasible, at least to make changes to improve the one we've got). This is the kind of paradigm I have been inviting us to use when comparing the conventional news system with the blogging system.

Unfortunately, as hinted earlier, matters are somewhat more complicated. One cannot associate with a system, institution, or mechanism a uniform propensity to generate a determinate level of knowledge. Much depends on the inputs to the system. What I have in mind by 'inputs', in the first instance, are patterns of psychological states of its users. The users' motivations for example, are an important subset of relevant inputs. If a system's users are highly motivated in certain ways, their use of the system may produce a high level of knowledge consequences. If they are less motivated, the resultant level of knowledge consequences may be lower (or perhaps higher).

How would this work in the case of blogging? Citizens who are highly polarized on the political spectrum will tend to want to make the opposition look bad. This seems to be true in today's America, where there is an unusually high level of polarization. One consequence of this polarization is that many people are highly motivated to gather evidence and report that evidence in a public forum, such as blogs. Assuming this evidence is genuine (true), the unearthing and publication of it over the Internet presumably increases the general level of knowledge on that particular subject. Less polarized citizens will be more passive; they won't devote as much energy to the collection of evidence, or they won't bother to transmit it over the Internet. So the epistemic power of blogging may depend in nontrivial ways on motivations that vary with the political climate. This is not equally true, arguably, with the conventional news system. In such a system, journalists and editors are motivated by their jobs and careers to perform well, and this doesn't change with the political wind. Blogging isn't a career, so the volume and intensity of blogging activity is more dependent on political drive, which is, plausibly, a more variable matter.

Another issue of motivation is people's precise reasons for reading news and news analysis in the first place. Posner (along with other commentators) claims that most people today aren't interested in knowing the truth whatever it may be, at least in political matters. In particular, they don't seek to be exposed to information that might force them to revise or overthrow their earlier opinions. They only want to have their prior opinions confirmed, or articulated more authoritatively, perhaps in order to help defend those views to others. This motivation would explain their propensity to consult only those channels or sites where they expect to find corroborating material. This isn't said to be everybody's motivation; it isn't a universal human trait. So we are talking about a kind of motivation that is variable across times and individuals.

If this is correct, it has a theoretical bearing on the kinds of statements that can or should be made by social epistemologists (of a veritistic stripe). Statements of the following simple sort should not (commonly) be made: 'System S is veritistically better (better in terms of knowledge-production) than system S*'. This may be taken to imply that S is better than S* across all sets of system inputs. Since this will rarely be the case, we shall usually want to confine ourselves to a more circumspect formula: 'System S is veritistically better than S* for sets of inputs of types $I_1, I_2, \ldots, I_k$'. Once this is clarified, the program of veritistic social epistemology can proceed as before, just more cautiously, or with greater qualification. This implies that it may be unwise to offer a categorical comparison, in veritistic terms, of conventional news versus blogging. Relativization to input sets is probably required. But this doesn't undermine the program of veritistic social epistemology; it just makes it more complex. That is hardly surprising.

References

Estlund, D. 1990. Democracy without preference. *Philosophical Review, 49,* 397–424.

Estlund, D. 1993. Making truth safe for democracy, in D. Copp, J. Hampton, and J. Roemer (Eds.), *The idea of democracy.* New York: Cambridge University Press, pp. 71–100.

Federal Rules of Evidence. St. Paul, MN: West Group.

Goldman, A. 1999. *Knowledge in a social world.* Oxford: Oxford University Press.

Goldman, A. 2002, What is social epistemology?: A smorgasbord of projects, in A. Goldman, *Pathways to knowledge, private and public.* New York: Oxford University Press, pp. 182–204.

Goldman, A. 2004. The need for social epistemology, in B. Leiter (Ed.), *The future for philosophy.* Oxford: Oxford University Press, pp. 182–207.

Goldman, A. 2005. Legal evidence, in M. P. Golding and W. A. Edmundson (Eds.), *The Blackwell guide to the philosophy of law and legal theory.* Malden, MA: Blackwell, pp. 163–175.

Goldman, A. 2007. Social epistemology, in E. Zalta, (Ed.), *Stanford encyclopedia of philosophy.* Retrieved August 1, 2007 from http://plato.stanford.edu/archives/spr2007/entries/epistemology-social/

Graham, G. 1999. *The Internet, A philosophical inquiry.* London: Routledge.

Grofman, B., and Feld, S. 1988. Rousseau's general will: A Condorcetian perspective. *American Political Science Review, 82,* 567–576.

Holmes, O. W. 1919. *Abrams v. United States* 250 U.S., 616 (dissenting).

List, C., and Goodin, R. 2001. Epistemic democracy: Generalizing the Condorcet jury theorem. *Journal of Political Philosophy, 9,* 277–306.

Milton, J. 1959. Areopagitica, a speech for the liberty of unlicensed printing (1644), in E. Sirluck, (Ed.), *Complete prose works of John Milton.* London: Oxford University Press.

Posner, R. 2005. Bad news. *New York Times,* July 31, book review, pp. 1–11.

Rousseau, J.-J. 1762. *The social contract,* in G. D. H. Cole (Trans.), *The social contract and discourses.* London: Everyman/Dent.

7

Plural Selves and Relational Identity

Intimacy and Privacy Online

Dean Cocking

INTRODUCTION

With unprecedented global access, speed, and relative anonymity with respect to how one is able to present oneself to and interact with others, computer-mediated communication (hereafter CMC) contexts provide many new worlds through which we may express and develop our identities as persons and form relationships with others. Through text-based e-mail and chat-room style forums, or Web site and Web cam technology, we may present or even 'showcase' ourselves to others, and we may enter and contribute to all sorts of communities, such as hobby and mutual interest groups, and develop various sorts of relationships with others. Indeed, for many people, significant aspects of key roles and relationships in their professional, business, and even personal lives are now conducted online.

It makes sense then, to consider if these CMC contexts, where people are increasingly presenting themselves to and undertaking various activities and relationships with others, might tailor the content of these relationships and the self that is presented to others online in any notable ways. For many, opportunities to express and form relationships have been enormously increased by computer communication technology. But what sorts of identities and relationships are really possible online? How might our pursuit of values that constitute and regulate our ideals of personal identity and various significant relationships be sensitive to such communication environments?

It is clear that contextual features of the setting within which we express ourselves to others can significantly influence the content and nature of our communication. Indeed, it is clear that the nature of the relationships one is able to have and the self one is able to communicate within those relationships can be seriously affected by the context of one's communication.[1] Perhaps certain contextual features of the environments provided by CMC enable and promote certain valuable kinds of relationships and self-expression. On the other hand, some values might be lost, perverted, or their pursuit limited by features of these communication environments.

One well-worn question in computer ethics has concerned whether or not computers can be persons. But, given the proliferation of computer communication in our lives, it now seems worth considering the extent and ways in which persons can be persons online. The general issue concerns the normative effects CMC contexts might have on values attached to our identities and our relationships with others. The particular aspect of this general issue I explore in this chapter concerns the effects of CMC contexts on intimacy and privacy.

I have argued elsewhere (Cocking and Matthews 2000) that, despite apparent 'real life' phenomena to the contrary, certain features of text-based online contexts largely rule out the development of close friendships exclusively in those contexts. One obvious feature to point the finger at here is the relative anonymity afforded, say, by text-based e-mail or chat-room formats. While each person may give quite a deal of information ostensibly about themselves, whether in fact this information is accurately representative is, of course, a separate question that one is unable to verify independently. If conditions allowing such anonymity, as Glaucon's tale of the Ring of Gyges[2] warned us, may tempt one to immorality (much less leave one without any reason to be moral at all), then we may understandably be very wary of trusting one another under such conditions.

But, even if we put aside worries regarding deliberate deception and so forth, the bare fact of information about one another being exclusively attained under conditions that allow such anonymity may seem sufficient to sink the idea that one could develop close friendships under such conditions. How could one become the close friend of another under conditions where, so far as one can tell, that other might not even exist? The 'other', for instance, may simply be a character someone has created or to which any number of writers regularly contribute. Of course, one may become quite attached to such a character. We do, after all, get attached to people in real life, only to discover they were not who they seemed, and we do become attached to characters, such as Daffy Duck, that we know do not exist. However, we typically think that those to whom we became quite attached but who turn out not to be who they seemed, were not after all our close friends. And, of course, while many of us might be quite fond of Daffy, he cannot be our close friend.

---

[1] For some detailed discussion of various ways in which I think the online communication context can affect such content, see Cocking and Matthews (2000).

[2] Plato's *Republic*, Book 11, pp. 359b–360b.

In response, it might be thought that the bare fact that communication conditions might allow such anonymity should not itself rule out close friendship. We could, for instance, simply add the condition that the parties to the virtual friendship in fact are the real characters they claim to be and that their interest in one another is sincere. Thus, I may believe that my Internet buddy is my close friend and, if he does exist and his communications to me are sincere, then he may in fact be my close friend. Against such a view, however, I claim that such online contexts nevertheless seriously limit the possible scope for the development of close friendships and, in particular, the intimacy found in such relationships. Not because of the range of possibilities for deception, or on account of the bare fact of anonymity, but on account of another distortion and limitation related to the relative anonymity afforded by such online contexts.

The key feature of CMC contexts to which I draw attention concerns the atypical dominance of high levels and kinds of choice and control in how one may present and disclose oneself afforded the person communicating online – one part of which is how CMC contexts makes one less subject to the thoughts and influence of others. In various virtual contexts, such as text-based e-mail and chat-room forums, one is able, for instance, to present a far more carefully constructed picture of one's attitudes, feelings, and of the sort of person one would choose to present oneself as than otherwise would be possible in various nonvirtual contexts.

In this chapter, I consider what effects such atypical control the individual is afforded over their own self-presentations may have for the possibility of developing the sort of intimacy found in close friendships. I also think. however, this focus is instructive and suggestive of a novel way to understand both online privacy and part of what is at stake in concern about privacy generally. For, while online contexts would seem to present a barrier to the development of intimacy, they also, at once, seem to facilitate the maintaining of a private self, insulated from the observations, judgments, and related interpretive interaction of others. Nevertheless, I will argue that the opportunity afforded online to insulate a private self from others would also seem to largely rule out certain ways of relating to one another in which we may respect one another's privacy.

In arguing my case here, I focus on the significance of aspects of self over which we exercise less choice and control, particularly in the context where they coexist with conflicting aspects of self over which we exercise more choice and control. Much contemporary literature in moral psychology has focused on the latter in order to provide accounts of our agency, our moral responsibility, and of our moral identities. Indeed, on many such accounts, uncooperative aspects of our conduct, over which we exercise less choice and control, are presented as key illustrations of failures of agency and moral responsibility and marginalized from the story given of our moral identities.[3] I do not here dispute that such aspects of conduct may illustrate failures of agency or moral responsibility. I think they may or may not. One may well be morally responsible for aspects of oneself over which one *now* exercises little or no choice or control because one may be responsible for aspects of one's character (e.g., one's selfishness, kindness, or courage) that motivate the action (or omission) with respect to which one could not have now, given one's character, exercised any choice or control to do otherwise. One thing this shows, I think, is that a highly voluntary, say, 'at-will', account of our moral responsibility for actions cannot generally be right because many of our actions – namely, those actions that issue from certain aspects of our character – will need an account of our moral responsibility for our character to explain our moral responsibility for actions or omissions that have issued from such a character. And one thing that does seem clear is that such a highly voluntary view of our responsibility for character cannot be right. We cannot in any 'at-will' way effectively choose to be, say, a kind character.

I will, however, not pursue the question of what determines our responsibility for character here. Instead, my concern in this chapter is to reject the marginalization of certain aspects of our selves[4] over which we are relatively passive (compared to other coexisting, uncooperative aspects of self) from the picture of our moral identities and of the evaluative phenomena relevant to worthwhile relations between people. And I want to resurrect the normative significance of such passive aspects of self, even if on a correct account of our responsibility for character, these aspects of self turned out to be features with respect to which we were not morally responsible. Because my account, then, is somewhat out of step with orthodoxy in the area, part of the burden of my discussion will be to support my view of the significance of such aspects of self and of relations with others. In making my case I will, in part, appeal to the case of certain online environments as a foil, where, as

---

[3] One general, standard view I have in mind here (within which there are many importantly distinct accounts) is the concept of a person limited to the view of free will and responsibility given by our identification with aspects of ourselves either through our second-order desires regarding our first-order desires or our evaluative judgments regarding the considerations that would move us to act. For the classic contemporary presentations of each of these views (respectively), see Frankfurt (1988) and Watson (1982). See also the centrality of choice and control to conceptions of unified agency thought to capture our moral identities in Korsgaard (1980) and Velleman (2000).

[4] It might be thought that I beg the question here by using such terms as 'aspects of self' or 'self-presentation' – rather than, say, simply 'conduct' – because the question is whether or not such conduct which is not the result of high levels of choice and control should be regarded as relevant to our moral identities, 'real' self, or our relationships. I thank Justin Oakley for presenting this problem to me. In fact, however, I take it that it is the justificatory burden of my discussion to convince the reader that the terms 'self-presentation' or 'aspects of self' can properly apply to *both* conflicting aspects of conduct to which I refer.

I claim, these aspects of self may be minimized or perverted – at least, with respect to intimacy and certain relational aspects of privacy.[5]

My discussion proceeds as follows. First, I provide some ordinary cases of nonvirtual self-presentation and interaction. Here I illustrate the sort of contrast between uncooperative aspects of self that I have in mind and put the case for their significance for intimacy and aspects of privacy. Second, I develop and support the contribution of my account by building upon and contrasting it to a recent account of the value of privacy from Thomas Nagel (1998). Third, I focus more directly on the case of certain online environments and develop my view of the nature and value of intimacy and certain relational aspects of privacy. Here, I argue that standard online environments afford those communicating online an atypical dominance of self-presentations of the more highly chosen and controlled variety and that this dominance largely eliminates the sort of values regarding identity and our relations with others I have canvassed.

I. ACTIVE AND PASSIVE SELVES

The identity of most of us consists in a bundle of plural selves or, at least, plural aspects of self. Given the range of interests, relationships, and the roles most of us have, and the range of contextual circumstances within which these are expressed, an identity without such plurality would be extraordinarily limited and ineffectual and unable to properly pursue various interests and properly engage in various relationships and roles across a range of contexts. Indeed, such cross-situational plurality of self commonly requires dispositional capacities that are significantly at odds with one another. At work, for instance, it may be appropriate that one is industrious and one's attention narrowly directed by the pursuit of quite specific goals, whereas this would be a very limiting, ineffectual, and inappropriate disposition to govern the enjoyment of values to do with relaxing at home or being with one's friends.[6]

Often however, plural and uncooperative aspects of self are presented within the context of *one* relationship, role, or encounter. Indeed, in ordinary nonvirtual contexts, such as at work or being out with friends, while I may exercise control over my self-presentations so that I do not actively present, say, my anger, competitiveness, envy, jealousy, or any other aspects of my character I am either unaware of, or would choose not to present, my more 'active' self-presentations need not be the most dominant, much less

---

[5] I give a fuller philosophical account of my rejection of what may be called the 'reflective choice and effective control' view of our moral identities, in an unpublished paper 'Identity, self-presentation and interpretation: The case of hypocrisy'.

[6] And sometimes, of course, our pursuit of plural values conflicts and the price of pursuing one is the cost of another – my pursuit of family life, for instance, suffers on account of the time, energy and/or temperament required for the pursuit of my working life.

the only, aspects of my behavior that are presented to others. Commonly, we communicate a lot with respect to our thoughts and feelings, through tone of voice, facial expression, and body movement that goes beyond and may well conflict with self-presentations that we might provide through, for instance, the literal meaning of the words we choose to speak or write. Such uncooperative conduct, over which one exercises less choice and control, we nevertheless also quite commonly regard as revealing of aspects of one's self, that is, one's attitudes, feelings, emotions, or character, and to provide fertile and appropriate grounds for interpretation of one's self, either from others, or one's own self-interpretation.

Thus, for instance, I notice my friend's enthusiasm for gossip, her obsession with food, or her anxiety when her expartner appears on the arm of his new love. Nevertheless, her enthusiasm, obsession, or anxiety, are not the result of her exercise of high levels of choice and control, and my interpretations of her attitudes and conduct may provide appropriate considerations to guide my interaction with her. Because of such interpretations I will, for example, be more attentive to my anxious friend when her expartner enters the room or try to lighten up the situation with a joke or some other strategy of distraction. Similarly, I might affectionately tease her regarding her interest in gossip or obsession with food. And she might joke at her own expense on any or all these counts.

Further, her attitudes and conduct here may be quite at odds with, and undermining of, the self-presentations she does intend as a matter of greater choice and control. Thus, although I interpret her as forcing her smile and putting on a brave face when her expartner unexpectedly turns up, she is not, as a matter of choice and control, presenting her smile as forced or presenting herself as putting on a brave face. On the contrary, this conduct conflicts with and to some extent undermines the self-presentation she chooses and aims to make effective – namely, to appear comfortable about seeing the expartner on the arm of his new love. Yet, not only are my interpretive interactions not confined to the self-presentations she chooses and aims to effect, if they were so confined she may rightly think me insensitive and as failing to react to her appropriately and form appropriate reasons with respect to her, for example, to engage in the distracting small talk or to provide cover for her to leave the room discreetly.

Such interpretive interactions, therefore, seem quite proper and commonplace to the realization of the friendship relationship and the intimacy found there. In both ordinary as well as significant ways, it is upon such interpretive interaction that the standard accepted features of the intimacy found in close friendship – namely, mutual affection, the desire for shared experiences, and the disposition to benefit and promote the interests of one's friend – are expressed. I express my affection for my friend when I playfully tease her about her food obsession; recognizing her enthusiasm for gossip leads me to notice a salacious story to pass on to her from the front page of a tabloid newspaper; my lightening up the situation when her expartner enters the room exhibits my concern for her welfare. In close friendship, we interpret these typically more 'passive' aspects of our close friend's conduct and our interpretations have an impact on the creation of the self in friendship, the reasons that emerge in it, and on the realization of the intimacy found in the relationship.[7]

Similarly, the presentation of more 'passive' aspects of our selves often provides the object for the expression of certain relational aspects of respect for another's privacy. For the purpose of respecting people's claim to keep certain of their thoughts and feelings to themselves and to have some choice and control over the 'self' they present to us for public engagement or scrutiny we can, and often should, choose to put aside what their conflicting, less chosen and controlled self-presentations might tell us. We can leave unacknowledged or unaddressed these thoughts and feelings we present and know about one another (either in general or more specific terms) for the purpose of getting along in such social encounters and to show respect for one another's claim to the public/private boundaries of the self we choose to present to one another. My friend's expartner, for instance, may no longer presume to engage in the private concerns of my friend, and so her anxiety and discomfort at their encounter, while recognized, may properly be set aside by the two of them and not be subjected to (his) unwelcome attention. In this way, then, relational aspects of our respect for the privacy of others can be shown.

The dissonance between self-presentations we affect more and less actively provide 'tells'[8] in communication and understanding. When, in some more highly chosen and controlled way, we present ourselves, say, as being pleased to see our expartner with his new love, but we do so in the face of quite contrary attitudes, emotions, feelings, and so forth, we do not present ourselves as we would in the absence of such conflict. The differ-ence in self-presentations is sourced in two ways. First, our self-directives regarding how we present ourselves have limited scope. Not all aspects of our self-presentation result as acts of highly chosen and controlled direction. For instance, my friend tries valiantly not to twitch and shuffle, but some

---

[7] For extended accounts of the interpretive process that I think are distinctive of friendship, see Cocking and Kennett (1998, 2000) and Cocking and Matthews (2000). The genesis of my focus here on interpretation that addresses both active and passive self-presentations and the import of this to our identity and related values can be seen in the latter article. The central examples I use here arguing for the significance of the passive to our moral identities and relationships were presented at the *Computing and Philosophy Conference*, Australian National University, Canberra, Australia, in December, 2003. I am especially indebted to Kylie Williams for our relentless discussions of the issues that have culminated in this and related work. I am also indebted to Justin Oakley, Seumas Miller, and Jeroen van den Hoven for their discussions and contributions to our ongoing related work.

[8] I take the term 'tells' from David Mamet's classic depiction of the conman's art in *House of Games*, (Good Times Entertainment, 1987).

twitching and shuffling gets through. Second, even putting these less chosen and controlled indicators aside, within the scope of the self-presentations we can affect in more highly chosen and controlled ways, these latter self-presentations do not replicate the former self-presentations they seek to mimic. We do not, for instance, use the same facial muscles when we direct ourselves to smile as we do when we more 'naturally' smile, say, because we are amused by a good joke.[9]

Moreover, the difference is often quite noticeable. My bitter colleague's smile through gritted teeth, for example, contrasts strikingly with her smirk as she offers her condolences at the knock-back I received for my latest book manuscript. Such 'tells' are of course not of a piece. Sometimes it is obvious what the dissonance signifies, but often it is not. Thus, communication and understanding in this regard may be as open to confusion as it is to clear insight. (Consider, for instance, the comic – and sometimes less so – experiences most of us have had romantically on account of failures of interpretation in this regard.) Often, as in the case of my friend and her expartner, good reasons may drive us to project self-presentations that are at odds with how we otherwise think or feel. Thus, such self-presentations may be appropriate, polite, kind, or even obligatory. Indeed, as many social scientists, psychologists, and philosophers have noted, without the capacity to choose and control self-presentation in the face of internal conflicting forces (in situations where it is necessary that we be able to get along with one another, such as in our working lives) much joint and social action would be impossible. Civilized society, in general, would be impossible. We would be jumping the queue at the deli, undermining our colleagues, and doing much worse things whenever we had the impulse to do so. Also, however, a person's highly chosen and controlled self-presentations may be inappropriate, pathetic, or give us the creeps – as, for example, with the self-deceived, conceited, or hypocritical.

Whether or not the dissonance between such plural and conflicting self-presentations tells us something of note, or even if it does, whether we should take note of what it tells us, depends significantly upon the context

---

[9] Separate neural systems are involved in governing our voluntary and involuntary facial expressions. Thus, for instance, certain stroke victims are able to laugh at a joke they find amusing but are unable to direct themselves to smile. The work of Paul Ekman in cataloguing thousands of facial 'micro-expressions' in his *Diogenes Project* and analysing their significance is especially substantial and fascinating. I thank Kylie Williams for bringing this work and many of the issues it raises to my attention. For some of Ekman's work, see Ekman and Friesen (1975) and Ekman and Rosenberg (1997). What is at least minimally clear is that we can use our neural-muscular system to voluntarily suppress and control various involuntary expressions and responses, but not all, and that, in many cases, our voluntary expressions differ recognizably from relevantly similar nonvoluntary ones. It also seems clear that although some differences provide quite clear 'tells', the ability to recognise such differences generally, easily, and with a high level of discrimination is a fairly rare talent that is not widely shared.

of the relation or role within which we are engaged. To show this it will be helpful to consider in more detail how interpretive interaction within relational contexts may in different ways appropriately address our plural and uncooperative self-presentations and, in part, create and sustain the self. In doing so, I shall contrast this approach with other accounts of the self and of its relations with others that focus largely, or exclusively, on the more highly chosen and controlled aspects of self, and which take such self-presentations to provide the uniquely proper object of our engagement and consideration.

II. RELATIONSHIPS, SELF-PRESENTATIONS, AND INTERPRETATIONS

As I have indicated, the case of personal relations, especially friendship, allows an extremely rich and broad range of self-presentations as appropriate territory for interpretive interactions. Unlike professional relations, our close friendships are not governed by relatively narrow purposes – such as to promote health for doctors, justice for lawyers, or education for teachers. The appropriateness of interpretations regarding plural and uncooperative self-presentations in professional–client relations is thus governed by a relatively limited scope of determinate considerations. Nevertheless, within the prism provided by appropriate conceptions of particular professional–client relations, interpretive interaction addressing both active and passive self-presentations remains. If, say, I am your boss or your teacher I may notice and interpret self-presentations conflicting with those you choose to present. In so far as my interpretations here are within a plausible conception of my proper interest, understanding, or engagement with you as your boss or teacher this may be appropriate territory for my interaction with you. So, for instance, more passive indicators of my student's demeanor may suggest she is having more serious trouble finishing her thesis than she chooses to present, and my interpretation here gives me reason to not leave her floundering and take more of an interest in how we might helpfully address the problem.

Just as well, the self-presentations that conflict with what you choose to present to me may be none of my business, be disrespectful for me to engage you with, or be relatively unimportant or irrelevant to the business at hand. When the checkout teller at the supermarket asks how my day has been, although I realize she is not likely to care either way, I need not snap: 'what do you care!' If my colleague is able to cooperate when he wants to compete and assert some superiority, I may still be able to work with him. When I notice the telling signs – for example, his looking away and talking up his own successes when someone congratulates me on my new book – so long as his competitive drives are under some control and not too intrusive, I can put them aside and we are able to work together.

Such examples are the territory of Thomas Nagel's recent account of how conventions of privacy, concealment, nonacknowledgement or of 'putting aside' various aspects of one another serve to provide a psychosocial environment that supports individual autonomy and enables civilized engagement with others (Nagel 1998, p. 4). As Nagel points out, social conventions of concealment are not just about secrecy and deception, but also reticence and nonacknowledgement. Such reticence and nonacknowledgement enable us to present ourselves for appropriate and fruitful interactions in our roles and relations with others without being overwhelmed by the influence of others or self-consciousness of our awareness of others – in particular, regarding distracting or conflicting aspects of ourselves over which we do not exercise much choice and control in presenting. We are thus not condemned or simply in receipt of unwelcome attention for aspects of ourselves we do not actively present for public engagement,[10] and we have a valuable space within which to engage in our own imaginary and reflective worlds – enabling, for instance, relaxation, enjoyment, self-development, and understanding.

Such social and relational conventions of privacy are thought, therefore, to support individual autonomy by supporting our capacity for some choice and control over the self that we present for engagement in our relations and roles with others. And clearly, as I have suggested, civil relations with others would be impossible for most of us without some robust capacity for putting aside distracting, annoying, or undesirable aspects of one another.[11] But while there are many cases where conventions of nonacknowledgement count toward respect for privacy, the value of our interpretive interactions regarding plural and often uncooperative self-presentations is not limited to, and would often be mischaracterized by, a singular focus on

[10] As I have indicated, on my account, the appropriateness or legitimacy of such claims needs to be understood within bounds of what might plausibly be thought (relatively) unimportant, unnecessary, or irrelevant with respect to the proper considerations governing the context of the relation or role at hand. Thus, so long as my colleague's bitter and competitive streak is not too extreme and intrusive, I can rightly put it aside as (relatively) unimportant to most of our joint tasks. On the other hand, as I discuss in the text ahead, the legitimacy of one's interactions with another based on certain interpretations, even where these interpretations are not welcomed by the other, may also be assessed in this way. Thus, for instance, insofar as my student's demeanour suggests she is in more trouble with her work than she chooses to present, my interactions with her may rightly be guided by my interpretation here.

[11] Similar observations by social scientists have long supported the necessity and value of such psycho-social environments. Ervin Goffman's work (Goffman 1959) on the social and contextual frames that govern and direct what we 'give' and 'give off' (or what we actively and passively present) has been especially influential here. Like Nagel, Goffman pointed to the importance of the acknowledged information for which the person accepts responsibility and the social and relational conventions discouraging focus on what is 'given off', rather than 'given', thus supporting presentations of self for public engagement over which we can claim sufficient responsibility, that is, over which we exercise sufficient choice and control.

nonacknowledgement and the respect for privacy shown by 'putting aside' aspects of self over which we exercise less choice and control.

First, when, for present purposes, I put aside my interpretation of my colleague's competitiveness I need not think my interpretation presents irrelevant information regarding the sort of person he really is. On the contrary, I may think it provides compelling and appropriate reason to not become any more involved with him than I need. Thus, although it may be appropriate in a given context and relationship or role that I respect privacy by observing conventions of nonacknowledgement, and putting aside certain aspects of another's conduct, this does not show that such aspects should be regarded as outside the proper domain, either of what is to counted as part of a person's character or of the interpretations of their character upon which one's interaction may more generally be guided. Second, although my colleague's overly competitive streak is not too intrusive and largely irrelevant to our relationship at work, it may be appropriate that I do not focus my attention on it too greatly and engage him on it, there may just as well be circumstances within our working relationship where it is appropriate that I do so. Thus, for instance, I may need to explain, say, to my boss, why I cannot trust my colleague with early drafts of my work.

The self a person chooses to present for our engagement is an important consideration it would often be disrespectful to ignore altogether. Similarly, however, it would be disrespectful to the limitations and fragility of, say, my friend's capacities for autonomy to ignore her anxiety and apparent desire to throw a drink in the face of her expartner when they unexpectedly meet. This concern for limited or fragile autonomy may be thought accommodated by the standard account of moral identity in terms of morally responsible agency and the exercise of (reflective) choice and (effective) control with respect to one's conduct. It may be accommodated as respect for the other's efforts in this regard, and this, it might be argued, can be evidenced by the implicit agreement of the other where she accepts such interpretive influence.

However, whether or not such interpretive influence counts as respect for such efforts, or is accepted by the person whose conduct is being interpreted, these considerations do not exhaustively answer the question as to whether or not one's interpretations are appropriate. One's interpretations may have been unacceptable to a person, but may nevertheless be appropriate and provide appropriate guidance in one's interaction with them. And one's interpretations need not evidence respect for the other's efforts to make effective some chosen presentation of self. Indeed, as with the self-deluded or hypocritical, one's interpretive interaction may be concerned to reject such presentations of self. Contrariwise, my *inappropriate* interpretations may have been acceptable to her, or be directed at supporting her more highly chosen and controlled self-presentations – as, for example, when I appeal to her vanity or her low self-esteem.

The concern then – commonly addressed in terms of respect for individual autonomy – to make effective one's reflective choices about how to be, engage with others and live, is not only the proper concern of the individual who may then keep from our influence what they may rightly regard as their choice. It is also the proper concern of others and is often significantly realized as a relational product of one's interpretive interactions with others. For often, what the individual may rightly regard as their choice, they simply cannot keep from our influence and, indeed, cannot realize without it. This is the situation with my interpretive interactions to the passive self-presentations of my friend (and just as well, again, with those between my friend and her expartner). By making the small talk and discreetly getting her out of the room in response to her discomfort and anxiety, I assist – perhaps crucially – her capacity to make effective her choices to put on the brave face and be civil. I (or her expartner) would not be respecting her efforts by not acknowledging or putting aside her passive self-presentations that threaten to derail how she (reasonably) chooses to present herself. We do not take the forced smiles to simply and solely represent smiles. Only the inconsiderate or inept would do that, and neither would be very helpful in respecting her efforts at self-presentation in the circumstances. Instead, her capacity to make her choices about how to present herself and engage with others is made (partly) effective and respected by our appropriate interpretive reactions to her efforts in light of the passive self-presentations we do see.

As many writers have claimed, much of the concern addressed by respect for privacy seems grounded upon the concern we have with the autonomy of persons.[12] The concern addressed by privacy, that is, to keep aspects of one's self private that one may rightly think are one's own business, seems significantly about allowing others some significant choice and control over how it is and to whom it is that one presents oneself. This concern however, should not be conceived as only the proper concern of the individual, who may then keep from our view and exclude from our engagement what they may rightly regard private. Rather, it is also often the proper concern of others and realized as a relational product of one's interpretive interactions with others. For again, as with my friend and her expartner, often what the individual may rightly regard as private they simply cannot keep from our view. Both my friend and her expartner may rightly regard their discomfort and anxiety at their chance meeting – a concern with which each may no longer presume to engage. Nevertheless, they cannot, or cannot very successfully, keep what they rightly regard private from one another's view. However, they can realize respect for one another's privacy as a relational product of their interpretive interaction.

---

[12] See, for instance, Rachels (1975) and Kupfer (1987). I thank Steve Matthews for passing on these references to me.

Moreover, contrary to what is claimed in virtue of the focus solely in terms of respect for individual autonomy, this relational respect for privacy is not simply a matter of not acknowledging or setting aside conflicting or uncooperative, more passive, aspects of self that one another sees. Instead, it is a matter of appropriate interpretive reactions in light of both the active and passive self-presentations one another does see. Thus, again, my friend and her expartner do not take the forced smiles to simply and solely represent smiles and so, for example, engage in an extended encounter delving into how each other is 'really' going – as they might in different circumstances or if they were old friends. Instead, in reaction to seeing the discomfort in one another, they respect privacy by such things as keeping eye contact fleeting, conversing only on nonconfronting subjects, and wrapping things up fairly quickly.

I now turn to the direct consideration of certain online environments and how these communication contexts might be thought to affect the sort of intimacy and aspects of privacy I have presented. Here I argue that, although standard online communication contexts favor our more highly chosen and controlled self-presentations and, thereby, tell against developing key aspects of intimacy, they would also seem to provide significant opportunities for maintaining a 'private' self in one's communication with others. At the same time, however, the favoring of such self-presentations would also seem to limit and pervert the value of privacy by largely ruling out some of the relational ways I have described in which we may respect one another's privacy.

III. THE DOMINANCE OF HIGHLY VOLUNTARY SELF-PRESENTATIONS ONLINE

So far I have argued that, although we may exercise significant choice and control over whom we allow in and exclude in everyday nonvirtual environments, we do not altogether do so over what we present and what we are subject to, and that the latter presentations of self and interactions with others are also crucial for key features of intimacy and certain relational aspects of privacy. We may, from privacy, choose to leave aside aspects of others and exclude others from aspects of ourselves. And from intimacy, we may choose to include others and allow more 'private' aspects of ourselves to be taken up by them. But, either way, the normal nonvirtual communication context provides us with a wide and often conflicting or problematic range of feelings and thoughts. Both privacy and intimacy depend not only upon our being able to exercise choices and controls regarding what we present for engagement by others and what we do not; who we exclude and who we do not, but also upon aspects of ourselves over which we exercise less choice and control being available to others as the subject of interpretive interactions reflecting, for instance, respect for privacy, efforts toward intimacy or both.

In various virtual contexts, such as text-based e-mail and chat-room forums, however, there is an atypical dominance of more highly chosen and controlled possibilities for self-presentation. As I mentioned earlier, one is able, for instance, to present a more carefully constructed picture of one's attitudes, feelings, and of the sort of person one would choose to present oneself as, than otherwise would be possible in various nonvirtual contexts. In ordinary nonvirtual contexts, such as at work or being out with friends, although I may exercise control over my self-presentations in the effort to not present, say, my anger, competitiveness, envy, jealousy, or any other aspects of my character I would choose not to present, such efforts at self-presentation need not be the most dominant, much less the only, aspects of my behavior that are presented to others. As I have described, we often communicate a lot with respect to our thoughts and feelings, through tone of voice, facial expression, and body movement that goes beyond, and may well conflict with, the more highly chosen and controlled self-presentations that we might provide through, for instance, the literal meaning of the words we speak or write.

Certainly, it is hard to see how, in standard online contexts, plural and conflicting, more and less active self-presentations can both be similarly represented and understood by others. Correspondingly, it is hard to see how we can be moved, as one often is in the nonvirtual case, in response to both the more and less active self-presentations of another. It is hard, for instance, to see how one might choose to put aside or exclude from public engagement and scrutiny another's self-presentations and disclosures *that are presented and so known to one* but which are not disclosed in the other's more highly chosen and controlled self-presentations. For, if the other gives expression online, say, to her anxiety over seeing the expartner, then she has – given such features of the communication context as being able to choose how and when, or indeed, if at all, she responds – been afforded much greater opportunity to only present herself in more highly chosen and controlled ways. It is much more likely, then, that if she has put her feelings on the table in this context, she has done so more as a matter of some relatively active choice and control in how she presents herself.[13] It is, for instance, hard to see how she could then sensibly expect the other to respect a claim not to have her feelings up for engagement or scrutiny when she has, say, written an e-mail telling them of her feelings. At least, it is hard to see how she can do so by presenting aspects of herself to the other which can and sometimes ought to be put aside without thereby making an issue of it – at least the putting aside – and so, without thereby encroaching the

---

[13] I do not rule out that one may communicate to others online in, say, quite unreflective and uncontrolled ways. My thought is that given the distinctive and additional opportunity to not do so, it is plausibly thought less likely in the sort of contexts and relations I have in mind – for instance, the pursuit of 'friendship' relations exclusively in, say, e-mail or chat-room formats.

public on to the aspects of herself, she would otherwise present passively and wish to be respected as private.

How one presents oneself and how one responds to that with which one is presented in standard online contexts would, therefore, seem able to avoid much of the lack of cooperation and the conflicts in plural self-presentations I have mentioned. My friend, for instance, had she got the news from her ex about his new love, say, by an inadvertent e-mail message, could have avoided her conflicting self-presentations altogether – perhaps she could have even convincingly sent her 'well-wishing'. Similarly, at work, my envious colleague could avoid presentations of her envy altogether, had she congratulated me on my promotion by e-mail rather than through 'gritted teeth' in the staff room. By enabling an atypical dominance, with respect to one's self-presentations, of the picture of self over which one does exercise higher levels of choice and control in presenting to others and by providing a minimization of the ways in which one is subject to the influence of those with whom one interacts, one is afforded the opportunity online to largely avoid the presentation of uncooperative passive aspects of one's self and one's related interaction. (Likewise, one may largely avoid the presentation of uncooperative passive aspects of self from others.)

In such ways then, online environments, rather than presenting a threat to privacy, may be thought to provide heightened opportunities to maintain a private self insulated from the interpretive interactions of others. Indeed, if online communication contexts do allow one to largely omit uncooperative, relatively passive, self-presentations from the picture of one's identity, then, in such cases, one might think privacy is better served than it is in the nonvirtual context. If the distinctive controls over self-presentation provided online may allow, say, my friend to present those aspects of self she may *rightly* only want to present to her ex, then it may have been better that she was able to do so. Because her anxieties or jealousies are now no longer any of his business, it may better serve her privacy – and be better all round – that she is able to exclude her private thoughts and feelings from his view altogether. Similarly, one might claim it would often be better for the purposes of one's, say, working relationship, that one is able to exclude one's skin color or acne from the other's view.

But it wouldn't be a good thing quite generally, if, as in standard online contexts, we could switch off and (largely) exclude from view, presentations of self other than those over which we exercise high levels of choice and control. For this would confine us to a monistic conception of the self and of how one's self-presentations can be engaged and developed in one's relationships that would, in part, limit and pervert the nature of various valuable aspects of self and its relations with others. Unlike outward aspects of one's 'self', such as one's skin color or acne, the aspects of intimacy and privacy to which I have referred and described as grounded on more passive aspects of self, represent aspects of a person's conduct and ways of relating, which are of positive normative significance.

First, consider privacy. As I argued above, the concern addressed by privacy is not just the proper concern of the individual who may rightly exclude us altogether. It is also relational and social in nature and value. As, for example, when dealing with your expartner, I can respect your privacy by putting aside your awkwardness. If, however, our contact is confined to online contexts, while I might not be able to violate your claim to this private self, because it may (largely) now be excluded from my view, I am not in a position to be able to show respect for such more private aspects of your self either.[14] I can't put aside and respect your claim to keep your own counsel on thoughts and feelings not presented to me, and I can't have them presented to me without encroaching on your claim to keep your own counsel on your private concerns – that is, by addressing these concerns as an object of my attention.

The concern addressed by privacy in the nonvirtual case enables a pluralism regarding identity and presentations of self, and it enables the relational and social good of civilized engagement that we may respect aspects of identity and self-presentation in others by putting these considerations aside. Privacy in the virtual case is secured at the expense of this pluralism about the self and at the loss of the relational and social good of respecting the privacy of others by not acknowledging or addressing aspects of the other's identity presented to us. This much one can glean from the accounts of Nagel and others regarding privacy. But the normative significance here is not limited to our 'making the best of a bad lot', whereby, because we often cannot keep what we may regard as private from another's view, we may engage in a morally civilized practice of nonacknowledgement. If it was, then online communication contexts might quite *generally*[15] serve privacy better by not putting us in the position of the more private aspects of ourselves being available to others.

What is missing from this approach, however, is a broader conception of the plural ways in which the availability of more passive aspects of self is important to how we understand and relate to others and ourselves. For the availability of such aspects of self provide important grounds, not only for how we may show respect for one another's privacy, but also for how we may thereby be moved either toward or away from developing other normatively

[14] I am especially indebted to Kylie Williams for suggesting this problem to me regarding the respect of privacy online.

[15] I do not rule out that in many *specific* cases it might be better that one's 'private' feelings, etc. are not available to others, as, for example, where my friend hears of her expartner's new love by an inadvertent e-mail message. This seems compatible with the claim that, as a general feature of our interactions, it would, nevertheless, not be a good idea due to the broad territory of aspects of self and interpretive interactions it would marginalise. Similarly, one may have concerns about anonymity if it were a general or quite global way in which we were to relate to others, but nevertheless think it a good thing in various specific instances.

significant aspects of sociality, such as goodwill and more intimate relations with another.

As I have indicated, in the nonvirtual case we present various aspects of ourselves other than what we more actively present, say, for the purposes of our working relationship. We may have a cordial and well-functioning work relationship with another, whom we nevertheless see as racked by bitterness and a lack of generosity toward the efforts of his colleagues. And, so long as this does not intrude too greatly upon our work relationship, I need not address these thoughts and feelings. I need not make them my business. On the other hand, I may make them my business in the sense that these considerations may well provide my reasons for having little interest in pursuing the relationship beyond our working lives together. I might respect their private thoughts and feelings as private, but these aspects of the other's character might also be my reasons for not pursuing more intimate relations with them. Thus, the availability of more passive aspects of self may be crucial to the development of such relations with another.

On the other hand, and just as well, most of us do manage to make a few friends amongst, say, our work colleagues. And an important avenue for the development of more intimate relations here are the more passive aspects of the other that do attract us. So, for instance, although I may respect my colleague's privacy and not make an issue out of the distress they are obviously going through on account of their relationship break-up, their distress may be the object of my developing concern and some affection for them. Similarly, though perhaps less morally admirable, other, more passive, features I notice, such as my colleague's wandering eye with women, may spark a developing affection and the development of more intimate relations between us. I need not present such interpretations to my colleague in too confrontational a way. I may leave room for such observations, and aspects of his conduct can be put aside. But presented, say, with some amusement and shared interest, my interpretive influence may spark more awareness and acceptance of his conduct by him, so that, for instance, with me he does not try to hide his wandering eye so much. Thus, he might take to my amusement, where previously he would deny identification with the trait. In such everyday ways, his character, in part, is shaped by, and a relational feature of, our developing friendship and the focus of our interaction is based on, and so requires the availability of aspects of self over which one does not exercise high levels of choice and control and which may well be uncooperative with those aspects of self over which one does exercise more active choice and control.

Our nonvirtual context of communication, then, enables plural self-presentations, the availability of which, in turn, enables a balancing act regarding who we let in and exclude. Contrarily, because it is hard to see how such plural, uncooperative self-presentations may be made available in, say, text-based e-mail or chat-room formats, these online environments would seem to force a choice between self-presentations – that is, where we either make the private unavailable altogether and rule out intimate interaction with respect to the private, or we make the private public in an attempt to establish intimacy primarily on the basis of one's own highly controlled and chosen self-disclosures.

Thus, there seems a distortion and loss of valuable aspects of a person's character and of the relational self ordinarily developed through those interactions which are weakened or eliminated by the dominance of more highly chosen and controlled forms of self-presentation and disclosure found in the virtual world. Moreover, these distortions and omissions are of important aspects of the self that provide much of the proper focus, not only of our interest and concern in nonvirtual friendships, but also of our understanding of others quite generally. Not only is it *proper* interaction between close friends that conduct or character traits, such as a wandering eye or competitive streak, are highlighted, interpreted, and may be transformed within friendship. It is also quite commonplace and proper that, say, my colleague's passive expression of his overly competitive streak provides me with reason not to move toward developing a more intimate relationship with him.

CONCLUSION

In summary, I have used the case of certain online environments as something of a 'real life' foil, in order to argue for the importance of certain aspects of self and of our relations with others, which seem minimized or largely eliminable within these environments. The aspects of self I have focused on concern those over which we exercise less choice and control in presenting, and I have focused on such attitudes or conduct especially in the context of their being uncooperative with other aspects of self over which we do exercise more choice and control. My claim has been that these plural, and often uncooperative, aspects of self we nevertheless commonly regard as indicative of the character, including the moral character, of persons and as providing relevant grounds for our interpretive interaction with one another. On the basis of my arguments in support of this claim, I have tried to show some of the inadequacies both of the pursuit of identity and relations with others in standard online contexts and the limitations of some contemporary moral psychological accounts of the nature of our moral identities and our interpretive interaction with one another.

References

Cocking, D., and Kennett, J. 1998. Friendship and the self. *Ethics, 108,* 3, 502–527.
Cocking, D., and Kennett, J. 2000. Friendship and moral danger. *Journal of Philosophy,* 97, 5, 278–296.

Cocking, D., and Matthews S. 2000. Unreal friends. *Ethics and Information Technology,* *2, 4,* 223–231.

Ekman, P., and Friesen, W. V. 1975. *Unmasking the face: A guide to recognizing emotions from facial cues.* Englewood Cliffs, NJ: Prentice Hall.

Ekman, P., and Rosenberg, E. L. 1997. *What the face reveals: Basic and applied studies of spontaneous expression using the facial action coding system (FACS).* New York: Oxford University Press.

Frankfurt, H. 1988. Freedom of the will and the concept of a person, in *The importance of what we care about.* Cambridge, UK: Cambridge University Press, pp. 11–25.

Goffman, E. 1959. *The presentation of self in everyday life.* New York: Doubleday Anchor.

Korsgaard, C. 1980. Personal identity and the unity of agency: A Kantian response to Parfit. *Philosophy and Public Affairs, 18,* 2, 101–132.

Kupfer, J. 1987. Privacy, autonomy, and self-concept. *American Philosophical Quarterly, 24,* 81–89.

Nagel, T. 1998. Concealment and exposure. *Philosophy and Public Affairs, 27,* 1, 3–30.

Rachels, J. 1975. Why privacy is important. *Philosophy and Public Affairs, 4,* 323–333.

Velleman, D. J. 2000. Well-being and time, in *The possibility of practical reason.* New York: Oxford University Press, pp. 56–84.

Watson, G. 1982. Free agency, in Watson, G (Ed.), *Free will.* Oxford: Oxford University Press, pp. 96–110.

8

Identity and Information Technology

Steve Matthews

INTRODUCTION

Advances in information technology (IT) should focus our attention onto the notion of personal identity. In this chapter, I consider the effects of IT on identity by focusing on two broad areas. First, the online environment provides a new virtual space in which persons interact almost exclusively via their computer terminals. What are the effects of this new space on our self-conceptions? In particular, given that such a large chunk of our work and recreational time is spent in a 'disembodied' mode online, how does this affect the ways human persons interact with one another and the kinds of persons we become as a consequence of those online relationships? Second, technological advances now and in the future raise the spectre of cyborgisation, the idea that human beings are subject to having their body parts replaced, enhanced, or added to. How might this affect the ways human beings respond to one another and how might these changed relations come to alter our self-image? This chapter will explore the notion of personal identity in the light of these actual and potential technological developments.

In the philosophical literature the concept of personal identity is used in two quite separate ways. The question of personal identity over time is a question about what makes an individual person considered at one time the *same* as one considered at another time. This question is sometimes put in terms of the conditions under which a person persists over time, or survives through some process. Notwithstanding its significance, in this chapter we will *not* be considering IT and personal identity understood in terms of the survival question.

A quite separate personal identity question addresses the notion of *character*. If we ask about a person's identity in this sense, we want to know what characterises him as a person, and so we are interested in his likes and dislikes, his interests, beliefs, values, his manner, and his social relations. A full understanding of a person's identity in this sense may come, not just from his own conception of himself (which may be inaccurate in many ways) but from the considered judgments of those around him, or from features of his personality he lacks insight about. It also comes, especially for us in the present analysis, from his physical presentation and manner. *Character identity* is a function of these heterogeneous aspects.[1]

In this chapter, we will consider how these specific aspects of IT – Internet communication and cyborgisation – affect the notion of character identity. We will consider the ways in which a consideration of persons in these contexts, and of the ways persons relate to other persons in these contexts, has implications for identity. The direction of analysis is thus world-to-person. But, because the notion of character identity is normatively loaded – our identities *ought* to have certain features – we need also to provide analysis in the other direction. Thus, the analysis here implies that there are design constraints for those IT systems which have the real potential to alter character identity in undesirable ways. What will loom large in this context is the role that embodiment plays in anchoring the values attaching to self-presentation. Our self-presentations depend a great deal on our embodied selves; thus, contexts which would systematically omit or distort the way we present ourselves are potentially morally problematic.

We will focus on the Internet and cyborgisation because, currently at any rate, these IT domains most saliently affect identity. They highlight, most significantly, changes in the way our identities are disclosed within the social space. Our identities depend to a large extent on the relations we bear to others, and, until recently, these relations have been mainly face-to-face relations. Computer-mediated communication (CMC) removes the human body from the communication transaction, thus removing the central vehicle in which our identities have hitherto been expressed. Our identities are partly a function of the relations we bear to *embodied* others; to alter our self-presentations to exclude these bodily aspects will tend to eliminate a rich source for the development of identity.

Cyborgisation affects identity by altering the modes by which we interact with the world, including especially the social world. By changing ourselves through the addition of bodily hardware, our self-conceptions must also incur changes.[2] The human body is the central 'site' marking the boundaries

---

[1] Some readers may be uneasy about my usage of 'character identity', given one construal of 'character' which refers to the moral qualities of temperament, such as courage, resolution, or self-reliance. But there is no word in English that really comes close to capturing this qualification on identity, as I am defining it. Oliver Black (2003, p. 145) uses the expression 'qualitative identity', but this is used for exact similarity in most contexts. Flanagan (1991, p. 134) uses the expression 'actual full identity', which is also misleading. My usage is perhaps closest to that of Williams (Smart and Williams 1973) in his integrity objection to utilitarianism as generating a disintegration of the self.

[2] Some, such as Andy Clark (1997, 2003), would argue there is no hard and fast distinction between a person using an Internet connection and a person with a bodily implant, for

for the human self. It is the vehicle within which we present ourselves as social and moral beings. The embodied self is recognised by others as the central place for determining who we are, for it is the central means of self-expression and the locus of human agency. Thus, processes that alter the quality, shape, or extent of bodily identity are implicated in changes to ourselves as moral and social beings.

One further preliminary is worth mentioning. I will claim that the notion of character identity has normative implications for design of IT systems, so it is worth noting an important sense in which character identity is normative. To state a thesis about personal identity understood as a view about character, one will be committed to an explicit rendering of identity in normative terms to the extent that one thinks the concept (person) is normative; but by this I mean something *in addition to* the standard Aristotelean or Kantian notions of, respectively, the thinking animal and the rational agent.[3] To possess a normative identity in this sense, one must at least possess the capacity for social communication and self-reflection. I cannot successfully reflect over who I am unless these reflections are sourced intersubjectively. My self-image is then partly a social ideal; so our interest in the effects of IT on identity consists largely in the effects of IT on social communication. To put it another way: the way I see myself depends often on the way I see myself through the interpretations of others, that is, in the way they see me. Thus, if IT affects the way others see me, especially in virtue of the ways it alters various modes of social communication, then it will come to affect the way I see myself.

ONLINE IDENTITY

Online interaction now provides a normal communication context for many people, and its growth in the future will almost certainly be exponential. The modes for online communication present quite a range, including, for example, live video (so-called Web cams). However, to simplify, I will consider the effects on identity of *text-based* communication. I will do so because this is overwhelmingly the most used mode of contact, and will serve as the right testing ground for the issues of self-presentation and identity. A further reason for this focus on text alone is that there is reason to think it is this mode of communication that will remain, despite the improvements in technology to Web cams and beyond. And this is because text-based

---

both count as mechanisms for cyborgisation; it is just that the Internet is an example of a 'portable' device. He is right about this. I divide these examples here for the theoretical convenience of analysing their effects on identity. Interestingly, these effects are similar in kind, and this is because of the effects on self-conception resulting from changes to the embodied self-affecting self-presentation.

[3] Aristotle, *De Anima*, iii, 4, 429a9–10, *Nicomachean Ethics*, vi, 8, 1143a35–b5; Immanuel Kant, 1956, *passim*.

communication has benefits that would be *undermined* if the technology permitted other (say visual) aspects of oneself to be presented. It is precisely such things as anonymity, the capacity to control how one presents, and the lack of pressure in time-delayed communication which confer the benefits of online text-based communication.

If we were to imagine a context in which we subtracted the fact of embodiment from communication we would, to a reasonable approximation, have the context of CMC. Thus, it provides a very useful analytical tool against which we may consider the role of human embodiment in our self-conceptions, especially as they feature in self-presentation, and the structure of relationships. The approach here will be to consider how the absence, online, of the embodied self affects our capacity to form relationships, and thus to examine the dynamic interplay between embodiment and relationships, and the way this role affects the development of identity.

Given our fundamental starting assumption that in CMC online self-presentations are circumscribed by textual content alone, those bodily aspects of ourselves that are normally (and, I claim, appropriately) in the arena of interpersonal contact are absent.[4] There are two effects of this absence corresponding to the fact that our self-disclosures in communication contain voluntary as well as nonvoluntary elements. Consider first the nonvoluntary. In communicating with a person face-to-face, the content of their self-presentation is facilitated within a space that permits all of the (communicating) senses to be engaged directly in the transaction. Because this is unavoidable in the face-to-face situation, there will inevitably be aspects of myself I am presenting to the other person that are not part of what I am choosing to exhibit. These nonvoluntary aspects divide into those of which I am indifferent, those of which I would prefer were not disclosed, and those of which I am unaware. For example, the colour of my eyes is a self-disclosure I may well have no thoughts about at all; but my speech impediment (say) may be a nonvoluntary intruder on a conversation which is quite unwanted. Thus, neither of these types of normally nonvoluntary self-disclosures intrudes upon an exchange in CMC, unless it is explicitly mentioned in the content of the communication. But in that case, it is no longer nonvoluntary. Talking about my blue eyes to someone in an e-mail requires a decision to disclose this information. That takes us to the second effect on self-presentation brought about by textually based communications alone.

This second effect that CMC has on the interpersonal relates to a person's *increased control* over their self-presentations online. This is, again, substantially a function of the very fact that the self I am disclosing online is contained largely by my text-based online interactions and descriptions, there,

---

[4] For a detailed account of the effects of online communication on close relationships, see Cocking and Matthews (2000) and Ben-Ze'ev (2004).

of who I am. Under these circumstances, it is inevitable that, as an embodied human agent sitting at a computer terminal, there is much less possibility that aspects of myself I would otherwise not allow to become public should leak out from my self-disclosing interaction.

There is a range of other considerations supporting the idea of increased control. First, the mere fact we have time to carefully consider how to present ourselves means we may concoct a carefully constructed identity. We may reflect more carefully about how we come across to the other person. There is time to filter out aspects of our offline selves we are unsure of. Perhaps in face-to-face communication there is a turn of phrase we use too often, or too crudely, or perhaps we can never find the right words to use under conditions where communication requires quick thinking. There may be myriad aspects of offline engagement that unavoidably feature in, or intrude on, our communicative capacities. Because of the increased power online to monitor these aspects, we may restrict their inclusion within the communicative space.

The question, then, is whether elimination of the nonvoluntary, and increases in our capacity to control whom we present, are desirable. Should our online selves partly constitute the identity we would, ideally, choose to present? If so, to what extent should they? To answer I will consider the effects online communication has on *relational* identity, that is, those aspects of character identity that are generated within the relationships we bear to significant others. In the normal case, the relations I bear to family, friends, colleagues, and workmates have an inevitable shaping effect on my character, and on the character I may aspire to become (and on theirs also). These effects may result from the actions of others in relation to what I *do* – for example, as a child my parents chose my school, not me; or they may result from the *thoughts* about myself that I have in relation to the attitudes of others towards me – for example, my friend's continued, and let's say justified, gibes about my strange dress sense may cause me consternation over an aspect of my social self-presentations (unless of course I simply don't care about fashion). In these, and innumerable other ways, our characters are shaped in relation to those around us.[5] If we assume that our relational identity constitutes an important social good – and after all our valued relations to significant others are *conditional* on our capacities for relational identity – then IT contexts that threaten our capacity for relational identity

---

5 Relational identity is not necessarily group identity, although the two are indirectly related. Roughly, group identity refers to those characteristics we possess in virtue of belonging to, adopting, or in some way being influenced by a social, political, or economic institution. Suppose I join a conservative political party, receive paraphernalia from its headquarters, and write letters to newspapers in defence of the beliefs of the party and so on. My character thus comes to reflect the conservative political facets of this institution, even though I may never have come under the direct influence of an individual human being who is part of this group.

also threaten this important social good. So let us consider what the effects of CMC on relational identity are.

First, a preliminary: there is here a noteworthy practical paradox, for there is a genuine sense that online communication facilitates certain relationships otherwise not possible offline because it eliminates unwanted and distracting aspects of the identity we present within the face-to-face environment. Think of someone with a speech difficulty, or someone deeply unhappy with some bodily feature, or mannerism, or the very shy or introverted person. In each of these cases, a feature of identity may often present a serious impediment to the formation or development of relationships. In that respect, the further development of that person's identity within a possible relationship, their *relational identity*, is made very difficult. It would seem that the possibility of eliminating such undesirable aspects of one's self-presentation through online communication would have the effect of enhancing the capacity for forming relationships that might then contribute to relational identity. This is certainly true for many people[6]. However, paradoxically the very mechanisms that allow this to happen are also the ones that constrict the development of relational identity in other cases.

If online disclosures conceal aspects of bodily self-presentation over which a person feels some inhibition, embarrassment, or shame, they also obscure aspects a person may feel some pride or attachment to. Someone who justifiably considers themselves beautiful in the offline world, perhaps even sometimes relying on this feature as an entry card for social interaction there, loses that card at the doors of cyberspace.[7] Thus CMC, in reducing identity disclosures to disclosures of text-based content, has a flattening, and an egalitarian effect. But in providing for (something approaching) equality of identity in these kinds of respects, the cost is a limitation on intimacy. Take friendship again. In offline friendship, since the embodied person is disclosed there – the fully extended self let's say – self-presentation within friendship is near-complete and highly nuanced. In particular it allows greatly for the possibility that one should come under the influence of one's friend. My friend, for example, may cause me to widen my interests in various ways I would never have considered. Or the influence may consist in advice about how to deal with an embarrassing or secret problem. More significantly, my friend sees me at close quarters and develops insights into my character that I can't see myself. Sometimes she may communicate these to me, or, if not, her responses to me may make it obvious that this is what she thinks. For example, I may have become so habituated to my impatience I could never

---

[6] There is support for this assertion from the social psychology literature. See, for example, Tidwell and Walther (2002).

[7] This should not be regarded necessarily as a bad thing. As Velleman (2001, p. 45) points out, the very beautiful may also feel shame in regard to this feature if they would prefer not to present themselves as beautiful: 'Even great beauty can occasion shame in situations where it is felt to drown out rather than amplify self-presentation.'

see this about myself, and it may well take my friend to shine a light on this aspect of my character. In all of these ways, my friend becomes a coauthor to my identity. Self-construction is in these ways a joint, ongoing production.[8] To apply a recent metaphor to these questions, other things being equal, the best continuing narrative for my self thus comes to include friends and, indeed, those significant others, such as family, who are also part of the self-story, and part-writers of that story. This picture of friendship and the self is one way of characterising the mechanism for intimacy. An intimate relation is one in which significant others are cowriters of the self-narrative.

Online life limits these possibilities for intimacy precisely because it undermines the possibility of the coauthored self.[9] The coauthored self requires identity feature-sharing in the social space which is not limited by the absence of the embodied agent. Intimacy is a matter of degree, and degrees of intimacy depend on our knowing each other in a certain kind of way. Quite plausibly, we might say that in order to really know who someone is, that person must be 'visible' in the fullest sense. It means we have access to the fully embodied person. There must be visibility across many channels, not merely the single channel of textual disclosure. Intimacy relies on being 'fully seen' within the relationship. It is only when this occurs that we can be said to have a stake in the relationship and to play a full role in developing that relationship, and, in so doing, develop relational identity there.

Being fully seen offline, the self that is normally, and appropriately, presented to the other combines both of the voluntary and nonvoluntary elements. In close friendship, for example, each party responds to these self-presentations through a process of mutual interpretation. In my interpretations of you, you come to see yourself through my eyes, so features of your character, even ones into which you have no insight, are made salient. Through this ongoing two-way process our identities may gradually come to be shaped by the relationship itself.[10] The problem of the online case is that this dynamic aspect of the formation of close relationships cannot really be simulated. The disembodied self inevitably will fail to disclose important elements of character identity. This will be so for the two reasons I have outlined: either my self-presentations are incomplete because of the absence of those nonvoluntary aspects; or, the heightened control over who it is I am presenting online will uncover a rather different self from what would otherwise be presented offline. The picture presented to the other of one's identity is thus impoverished and distorted, and for those reasons

---

[8] This account of friendship is due to Cocking and Kennett (1998).

[9] I have focused here on friendship to make this general point, but it can be made for other kinds of relationship. Elsewhere (Matthews, 2006), I have argued that professional identity is stifled by online interaction. The online environment fails to provide a context for professional character traits to emerge and develop because the online space limits the conditions under which the professional–client relationship may properly flourish.

[10] The interpretation point is due to Cocking and Kennett (1998).

an online identity is far less disposed to engaging in the normal dynamics of intimate relationships.

Let me sum up the argument thus far. An important source of character identity derives from social agency. Such agency depends both on my capacities for self-presentation, and on those aspects of who I am in the social space that are disclosed nonvoluntarily. It is in virtue of my presentations as an embodied agent that I am able to present socially as a fully extended self, and only in that mode of self-presentation can the self develop in relation to others fully and appropriately. Thus, online life is an impoverished context for the development of identity because it fails as a source for the social agential characteristics of identity. It excludes important aspects of self-presentation which are normally and appropriately the subject matter for the development of relational identity.

CYBORGS

Different IT domains raise different, but in a sense related, problems of identity. Selves in cyberspace are disembodied communicators, and this limits the possibility of intimacy and the development of relational identity. The self in this context is clearly and directly embedded in the IT context of Web-based communication. Yet, there is a sense in which the embodied person – a self in real space – is, itself, something that is embedded in an IT context, for it is what we might call an informational self, or, in a sense to be explained presently, a *cybernetic organism*. The problems for identity here are not raised by the lack of embodiment but rather by the mode of embodiment by which the self presents itself. In so far as this is the case, questions are raised again for our identity qua relational beings. In this section, then, I will discuss the implications for identity raised by the idea that human beings are, to put it generally, informational organisms. Specifically, I will address issues of identity raised by the idea of human beings as cybernetic organisms, or cyborgs.

A *cyborg*, as I will define it, is a reflexive agent. Think here of a simple operation involving say the picking up of a glass from a table. The goal is to pick up the glass; as the hand moves closer to the glass, information feeds back to the agent regarding its position; adjustments to movement are made by comparing the position the hand should be in, given the goal, and its actual position. Information continues to be fed back into the system until the operation is complete. (Of course, in the real world all of this happens automatically, spontaneously, and noninferentially.) Extrapolating, the agency of the cyborg is a product of external features of its environment (including extensions to its own body) working in tandem with itself. Given this minimal description it is clear that functioning human beings count as cyborgs just as they are. Of course popular culture has its own sense of what a cyborg should be – think for example of the series of *Terminator* films – and the typical cyborg in this sense is a creature functioning according to the cybernetic principles just outlined but typically incorporating both biological and machine parts.[11] The identity issues that are raised come into focus especially when we consider the possibility of biomechanical hybrids, so we will consider these as central in what follows.[12]

The concept of character identity, as I have argued, is ineliminably normative, and inherently dynamic. The interplay between our actual identities and self-constituting capacities invokes thoughts about who we are, and who we think we should be, in an ongoing story connecting ourselves to others and the natural world. This inevitable normative feature of identity provides the clue to issues about identity and cyborgisation. The question is about the extent to which we should proceed down a path in which biomechanical selves are increasingly normalised. Moreover, the rationality of the tendency in that direction must depend on the *purpose* for which it is intended. So let me distinguish four different kinds of cases here, associated with different motivations.

First, anyone who has a pacemaker, prosthetic limb, or even spectacles is centrally motivated by the need to *restore to themselves what they take to be a normal function of a human being.* Second, anyone who has had a facelift, liposuction, or some kind of body implant is motivated centrally by the desire for cosmetic changes aiming at *restoration or enhancement of their bodily self-image.* Third, consider the case of Stelarc. Stelarc is a performance artist with a third hand.[13] The main consideration for this seems to be *aesthetic, and perhaps more generally an intellectual curiosity.* Fourth, consider the possibility of inserting silicon chips into the brain, or of devices, or drugs (not a mere possibility) that *enhance neural function* in some way, say to improve memory, relieve anxiety, or to manipulate emotions.[14] The motivation here might be through the range already considered: my aim might be to repair mental

---

[11] *The Terminator* (1984), directed by James Cameron, starring Arnold Schwarzenegger.

[12] Clark (2003) and others consider that persons in unadulterated human form are still cyborgs, hence the title of his book, *Natural-Born Cyborgs.* The mere fact that we use language, or that we externalise our agency through, for example, the use of pen and paper to complete arithmetic provides a sufficient motivation to regard human persons as cybernetic organisms. I will not dispute this claim. However, if we are already cyborgs in this sense, then no particularly new problem of identity is raised through a consideration of the new IT technologies. The more interesting cases that problematise identity are those in which the human form is altered in certain ways, and for certain kinds of motivation; so, these are the cases I think should be addressed. Thus, it is not cyborgisation per se that raises the problem of identity; rather it is the degrees and qualities of certain cyborgisation processes that do.

[13] I will describe this case in more detail later in this chapter.

[14] The division into four kinds of motivation is one way of carving the logical space, but not the only way. Notice, for example, that my social confidence might be improved either through some cosmetic surgery, or with some neural manipulation. So, what is the best description for the purpose here? We have here the problem of distinguishing means and ends, and in some cases the same end may be achieved with different means. My taxonomy is simply designed to recognise ends that are central.

dysfunction in this way; or my aim might be to improve my self-presentation skills for social occasions; or my aim might be to enhance my intellectual skills to solve new problems.

I wish to focus on cases in which the process of cyborgisation is implicated in our self-presentations in so far as these constitute conspicuous problems for character identity. Here, as a springboard to the analysis, I want to help myself to a point made by Harry Frankfurt. He talks about a human as being responsive to his or her own condition, to the risks of existence, and to the conflicts with others. He writes:

> There is [a sort] of reflexivity or self-consciousness, which appears [...] to be intelligible as being fundamentally a response to conflict and risk. It is a salient characteristic of human beings, one which affects our lives in deep and innumerable ways, that we care about what we are. This is closely connected both as cause and as effect to our enormous preoccupation with what other people think of us. We are ceaselessly alert to the danger that there may be discrepancies between what we wish to be (or what we wish to seem to be) and how we actually appear to others and ourselves. (Frankfurt 1988, p. 163)

Frankfurt's basic insight here is that we care about who we are partly because we care about what others think of us, so we are motivated to present the kind of self that is not at odds with what we hope others will think of us. My purpose in the light of this comment is to set up what I take to be a fundamental structural feature of identity. I have a set of beliefs (or story) about my actual character identity, captured by thoughts such as 'this is how I really am'. I have a set of beliefs (or story) generated by the image I project both to myself and others, captured by thoughts such as 'this is how I am coming across'. Finally I have a set of beliefs (or story) about the person I would ideally like to be, captured by thoughts such as 'this is how I really want to be'.[15] Frankfurt is right that an important corrective to the possibility of getting all three stories wrong is that we care about the character we present to others. I would add that we care about its presentation because, unless we are constitutively deceitful or manipulative, we care about the character we in fact possess, and we care to display the character we in fact possess.

Now unfortunately this simplifies the picture somewhat. For, although I think it is analytic that, in an ideal possible world, the character I really want to have is the character I really possess, there are many possible circumstances in which it is desirable for me to project a certain kind of identity I do not in fact have, or believe myself to have. It is a commonplace, for example, that, in order to change oneself, one needs to deliberately play a role inconsistent with your current conception of who you are. In order to become a certain kind of person you need, for a while, to act like that kind of person. You need to 'fake it till you make it' as is sometimes said.

---

[15] Equating sets of beliefs with the notion of a story connects the former notion with the narrative theory of the self that I referred to earlier.

Thus, we have a model of the psychological structure that underpins the construction of identity. The question now is what, normatively speaking, ought to inform the model. To address this question we should point to certain features of human embodiment we regard as important to identity which place normative limits on their possible design. Roughly, these features are ones which enhance or permit those practices we regard as important to our relational identity, because our self-presentations play a crucial role in social recognition. IT bodily add-ons that would be disruptive to our social recognition would thus have a clear impact on character identity. In order to develop this idea, I will sketch the theoretical normative account a little more by arguing that if we stray too far from the human form, we lose touch with ourselves as the narrative agents in which the human body is best seen as the appropriate locus of relationships – the normative source of relational identity.

With this in place, let us return to the applied arena and consider a slightly fanciful case based on Stelarc. Andy Clark discusses Stelarc, an Australian performance artist who has a prosthetic third hand.[16] The hand can be attached to Stelarc's right arm by mechanical clamps and has grasping, pinching, and rotation motor control. It is controlled by Stelarc via the indirect route of muscle sites located on his legs and abdomen. When these sites are engaged, the signals are picked up by electrodes which are then sent to the metal prosthesis. Initially Stelarc moved his third hand with some difficulty, since the movement required thought about how, for example, an abdominal muscle movement translated to a hand movement. Now, after many years, Stelarc moves his third arm effortlessly, automatically, and with some precision. (Anyone who has mastered some very complex motor skills – playing a musical instrument, or indeed, adjusting to a prosthetic that restores normal function – will have some insights into the process of the development of motor coordination.)

Let uss consider a variation of Stelarc – Stelarc 3 – who, we may imagine, has decided never to remove his third hand. From his point of view it is now permanently incorporated as part of himself, and he comes to regard his third hand as being on *his* side when thinking about the boundary between himself and the world. His motivations for the move to permanency may be quite mixed and might include aesthetic as well as functional reasons. We should think that it matters what purpose Stelarc 3 has in mind in adopting a third hand as his identity, but, more importantly, the fact that a person should adopt the new technology permanently means that at some level they have decided, quite simply and without qualification, *to make it a part of themselves*. And it is this more global motivation to radically transform oneself into something else that swamps all other specific considerations of function, aesthetics, personal advantage, or whatever.

[16] See Andy Clark (2003: 115–119). Stelarc has his own Website at http// :www.stelarc.va. com.au/, viewed July 3, 2006.

Thus we can imagine that Stelarc 3 has made a decision about himself, namely to present a new three-handed self to the world. Why does this matter? There are many obvious responses to be made at this point, which I will just mention, but I think we want to draw as general a lesson as we may from the example. I begin, then, with the obvious responses. First, no doubt Stelarc 3's self-presentation would engender a visceral repulsion, at least in some. A visit to Stelarc's Web site should leave no doubt that the possession of a third hand is aesthetically strange, so much so that, in the normal course of life, it might be hard to know where to look were one to (say) share a drink with Stelarc 3 at a lounge bar. Second, the inclusion of a third hand might be distracting, or even illegal, in the context of certain conventional practices. Consider the time-honoured practice of two-handed clapping; or consider competitive sports in which the addition of a third hand would confer some distinct material advantage. Third, consider the effect of a third hand on sexual attractiveness. At the very least, such an addition might well create too much of a distraction from (let's say) an otherwise beautiful body. Fourth, we might wonder about the state of a person who comes to have such a motivation in the first place. Why would anyone wish to radically transform themselves this way? What was it about this person before the change that motivated a need to drastically alter their appearance? Was it mere attention-seeking? Were they so unhappy about their former appearance that they were driven to this? What might be next? And so on. Thus, the addition of a permanent third hand might raise questions about the state of the person prior to this action, even if such questions had apparently acceptable answers.

So, more generally now, why might it matter that someone should go down the path of cyborgisation in the way our imagined Stelarc has done?[17] There are two points to be made at this general level. First, our self-presentations affect the nature of the relationships we are in, and so there are intrinsic effects of self-presentation on our existing relationships. Second, our self-presentations affect who it is that we have relationships with in the first instance; this is an extrinsic effect.

So, consider first the intrinsic point. The interpersonal relations that matter to human beings most are those relations we choose in our capacities as normative agents. If someone cares about their relations to nearest and

[17] In this chapter, I have focused on cases in which self-presentation is an issue. Space prevents me from considering the interesting cases in which neural implants alter aspects of one's personality or cognitive capacities. Just as interesting are cases of shared agency in which, for example, a person affects an action in a different person via a 'wire tapping' apparatus in which nerve signals from the former are diverted to muscle sites in the latter. Finally, there is, mooted in the literature, the possibility of shared experiences in which a person might come to remember an experience had by a different person, or experience similar feelings to a person performing an action elsewhere. These cases raise not only questions of character identity but connect also to the issue of survival. For example, Shoemaker (1970) and Parfit (1984) have talked about the latter kinds of cases in their discussions of quasimemory.

dearest then they ought to be motivated to act in ways in which the self they present within these relations aims at preserving or nurturing them. This is not just a moral point about the requirements of such relationships, but rather a more general point that the value of our relations to others enjoins us to consider carefully how we are within them. How we are within relationships turns out to be a function of the quality of that relationship itself. How we relate to friends, family, work colleagues, and so on has an important impact on our identities, and so, in turn, on the quality of those relationships. This point emerged earlier in the discussion of online communication. Our identities are constructed in the social space partly as a result of feature-sharing within that space which is then internalised as part of the three-pronged model set out above. A lack of embodiment removes a range of features available for the construction of identity. Thus, changes to embodiment of the radical sort in the case of our imagined Stelarc, would contribute a new feature into the social space. In so far as such a feature – or its lack – alters the ordinary dynamics of those relations we care most deeply about, it raises a question concerning the appropriateness of its inclusion.

Consider now the extrinsic point. This emerged earlier when considering the effects of self-presentation on social attraction. In this connection, consider someone with multiple body-piercing or tattoos in a culture where such practices are outside the mainstream. In choosing to present myself outside the mainstream in such a way, I do in the first instance exclude the possibility of relationships with certain kinds of people. There are many contexts where such exclusion may take place – for example, I make it very unlikely I will work in an office environment in which such self-presentation is conventionally ruled out – and there are many different mechanisms determining the way it occurs; however, the central point is simply that, to a large extent, choosing to present as a certain kind of person constitutes choosing the kinds of relationships we may have, and so, in turn, the kinds of people we may become by then being part of that group. The extrinsic point in relation to self-presentation is a point about group identity (see note 6).

In summary, then, the central normative points that must be raised in any discussion of the effects of cyborgisation concern the way it may alter the dynamics of existing relationships (intrinsic point), and the way self-presentation may automatically select the kinds of relationships we will tend to have (extrinsic point).

CHARACTER IDENTITY

The position developed so far is that our character identity derives importantly from our public roles as embodied self-presenting agents; but what kind of agents? And how, exactly, is our agency implicated in our identity? What are the normative sources for this identity, and how are the features of our identity organised around our agency? In this section, I say something brief about these general issues surrounding character identity before returning to the main argument.

I am going to distinguish between the identities we in fact have, including the factors that determine those actual identities, and the identities we ought to have which we can label 'normative identities'. It is important to distinguish actual from normative identity for at least two reasons. First, as reflective beings, we measure our self-conceptions against a conception of who we aspire to be. A significant mechanism in personality development lies in the tension between a person's real self-image and her ideal self-image. One's ideal self-image is simply the image one has of the sort of person one would like to be. One's real self-image is constituted by the set of beliefs about oneself that one actually possesses. A premise in much of this literature is that the dynamics of personality development are explained by reference to the gap between the real and ideal self-image.[18] In our terms, one's ideal self-image will be informed saliently by the range of considerations arising from one's social relations, as described in the previous section.

The second reason for distinguishing normative and actual identity is that identity (simpliciter) just *is* a dynamic construction: as normative agents our identity is something we work on, both for ourselves and for others. Thus, it is important to have a picture both of how identity is constructed, and of the normative frameworks within which such construction takes place. Our identities have significant connections to practical deliberation, and, as such, thinking about identity importantly determines what our ends will be, and how we treat others. In addition, as reflective beings it is in our nature to consider who we are, how we think others perceive us, and to ask whether a certain kind of person is what we wish to aim at being. It is in this context that it is critical to consider what effects there are on identity development and construction. Typically, the question arises in the social or political sphere. In the context of IT, it is similarly pressing.

Why might we think a normative consideration provides one with a legitimate identity-constituting reason for action? Acting from a normative consideration unifies a person understood as a narrative agent. What does this mean? A *narrative* agent is a person whose self-conception consists in narrating and acting in a story 'written' by the agent.[19] According to the narrative account the normativity attaching to one's reasons emerges from considerations about how those reasons will best serve in the continued construction of one's life. They will do so when the best continuation is a story that coheres with one's past so as to generate well-being, achieved through such

---

[18] See, for example, Leahy (1985, especially chapter 1), and Stagner (1974, p. 188).

[19] The recent literature contains many expressions of the narrative theory of the self. See, for example, Dennett (1992), Velleman (2005) and also a special 2003 issue of *Philosophy, Psychiatry, and Psychology* titled 'Agency, Narrative and Self', *10*, 4 (December).

goods as long-term relationships, careers, or roles that are available to agents who are unified over time. Once we recognise the close connection between humanly embodied agency and narrative agency we see that, ceteris paribus, the best continuing story cannot diverge too far, too quickly, from that kind of embodiment.

A *unified* agent is one whose reasons for action project her into the future by connecting them to her ends.[20] As Christine Korsgaard (1999, p. 27) puts it, '...deliberative action by its very nature imposes unity on the will...whatever else you are doing when you choose a deliberate action, you are also unifying yourself into a person...action is self-constitution'. Korsgaard's view of identity is practical: one's identity consists in the fact that as rational beings who act over time we construct who we are in virtue of the choices we make about what to do. When an agent acts for reasons she both constitutes herself at a time and projects herself into the future. As Korsgaard says (1989, pp. 113–114) '[t]he sort of thing you identify yourself with may carry you automatically into the future...Indeed the choice of any action, no matter how trivial, takes you some way into the future. And to the extent that you regulate your choices by identifying yourself as the one who is implementing something like a particular plan of life, you need to identify with your future in order to be *what you are even now*'.

What connects the narrative and self-constitution accounts is the central idea that operative reasons necessarily project one into the future, and, in this way, they are critical to identity construction. These accounts point to the ways in which choices for identity might matter. The narrative view is concerned with coherence and well-being: to the extent my life is an incoherent, fragmented story, depriving me of the capacity to build and develop a life containing a range of social goods, well-being will be lacking. The self-constitution view connects choices for determining the character of my identity much more closely with autonomy itself. The failure to act consistently on my reasons results in a failure to be an effective self-governing being. Bringing the two together, we can say that a significant aspect of identity just *is* the capacity to construct one's life according to the best continuation of its narrative features to that point. Who we are, then, depends on the capacity for the right kind of self-unification. The value that attaches to our identity depends on our continuing capacity to construct ourselves according to the right story.

Of course there is no single right story, but there are clues to the right *kind* of story once we see what is lacking in disunified, or disrupted agency: a person who fails to unify herself over time simply lacks the resources for constructing the kind of self narrative we regard as valuable. Much of what we regard as valuable derives from an agent's capacity to access the social goods. Continuing relationships, the occupation of valued social roles, the completion of goals, the keeping of commitments, and so forth are all

[20] See Korsgaard (1989, 1999).

examples of these.[21] Thus a central consideration in the design of IT is its effect on identity to the extent that it may undermine extended narrative agency.

Our control over who we are is something we work at by constructing a self which is hopefully not so besotted by technology that it would undermine our sense that our lives hang together within a single narrative. If we become too dependent on, or too distracted by, the offerings of a technologically rich and tempting world, we may well tend to lose ourselves in the technology. We will tend less to be sensitive to other human beings who had hitherto engaged with us in the kinds of relationships that engender value both in them and in the identities that develop in relation to them. We saw this perhaps most aptly in the analysis of online identity and friendship in which our identity within friendship-like relations is effectively obscured. In the remaining section, I intend to bring together the threads of the discussion so far and then finish with some remarks on the implications these ideas have for the design of IT systems.

THE IMPORTANCE OF SELF-PRESENTATION TO IDENTITY

The argument so far has been complex, so it will be useful at this point to tie together the various strands in order to see where we stand. I have attempted, where possible, to divide the discussion of identity between descriptive structural aspects on the one hand, and normative aspects on the other. Let us begin with the descriptive. I have claimed that who we are depends in large part on our significant relationships and how we think and act within those relationships. How we think and act there depends largely on the responses we make to others' attitudes towards, and influence over us. A measure of those responses can be gleaned from our shared understandings of how we come across to each other as social agents. The central and appropriate mode for how we come across socially is in our body and bodily behavioural self-presentations. Thus, the connection between IT and identity, descriptively speaking, boils down to the effect IT has on those self-presentation elements which structure identity given this social dimension of identity formation.

Turning to the normative I have tried to show the connection between these facts about identity construction with normativity by arguing that, as self-reflective beings, we have a sense not just of who we are, but of the ideal person we might strive to become. I have further connected that idea with contemporary views about identity and agency; as narrative agents we provide reasons for our future selves to best continue the story we have so far established for ourselves. Although I have only hinted at this, I think this theory of narrative agency is inadequate unless it recognises the possibility that autonomy comes in degrees. Our identities are almost never fully under

---

[21] See Kennett and Matthews (2003).

our own control, and there are innumerable explanations of why they are not; some of these point to circumstances that are undesirable – think of the many cases of mental illness, social dislocation, or criminal influence, for example – but some explanations allude to, for example, relationships that constitute robust social goods – we have considered the influence on identity between good and true friends, but a longer list might include such relationships as teacher–pupil, or patient–doctor, in which the subordinate individual gives up autonomy; in deferring to expert opinion, I place myself, to a limited extent anyway, in the hands of someone else. Who we are depends on our social agency in which others become identity coauthors. We, thus, have a normative theoretical framework for considering IT and identity.

What, then, are the lessons this account of identity has for IT design? First, it has to be noted that no philosophical theory of identity construed at this level of generality can provide specific prescriptive parameters for technology design. What it can do, however, is to register some general *constraints* on the design of technologies in which the mode of self-presentation prevents the values of the normative self being expressed. Thus, given the connection I have drawn between identity and our capacity to shape who we are as narrative agents, there is an overarching constraint which is the avoidance of technologies which prevent us both from continuing acts of self-creation, but also, technologies that would obscure from us the knowledge that this is what we are. Still, we can be more specific than this, and I want to return to the theme of relationships and self-presentation.

Consider again intimate relationships such as close friendship. These are relationships in which there is deep mutual affection, a disposition to assist in the welfare of the other, and a continuing desire to engage with the other in shared activities. True friendship, however, departs from these baseline features in which the object of desire appears to be some nonpersonal value – affection, welfare, activities – to include the person himself. I have argued here that a significant source of our character identity emerges from our social agency, and this has its most significant expression in our close relationships. Technologies which eliminate or distort our capacities to present ourselves to the social world fully, so that we may fully engage in social relations, including especially, but not limited to, love and friendship, will thus act to dry up an important source for character identity. Technology that would tend to reduce the object of a potential love to some kind of natural feature, a thing, or an aesthetic device, will tend in this direction. It seems to me that this point gets to the core of the relation between identity and IT. Technology that disables our capacity to both be seen, and to see the other, within a relationship, for the good of that relationship, and which enables us to come across as something we are not within a relationship, risks its derailment; in such cases, technology also risks something that is a *proper* source for identity construction.

Note that this position is compatible with technologies that would instantly alter a person's mode of self-presentation across *some* dimensions. Suppose technology existed which could instantly eliminate an unwanted feature of identity such as a stutter, facial tic, a blushing disposition, or some nonvoluntary personal attribute that tended to disrupt one's capacity for social intercourse. The removal of that attribute would *enhance* one's participation as a social agent. This would be technology which led to a person's being more fully seen for what they ideally would like to be, if the unwanted attribute had hitherto prevented the person from successfully engaging with others in the social world. Thus the position I am advocating is not monolithically opposed to technologies *merely* because they have the potential to alter the character of our social selves. On the contrary, I would only be arguing for such a position if the technologies referred to here were to become the main mode of communication. I am not, of course, suggesting (for example) the elimination of e-mail. The central point is that our identities are indeed sensitive to modes of self-presentation which are in turn determined by the technological contexts of communication and embodiment. We currently retain choices over the uses of technology (both its extent and the mode of use), and their uses can facilitate the appropriate elimination of undesirable identity-constituting features; but just as technologies can do this, they can also eliminate, obscure, or distort what we regard as important to our social relationships and our social agency.

CONCLUSION

The IT domains discussed here raise questions about character identity. Because we are reflective narrative agents who care about our embodied selves, and how they come across to others, IT that undermines or distorts our (embodied) self-presentations inevitably feeds into our self-conceptions. What we will really become will tend to follow on from how we project ourselves intersubjectively and in the public sphere. This is problematic in so far as it disrupts or even destroys those human relationships that have hitherto served us well, ethically and, more broadly, normatively. If this is the case, then technology that affects our identity via this path must consider the ways in which it will impact on our embodied self-presentations, or, indeed, the extent to which it will omit embodiment completely as is the case with the Internet.

References

Aristotle. 1984. *The complete works of Aristotle: The revised Oxford translation.* Jonathan Barnes (Ed.). Oxford: Oxford University Press.

Ben-Ze'ev, A. 2004. *Love online.* Cambridge, UK: Cambridge University Press.

Black, O. 2003. Ethics, identity and the boundaries of the person. *Philosophical Explorations, 6,* 139–156.

Clark, A. 1997. *Being there: Putting brain, body, and world together again.* Cambridge, MA: MIT Press.

Clark, A. 2003. *Natural-born cyborgs: Minds, technologies, and the future of human intelligence.* Oxford: Oxford University Press.

Cocking, D., and Kennett, J. 1998. Friendship and the self. *Ethics, 108,* 502–527.

Cocking, D., and Matthews, S. 2000. Unreal friends. *Ethics and Information Technology,* 2, 223–231.

Dennett, D. 1992. The self as a center of narrative gravity, in F. Kessell, P. Cole, and D. Johnson (Eds.), *Self and consciousness: Multiple perspectives.* Hillsdale, NJ: Erlbaum.

Flanagan, O. 1991. *Varieties of moral personality.* Cambridge, MA: Harvard University Press.

Frankfurt, H. 1988. *The importance of what we care about.* Cambridge, UK: Cambridge University Press.

Kant, Immanuel. 1956. *Groundwork of the metaphysic of morals,* H. J. Paton (Ed.). New York: Harper and Row.

Kennett, J., and Matthews, S. 2003. The unity and disunity of agency. *Philosophy, Psychiatry and Psychology, 10,* 302–312.

Korsgaard, C. 1989. Personal identity and the unity of agency: A Kantian response to Parfit. *Philosophy and Public Affairs, 18,* 2, 101–132.

Korsgaard, C. 1999. Self-constitution in the ethics of Plato and Kant. *Journal of Ethics, 3,* 1–29.

Leahy, R. L. (Ed.) 1985. *The development of the self.* Orlando, FL: Academic Press.

Locke, J. 1690/1984. *An essay concerning human understanding.* Glasgow: Collins.

Matthews, S. 2006. On-line professionals. *Ethics and Information Technology, 8,* 1, 61–71.

Parfit, D. 1984. *Reasons and persons.* Oxford: Clarendon.

Shoemaker, S. 1970. Persons and their pasts. *American Philosophical Quarterly, 7,* 4, 269–285.

Smart, J. J. C., and Williams, B. A. O. 1973. *Utilitarianism: For and against.* Cambridge, UK: Cambridge University Press.

Stagner, R. 1974. *Psychology of personality.* New York: McGraw-Hill.

Stelarc, 2006. http://www.stelarc.va.com.au.

Tidwell, L. C., and Walther, J. B. 2002. Computer-mediated communication effects on disclosure, impressions, and interpersonal evaluations: Getting to know one another a bit at a time. *Human Communication Research, 28,* 317–348.

Velleman, J. D. 2001. The genesis of shame. *Philosophy and Public Affairs, 30,* 1, 27–52.

Velleman, J. D. 2005. *Self to self.* New York: Cambridge University Press, chapter 8: The self as narrator.

9

Trust, Reliance, and the Internet[1]

Philip Pettit

Words such as 'trust' and 'reliance' are used as context requires, now in this way, now in that, and they serve to cover loose, overlapping clusters of attitudes and actions. Here I invoke some theoretical licence, however, and use the terms to tag distinct phenomena: 'reliance', a generic phenomenon, and 'trust', a species of that genus. I want to argue that, while the Internet may offer novel, rational opportunities for other forms of reliance, it does not generally create such openings for what is here called trust.

The chapter is in three sections. In the first, I set up the distinction between trust and reliance. In the second, I outline some different forms that trust may take. And then, in the final section, I present some reasons for thinking that trust, as distinct from other forms of reliance, is not well-served by interactions on the Internet, at least not if the interactants are otherwise unknown to one another. The chapter follows up on a paper I published in 1995; it draws freely on some arguments in that piece (Pettit 1995).

The Internet is exciting in great part because of the way it equips each of us to assume different personas, unburdened by pregiven marks of identity like gender, age, profession, class, and so on. A very good question, then, is whether people can develop trust in one another's personas under the shared assumption that persona may not correspond to person in such marks of identity. Suppose that you and I appear on the Internet under a number of different names, developing a style that goes with each. I am both Betsy and Bob, for example; you are both Jane and Jim. The question is whether you as Jane can trust me as Bob, I as Betsy can trust you as Jim, and so on. But good though it is, I should stress that this is not the question that I try to deal with here (Brennan and Pettit 2004b; McGeer 2004a). My focus

[1] This chapter was originally published in 2004 in *Analyse & Kritik*, 26, 1, 108–121. My thanks to Geoffrey Brennan and Victoria McGeer for background discussions, to those attending the conference on 'Trust on the Internet' held in Bielefeld, Germany in July 2003 for helpful comments, and to Michael Baurmann for a very insightful set of queries and suggestions.

is rather on how far real-world, identity-laden persons may achieve trust in one another on the basis of pure Internet contact, not just how the Internet personas they construct can achieve trust in one another on that basis.[2]

1. TRUST AND RELIANCE

Trust and reliance may be taken as attitudes or as actions, but it will be useful here to take the words as primarily designating actions – the actions whereby I invest trust in others or place my reliance in them. So, what then distinguishes relying on others in this sense from trusting in them?

To rely on others is just to act in a way that is premised on their being of a certain character, or on their being likely to act under various circumstances in a certain way. It won't do, of course, if the guiding belief about others is just that they have a low probability of displaying the required character or disposition. The belief that others will prove amenable to one's own plans must be held with a degree of confidence that clearly exceeds 0.5. To rely on others, as we say, is to manifest confidence in dealing with them that they are of the relevant type or are disposed to behave in the relevant way.

I may rely on others in this sense in a variety of contexts. I rely on automobile drivers to respect the rules of the road when I step out on to a pedestrian crossing. I rely on my doctor being a competent diagnostician when I present myself for a medical examination. I rely on the police to do their duty when I report a crime I have just witnessed. In all of these cases, reliance is a routine and presumptively rational activity. If we are Bayesians about rationality, then we will say that such acts of reliance serve to promote my ends according to my beliefs, and, in particular, that they serve to maximize my expected utility.

Relying on others, in the sense exemplified here, is not sharply distinguishable from relying on impersonal things: relying on the strength of the bridge, relying on the accuracy of the clock, and so on. True, the reliance is something I may expect those on whom I rely to notice, but this does not appear to be essential. The important point in the cases surveyed is that relying on someone to display a trait or behaviour is just acting in a way that is shaped by the more or less confident belief that they will display it. And relying on a person in that sense is not markedly different from relying on a nonpersonal entity like a bridge or a clock or, perhaps, just the weather.

Acts of rational reliance on other people, such as our examples illustrate, do not count intuitively as acts of trust; certainly, they do not answer to

---

[2] Although this question is more mundane than the question that I ignore, it is, in one respect, of greater importance. A form of trust is intuitively more significant, the greater the potential gains and losses with which it is associated. And by this criterion, person-to-person trust is likely to be of more significance than trust between personas. It may put one's overall fortune at stake, where persona-to-persona trust will tend to involve only stakes of a psychological kind.

the use of the word 'trust' that I treat here as canonical. Trusting someone in the sense I have in mind – and it is a sense of trust that comes quite naturally to us – means treating him or her as trustworthy. And treating someone as trustworthy involves assuming a relationship with the person of a kind that need not be involved in just treating someone as reliable. To treat someone as reliable – say, as a careful driver, a competent doctor, a dutiful police officer – means acting on the confident belief that they will display a certain trait or behaviour. It would be quite out of place to say that, whenever I treat a person as reliable in this way, I treat them as trustworthy. Thus, I might be rightly described as presumptuous if I described my attitude towards the driver or doctor or police officer as one of treating the person as trustworthy. The washerwomen of Koenigsberg might as well have claimed that they treated Kant as trustworthy when they relied on him for taking his afternoon walk at the same time each day.

The cases of reliance given, which clearly do not amount to treating someone as trustworthy, are all instances of rational reliance, as we noticed. Does this mean that when I go beyond mere reliance and actually trust a person – put my trust in the person – I can no longer be operating in the manner of a rational agent? Does it mean, as some have suggested, that trust essentially involves a leap beyond rationality, a hopeful but rationally unwarranted sort of reliance – if you like, a Hail Mary version of the practice? This suggestion would leave us with a paradox that we might phrase as follows. If trust is rational, then it is not deserving of the name of 'trust' – not at least in my regimented sense – and, if it deserves the name of 'trust', then it cannot be rational.

Happily, however, there is an alternative to this suggestion, and a way beyond this paradox. The assumption behind the suggestion is that the only factor available to mark off ordinary reliance from trust is just the rationality of the reliance. But this is mistaken. The acts of reliance considered are distinguished, not just by being rational, but also by being, as I shall put it, interactively static. And what distinguishes trust from reliance is the interactively dynamic character of the reliance displayed – not any necessary failure of rationality. So this, at any rate, is what I argue.[3]

My relying on others will count as interactively dynamic when two special conditions are fulfilled; otherwise it will be static in character. The first condition required is that the people on whom I rely must be aware of that fact that I am relying on them to display a certain trait or behaviour; that awareness must not be left to chance – in the paradigm case, indeed, I will have ensured its appearance by use of the quasiperformative utterance 'I'm

---

[3] In putting this argument, I do not want to legislate for the use of the word 'trust'. I am perfectly happy to acknowledge that the characterization I provide of interactively dynamic trust does not catch every variation in usage, even in the usage of the word beyond the limit where it clearly means little more than 'rely'. My primary interest is in demarcating a phenomenon that is clearly of particular interest in human life.

trusting you to. . . . '. And the second condition required is that, in revealing my reliance in this manner, I must be expecting that it will engage the dispositions of my trustees, giving them an extra motive or reason for being or acting as I am relying on them to be or act.[4]

I think that trust involves dynamic reliance of this kind, because the dynamic aspect provides a nice explanation for why trusting people involves treating them as trustworthy. If I am said to treat you as trustworthy, then I must be treating you in a way that manifests to you – and to any informed witnesses – that I am relying on you; otherwise it would not have the gestalt of treating you as trustworthy. And if I am said to treat you as trustworthy, then, in addition, I must be manifesting the expectation that this will increase your reason for acting as I rely on you to act. The implication of anyone's saying that I treat you as trustworthy is that I expect you to live up to the trust I am investing in you; that is, I expect that the fact that I am relying on you – the fact that I am investing trust in you – will give you more reason than you previously had to display the trait or behaviour required.

Relying on others is a generic kind of activity; trust, in the sense in which I am concerned with it, is a specific form of that generic kind. The difference that marks off trust from reliance, contrary to the suggestion mentioned, is not that trust is a nonrational version of reliance. Rather, it is that trust is interactively dynamic in character. It materializes so far as the act of reliance involved is presented as an act of reliance to the trustee and is presented in the manifest expectation that that will give the trustee extra reason to conform to the expectation.

What of the connection to rationality? I argue that both reliance, in general, and trust, in particular, may be rational or irrational. While we illustrated reliance on other people by instances that were intuitively rational in character, nothing rules out cases of irrational reliance. Reliance will be irrational so far as the beliefs on which it is based are not well grounded or, perhaps a less likely possibility, so far as they do not provide a good ground for the reliance that they prompt. Trust is the species of reliance on other people that is interactively dynamic in the sense explained and, while this may certainly be irrational, it should be clear that it may be rational too. There may be good reason to expect that others will be motivated by my act of manifest reliance on them, and so, good reason to indulge in such reliance. I may think that they are not currently, independently disposed to act as I want them to act, for example, but believe that my revealing that I am relying on their acting in that way will provide them with the required motive to do so.

---

[4] Providing an extra motive or reason, as discussed in Pettit (1995), need not mean making it more likely that the person will behave in the manner required; he or she may already have enough reason and motive to ensure that they will behave in that way. I can raise the utility that a certain choice has for you, even when it already has much greater utility than any alternative.

The results we have covered are summed up in the following tree diagram and I hope that this will help to keep them in mind.

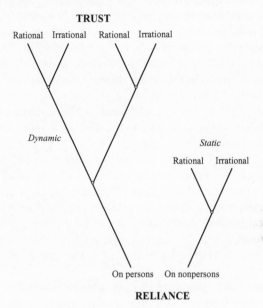

TRUST

2. TWO FORMS OF TRUST

There are two broadly contrasted sorts of beliefs, on the basis of which you might be led to trust others in a certain manner – say, trust them to tell the truth on some question, or to keep a promise, or to respond to a request for help.

You might believe that certain others are indeed trustworthy, in the sense of being antecedently disposed to respond to certain manifestations of reliance. They may not be disposed antecedently to display the trait or behaviour you want them to display, but they are disposed to do so, other things being equal, should you manifestly rely on them to do so. They are possessed of stable, ground-level dispositions that you are able to engage by acts of manifest reliance.

The dispositions in which you believe, in this case, would constitute what we normally think of as virtues. You might believe that it is possible to engage some people by manifesting reliance on them because they are loyal friends or associates, for example; or because they are kind and virtuous types who won't generally want to let down someone who depends on them; or because they are prudent and perceptive individuals who will see the long-term benefits available to each of you from cooperation and will be prepared, therefore, to build on the opportunity you provide by manifesting reliance on them.

But there is also a quite different sort of belief that might prompt you to trust certain others, manifesting reliance in the manifest expectation that they will prove reliable. You might think, not that those people are currently disposed to respond appropriately, but rather that they are disposed to form such a disposition under the stimulus provided by your making a relevant overture of trust. You might think that they are metadisposed in this fashion to tell you the truth, or to keep a promise you elicit, or to provide some help you request. They may not be currently disposed in such directions but they are disposed to become disposed to respond in those ways, should you make the required overture.

This second possibility is less straightforward than the first, and I will devote the rest of this section to elucidating it. The possibility is not just a logical possibility that is unlikely to be realized in practice. It materializes in common interactions as a result of people's desiring the good opinion of others and recognizing – as a matter of shared awareness, however tacit – that this is something that they each desire. It has a salient place within what Geoffrey Brennan and I describe as the 'economy of esteem' (Brennan and Pettit 2004a).

There are two fundamentally different sorts of goods that human beings seek for themselves. The one kind may be described as attitude-dependent, the other as action-dependent (Pettit 1993, Chapter 5). Attitude-dependent goods are those which a person can enjoy only so far as they are the object of certain attitudes, in particular certain positive attitudes, on the part of others, or indeed themselves. They are goods like being loved, being liked, being acknowledged, being respected, being admired, and so on. Action-dependent goods are those which a person can procure without having to rely on the presence of any particular attitudes in themselves or others; they are attained by their own efforts, or the efforts of others; and they are attained regardless of the attitudes at the origin of those efforts.

Action-dependent goods are illustrated by the regular sorts of services and commodities and resources to which economists give centre stage. But it should be clear that people care also about goods in the attitude-dependent category; they care about being cherished by others, for example, and about being well regarded by them. Thus, Adam Smith, the founding father of economics, thought that the desire for the good opinion or esteem of others, the desire for standing in the eyes of others, was one of the most basic of human inclinations:

Nature, when she formed man for society, endowed him with an original desire to please, and an original aversion to offend his brethren. She taught him to feel pleasure in their favourable, and pain in their unfavourable regard. She rendered their approbation most flattering and most agreeable to him for its own sake; and their disapprobation most mortifying and most offensive (Smith 1982, p. 116).

In arguing that people care about the esteem of others, Smith was part of a tradition going back to ancient sources, and a tradition that was particularly powerful in the seventeenth and eighteenth centuries (Lovejoy 1961). I am going to assume that he is right in thinking that people do seek the good opinion of others, even if this desire is not any more basic than their desire for material goods. More particularly, I am going to assume that while the good opinion of others is certainly instrumental in procuring action-dependent goods, it is not desired just as a currency that can be cashed out in action-dependent terms. People will naturally be prepared to trade off esteem for other goods, but the less esteem they have, the more reluctant they will be to trade; esteem is an independently attractive good by their lights, not just a proxy for material goods.[5]

The desire for esteem can serve in the role of the metadisposition of which I spoke earlier. Let people want the esteem of others and they will be disposed to become disposed to prove reliable in response to the trusting manifestation of reliance. Or, at least, that will be the case in the event that the trusting manifestation of reliance normally serves to communicate a good opinion of the trustee. And all the evidence suggests that it does serve this purpose, constituting a token of the trustor's esteem.

The act of relying on others in a suitable context is a way of displaying a belief that they are not the sort to let you down; they are trustworthy, say in the modality of loyalty or virtue or prudence/perception. The trustor does not typically utter words to the effect that the trustees are people who will not let the needy down, that the trustees, as we say, are indeed trustworthy individuals. But what the trustor does in manifesting reliance is tantamount to saying something of that sort. Let the context be one where, by common assumption, the trustor will expect the trustees to prove reliable in a certain way, only if they have a modicum of trustworthiness – only if the trustees are loyal or virtuous or prudent/perceptive or whatever. Under such a routine assumption – more below on why it is routine – the act of trust will be a way of saying that the trustees are, indeed, of that trustworthy sort.

Indeed, since words are cheap and actions dear, the act of trust will be something of even greater communicative significance. It will communicate in the most credible currency available to human beings – in the gold standard represented by action – that the trustor believes the trustees to be truly trustworthy, to be truly the sorts of people who will not take advantage of someone who puts himself or herself in their hands. It does not just record the reality of that belief; it shows that the belief exists. Thus Hobbes (1991, p. 64) can write: 'To believe, to trust, to rely on another, is to Honour him:

---

[5] It may be that esteem is desired intrinsically, as a result of our evolutionary priming; or it may be that it is desired instrumentally, where one of the goods it instrumentally promotes is the nonmaterial good of facilitating self-esteem. I abstract from such issues here (see Brennan and Pettit 2004a, chapter 1).

sign of opinion of his virtue and power. To distrust, or not believe, is to Dishonour.'

When it connects in this way with the desire of a good opinion, the act of trust has an important motivating aspect for the trustees. It makes clear to them that they enjoy the good opinion of the trustor – the belief that they are trustworthy – but that they will lose that good opinion if they let the trustor down. This means that the trustor has a reason to expect the manifestation of reliance to be persuasive with the trustees, independently of any belief in their preexisting loyalty or virtue or prudence. If the trustees value the good opinion of the trustor, which the manifestation of reliance reveals, then that is likely to give them pause about letting the trustor down, even if they are actually not particularly loyal or virtuous or prudent/perceptive in character. Let the trustor down, and they may gain some immediate advantage or save themselves some immediate cost. But let the trustor down, and they will forfeit another immediate advantage, the salient benefit of being well regarded by the trustor, as well as the other benefits associated with enjoying such a status.

But there is also more to say. When I display trust in certain others, I often demonstrate to third parties that I trust these people. Other things being equal, then such a demonstration will serve to win a good opinion for the trustees among those witnesses; the demonstration will amount to testimony that the trustees are trustworthy. Indeed, if the fact of such universal testimony is salient to all, the demonstration may not just cause everyone to think well of the trustees; it may cause this to become a matter of common belief, with everyone believing it, everyone believing that everyone believes it, and so on. Assuming that such facts are going to be visible to any perceptive trustees, then, the existence of independent witnesses to the act of trust will provide further esteem-centred motives for them to perform as expected. Let the trustor down and not only will trustees lose the good opinion that the trustor has displayed; they will also lose the good opinion and the high status that the trustor may have won for them among third parties.

The belief that someone is loyal or virtuous or prudent/perceptive may explain why the risk-taking that trust involves may actually be quite sensible or rational. Certainly there is a risk involved in this or that act of trust, but the risk is not substantial – it is, at the least, a rational gamble – given that the trustee has those qualities.[6] What we now see is that the belief that certain

[6] For the record, I think that the risk involved in the act of trust need not be a risk of the ordinary, probabilistic kind (Pettit 1995). Take the case where I am dealing with others whom I believe to be more or less certain of responding appropriately to an act of manifest reliance on my part; let my degree of confidence that they are reliable in this way be as near as you like to one. I can still be said to trust such people, so far as I put my fate in their hands when I rely on them. I do not expose myself to a significant probability that they will betray me – that probability may approach zero – but I do expose myself to the accessibility of betrayal to them; I expose myself to their having the freedom to betray me. Here, I break with Russell Hardin (1992, p. 507) and join with Richard Holton (1994).

parties desire esteem and that responding appropriately to an overture of trust will secure esteem for them, may equally explain why it is rational to trust those people.[7] It does not direct us to any independent reason why the trustees may be taken to be antecedently reliable – any reason of objective trustworthiness – but it reveals how the act of trust can transform the trustee into reliable parties, eliciting the disposition to perform appropriately. To manifest trusting reliance is to provide normal, esteem-sensitive trustees with an incentive to do the very thing that the trustor is relying on them to do. It is a sort of bootstraps operation, wherein the trustor takes a risk and, by the very fact of taking that risk, shifts the odds in his or her own favour.

Believing that certain individuals are loyal or virtuous or prudent/ perceptive is quite consistent, we should notice, with believing that still in some measure they desire the esteem of others. This is important because it means that people may have double reason for trusting others. They may trust them both because they think that they are trustworthy and – a back-up consideration, as it were – because they think that they will savour the esteem that goes with proving reliable and being thought to be trustworthy. I said earlier that to trust certain others is to treat them as trustworthy. When one trusts them in the standard way, one treats them as trustworthy in the sense of acting out of a belief that they are trustworthy. When one trusts them on the esteem-related basis, one treats them as if they were trustworthy, whether as a matter of fact they are trustworthy or not.

One final issue: the esteem-related way in which trust may materialize depends on its going without saying – its being a matter of routine assumption shared among people – that, when a trustor invests trust in a trustee, that is because of taking the trustee to be trustworthy. But isn't it likely that people will recognize that in many cases the trustor invests trust because of taking the trustee to want his or her esteem, or the esteem of witnesses, not because of taking the person to be antecedently trustworthy? And, in that case, won't the mechanism we have been describing be undermined? People are not going to expect to attract esteem for proving reliable, if they expect that their proving reliable will be explained by the trustor, and by witnesses, as an effect of their wanting to win that esteem. They will expect to attract esteem only if they think that their proving reliable will be generally explained by the assumption that they are trustworthy types: by the attribution of stable dispositions like loyalty or virtue or prudence or perception.

Is there any special reason to think that the system won't unravel in this way, and that it will continue to go without saying – it will continue to be a matter of common assumption – that people who prove reliable under overtures of trust will enjoy the attribution of estimable, trustworthy dispositions?

---

[7] I have come to realize, from discussions with Victoria McGeer, that the role of belief here may be played by the attitude of hope, as I have characterized it elsewhere (Pettit 2004). For an exploration of this idea see (McGeer 2004b).

I believe there is. The assumption is going to remain in place as long as people are subject to the 'fundamental attribution error or bias', as psychologists call it, and so are likely to expect everyone to conform to that pattern of attribution. And a firm tradition of psychological thought suggests that the bias is deeply and undisplaceably ingrained in our nature.

E. E. Jones (1990, p. 138) gives forceful expression to the view that the bias has this sort of hold upon us: 'I have a candidate for the most robust and repeatable finding in social psychology: the tendency to see behavior as caused by a stable personal disposition of the actor when it can be just as easily explained as a natural response to more than adequate situational pressure'. This finding – that people are deeply prone to the fundamental attribution bias – supports the idea that, even if they are conscious of their own sensitivity to a force like the desire for esteem (Miller and Prentice 1996, p. 804), people will be loath to trace the behaviour of others to such a situational pressure. They are much more likely to explain the behaviour by ascribing a corresponding disposition to them. And that being so, they are likely to expect each to do the same, to expect that each will expect each to do the same, and so on in the usual hierarchy. Thus they are likely to expect that trustors will invest trust in certain others only so far as they take those others to have the stable personal dispositions associated with trustworthiness.[8]

3. THE INTERNET

And so, finally, I come to the connection between trust and the Internet. The question that I want to raise is whether the Internet offers a milieu within which relations of trust – trust as distinct from reliance – can rationally develop. There is every reason, of course, why people who already enjoy such relations with one another should be able to express and elicit trust in one another over the Internet. But the question is whether the Internet offers the sort of ecology within which trust can rationally form and strengthen in the absence of face-to-face or other contact. Is it a space in which I might rationally make myself reliant on others by sharing difficult secrets, asking their advice about personal problems, exposing myself financially in some proposal, and so on?

We distinguished in the last section between two sorts of bases on which trust may emerge in general. The primary basis for trust is the belief that

[8] A related problem arises with the trustor as distinct from the trustee. Why should the trustor expect that the trustee and other witnesses will take them to be moved, not by a wish to signal esteem and thereby motivate the trustee, but rather by the attribution of a trustworthy disposition to the trustee? The answer, I think, is that to the extent that people tend to explain the esteem-seeking behaviour of others by attributing stable dispositions they will also tend to explain the relevant sort of esteem-signalling behaviour as springing from the attribution of such dispositions. They will display, not just an attribution bias, but a meta-attribution bias: a tendency to take people to employ an attributionist heuristic in interpreting and in dealing with others.

certain people are trustworthy: that is, have stable dispositions like loyalty and virtue and prudence or perception. Primary trust will be rational just in case that belief is rational and serves rationally to control what the trustor does. The secondary basis for trust is the belief that even if the people in question are not trustworthy – even if they do not have stable dispositions of the kind mentioned – they are metadisposed to display the trait or behaviour that the trustor relies on them, now in this instance, now in that, to display. More concretely, they desire esteem and they can be moved by the esteem communicated by an act of trust – and perhaps broadcast to others – into becoming disposed to be or act as the trustor wants them to be or act. The secondary form of trust that is prompted in this manner will be rational, just in case the belief in the esteem-seeking metadisposition is rational and serves rationally to shape the trustor's overture.

Does the Internet offer a framework for the rational formation of primary trust? In particular, does it provide an environment where I may rationally come to think that someone I encounter only in that milieu is likely to respond as a loyal or virtuous or even prudent/perceptive person? Or does it offer a framework for the rational formation of secondary trust? Does it enable me to recognize and activate another's desire for esteem, creating a ground for expecting that he or she will respond favourably to my trusting displays of esteem?

There is no problem with the possibility of the Internet facilitating rational reliance, as distinct from trust. Suppose I become aware of someone over e-mail or in a chat room or via the Web. And imagine that an opportunity arises where I will find it rational to do something – say, go to a proposed meeting place – only if there is reason to believe that the other person will act in a certain way: in this way, be at the proposed place to meet me. I may not have very much solid evidence available about that person over the Internet – deception is not easily detectable – but there is nothing to block the possibility that what evidence I have makes it rational for me to rely on their doing this or that; what evidence I have makes that a rational gamble.

But reliance is one thing, trust another. Take the question of primary trust first of all. Is it ever likely to be the case, with the individuals I encounter on the Internet, and on the Internet only, that I can come to think of them as loyal or virtuous or even prudent/perceptive, that is, capable of recognizing and responding to a sense of the long-term interests that they and I may have in cooperating with one another? And is it ever likely to be possible for me to invest trust rationally in such contacts?

I think not. Consider the ways in which I come to form beliefs about loyalty and virtue and prudence/perception in everyday life. I may rely in the formation of such beliefs on at least three distinct sources of evidence. First, the evidence available to me as I see and get cued – no doubt at subpersonal as well as personal levels of awareness – to the expressions, the gestures, the words, the looks of people, in a phrase, and their bodily presence. Call this the evidence of face. Second, the evidence available to me as I see the person in interaction with others, enjoying the testimony of their association and support: in particular, I see them connecting in this way with others whom I already know and credit. Call this the evidence of frame. And third, the evidence that accumulates in the record that I will normally maintain, however unconsciously, about their behaviour towards me and towards others over time. Call this the evidence registered in a personal file on the people involved.

The striking thing about Internet contact is that it does not allow me to avail myself of such bodies of evidence, whether of face, frame, or file. The contact whose address and words reach my screen is only a virtual presence, albeit a presence I may dress up in the images that fantasy supplies. I cannot read the face of such a contact; the person is a spectral, not a bodily presence in my life. Nor can I see evidence of his or her character – and I won't be able to establish independently whether 'his' or 'her' is appropriate – in the interactions the person enjoys with other persons familiar to me, assuming that such witnesses will be themselves only spectral presences in my experience. And nor, finally, will I be able to keep a file on the performance of the person over time, whether with me or with others. There won't be any way of tracking that person for sure, because a given person may assume many addresses and the address of one person can be mimicked by others.

Not only do these problems stand in the way of my being able to judge that a pure Internet contact is loyal or virtuous or prudent/perceptive. They are compounded by the fact that such problems, as I am in a position to see, will also stand in the way of others when they try to read and relate to me. For them I will be just a spectral presence, as they are spectral presences for me. Our voices may call out over the Internet, but it won't ever be clear where they come from or to whom they belong. They will be like a chorus of lost cries, seeking in vain to pin one another down. Or, at least, that is what they will be like, absent the illusions that fantasy may weave as it claims to find structure and stability in the shifts of the kaleidoscope.

On the Internet, to put these problems in summary form, we all wear the Ring of Gyges. Plato took up an old myth in asking whether we would be likely to remain virtuous, should we have access to a ring that would give us power, on wearing it, to become invisible and undetectable to others. That myth becomes reality on the Internet for, with a little ingenuity, any one of us may make contact with another under one address and then, slipping that name, present ourselves under a second or third address and try to manipulate the other's responses to the first. That we exist under the second or third address may not be undetectable to the other in such a case, but that it is we who do so – that we have the same identity – certainly will be undetectable.

In view of these difficulties, I think that the possibility of rational, primary trust in the virtual space of the Internet is only of vanishing significance. It is a space in which voices sound out of the dark, echoing to us in a void where it is never clear who is who and what is what. Or at least that is so when we enter the Internet without connection to existing, real-world networks of association and friendship.

But what of secondary trust? Are the prospects any better here that we will be able to reach out to one another in the environment of the Internet and forge relationships of trust? I think not. I may be able to assume, as a general truth about human nature, that those with whom I make contact are likely to savour esteem, including the esteem of someone like me that they don't yet fully know. But how can I think that anything I do in manifesting reliance will seem to make esteem available to them, whether it be my own esteem or the esteem of independent witnesses?

The problem here derives from the problems that jeopardize the possibility of primary trust. I am blocked from rationally forming the belief that an Internet contact is loyal or virtuous or prudent/perceptive, as we saw. Since that blocking is something that anyone is in a position to recognize, others will see that it is in place, and I will be positioned to recognize that they will see this. And that being so, I will have no ground to think that others – other pure Internet contacts – are likely to take an act of manifest reliance on my part as an expression of the belief that they are people of proven or even rationally presumed loyalty or virtue or prudence/perception. I will have no ground for expecting them to take my act of trust as a token of personal esteem.

There is not any way out of this difficulty because of the lack of witnesses. For, as those on whom I bestow trust will be unable to see my manifestation of reliance as a token of esteem, so the witnesses to my act will be equally prevented from viewing it in that way. The addressees and the witnesses of my act may see it as a rather stupid, perhaps even pathetic attempt to make contact. Or if the act promises a possible benefit to me at a loss to the addressees – as in the case of e-mails that propose various financial scams – they may see it as a rather obvious attempt at manipulation and fraud. And that just about exhausts the possibilities. If I try to invest trust in others unknown to me outside the Internet, then the profile I assume will have to be that of the idiot or the trickster. Not a happy choice.

The claims I have been making may strike some as exaggerated. But if they do, that may be because of a confusion between what I described at the beginning of the chapter as Internet trust between real people – my topic here – and Internet trust between Internet people, that is, between personas that we real individuals construct on Internet forums. If I construct an agony aunt persona on an Internet forum, then in that persona I may succeed over time in earning – earning, not just winning – the trust of those who, in the guise of other Internet identities, seek my guidance. This form of trust is of great interest and opens up possibilities of productive human relationships, but it is not the phenomenon that I have been discussing here. My concern has been with how far real people can manage, on the basis of pure Internet contact, to establish trust in one another. And the answer to which I am driven is that they cannot effectively do so. The message of the chapter, in a word used by Hubert Dreyfus (2001), is that 'telepresence' is not enough on its own to mediate the appearance of rational trust between real people.

One concluding word of caution, however: I have argued for this claim on the assumption that telepresence will remain as Gygean as it currently is, that it will continue to lack the facial salience, the framed support, and the fileable identities available in regular encounters with other people. I am no futurist, however, and I cannot say that telepresence will always remain constrained in these ways. Perhaps lurking out there in the future of our species is an arrangement under which telepresence can assume firmer, more assuring forms and can serve to mediate rational trust. I do not say that such a brave new world is logically impossible. I only say that it has not yet arrived.

References

Brennan, G., and Pettit, P. 2004a. *The economy of esteem: An essay on civil and political society.* Oxford: Oxford University Press.

Brennan, G., and Pettit, P. 2004b. Esteem, identifiability, and the Internet. *Analyse & Kritik, 26,* 1, 139–157.

Dreyfus, H. 2001. *On the Internet.* London: Routledge.

Hardin, R. 1992. The street-level epistemology of trust, *Politics and Society, 21,* 4, 505–529.

Hobbes, T. 1991. *Leviathan.* Cambridge, UK: Cambridge University Press.

Holton, R. 1994. Deciding to trust, coming to believe, *Australasian Journal of Philosophy, 72,* 63–76.

Jones, E. E. 1990. *Interpersonal perception.* New York: Freeman

Lovejoy, A. O. 1961. *Reflections on human nature.* Baltimore: Johns Hopkins Press

McGeer, V. 2004a. Developing trust on the Internet, *Analyse & Kritik, 26,* 1, 91–107.

McGeer, V. 2004b. Trust, hope and empowerment. Princeton University, Dept of Philosophy. Unpublished ms.

Miller, D. T., and Prentice, D. A. 1996. The construction of social norms and standards, in E. T. Higgins and A. W. Kruglanski (Eds.), *Social psychology: Handbook of basic principles.* New York: Guilford Press, pp. 799–829.

Pettit, P. 1993. *The common mind: An essay on psychology, society and politics,* New York: Oxford University Press.

Pettit, P. 1995. The cunning of trust. *Philosophy and Public Affairs, 24,* 202–225.

Pettit, P. 2004. Hope and its place in mind. *Annals of the American Academy of Political and Social Science, 592,* 1, 152–165.

Smith, A. 1982. *The theory of the moral sentiments.* Indianapolis: Liberty Classics

10

Esteem, Identifiability, and the Internet[1]

Geoffrey Brennan and Philip Pettit

1. ESTEEM, REPUTATION, AND THE 'COMPOUNDING EFFECT'

Nature, when she formed man for society, endowed him with an original desire to please, and an original aversion to offend his brethren. She taught him to feel pleasure in their favourable, and pain in their unfavourable regard.

(Adam Smith 1759/1982, p. 116)

We assume in this chapter, in line with what we have argued elsewhere (Brennan and Pettit 2004), that people desire the esteem of others and shrink from their disesteem. In making this assumption, we are deliberately associating ourselves with an intellectual tradition that dominated social theorizing until the nineteenth century, and specifically until the emergence of modern economics. That tradition includes Adam Smith, Thomas Hobbes, John Locke, the Baron de Montesquieu, David Hume – indeed, just about everyone who is recognized as a forebear of modern social and political theory, whether specifically in the economistic style or not. There is scarcely a social theorist up to the nineteenth century who does not regard the desire for esteem as among the most ubiquitous and powerful motives of human action (Lovejoy 1961). Smith's elegantly forthright formulation, offered as the epigraph to this section, simply exemplifies the wider tradition.

We can think of a minimalist version of the basic esteem relationship as involving just two individuals – actor A and an observer, B. The actor undertakes some action, or exhibits some disposition, that is observed by B. The observation of this action/disposition induces in B an immediate and spontaneous evaluative attitude. That attitude can be either positive (esteem) or negative (disesteem). B has this response, we think, simply as a

---

[1] This chapter was originally published in 2004 in *Analyse & Kritik*, *26*, 1, 139–157. Its writing was stimulated by our participation in a conference on 'Trust on the Internet' held in Bielefeld, Germany in July 2003. The current version owes much to Michael Baurmann for excellent editorial comments.

result of her being the kind of evaluative creature that humans are.[2] Crucially for the 'economy of esteem', *B*'s evaluative attitude is itself an object of *A*'s concern; as the economist might put it, *B*'s attitude is an argument in *A*'s utility function – positively valued by *A* in the case of esteem, and negatively valued in the case of disesteem. In short, *A* cares what *B* thinks of him, and is prepared to act in order to induce *B* to think better (or less badly) of him. To the extent that prevailing values are matters of common awareness, *A*'s desire for positive esteem (and the desire to avoid disesteem) will induce *A* to behave in accord with those values.

The esteem that accrues and the corresponding behavioural incentive will be greater:

- the greater the likelihood that *A* will be observed – at least over a considerable range. The significance of the proviso we shall explore in Section 4;
- the larger the size of the relevant audience; and
- the higher is audience quality – with 'quality' here understood in terms of attentiveness, capacity to discriminate, capacity to provide valued testimony, and so on. Audience quality is also a matter of the esteem which observers themselves enjoy in the relevant domain. If more esteemed observers esteem you, that both tends to augment the self-esteem you enjoy and also gives greater credibility and effect to any testimony those observers provide on your behalf.

Now, it should be clear that the Internet is a setting in which observation is assured, where there is a large audience on offer, and where at least some proportion of that audience can be assumed to be 'high quality' in the sense indicated. So, for example, if you post a solution to a difficult software problem on the mailing list of Linux experts,[3] you will immediately have a very large audience, and moreover one composed of highly qualified and highly attentive readers. The technology provides relatively open access to much larger, and more dedicated, audiences than are typically available in the real world. This fact immediately suggests that esteem may play an especially important role on the Internet; and that the behavioural incentives to act 'properly', as prevailing values understand that term, will be especially potent in the Internet setting.

There is, however, an interesting feature of Internet relations that might moderate the strength of these audience effects, and is, in any event, worth some detailed exploration in its own right. To focus on what is at stake, it is necessary to say a little about the relation between esteem and reputation.

---

[2] In particular, *B* develops her evaluative attitude independently of any utility gain or loss that she may sustain in enduring the spectacle of *A*'s performance.

[3] The example is Michael Baurmann's.

Reputation in the sense of brand name recognition can clearly materialize without esteem or disesteem. Equally, esteem or disesteem can accrue without any reputational effects. When you behave badly by prevailing standards, observers who witness your conduct will think ill of you whether or not they will be able to identify you in the future, and whether or not you are ever likely to meet them again. And this fact can induce you to behave better – without any reputational effects as such.

However, reputational effects do serve to increase the esteem stakes. If the observer can recognize you in the future, then you stand to enjoy esteem (or suffer disesteem) not only at the point of actual performance but also later when you are recognized as 'the person who did X'. And further, if your identity is communicable to others, then you can be recognized as 'the one who did X' by all those within the community of discourse, and specifically by those who were not witnesses of the original action. Both properties – future recognition and communicability – are involved in reputation. In this sense, reputation serves to extend the time frame and the effective audience over which the esteem/disesteem can be sustained, and to magnify the corresponding esteem incentive to behave in accord with prevailing values.

In what we take to be the 'normal case', esteem and disesteem, *and* reputation good or bad, will accrue in a process in which the individual's identity is clear and unproblematic. But the Internet is often – perhaps typically – not a 'normal case' in this sense. For it is a routine feature of many forms of Internet interactions that individuals develop *Internet-specific* identities. That is, many people choose to operate on the Internet under an alias and have 'virtual' identities which are distinct from their 'real' identities. And this phenomenon of multiple identities is something of a puzzle in the esteem context because it seems to stand against what we take to be an important feature of the structure of esteem. This feature we shall term the 'compounding effect', and we turn immediately to explain what it is.

Esteem and disesteem accrue to the actor by virtue of performance in one or other of the entire range of evaluated dispositions or actions. One is esteemed for one's benevolence, or one's courage or one's musical prowess or one's putting ability. Reputations are similar: one develops a reputation *for* something. Esteem and reputation, both, are activity-specific. This does not mean, though, that we cannot give sense to the idea of the esteem a person enjoys *in toto*, or to his reputation overall. The esteem acquired in each field will be aggregated in some way to form overall esteem. The reputation in the various domains will add up to the person's overall reputation. The precise way in which these activity-specific reputations aggregate to form overall reputation is an important matter; and the specific assumption we shall make in this connection is this: *other things equal, positive (and negative) reputations compound across domains.* So if A enjoys a fine reputation within his profession, and a fine reputation in the particular sporting and artistic avocations he pursues, and has a reputation for honesty, generosity, and so on, then his overall reputation will be better by virtue of the variety. Each element in his reputation serves to augment the other elements in such a way that the whole tends to be larger than the sum of the parts. Obversely, if A's reputation in a range of areas is negative or merely mediocre, these reputational elements will also tend to be mutually supportive, although in a negative direction.

It might be helpful here to think of overall esteem or overall reputation in terms of a functional form that reflects the relevant property. So let A's total reputation be Ω_A, where:

$$\Omega_A = R_A(X) + R_A(Y) + c \cdot R_A(X) \cdot R_A(Y) \qquad (1)$$

where $R_A(X)$, $R_A(Y) > 0$,

and c is some positive constant.

A person who had a positive reputation in some domains and a negative one in others would have the positive and negative elements separately combined as in Equation (1) and simply added.

The force of this assumption in the current context is that it creates a presumption in favour of A's having a single identity for reputational purposes. Having a positive reputation for X somehow maintained separately from the positive reputation for Y involves forgoing the benefits associated with the final term of Equation (1) – the 'compounding effect', as we denote it. Of course, the benefits of compounding may be offset by other considerations in special cases. But our formulation means that these 'other considerations' have to be specified.

The problem we face is to explain how it could make sense for people on the Internet to multiply their identities in this way, putting out a variety of personas in place of their real, universally identifiable self. The problem, in particular, is to explain this under the assumption that people desire esteem and reputation. Is the phenomenon to be explained by technical features of the Internet? Or does it have a large life in the economy of esteem? Whatever its source, what effect does multiple identity have on the behavioural incentives associated with esteem? These are the questions with which this chapter will be concerned.

Our strategy in addressing them is somewhat indirect. We begin by considering three cases in which identity is an apparently critical factor, but where the distinctive technical features of the Internet are not present. This task occupies us in Section 2. We then examine in some detail the variety of motives that seem to be in play in those cases. In Section 3, we explore the use of (or effects of) anonymity as an insurance strategy; in Section 4, the use of anonymity as an esteem-optimising strategy; and in Section 5, a variety of other considerations that seem to be in play when anonymity is invoked.

In Section 6, we seek to examine the relevance of this analysis drawn from these cases for the Internet case specifically; and draw some appropriately tentative conclusions.

2. THREE CASES SOMEWHAT ANALOGOUS TO THE INTERNET

The cases we consider all involve identity and reputational issues but are not subject to the technical peculiarities of the Internet setting. The cases are:

- the use of the pseudonym;
- the resort to name change; and
- the creation of a secret society.

Of these, the pseudonym seems to offer the closest analogue to what happens on the Internet. But the case of name change is similar in some respects and may offer some insight into motives for use of pseudonyms on the Internet. And, as we shall try to show, consideration of the secret society cases, though somewhat removed, can also offer some insight into motives for, and/or the consequences of, the use of Internet pseudonyms.

2.1. Pseudonyms

The characteristic feature of the pseudonym case is that individuals operate under a variety of names simultaneously. Each of these names can give rise to a reputation and each of those reputations can be a source of public esteem. There is, in fact, an interesting variety of cases; and it will be useful here to provide some examples.

In theatrical and cinematic circles, the practice of the 'professional stage name' is so familiar as to be unremarkable. Indeed, operating under one's original birth name seems to be the exception. In some small number of cases, the reason for adopting a stage name (different from one's birth name) is that the birth name is already in use as a stage name by someone else. So for example, James Stewart (birth name) adopted a screen name (James Cagney) because Jimmie Stewart was already an established screen personality. In general, however, the motivation is quite different: it is to secure a name with the right combination of salience and associative properties, much like the choice of brand name or name for a new product.

In the screen cases, the screen persona is such a dominant aspect of the actor's life, and so constitutive of the actor's reputation, that the individuals are usually known by their screen names offscreen as well as on. The choice of pseudonym in such cases is then more like a name change, and probably ought to be considered in that setting.

The literary context is another in which the use of pseudonyms is common – or at least has been so at some periods of literary history. But here the specifically *multiple*-identity property seems more relevant.

In the eighteenth century, the practice of writing under a nom de plume (interestingly a 'nom du guerre' in French) seems to have been the rule rather than the exception – though more for novelists than poets.[4] Just how extensive a practice this has been can be gauged by consulting one or another of the several dictionaries of pseudonyms that are now available – dictionaries that run to hundreds of pages and contain thousands of entries (e.g., Carty [1996/2000] and Room [1989] [5]).

Some examples will serve to illustrate the variety:

- Throughout the eighteenth century, most commentators on political affairs, including the authors of much significant political theory, wrote under pseudonyms. Hamilton, Jay, and Madison writing as *Publius* is only one notable example of a very widespread practice. The so-called *Cato* letters are another. John Adams wrote as *Marcellus* (among the eighteenth century political essayists, classical names, even invented ones, were popular). In many such cases, the authors were themselves political figures and the pseudonym might have served partly to protect them in their political roles from criticism associated with their published views.

- Female novelists through eighteenth and nineteenth centuries frequently wrote under male pseudonyms. So, for example, the famous cases of Mary Ann Evans ('George Eliot') and the Bronte sisters writing their early efforts as the brothers Bell (Acton, Currer, and Ellis). It is natural to think that the motive here was primarily to avoid gender prejudice. However, interestingly, Jane Austen published *Sense and Sensibility* under the authorship of 'a Lady' – specifically not 'a Gentleman' – indicating the presence of other considerations. Perhaps to be identified as an author was not a source of positive esteem in all the quarters in which Austen moved.

- Walter Scott wrote his first historical novel *Waverley* anonymously, and his next few efforts in the genre were published under the epithet 'by the author of Waverley'. At the time *Waverley* appeared, Scott had already something of a reputation as a writer of heroic and romantic poetry, and is reputed to have been concerned that the historical novels might tarnish his reputation in the poetic field. In the same spirit, Thomas Hardy's early novels *Desperate Remedies*, and then, three years later, *Far From the Madding Crowd*, were written anonymously – again at a time when Hardy aspired to a reputation primarily as a poet.

[4] Perhaps this term was used for poets because writing poetry was considered to be more prestigious. The case of Walter Scott might seem to lend support to this consideration. We deal with Scott's case in some detail below.

[5] Room (1989) deals with name changes as well as pseudonyms; it includes accounts of the circumstances and possible motivations for the name choices in the entries. There is also a set of interesting brief essays on various aspects of name choice at the beginning of the volume.

- David Cornwell, a civil servant in the British Foreign Office, through the 1960s and 1970s, wrote his espionage novels under the pseudonym, John le Carre, presumably to protect his employers from any taint of association.
- Charles Dodgson, Oxford mathematician and precursor of modern social choice theory, published his literary inventions, told originally as stories to the daughter of friends, under the pseudonym Lewis Carroll.
- Especially interesting in the current context are the cases of Stendhal and Voltaire. Voltaire (real name Francois Marie Arouette) wrote under no fewer than 176 different pseudonyms. Stendhal (Marie Henri Beyle) had as many as 200, including Henri Brulard, under which he published his autobiography! Among English novelists, Thackeray probably holds the record, with a portfolio of pseudonyms running to about seventy or so (but clearly well-short of the Stendhal/Voltaire standard).

In lots of these cases, the motives for the use of pseudonyms have been matters of (subsequent) public disclosure by the authors involved. But, of course, such disclosures are not always to be taken at face value. And in many other cases, the motives remain mysterious and can only be the object of speculation. In particular, the use of a very large number of pseudonyms, all for writings that are essentially alike in audience and character, seems bizarre. It is as if the author wished to set aside the benefits of esteem and reputation – for any of the individual personas adopted. Presumably, in some cases, the multiplicity of names is just evidence of a playful spirit. In some, the choice of authorial persona becomes itself an element in the entire fictional effort: an author name operates as a kind of imaginative framing of the larger narrative. Nevertheless, there is a puzzle here for the analysis of esteem, especially in cases where the esteem attached to the pseudonym is considerable.

2.2. Name Changes

Name change is different from the use of a pseudonym because the pseudonymous person operates by their original name in at least some circles. A pseudonym involves in that sense 'multiple identities' among the various publics in which the individual operates. Name change involves the choice of a new identity. A few illustrative examples will again be helpful:

- Joseph Stalin [Iosif Vissarionovich Dzhugashvili], perhaps following Lenin's example, altered his name – probably with an eye to the reference to steel ('stal'). Salience and memorability are relevant characteristics in a name for an overweening ambition, whether on stage or in politics.
- The British Royal family altered their names during the First World War – from Wettin to Windsor, Beck to Cambridge, Battenberg to Mountbatten – to distance themselves from their German cousins (and common

grandfather). In fact they did so remarkably late in the War – after American entry – and reportedly with great reluctance, only after considerable political pressure had been brought to bear.

• Countless immigrants to the United States had name changes thrust upon them by immigration officials impatient with the eccentricities of 'unpronounceable' names. Presumably, some victims were complicit in this process, seeking to establish a more 'local' identity. The practice of Jews changing their names is not unfamiliar and the motivations for doing so presumably reflect a desire for assimilation into 'mainstream' society.

• The ecclesiastical practice (mainly Roman) of individuals changing names as they enter orders, or become popes, is worth noting here. In this context, the name change is taken to be sacramental: it signifies the new identity associated with the 'new life' on which the individual is taken to be embarking. Presumably a similar symbolic element is at stake in the (increasingly contested) practice of women changing surnames at marriage: the change is designed to signify the 'new life' that the partners take on in their joint enterprise. Currently common variants involve both parties altering their names to some amalgam of the originals – often a simple hyphenated version of both surnames – or, occasionally, the male partner taking his wife's surname. This latter practice indicates that, although the tradition of the female partner's identity being absorbed into the male's is now often identified as objectionable on gender-equity grounds, the practice of name change as such can have independent significance.

2.3. Secret Societies

The case of the secret society may seem to be rather different in character from that of individual pseudonyms and name changes, but, from an esteem perspective, there are some significant similarities. Societies, like individuals, can bear reputations; members often derive significant esteem (or disesteem) from the associations of which they are part. When the membership of the society is secret, however, the esteem connections to members are blocked. So, by 'secret' here, we have in mind the case in which the *membership* of the society is secret – not the case in which the existence of the association is secret.

In the case of societies that have a negative reputation, or that have essentially underhand activities to pursue, the reasons for secrecy are clear enough. Members prefer to avoid the disesteem that would attach to them if their membership of the society were known. But not all secret societies are the object of disesteem.

Take two examples. 'The Apostles' at Cambridge University is a society of the putatively most clever and accomplished students at the University. It is a very considerable honour to be a member. But the membership is entirely secret. At least on the face of things, members would seem to do better in the esteem stakes if their membership were to become public. If the desire for esteem is ubiquitous, as we have claimed, why would the individual Apostles rationally forgo esteem they might otherwise accrue? Why would they vote to retain rules of secrecy? The case is, on the face of things, puzzling.

Or consider the Bourbaki case. 'Nicolas Bourbaki' was a collective pseudonym adopted by a group of French mathematicians writing during the 1930s, 1940s, and 1950s. To the scholarly community, it appeared that Bourbaki was a single scholar – and one of very considerable distinction, because much foundational work in algebra was perpetrated at 'his' hands. As in the Apostles' case, those who constituted the Bourbaki membership seem to have forgone much esteem that would have been on offer had their identity been made public. If, as we have claimed, esteem is indeed an object of desire, why the secrecy?

This question seems a serious puzzle for the esteem account, and so we will address it in greater detail in the ensuing three sections. Before doing so, however, it is worth emphasizing that not all name modifications connect to anonymity, either partial or total.

Many name changes seem to be either a quest for something memorable (as in the film star or Stalin examples) or a desire to dissociate from an earlier identity (as in the assimilation cases or more mundane cases of ex-convicts – the Jean Valjean case, to take a literary example). Equally, the desire to associate specifically with a new identity – as in the papal or marital examples. All of these cases can be explained in reputational and esteem terms; they clearly present no challenge to the esteem account.

Equally, where one operates pseudonymously, because the activity in which one is involved is likely to reflect poorly on one's reputation in some other more significant arena, there is no esteem-related puzzle. This is simply a case of partial secrecy, where the secrecy can itself be explained as an esteem-augmenting strategy.[6] The puzzle arises only where the activity is a (possibly significant) source of positive esteem, and yet the pseudonym is retained. This case seems more like the secret society case, and demands further exploration.

3. ANONYMITY AS AN INSURANCE STRATEGY

The first line we take in resolving the question raised is to observe that seeking anonymity, whether in the pseudonym, the name change or the secret society cases, can have important value as an insurance strategy. We

---

[6] Of course, the secrecy does moderate esteem incentives in the performance domain. In the absence of access to a pseudonym, the individual would have been more constrained by prevailing norms.

illustrate the idea with reference to the pseudonym though it clearly extends, with obvious amendments, to the other cases.

Whatever the precise motives for adopting a pseudonym, it is clear that doing so has certain consequences; and one of the more important of these involves attitude to risk. Consider the case mentioned above of Walter Scott. As he embarks on *Waverley*, it is not that he is convinced that the admirers of his poetry will necessarily think that historical novels are an inferior genre. They may; but he just doesn't know. More generally, he doesn't know how the novel will be received. It is an experiment. If it works well, it will doubtless redound to his credit. But if it works badly, his reputation will suffer.

The pseudonym is a mechanism for managing this risk. If the novel is poorly received in general, or if it is poorly regarded by Scott's literary peers, in particular, he can simply give up writing novels and stick to poetry, with no effect on his reputation one way or the other. Or he may continue to write the novels but do so anonymously or pseudonymously (as 'the author of Waverley'). If, on the other hand, the novel is a huge literary success, he can declare his identity and turn to writing novels in a more public way. There is a potential upside to benefit if successful, but no downside loss if not. The pseudonym (or anonym) operates as an insurance policy. Like most insurance policies, it costs something. In Scott's case, for example, his reputation as a poet may well have been expected to sell a few more copies of the book. Forgoing this market advantage is a price that pseudonymity imposes; but it is a small price to pay to avoid the possibility of ridicule from one's peers.

The dictionaries of pseudonyms do not record the (probably vast) number of authors whose pseudonymously written books sold only a few copies and who sank into obscurity. There must have been many. We do not know of them, precisely because their failures as authors were not matters of which they themselves ever made much ado – for good esteem-based reasons. The great advantage of the pseudonym is that it can be discarded should things not work out. Perhaps the failing author will try again under another pseudonym; it can be no advantage to advertise one's work as by the author of some notorious flop. The best strategy seems to be to just move on to another persona until one of one's works takes off. And if no works do take off, we will never hear of the pseudonym, or the real identity that lies behind it.

Of course, once the reputation has been secured, whether pseudonymously or otherwise, the propensity to take risks is largely removed. The pseudonym provides an insurance policy only in the case where one has nothing to lose by failure. Once the reputation is established, a failure costs something in terms of diminished reputation. Even if the reputation attaches only to the pseudonym (so that the author's real identity remains undisclosed), that reputation is still valuable to its generator and still a source of genuine esteem. If one is seriously worried about the success of one's newest book, then one might well choose to write under a different pseudonym from one's earlier successful efforts; but then one forgoes the ex ante reputational advantages for sales. Once the reputation is established, that particular pseudonym cannot act as an insurance policy any further. One might, though, having established a reputation under one pseudonym, use another for one's next book. One can always announce ex post that pseudonym 1 and pseudonym 2 are the same person, even if the real identity remains undisclosed.

There remains an obvious question, however. Why not disclose the real identity? It is hardly surprising that, in cases like Scott's and Hardy's where the risky action paid off, anonymity was immediately discarded. When an insurance policy no longer protects you, it is not sensible to continue to pay the premiums. So though insurance motives can explain the adoption of a pseudonym, they cannot explain the retention of one. For that, we have to look to other considerations. And we shall explore some further possibilities in the ensuing sections.

In the meantime however, we should emphasize that the pseudonym encourages much action that would not be undertaken. We do not know whether Scott would have embarked on the Waverley novels and their sequels if he had not had the protection of doing so anonymously. If prevailing regulations or literary conventions had required total disclosure of authorship, it seems at least conceivable that those novels would never have seen the light of day. In this way, the protection of reputation against failure that the pseudonym provides may well be responsible for much genuine creativity. The pseudonym liberates the author from low-level inhibitions. Of course the fact that access to the pseudonym strategy can be good for literature does not explain its use by the authors concerned. Such explanation has to look to the individual authors' motives – including, specifically, their concern for esteem. On the other hand, the good consequences of pseudonymity in certain contexts might explain why institutional designers and policy makers might want to establish or support the availability of that option.

4. ANONYMITY AS AN ESTEEM-OPTIMIZING STRATEGY

In many, perhaps most, cases in which esteem is attached to an activity, it is somewhat disesteemable to be seen to be pursuing that activity for the express purpose of securing the esteem. 'The general axiom in this domain', as Jon Elster (1983, p. 66) puts it, 'is that nothing is so unimpressive as behaviour designed to impress'. Elster's formulation is, we think, extreme, but there is a partial truth here that needs to be acknowledged. The esteem-maximizer will do well to disguise his motives in lots of cases. There are several reasons why this may be so:

- It may be that the esteem attaches not only to an action, but also to the disposition to undertake that action. So, for example, someone who acts beneficently may be esteemed both because she so acts, and because the action reveals that she is a benevolent person. Suppose we discover of a particular actor that she is acting beneficently mainly to secure esteem. We might, for example, discover that she is much less likely to act beneficently when she believes she is not being observed. She would then receive less esteem from us, and may receive no esteem at all. This may be because we approve of beneficent action and want it to be counterfactually robust (and not just dependent on whether there are people around to applaud). Or it might be that we are attracted to personal qualities intrinsically. Either way, the best strategy for her to maximize her esteem may be for her to disguise her esteem-motives.

* Alternatively and somewhat independently, it may be that people think less well of you when you show off, or blow your own trumpet. A charming modesty is more estimable than an overweaning self-aggrandisement. The eighteenth century satirist, Edward Young, puts the point very neatly: 'The Love of Praise, howe'er conceal'd by art, Reigns, more or less, and glows in every heart: The proud, to gain it, toils on toils endure; The modest shun it, but to make it sure' (Young 1968, pp. 348–349).

If either of these considerations is in play, then the management of one's pursuit of esteem requires some subtlety. If there is literally no audience at all, ever, then one's esteem is restricted to self-esteem. That cannot be best for the esteem-seeker if her performance is such as to justify positive esteem in observers. On the other hand, maximal publicity might not be best either. If one were to be discovered acting in a beneficent way in circumstances where the ex ante chances of detection were low, then the esteem that accrued might well be considerably larger, because observers will believe you to be genuinely benevolent or modest or both. If so, then you have grounds for preferring contexts with somewhat *less* than maximal publicity. Clearly, some trade-off between actual publicity and ex ante probability of being observed is involved here.

A simple model will make the point. Suppose that, in all cases, the probability of being observed is a context-specific parameter, P, and that this probability is always going to be a matter of common awareness. Now, the value of the esteem that will accrue if you are observed is E, and E is negatively related to P: you get more esteem, E, if you act in an environment where you are less likely to be observed. Suppose that as P tends to zero, E takes value A and that when P is one, E takes value B. We take it as given that $A > B$. That is, the esteem that is forthcoming if you are observed is larger the smaller the likelihood ex ante that you would be observed. On this basis,

$$E = A - (A - B) \cdot P.$$

This equation is consistent with our stipulation that when $P = 0$, $E = A$, and when $P = 1$, $E = B$.

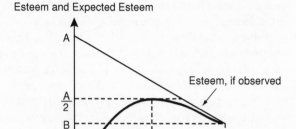

FIGURE 10.1. Optimal probability of being observed.

Now, what value of P_i would maximize expected esteem? On the one hand, esteem is higher if the probability of being observed is lower; but then there is a chance that you won't be observed at all, and then you will not enjoy esteem. So it can't be the case that it is best for you when P is zero. But equally, expected esteem is not necessarily maximized when the probability of being observed is one.

Expected esteem is:

$$P \cdot E = P\{A - (A - B)P\},$$

which is maximized: either when $P = 1$; or when $P = A/2(A - B)$, which value of P we denote P^*.

In this latter case, the optimal value of expected esteem is $A/2$. In the former case, the value of esteem is B. So if $B > A/2$, then it will be desirable to have P as high as possible. But if $B < A/2$, then there is a range where expected esteem and probability of being observed are inversely related.

A diagram may help here. Consider Figure 10.1. On the horizontal axis we show the value of P, ranging from zero to one. On the vertical axis we depict both the value, E, of the esteem accruing, if observed, and the expected value of the esteem – the product of P and E. We can see by appeal to the diagram that if $B < A/2$, we have an interior solution, with P^* less than 1. If $B > A/2$, we have a corner solution in which the highest expected esteem occurs when P is 1. In Figure 10.1, we have shown the former case, where $B < A/2$.

So far, we have taken it that the probability of being observed is an exogenous factor. But individuals can work to alter the probability of being observed; they can thrust themselves into the light – they can blow their own trumpet. Or they can hide their light under a bushel, or modestly change the subject when their accomplishments become the topic of conversation.

These strategies are themselves esteem-relevant: modesty tends to be positively esteemed; self-aggrandisement and bragging tend to be disesteemed.

This fact introduces a further complication. Consider, for example, the case where P happens to fall precisely at P^*. Then the esteem-maximising individual reason will act to *reduce* the probability of being observed, because his modesty will earn him further esteem. Indeed, those incentives will be operative even if P is originally somewhat below P^*, provided that P lies not too far below.[7] At the same time, if P is low, it will pay the esteem-maximising individual to work to increase observability, despite the esteem cost of the self-aggrandising actions involved.

These considerations explain why it may be in the (esteem) interests of an individual to court some measure of secrecy, even when the acts undertaken are esteem-worthy ones. There is no puzzle involved when a person who engages in scurrilous conduct seeks secrecy; such a person has an interest in minimizing the likelihood of discovery. But the thought that secrecy can be an esteem-maximising strategy in cases where the action reflects credit on the actor is a mildly puzzling one. This possibility is, however, perfectly consistent with plausible assumptions about the nature of esteem and its pursuit.

Consider, in the light of this discussion, the situation of a person who writes under a pseudonym and acquires thereby a first-class reputation as an admirable writer. It is not self-evident that the best strategy in maximizing esteem is to declare one's 'true identity' immediately. Perhaps people will think that you are self-aggrandising. Perhaps they will be less inclined to buy your books once it is revealed that their author is just grey old you. Best, of course, if people come to discover that you are the 'famous author' more or less by accident – or later, when you are ready to retire and have built up a reputation, not just for your writing but, by implication, for your modesty. After all, you always have the option of revealing your identity at any point. You can, if you choose to keep your esteem in reserve – stored at the bank rather than spent, as it were. It need not be the best strategy to go public immediately.

5. ANONYMITY AS AN AD HOC STRATEGY

Apart from the general considerations related to insurance and modesty, there is a variety of more or less ad hoc reasons, some more relevant in one of our three sorts of cases than in the others, why people might be prompted to seek anonymity; in particular, why they might be prompted to seek anonymity out of a concern for their esteem and reputation. We look at two.

---

[7] These considerations also bear in the case where $B > A/2$ and hence $P^* = 1$.

5.1. In-Group Esteem

Consider first the case of the secret society. Within any such society, members operate both as performers and as privileged observers. They earn esteem from each other *and from no-one else*. That is, outsiders cannot provide esteem for me by virtue of my being a member of the Bourbaki group, because they don't know that I am one. Keeping membership secret is then a mechanism for declaring to all members that theirs is the only esteem that counts as far as each member is concerned. But this declaration can be a very significant source of esteem to members. It is a commonly observed property of esteem that people especially value the esteem of those that they esteem. Hume (1978, book 2, chapter 9) puts it thus in his discussion of fame: 'though fame in general be agreeable, yet we receive a much greater satisfaction from the approbation of those whom we ourselves esteem and approve of, than of those whom we hate and despise'.

So, when asked to join the secret society, I discover that my esteem matters to these people whom I know I have reason to esteem. And if my esteem matters to them, then that is in itself a source of esteem for me. Further, all members are quite special in this regard. These others whom I esteem apparently care not a whit about the esteem of outsiders; they seem to care only about the esteem they get from me and the other members.

Return now to the pseudonym case. My identity as 'the famous author' is almost always known to *some* people – the editor, my agent, my inner circle of friends and family. And I always have the option of telling the secret to special others, of course swearing them to secrecy in the process. Those in the know form a secret society of a kind. It is not just that they are party to a secret – that they know something that others do not know and perhaps would like to know. It is also that, when I admit them to my inner circle, I declare to them that their esteem is especially valuable to me. Given the reciprocal nature of esteem, this is a signal that I especially esteem them. In this way, secrecy affords me the capacity to give special signals of esteem.

A related benefit of secrecy is that while those who belong with me in a secret society, or those I let know of my fame under a pseudonym, will be bound to respect the confidence involved, they need not be inhibited from speaking well of me more generally. Thus, there can be a powerful benefit in the likely testimony that such people will give me for embracing the hidden bonds that bind me to them. And this benefit is the greater because the testimony thus offered is not seen to redound to their own glory.

5.2. Segmented Audiences

The case of segmented audiences invokes somewhat similar considerations to those already canvassed. Consider the case where A is a good performer in two separate arenas, where those two arenas appeal not just to separate audiences but to somewhat opposing ones. I am a good author, and also Jewish. I recognize well enough that being Jewish is an object of general disesteem in the population in which I am located, or at least is so among some people. Actually I despise such people for their prejudice. And I relish my Jewish identity. On the other hand, I want people to buy my books and to read them 'without prejudice', as we might put it. If it became known in the Jewish community that I was writing as if a gentile, then this would not be approved within that community and might be regarded as outrageous by some.

In such a case, the logic of a pseudonym seems clear. I want to segment the relevant arenas in which I can earn esteem. On the one hand, I want to develop my talent and be appreciated simply as an author. On the other, I want to be recognized as a decent committed member of my cultural and religious community.

This situation arguably describes the George Eliot case. Mary Ann Evans was a controversial individual, with a somewhat dubious public reputation. She was living out of wedlock with a married man; she had strongly expressed unconventional religious views. She was not exactly infamous, but might have become so were she to come to more extensive public attention. Better to avert such a risk by writing under a pseudonym. And better to do so under a pseudonym that does not declare itself immediately as such – such as, 'a Lady', or 'Boz', or 'Publius', or 'Mark Twain' (a name that would have declared its pseudonymous qualities at least to anyone familiar with Mississippi riverboat calls).

Now, it need not be the case that the 'natural audiences' in the two arenas disesteem each other. Perhaps the disesteem is only in one quarter. Or perhaps the disesteem is not general, but only occurs within a minority of those involved in one activity or the other. Still, in these cases, it can be esteem-maximising to segment the audiences, and the pseudonym provides a mechanism for securing that segmentation.

It should also be recognised that audiences sometimes segment naturally. You are, let us suppose, a singer and a golfer, and the overlap between the groups who are expert in these fields, and whose esteem is really worth something, may be very small. Segmentation of audiences just occurs automatically. Nevertheless, your esteem will be magnified if your golfing colleagues are aware that you have some prowess as a singer, and vice versa. Positive esteem is likely to 'compound', in the sense stipulated in the introductory section. In this kind of case, you will not rationally work to keep the audiences separate unless some of the considerations we have explored earlier (secrecy effects, or risk management issue) come into play – or unless golfers tend to hold singers in contempt (and/or vice versa). On the other hand, segmentation in such cases is unlikely to cost you much. If experts count disproportionately for esteem and expert groups are totally disjoint, the 'compounding effect' does not generate much additional esteem – or more accurately, the additional esteem is not worth very much, coming as it does from a group that is uninformed about one or other of your accomplishments.

6. BACK TO THE FUTURE: THE INTERNET CONTEXT

The aim in this chapter has been to explore some of the implications of a desire for esteem and for esteem-based reputation, for the operation of Internet relations.

One of the features, we have said, of Internet relations is that they are often pseudonymous. Many individuals conduct their most significant Internet transactions via e-specific identities. Perhaps in some cases, the adoption of such e-specific identity is necessary because offline names contain too many characters or are not unique; but it is increasingly just an emergent convention. Many of the pseudonyms are clearly recognisable as pseudonyms; names like '#9**ms' or even 'hotchick-in-fairfax' are not for offline use. But there is scope for use of pseudonyms that might be interpreted as 'real' names, and, in this respect, scope for some measure of deception. Such deception possibilities may make one generally anxious about Internet relations.

And there are, of course, contexts in which such anxieties may well be justified. In economic trading settings for example, the rewards of deception can be considerable. And some commentators fear for the long-term viability of e-trading precisely because of these sorts of difficulties with verifying identity.

However, even in these cases, the problems can be overstated. Even in market contexts, agents seem to care about their reputations for trustworthiness and honest dealing as an end in itself (or more accurately, as a means to greater esteem), as well as for economically instrumental reasons. More generally, the Internet seems to be an especially fruitful source of possible esteem. It offers potentially large audiences of an appropriately fine-grained kind. What is crucial, of course, for the effectiveness of esteem on the Internet is that agents care about the reputations that their e-identities secure. The fact that such e-identities are often pseudonymous – and where not, are difficult to check – certainly moderates the forces of disesteem for some range of actions and actors. The kind of anonymity involved means that e-identities that lack reputation have nothing to lose by acting in a disesteemable manner. However, the same is not true for e-identities who have established a reputation already; they have esteem to lose. And even those without a (positive) reputation aspire to have one. Behaving poorly on the Internet always means positive esteem for behaving exceptionally well *forgone*.

And there is no reason to believe that real actors do not care about their virtual reputations. That is something that we think the analogy with the use of pseudonyms in literature establishes quite clearly. There is no reason to think that pseudonymous reputations cannot be a source of esteem to the generator of the pseudonymous material. George Eliot has a reputation as an author; people esteem George Eliot in that connection; and Mary Ann Evans has every reason to care about that reputation and to act in whatever way she can to sustain and augment it. There may be a cost in esteem terms of the pseudonymous strategy, of course – namely, that in the normal case, the esteem that an individual derives from the multitude of activities she engages in tends to be more than the simple sum of separate pieces. I will esteem you more when I observe your estimable qualities across a wide range of arenas. If this is so, then, in the general case, esteem considerations would encourage individuals to operate under a single identity. And the adoption of a separate e-identity might on such grounds be seen to take on a sinister cast.

However, as we have been at pains to show in the forgoing discussion, there can be countervailing, esteem-based reasons for maintaining separate identities – and for a separate e-identity specifically.

For example, having a distinct e-identity can be a risk-management strategy, in the sense that one's offline esteem is protected from the consequences of e-actions. If one's initial e-actions turn out to produce disesteem, the reputational cost is negligible. One can simply jettison that particular e-identity and begin e-life anew with another. The resultant removal of downside risk can be highly liberating. One can be more adventurous, more speculative, in one's initial e-interactions precisely because one's reputation elsewhere is protected. One's inhibitions are lowered. Rather like the eighteenth century masked ball – an institution that seems to have been invented precisely with the intent of lowering inhibitions and promoting general licence – participants do things they would otherwise not do. But in the Internet setting, at least, there seems no general reason to fear the effects of this removal of inhibition. If our reasoning is broadly right, individuals will be seeking positive esteem in their Internet transactions; they will not in most cases be using the cloak of pseudonymity to do outrageous things. But they may well experiment with things that they would be inhibited from pursuing in offline life, and some of those experiments will prove successful. In these successful cases, e-life can have a quality, and constitute a source of considerable positive esteem, that offline life lacks. And indeed, we would expect that most ongoing Internet relations will have these characteristics; those whose e-life does not have them will have less incentive to maintain their e-life.

Of course, once one's e-life proves successful, there will be some incentive to integrate reputations, and the maintenance of separate real and virtual identities seems on that basis to represent a residual puzzle. What we have tried to argue in the forgoing discussion, is that this is less of a puzzle than it might seem. Esteem maximization does not always call for identity integration. And it will be a useful way of summarizing our argument to enumerate the reasons as to why it might not. First, if one's e-reputation is strong and one's offline reputation lacklustre, it may diminish one's overall esteem to integrate online and offline identities. One's online reputation may be damaged by one's offline mediocrity (and, a fortiori, if one's offline reputation is a source of disesteem). Better then to keep one's e-reputation unsullied.

Second, there is some presumption that those who develop online relations will think that online activities are estimable. Not all those who admire you in ordinary life will necessarily share that view. And perhaps not all those who operate on the Internet will think that being a successful stockbroker or a well-reputed clergyman is such a big deal. In all discretionary activities, there is a presumption that those who are involved think the activity to be worthwhile and success in it to be highly estimable. But those not involved may have other attitudes. Perhaps it would be better to keep one's audiences segmented.

Third, even in the contrary case where one's offline and online reputations are rather impressive, declaration might seem to be self-aggrandising and, therefore, serve to diminish one's esteem. Although integration would add to your reputation and esteem overall if it were to occur by accident, deliberate action on your part to bring that integration about, runs the risk of seeming immodest. A little cultivated modesty may be esteem-enhancing.

Finally, retaining separate identities *in general* allows me to share the secret *in particular*. I can admit specially selected e-persons to the inner circle of those who 'know who I really am'; I can reveal to special personal friends my online activities. This can be an added source of esteem to me in itself; but it also provides a source of esteem to *them*, and, thereby, is likely to induce some measure of reciprocal esteem. Effectively, one is creating a kind of small 'secret society' around the dual identities, and secret societies can be the source of special esteem benefits.

The bottom line here is that Internet activities can be a significant source of esteem for those who operate 'well' in virtual space. Agents have reason to care about their e-reputations, even where those reputations attach to a pseudonymous e-specific identity. This being so, the desire for esteem will play a significant role in stabilising decent communication practices and supporting the operation of other social norms on the Internet. In this respect, there is no reason to think that the Internet context will be significantly different from interactions in the 'real' world.

References

Brennan, G., and Pettit, P. 2004. *The economy of esteem: An essay on civil and political society*. Oxford: Oxford University Press.

Carty, T. 1996/2000. *A dictionary of literary pseudonyms in the English language* (2nd ed.). New York: Mansell.

Elster, J. 1983. *Sour grapes: Studies in the subversion of rationality.* Cambridge, UK: Cambridge University Press.

Hume, D. 1978. *A treatise of human nature.* Oxford: Clarendon Press.

Lovejoy, A. O. 1961. *Reflections on human nature.* Baltimore: Johns Hopkins University Press.

Room, A. 1989. *A dictionary of pseudonyms and their origins, with stories of name changes* (3rd ed.). Jefferson, NC: McFarland.

Smith, A. 1759/1982. *The theory of the moral sentiments.* Indianapolis: Liberty Fund.

Young, E. 1968. *The Complete Works, Poetry and Prose* (Vol. 1). J. Nichols (Ed.). Hildesheim: Georg Olms.

11

Culture and Global Networks

Hope for a Global Ethics?

Charles Ess

INTRODUCTION

1. From Global Village to Electronic Metropolis

At the height of 1990s, optimism regarding the rapidly expanding Internet and World Wide Web, Marshall McLuhan's vision of a global village seemed within more or less easy reach. By wiring the world, it was argued in many ways, we would enter into the 'secondary orality of electronic culture' (Ong 1988) and thereby open up an electronic information superhighway that would realize a genuinely *global* village – one whose citizens would enjoy the best possibilities of democratic politics, social and ethical equality, freedom of expression, and economic development.

This optimism, however, was countered by increasing tensions in the economic, political and social arenas between two contrasting developments. On the one hand, the phenomena of globalization – including, for example, growing internationalization and interdependencies of markets – appear to lead to increasing cultural *homogenization*. As terms for this homogenization such as 'McWorld' (Barber 1995) or 'Disneyfication' (Hamelink 2000) suggest, it is strongly shaped by the consumer and entertainment cultures of Western nations. On the other hand, and at least in part in reaction against real and perceived threats to given cultural traditions and identities, new (or renewed) efforts to defend and sustain these identities and traditions were seen by some to lead to fragmentation and indeed violence – most famously and disastrously, of course, in the attacks of September 11, 2001 against the World Trade Towers and the Pentagon.

Indeed, parallel to these real-world developments, a range of emerging research and scholarship began to call into serious question the rosy vision of an electronic global village. To begin with, as the Internet indeed spread rapidly around the globe, it gradually became clear that not every country and culture would embrace without question the *values* at work in the McLuhanesque vision, whether ethical (e.g., rights to freedom of expression), political (e.g., the preferences for democracy and equality), and/or economic (e.g., the belief that untrammeled markets would inevitably lead to greater economic prosperity for all). On the contrary, as a range of *cultural collisions* between Western computer-mediated communication (CMC) technologies and various 'target' cultures make clear, and contrary to the belief that these technologies are somehow neutral – that they serve as mere tools that favor no particular set of cultural values (the claim of technological instrumentalism) – varying degrees of conflict emerged between the cultural values and communicative preferences of a specific culture and those embedded in and fostered by the technologies of the Web and the Net. At the same time, more fruitful *collusions* can be documented in which persons and communities find ways to resist and reshape Western-based CMC, so as to create new, often hybrid systems and surrounding *social contexts of use* that work to preserve and foster the cultural values and communicative preferences of a given culture.[1]

By the same token, research on computer-mediated communication – especially with regard to *virtual communities* and the role of *embodiment* in shaping online practices and behaviors (Ess 2004a) – increasingly argues the point that, contra enthusiasms of the 1990s for a liberation of disembodied (and thereby ostensibly free and equal) minds in cyberspace, our online identities and interactions remain deeply rooted in our identities as embodied members of real-world communities. This means, in turn, that as the Internet and the Web come to connect more and more people and cultures outside their origins in the United States, these domains increasingly reflect an extensive diversity, if not cacophony, of cultural identities, traditions, voices, views, and practices. As Roger Silverstone (2002) has put the point, there is, to be sure, the 'major cosmopolitanism' of global capitalism. But in its shadow, he adds, are the growing 'minor cosmopolitanisms' of diaspora and immigrant communities. Indeed, Stig Hjarvard argues that, instead of the McLuhanesque global village, global media rather effect a cultural and mental urbanization; any emerging 'global' society made possible by the rapidly expanding nets of electronic communication rather resembles a metropolis, not a simple village (Hjarvard 2002).

2. From Computer Ethics to Global Ethics? Convergences, Divergences, and Critical Meta-questions

These distinct but parallel contexts raise questions as old as the Pre-Socratics. Much of Western philosophy revolves around the effort to discern through

---

[1] These collisions and collusions are the focus of my work with Fay Sudweeks (Murdoch University, Australia) in the biennial conferences on Cultural Attitudes towards Technology and Communication (CATaC), first held in London in 1998. For a representative overview of such collisions and collusions as we can now document them from the United States, Europe and Scandinavia, Africa, the Middle East, much of Asia, Australia, and among indigenous peoples, see Ess (2001, 2002a, 2002b) and Ess and Sudweeks (2003, 2005).

reason a view of the universe – including human beings and their social and ethical practices – that might indeed go beyond the *ethos* (originally the habits and practices) of a given *local* community or society (*ethnos* in Greek). From Plato's allegory of the cave (*Republic*, Book VII, 514a/193ff.)[2] through the Stoic vision of the *cosmo-politan* (the 'citizen of the world') to the United Nations Declaration of Universal Human Rights (1948), the hope is that local differences – especially as these foster ethnocentrisms that issue in hatred of 'the other' (including women), bigotry, and war – may be surmounted in a shared *rational* understanding of the world and human nature that might lead to more pacific (indeed, in the modern era, democratic) modes of living with one another.

As the title of the UN Declaration makes explicit, such visions have classically entailed notions of *universally* valid norms and values – that is, norms and values that are ostensibly legitimate and morally compelling for *all* human beings (more or less) in all times and places, not simply the *ethos* of a specific group of human beings in a specific time and place. But of course, the ancient and modern efforts to discern universal values have famously encountered difficulties, as everyone from the sophists through to the postmodernists of the 1990s happily point out. As crystallized, however, in the debate between Jürgen Habermas (defending the possibility of discerning at least quasi-universal norms through the procedures of discourse ethics) and postmodernists such as Lyotard and Foucault (who appear to argue that all norms can be reduced to expressions of power), those who critique the efforts to develop universal norms run the risk of committing us instead to a moral *relativism*. That is, for the ethicists and others, who seek universally valid norms as a basis for a more just and peaceful society, to argue against the possibility of such norms appears to commit one to the view that, because no such universal norms exist, *any* value, or set of values, is as legitimate as any other – relative to a given individual, culture, time/place. As Habermas and others are quick to argue, however, such relativism plays directly into the hands of various authoritarianisms, including fascism (suggested, nicely enough, by the commonplace version of ethical relativism, 'when in Rome, do as the Romans do').[3] By contrast, a central worry of the critics, argued with particular force in postmodernist critiques of the Enlightenment, is that the philosophers' quest for universal values, however benignly intended, will rather degenerate into ethical *dogmatism*,

---

[2] *Republic* references are first to the standard Stephanus pagination, followed by reference to page numbers in Allan Bloom's translation (1991).

[3] John Weckert has offered the further, much more contemporary – and more chilling – example, from no less an expert on fascism than Benito Mussolini: 'If relativism signifies contempt for fixed categories and men who claim to be the bearers of an objective, immortal truth . . . then there is nothing more relativistic than Fascist attitudes and activity . . . From the fact that all ideologies are of equal value, that all ideologies are mere fictions, the modern relativist infers that everybody has the right to create for himself his own ideology and to attempt to enforce it with all the energy of which he is capable' (Veatch 1971, p. 27).

that is, the belief that one value, or set of values, is correct and universally valid for all peoples and all times. Although philosophers, especially in the modern Enlightenment, may intend for universal reason to move us away from the bigotry and warfare affiliated with tribalism and custom, the critics argue that their version of putatively universal values can issue in much the same authoritarianism and intolerance as the more ethnocentric customs and traditions they seek to replace (cf. Ess 1996).

In this light, the cultural conflicts and collusions of computer-mediated communication noted above thus force the meta-ethical question for an information ethics[4] that engages with the issues and topics surrounding computer technologies and networks as global communication media, especially as our efforts to resolve diverse ethical issues evoked by information technologies increasingly implicate a global range of ethical and cultural traditions. Do these efforts point in the direction of genuine universals, and/or do these efforts in fact end in ethical relativism?

In the following I will outline two threads of recent responses to these questions. The first, 'Convergences', is a series of ethical developments and resolutions that establish norms and values as legitimate for more than a single culture or national tradition of ethical decision making. They do so, moreover, by tracing out important *pluralistic* middle grounds between homogenizing universalism and fragmenting relativism. Somewhat more carefully, we will see that such middle grounds are developed in various forms, including what I call Platonic interpretative pluralism, Aristotle's notion of the *pros hen* equivocal, Lawrence Hinman's notion of 'robust pluralism' (as entailing the *possibility* of compatibility) and Charles Taylor's notion of 'robust pluralism' that emphasizes the way(s) in which the strengths of given views, claims, and approaches can offset weaknesses of other views, claims, and approaches as thus conjoined together in a *complimentarity*.[5]

---

[4] As the essays in this volume attest, the literature of computer ethics, especially in the form of information ethics and including research ethics, is growing rapidly. Other authors in this volume will provide a far more comprehensive overview of information ethics than I. For representative work in online research ethics, see Buchanan (2003), Johns, Chen and Hall (2003), Thorseth (2003), and cf. Floridi and Sanders (2004).

[5] My primary use and understanding of the term 'pluralism' begins with what I call 'Plato's interpretive pluralism', developed primarily in the analogy of the line in *The Republic*, as part of his (putative) theory of ideas: just as a single object may cast multiple shadows as it is illuminated by different sources of light – so the Ideas, including the Ideas of the Good, Justice, and so forth – allow for diverse interpretation, understanding, and so forth (pp. 509d–511e). This understanding of the ideas thus demarcates both an epistemological and ethical middle ground between ethical and epistemological relativisms (that assert that diversity and difference can only mean the lack of a single truth/value) and dogmatisms (that insist on the homogenous application of a single ethical value and/or epistemological claim to truth – such that any *different* values and/or truth claims must be wrong/false) (cf. Jones 1969, pp. 126–136). Aristotle systematizes this notion, in turn, in terms of language – specifically with his account of the *pros hen* equivocals. The *pros hen* – 'towards one' – equivocals likewise

What is common to each of these forms of pluralism is their conjunction of the irreducible differences defining diverse traditions, values, interpretations, etc., with a connection, for example, in the form of a shared referent (as in Plato's interpretive pluralism), compatibility (Hinman), or complimentarity (Taylor). In doing so, they avoid both ethical dogmatism that insists on a homogeneous unity (one set of universal values applied without

demarcate a middle ground between homogenous *univocation* (a term can have one and only one meaning) and pure equivocation (a term holds multiple meanings entirely unrelated – sheerly different) from one another. One of his most central examples is the word/reality 'Being': 'there are many senses in which a thing is said to 'be,' but all that 'is' is related to one central point, one definite kind of thing, and is not said to 'be' by a mere ambiguity' (*Metaphysics* 1003a33 (Burrell 1973, p. 84)). This structure of difference (diverse senses/ways of being) and connection (unified through reference to one primary sense/mode of Being) directly echoes Plato's interpretive pluralism used on both epistemological and ontological levels. And for both Plato and Aristotle, these pluralisms are at least intended to hold together both unity and irreducible difference, and thereby to establish a middle ground between unity as sheer homogeneity and irreducible differences thought to exclude all forms of connection and coherency. Such pluralisms subsequently appear in Aquinas and Kant, for example, who follow Plato and Aristotle in seeking to exploit these structures of connection alongside the irreducible differences within their metaphysics (Ess 1983).

More recently, similar pluralisms – apparently related to, if not always explicitly rooted in, these historical antecedents – have emerged as central features of contemporary ethical and political discourse. To begin with, for example, the eco-feminist Karen Warren (1990) and the business ethicist Richard T. De George (1999) argue for pluralisms in ethics that, precisely as I argue here, function as structures of connection and difference that strike a middle ground between ethical relativism and ethical dogmatism. Lawrence Hinman, in particular, seeks to develop what he calls an ethics of 'robust pluralism', one rooted in the work of Bernard Gert and Amélie Rorty, and which ' . . . entertains the possibility not only that we may have many standards of value, but also that they are not necessarily consistent with one another. This position, which we will call *robust pluralism*, does not give up the hope of compatibility, but neither does it make compatibility a necessary requirement' (Hinman 1998, p. 66). (Hinman's chapter 2, pp. 32–71, is especially helpful for its overview of classic and contemporary sources of pluralism in ethics.)

In their anthology, which collects both religious and secular views on pluralism (the most recent and comprehensive treatment of ethical pluralism known to me), Madsen and Strong develop still more fully these contrasts between ethical relativism, ethical dogmatism, and ethical pluralism – distinguishing first of all between levels of ethical pluralism (the existential or individual, the cultural, and the civilizational). Acknowledging that 'ethical pluralism' is itself used in a variety of senses, they suggest that the term be reserved to refer to the cultural level of ethical pluralism, in which incommensurable values and traditions of ethical decision making mark the differences (and sometime agreements) between cultures. 'Culture', in turn, is an exceptionally ambiguous term – one they define here as 'the assemblages of lived practices' (Madsen and Strong 2003, p. 4). In addition, Madsen and Strong argue for an ethical pluralism that seeks to do more than simply acknowledge differences and tolerate these (at least up to a point). Rather, they specifically hope for a robust, positive form of ethical pluralism – one characterized in the work of Charles Taylor, whom they cite as follows: 'The crucial idea is that people can bond not in spite of but because of difference. They can sense, that is, that their lives are narrower and less full alone than in association with each other. In this sense, the difference defines a complimentarity' (Taylor 2002, p. 191, cited in Madsen and Strong 2003, p. 11). As they comment, 'According to this approach one needs to strive qualification equally and everywhere) and ethical relativism (that insists, in effect, that the irreducible differences between diverse ethical traditions, values, etc. forbid any connection or coherency with others whatsoever). At the same time, however, balancing this trajectory towards at least pluralistic forms of universal values and norms is a second series of issues and problems – 'Divergences' – that rather highlight the apparently intractable differences between diverse cultural and ethical traditions.

This approach then seeks to argue that, on the one hand, there are real-world, practical examples of moving beyond the boundaries of a given cultural or ethical tradition, towards at least approximations of *pluralistic* universal values and norms that move beyond relativism while simultaneously avoiding homogenous universals, their affiliated colonizations, and so forth. At the same time, however, the equally significant divergences make the point that any effort to establish such universal norms and values in the domain of information ethics may remain only partly successful and delimited by irreducible differences between diverse cultures that must be acknowledged in the name of respecting cultural integrity. In other words, although the relativist's story is not the whole story, neither is it clearly a false story. More broadly, the tension between pluralistic universals and perhaps irresoluble differences in cultural and ethical traditions means that any hope for a (pluralistic) universal information ethics will only be answered

for a full understanding of the other, because without such an understanding, one cannot truly know oneself'.

J. Donald Moon seeks to provide an overview of the religious and secular perspectives on pluralism represented in this extensive collection, and comments along the way that classical liberalism and critical theory represent the most capacious perspectives on pluralism – but by no means to the exclusion of religious traditions, both East and West, which also, contra their Fundamentalist interpreters, also develop resources for taking up and preserving incommensurable differences (2003, pp. 344f., 350f.). He further characterizes liberalism and critical theory as forms of 'perspectival pluralism' – that is, a form of ethical pluralism that acknowledges the possibility of reasonable disagreement between ' . . . the frameworks within which ethical issues are framed . . . ' (2003, p. 344).

As we will see in what follows, I follow Madsen and Strong, especially with regard to using 'ethical pluralism' to refer to a pluralism that seeks to bridge primarily *cultural* differences. Moreover, my examples of convergences all fit Hinman's definition of robust pluralism, insofar as they outline examples of possible *compatibility* between diverse ethical traditions. My first three examples – Stahl's notion of reflexive responsibility, diverse research ethics traditions, and the resonances between Western virtue ethics/ethics of care and Confucian thought – in fact stand as examples of the robust pluralism described by Charles Taylor, that is, one in which differences can *compliment* one another in crucial ways, rather than merely stand as obstacles to communication, collaboration, and so forth. Finally, the first convergence I examine – that of Bernd Carsten Stahl's notion of reflexive responsibility – specifically entails what Moon calls *perspectival pluralism* as it invokes critical theory the procedural discourse ethics of Habermas. But this means, in fact, a (re)turn to Plato's interpretative pluralism: discourse ethics facilitates precisely the development of norms that are then interpreted, applied, and understood in diverse ways by diverse communities. We will see this interpretive pluralism, in fact, in each of my examples.

by further efforts to determine – in both theory and praxis – whether such an ethics can in fact be established beyond the current, limited successes.

CONVERGENCES?

1. Responsibility As a Unifying Ethical Concept?

In his recent book, Bernd Carsten Stahl seeks to develop a synthesis of especially two distinctive ethical traditions, the German and the French, as part of a larger argument that develops a specific notion of *responsibility* as a key, highly *practical* ethical focus for information ethics (Stahl 2004).

As Stahl characterizes it, the German tradition, exemplified by Kant and Habermas, is strongly *deontological*.[6] Whether in the expression of Kant's Categorical Imperative ('Act only according to that maxim whereby you can at the same time will that it should become a universal law' (Kemerling 2000) or Habermas' discourse ethics as it seeks universal, or at least, quasi-universal (Benhabib 1986, p. 263), norms that emerge from consensus in an ideal speech situation (Habermas 1981, 1983, 1989). German deontological ethics thus stress the development of universal norms, based in reason (Kant) and/or intersubjective rationality (Habermas), that include fundamental rights as rooted in absolute respect for the human *person* as a rational autonomy (cf. Ess 2004b).

---

[6] As Deborah Johnson defines them, 'deontological theories put the emphasis on the internal character of the act itself, and thus focus instead on the motives, intentions, principles, values, duties, etc., that may guide our choices' (Johnson 2001, p. 42). For deontologists, at least some values, principles, or duties require (near) absolute endorsement – no matter the consequences. As we will see in the context of research ethics, deontologists are thus more likely to insist on protecting the fundamental rights and integrity of human subjects, no matter the consequences – for example, including the possibility of curtailing research that might threaten such rights and integrity. Utilitarians, by contrast, might argue that the potential benefits of such research outweigh the possible harms to research subjects: in other words, the greatest good for the greatest number would justify overriding any such rights and integrity.

Of course, these distinctions are not as absolute as they might first appear. On the contrary, it is hard to see, for example, how Kantian deontology can work without considering consequences – that is, whether or not a given act, if universalized, would lead to greater or lesser moral order. And at least since John Stuart Mill, utilitarianism has sought to incorporate at least some aspects of deontological emphases on rights, and so forth (Mill 1913, chapter 1).

Finally, as argued by Hinman (1998) and many others, especially in the real-world, day-to-day experience of making ethical choices, most of us use some mixture of deontology and utilitarianism, using the strengths of one to offset the weaknesses of the other. Such a complimentarity and conjunction of ethical theories, of course, is itself another form of ethical pluralism (see Note 5). Indeed, as we are about to see, Stahl's notion of responsibility, as it conjoins deontology and teleology in ways that the strengths of one offset the weaknesses of the other, provides a specific example of how these two approaches may compliment one another in what Taylor would identify as a robust form of ethical pluralism.

By contrast, Stahl characterizes French ethical tradition, represented by Montaigne and Ricoeur, as a moralism that is first of all skeptical of the possibility of establishing a universal foundation for ethics; rather, ethical norms and values are justified primarily by a *teleological* orientation – what will promote peace and minimize violence? This tradition, with roots in Cicero, stoicism, and Aristotle, for whom *ethics* is concerned with the pursuit of the good life as its teleological goal, at the same time recognizes more deonto-logical forms of duties and obligations – namely those that are necessary for members of a society to pursue their conceptions of the good life without interference and/or with the assistance of others. Nevertheless, on Stahl's showing, this deontological dimension is subordinated to the teleological; that is, in contrast to the German tradition, which begins with universal duties and rights as a framework defining any individual pursuit of the good life, French moralism reverses this to make teleological goals primary, as these then define duties and rights as necessary conditions for achieving those goals (see Stahl 2004, chapter 3).

Despite these contrasts – along with that represented, finally, by the even more teleological emphases of Anglo-American utilitarianism – Stahl nonetheless argues that a notion of reflexive responsibility can bridge these otherwise diverse traditions. I cannot do justice in this space to Stahl's argument, but, for our purposes, it suffices to note that his concept of responsi-bility conjoins both teleology (e.g., the intended outcomes or consequences of those acts for which one is responsible) and deontology (beginning with precisely the recognition that, whatever else one may think about ethics, etc., people are responsible for their decisions and acts). Moreover, his notion takes up the formalistic character of especially Habermasian dis-course ethics, insofar as specific notions of individual and corporate respon-sibility, of the good life as pursued by the individual and/or the corporation and of the means for achieving these goals are *not* prescribed, but are rather left free to emerge from the communicative processes at work in developing these notions (see Stahl 2004, chapter 4).

If Stahl's notion of responsibility succeeds as intended, then it will stand as an important example of an ethical concept that manages to move beyond the boundaries of at least three major ethical traditions and cultures. In doing so, it would serve as an important counterexample to the claims of ethical relativism – that is, that norms and values are entirely defined within and thus relative to a specific culture or tradition. Rather to the con-trary, Stahl's notion of responsibility would support especially the Stoic and Enlightenment projects, exemplified in Kant and Habermas, of establishing universal norms based on reason.[7]

---

[7] For additional notions of responsibility intended to function on a global scale, see O'Neill (2001) and Scheffler (2001). Although significant and influential, however, both develop notions of responsibility that seem more straightforwardly universalistic rather than

Moreover, Stahl's notion stands as a significant example of robust ethical pluralism along the lines described by Charles Taylor (2002).[8] That is, Stahl moves us from the simple differences between German, French, and Anglo-American ethical traditions to a notion of responsibility that seeks to use elements of each in *complimentary* ways. Most centrally, his conjunction of teleology with deontology first offsets the tendency of deontologies, in their emphases on rights, duties, obligations, etc. to downplay the consequences of ethical decisions; at the same time, the inclusion of deontology offsets the tendency of consequentialist theories to override basic rights in the name of the greater good for the greater number.

Finally, Stahl's account of responsibility, as appropriating the procedural approach of critical theory, thereby allows it to function as what I have called an interpretive pluralism – one that facilitates the developments of diverse understandings, interpretations and applications of a shared notion of responsibility: see especially his chapter 6 for examples of how this notion may be applied in diverse contexts (Stahl 2004, pp. 153–215).

2. A Global Research Ethic?

In December 2000, the Association of Internet Researchers (AoIR) began developing ethical guidelines for online research. Despite the realities of the digital divide, the Internet has grown rapidly from a communication technology dominated by the U.S. middle class to an increasingly global medium.[9] Thus, the original members of the AoIR ethics working committee represented eleven countries, including Thailand and Malaysia. The charge of the committee – to develop ethical guidelines that recognized and respected the intractable differences as well as agreements between the traditions of research ethics in the United States, the United Kingdom, the European Union and Scandinavia, and Asia – was thus shaped from the outset by a still broader cultural and ethical scope than we find in Stahl.

In point of fact, over the following two years, a set of guidelines emerged that reflected consensus among the AoIR ethics working committee and

pluralistic in the fashion developed by Stahl. That is, O'Neill and Scheffler appear to argue for single conceptions that should apply universally, but which do not seem to allow for pluralism in the form of diverse interpretation, understanding, and application of these conceptions. I am grateful to John Weckert for pointing me to these sources.

[8] See Note 5.

[9] As late as 1998, about 85 percent of all Internet users resided within the United States: of these, 87 percent were white and 66 percent were male. The considerable majority (ca. 68 percent) enjoyed household incomes of $30,000/year or greater: the 17.3 percent who did not report income thus left a user base of 14.8 percent from households with less than $30,000/year (GVU Center 1998). By contrast, according to current estimates, there are now more people in Asia and the Pacific Rim using the Internet (187.24 million) than in the Northern Hemisphere (182.67 million), its source and origin (NUA 2003).

was approved by the AoIR membership in November 2002 (AoIR 2002; cf. Ess 2003; NESH 2003). This achievement in marking out the first international guidelines for online ethics, of course, required successfully resolving a range of significant differences in the ethical traditions of various countries. For example, it became clear that the United States and the European Union approached these issues in distinctive ways. As a primary example, the European Union has developed data privacy protection laws that emphasize the primary rights of the individual to privacy and control over his or her personal data (European Parliament 1995). Within the context of research ethics in particular, these laws lead to a strong emphasis on such standard Human Subjects Protections as guarantees of anonymity, confidentiality, informed consent, and so forth, including the requirement that personal data collected in the European Union *not* be transmitted to countries with less stringent data privacy protection. As researchers know from experience, however, following the ethical requirements of Human Subjects Protections often conflicts with the design of specific research projects. For example, informed consent is notoriously difficult to acquire especially in the context of Internet research – as it is in more traditional research, for example, when working with children. These difficulties occasionally force researchers into the difficult ethical dilemma: to fulfill the Human Subjects Protections requirements may make their research, and its potential benefits, impossible to pursue. In the face of this conflict, the European Union Data Privacy Protection laws and other national ethical codes for research such as the Norwegian research guidelines (NESH 2001) – take a *deontological* stance: the rights of individuals must be protected, *no matter the consequences* (including the loss of the research project and its potential benefits). By contrast, a *utilitarian* approach would consider rather whether violating these rights would be justified if the *consequences* of doing so – primarily in the form of potential benefits to individuals and society at large to be gained by research – were by some calculus to outweigh the 'costs' of violating such rights. In point of fact, although the United States certainly has its own tradition of Human Subjects Protection codes (most importantly, the Code of Federal Regulations (National Institutes of Health, Office of Human Subjects Research 2005), both law and practice in the United States takes a utilitarian approach that emphasizes *not* absolute protection of human autonomy, privacy, etc., but rather, minimizing the *risks* to these basic rights in research – ostensibly because such risks, if kept minimal, are thereby outweighed by the social benefits of research.

This contrast can be seen still more sharply vis-à-vis the Norwegian research guidelines, as these require researchers to respect not only the individual, but also 'his or her private life and close relations' (NESH 2001). That is, the researcher must consider the possible harms that might come to both the individual *and* his or her close relations if personal information were to become public. By contrast, U.S. law and practice requires researchers to consider *only* the possible harms that such publication of personal information would entail for the *individual.*

This large contrast between a U.S. preference for *utilitarian* approaches and European and Scandinavian emphases on *deontological* approaches has been noted by other ethicists (e.g., Burkhardt, Thompson, and Peterson 2002, p. 329). In particular, Aguilar (2000) observes that this contrast reflects a U.S. orientation towards *utilitarian* interests in sustaining a strong economy. That is, as weaker U.S. laws favor the economic interests of corporations over the rights of the individual, they present to U.S. corporations fewer obstacles to economic activity and competition. From a *laissez-faire* free-market perspective, greater economic activity and competition will generate the greatest good for the greatest number in terms of economic efficiencies, growth, and so forth.[10] By contrast, greater *deontological* emphasis on basic human rights to autonomy, privacy, confidentiality, etc. in Europe and Scandinavia insists that these rights cannot be put at risk (even minimal risk) for the sake of larger benefits, whether social, economic, or scientific.

At first glance, then, it would appear that there is a deep, perhaps intractable ethical divide between the United States and the European Union. For the ethical relativist, this divide stands as but one more example of significant ethical difference between diverse nations and cultures, and thus as support for the claim that there are no universal values; rather, values and norms are legitimate solely in relation to a given culture or tradition. By contrast, the ethical dogmatist would be forced to assume an either/or. Given that there can be only one universal set of codes and values, this conflict means that one approach must be right and the other wrong.

But again, there is a middle ground between these positions – namely, an interpretive ethical *pluralism* that takes the view that *some* value(s) are arguably more legitimate than others, and that many apparent ethical

---

[10] Joel Reidenberg has further described this contrast as one between 'liberal, market-based governance or socially protective, rights-based governance.' (2000, p. 1315)

In particular, the European model is one in which 'omnibus legislation strives to create a complete set of rights and responsibilities for the processing of personal information, whether by the public or private sector. First Principles become statutory rights and these statutes create data protection supervisory agencies to assure oversight and enforcement of those rights. Within this framework, additional precision and flexibility may also be achieved through codes of conduct and other devices. Overall, this implementation approach treats data privacy as a political right anchored among the panoply of fundamental human rights and the rights are attributed to "data subjects" or citizens' (p. 1331f). By contrast, the United States' approach presumes that 'the primary source for the terms and conditions of information privacy is self-regulation. Instead of relying on governmental regulation, this approach seeks to protect privacy through practices developed by industry norms, codes of conduct, and contracts rather than statutory legal rights. Data privacy becomes a market issue rather than a basic political question, and the rhetoric casts the debate in terms of 'consumers' and users rather than 'citizens' (p. 1332). Again, this latter approach appears in ethical terms to be a *utilitarian* approach that emphasizes the greater social benefit of a robust economy over possible risks to individual privacy.

differences reflect diverse *interpretations, applications* and/or *understandings* of a *shared* value. Again, such pluralism seeks to establish a middle ground between ethical relativism (and fragmentation) and moral absolutism (and ethnocentrism/colonization).

Such a pluralism is argued, to begin with, by Reidenberg (2000), as he shows that these differences in fact reflect a 'global convergence' on what he calls the First Principles of data protection.[11] On this argument, the differences between the United States and the European Union amount to differences in how each society will implement and apply the *same* set of shared values (first of all, privacy and informed consent) – differences he characterizes in terms of '... either [current U.S.-style] liberal, market based governance or [current E.U.-style] socially protective, rights-based governance' (2000, p. 1315). In the same way, Diane Michelfelder shows the ways in which a *shared* conception of fundamental human rights – conceptions articulated both in the 1950 European Convention for the Protection of Human Rights and in the U.S. Constitution itself – roots both U.S. and European law on data privacy (Michelfelder 2001, p. 132).

In light of these arguments, the significant differences between diverse national and cultural ethical traditions are thus encompassed within a larger framework of interpretive pluralism, one in which these differences constitute different interpretations and applications of shared values and norms. Such shared values and norms thus approximate a more universally valid set of norms and values, countering the relativist's claim that no such values and norms exist. At the same time, however, recognizing the legitimacy

---

[11] Reidenberg argues that these First Principles 'revolve around four sets of standards: (1) data quality; (2) transparency or openness of processing; (3) treatment of particularly sensitive data, often defined as data about health, race, religious beliefs and sexual life among other attributes; and (4) enforcement mechanisms' (2000, p. 1327). These include, in particular, the ten elements recommended by the 1972 Younger Committee in the United Kingdom, namely that an organization:

Must be *accountable* for all personal information in its possession;
Should *identify the purposes* for which the information is processed at or before the time of collection;
Should only collect personal information with the *knowledge and consent* of the individual (except under specified circumstances);
Should *limit the collection* of personal information to that which is necessary for pursuing the identified purposes;
Should not use or disclose personal information for purposes other than those identified, except with the consent of the individual (the *finality principle*);
Should *retain* information only as long as necessary;
Should ensure that personal information is kept *accurate, complete and up to date*;
Should protect personal information with appropriate *security safeguards*;
Should be *open* about its policies and practices and maintain no secret information systems; and
Should allow data subjects *access* to their personal information with an ability to amend it if necessary.

of interpreting and applying these norms and values through the lenses of diverse ethical and cultural traditions thereby preserves the integrity of these traditions, countering the dogmatist's insistence that moral legitimacy can be achieved only through agreement upon a single set of norms and values. In this way, ethical pluralism steers a middle course between sheer relativism (and fragmentation) and a universalism that, as monolithic and dogmatic, is historically affiliated with intolerance, homogenization, and colonization.

Both Stahl's notion of responsibility and the AoIR guidelines, along with the examples discussed by Reidenberg and Michelfelder, thus stand as significant examples of resolving distinctive ethical traditions within diverse cultures and countries into larger frameworks of interpretive (and sometimes robust, complimentary) ethical pluralism. But, as powerful as these examples may be, they remain squarely within a Western cultural framework and thus force the question: Is it possible to find analogous pluralisms that might resolve the still greater ethical differences between East and West[12] – again, pluralisms that would run between sheer relativism and dogmatism?

3. Convergence re Virtue Ethics/Ethics of Care – Confucian Ethics

Building on the insights of philosophers working especially in phenomenological traditions (Borgmann 1999; Becker 2000, 2001, 2002; Dreyfus 2001) and others (e.g., Hayles 1999), I have argued that there is a turn in contemporary philosophy and the literature of computer-mediated communication

---

[12] It must be stressed that such cultural generalizations, beginning with the very categories 'Western' and 'Eastern', are highly problematic. To begin with, even as geographical references, they are themselves, of course, thoroughly relative. That is: despite their appearance as 'objective' – because ostensibly rooted in the facts of geography – the terms rather have meaning primarily as defined by the standpoint/location of the observer/speaker (Hongladarom 2004; cf. Solomon and Higgins 1995, pp. xxxviii–xlii). More specifically, post-colonial and post-post-colonial studies have amply demonstrated that these terms are primarily the product of 'Western' colonialism from the late 1400s CE through the conclusion of the Cold War. Such studies rightly challenge these categories and hope to create new frameworks that more faithfully reflect the beliefs, practices, and traditions of specific peoples and cultures. At this time, however, no agreement on such a framework has yet emerged. Therefore, I use the terms 'East' and 'West' here only as convenient shorthand. I hope to offset the risk of re-instantiating an untenable and misleading distinction by using it only to introduce a discussion focused more narrowly on differences at a much more specific level. So, in the example of *convergence* we're about to take up, I will discuss Socratic and Aristotelian virtue ethics, feminist ethics of care, and Confucian ethics as important examples of what can be initially characterized as Western and Eastern ethical traditions. Similarly, in the third example of *divergence*, I will take up Danish privacy law vis-à-vis research ethics in Japan and Thailand, as particular examples of a greater emphasis on consensus among the larger group often associated with Eastern societies vis-à-vis a more individualist orientation associated with Western societies.

from a Cartesian/modern conception of human beings as minds radically divorced from bodies (a view apparent especially in 1980s' and 1990s' visions of 'liberation in cyberspace') *to* nondual conceptions. These nondual conceptions, as Barbara Becker's neologism 'BodySubject' (LeibSubjekt) suggests, stress that our understandings of self and personal identity are inextricably interwoven with our bodies as possessed of their distinctive materiality (according to Becker), as defining the centering point of our perspectival experience of the world, and as the vehicle through which we 'get a grip' on the world (Dreyfus 2001; Ess 2004a; cf. Barney 2004).

An important consequence of this turn from Cartesian modernity is that these nondual understandings of human beings allow us to return to older, pre-modern conceptions of human beings, such as those developed by Socrates and Aristotle. At the same time these nondual understandings of human beings thereby cohere more directly with especially Socratic and Aristotelian virtue ethics, as well as more contemporary ethics of care as elaborated by feminists, beginning with Carol Gilligan (1982). (See Rachels 1999, pp. 162–174, and Boss 2004, pp. 212–217, 396–405, for an overview and suggestions for further reading). Moreover, following the works of a number of comparative philosophers (for example, Ames and Rosemont 1998; Yu and Bunnin 2001; Li 2002), I have argued that in doing so, this turn simultaneously brings Western ethical reflection closer to those Eastern traditions that likewise build ethical considerations on nondual conceptions of human beings – most notably, for my purposes, Confucian thought.

To take a first example: both Socratic virtue ethics and Confucian thought emphasize first of all the importance of seeking virtue – excellence or *arête* – first. So the *Analects* tell us:

4.5 The Master said, 'Wealth and honor are what people want, but if they are the consequence of deviating from the way (*dao*), I would have no part of them. Poverty and disgrace are what people deplore, but if they are the consequence of staying on the way, I would not avoid them'.

And:

4.11: The Master notes, 'Exemplary people cherish their excellence; petty persons cherish their land. Exemplary persons cherish fairness; petty persons cherish the thought of gain'.

In the same way, Socrates insists on putting the pursuit of excellence before the pursuit of wealth,

I have gone about doing one thing and one thing only – exhorting all of you, young and old, not to care for your bodies or for money above or beyond your souls and their welfare, telling you that virtue does not come from wealth, but wealth from virtue (αρετε), even as all other goods, public or private, that man can need (*The Apology*, 29d–30b: cf. *The Republic*, 608b/291 and 618b–619a/301).

Broadly, then, both Confucius and Socrates focus on ethics as a matter of achieving human excellence as embodied human beings – that is human beings both capable of excellence and subject to death.

As a second point: Tu Wei-Ming shows that the Confucian emphasis on *embodied* humanity further entails an understanding of the self as a *relational* self – that is, one inextricably interrelated with community, nature, and Heaven (*Tian*) (Tu 1999, p. 33). From this follows the primary Confucian *ethos* of filial piety, 'as an authentic manifestation of embodied love'. Filial piety, as refracted through these nodes of interrelationship, then expresses itself in the primary postures of *gratitude* and *thanksgiving* 'to those to whom we owe our subsistence, development, education, well-being, life and existence', namely, 'Heaven, Earth, Ruler, Parents and Teachers' (Tu 1999, p. 34). There is thus a close resonance between a Western ethics of care and the Confucian *ethos* of a sense of fidelity and fiduciary responsibility to a community that begins in family and ultimately encompasses the world (Tu 1999, p. 35).

Of course, the complexities and difficulties of comparisons of this sort are well known. As a rule, first of all, such apparent resonances will always be accompanied by important differences as well (Pohl 2002; Gupta 2002). Even so, at least some of these differences may be seen to be complimentary, rather than oppositional. For example, in his analysis of Aristotelian virtue ethics and the Confucian notion of *ren*,[13] Ji-Yuan Yu suggests that, just as 'an Aristotelian revival would do well to borrow the Confucian insight of filial love, a Confucian revival could hardly be constructive without developing an Aristotelian function of rationality in weighing and reanimating the tradition' (Yu 2003, p. 30). In this way, Yu again supports the resonance and *complimentarity* between the Confucian stress on filial love and a Western ethics of care that we see in Tu and is further developed by Henry Rosemont (2001).

Indeed, this impulse towards complimentarity is itself an expression of the Confucian *ethos* as an orientation towards harmony (*he*) rather than sameness (Analect 13.23).[14]

Although striking, these resonances between Eastern and Western ethics of care have not been applied, to my knowledge, to matters of online

---

[13] As Ames and Rosemont put it, '*ren* is one's entire person: one's cultivated cognitive, aesthetic, moral, and religious sensibilities as they are expressed in one's ritualized roles and relationships. It is one's 'field of selves', the sum of significant relationships, that constitute one as a resolutely social person. *Ren* is not only mental, but physical as well: one's posture and comportment, gestures and bodily communication' (1998, p. 49).

[14] As Ames and Rosemont note with regard to Analect 1.12: 'Ancestor reverence as the defining religious sensibility, family as the primary human unit, authoritative humanity (perhaps more literally, 'co-humanity,' *ren*) and filiality (*xiao*) as primary human values, ritualized roles, relationships and practices (*li*) as a communal discourse, are all strategies for achieving and sustaining communal harmony (*he*)' (1998, p. 30).

research. But just such an application, as a way of testing theory through *praxis* (an approach, moreover, consistent with both Aristotelian and Confucian thought), would be an important step in further development of a global ethics. Absent such a development, these resonances nonetheless stand as an important counterexample to the relativist's claim that no universally valid values and norms may be found. On the contrary, these resonances stand as important convergence points for human, and 'cooperatively humane' (*ren*), ethics – that is, shared points of focus that go beyond even the considerable boundaries of classical China and ancient Greece. At the same time, these resonances fail to collapse into a single monolithic ethical standard as sought by the ethical dogmatist. That is, as with the earlier pluralisms we have seen, these resonances – including a strong complimentarity – between Confucian ethics and Western ethics of virtue and care likewise constitute a pluralism, one that is first of all an instance of Platonic interpretive pluralism, as well as of Aristotle's *pros hen* equivocal: the considerable difference between Western and Eastern forms of virtue ethics and ethics of care are balanced precisely by a shared focus (*pros hen*) on human excellence and care. Their complimentarity, moreover, thus instantiates the sort of robust pluralism hoped for by Charles Taylor. In these ways, these pluralisms again constitute a middle ground between the sheer fragmentation of ethical relativism and the monolithic universalism of ethical dogmatism (cf. Boss 2004, pp. 383–419).[15]

[15] We can amplify these resonances in at least two additional ways. To begin with, Chan points out that 'Insofar as the framework of *ren* and rites remains unchallenged, Confucians are often ready to accept a plurality of diverse or contradicting ethical judgments' (2003, p. 136). Indeed, Chan's description of how this can occur is strongly reminiscent of what I have called Plato's interpretive pluralism – that is, that the same ethical standard (in this case, *ren*) can be interpreted, applied, or understood in more than one way: 'If after careful and conscientious deliberation, two persons equipped with *ren* come up with two different or contradictory judgments and courses of action, Confucians would tell us to respect both of the judgments' (2003, p. 137). Insofar as this understanding of possible diversity of judgments regarding the application/interpretation/application of the same ethical standard indeed parallels the Platonic example (as well as Aristotle's notion of *phronesis*, the practical judgment whose task is precisely to determine how to best apply such standards), then we see here a further element of ethical pluralism *between* these two traditions – that is, precisely as both share an understanding of the possibility of ethical pluralism *within* each tradition, as each recognizes the possibility of an interpretive pluralism that applies and interprets central ethical standards in different ways.

A similar ethical pluralism *between* these two traditions holds at the meta-ethical level. As Elberfeld points out, notions of harmony and resonance appear within Western traditions, beginning with the Pythagoreans and including Socrates' comments about music and education in *The Republic*, 401d (cf. 443d) *and* East Asian traditions, including just the notion of harmony [*he*] that we have seen to be central to Confucian thought (Elberfeld 2002). Moreover, in both traditions, these notions of harmony and resonance – as notions of *different* musical notes that, as harmonious and/or resonant, thereby compose a unity that includes their irreducible difference – serve as metaphors and analogues to the notions of ethical pluralism (precisely as structures of unitary foci that include diverse, even contradictory,

4. Convergences 'on the Ground'? – Emerging Notions of Privacy in China and Hong Kong

Information ethics is a comparatively young field in both Japan and China – the first book devoted to Chinese information ethics was published in 2002 (Lü 2002). Even so, the central topics of emerging conceptions of privacy and data privacy protection laws provide a striking example of pluralism across the differences between Eastern and Western approaches.

Broadly speaking, 'privacy' is a distinctively Western cultural value, affiliated with individual rights, rule of law, and limited government as defining elements of liberal democratic societies (Ramasoota 2005). Indeed, the very term 'privacy' is introduced, for example, into Thai and Japanese, as a loan word. Not surprisingly, the justifications for privacy, and thus data privacy protection, in Western countries such as the United States and Germany are *almost* entirely incompatible with the cultural and political traditions of many Asian countries. Briefly, these justifications center on privacy as necessary for developing a sense of an autonomous self, where such autonomy and allied rights to freedom of expression, and so forth are seen as the elements necessary for human beings if they are to function effectively as citizens in liberal democratic societies (Johnson 2001; Bizer 2003). Nevertheless, at least limited rights to privacy, including data privacy rights, have been gradually recognized by both China and Hong Kong. In both cases, the primary justification for such privacy rights is their necessity for the sake of developing e-commerce (Tang 2002; Chen 2005).

Ole Döring has observed that 'China has engaged in formulating, and has eventually accepted, the main relevant international declarations and guidelines in bioethics and medical ethics' as these have been required by its recent admittance to the World Trade Organization. But in doing so, 'China attempts to build the new regulations based on a universal common ground – yet with 'Chinese particularities' – to honour the special features of China's culture and society' (2003, p. 233). Such a conjunction of both initially Western conceptions of Human Subjects protections with distinctively Chinese approaches (recognizing first of all the 'co-relational' sense of the person (Döring 2003, p. 235f)) is a clear example of the sort of ethical *pluralism* that I have identified with Plato and Aristotle – one that sees basic values agreements nonetheless implemented in diverse ways as these values are refracted through the specific practices and traditions of diverse cultures. Similarly, it appears that the emerging conceptions of privacy and data privacy protection in China and Hong Kong are both recognizably 'Western' in their efforts to provide some measure of protection to personal information in online contexts such as banking, purchasing, and so

interpretation). This shared understanding of notions of harmony and resonance *between* these two traditions thus stands as still another element of ethical pluralism between the two.

forth, and distinctively Chinese and Hong Kongese in their justifications and implementations, as these remain strongly tied to and shaped by the specific cultural, historical, political, and legal traditions of each country. These emerging elements of information ethics in China and Hong Kong thus support a pluralistic resolution to the tension between preserving local cultural traditions and more global ethical norms – precisely between the rather large divide between Western and Eastern countries.

CHALLENGES TO GLOBAL ETHICS

These important ethical convergences – in particular, in the form of a pluralism that conjoins diverse implantations with agreement on shared values – stand as significant examples of convergences of either actual or potential use in a global information ethics. At the same time, however, there remains a series of deep conflicts and divergences in global ethics that may resist pluralist interpretation and, thereby, counter the optimistic view that a global ethics might be developed.

1. Divergences: Technology Assessment

As I have argued elsewhere (Ess 2004b), the divide between deontological and utilitarian approaches remains especially sharp in the area of technology assessment (TA). Briefly, TA grows out of the recognition that, in a democratic society, citizens have the right to shape important decisions concerning those developments that affect them in important ways. In societies deeply shaped by new technologies, citizens thereby should have considerable decision-making power over the development and deployment of these technologies. TA takes central expression in consensus conferences, as first developed in the United States in the 1970s and then in Europe, beginning in Denmark (Jacoby 1985; Fixdal 1997). These conferences are constituted by carefully structured study and dialogue among lay persons, political representatives, and experts from the sciences and business, and have focused on the ethical issues evoked by the Human Genome Project and the development of genetically modified foods, as well as issues in information technology (Anderson and Jæger 1997).

Interestingly, a number of philosophers have argued that such consensus conferences are at least imperfect realizations of a Habermasian discourse ethics (e.g., Skorupinski and Ott 2002). Such conferences can be documented precisely in the Germanic countries (e.g., beyond Denmark, the Netherlands (Keulartz et al. 2002), Austria (Torgersen and Seifert 1997), Norway (Sandberg and Kraft 1997)). Somewhat more broadly, these conferences reflect what is now a recognizably deontological commitment to the basic rights and duties of citizens in a democratic society over more utilitarian concerns, say, for example, for market efficiencies. So, for example, in their description of the frameworks of Danish consensus conferences, Anderson and Jæger observe that 'market forces should not be the only forces involved' in decisions regarding the design and deployment of information technology. Rather, such design and deployment must further observe the deontological values of 'free access to information and exchange of information' and 'democracy and individual access to influence' (1997, p. 151). To say it another way, such consensus conferences exemplify what Reidenberg has described precisely as the European emphasis on 'socially-protective, rights-based governance', in contrast with U.S. utilitarianism, including strong preferences for market-oriented approaches.

Consistent with these differences, the United States abolished its federally funded Office of Technology Assessment in 1997. By contrast, the European Union continues to fund important initiatives in TA, including issues surrounding human cloning, stem cell, and cloning research, as well as research ethics (primarily biomedical ethics (europa.eu.int/comm/research/science-society/ethics/rules_en.html)). Whether or not these differences can be resolved, as Reidenberg has argued in the case of information ethics, into a pluralism that holds the U.S. and E.U. approaches in a larger framework of shared norms and values remains very much an open question – not only in ethical, but also in political terms.

2. Online Research: National Differences Revisited – The RESPECT Guidelines

By the same token, a current European Commission project to develop guidelines for socioeconomic research – the RESPECT Project (2004) – illustrates a similar tension between the *deontological* traditions of especially the Germanic countries and the more *utilitarian* tradition of the United Kingdom.

In their current form, the guidelines begin with professional ethics (my term) – that is, the obligations of professional researchers to uphold the standards of scientific research. The guidelines then emphasize the importance of compliance with the law, including relevant data protection and intellectual property laws. In contrast with what thus might be taken as *deontological* emphases, the guidelines then turn to a *utilitarian* discussion of the importance of minimizing risks and avoiding social harm in the pursuit of research that presumably has social benefit. Finally, the guidelines recognize the *deontological* obligation to uphold standard Human Subjects protections, for example, voluntary participation, informed consent, protection of the vulnerable, the (Habermasian point) that all relevant stakeholders' views and interests must be taken into account, and, finally, that research results are disseminated in a manner that is accessible to relevant stakeholders.

It appears that the RESPECT guidelines thus intend to incorporate *both* deontological and utilitarian approaches – ostensibly in the effort to recognize the legitimacy of the range of ethical approaches and traditions at work in the European Union. If the guidelines are indeed adopted by the European Commission, then arguably they will have succeeded in striking the necessary balance to achieve consensus among researchers in the European Union. In this direction, the RESPECT guidelines would then stand as another important example of a *convergence* that resolves national and cultural traditions within a larger consensus framework.

At the same time, however, the RESPECT guidelines themselves contrast with other national guidelines – most notably, the NESH guidelines (2001). Although the RESPECT guidelines acknowledge the *utilitarian* consideration of seeking only to *minimize* risk to research subjects, the NESH guidelines emphasize the absolute *deontological* importance of protecting human subjects *and* their close relations, *no matter the consequences* of doing so (including possible loss of research). In this way, the NESH guidelines clearly reflect the Norwegian cultural emphases on deontological ethics and the importance of the community in the form of the 'web of relationships' connected to a given individual.

Whether or not these differences may be resolved within a larger framework of research ethics remains an open question.

3. Divergences East–West – A Case Study in Research Ethics

In light of these stubborn differences within Western cultures and traditions, it is not surprising that even greater differences can be found between Eastern and Western approaches. One way of illustrating these differences is with a recent example of a project proposed by an Asian researcher.[16]

In this project, a mobile service provider wants to determine what service(s) of next-generation networks will be attractive to consumers, in order to help guide the company to develop and market the most successful products. To accomplish this, the researcher proposes developing an online game that invites users/consumers to play with a range of possible services – perhaps with a lottery prize as an incentive. Before users/consumers are allowed to play the game, however, they must first provide personal information, including age, education, gender, profession, and income. This information will be used as demographic information vis-à-vis the preferences users subsequently express for a given possible product. No IP addresses or other information will be collected that could be used to identify specific individuals. Consumers are never told why this information is collected – that is, that it is to help the company design products and services deemed

---

[16] This example is based on a student project developed at IT-University during the fall of 2003. I have anonymized it and presented it in the form seen here to the project developer who has kindly granted permission to use this example here. See Note 13 for the provisos regarding use of the terms 'East'and 'West'.

desirable. They are neither asked for their consent to use this information in this way, nor are they assured that this information will be protected in any way. Such a design, for what appears to be a free online game that actually works to collect demographic information and consumer preferences that will, in the first instance, benefit the company, is morally unproblematic in the home country of the company involved.

To begin with, this project may seem ethically unproblematic within a Western framework. Because it does *not* collect clearly personal information (names, addresses, etc.), it may not seem to constitute a threat to the basic human subjects rights to personal privacy, autonomy, and confidentiality. At the same time, however, such a design raises other ethical concerns – for example, that it fails to provide explicit information regarding the purpose of the game, that it fails to ask for informed consent to use the demographic data users provide, and that it makes no provision for protecting that data.

Much turns here, then, on the definition of 'personal information'. Under the Danish law regarding personal data (*Persondataloven* 2000, 2001), for example, personal information *includes* such demographic information as age, profession, income, and gender.[17] If, for the sake of argument, we use the Danish definition – a real possibility that would follow if, for example, this project were outsourced to employees in Denmark – then this project would violate Danish law.

But from the perspective of the researcher, this project is both ethically and legally unproblematic. This perspective may be understood in terms of the Confucian emphasis on *harmony* [*he*], and, more generally, as has been documented by Hofstede (2001) and Hofstede and Bond (1988)[18], the greater emphasis in many non-Western societies on developing a consensus regarding specific choices that reflects the views of the group, not simply those of the individual. Again, we must be careful of overly simple generalizations regarding differences between East and West.[19] At the same time, however, there does seem to be a general pattern. In many

---

[17] Line Gulløv Lundh (2003) has observed: 'Lars Stoltze (2001) states that the personal data law in principle differentiates between three kinds of personal information: (1) sensitive information (as mentioned in § 7), (2) semi-sensitive information (as mentioned in § 8) (3) and ordinary information "almindelige oplysninger"). According to Stoltze (2001, p. 271) the "ordinary personal information" includes all the information which doesn't fall within § 7 and § 8, such as names, addresses, e-mails, age, economical relations, etc. The treatment of this kind of "ordinary personal information" must only be carried out if one of the seven conditions in § 6 is fulfilled'.

[18] Hofstede, of course, has his critics, and I do not mean to present him as a final authority on matters of culture. At the same time, however, his frameworks, whatever their deficits, remain at least useful starting points for discussing cultural differences. For an overview of the debate and a moderate defense of Hofstede, see Søndergaard (1994) and his more recent online discussion (www.international-business-center.com/geert-hofstede/Sondergaard.shtml, accessed 19 December 2003).

[19] See Footnote 13.

non-Western societies the rights and interests of the individual are seen as more interwoven with those of the group, so that, for example, ethical concerns regarding informed consent implicate both the individual and the group. As one instance, in the rural villages of Thailand, a researcher must request the consent of both the individuals and the village head (Hongladarom 2004). Indeed, in Japan, a researcher would ask a superior for permission to interview employees – not the employees themselves (Kawasaki 2003). In this light, our project researcher may feel, especially given that no personal information in the form of names, addresses, and so forth, will be collected, that because the project will likely result in benefits both to the company and to its future customers (that is, the group at large), there is no need to be concerned with informed consent.

But in light of these contrasts between Danish privacy law, on the one hand, and the ethical sensibilities at work in this example, it appears that the resonances we have seen earlier between a Confucian ethics and Western ethics of care and virtue, along with emerging, if comparatively limited, rights to data privacy in China and Hong Kong, are countered by remaining differences between the greater emphasis on individual rights in many Western countries and the interweaving of those rights with those of the larger collective in many Asian, as well as African, Middle-Eastern, and other traditional societies.[20]

4. Divergences: Online and Offline Ethical Behavior – Minority/Immigrant/Diaspora Media Use

Finally, we can note that a number of recent studies reiterate a crucial point concerning our sense of identity and, thus, our behavior in the online world: again, contrary to earlier Cartesian/modernist notions of a primarily *disembodied* experience in a range of *virtual* worlds. These studies rather point to the fact that we do not leave our bodies behind when we go online. This means, in turn, that our online experiences and interactions with others remain deeply rooted in our *bodily* existence. As such, these experiences and interactions are thus deeply shaped by nothing less than the entire spectrum of human communities, cultures, traditions, histories, and, thus, by the particular ethical and cultural norms of the persons who enter online worlds.

As a first example, in a cross-cultural study of Japanese, Singaporean, and U.S. users of the Internet, Nara and Iseda (2004) have found close correlations between persons' ethical sensibilities and orientations and their online

[20] As a starting point, for readings in African philosophy, see Serequeberhan (1991), Bonevac, Boon, and Phillips (1992), Part I, Bonevac and Phillips (1993, Part I), Solomon and Higgins (1995, chapter 8). For additional examples of comparative approaches and overviews, see Blocker (1999) and Mall (2000).

ethical behaviors. This is to say that, on the one hand, persons with a high ethical awareness and behavior in their 'everyday ethics' also demonstrated a high ethical awareness and behavior online. By the same token, on the other hand, persons with a low everyday ethical awareness and behavior demonstrated a low ethical awareness and behavior online. Nara and Iseda note that 'A natural interpretation of the results suggests that everyday ethics would be the baseline for proper information ethics' (2004, p. 170).

These results are consistent with a large body of research that shows, for example, that our gender continues to be apparent in our discourse online (Herring 1999, 2001), that our online activities deeply reflect race and ethnicity (Kolko et al. 2000), and that contra the rhetoric of an electronic global village, a great deal of Internet use in fact remains within the cultural and geographical borders of nation states (Halavais 2000).

Indeed, more recent research on media use, including use of the Internet, by minority and diaspora communities makes very clear that the spectra of media utilized (e.g., newspapers, radio, mobile phones, and various Internet applications, such as chat and e-mail) and the ways in which media are used are distinctive for each group. For example, in her research on both old immigrant groups (white Protestant, white Jewish, African American) and new immigrant groups (Chinese, Central American, Korean, and Mexican), Mary Wilson has found that, with the exception of recent Chinese immigrants, Internet use among new and old immigrant groups is relatively low. In particular, although white Protestant and white Jewish groups report a high confidence in the importance of the Internet, their actual use of the Internet is below that of recent Chinese immigrants. By contrast, and not surprisingly, other immigrant groups with low literacy rates (Central American, Mexican) make very little use of the Internet or print media (Wilson 2002, p. 82).

In ways parallel to Wilson, Thomas Tufte has found that second-generation immigrant Danes likewise make relatively low use of the Internet, despite considerable access both at school and in public libraries. Rather, the mobile phone is the medium of choice. Moreover, contra hopes of community activists and supporters of governmental efforts to integrate newcomers into mainstream Danish society, these young Danes are not using media to develop social networks with mainstream Danes. At the same time, however, neither are they using the Internet, as happens in many diaspora communities, to sustain a diaspora identity (for example, through maintaining contacts with friends and relatives in the homeland). Rather, they use the new technologies to foster and maintain a social network largely within their neighborhood and thereby to create a third identity between that of their immigrant parents and the mainstream Danish society (Tufte 2002).

Thus, Tufte shows that the very media that optimists hoped would foster greater global communication, understanding, and harmony work equally well to foster and reinforce a rapidly growing diversity of distinctive cultural mixtures that both reflect specific patterns of immigration and mobility and foster cultural and political obstacles to integration. Similarly, Wilson's research shows that, in the case of those immigrant communities that culturally prefer oral rather than literate forms of communication, for example, they are likely to likewise remain as communities that are literally disconnected from mainstream society, and thus remain trapped with the various economic and political disadvantages they face as new immigrants. In these ways, and as noted at the outset, media scholar Stig Hjarvard has observed that, contra rosy visions of a McLuhanesque electronic global village, global media rather issue in a cultural and mental urbanization that directly reflects the urbanization of the social and physical world (Hjarvard 2002).

CONCLUSION

More broadly, it seems clear, consistent with earlier research on cultural collisions between Western CMC technologies and initial 'target' cultures, especially in non-Western societies, that indeed, our offline identities, ethical values, communities, histories, and cultures deeply shape our online behaviors, expectations, and experiences. Given these intimate relationships between our offline and online worlds, a global ethic that would guide our interactions online, in ways that would be recognized as legitimate by at least most cultures and ethical traditions, thus faces nothing less than the stubborn resistance of the fine- and coarse-grained differences between these cultures and traditions, *including* the emerging, complex hybrids of immigrant and diaspora communities.

On the one hand, I would suggest that the sorts of successes in developing international norms both for the offline worlds of economy (including property and copyright protection) and politics (including recognition, however tenuous and varying it may be, of universal human rights) and for online worlds (in the case of the AoIR guidelines for online research and emerging rights to data privacy protection in Asian countries such as China and Hong Kong) clearly stand as encouraging indications that global ethics is possible. At the same time, this optimism must be countered by the clear-eyed recognition of the fine- and coarse-grained differences between ethical and cultural traditions that cannot always be resolved through strategies of ethical pluralism and notions of resonance.

UNSCIENTIFIC POSTLUDE

As some remember, Plato uses the κυβερνήτησ [*cybernetes*] – a steersman, helmsman, or pilot – as a primary model or example of the just human being and just rulers (*Republic* I, 332e–c; VI, 489c). The image of the *cybernetes* is then taken up by Norbert Wiener (1948) as the root concept of 'cybernetics'. It is helpful, however, to recall Plato's description of the *cybernetes*:

a first-rate pilot or physician, for example, *feels* [διαισθάνεται] the difference between the impossibilities and possibilities in his art and attempts the one and lets the others go; and then, too, if he does happen to trip, he is equal to correcting his error. (*Republic*, 360e–361a)

This is to say that a primary capacity of the *cybernetes* is not simply *informational* self-direction, as cybernetics later came to mean, but more fundamentally the capacity for *ethical* self-direction. Moreover, as Plato reminds us here, and echoed in Aristotle's notion of *phronesis* as a kind of practical judgment, the *cybernetes* is not guaranteed success at every effort. Rather, our development of ethical judgment necessarily entails both success and failure, where both help us refine and improve our understanding and capacities. Whether or not Plato's *cybernetes* might find a global ethic that would guide ethical navigation in all waters and conditions, I have tried to suggest, is precisely a matter of making the attempt, and learning from both failure and success.

By the same token, Confucius reminds us that the exemplary person (*junzi*) seeks harmony, not sameness (Analect 13.23). Such harmony – neither sheer fragmentation of pure difference, nor sheer identity of single norms and views – is a promising model for a global ethics as such harmony thus seeks to preserve the ethical sensibilities and traditions of diverse nations and peoples while pursuing the impulse of overcoming ethnocentrism and fragmentation. But again, as multiple ethical and cultural divergences make clear, following the impulse towards a global ethics is neither easy nor sure of success. Following this impulse, however, is virtually required by the growth of computer-mediated communication as a global medium. And here Confucius provides a further model: he is known as the one who keeps on trying, even when he knows it's no use (Analect 14.38).

References

Aguilar, J. R. 2000. Over the rainbow: European and American consumer protection policy and remedy conflicts on the Internet and a possible solution. *International Journal of Communications of Law and Policy, 4*, 1–57.

Ames, R., and Rosemont, H. 1998. *The Analects of Confucius: A philosophical translation.* New York: Ballantine Books.

Anderson, I.-E., and Jæger, B. 1997. Involving citizens in assessment and the public debate on information technology, in A. Feenberg, T. H. Nielsen, and L. Winner (Eds.), *Technology and Democracy: Technology in the Public Sphere – Proceedings from Workshop 1*, Center for Technology and Culture, Oslo, pp. 149–172.

AoIR (Association of Internet Researchers) 2002. *Decision-making and ethical Internet research.* Retrieved January 10, 2006 from http://www.aoir.org/reports/ethics.pdf.

Barber, B. 1995. *Jihad versus McWorld.* New York: Times Books.

Barney, D. 2004. The vanishing table, or community in a world that is no world, in A. Feenberg and D. Barney (Eds.), *Community in the digital age: Philosophy and practice.* Lanham, MD: Rowman & Littlefield.

Becker, B. 2000. Cyborg, agents and transhumanists. *Leonardo, 33*, 5, 361–365.

Becker, B. 2001. The disappearance of materiality? in V. Lemecha and R. Stone (Eds.), *The multiple and the mutable subject.* Winnipeg: St. Norbert Arts Centre, pp. 58–77.

Becker, B. 2002. Sinn und Sinnlichkeit: Anmerkungen zur Eigendynamik und Fremdheit des eigenen Leibes, in L. Jäger (Ed.), *Mentalität und Medialität,* München: Fink, pp. 35–46.

Benhabib, S. 1986. *Critique, norm and utopia: A study of the foundations of critical theory.* New York: Columbia University Press.

Bizer, J. 2003. Grundrechte im Netz: Von der freien Meinungsäußerung bis zum Recht auf Eigentum [Basic rights on the net: from the free expression of opinion to property right], in C. Schulzki-Haddouti (Ed.), *Bürgerrechte im Netz [Civil rights online],* Bonn: Bundeszentrale für politische Bildung, pp. 21–29. Available at http://www.bpb.de/publikationen/UZX6DW,0,B%fcrgerrechte_im_Netz.html.

Blocker, H. G. 1999. *World philosophy: An East-West comparative introduction to philosophy.* Upper Saddle River, NJ: Prentice-Hall.

Bonevac, D., Boon, W., and Phillips, S. 1992. *Beyond the Western tradition: Readings in moral and political philosophy.* Mountain View, CA: Mayfield.

Bonevac, D., and Phillips, S. 1993. *Understanding non-Western philosophy: introductory readings.* Mountain View, CA: Mayfield.

Borgmann, A. 1999. *Holding onto reality: The nature of information at the turn of the Millennium.* Chicago: University of Chicago Press.

Boss, J. A. 2004. *Ethics for life: A text with readings.* New York: McGraw Hill.

Buchanan, E. (Ed.) 2003. *Readings in virtual research ethics: Issues and controversies.* Hershey, PA: Idea Group.

Burkhardt, J., Thompson, P. B., and Peterson, T. R. 2002. The first European Congress on Agricultural and Food Ethics and follow-up Workshop on Ethics and Food Biotechnology: A US perspective, *Agriculture and Human Values, 17,* 4, 327–332.

Burrell, D. 1973. *Analogy and philosophical language.* New Haven: Yale University Press.

Chan, J. 2003. Confucian attitudes towards ethical pluralism, in R. Madsen and T. B. Strong (Eds.), *The many and the one: Religious and secular perspectives on ethical pluralism in the modern World.* Princeton: Princeton University Press, pp. 129–153.

Chen, Y. 2005. *Privacy in China.* Unpublished Master's thesis, Nanyang Technological University, Singapore.

De George, R. T. 1999. *Business ethics* (5th ed.). Upper Saddle River, NJ: Prentice Hall.

Döring, O. 2003. China's struggle for practical regulations in medical ethics. *Nature Reviews Genetics, 4,* 3, 233–239.

Dreyfus, H. 2001. *On the Internet.* London: Routledge.

Elberfeld, R. 2002. Resonanz als Grundmotiv ostasiatischer Ethik [Resonance as a fundamental motif of East Asian ethics], in R. Elberfeld and G. Wohlfart (Eds.), *Komparative Ethik: Das gute Leben zwischen den Kulturen.* München: Chora, pp. 131–141.

Ess, C. 1983. *Analogy in the critical works: Kant's transcendental philosophy as analectical thought.* Ann Arbor, MI: University Microfilms International.

Ess, C. 1996. The political computer: democracy, CMC and Habermas, in C. Ess (Ed.), *Philosophical perspectives on computer-mediated communication.* Albany, NY: State University of New York Press, pp. 197–230.

Ess, C. (Ed.) 2001. *Culture, technology, communication: Towards an intercultural global village,* with Fay Sudweeks, foreword by Susan Herring. Albany, NY: State University of New York Press.

Ess, C. 2002a. Cultures in collision: Philosophical lessons from computer-mediated communication, in J. H. Moor and T. W. Bynum (Eds.), *CyberPhilosophy: The intersection of philosophy and computing.* Oxford: Blackwell, pp. 219–242.

Ess, C. 2002b. Liberation in cyberspace ... or computer-mediated colonization? / Liberation en cyberspace, ou colonisation assistee par ordinateur? *Electronic Journal of Communication/La Revue Electronique de Communication, 12,* 3 & 4. Available at: http://www.cios.org/www/ejc/v12n34.htm.

Ess, C. 2003. The cathedral or the bazaar? The AoIR document on Internet research ethics as an exercise in open source ethics, in M. Consolvo (Ed.), *Internet Research Annual Volume 1: Selected papers from the Association of Internet Researchers Conferences 2000–2002.* New York: Peter Lang.

Ess, C. 2004a. Beyond *Contemptus Mundi* and Cartesian dualism: Western resurrection of the bodysubject and (re)new(ed) coherencies with Eastern approaches to life/death, in G. Wohlfart and H. Georg-Moeller (Eds), *Philosophie des Todes: death philosophy east and west,* Munich: Chora, pp. 15–36.

Ess, C. 2004b. Discourse ethics. in C. Mitcham et al. (Eds), *Encyclopedia of science, technology and ethics.* New York: MacMillan Reference.

Ess, C., and Sudweeks, F. 2003. Introduction and special issue on liberatory potentials and practices of CMC in the Middle East. *Journal of Computer-Mediated Communication, 8,* 2. Available at: http://jcmc.indiana.edu/vol8/issue2/essandsudweeks.html.

Ess, C., and Sudweeks, F. 2005. Culture and computer-mediated communication: Toward new understandings. *Journal of Computer-Mediated Communication, 11,* 1. Available at: http://jcmc.indiana.edu/vol11/issue1/ess.html.

European Parliament 1995. *Directive 95/46/EC of the European Parliament and of the Council of 24 October 1995 on the Protection of Individuals with Regard to the Processing of Personal Data and on the Free Movement of Such Data.* Retrieved 16 May 2006 from: http://eur-lex.europa.eu/smartapi/cgi/sga_doc?smartapi!celexapi!prod!CELEXnumdoc&lg=EN&numdoc=31995L0046&model=guichett.

Fixdal, J. 1997. Consensus conferences as extended peer groups, in A. Feenberg, T. H. Nielsen, and L. Winner (Eds), *Technology and Democracy: Technology in the Public Sphere – Proceedings from Workshop 1.* Oslo: Center for Technology and Culture, pp. 75–94.

Floridi, L., and Sanders, J. W. 2004. Internet ethics: The constructionist values of *homo poeticus,* in R. Cavalier (Ed.), *The Internet and our moral lives.* Albany, NY: State University of New York Press.

Gilligan, C. 1982. *In a different voice: Psychological theory and women's development.* Cambridge, MA: Harvard University Press.

GVU Center (College of Computing, Georgia Institute of Technology) 1998. *GVU's 10th WWW User Survey.* Retrieved 25 November 2003 at: http://www.gvu.gatech.edu/user_surveys/survey-1998-10/.

Gupta, B. 2002. *Ethical questions: East and West.* Lanham, MD: Rowman & Littlefield.

Habermas, J. 1981. *Theorie des Kommuikativen Handelns.* 2 vols. Suhrkamp, Frankfurt. Translated by T. McCarthy as *The theory of communicative action.* Boston: Beacon Press, 1984 (Vol. 1) and 1987 (Vol. 2).

Habermas, J. 1983. Diskursethik: Notizen zu einem Begründungsprogram, in *Moralbewusstsein und kommunikatives Handeln*. Frankfurt: Suhrkamp. Translated by C. Lenhardt and S. W. Nicholsen, as Discourse ethics: Notes on philosophical justification, in *Moral consciousness and communicative action*. Cambridge, MA: MIT Press, 1990, pp. 43–115.

Habermas, J. 1989. Justice and solidarity: On the discussion concerning stage 6, in T. Wren (Ed.), *The moral domain: Essays in the ongoing discussion between philosophy and the social sciences*. Cambridge, MA: MIT Press, pp. 224–251.

Halavais, A. 2000. National borders on the World Wide Web. *New Media and Society*, 2, 1, 7–28.

Hamelink, C. 2000. *The ethics of cyberspace*. London: Sage.

Hayles, K. 1999. *How we became posthuman: Virtual bodies in cybernetics, literature and informatics*. Chicago: University of Chicago Press.

Herring, S. 1999. Posting in a different voice: Gender and ethics in computer-mediated communication, in P. A. Mayer (Ed.), *Computer media and communication: A reader*, New York: Oxford University Press, pp. 241–265.

Herring, S. 2001. *Gender and power in online communication*. Center for Social Informatics Working Papers, WP01–05B. Retrieved 15 December 2003 from: http://www.slis.indiana.edu/csi/WP/WP01–05B.html.

Hinman, L. M. 1998. *Ethics: A pluralistic approach to moral theory*. Fort Worth: Harcourt Brace.

Hjarvard, S. 2002. Mediated encounters: An essay on the role of communication media in the creation of trust in the global metropolis, in G. Stald and T. Tufte (Eds.), *Global encounters: Media and cultural transformation*. Luton: University of Luton Press, pp. 69–84.

Hofstede, G. 2001. *Culture's consequences: Comparing values, behaviors, institutions and organisations across nations* (2nd ed.). Thousand Oaks, CA: Sage.

Hofstede, G., and Bond, M. H. 1988. The Confucius connection: From cultural roots to economic growth. *Organisational Dynamics, 16*, 4–21.

Hongladarom, S. 2004. Personal communication, 20 January.

Jacoby, I. 1985 The Consensus Development Program of the National Institutes of Health. *International Journal of Technology Assessment in Health Care, 1*, 420–432.

Johns, M. Chen, S., and Hall, J. (Eds.). 2003. *Online social research: Methods, issues and ethics*. New York: Peter Lang.

Johnson, D. G. 2001. *Computer ethics* (3rd ed.).Upper Saddle River, NJ: Prentice-Hall.

Jones, W. T. 1969. *The Classical mind: A history of Western philosophy* (2nd ed.), Vol. 1). New York: Harcourt, Brace & World.

Kawasaki, L. T. 2003. Personal communication, December.

Kemerling, G. 2000. *Kant: The moral order*. Retrieved 13 June 2006 from: http://www.philosophypages.com/hy/5i.htm.

Keulartz, J., Korthals, M., Schermer, M., and Swierstra, T. (Eds) (2002). *Pragmatist ethics for a technological culture*. Dordrecht: Kluwer.

Kolko, B., Nakamura, L., and Rodman, G. B. (Eds.). 2000. *Race in cyberspace*. New York: Routledge.

Li, C. 2002. Revisiting Confucian Jen ethics and feminist care ethics: A reply. *Hypatia: A Journal of Feminist Philosophy, 17*, 1, 130–140.

Lü, Y. 2002. *Xin Xi Lun Li Xue* [Chinese information ethics]. Hunan: Middle South University.

Lundh, L. G. 2003. Personal communication, 15 December.

Madsen, R., and Strong, T. 2003. *The many and the one: Religious and secular perspectives on ethical pluralism in the modern world.* Princeton: Princeton University Press.

Mall, R. A. 2000. *Intercultural philosophy.* Lanham, MD: Rowman & Littlefield.

Michelfelder, D. 2001. The moral value of informational privacy in cyberspace. *Ethics and information technology, 3,* 2, 129–135.

Mill, J. S. 1913. *Utilitarianism.* Chicago: University of Chicago Press.

Moon, J. D. 2003. Pluralisms compared, in R. Madsen and T. B. Strong (Eds.), *The many and the one: Religious and secular perspectives on ethical pluralism in the modern world.* Princeton: Princeton University Press, pp. 343–359.

Nara, Y., and Iseda, T. 2004. An empirical study on the structure of Internet information ethics behaviors: Comparative research between Japan, US and Singapore, in A. Feenberg and D. Barney (Eds.), *Community in the digital age: Philosophy and practice.* Lanham, MD: Rowman & Littlefield, pp. 161–179.

National Committee for Research Ethics in the Social Sciences and the Humanities (Den nasjonale forskningsetiske komité for samfunnsvitenskap og humaniora [NESH], Norway) 2001. Guidelines for research ethics in the social sciences, law and the humanities. Retrieved 15 May 2006 from http://www.etikkom.no/ Engelsk/NESH/Publications/NESHguide.

National Committee for Research Ethics in the Social Sciences and the Humanities (Den nasjonale forskningsetiske komité for samfunnsvitenskap og humaniora [NESH], Norway) 2003. Research ethics guidelines for Internet research. Translated by L. G. Lundh and C. Ess. Retrieved 15 May 2006 from http://www. etikkom.no/Engelsk/Publications/Internet03/.

National Institutes of Health, Office of Human Subjects Research. 2005. *Code of Federal Regulations Title 45, Department of Health and Human Services, Part 46, Protection of Human Subjects.* Retrieved 15 May 2006 from http://ohsr.od.nih.gov/ guidelines/45cfr46.html.

NUA Internet Surveys. 2003. *How Many Online?* Retrieved 15 December 2003 from http://www.nua.com/surveys/how_many_online/index.html.

O'Neill, O. 2001. Agents of justice, in T. Pogge (Ed.), *Global justice.* Oxford: Blackwell, pp. 188–203.

Ong, W. 1988. *Orality and literacy: The technologizing of the word.* London: Routledge.

Persondataloven [Personal Data Law, Denmark]. Lov. nr. 429 af 31. maj 2000 som ændret ved lov. nr. 280 af 25. april 2001. Retrieved 2 December 2003 from http://147.29.40.90/_GETDOC_/ACCN/A20000042930-REGL; English version: http://www.datatilsynet.dk/eng/index.html.

Plato. 1991. *The Republic of Plato.* Translated by Allan Bloom. New York: Basic Books.

Pohl, K.-H. 2002. Chinese and Western values: Reflections on a cross-cultural dialogue on a universal ethics, in R. Elberfeld and G. Wohlfart (Eds.), *Komparative Ethik: Das gute Leben zwischen den Kulturen.* München: Chora, pp. 213–232.

Rachels, J. 1999. *The right thing to do: Basic readings in moral philosophy.* New York: McGraw Hill.

Ramasoota, P. 2005. Thai Webmasters Association Code of Ethics. Second Asian-Pacific Computing and Philosophy Conference, Bangkok, Thailand, 8 January 2005.

Reidenberg, J. R. 2000. Resolving conflicting international data privacy rules in cyberspace. *Stanford Law Review, 52,* 1315–1376.

RESPECT Project. 2004. Institute for Employment Studies. Retrieved 16 May 2006 from http://www.respectproject.org/main/index.php.

Rosemont, H. 2001. *Rationality and religious experience: The continuing relevance of the World's spiritual traditions* (The First Master Hsüan Memorial Lecture), with a commentary by Huston Smith. Chicago and La Salle, IL: Open Court.

Sandberg, P., and Kraft, N. (Eds.). 1997. Fast salmon and technoburgers. Retrieved 15 May 2006 from http://www.etikkom.no/Etikkom/Etikkom/Engelsk/Publications/fast.

Scheffler, S. 2001. *Boundaries and allegiances: Problems of justice and responsibility in liberal thought.* Oxford: Oxford University Press.

Serequeberhan, T. 1991. *African philosophy: The essential readings.* New York: Paragon House.

Silverstone, R. 2002. Finding a voice: Minorities, media and the global commons, in G. Stald and T. Tufte (Eds.), *Global encounters: Media and cultural transformation.* Luton: Luton University Press, pp. 107–122.

Skorupinski, B., and Ott, K. 2002. Technology assessment and ethics, *Poiesis and Praxis: International Journal of Technology Assessment and Ethics of Science, 1,* 2, 95–122.

Solomon, R. C., and Higgins, K. M. 1995. *World philosophy: A text with readings.* New York: McGraw-Hill.

Søndergaard, M. 1994. Hofstede's Consequences: A study of reviews, citations and replications. *Organization Studies, 15,* 3, 447–456.

Stahl, B. C. 2004. *Responsible management of information systems.* Hershey, PA: Idea Group.

Stoltze, L. 2001. *Internet ret* [Internet law]. Copenhagen: Nyt Juridisk Forlag.

Tang, R. 2002. *Approaches to privacy – The Hong Kong experience.* Retrieved 16 May 2006 from http://www.pco.org.hk/English/infocentre/speech_20020222.html.

Taylor, C. 2002. Democracy, inclusive and exclusive, in R. Madsen, W. M. Sullivan, A. Swiderl, and S. M. Tipton (Eds.), *Meaning and modernity: Religion, polity and self.* Berkeley: University of California Press.

Thorseth, M. (Ed.). 2003. *Applied ethics in Internet research.* Programme for Applied Ethics, Norwegian University of Science and Technology, Trondheim.

Torgersen, H., and Seifert, F. 1997. How to keep out what we don't want: On the assessment of 'Sozialvergträglichkeit' under the Austrian Genetic Engineering Act, in A. Feenberg, T. H. Nielsen, and L. Winner (Eds.), *Technology and democracy: technology in the public sphere – Proceedings from Workshop 1,* Center for Technology and Culture, Oslo, pp. 115–148.

Tu, W.-M. 1999. Humanity as embodied love: Exploring filial piety as a global ethical perspective, in M. Zlomislic and D. Goicoechea (Eds.), *Jen Agape Tao with Tu Wei-Ming.* Binghamton, NY: Institute of Global Cultural Studies, pp. 28–37.

Tufte, T. 2002. Ethnic minority Danes between diaspora and locality – Social uses of mobile phones and Internet, in G. Stald and T. Tufte (Eds), *Global encounters: Media and cultural transformation.* Luton: Luton University Press, pp. 235–261.

United Nations. 1948. *Universal Declaration of Human Rights.* Retrieved 16 May 2006 from http://www.un.org/Overview/rights.html.

Veatch, H. 1971. A Critique of Benedict, in J. R. Weinberg and K. E. Yandell (Eds.), *Theory of knowledge.* New York: Holt, Reinhart & Winston.

Warren, K. J. 1990. The power and the promise of ecological feminism. *Environmental Ethics. 12*, 2, 123–146.

Weiner, N. 1948. *Cybernetics, or Control and communication in the animal and the machine.* New York: John Wiley.

Wilson, M. 2002. Communication, organizations and diverse populations, in F. Sudweeks and C. Ess (Eds), *Proceedings: Cultural Attitudes Towards Communication and Technology 2002, Université de Montréal,* School of Information Technology, Murdoch University, Perth, WA, pp. 69–88. Available online: http://www.it.murdoch.edu.au/~sudweeks/catac.

Yu, J. Y. 2003. Virtue: Confucius and Aristotle, in X. Jiang (Ed.) *The examined life: The Chinese perspective.* Binghamton,NY: Global Publications, pp. 1–31.

Yu, J. Y., and Bunnin, N. 2001. Saving the phenomena: An Aristotelian method in comparative philosophy, in M. Bo (Ed.), *Two roads to wisdom? – Chinese philosophy and analytical philosophy.* LaSalle, IL: Open Court, pp. 293–312.

12

Collective Responsibility and Information and Communication Technology

Seumas Miller

Recently, the importance of the notion of collective moral responsibility has begun to be realised in relation to, for example, environmental degradation and global poverty. Evidently, we are collectively morally responsible for causing environmental damage of various kinds and degrees; and, arguably, we have a collective responsibility to assist those living in extreme poverty. However, thus far, the focus in theoretical and applied ethics has been on collective responsibility for actions and omissions, that is, for outward behaviour. There has been scant attention paid to collective responsibility for knowledge acquisition and dissemination, that is, for inner epistemic states. Further, although the notion of individual responsibility in relation to computer technology has been the subject of a certain amount of philosophical work, this is not so for collective responsibility. In this chapter, I seek to redress these imbalances somewhat by examining the notion of collective responsibility in so far as it pertains to the communication and retrieval of knowledge by means of information and communication technology.

The chapter is in two main parts. In Part A, I apply my collective end theory (Miller 2001, chapters 2 and 5) of joint action, and its associated technical notions of joint procedures, joint mechanisms, and collective ends, to the process of the acquisition of certain forms of social knowledge.[1] The focus here is on analysing the communication, storage, and retrieval of knowledge by means of information and communications technology (ICT) in terms of the collective end theory. In Part B, I apply my theory of collective responsibility to the communication, storage, and retrieval of morally significant knowledge by means of ICT.

Accordingly, we need to distinguish between the genus, joint action, and an important species of joint action, namely, what I will call joint *epistemic*

[1] So my task here is in within the general area demarcated by, for example, Alvin Goldman (1999).

action. In the case of the latter, but not necessarily the former, participating agents have epistemic goals, that is, the acquisition of knowledge.

We also need to distinguish between actions, whether individual, joint, or epistemic actions (including joint epistemic actions), that do not make use of technology and those that do. For example, A and B might travel to work together by walking. Alternatively, A and B might travel to work together by taking a train. Again, A might communicate to B the proposition that A is not going to work today, and do so by uttering the English sentence, 'I am not going to work today'. Alternatively, A might send an e-mail to B to this effect. The e-mail to B, but not A's speech act involves the use of technology, as was the case with travelling together by train.

So there are two major hurdles for the attempt to apply my collective end theory of joint action to joint epistemic action that makes use of technology – and specifically of ICT. The first hurdle is to see how the communication, storage, and retrieval of knowledge could reasonably be conceived of as joint action at all. The second hurdle is to see how the communication, storage, and retrieval of knowledge by means of ICT, in particular, could reasonably be conceived of as joint action.

Likewise, there are two major hurdles for my attempt to apply my account of collective moral responsibility to joint epistemic action that makes use of ICT. The first hurdle is to see how agents could be collectively responsible for the communication, storage, and retrieval of morally significant knowledge. The second hurdle is to see how agents could be collectively responsible for the communication, storage, and retrieval of morally significant knowledge by means of ICT, in particular.

PART A: APPLICATION OF THE COLLECTIVE END THEORY TO SOCIAL KNOWLEDGE ACQUISITION

Joint Action

Joint actions are actions involving a number of agents performing interdependent actions in order to realise some common goal (Miller 2001, chapter 2). Examples of joint action are: two people dancing together, a number of tradesmen building a house, and a team of researchers conducting an attitudinal survey. Joint action is to be distinguished from individual action on the one hand, and from the 'actions' of corporate bodies on the other. Thus, an individual walking down the road or shooting at a target are instances of individual action. A nation declaring war or a government taking legal action against a public company are instances of *corporate* action.[2] My concern in this chapter is only with joint action.

---

[2] I have argued elsewhere that, properly speaking, there are no such things as corporate actions (Miller 2001, chapter 5).

The concept of joint action can be construed very narrowly or more broadly. On the most narrow construal, we have what I will call *basic* joint action. Basic joint action involves two co-present agents, each of whom performs one basic individual action, and does so simultaneously with the other agent, and in relation to a collective end that is to be realised within the temporal horizon of the immediate experience of the agents. A basic individual action is an action an agent can do at will without recourse to instruments other than his or her own body. An example of a basic individual action is raising one's arm; an example of a basic joint action is two people greeting one another by shaking hands.

If we construe joint action more broadly, we can identify a myriad of other closely related examples of joint action. Many of these involve intentions and ends directed to outcomes outside the temporal horizon of the immediate experience of the agents, for example, two people engaging in a two-hour long conversation or three people deciding to build a garden wall over the summer break. Others involve intentions and ends directed to outcomes that will exist outside the spatial horizon of the immediate experience of the agents, and involve instruments other than the agents' bodies. Thus two people might jointly fire a rocket into the extremities of the earth's atmosphere. Still, other joint actions involve very large numbers of agents, for example, a large contingent of soldiers fighting a battle (Miller 2001, chapter 6).

Recent developments in ICT have greatly extended the range of joint actions. For example, new forms of joint work have arisen, such as Computer Supported Collaborative Work (CSCW or Groupware). (See, for example, Bentley et al. 1997.) Workers located in different parts of the world can over lengthy time periods function as a team working on a joint project with common goals. The workers can make use of a common electronic database, their communications with one another via e-mail and/or video-teleconferencing can be open to all, and the contributing actions of each can be a matter of common knowledge, for example, via a Basic Support for Cooperative Work (BSCW) Shared Workspace system. Moreover, there can be ongoing team discussion and a coordinated team response to problems as they arise via such systems.

Joint Procedures (Conventions)

Basic joint actions can also be distinguished from what I will call joint procedures. An agent has a joint procedure to x, if he x-s in a recurring situation and does so on condition that other agents also x. (Procedures are distinct from repetitions of the same action in a single situation, for example, rowing or skipping.) Thus, Australians have a procedure to drive on the left-hand side of the road. Each Australian drives on the left whenever he drives, and he drives on the left on condition the other agents drive on the left. Moreover, joint procedures are followed in order to achieve collective goals, for example, to avoid car collisions. Joint procedures are in fact conventions (Miller 2001, chapter 3).

It is important to distinguish conventions from social norms. Social norms are regularities in action involving interdependence of action among members of a group, but regularities in action that are governed by a moral purpose or principle (Miller 2001, chapter 3). For example, avoiding telling lies is a social norm. Some regularities in action are both conventions and social norms, for example, driving on the left-hand side of the road.

Joint Institutional Mechanisms

We can also distinguish between joint procedures (in the above sense) and what I will call joint mechanisms.[3] Examples of joint mechanisms are the device of tossing a coin to resolve a dispute and voting to elect a candidate to office.

In some cases, that these joint mechanisms are used might be a matter of having a procedure in my earlier sense. Thus, if we decided that (within some specified range of disputes) we would always have recourse to tossing the coin, then we would have adopted a procedure in my earlier sense. Accordingly, I will call such joint mechanisms, joint *procedural* mechanisms.

Joint mechanisms (and, therefore, joint procedural mechanisms) consist of: (a) a complex of differentiated but interlocking actions (the input to the mechanism); (b) the result of the performance of those actions (the output of the mechanism); and (c) the mechanism itself. Thus, a given agent might vote for a candidate. He will do so only if others also vote. But further to this, there is the action of the candidates, namely, that they present themselves as candidates. That they present themselves as candidates is (in part) constitutive of the input to the voting mechanism. Voters vote *for candidates*. So there is interlocking and differentiated action (the input). Furthermore, there is some result (as opposed to consequence) of the joint action; the joint action consisting of the actions of putting oneself forward as a candidate and of the actions of voting. The result is that some candidate, say, Jones is voted in (the output). That there is a result is (in part) constitutive of the mechanism. That to receive the most number of votes is to be 'voted in' is (in part) constitutive of the voting mechanism. Moreover, that Jones is voted in is not a collective end of all the voters. (However, it is a collective end of those who voted for Jones.) However, that the one who gets the most votes – whoever that happens to be – is voted in, is a collective end of all the voters.

---

[3] Joint procedures and joint mechanisms are not mutually exclusive.

Collective Ends

Joint actions are interdependent actions directed toward a common goal or
end. But what is such an end? This notion of a common goal or, as I shall
refer to it, a collective end, is a construction out of the prior notion of an
individual end. Roughly speaking, a collective end is an individual end that
more than one agent has, and which is such that, if it is realised, it is realised
by all, or most, of the actions of the agents involved; the individual action
of any given agent is only part of the means by which the end is realised.
The realisation of the collective end is the bringing into existence of a state
of affairs. Each agent has this state of affairs as an individual end. (It is
also a state of affairs aimed at under more or less the same description by
each agent.) So a collective end is a species of individual end (Miller 2001,
chapter 2).

An interesting feature of the above-mentioned CSCW systems is their
capacity to structure pre-existing relatively unstructured practices, such as
group decision making, in the service of the collective ends of efficiency and
effectiveness. For example, Group Decision Support Systems can provide
for simultaneous information sources for the participants in the decision-
making process, assure equal time for the input of participants, establish
key stages and time frames for the decision-making process, and so on.

Assertion, Information, and Joint Action

Thus far we have been discussing joint action in general terms. Now I want to
consider a particular category of joint actions, namely, joint actions involved
in the communication, storage, and retrieval of information. So my concern
is principally with various kinds of linguistic or speech acts, and with various kinds of cognitive or epistemic actions, namely, so-called truth-aiming
attitudes or actions.

I will assume in what follows that information is: (i) the propositional
content of truth-aiming attitudes, for example, beliefs, and of truth-aiming
actions, for example, assertions; and (ii) true propositional content. Accordingly, false assertions do not convey information, in my sense of the term;
so there is no such thing as false information. Moreover, propositions in the
abstract, for example, propositions that no-one has ever, or will ever, express
or think of, do not constitute information. Propositions in the sense of content that is not, as such, truth-aiming, and, therefore, not assessable as true or
false, for example, content of the form 'whether or not the cat is on the mat'
or 'the cat's being on the mat' (as distinct from 'the cat *is* on the mat') do not
constitute information either. Finally, information, thus defined, is suitable
for use as an element(s) in inference-making, for example, as the premise
in a deductive argument. For so-called information that is communicated,

stored, or retrieved, but which is false or nonpropositional in the above sense, I will use the term 'data'.

Naturally, many truth-aiming attitudes or actions, such as beliefs, inferences, perceptual judgments, assertions to oneself, and so on, are individual, not joint, actions or attitudes. Moreover, I am not an advocate of collective beliefs (Gilbert 1992, chapter 5) or of collective subjects that engage in some form of irreducibly, nonindividualist reasoning or communication (Pettit 2001, chapter 5).[4] However, I contend that speech acts, and truth-aiming speech acts, in particular, are principally a species of joint actions (in my sense). Further, I contend that the activities of communicating, storing and retrieving knowledge in the context of the new communication and information technologies involve joint action at a number of levels. One such level involves the speech act of assertion.

Assertion

Assertion is a fundamental form of speech act in ordinary face-to-face interaction. Moreover, the practice of assertion has been transposed to communication and information systems, such as the Internet. Assertion typically involves a speaker (assertor) and a hearer (audience). Moreover, there is a collective end, namely, the audience coming to grasp a true belief. So assertions are candidates for being joint actions. But let us get clearer on the speech act of assertion.

The practice of assertion involves, I suggest, three connected features. First, assertions have a communicative purpose or end; they are acts performed in order to transmit beliefs, and typically knowledge, that is, true belief (and, therefore, information). Second, they are acts at least constrained by considerations of truthfulness. It is central to the practice of assertion that participants (in general) aim at the truth, or at least try to avoid falsity. Third, speakers not only aim at the truth but purport to be, or represent themselves as, or make out that they are, aiming at the truth. Indeed, they make out not only that they are aiming at the truth, but also that they have succeeded in 'hitting' the truth.

I offer the following modified Gricean[5] analysis of the speech act of assertion (Miller 1985). Utterer U in producing utterance x asserts that p to audience A, if, and only if, U utters x intending: (1) to produce a belief in A that p;[6] (2) A to recognise intention (1) (in part on the basis of x);

---

[4] For criticisms see Miller and Makela (2005).

[5] See Grice (1989, chapter 6) and, for a modified Gricean account of assertion, see Miller (1985).

[6] Or a belief in A that U believes that p (See Grice 1989).

(3) A to fulfil intention (1) on the basis of; (a) fulfilling intention (2); and (b) A's belief that speaker U intends to avoid producing a false belief in A.[7]

Conditions (1), (2), and (3a) express the communicative element of assertion (and Grice's theory of assertoric speaker-meaning), and condition (3b) the truth-aiming element (although not as Grice envisaged it). Note that there will need to be a further condition attached to (3b), namely, that it is common knowledge between A and U that U intentionally provided a good reason for A believing that U intends to avoid producing a false belief in A. Condition (3b), in the context of this further common knowledge condition, provides for the 'making out that what one says is true' element of assertion.

This account of assertion is a minimalist one. Specifically, it defines a form of assertion stripped of its institutional raiments, such as linguistic conventions and social norms, for example, the truth-telling norm. However, even in this minimal form, assertion involves joint action, or so I will argue. Moreover, such conventions and social norms strengthen the validity of inference-making on the part of the audience in relation to the speaker's intentions and beliefs. For example, if it is common knowledge that speakers are committed to the social norm to avoid telling falsehoods, then a speaker who asserts that p has clearly made out that he or she believes that p, or has otherwise represented himself as believing that p, by virtue of being a party to that norm.

Assertion and Joint Action

In the first place, the act of assertion involves a speaker and a hearer who each do something. The speaker intentionally produces an utterance with a complex intention to get the hearer to believe something (by various means). The hearer intentionally listens to the utterance, draws inferences from it, and, in the standard case, comes to believe something. (The hearer often does much of what s/he does more or less automatically, for example, inference-making on the basis of knowledge of linguistic conventions; but from this it does not follow that what s/he did was not an intentional action.) Moreover, there is a collective end, namely, that the hearer receive information (in my above sense), that is, the hearer comes to believe some true proposition that the speaker intends the hearer to come to believe. So an act of assertion is a basic form of joint action, or at least typically is such.

So far, so good, for many, if not most, assertions. But what of those assertions in which the speaker intends the hearer to believe what is false or in

---

[7] Note also that, as Grice (1989) points out, there needs to be an exclusion clause such as: 'There is no inference element, e, such that A is intended by U to use e, and such that U intends A to think U does not intend A to rely on e.'

which the hearer does not accept what the speaker says? In these cases, that the hearer receives information from the speaker is *not* the collective end of the speaker and hearer. So we need to make a slight adjustment in relation to our conception of assertion as joint action. That the hearer receive information from the speaker is, *normatively* speaking, the collective end of assertions. In short, the point of assertion is for the speaker to transmit information to the hearer. This is consistent with this collective end not being realised, or even not being pursued, on some occasions. However, if in general speakers and hearers did not have this as a collective end – and did not in general realise this end – then the practice of assertion would collapse. Hearers would cease to listen, if they did not trust speakers to speak the truth; speakers would not speak, if they believed hearers did not trust them to speak the truth.

It might be argued that one cannot freely choose to believe a proposition and that, therefore, the hearer coming to believe some true proposition that the speaker intends the hearer to believe is not an action. Accordingly, assertion is not a joint action, because one of the alleged individual actions, that is, the hearer's coming to believe some proposition, is not really an action. Doubtless, many comings to believe are not under the control of the believer, that is perceptual beliefs. However, many acts of judgment in relation to the truth of certain matters are akin to judgments in relation to what actions to perform. The hearer, I suggest, is typically engaged in an act of judgment in relation to what a speaker asserts for the simple reason that the hearer is engaged in a process of defeasible inference-making, first, to the speaker's intentions and beliefs and, second, from those intentions and beliefs to the truth of the proposition asserted. In particular, the hearer knows that in principle the speaker might be insincere, or might be sincere but mistaken.

Sincerity is itself often an act of will; one can simply *decide* to tell a lie. Accordingly, an audience needs to *trust* a speaker. Trust in this sense is not simply reliance; it is not simply a matter of the audience reasonably believing on the basis of, say, inductive evidence that the speaker will not tell a lie. For the speaker can make a decision to tell a lie on this occasion here and now, notwithstanding his history of telling the truth, and the audience knows this. So, at least in the typical case, the audience over time in effect *decides* to trust the speaker.[8] In so doing, the audience takes a leap of faith, albeit one grounded in part in justificatory reasons; however, the reasons can only take the audience so far, given the ongoing capacity of the speaker simply to lie at will. At any rate, my general point is that the possibility of the speaker lying at will ensures that the audience's trust and, therefore, the audience's

---

[8] This is consistent with trust being a default position in the sense that one trusts unless one has reason not to. For even in the latter case a reason-based decision to, for example, continue to trust because one has no good reason not to, is called for from time to time.

coming to believe the speaker, has an element of will itself; trust in this sense is in part a matter of decision making.

Moreover many, if not most, communications involve a process of reflective reasoning on what the speaker has asserted; this reasoning is in part a process of testing the truth and/or validity of the propositions being advanced by the speaker (and believed by the speaker to be true). Indeed, the speaker often expects the audience to engage in such reflection and testing.

The upshot of all this is that the hearer's coming to believe what the speaker asserts is a process mediated by an act of inferential judgment with an element of volition; for this reason the comings to believe in question are appropriately described as *the result* of a joint action, the main component actions of which are; (a) the speaker's complex intention to get the hearer to believe some proposition; and (b) the hearer's judgment that the proposition being advanced is true (a judgment based in part on the inference that the speaker intends the hearer to believe the proposition and would not intend to get the hearer to believe a false proposition).

It is consistent with this conception of assertions as joint actions that assertions, nevertheless, are joint actions in an importantly different – indeed weaker – sense from joint actions that do not have as their collective end the transmission of cognitive states.

Moreover, typically assertion is joint action in some further senses. For one thing, assertion normally involves conventions, that is, joint procedures. Thus, there is a convention to utter the term 'Sydney' when one wants to refer to Sydney, and to utter 'is a city' when one wants to ascribe the property of being a city.

Further, assertion is a joint action normally involving joint mechanisms and, specifically, joint institutional mechanisms. As we have seen, joint mechanisms have the characteristic of delivering different actions or results on different occasions of application. Typically, this involves a resultant action.[9]

Language, in general, and assertion, in particular, appears to consist in part of joint mechanisms involving resultant actions.[10] Assume that there are the following joint procedures in a community: utter 'Sydney' when you have as an end reference to Sydney; utter 'Paris' when you have as an end reference to Paris; utter 'is a city' when you have as an end ascription of the property of being a city; and utter 'is frequented by tourists' when you have as an end ascription of the property of being frequented by tourists. Then there might be the resultant joint action to utter 'Paris is a city' when you have as an end ascription to Paris of the property of being a city; and there might be the second and different, resultant joint action to utter

[9] Grice (1989, p. 129) first introduced this notion.
[10] Grice (1989, p. 129f) developed his notion of a resultant procedure (as opposed to a resultant action) for precisely this purpose.

'Sydney is frequented by tourists' when you have as an end ascription to Sydney of the property of being frequented by tourists. It is easy to see how, by the inclusion of a conjunctive operation indicated by 'and', additional linguistic combinations might yield multiple additional resultant actions, for example, the communication effected by uttering 'Paris is a city and Paris is frequented by tourists'.

So assertions consist of joint actions at a number of levels. Assertions are, or can be, basic joint actions, and assertions (typically) are performed in accordance with joint procedures (conventions) and with joint procedural mechanisms. Accordingly, information and communication systems, to the extent that they involve the practice of assertion, involve joint actions of these three kinds. But to what extent do information and communication technology (ICT) systems, in particular, involve the practice of assertion? I will consider three broad areas: communication of information; storage of information; and retrieval of information.

COMMUNICATION, STORAGE, AND RETRIEVAL OF INFORMATION BY MEANS OF ICT

Communication, Storage, and Retrieval of Information

As I have argued, assertion is a species of joint action. Thus far we have considered only assertion in face-to-face contexts. However, an assertion in written form is also joint action; it is simply that the relevant speaker intentions are embodied in written, as opposed to spoken, form. Here we should also note that one and the same assertion can be directed to multiple hearers. Moreover, the multiple hearers can constitute a single audience by virtue (at least in part) of their common knowledge that each is an intended audience of the assertion. Further, each of these multiple hearers, whether they collectively constitute a single 'audience' or not, can 'hear' the assertion at different times and/or at different spatial locations. Indeed, written language enables precisely this latter phenomenon; a speaker can assert something to an audience which is in another part of the planet, for example, by means of an air-mail letter, or indeed in another historical time period, for example, an assertoric sentence written in a history book authored a hundred years ago. Finally, 'a speaker' can consist of more than one individual human being. Consider a selection committee that makes a recommendation that Brown be appointed to the position in question. Each of the members of the committee is taken to be endorsing the proposition that Brown ought to be appointed. This endorsement is expressed in a written statement, let us assume, that is signed by each of the members of the committee. Note here that such an assertion made by a collective body is to be understood as involving a joint institutional mechanism in my above-described sense of that term. The input consists in each member of the committee putting forward his or her views in relation to the applicants, including the reasons for those views. The output consists in the endorsement of Brown by all of the members of the committee. The mechanism is that of deliberation and argument having as a collective end that one person is endorsed by everyone. Accordingly, there is no need to invoke mysterious collective agents that perform speech actions and have mental states, for example, intentions, that are not simply the speech acts and mental states of individual human beings.

Once assertions can be embodied in written form they can be stored in books and the like. Once stored, they can be retrieved by those with access to the book store-house in question. For example, assertions can be written down in book format and the resulting book stored with other such books in a library.

Such assertions and structured sets of assertions and other speech acts, that is, books and other written documents, that are accessible in this way constitute repositories of social knowledge; individual members of a social group can come to know the propositions expressed in these written sentences, and can come to know that others know these propositions, that is, there is common knowledge of the propositions in question.[11]

Most important for our purposes here, such storage and retrieval of information in libraries and the like is an institutional arrangement serving collective ends, for example, the ends of the acquisition of common knowledge and of multiple-'hearer' acquisition of knowledge. Moreover, the procedures by means of which such knowledge is stored and retrieved typically involve joint procedures (conventions) and joint procedural mechanisms. An example of this is classificatory systems used in libraries. The system itself consists in part of a set of conventions that ascribe numbers to designated subject areas and in part of an ascription to each book of a number; the latter number being based on matching the content of the book with one of the subject areas. However, both librarians and borrowers jointly use the system. The library staff stores books in accordance with the system and borrowers retrieve books in accordance with the system. So the input of the joint mechanism is the storage of a book in accordance with the classificatory system. The output is the retrieval of that book by means of the same system. Note that, in the case of paper-based books, there is a physical location (a shelf space) associated with each number and each book; each book is stored in and retrieved from that shelf space.

Communication, Storage, and Retrieval of Information by Means of ICT

ICT systems, such as the Internet, enable assertions to be performed more rapidly and to far greater numbers of 'hearers'. In so doing, an important

---

[11] On the concept of common knowledge, see, for example, Heal (1978).

difference has arisen between such technology-enabled communication and ordinary face-to-face communication. In the latter case, the speaker and the hearer are simply performing so-called basic actions, that is, actions that they can perform at will and without the use of a mediating instrument or mediating technology. Like raising one's arm, speaking is in this sense a basic action, albeit in the context of an audience a basic joint action. On the other hand, driving in a screw by means of a screwdriver, or sending an assertion by e-mail, are not basic actions in this sense (Goldman 1999, chapter 6).

As we shall see in the next section, the fact of this technological intermediary, ICT, raises issues of moral responsibility in relation to the design, implementation, maintenance, and use of this technology-enabled communication; issues that do not, or might not, arise for face-to-face acts of assertion. Consider, for example, the possibility of communicating instantaneously to a large number of people or of filtering out certain addresses and communications. At each of these stages there is joint action, such as that of the team of designers. Moreover, there are new conventions and norms, or new versions of old ones, governing these joint actions at each of these stages, for example, the norm not to continue to send advertisements to an e-mail recipient who has indicated a lack of interest.[12]

ICT also enables the storage and retrieval of databases of information and the integration of such databases to constitute ever larger databases. Such electronic databases enable the generation of new information not envisaged by those who initially stored the information in the database, for example, by combining elements of old information. Such generation of new information on the part of a 'retriever' can be an instance of a joint procedural mechanism.

Consider a large database of police officers in a police organisation. The database consists of employment history, crime matters reported and investigated, complaints made against police, and so on. A large number of people, including police and administrative staff, have stored, and continue to store, information in this database. This is joint action. Moreover, when another police officer accesses the database for some specific item of information this is also joint action; it is, in effect, an assertor informing an audience, except that the assertor does not know who the audience is, or even if there is to be an audience.

Now consider a police officer engaged in an anti-corruption profiling task. He first constructs a profile of a corrupt police officer, for example, an officer who has at least five years of police experience, has had a large number of complaints, works in a sensitive area such as narcotics, and so on. At this stage, the officer uses an ICT search engine to search the database

---

[12] On moral problems of computerised work environments, including what he calls 'epistemic enslavement', see Van den Hoven (1998).

for officers that fit this profile. Eventually, one police officer is identified as fitting the profile, say, Officer O'Malley. This profiling process is the operation of a joint procedural mechanism. First, it relies on the differentiated, but interlocking, actions of a number of agents, including those who initially stored the old information from which the new information is derived, and the anti-corruption officer who inserted the profile into the search engine. Moreover, as is the case with all joint *procedural* mechanisms, this profiling process is repeatable and repeated, for example, different profiles can be and are searched for. Second, the new information, namely that O'Malley fits the profile, is the resultant action; it is derived by means of the profiling mechanism from the inputs of the profile in conjunction with the stored data. However, that O'Malley fits a certain profile is not in itself part of the profiling mechanism per se. Third, there is the profiling mechanism itself.

The resultant action of the use of the profiling mechanism is akin to the resultant action of the use of a voting system and to the resultant action involved in ascribing a property to the subject referred to in a subject-predicate sentence. As with the voting and the ascription of property cases, at one level of description identifying O'Malley was an intentional action, that is, it was intended that the person(s) who fits this profile be identified. (As it was intended that the person with the most votes win the election, and it was intended that Paris be ascribed the property of being a city.) At another level of description it was not intended, that is, it was not intended or known that O'Malley would fit the profile. (As it was not intended by all the voters that Jones win the election; and it was not intended by the *audience* that he or she comes to believe that the speaker believes that Sydney is a city, given that the speaker has (a) referred to Sydney, and (b) ascribed the property of being a city.)

A further example of a joint procedural mechanism in ICT is a so-called expert system (Cass 1996). Consider the following kind of expert system for approving loans in a bank. The bank determines the criteria, and weightings thereof, for offering a loan and the amount of the loan to be offered; the bank does so for a range of different categories of customer. These weighted criteria and associated rules are 'designed-in' to the software of some expert system. The role of the loans officer is to interview each customer individually in order to extract relevant financial and other information from them. Having extracted this information, the loans officer simply inserts it as input into the expert system. The expert system processes the information in terms of the weighted criteria and associated rules designed into it and provides as output whether the customer does or does not meet the requirements for a loan of a certain amount. (Naturally, the decision whether or not to approve the loan is an additional step; it is a decision based on the information that the customer meets, or does not meet, the requirements for being offered a loan.) The loans officer then tells the customer his loan request has either been approved, or not approved, based on the information provided by the expert system. I am assuming that the overall context of this scenario is customers and banks seeking to realise a collective end, namely, the provision of bank loans to appropriate customers.[13] This is a series of joint actions involving information input from customers and the application of criteria to that information by the bank. However, it is also the application of a joint procedural mechanism because there is differentiated, but interlocking, input (information from the customer, application of criteria on the part of the bank) and a derived resultant action (customer does or does not meet the requirements for a loan) that can, and does, differ from one application of the mechanism to the next. In our example, the joint procedural mechanism has been embodied in the expert system.

PART B: COLLECTIVE RESPONSIBILITY OF THE COMMUNICATION, STORAGE, AND RETRIEVAL OF KNOWLEDGE BY MEANS OF ICT

Responsibility

Let me now apply my account of collective responsibility to the communication, storage, and retrieval of knowledge by means of ICT. We need first to distinguish some different senses of responsibility.[14] Sometimes to say that someone is responsible for an action is to say that the person had a reason, or reasons, to perform some action, then formed an intention to perform that action (or not to perform it), and finally acted (or refrained from acting) on that intention, and did so on the basis of that reason(s). Note that an important category of reasons for actions are ends, goals, or purposes; an agent's reason for performing an action is often that the action realises a goal the agent has. Moreover, it is assumed that in the course of all this the agent brought about or caused the action, at least in the sense that the mental state or states that constituted his reason for performing the action was causally efficacious (in the right way), and that his resulting intention was causally efficacious (in the right way).

I will dub this sense of being responsible for an action 'natural responsibility'. It is this sense of being responsible that I will be working with in this chapter, that is, intentionally performing an action, and doing so for a reason.

On other occasions what is meant by the term, 'being responsible for an action', is that the person in question occupies a certain institutional role and that the occupant of that role is the person who has the institutionally determined duty to decide what is to be done in relation to certain

---

[13] I will ignore the inherent elements of conflict, for example, some customers who want loans are unable to afford them, banks often want to lend at higher rates of interest than customers want to pay.

[14] The material in this and the following sections is derived from Miller (2001, chapter 8).

matters. For example, the computer maintenance person in an office has the responsibility to fix the computers in the office, irrespective of whether or not he does so, or even contemplates doing so.

A third sense of 'being responsible' for an action, is a species of our second sense. If the matters in respect of which the occupant of an institutional role has an institutionally determined duty to decide what is to be done, include ordering other agents to perform, or not to perform, certain actions, then the occupant of the role is responsible for those actions performed by those other agents. We say of such a person that he is responsible for the actions of others persons in virtue of being the person in authority over them.

The fourth sense of responsibility is in fact the sense that we are principally concerned with here, namely, moral responsibility. Roughly speaking, an agent is held to be morally responsible for an action if the agent was responsible for that action in one of our first three senses of responsible, and that action is morally significant.

An action can be morally significant in a number of ways. The action could be intrinsically morally wrong, as in the case of a rights violation. Or the action might have moral significance by virtue of the end that it was performed to serve or the outcome that it actually had. We can now make the following preliminary claim concerning moral responsibility:

(Claim 1) If an agent is responsible for an action in the first, second, or third senses of being responsible, and the action is morally significant, then – other things being equal – the agent is morally responsible for that action, and can reasonably attract moral praise or blame and (possibly) punishment or reward for performing the action.

Here the 'other things being equal' clause is intended to be cashed in terms of exculpatory conditions, such as that he was not coerced, he could not reasonably have foreseen the consequences of his action, and so on.

Having distinguished four senses of responsibility, including moral responsibility, let me now turn directly to collective responsibility.[15]

Collective Moral Responsibility

As is the case with individual responsibility, we can distinguish four senses of collective responsibility. In the first instance, I will do so in relation to joint actions.

Agents who perform a joint action are responsible for that action in the first sense of collective responsibility. Accordingly, to say that they are collectively responsible for the action is just to say that they performed the joint action. That is, they each had a collective end, each intentionally performed their contributory action, and each did so because each believed

---

[15] On the notions of joint and collective responsibility, see Zimmerman (1985) and May (1991).

the other would perform his contributory action, and that therefore the collective end would be realised.

Here it is important to note that each agent is individually (naturally) responsible for performing his contributory action, and responsible by virtue of the fact that he intentionally performed this action, and the action was not intentionally performed by anyone else. Of course the other agent or agents *believe* that he is performing, or is going to perform, the contributory action in question. But mere possession of such a belief is not sufficient for the ascription of responsibility to *the believer* for performing the individual action in question. So what are the agents *collectively* (naturally) responsible for? The agents are *collectively* (naturally) responsible for the realisation of the (collective) *end* which results from their contributory actions. Consider two agents jointly lifting a large computer onto a truck. Each is individually (naturally) responsible for lifting his side of the computer, and the two agents are collectively (naturally) responsible for bringing it about that the computer is situated on the truck.

Again, if the occupants of an institutional role (or roles) have an institutionally determined obligation to perform some joint action then those individuals are collectively responsible for its performance, in our second sense of collective responsibility. Here there is a *joint* institutional obligation to realise the collective end of the joint action in question. In addition, there is a set of derived *individual* obligations; each of the participating individuals has an individual obligation to perform his or her contributory action. (The derivation of these individual obligations relies on the fact that if each performs his or her contributory action then it is probable that the collective end will be realised.)

There is a third sense of collective responsibility that might be thought to correspond to the third sense of individual responsibility. The third sense of individual responsibility concerns those in authority. Suppose the members of the Cabinet of country A (consisting of the Prime Minister and his Cabinet Ministers) collectively decide to exercise their institutionally determined right to relax the cross-media ownership laws in the light of an increase in the number and forms of public electronic communication. The Cabinet is collectively responsible for this policy change.

There are a couple of things to keep in mind here. First, the notion of responsibility in question here is, at least in the first instance, institutional – as opposed to moral – responsibility.

Second, the 'decisions' of committees, as opposed to the individual decisions of the members of committees, need to be analysed in terms of the notion of a joint institutional mechanism introduced above. So the 'decision' of the Cabinet can be analysed as follows. At one level, each member of the Cabinet voted for or against the cross-media policy. Let us assume that some voted in the affirmative, and others voted in the negative. But at another level each member of the Cabinet agreed to abide by the outcome of the vote; each voted having as a collective end that the outcome with a majority of the votes in its favour would be pursued. Accordingly, the members of the Cabinet were jointly, institutionally responsible for the policy change, that is, the Cabinet was collectively institutionally responsible for the change.

What of the fourth sense of collective responsibility: collective *moral* responsibility? Collective moral responsibility is a species of joint responsibility. Accordingly, each agent is individually morally responsible, but conditionally on the others being individually morally responsible; there is interdependence in respect of moral responsibility. This account of collective moral responsibility arises naturally out of the account of joint actions. It also parallels the account given of individual moral responsibility.

Thus, we can make our second preliminary claim about moral responsibility:

(Claim 2) If agents are collectively responsible for the realisation of an outcome, in the first or second or third senses of collective responsibility, and if the outcome is morally significant, then – other things being equal – the agents are collectively morally responsible for that outcome, and can reasonably attract moral praise or blame, and (possibly) punishment or reward for bringing about the outcome.

Collective Responsibility for the Communication, Storage, and Retrieval of Information

As is probably by now evident, I reject the proposition that nonhuman agents, such as institutions or computers, have mental states and can, properly speaking, be ascribed responsibility in any noncausal sense of that term. Specifically, I reject the notion that institutions per se, or computers, can legitimately be ascribed moral responsibility, either individual or collective moral responsibility.[16] Accordingly, in what follows I am going locate moral responsibility for morally significant communication, storage, and retrieval of information with individual human beings.

Moral responsibility for epistemic states is importantly different from moral responsibility for actions as such. Nevertheless, it is legitimate to ascribe moral responsibility for the production of morally significant epistemic states. In particular, it is legitimate to ascribe collective moral responsibility for morally significant epistemic states that are, at least in part, the collective ends of joint actions, for example, of assertions.

Many epistemic states are, or ought to be, dependent on some rational process such as deductive inference. In this sense, the epistemic state is 'compelled' by the evidence for it; there is little or no element of volition. Accordingly, there is a contrast with so-called practical decision making.

---

[16] For an outline of this kind of view, see Ladd (1988).

The latter is decision making that terminates in an action; the former is inference-making that terminates in an epistemic state.

However, this contrast can be exaggerated. For one thing, the compulsion in question is not necessarily, or even typically, such as to guarantee the epistemic outcome; nor is it necessarily, or even typically, a malfunction of the process if it does not guarantee some epistemic outcome. For another thing there are, or can be, volitional elements in inference-making that terminates in epistemic states; we saw this above in relation to an audience's decision to trust in a speaker's sincerity.

At any rate, my general point here is that theoretical reasoning is sufficiently similar to practical reasoning for it to be possible, at least in principle, to ascribe responsibility to a theoretical reasoner for the epistemic outcomes of their theoretical reasoning. One can be held responsible for the judgments one makes in relation to the truth or falsity of certain propositions, given the need for conscientious inference making, unearthing of facts, and so on. Therefore, one can be held morally responsible for such judgments, if they have moral significance.[17]

The principle that a rational adult is morally responsible for their morally significant beliefs has a certain intuitive appeal in relation to their beliefs about moral values and principles; after all, if you are not responsible for your belief that it is acceptable for, say, paedophiles to stalk children on the Internet, then who is? And the same point holds true of one's beliefs about the best way to spend one's own life; surely, you have to be held morally responsible for, say, your belief that it is best for you to abandon your career as a philosopher in favour of making money through online gambling.

What of your beliefs in respect of the moral character of other persons? Suppose C asserts to A that a person known to A, namely B, is dishonest. Presumably, some weight ought to be given to, for example, written character references from former employers that have been stored in an official administrative database. On the other hand, A's belief in respect of B's character is surely not something that A should arrive at entirely on the basis of what other persons assert about B, and certainly not on the basis of what *one* other person asserts about B. In this respect, assertions about moral character are different from assertions about simple matters of fact such as, for example, that it is now raining outside.

One can also be morally responsible for coming to have false beliefs in relation to factual matters. Consider a scientist who comes to believe that

---

[17] I accept the arguments of James A. Montmarquet (1993, chapter 1) to the conclusion that one can be *directly* responsible for some of one's beliefs, that is, that one's responsibility for some of one's beliefs is not dependent on one's responsibility for some action that led to those beliefs. In short, doxastic responsibility does not reduce to responsibility for actions. However, if I (and Montmarquet) turn out to be wrong in this regard, the basic arguments in this chapter could be recast in terms of a notion of doxastic responsibility as a form of responsibility for actions.

the universe is expanding, but he or she does so on the basis of invalid, indeed very sloppy, calculations. Such a scientist would be culpable in a further sense, if he communicated this falsity to others or stored the data in a form accessible to others. Moreover, a second scientist who retrieved the data and came to believe it might also be culpable if, for example, he failed to determine whether or not the data had been independently verified by other scientists.

Now suppose that it is not an individual scientist who engages is such invalid and sloppy work, but a team of scientists. This is an instance of collective moral responsibility for scientific error. Again, there would be culpability in a further sense, if the team communicated the falsity to others, or stored the data in a form accessible to others. Moreover, other scientists who retrieved the data and came to believe it might also be culpable if, for example, they failed to determine whether or not the data had been independently verified by other teams of scientists.

A further category of morally significant data is information in respect of which there is, so to speak, a duty of ignorance. This category may well consist of true propositions. However, the point is that certain persons ought not have epistemic access to these propositions. Examples of this are propositions governed by privacy or confidentiality rights and duties.

So a person can reasonably be held morally responsible for coming to believe, communicating, storing, or retrieving false propositions where the basis for this ascription of moral responsibility is simply the moral significance that attaches to false propositions; other things being equal, falsity ought to be avoided. In addition, a person can reasonably be held morally responsible for coming to believe, communicating, storing, accessing, or retrieving true propositions in respect of which he or she has a duty of ignorance. Moreover, such moral responsibility can be individual or collective responsibility. What of beliefs that are morally significant only because they are necessary conditions for morally unacceptable actions or outcomes?

Moral responsibility for adverse outcomes is sometimes simply a matter of malicious intent; it is in no way dependent on any false beliefs. Suppose that A fires a gun intending to kill B and believing that by firing the gun he will kill B. Suppose further that A does in fact kill B, and that it is a case of murder. A's wrongful action is dependent on his malicious intention. It is also dependent on his true belief; however, there is no dependence on any false beliefs. Here, it is by virtue of A's malicious intention that his action is morally wrong and he is morally culpable.

Now assume that A does not intend to kill B but A, nevertheless, kills B because A fires the gun falsely believing that it is a toy gun. Here, A is culpable by virtue of failing to ensure that he knew that the gun was a toy gun. That is, it is *in part* by virtue of A's epistemic mistake that he is morally culpable. A did not know that it was a real gun, but he should have known this.

Let us consider a similar case, but this time involving a third party who provides information to A. Suppose C asserts to A that the gun is a toy gun and that, therefore, if A 'shoots' B with the gun A will not harm, let alone kill, B. Agent A has reason to believe that C is telling the truth; indeed, let us assume that C believes (falsely) that the gun is a toy gun. C is at fault for falsely asserting that the gun is a toy gun. However, A is also at fault for shooting B dead, albeit in the belief that it was a toy gun. For A should have independently verified C's assertion that the gun was a toy gun; A should not simply have taken C's word for it. Indeed, the degree of fault A has for killing B is not diminished by the fact that C told A that it was a toy gun.

Now consider a scenario similar to the above one, except that C is a doctor who gives A some liquid to inject into B. B is unconscious as a consequence of having been bitten by a snake, and A asserts sincerely, but falsely, to B that the liquid is an antidote. Assume that the liquid is in fact a poison and that B dies as a consequence of A's injection of poison. Assume further that the snake venom is not deadly; it would only have incapacitated B for a period. C is culpable by virtue of his epistemic error; he is a doctor and should have known that the liquid was poison. What of A? He relies on his belief that C's assertions in relation to medicine are true; and that belief has a warrant, namely the fact that C is a doctor. Presumably, A is not morally culpable, notwithstanding his epistemic error.

However, consider the case where C is not a doctor but is, nevertheless, someone with a reasonable knowledge of medicines, including antidotes; he is a kind of amateurish 'doctor'. Here we would be inclined, I take it, to hold that both A and C were jointly morally responsible for B's death. For whereas A was entitled to ascribe to C's assertion a degree of epistemic weight, he was not entitled to ascribe to it the kind of weight that would enable him (A) to avoid making his own judgment as to whether or not to inject the liquid into B.

The upshot of the discussion thus far is that in relation to harmful outcomes arising from avoidable epistemic error on the part of more than one agent, there are at least three possibilities. First, the agent who *directly* – that is, not via another agent – caused the harm is individually and fully culpable; the culpability in question being negligence. Second, the agent who *directly* caused the harm is not culpable. Third, the agent who *directly* caused the harm and the agent who *indirectly* caused it (by misinforming the agent who directly caused it) are jointly culpable. The question remains as to whether each is fully culpable, or whether their responsibility is distributed and in each case diminished. Here, I assume that there can be both sorts of case.

Thus far we have been discussing situations involving harmful outcomes arising from avoidable epistemic error. But we need also to consider *some* cases involving harmful outcomes that have arisen from true beliefs. Assume that an academic paper describing a process for producing a deadly virus exists under lock and key in a medical library; the contents of the paper have not been disseminated because there are concerns about bioterrorism. Assume further that the scientist who wrote the paper decides to communicate its contents to a known terrorist in exchange for a large amount of money. The scientist is morally culpable for communicating information, that is, true propositions. This is because of the likely harmful consequences of this information being known to terrorists, in particular. Here we have the bringing about of a morally significant epistemic state for which an agent is morally culpable; but the epistemic state in question is a *true* belief.

So there is a range of cases of morally significant epistemic states for which agents can justifiably be held morally responsible, and these include epistemic states for which agents can justifiably be held collectively morally responsible.

This being so, it is highly likely that in some cases the individual and collective responsibility in question will not only be for the communication of false beliefs, but also for the storage and retrieval of false data. Given that speakers can be, individually or collectively, morally responsible for communicating falsehoods that cause harm, it is easy to see how they could be morally responsible for storing falsehoods that cause harm. For example, a librarian who knows that an alleged medical textbook contains false medical claims that if acted upon would cause death might, nevertheless, choose to procure the book for her library and, thereby, ensure that it will: (a) be read, and (in all probability) (b) be acted upon with lethal consequences. What of responsibility for the retrieval of information?

Let us recall the example of an academic paper describing a process for producing a deadly virus exists under lock and key in a medical library; the contents of the paper have not been disseminated because there are concerns about bioterrorism. Now suppose that in exchange for a large amount of money the librarian (not the scientist who wrote the paper) forwards a copy of the paper to a known terrorist.

I have been speaking of moral culpability for morally significant communication, storage, or retrieval of information; however, the moral significance has consisted in the harmfulness attendant upon the communication, storage, or retrieval of the information in question. Naturally, moral responsibility could pertain to morally *desirable* communication, storage, and retrieval of information.

COLLECTIVE RESPONSIBILITY FOR THE COMMUNICATION, STORAGE, AND RETRIEVAL OF INFORMATION BY MEANS OF ICT

Thus far I have provided an account of collective responsibility for the communication, storage, and retrieval of information. Finally, I turn to the special case of collective moral responsibility for the communication, storage, and retrieval of information by means of ICT.

We have already seen that assertions are a species of joint action, and in the case of morally significant assertions, speakers and audiences can reasonably be held collectively morally responsible for the comings to believe consequent upon those assertions. In so far as ICT involves the communication, storage, and retrieval of morally significant assertions, users of ICT who are speakers and audiences can likewise reasonably be held collectively morally responsible for the comings to believe consequent upon those computer-mediated assertions.

Expert systems provide a somewhat different example. We saw above that many expert systems are joint procedural mechanisms. In cases in which the resultant action of a joint mechanism is morally significant, then those who participated in the joint mechanism can reasonably be held collectively morally responsible, albeit some might have diminished responsibility, others full responsibility. Thus, voters can be held responsible for the fact that the person with the most votes was elected. Likewise, the customers and the bank personnel – including those who determine the criteria for loan approvals – can be held collectively morally responsible for a loan being approved to, say, a person who later fails to make his/her payments. And the police who enter data into a police database, the police who develop and match profiles against stored data, and the senior police who orchestrated this profiling policy can be held collectively morally responsible for the coming to believe on the part of some of the above that, say, O'Malley fits the profile in question. Naturally, the degree of individual responsibility varies from officer to officer, depending on the precise nature and extent of their contribution to this outcome.[18]

An additional point in relation to moral responsibility and expert systems is that the designers of any such system can, at least in principle, be held jointly morally responsible for, say, faults in the system or indeed for the existence of the system itself. Consider a team that designs a computerised delivery system for nuclear weapons.

In conclusion, I make two general points in relation to moral responsibility and ICT expert systems, in particular. First, there is an important distinction to be made between the application of mechanical procedures, whether by humans or computers, on the one hand, and the *interpretation* of moral principles, laws, and the like, on the other hand. This point is in essence a corollary of the familiar point that computers and other machines do not mean or interpret anything; they lack the semantic dimension. So much John Searle (1984) has famously demonstrated by means of his Chinese rooms scenario. Moreover, computers do not assert anything

---

[18] There are a host of other issues of moral responsibility raised by expert systems, including in relation to the responsibility to determine who ought to have access to what sources of information. The provision to library users of computer-based information directly accessible only to librarians is a case in point, for example, sources of information potentially harmful to third parties. For a discussion of these issues, see Ferguson and Weckert (1993).

or come to believe anything. Specifically, assertions and propositional epistemic states are truth-aiming and, as such, presuppose meaning or semantics. In order to assert that the cat is on the mat, the speaker has to refer to the cat and ascribe the property of being on the mat. However, asserting that the cat is on the mat is an additional act to that of meaning something in the sense of expressing some propositional content by, say, uttering a sentence.

At any rate laws, but not mechanical procedures, stand in need of interpretation and, therefore, require on occasion the exercise of interpretative judgment. The law makes use of deliberately open-ended notions that call for the exercise of discretion by judicial officers, police and so on, for example, the notion of reasonable suspicion. And some laws are deliberately framed so as to be left open to interpretation – so-called fuzzy laws. The rationale for such laws is that they reduce the chances of loopholes being found; loopholes of the kind generated by more precise, sharp-edged laws. Moreover, laws often stand in need of interpretation in relation to situations not encountered previously or not envisaged by the law-makers. Consider a well-known South African case in which a policeman arrested a man for speaking abusively to him over the phone, claiming the offence had been committed in his presence. The court ruled that the place at which the offence was committed was in the house of the defendant and that therefore the crime had not been committed in the presence of the policeman. So the ruling went against the police officer. But it was not obvious that it would. At any rate, the interpretation of laws is not always a straightforward matter, yet, it is a matter that will be adjudicated. Accordingly, judicial officers, police, and indeed citizens, necessarily make interpretative judgments which can turn out to be correct or not correct. There is no such room for interpretative judgment in the case of mechanical procedures. Either the procedure applies or it does not, and, if it is not clear whether or not it is to be applied, the consequence is either recourse to a default position, for example, it does not apply, or to a malfunction. The implications of this discussion are: (a) many laws are not able to be fully rendered into a form suitable for mechanical application; and (b) expert systems embodying laws might need additional ongoing interpretative human expertise. Accordingly, such expert systems ought to be designed so that they can be overridden by a human legal expert.[19]

Second, conformity to conventions, laws, and mechanical procedures is importantly different from conformity to moral principles and ends. It is just a mistake to assume that what morality requires or permits in a given situation must be identical with what the law requires or permits in that situation, much less with what a mechanical procedure determines. Let me explain.

---

[19] For more detail on this kind of issue, see Kuflik (1999).

The law, in particular, and social institutions, in general, are blunt instruments. They are designed to deal with recurring situations confronted by numerous institutional actors over relatively long periods of time. Laws abstract away from differences between situations across space and time, and differences between institutional actors across space and time. The law, therefore, consists of a set of generalisations to which the particular situation must be made to fit. Hence, if you exceed the speed limit you are liable for a fine, even though you were only 10 m.p.h. above the speed limit, you have a superior car, you are a superior driver, there was no other traffic on the road, the road conditions were perfect, and therefore the chances of you having an accident were actually less than would be the case for most other people most of the time driving at or under the speed limit.[20] This general point is even more obvious when it comes to mechanical procedures.

By contrast with the law and with mechanical procedures, morality is a sharp instrument. Morality can be, and typically ought to be, made to apply to a given situation in all its particularity. (This is, of course, not to say that there are not recurring moral situations in respect of which the same moral judgment should be made, nor is it to say that morality does not need to help itself to generalisations.) Accordingly, what might be, all things considered, the morally best action for an agent to perform in some one-off,that is, nonrecurring, situation might not be an action that should be made lawful, much less one designed in to some computer or other machine. Consider the well-worn real-life example of the five sailors on a raft in the middle of the ocean and without food. Four of them decide to eat the fifth – the cabin boy – in order to survive.[21] This is a case of both murder and cannibalism. Was it morally excusable to kill and eat the boy given the alternative was the death of all five sailors? Arguably, it was morally excusable and the sailors, although convicted of murder and cannibalism, had their sentence commuted in recognition of this. But it would be absurd to remove the laws against murder and cannibalism, as a consequence of this kind of extreme case. Again, consider an exceptionless law against desertion from the battlefield in time of war. Perhaps a soldier is morally justifiable in deserting his fellow soldiers, given that he learns of the more morally pressing need for him to care for his wife who has contracted some life-threatening disease back home. However, the law against desertion will not, and should not, be changed to allow desertion in such cases.

The implication here is that by virtue of its inherent particularity moral decision making cannot be fully captured by legal systems and their attendant processes of interpretation, much less by expert systems and their

---

[20] Frederick Schauer (2003) argues this thesis in relation to laws and uses the speed limit as an example. As it happens, I believe Schauer goes too far in his account of laws and in insisting that the law is blunter than it needs to be. However, that does not affect what I am saying here.

[21] Andrew Alexandra reminded me of this example.

processes of mechanical application of procedures. Moral decision making has an irreducibly discretionary element. Accordingly, expert systems embodying moral principles ought to be designed to as to be able to be overridden by a morally sensitive human being, if not by a human moral expert (Kuflik 1999).

References

Bentley, R., Appelt, W., Busbach, U., Hinrichs, E., Kerr, D., Sikkel, K., Trevor, J., and Woetzel, G. 1997. Basic Support for Cooperative Work on the World Wide Web. *International Journal of Human-Computer Studies, 46,* 6, 827–846.

Cass, K. 1996. Expert systems as general-use advisory tools: An examination of moral responsibility. *Business and Professional Ethics Journal, 15,* 4, 61–85.

Ferguson, S., and Weckert, J. 1993. Ethics, reference librarians and expert systems. *Australian Library Journal, 42,* 3, 3–13.

Gilbert, M. 1992. *Social facts.* Princeton, NJ: Princeton University Press.

Goldman, A. 1999. *Knowledge in a social world.* London: Oxford University Press.

Grice, P. 1989. *Studies in the way of words.* Cambridge, MA: Harvard University Press.

Heal, J. 1978. Common knowledge. *Philosophical Quarterly, 28,* 116–131.

Kuflik, A. 1999. Computers in control: Rational transfer of authority or irresponsible abdication of autonomy? *Ethics and Information Technology, 1,* pp. 173–184.

Ladd, J. 1988. Computers and moral responsibility: A framework for an ethical analysis, in C. Gould (Ed.), *The Information web: Ethical and social implications of computer networking.* Boulder, CO: Westview Press.

May, L. (Ed.). 1991. *Collective responsibility.* Lanham, MD: Rowman and Littlefield.

Miller, S. 1985. Speaker-meaning and assertion. *South African Journal of Philosophy, 2,* 4, 48–54.

Miller, S. 2001. *Social action: A teleological account.* Cambridge, UK: Cambridge University Press.

Miller, S., and Makela, P. 2005. The collectivist approach to collective moral responsibility. *Metaphilosophy, 36,* 5, 634.

Montmarquet, J. A. 1993. *Epistemic virtue and doxastic responsibility.* Lanham, MD: Rowman and Littlefield.

Pettit, P. 2001. *A Theory of freedom.* Cambridge, UK: Polity Press.

Schauer, F. 2003. *Profiles, probabilities and stereotypes.* Cambridge MA: Belknap Press.

Searle, J. 1984. *Minds, brains and science.* London: Pelican.

van den Hoven, J. 1998. Moral responsibility, public office and information technology, in I. Snellen & W. van de Donk (Eds.), *Public administration in an information age.* Amsterdam: IOS Press.

Zimmerman, M. J. 1985. Sharing responsibility. *American Philosophical Quarterly, 22,* 2, 115–122.

13

Computers as Surrogate Agents

Deborah G. Johnson and Thomas M. Powers

Computer ethicists have long been intrigued by the possibility that computers, computer programs, and robots might develop to a point at which they could be considered moral agents. In such a future, computers might be considered responsible for good and evil deeds and people might even have moral qualms about disabling them. Generally, those who entertain this scenario seem to presume that the moral agency of computers can only be established by showing that computers have moral personhood and this, in turn, can only be the case if computers have attributes comparable to human intelligence, rationality, or consciousness. In this chapter, we want to redirect the discussion about agency by offering an alternative model for thinking about the moral agency of computers. We argue that human surrogate agency is a good model for understanding the moral agency of computers. Human surrogate agency is a form of agency in which individuals act as agents of others. Such agents take on a special kind of role morality when they are employed as surrogates. We will examine the structural parallels between human surrogate agents and computer systems to reveal the moral agency of computers.

Our comparison of human surrogate agents and computers is part of a larger project, a major thrust of which is to show that technological artifacts have a kind of *intentionality*, regardless of whether they are intelligent or conscious. By this we mean that technological artifacts are directed at the world of human capabilities and behaviors. It is in virtue of their intentionality that artifacts are poised to interact with and change a world inhabited by humans. Without being directed at or being about the world, how else could technological artifacts affect the world according to their designs? Insofar as artifacts display this kind of intentionality and affect human interests and behaviors, the artifacts exhibit a kind of *moral agency*. If our account of technology and agency is right, the search for the mysterious point at which computers become intelligent or conscious is unnecessary.

We will not rely, however, on our broader account of the intentionality of all technological artifacts here. In this chapter, our agenda is to show that computer systems have moral agency in a narrower sense. This agency can be seen in the structural similarities of human and computer surrogate agents, and in the relationship between computer systems and human interests. Both human and computer surrogate agents affect human interests in performing their respective roles; the way they affect interests should be constrained by the special morality proper to the kind of surrogate agents they are. To reveal the moral agency of computer systems, we begin by discussing the 'role morality' of human surrogate agency and the nature of agency relationships (Part 1). We then turn our attention to specifying more carefully the object of our attention: computers, computer programs, and robots (Part 2). The next part of our account draws out the parallels between human surrogate agents and computer systems and maps the moral framework of human surrogate agency onto the agency of computer systems (Part 3). This framework allows us to identify the kinds of interests that human and computer surrogate agents pursue and also leads to an account of the two ways in which surrogate agents can go wrong. Finally, we review the account we have given and assess its implications (Part 4).

1. HUMAN SURROGATE AGENCY

In standard accounts of agency, moral agents are understood to be acting from a first-person point of view. A moral agent pursues personal desires and interests based on his or her beliefs about the world, and morality is a constraint on how those interests can be pursued, especially in light of the interests of others. In this context, human surrogate agency is an extension of standard moral agency. The surrogate agent acts from a point of view that can be characterized as a 'third-person perspective'. In acting, the surrogate agent considers not what he or she wants, but what the client wants. While still being constrained by standard morality in the guise of such notions as duty, right, and responsibility, human surrogate agents pursue a subset of the interests of a client. But now, they are also constrained by role morality, a system of conventions and expectations associated with a role.[1] Examples of surrogate agents are lawyers, tax accountants, estate executors, and managers of performers and entertainers. Typically, the role morality entails responsibilities and imposes duties on the agents as they pursue the desires and interests of the client. For example, lawyers are not supposed to represent clients whose interests are in conflict with those of another client; tax accountants are not supposed to sign for their clients; and estate

---

[1] See Goldman (1980) for a theory of role morality and the justification of special moral rights and responsibilities attached to professional roles.

executors are not supposed to distribute the funds from an estate to whomever they wish.

To say that human surrogate agents pursue the interests of third parties is not to say that they have no first-person interest in their actions as agents. Rather, the surrogate agent has a personal interest in fulfilling the role well, and doing so involves acting on behalf of the client. Failure to fulfill the responsibilities of the role or to stay within its constraints can harm the interests of the surrogate agent insofar as it leads to a poor reputation or being sued for professional negligence. Conversely, success in fulfilling the responsibilities of the role can enhance the reputation and market worth of the surrogate agent and may, thereby, fulfill some of his or her own goals.

Although surrogate agents pursue the interests of their clients, they do much more than simply take directions from their clients. To some extent, stockbrokers are expected to implement the decisions of their clients, but they are also expected to provide advice and market information relevant to making informed decisions.[2] In addition, stockbrokers form investment strategies based on a client profile of risk aversion, liquidity, goals, and so forth and not based on generic investment strategies. The surrogate role of tax accountants is not merely to calculate and file a client's taxes but also to find the most advantageous way for the client to fulfill the requirements of the tax code.[3] Estate executors provide a unique case of surrogate agents because they must pursue the expressed wishes of their clients after the clients are deceased. The client's will is comparable to a closed-source program; it is a set of instructions to be implemented by the executor, and not to be second-guessed or improved upon.

Generalizing across roles and types of human surrogate agents, we find at least two different ways that surrogate agents can do wrong. First, they can act incompetently and in so doing fail to further the interests of their clients. Imagine a stockbroker who forgets to execute a client's request to buy 500 shares of IBM stock at a target price; the stock soars and the client loses the opportunity to obtain the shares at an attractive price. Or imagine a tax accountant who, in preparing a client's annual income tax, fails to take advantage of a tax credit for which the client is fully qualified. Finally, imagine the estate executor who neglects to include the appropriate parties in the meeting to read the will and, as a result, the will is thrown into probate court. These are all cases in which the surrogate agent fails to implement an action or achieve an outcome because of incompetence on the part of the agent. Such failures are generally unintentional, but, nevertheless, the surrogate agent fails to do what is in the interest of the client.

[2] The practice of electronic trading has changed or eliminated the moral relations between investors and stockbrokers to a large extent.

[3] Tax accountants are important in our analysis because they can be compared to software programs that individuals use to prepare their annual income taxes.

Second, surrogate agents can do wrong by intentionally violating one of the constraints of the role. We will refer to this form of doing wrong as misbehavior. Imagine the stockbroker encouraging a client to buy shares in a company and lying about the last dividend paid by the company or the company's price-to-earnings ratio. Worse still, consider the real case in which a major investment firm advocated the purchase of stock in a troubled company in order to gain the investment banking business of the company – at the expense of the interests of their investors.[4] Imagine the tax accountant violating confidentiality by giving out information about a client to a philanthropic organization; or imagine the estate executor giving money to the client's children despite the fact that the client specified that they were to receive none. These are all cases in which the agent does wrong by violating the duties or constraints of the role. In most cases of misbehavior, the surrogate agent pursues someone else's interests, for example, the agent's or other third parties, to the detriment of the interests of the client. In this way, the surrogate agent intentionally fails to fulfill one crucial expectation associated with the role: to take the (third-person) perspective of the client.

2. COMPUTERS, COMPUTER PROGRAMS, AND ROBOTS

Up until now, we have used the phrase 'computers, computer programs, and robots' to identify the object of our focus. Because our primary interest is with the activities engaged in by computers as they are deployed and their programs are implemented, it is best to refer to them as computer systems. Users deploy computer systems to engage in certain activities and they do so by providing inputs of various kinds to the system – turning the system on, modifying the software, setting parameters, assigning values to variables, and so on. The user's input combines with the computer system's functionality to produce an output. Furthermore, every computer system manifests a physical outcome, even if it is the mere illumination of a pixel on an LCD screen.

In this context, robots are distinctive only in the sense that they have mobility and sensors that allow them to perform complex tasks in an extended space. Typically robots are responsive to their physical environment and they have motors that allow locomotion. This special functionality allows robots to engage in activities that most computer systems cannot

---

[4] A class action lawsuit settled in May of 2002 involved Merrill Lynch & Co. and the state of New York. The settlement required the investment firm to pay $100 million for misleading investors by giving them 'biased research on the stocks of the company's investment banking clients'. (See 'Merrill Lynch, NY reach $100M Settlement', Frank Schnaue, UPI: 05/21/02.) The Merrill Lynch agreement was the basis for many other settlements of suits against investment houses that had done basically the same thing – trade-off the interests of individual investors for the interests of their investment banking business.

achieve. Robots are, nevertheless, computer systems; they are a special type of computer system.

For quite some time computer enthusiasts and cognitive scientists have used the language of agency to talk about a subset of computer systems, primarily search engines, Web crawlers, and other software 'agents' sent out to look for information or undertake activities on the Internet. The term 'bot' has even been introduced for software utilities that search and destroy invading forms of software or 'spyware' on a resident computer system. Hence, the idea that computer systems can be thought of as agents is not novel.[5] However, we are extending the idea that software utilities and robots are agents to include all computer systems as agents.

Because of the similarities of some computer system behaviors to human thinking, mobility, and action, the simile of computer surrogate agency may seem strikingly obvious. However, our argument does not turn on functional similarities of computers and humans, such as mobility, responsiveness, or even logical sophistication. Rather, we want to focus on the relationship of computer systems (when in use) to human interests; that is, we want to see the relationship in its social and moral context. It is there where we locate the key to seeing computer systems as moral agents.

Computer systems are designed and deployed to do tasks assigned to them *by* humans. The search engine finds online information by taking over a task similar to the task humans used to undertake when they rummaged through card catalogs and walked through stacks. Computer systems also take over tasks that were previously assigned to other mechanical devices. For example, an automobile braking system used to work mechanically (although not reliably) to prevent the caliper from locking the pad onto the rotor, which causes the road-wheel to slide in a severe braking maneuver. Now the mechanics of the caliper, pad, and rotor are changed, and an added ABS computer makes the caliper pressure vacillate very quickly in order to prevent road-wheel lockup. Technically, the same outcome could have been achieved by the driver pumping the brake very rapidly in a panic braking situation. However, given the psychology of panic, the automated system is more reliable than the system of driver-and-mechanical-device.

In addition to aiding humans and machines in doing what was formerly possible but still difficult or tedious, computer systems often perform tasks that were not possible for individuals and purely mechanical devices to achieve. Before fuel injection computers, a driver in a carbureted automobile could not vary the air/fuel mixture to respond to momentary changes in air and engine temperature and barometric pressure. Now, computers make all of these adjustments, and many more, in internal combustion engines. Similarly, an individual could never edit a photograph by changing

---

[5] Software agents have been seen as agents of commerce and contract, in the legal sense. See Ian R. Kerr (1999).

resolution, colors, and dimensions, and erase all of those changes if not desirable, without the aid of a computer program. Now a child can do these things to a digital image. In all of these cases, users deploy computers to engage in activities the user wants done.

The conception of computer systems as agents is perhaps obvious in the case of search engines deployed on behalf of their users to find information on a certain topic, and in the case of tax software that does more or less what tax accountants do. But the comparison really encompasses a continuum: some computer systems replace human surrogates; other systems do tasks that humans did not do for one another; and still other systems perform tasks that no human (unaided) could ever do. We intend that our account will work just as well for the automotive tasks described above as for other activities such as wordprocessing, database management, and so on. The user deploys the system to accomplish certain tasks, and we now talk freely of the computer 'doing things' for the user.

Depending on the system and the task, the computer system may do all or some of a task. Spreadsheet software, for example, does not gather data, but it displays and calculates. Wordprocessors do not help generate ideas or words or help get the words from one's mind to one's fingers. But the wordprocessing system does help get the words from someone's fingers to a visible medium, and it facilitates, and sometimes automates, change and reconsideration. Insofar as they do things at all, computers act as agents on behalf of humans. Thus, it seems plausible to think of computer systems as agents working on behalf of humans. Sometimes the computer system is deployed on behalf of an individual; at other times it is deployed on behalf of groups of individuals, such as corporations or other kinds of organizations. As we have suggested, when computer systems are deployed on behalf of humans, the activities undertaken involve varying degrees of automation and human involvement. Outcomes are achieved through a combination of human performance and automation. This is what happens with the automobile braking systems, as described above, as humans move their bodies in various ways in relation to automobile levers. This is also what happens with search engines and spybots, where humans manipulate keyboards (or other input devices) and set computers in motion. Tasks are accomplished by combinations of human and machine activity but in pursuit of the interests of humans.

Can't the same be said about all technological artifacts? Aren't all technological artifacts deployed by users to pursue the interests of the users? Not only is this an accurate characterization of all technologies, it seems to define technology.[6] All technological artifacts receive input from users and transform the input into output, even though every artifact has distinctive features. Computer systems are a particular kind of technological artifact.

---

[6] See Pitt (2000) in which Pitt argues for a definition of technology as 'humanity at work'.

Their distinctiveness can be characterized in any number of ways. Unlike many artifacts, they respond to syntactically structured and semantically rich input and produce output of the same kind; they are more complex and more malleable than most artifacts; and, the operations they perform seem to exhibit a high degree of intelligence and automaticity.

The apparent intelligence exhibited by computer systems has led some scholars to argue that they have at least a minimal kind of autonomy. Our argument does not depend on the autonomy of computer systems; it circumvents the AI debate altogether. We argue instead that the connection between computer systems and human interests brings computer systems into the realm of morality and makes them appropriate for moral evaluation.

3. COMPUTER SYSTEMS AS SURROGATE AGENTS

Computer systems, like human surrogate agents, perform tasks on behalf of persons. They implement actions in pursuit of the interests of users. As a user interacts with a computer system, the system achieves some of the user's ends. Like the relationship of a human surrogate agent with a client, the relationship between a computer system and a user is comparable to a professional, service relationship. Clients *employ* lawyers, accountants, and estate executors to perform actions on their behalf, and users *deploy* computer systems of all kinds to perform actions on their behalf. We claim that the relationship between computer system and user, like the relationship between human surrogate and client, has a moral component. How is this possible?

Admittedly, human surrogate agents have a first-person perspective independent of their surrogacy role, but computer systems cannot have such a perspective. They do not *have* interests, properly speaking, nor do they have a self or a sense of self. It is not appropriate to describe the actions of computers in terms that imply that they have a psychology. This comparison of agents, interests, and perspectives helps to clarify one of the issues in the standard debate about the moral agency of computers. Those who argue against the agency of computers often base their arguments on the claim that computers do not (and cannot be said to) have desires and interests.[7] This claim is right insofar as it points to the fact that computer systems do not have first-person desires and interests. In this respect, they cannot be moral agents in the standard way; that is, they do not have a rich moral psychology that supports sympathy, regret, honor, and the like.

However, the special moral constraints that apply to human surrogate agents do not rely on their first-person perspective. Although human

---

[7] A similar argument against the intelligence of search engines is used by Herbert Dreyfus (2001).

surrogate agents do not step out of the realm of morality when they take on the role of lawyer or tax accountant or estate executor, they do become obligated within a system of role morality; they become obligated to take on the perspective of their clients and pursue the clients' interests. Human surrogate agents are both moral agents of a general and a special kind. They are moral agents as human beings with first-person desires and interests and the capacity to control their behavior in the light of its effects on others; they are a special kind of moral agent insofar as they act as the agent of clients and have a duty to pursue responsibly their clients' interests and to stay within the constraints of the particular role.

This special kind of moral agency best describes the functioning of computer systems when they are turned on and deployed on behalf of a user. Surrogate agency, whether human or computer, is a special form of moral agency in which the agent has a 'third-person perspective' and pursues what we will call 'second-order interests' – interests of clients or users.

What exactly are the second-order interests of a surrogate agent? By definition, they are interests in or about other interests. Human surrogate agents have second-order interests (not their personal interests) when they pursue, by contractual agreement, the interests of a client. Computer systems take on and pursue second-order interests when they pursue the interests of their users. Computer systems are designed to be able to represent the interests of their users. When the computer system receives input from a user about the interests that the user wants the system to pursue, the system is poised to perform certain tasks for that user. As such, when a computer system receives inputs from a user, it is able to pursue a second-order interest.[8]

Let us be clear that we are not anthropomorphizing computer systems by claiming that they pursue second-order interests, when put to use. Without being put to use, a computer system has no relation to human interests whatsoever. But when a user interacts with the system and assigns it certain tasks, the computer system takes up the interests of the user. These second-order interests can be identified from the behavior of the computer system. For example, when a user commands a browser to search for a map of a destination – the destination to which the user is *interested* in traveling – the browser calls up just that map, and not the map that some other human might want to see. When the browser searches for the map the user wants, the browser pursues a second-order interest in finding that map. That second-order interest is determined by the combination of the program and the input from the user; the interest cannot be pursued until the user 'hires' the computer system to find the map.

---

[8] We are tacitly claiming what may seem to be an unlikely psychological thesis: that having first-order interests is not a necessary condition for pursuing second-order interests.

When a tax accountant has an interest in minimizing a client's income tax burden, the accountant has a second-order interest. As indicated earlier, the first-order interests of human surrogate agents are not eliminated when they act in role; rather, some of the first-order interests of the human surrogate agent become temporarily aligned (in a limited domain) with the interests of a client. In other words, the human surrogate agent has self-interested reasons for seeing that some subset of the client's interests are successfully pursued. The tax accountant wants the client's tax burden to be reduced, both for the good of the client and for his or her own good. There is a temporary alignment between some of the first- and second-order interests of the human surrogate agent.

With computer surrogate agents, there can be no alignment because computer systems do not have first-order interests. This is one important difference between human surrogate agents and computer systems and we do not mean to underestimate the significance of this difference. Computer surrogate agents also do not 'have' second-order interests but they are able to pursue the second-order interests of others without having interests of their own. Users have a first-person perspective and interests – complex interests at that. Users employ computer systems to operate in specific ways that pursue the users' interests. In this way, computer systems pursue second-order interests that require a first-order interest to activate them.

The differences between human and computer surrogate agents are important, but not as significant as many would think. Consider, for instance, the issue of expertise. It is important to acknowledge that in many cases of human surrogate agency, the client may not fully understand what the agent does. But this is true of users and their computer systems too. Indeed, in the cases we have discussed, the client/user has deployed the agent because the client/user does not have the requisite expertise or does not want to engage in the activities necessary to achieve the desired outcome. In the case of hiring a tax accountant, as well as the case of using an income tax software package, the client/user does not need to understand the details of the service that is implemented. The user of the software package need not understand the tax code or how computer systems work; the client of the tax accountant need not understand the tax code or how accountants do their work. In both cases, the client/user desires an outcome and seeks the aid of an agent to achieve that outcome.

Our comparison of human surrogates and computer systems reveals that both kinds of agents have a third-person perspective and pursue second-order interests. We have pointed out that the primary difference between human and computer surrogate agents concerns psychology and not morality; human surrogate agents have first-order interests and a first-person perspective, while computer systems do not. Note, however, that when it comes to moral evaluation of the surrogate agent's behavior qua surrogate agent, these first-order interests and the first-person perspective are irrelevant. The primary issue is whether the agent is incompetent or misbehaves with respect to the *clients'* interests. In other words, does the surrogate agent stay within the constraints of the special role morality?

It will now be useful to look in more detail at the ways in which human and computer surrogate agents can go wrong and see how this account of the moral agency of computer systems plays out. We will have to do so, however, without recourse to a specific role morality. The particular constraints of the role morality will depend on just what role is under consideration, and so our discussion here is necessarily general and abstract. The moral constraints of a tax accountant, for instance, differ significantly from those of an estate executor. Likewise, if our account is correct, the moral constraints on personal gaming software will differ from those on software that runs radiation machines, or secures databases of medical information, or guides missile systems.[9]

3.1. Incompetence

Both income tax accountants and income tax software system can perform incompetently. Just as the incompetence of the accountant might derive from the accountant's lack of understanding of the tax code or lack of understanding of the client's situation, a computer system can inaccurately represent the income tax code or errantly manipulate the input from a user. In both cases, the surrogate agent may not have asked for the right input or may have misunderstood or errantly assigned the input provided.

The outcome or effect on the client/user is the same in both cases. That is, whether it is a human surrogate agent or a computer system, incompetence can result in the client/user's interest not being fully achieved or not achieved to the level the client/user reasonably expected. For example, the incompetence of agents of either kind may result in the client/user missing out on a filing option in the income tax code that would have reduced the client/user's taxes. These are some of the morally relevant effects to which we referred in the opening section.

Admittedly, ordinary language often treats the two cases differently; we say of the tax accountant that he or she was 'incompetent', and we say of the software package that it was 'faulty' or 'buggy'. This linguistic convention acknowledges that the one is a person and the other a computer system. No doubt, critics will insist here that the wrong done to the user by the computer system is done by (or can be traced back to) the designers of the software package. Indeed, the *de facto* difference between the two cases is in the way the legal system addresses the incompetence in each case. A client sues a human surrogate agent for negligence and draws on a body of law

---

[9] See, for example, Leveson (1995) and Cummings and Guerlain (2003).

focused on standards of practice and standards of care. Software users can also sue, but they must use a different body of law; typically software users will sue a software company for defective (error-ridden) software and will do so only if the errors in the system go beyond what the software company disclaims in the licensing agreement.[10]

There is a special kind of incompetence in designing computer systems that goes beyond programming errors. Problems can emerge when otherwise good modules in software/hardware systems are combined in ways that bring out incompatibilities in the modules.[11] It is hard to say where exactly the error lies; parts of the system may have functioned perfectly well when they were in different systemic configurations. Software packages and computer system configuration are generally the result of complex team efforts, and these teams do not always work in concert. Error can be introduced in any number of places including in the design, programming or documentation stage. Thus, it will take us too far afield to identify and address all the different causes leading to a computer system performing, incompetently. But certainly there is some level of incompetence when a computer system is put together without testing the compatibility or interoperability of its components through various state-changes in the system.

3.2. Misbehavior

The second way in which a human surrogate agent can go wrong is through misbehavior. Here, the agent uses the role to further the interests of someone besides the client, and in a way that neglects or harms the interests of the client.[12] As we have already indicated, computer systems cannot take a first-person perspective. Hence, it would seem that computer systems cannot misbehave. Indeed, it is for this reason that many individuals and corporations prefer computer systems to human agents; they prefer to have machines perform tasks rather than humans, believing that computers are

---

[10] Standard end-user license agreements agreements make it exceedingly difficult for users of software to get relief from the courts for faulty software. In this section, we suggest that one way for computer surrogate software to be faulty is for it to be incompetent in pursuing the interests of the client/user. If our argument about the human–computer surrogacy parallel is correct, it should be no more difficult to win a suit against a computer than against a human surrogate agent. We should add here that the two cases are alike from the perspective of the U.S. Internal Revenue Service; the client/user is always responsible for errors in their tax returns. The comparison between the two cases is also complicated because currently most income tax accountants use software packages to prepare their clients' tax returns.

[11] We would like to thank David Gleason for bringing this special kind of incompetence to our attention.

[12] If the computer system merely neglects, but does not harm, the interests of the user, and the user has paid for or rented the system in order to further his or her interests, then it is still reasonable to say that the user has borne a cost to his or her interests. That is, both opportunity costs and real costs to interests will count as harms.

programmed to pursue only the interests of the user. Of course, machines break down, but, with machines, the employer does not have to worry about the worker getting distracted, stealing, being lazy or going on strike. Computer systems do exactly what they are told (programmed) to do.

Computer systems cannot misbehave by pursuing *their* personal interests to the neglect or detriment of their users. On the other hand, although computers do not have (and, hence, cannot pursue) their own interests, computer systems can be designed in ways that serve the interests of people other than their users. They may even be designed in ways that conflict with or undermine the interests of their users. As indicated earlier, computer systems have a way of pursuing the interests of their users, or of other (third) parties. Misbehavior can occur when computer systems are designed in ways that pursue the interests of someone other than the user, and to the detriment of the interests of the user. Consider the case of an Internet browser that is constructed so that it pursues the interests of other third parties. Most browsers support usage-tracking programs (cookies, pop-ups, or adware), keyloggers (which transmit data about your computer use to third parties), and other forms of spyware on a personal computer. Most of this noxious software is installed without the user's expressed, or at least informed, consent. Accordingly, we might say that an Internet browser is the surrogate agent of the end-user (client), when it searches the Internet for information, but at the same time acts as the surrogate agent of other clients, such as advertisers, corporations, hackers, and government agencies, when it allows or supports invasions of privacy and usurpation of computer resources.

Such misbehavior is embodied in other parts of computer systems. In the mid-1990s, Microsoft marketed a version of their platform for personal computers that was advertised to consumers as more flexible than it really was. Although Microsoft claimed, in particular, that their Internet Explorer version 4.0 would operate smoothly with other Sun JAVA™ applications, in fact Microsoft had programmed IE version 4.0 and other types of software with a proprietary form of the JAVA code.[13] The nonproprietary JAVA programming technology was, per agreement, to be supported by Microsoft, and in exchange Microsoft could advertise that fact on its software products. Hence, consumers thought that they were getting products that would be compatible with all or most of Sun JAVA applications, when, in fact, they were getting software that was reliable only with proprietary versions of JAVA. The expectation of broader interoperability was bolstered by the very public nature of the agreement between Sun and Microsoft. Here, the

---

[13] Sun and Microsoft agreed that the Microsoft would support JAVA in its operating system and applications in March of 1996. Subsequently, Microsoft seems to have reneged on the deal but still advertised that their products were 'Sun JAVA compatible'. The case was settled in favor of Sun Microsystems. The complaint can be accessed at http://java.sun.com/lawsuit/complaint.html. This is one of many lawsuits initiated over JAVA by Sun, not all of which were successful.

users' interests in interoperability were undermined by Microsoft's interests in getting users to use only Microsoft applications – the very applications that would work with the Microsoft proprietary JAVA. In the courts, it appeared as though the problem was just a legal one between Microsoft and Sun, but in the technology itself users were confronted with a system that would not support at least some of the users' interests in using non-Microsoft products. Not surprisingly, the users were not informed of Microsoft's use of proprietary JAVA code, but would discover this fact when they tried (unsuccessfully) to use some Sun JAVA programs with their Microsoft computing platforms.

There are many kinds of misbehavior to be found in the activities of human surrogate agents. Imagine hiring a lawyer to represent you and later finding that, although the lawyer represents you well, he or she is selling information about you to fundraising or advertising organizations. Here, the agent's activities introduce the possibility of conflict between the agent's interests and third-party interests. Consider also the case of the Arthur Anderson auditors who were supposed to ensure that Enron stayed within the laws of corporate accounting. They can be thought of as agents of Enron stockholders. They misbehaved by allowing their judgment on behalf of Enron to be distorted by their own (Arthur Anderson's) interests. In parallel, users deploy a computer system such as a browser to seek out information they desire, believing that the browser will serve their interests. The browser, however, has been designed not just to serve the interest of the user but also to serve the interests of the software producer, or advertisers, or even hackers. The information delivered by the browser may or may not serve the interest of the user. In the literature on conflict of interest, these cases can be seen as classic conflicts of interest in which the agent's judgment is tainted by the presence of a conflicting interest. The client believes the agent is acting on his or her behalf and discovers that the agent has interests that may interfere with that judgment. In the case of pop-ups, adware, and the like, the user typically has no interest in the functions that have been added to the computer system. Hence, from the perspective of the user, these aspects of browsers are a kind of misbehavior or, at the least, a candidate for misbehavior.

When a surrogate agent is hired by a client, the agent is authorized to engage in a range of activities directed at achieving a positive outcome for the client. Similarly, computer agents are put into operation to engage in activities aimed at an outcome desired by the user, that is, the person who deployed the computer program. Not only are human surrogate agents and computer agents both directed towards the interest of their client/users, both are given information by their client/users and expected to behave within certain constraints. For human surrogate agents, there generally are social and legal understandings such that, when the behavior of a surrogate agent falls below a certain standard of diligence, authority, or disclosure, the client can sue the agent and the agent can be found liable for his or her behavior. This suggests that standards of diligence and authority should be developed for computer agents, perhaps even before they are put into operation.

3.3. Differences between Computer Systems and Human Surrogate Agents

We want to be clear about the precise scope of the computers-as-surrogates simile that lies at the heart of our argument. The most fruitful part of the simile comes in the way it reveals moral relations between human surrogate agents and clients, on the one hand, and computers and users, on the other. But we are not claiming that all computer systems are like *known* surrogate agents. Likewise, not all human surrogate agents engage in activities that could be likened to the operation of a computer system. There may be some human surrogate agents, for instance, who rely on certain cognitive abilities, in the performance or their roles, which are in no way similar to the computational abilities of computer systems. Many skeptics about the human-computer comparison rely on a particular dissimilarity: humans use judgment and intuition, while computers are mere algorithmic or heuristic 'thinkers'.

If the surrogacy role always and essentially depended on the agent exercising judgment or guiding the client by using intuition, then computers could not be surrogate agents because they lack these mental capacities. But what reasons do we have for thinking that human surrogate agents rely principally or exclusively on judgment or intuition, and not on codified rules of law and standard practice – rules a computer system can also follow? Certainly the rules of the federal taxing and investment authorities, such as the Internal Revenue Service and the Securities and Exchange Commission in the United States, and the statutes concerning estates and probate and other laws can be programmed into a computer system. The best computer surrogate agents, then, are likely to be expert systems, or perhaps even 'artificially' intelligent computers, that can advise clients or users through a maze of complex rules, laws, and guidelines. For those roles where the human surrogate cannot define such formal components of the agency – roles such as 'educational mentor', 'spiritual guide', or 'corporate raider' – perhaps there will never be computer surrogates that might take over.

Of particular importance is the role of information in the proper functioning of a surrogate agent. An agent can properly act on behalf of a person only if the agent has accurate information relevant to the performance of the agent's duties. For human surrogate agents, the responsibility to gather and update information often lies with those agents. For computer agents, the adequacy of information seems to be a function of the program and the person whose interests are to be served. Of course, the privacy and security of this information, in digitized form, are well-known concerns for computer ethics. A new aspect of information privacy and security is raised by computer surrogate agency: can computer programs 'know' when it is appropriate to give up information (perhaps to governments or marketing agencies) about their clients? Discovering the proper moral relations between computers and users may depend in part upon further inquiries in information science.

A complete account of the cognition and psychology of human surrogate agency is beyond the scope of this chapter. In lieu of such an account, it should be enough to note that there are many forms of human surrogate agency that pursue the interests of clients, which are prone to the kinds of misbehavior and incompetence we described earlier and do not rely on non-formalizable 'judgment' or 'intuition'. Likewise, there are many computer systems that serve the same role for their users.

4. ISSUES OF RESPONSIBILITY, LIABILITY, AND BLAME

Because our conception of computer systems as surrogate agents has wide-ranging implications, we will briefly focus on one particular area of concern that is likely to be raised by the human surrogate–computer surrogate comparison. Foremost in the traditional analysis of role moralities are questions about rights and responsibilities. Many professional societies, in writing professional codes of ethics, have struggled with articulating the rights and responsibilities of human surrogate agents and their clients. How far can surrogate agents go to achieve the wishes of the client? If the surrogate agent acts on behalf of a client and stays within the constraints of the role, is the agent absolved of responsibility for the outcomes of his or her actions on behalf of the client?

Thus, the implications of our thesis for issues of responsibility, liability, and blame seem important. Because we claim that computer systems have a kind of moral agency, a likely (and possibly objectionable) inference is that computer systems can be responsible, liable, and blameworthy. This inference is, however, not necessary and should not be made too quickly. There are two issues that need further exploration. First, we must come to grips with issues of responsibility, liability, and blame in situations in which multiple and diverse agents are at work. In cases involving computer systems, there will typically be at least three agencies at work – users, systems designers, and computer systems; and, second, we must fully understand the kind of agency we have identified for computer systems.

In addressing the first issue, it is important to note that we have *not* argued that users or system designers are absolved of responsibility because computer systems have agency. We anticipate that the standard response to our argument will be that the attention of moral philosophers should remain on system designers. Of course, computer systems are made by human beings, and, hence, the source of error or misbehavior in a computer system can be traced back, in principle, to human beings who made decisions about the software design, reasonable or otherwise. Similarly, when lawyers consider legal accountability for harm involving a computer system, they focus on users or system designers (or the companies manufacturing the computer system). In making these claims, however, moral philosophers and lawyers push computer systems out of the picture, treating them as if they were insignificant. This seems a serious mistake. A virtue of our analysis is that it keeps a focus on the system itself.

To understand computer systems merely as designed products, without any kind of moral agency of their own is to fail to see that computer systems also behave and their behavior can have effects on humans and can be morally appraised independently of an appraisal of their designers' behavior. What the designer does and what the computer does (in a particular context) are different, albeit closely related. To think that only human designers are subject to morality is to fail to recognize that technology and computer systems constrain, facilitate and, in general, shape what humans do.

Nevertheless, the point of emphasizing the moral character of computer systems is not to deflect responsibility away from system designers. Because computer systems and system designers are conceptually distinct, there is no reason why both should not come in for moral scrutiny. Ultimately, the motivation to extend scrutiny to computer systems arises from the fact that computer systems perform tasks and the way they do so has moral consequences – consequences that affect human interests.

This brings us to the second issue: because computer systems have a kind of moral agency, does it make sense to think of them as responsible, liable, or blameworthy? We do not yet have the answer to this question, though we have identified some pitfalls to avoid and a strategy for answering it. First, although we have argued that computer systems are moral agents, we have distinguished this moral agency from the moral agency of human beings. Hence, it is plausible that the moral agency of computer systems does not entail responsibility, liability, or blame. We have acknowledged all along that computer systems have neither the first-person perspective nor the moral psychology and freedom that are requisite for standard (human) moral agency. Computer systems are determined to do what programs tell them to do. Instead, we have proposed a kind of moral agency that has features in common with human surrogate agency but is also different from it. Before proclaiming that notions of responsibility, liability, and blame can or cannot be used in relation to computer systems, we need a more complete analysis of human surrogate agency and responsibility, liability and blameworthiness of individuals acting in such roles.

The surrogacy comparison should go some distance in helping us here. For example, in the case of a trained human surrogate agent, a failure of incompetence would reflect poorly on the source of the training. A professional school that trains accountants for the Certified Public Accountant (CPA) license, for instance, would be accountable if it regularly taught improper accounting methods. The designer of a computer accounting system, on the other hand, would be to blame if the computer program used the wrong database in calculating a user's tax rate. But the professional school would not be accountable if its graduates regularly forgot the proper accounting method (a form of incompetence), or diverted funds from the client's account to his or her own (a form of misbehavior). Likewise, the designer of the computer system would not be to blame if an unpredictable power surge changed a few variables while the user was calculating the tax rate (still, an incompetence in the computer system). And the designer would not be to blame for every bug in a very complex computer program, on the assumption that complex programs cannot be proven 'correct' or bug-free within the lifetime of the user (Smith 1995). The possibility of bugs in tax-preparation software, like the chance of cognitive breakdowns in the CPA, must be assumed as a risk of hiring another to pursue one's proper interests. On the other hand, the designer would be to blame for deliberately programming a routine that sent e-mail summaries of one's tax returns to one's worst enemies – certainly a form of misbehavior.

We do not claim to have figured out whether or how to adjust notions of responsibility, liability, and blame to computer systems. We leave this daunting task as a further project. Our point here is merely to suggest that computer systems have a certain kind of moral agency and this agency and the role of this agency in morality should not be ignored. In other words, although we have not fully worked out the implications of our account for issues of responsibility, they are worth facing in light of the virtues of the account.

5. CONCLUSION

What, then, do we gain from thinking of computer systems as having a kind of moral agency? From thinking of them as surrogate agents? The simile with human surrogate agency brings to light two aspects of computer systems that, together, ground the claim for a kind of moral agency. First, computer systems have a third-person perspective as they pursue second-order interests. Second, the tasks performed by computer systems, as they function with users, have effects on human interests. The character of computer systems (that is, the features they exhibit) is not random or arbitrary. Computer systems are designed and could be designed in other ways. What users are able to do, which of their interests are furthered and how, and what effects there are on others are a function of the design of computer systems. This is the kind of agency that computer systems have.

What we gain from acknowledging this kind of agency is a framework for thinking about the moral character of computer systems, a framework in which computer systems can be morally evaluated. Using the framework of surrogate agency, we can evaluate computer systems in much the same way we scrutinize the pursuit of second-order interests by human surrogate agents. In such an evaluation, we are able to apply to computer systems the concept of morality as a set of constraints on behavior, based on the interests of others. As surrogate agents, computer systems pursue interests, but they can do so in ways that go beyond what morality allows.

Recognizing that computer systems have a third-person perspective allows us to evaluate systems in terms of the adequacy of their perspective. Just as we evaluate human surrogate agents in terms of whether they adequately understand and represent the point of view of their clients, we can evaluate computer systems in terms of how they represent and pursue the user's interests. Such an evaluation would involve many aspects of the system, including what it allows users to input and how it goes about implementing the interests of the user. Consider the search engine surrogate that pursues a user's interest in Web sites on a particular topic. Whether the search engine lists Web sites in an order that reflects highest use, or one that reflects how much the Web site owner has paid to be listed, or one that reflects some other listing criteria, can have moral implications (Introna and Nissenbaum 2000). Recognizing the third-person perspective allows us, then, to ask a variety of important questions about computer systems: does the system act on the actual user's interests, or on a restricted conception of the user's interests? Does the system competently pursue the users' interests, without pursuing other, possibly illegitimate interests such as those of advertisers, computer hardware or software manufacturers, government spying agencies, and the like?

Throughout this chapter, we have provided a number of analyses that illustrate the kind of evaluation that can be made. Tax preparation programs perform like tax advisers; contract-writing programs perform some of the tasks of attorneys; Internet search engines seek and deliver information like information researchers or librarians. Other types of programs and computer systems serve the interests of clients, but there are no corresponding human surrogate agents with whom to compare them. Spyware programs uncover breaches in computer security, but when they do so for the user, they do not replace the tasks of a private detective or security analyst. Increasingly, our computers do more for us than human surrogates could do. This is why it is all the more important to have a framework for morally evaluating computer systems, especially a framework that acknowledges that computer systems can do an incompetent job of pursuing the interests of their users and can misbehave in their work on behalf of users.

In some ways, the need to give a moral account of computer systems arises from the fact that they are becoming increasingly sophisticated, in both technical and social dimensions. Although they may have begun as simple utilities or 'dumb' technologies to help humans connect phone calls, calculate bomb trajectories, and do arithmetic, they are increasingly taking over roles once occupied by human surrogate agents. This continuous change would suggest that, somewhere along the way, computer systems changed from mere tool to agent. Now, it can no longer be denied that computer systems have displaced humans – both in the manufacturing workforce, as has long been acknowledged, and, more recently, in the service industry. It would be peculiar, then, to recognize that computers have replaced human service workers who have always been supposed to have moral constraints on their behavior, but to avoid the ascription of similar moral constraints to computer systems.

References

Cummings, M. L., and Guerlain, S. 2003. The tactical tomahawk conundrum: Designing decision support systems for revolutionary domains. IEEE Systems, Man, and Cybernetics Society conference, Washington DC, October 2003.

Dreyfus, H. 2001. *On the Internet.* New York: Routledge.

Goldman, A. 1980. *The moral foundation of professional ethics.* Totowa, NJ: Rowman and Littlefield.

Introna, L. D., and Nissenbaum, H. 2000. Shaping the Web: Why the politics of search engines matters. *The Information Society, 16,* 3, 169–185.

Kerr, I. R. 1999. Spirits in the material world: Intelligent agents as intermediaries in electronic commerce. *Dalhousie Law Journal, 22,* 2, 189–249.

Leveson, N. 1995. *Safeware: System safety and computers.* Boston: Addison-Wesley.

Pitt, J. C. 2000. *Thinking about technology.* New York: Seven Bridges Press.

Smith, B. C. 1995. The limits of correctness in computers. CSLI 1985. Reprinted in D. Johnson and H. Nissenbaum (Eds.), *Computers, ethics, and social values,* Saddle River, NJ: Prentice Hall.

14

Moral Philosophy, Information Technology, and Copyright

The Grokster Case[1]

Wendy J. Gordon

INTRODUCTION

A plethora of philosophical issues arise where copyright and patent laws intersect with information technology. Given the necessary brevity of the chapter, my strategy will be to make general observations that can be applied to illuminate one particular issue. I have chosen the issue considered in *MGM v. Grokster*,[2] a recent copyright case from the U.S. Supreme Court. Grokster, Ltd., provided a decentralized peer-to-peer technology that many people, typically students, used to copy and distribute music in ways that violated copyright law. The Supreme Court addressed the extent to which Grokster and other technology providers should be held responsible (under a theory of 'secondary liability') for infringements done by others who use the technology.

In its *Grokster* opinion, the U.S. Supreme Court ducked difficult questions about the consequences of imposing liability on such a technology provider, and instead chose to invent a new doctrine that imposed secondary liability on the basis of a notion of 'intent'. The judges have been accused of sidestepping immensely difficult empirical questions and instead taking the 'easy way out' (Wu 2005, p. 241). This chapter asks if the Court's new doctrinal use of 'intent' is in fact as deeply flawed as critics contend. To examine the issue, the chapter employs two broadly defined ethical approaches to suggest an interpretation of what the Court may have been trying to do. The first is one that aims at impersonally maximizing good consequences; the chapter

---

[1] Copyright © 2007 by Wendy J. Gordon. For comments on the manuscript, I thank Iskra Fileva, David Lyons, Russell Hardin, Ken Simons, Lior Zemer, the members of the Boston University Faculty Workshop, and the editors of this volume. For helpful discussion, I thank Seana Shiffrin, and I also thank the audience at the Intellectual Property Section of the 2006 Annual Meeting of the American Association of Law Schools, where a version of the *Grokster* discussion was presented. Responsibility for all errors, of course, rests with me.
[2] *Metro-Goldwyn-Mayer Studios, Inc. v. Grokster, Ltd.*, 545 U.S. 913, 125 S. Ct. 2764 (2005).

uses the term 'consequentialist' for this approach. The second is neither maximizing nor impersonal; the chapter uses the term 'deontological' for this second approach.

The chapter addresses the role 'intent' can play in each category. The chapter then draws out implications for the *Grokster* case, arguing that the Court neither fully explored the consequentialist issues, nor provided an adequate account of its nonconsequentialist approach.[3] The chapter then draws on a deontological strand in John Locke's theories of property to see what might be said in defense of the Court's approach in *Grokster*. It concludes that Lockean theory fails to provide a justification for the Court's approach, and that the critics (notably Tim Wu) are right. The Court's mode of analysis in *Grokster* still stands in need of justification.

CONSEQUENTIALISM

The overall topic of this chapter is to examine the moral implications that computers and the Internet hold for copyright. At first, this seems like an odd question. We think of morality as independent of happenstance, so how can a change in technology alter one's moral judgments about whether a given act is wrong or right?

One response is to examine whether one's moral judgments are indeed independent of circumstance. There is a species of morality, consequentialism, which makes the rightness or wrongness of an action depend on outcomes. One is even tempted to say that for consequentialists (such as Benthamite utilitarians[4]) morality is totally dependent on circumstance.

But that would be an overstatement. Consequentialists must answer crucial questions whose answers cannot be 'read off' factual reality the way we can 'read off' the color of paint simply by looking at it. For example, consider this question: what kind of consequences should count (pleasure? progress? what about sadistic pleasures, or material progress that dehumanizes?). Such questions are answered by moral reasoning. Although the reasoner's conditions of life (some of which will be happenstance) will inevitably color her moral reasoning, circumstances do not 'dictate' what their moral significance or insignificance will be – the reasoner chooses which circumstances will count, and why.

---

[3] In stipulating these definitions, I follow an old pattern: 'For the last two centuries ethicists have focused, almost exclusively, on just two theoretical possibilities: deontology [i.e., agent-relative nonconsequentialism] and utilitarianism [i.e., agent-neutral consequentialism]' (Portmore 2001, p. 372). The landscape of today's ethical theory is of course more complex. Nevertheless, these two classic possibilities will suffice to illuminate the unsatisfactory nature of the reasoning in the *Grokster* decision.

[4] Although there are nonutilitarian consequentialist theories, this chapter will generally focus on Benthamite utilitarianism.

One might adopt a consequentialist approach that seeks to maximize the welfare of only a limited group of people – a society's aristocrats, say, or one's self.[5] But most consequentialist theories treat all persons as equals, and the 'good' that each person experiences (however 'good' is defined) has equal moral importance to the 'good' any other person experiences. It is the total good that most consequentialists seek to maximize. Consequentialism can be seen as combining a theory of value with a theory about how its promotion is related to rightness or obligation.[6]

It is sometimes said that consequentialists are 'agent neutral' in ways that some nonconsequentialists are not,[7] in the sense that reasons for action are agent-neutral in most consequentialist theories,[8] not varying with who one is. Thus, in Benthamite and other kinds of maximizing consequentialism, everyone has the same duty to maximize the net of good over bad results, and our positions affect only our abilities to execute the duty. By contrast, 'agent-relative' theories include notions of duty that vary with the identity of the persons involved. 'Deontological reasons have their full force against your doing something – not just against its happening' according to Nagel (1986, p. 177).

For example, in the commands, 'honor thy father and thy mother' or 'respect your teachers', I am an agent who owes a duty to my parents and teachers that you, as a differently situated agent, do not have. The duty is 'mine'. Even if you are in a position to affect the welfare of my parents or teachers more directly than I am, an agent-relative approach would not impose upon you a duty of the same kind I have toward them. You would have a duty to them simply as persons, not as parents or teachers, and on an agent-relative view you probably owe them less – or something different – than I do.[9]

Similarly, 'agent-relative' theories may be sensitive to what individuals *do*. The person who copies a work of authorship may morally owe something to the author that would not be owed by a third party who has not himself copied the authored work. The act of the copyist could distinguish him from the party who has not chosen to make such a copy. Yet, the copyist may be hard to locate, while the copyright owner might easily identify a third

---

5 For an overview, see Frankena (1988).

6 I am indebted to David Lyons for this last sentence.

7 Discussion here is indebted to Thomas Nagel (1986, pp. 165–188).

8 I am obviously simplifying the discussion. Some consequentialist theories are agent-relative, and some deontological theories are agent-neutral. See, for example, Broome 1995, p. 6. In the *Grokster* case, the Court indicated that copyright law should treat two different technology providers differently depending on their intent (an agent-relative consideration). Thus, the Court's approach could impose liability on one technology provider because it had a particular 'intent', and free another from liability if it lacked the 'intent', even if the *consequences* of putting liability on the two technologies would be the same. This is an agent-relative position.

9 I use the example of obligations to relatives for ease of exposition. Nagel (1986, p. 165) notes that obligations to such persons might not 'resist agent-neutral justification'.

party – perhaps an Internet service provider, perhaps an entity like Napster or Grokster – possessed of some potential leverage that could be exerted over the controverted activity. Nevertheless, under 'agent-relative' approaches, the fact that the third-party technology provider could be located, and was well situated to change copying behavior, would not in itself justify a duty on the technology provider; additional questions about what constituted good grounds for responsibility would need to be asked.

By contrast, under an 'agent-neutral' theory, the questions would be complex also, but much of the complexity would be empirical in nature; moral duties and rights would be arranged according to how best to achieve a chosen goal. For example, if the goal was to encourage authorship, and if to accomplish this goal peer-to-peer copying had to be discouraged (a big and controversial 'if'), then under an agent-neutral approach, moral duties to monitor or to pay might be placed on the third-party technology provider, or even on a more distant entity, if somehow that entity had the power to control copying.

For an example of such distant entities, consider Guido Calabresi's observation about who should bear the costs of automobile accidents. Judge Calabresi noted that if an 'arbitrary third party, e.g., television manufacturers', were somehow situated so that they were the people best able to effectuate accident-avoiding precautions, from a consequentialist perspective it would be appropriate to put liability for auto accidents upon the television manufacturers rather than upon speeding drivers (Calabresi 1970, p. 136).[10] Similarly, if speeding drivers, or any other third party, were somehow situated so that they were the people best able to encourage the composition of art works and computer programs, a consequentialist might argue for giving copyright ownership to them rather than to authors.

It strains our credulity to imagine that this could happen. Even if drivers could somehow bribe or threaten artists and programmers to work harder, giving copyright ownership to drivers is less likely to be productive than giving copyright ownership to the people who make the works of authorship. But our incredulity at *possible* results does not mean that Benthamite consequentialism is wrong.

To the contrary: according to followers of Jeremy Bentham, it is just the low odds of such bizarre possibilities (such as television makers having more ability to control traffic safety than drivers do, or drivers having more ability to control television content than TV producers do) that create our senses of expectation and incredulity. The *likely* coincidence between consequentialist result and commonsense notions of responsibility, Bentham would say, makes us miss the consequentialist basis of our commonsense notions. Thus, those notions may be conditioned patterns of stimulus-response, rather than

---

[10] Calabresi (1970, pp. 136–152) goes on to explain why such an 'arbitrary third party' is unlikely to be appropriately situated for such imposition of liability to be effective.

morally-reliable guides. A consequentialist would argue that, if and when circumstances change, we need to be ready to change our notions of responsibility and desert. A person who has the ability to control the behavior of another may be as good a candidate for consequentialist moral duty as is the actor himself – or even a better candidate. Under a consequentialist approach, the law might make the producers of a new technology liable for copyright infringements that third parties accomplished through use of the technology, even if under some deontological notions, the technologists would seem to lack personal responsibility.

A consequentialist approach can therefore drive a wedge between usual notions of cause and effect, or at least, change our notion of how we should give moral attribution to cause and effect. Instead of asking questions like, 'you did harm, do you deserve to pay damages?', or 'you created a benefit, do you deserve to be rewarded?', we ask, 'what kinds of rules[11] about damages and rewards would create, in the long run, the greatest excess of good over bad consequences.'

That an actor intends something to happen has no *per se* importance for a consequentialist analysis. This is not to deny that intent can be relevant to the extent that intent changes consequences; among other things, intention can make something more likely to occur (Simons 1992).[12] But intention in itself does not make an act rightful or wrongful for a consequentialist; from most consequentialist perspectives, whether the act is rightful or wrongful depends on its results. By contrast, many deontological views emphasize the wrongfulness of intentionally doing harm to another (Nagel 1986), even if doing the harmful act has substantial beneficial effects.

Consequentialist approaches to copyright typically have two primary emphases – inducing creativity and encouraging dissemination of what is created. The divergence between consequentialist and nonconsequentialist approaches can be visualized if we consider the case of the compulsive creator.[13]

---

[11] In this chapter, I elide the differences between act and rule utilitarianism, and many other subtleties.

[12] Regarding mental state, Kenneth Simons (1992, p. 504) summarizes 'six significant conclusions of utilitarian and economic analyses' as follows:

'(1) If an actor's mental state reflects a greater likelihood of success in causing harm, a higher sanction is warranted in order to deter him; (2) If an actor lacks a minimal awareness of the nature or likely results of his conduct, he cannot be deterred and should not be punished; (3) If a mental state reflects a higher private benefit to the actor, a higher sanction is necessary to deter him; (4) Some mental states, such as sadistic desires, reflect a private benefit that lacks social value; (5) Criminalizing some mental states would create 'steering clear' costs, inducing socially costly efforts to avoid liability; and (6) Inflicting harm with an aggravated mental state sometimes thereby aggravates the harm to the victim.'

[13] There is a parallel case of the compulsive bad driver. If nothing we can do will make the bad driver slow down – it might be better to encourage the pedestrians and all the other

According to most accounts, Picasso was a compulsive creator. His hands would turn out paintings, sculptures, collages, and prints, so long as he had shelter, supplies and enough energy to work. Let us say that sale of his individual art works would give him enough money to cover these basic needs. Should the law give him also the right to profit from people *copying* his works?

Commonsense notions of desert suggest that the answer should perhaps be 'yes'. Yet, from a consequentialist perspective, giving Picasso a right to control copying would not, ex hypothesis, make him work any harder or any more creatively. Further, giving Picasso that right would cause fewer copies to be distributed (and to bring less joy or insight) than would occur in the absence of giving him such a right. Therefore, a consequentialist might argue that, so long as an absence of right in Picasso didn't demoralize other artists into lessening their production[14] and, so long as the institutional costs of distinguishing the Picassos from ordinary creators were not too high, a prosperous compulsive creator such as Picasso should not have copyright. Putting Picasso's various collocations of shape and color into the public domain immediately, for purposes of inexpensive copying and adaptation, would make the society better off than would giving Picasso copyright in them.

For the consequentialist, then, the key question is, what rule (or choice of act) will make for better results? The perspective is looking forward, rather than looking backward at who has done what.

Thus, the copyright consequentialist begins not by asking questions that look backward, such as, 'Who created this work of art?', but rather questions, such as this, that look forward: 'To whom should we give rights in this if we want to encourage creativity in the future?' or 'How should we allocate rights in this if we want to encourage happiness (or economic prosperity, or reciprocal respect among creative people and their audiences, or some other notion of the good)?'

---

drivers to take care – by, for example, making those people bear any costs resulting from colliding with the bad driver. One might imagine requiring the bad driver to post a badge of identification on his car that alerts others, that here is someone who won't have to pay damages. Of course, this might not work out beneficially in practice for a multitude of reasons – not least because third alternatives, such as confiscating the bad driver's car, may be far more effective in reducing accidents than would relieving the compulsively bad driver of the responsibility to pay damages. But the counterintuitive example – that the worst driver might be the one we'd relieve of a duty to pay damages – suggests the kind of untethering from usual notions of desert that consequentialism can cause.

[14] Frank Michelman (1967, p. 1165) has suggested that utilitarians may protect rights more stringently than some other varieties of moralists because what happens to an individual can demoralize (i.e., reduce the effectiveness of positive incentives on) onlookers. A demoralization argument might support giving Picasso a copyright, not for his own sake, but for the sake of the audiences who might benefit from the arts to be produced by persons who, observing Picasso's fate, will be disheartened.

In the law of copyright, a person who copies is potentially liable as a 'direct infringer'. Someone else, who does not directly violate copyright law, may nevertheless be in a position to affect whether the law is violated. Deciding whether to make this other person liable is known as the question of 'secondary liability'.[15] As will appear, there can be both consequentialist and nonconsequentialist approaches to deciding secondary liability issues.

SEA CHANGES

So far, our most general point is this: if there is a sea change in the pattern of likely consequences – and arguably the advent of computers and the Internet constitutes such a sea change – the utilitarian consequentialist will alter his recommendation of what acts and rules are likely to be good, and which bad.

What are some of the sea changes? I will mention some of the grossest changes, and then proceed to some more subtle.

First, there is a great increase in value of 'content'. A story or song that could have reached X people in the analog world, can reach X plus Y people now, and, with each additional person reached, the value they experience adds to the world's stock of value. This potential increase in the world's stock of 'good' may shift preexisting balances.

Second, the union of digitization and the Internet causes arguably greater vulnerability to unconsented copying. Not only is copying and distribution easy; enforcement is difficult. Because of the privacy with which one typically employs computers, and because copying by computer is so widespread that any individual faces a low chance of being sued, potentially unlawful copying may increase.[16] Such copying can decrease the value of old markets and the profitability of old business models, and make it difficult for businesses to capture the same revenues in digital markets.

Third, the same union of digitization and Internet causes a drastic decrease in the costs of distribution and access. Instead of printing and binding tons of paper and sending them out in trucks to be purchased in stores located on expensive real estate, the Internet can distribute works at minimal or no cost.

---

[15] Sometimes secondary liability can be masked as something else. Thus, the U.S. copyright statute includes among the acts that constitute direct infringement, the act of distributing the copyrighted work to the public: 17 USC §106(3). A store owner who doesn't realize he is selling unlawful copies is nevertheless guilty of violating the distribution right. Congress could have relied on secondary liability as a basis for copyright owners going after store owners who sell unlawful copies; by instead using a 'distribution' right, Congress made the store owners' liability primary, and made it easier for plaintiffs to take action.

[16] See also Moor (1985, p. 266) for a discussion of aspects of computer use that may affect ethics.

Because it is hard to know, empirically, what the 'best' mixture of activities might be, some commentators have reasoned from the status quo that prevailed before the ubiquity of the personal computer. One might compare the postdigital with the predigital world.[17]

From this vantage point, consider the three major developments I have mentioned. First, consider the increase in the monetary value of copyrighted works. The increase means that the same amount of money can flow to artists, even if the percentage of value they can capture decreases. That suggests, on the one hand, that post–Internet copyright can safely decrease the scope of its protection. On the other hand, the potential increase in all works' *social* value may warrant an increase in authorial productivity, and conceivably authors would create more or better works if the amount of money they received were increased. There is undoubtedly an upper limit on this responsiveness; an infinite amount of royalties will not produce an infinite supply of perfect works.[18] Nevertheless, the two forces pull in somewhat different directions; the Internet-induced increase in monetary value means that authors will retain their status-quo revenues even if their ability to employ copyright is decreased, but the increase in monetary value may mean that authors should begin obtaining more than their status-quo revenues, in order to induce an increase in the number of works.

Second, consider the increased vulnerability to copying. This may be tolerable, because the rise in overall value will preserve incentives, even in the face of decreased per-copy compensation. Or it may be dangerous in reducing incentives below a desired level. From the latter perspective, some scholars urge increasing the private use of contractual limits and 'automated rights management' technologies to limit copying (Bell 1998), or increasing centralized legal controls over copying technology.[19] By contrast, writers like Julie Cohen point out that securing additional protections for copyright owners will affect users in negative ways that prior regimes did not – and erode effective access to the public domain as well.[20]

[17] This is a methodology used by Trotter Hardy, to quite different results (Hardy 2002, pp. 226–228).

[18] See Glynn Lunney (1996, p. 483) for an intriguing discussion of other reasons why it would be unwise for the law to seek to give copyright owners all the value that their efforts generate.

[19] Thus, the Digital Millennium Copyright Act (DMCA) supplements technological barriers. The DMCA makes it unlawful to make or circulate technology that enables consumers to bypass cryptolopes and other technological access barriers that block access to copyrighted work. Similarly, as I will discuss, there is pressure to make copying technologies themselves liable for copying. On this development, see Trotter Hardy (1996, pp. 249–252).

[20] See Julie Cohen et al. (2002, p. 10) and Cohen (2005, p. 347). Decentralized methods such as contracts are not only available to make copying harder. They also can be used for the opposite result. Richard Stallman (2002) has shown individual copyright owners how to use contract (and copyright law) to make sharing conditionally mandatory. (See also the material collected by the GNU Project at http://www.gnu.org/philosophy/.) Under a 'copyleft' license of the kind Stallman developed, the author of a computer program can

Third, consider the decrease in the costs of distribution and access. In the past, much copyright revenue has been used to cover those costs. For example, as between music companies and composers or performers, the music companies often receive the bulk of the revenue. If distribution costs are drastically reduced by the Internet, and the costs of printing or making CDs are shifted to the home user, copyright and its associated revenues may be less necessary (see, for example, Litman 2004).

A host of more subtle effects are also occurring. For example, copyright law impacts on individuals in their homes and friendships in new, unexpected ways (Lange 2003, Palmer 2002). Acts that feel natural and community-building (such as sharing) may for the first time be prohibited. Old behaviors may become no longer acceptable as laws change, and as familiar choices (like a decision to share)[21] take on a digital form (Litman 1994, 2004).

In addition, the advent of computers and Internet causes a change in the 'fit' of law. Copyright law was adapted to commercial users, and is ill-equipped for noncommercial copiers (Litman 2001). The question arises, whether this new lack of 'fit' changes whatever might otherwise be a prima facie moral obligation to obey the law.[22]

Much of the debate revolves around the private person, sitting at home with his or her computer, deciding whether to make a copy of something she purchased (such as a music CD) or something she obtained from the Internet. The legal status of space-shifting, sampling, or individual downloading, is still somewhat murky, even in the United States (Cohen 2005, p. 347).

A consequentialist would ask about effects. For example, will putting a restraint on a home copyist increase the likelihood of creativity, and will that be worth more than the costs? The costs include the decrease in access, the decrease in follow-on activity, the increase in home surveillance, the loss of a sense of control over one's CD and computer, the loss of spontaneity, and the loss of a sense of 'protected space' at home.

---

specify that she grants permissions to anyone to copy and adapt her program – but she makes this permission conditional on the next person's imposing the same license on all those who wish to copy and adapt downstream.

[21] For example: sending our copy of an interesting book to a friend does not violate the copyright owner's 'distribution right' because any owner of a lawfully made copy has a liberty to give, sell, or rent that copy. See 17 USC §109. This liberty, a product of the limits that the 'first sale doctrine' places on the copyright owner's distribution right, continues to be valuable in the nondigital world. However, in the digital world, sharing an interesting article with a friend usually involves copying the article, and in the United States, the first sale doctrine does not apply to the copyright owner's 'right of reproduction'. Although, in some circumstances, the act of digital sharing might nevertheless be sheltered (as by the fair use doctrine), the legal analysis and result may differ. Therefore, acts with identical effects (sharing a physical paper copy and sharing a digital copy) may receive different legal treatment.

[22] On the issue of copyright civil disobedience, see Lunney (2001, p. 893–910).

Although the U.S. Supreme Court occasionally talks about 'fair return',[23] the American copyright and patent systems are generally understood to be consequentialist in nature. According to the U.S. Constitution, Art. I Cl. 8, Congress is given power to grant rights 'for limited times' to 'authors and inventors' to 'promote the progress of Science and the useful arts'. Given the great uncertainty about the empirical issues, the consequentialist moralist may turn to issues of process and institutional competence: how expert is Congress at making these difficult empirical judgments? To what extent does the legislature deserve our deference on grounds of its superior ability to process information?

Observers of the copyright lawmaking process in the United States suggest the legislature used little of its potential expertise. Jessica Litman, the 'dean of the observational corps', argues that Congress does not make most copyright policy. Rather, Congress delegates authority to industry actors who hammer out legislative provisions behind closed doors – provisions that might accommodate everyone sitting at the table, but it's a table at which the public rarely sits (Litman 2001).

SECONDARY LIABILITY: TECHNOLOGY PROVIDERS

One of the most important issues concerns the intersection of copyright and technology, namely, to what extent should the makers of a technology that enables copying and distribution be liable as 'secondary infringers' for the acts of strangers who utilize the technology to commit copyright infringement? The social stakes are large. Consider, for example, what is at issue in regard to decentralized peer-to-peer technology.

Distribution and copying technologies have great potential for disseminating culture and stimulating new thoughts and new work to come into being. Particularly when coupled with the Internet, such technologies also have significant potential for enabling copyright infringement.

The U.S. Supreme Court, in the recent *Grokster* case, had to decide whether the law should permit or restrain such a technology.[24] This is a particularly important question when the technology at issue is (like *Grokster*'s) a decentralized peer-to-peer system that allows communication among separate computer users who can copy and transmit without having to go through a central controller or hub. Such a pure peer-to-peer technology offers potential for preserving privacy and for fostering democratic grassroots development free of Big Brother supervision.[25]

---

[23] 'The rights conferred by copyright are designed to assure contributors to the store of knowledge a fair return for their labors'. *Harper & Row, Publishers v. Nation Enterprises,* 471 U.S. 539, 546 (1985).

[24] *Metro-Goldwyn-Mayer Studios Inc v. Grokster, Ltd.,* U.S. 125 S. Ct. 2764 (2005).

[25] In George Orwell's *1984*, 'Big Brother' was the superficially paternalistic governmental figure that had electronic access to all homes and could stop any talk of dissatisfaction before it spread.

From the perspective of democracy, what kinds of files might one want to be able to share and send widely? In the United States, one thinks of the Zapruder film that contained the sole visual recording of the Kennedy assassination, or of the Pentagon Papers, the multi-volume secret study that opened the eyes of many regarding the Vietnam War. In considering the old USSR, one thinks of suppressed texts circulated through *samizdat*. In any context, one thinks of evidence, such as records of pollution and corporate cover-ups. To keep our governments honest and our private sectors responsive, the possibility of private circulation of truth-material must be maintained. And as we come increasingly to depend on the Internet for communication, alternative sources may atrophy, increasing the importance of keeping the Internet usable.

A devil's advocate might say that the current judiciary will protect the circulation of such information, that we needn't preserve special technology to do so. Thus, in the United States, the *New York Times* and the *Washington Post* published the Pentagon Papers despite governmental opposition,[26] and when the copyright owner of the Zapruder film sued a scholar who copied it, the defendant was held free of liability under the 'fair use' doctrine.[27] Therefore (says a devil's advocate), the courts will keep us able to communicate with each other, regardless of whether decentralized and hidden modes of Internet communication are available. But we're talking about legal rules that can control technology for the indefinite future; we are talking about crafting a structure that might create a permanent block on technology. Who knows how responsive courts will be to free speech arguments in various nations at various times in the future?[28]

As Lawrence Lessig (1999) points out, computer code can be even more binding than legal code, because it changes the *physical* world. A law saying 'do not cross this river' is a less effective restraint than dismantling the bridge. In addition, as Lessig recognizes, law can also change the physical world; law can order the bridge taken down. And once the bridge is down, whatever the reasons motivated its destruction, it is unavailable for good purposes as well. Enjoining decentralized copying and distribution technology may mean that we will have systematically less privacy than we need to guard our civil liberties and our democracies. So the issues are vital, and the consequences are of immense importance.

---

[26] *New York Times Co. v. United States*, 403 U.S. 713 (1971).

[27] *Time Inc. v. Bernard Geis Assocs.*, 293 F. Supp. 130 (SDNY 1968).

[28] In addition, of course, it might be argued that utilizing the first amendment and related doctrines like 'fair use' involves uncertainty, and resolving that uncertainty requires the use of expensive lawyers. Thus, Lawrence Lessig sometimes asserts that, '"Fair use" in America is the right to hire a lawyer.' (http://lessig.org/blog/2004/03/talkback_manes.html) The resulting uncertainty can chill lawful expression. However, it is possible to overstate the chilling effect of copyright law. The recent *Documentary Filmmakers' Statement of Best Practices in Fair Use* (http://www.centerforsocialmedia.org/resources/publications/statement_of_best_practices_in_fair_use/) suggests an even more vigorous future for fair use.

The same characteristic that makes decentralized peer-to-peer technology socially valuable – the breathing room it provides through its lack of a central clearinghouse or bottleneck – makes it costly for copyright owners. Because such technology is decentralized, it provides no easy way to stop copyright infringement, even when it's happening. That makes it hard to integrate a decentralized system in to a pay-to-play system. There's no central location at which to check that payment is being made, or to stop the copying if payment is lacking.

The lack of centralized control also makes it questionable to impose liability on the technology's developers when its users copy without paying. Because the developers likely do not even know of the infringing behavior prior to its occurring, and may never learn of it, they may have no way to stop the infringement.[29] Yet, from a consequentialist perspective, their lack of knowledge or control over individual infringing acts may be irrelevant.[30] As the U.S. Supreme Court wrote: 'When a widely shared service or product is used to commit infringement, it may be impossible to enforce rights in the protected work effectively against all direct infringers, *the only practical alternative* being to go against the distributor of the copying device for secondary liability on a theory of contributory or vicarious infringement' (*Grokster* at 125 S. Ct. 2776; emphasis added).

GROKSTER

As mentioned above, decentralized systems have immense positive potential, but they can indeed also empower massive copyright violations. In *Grokster* the U.S. Supreme Court thus had to face a difficult set of conflicting imperatives. How important is copyright after all? Should copyright be a tail that wags the cultural/political dog? Did the Court want to outlaw *any* technology that uses the privacy-preserving technology of decentralized peer-to-peer? Did it want to preserve such technologies, so long as they were capable of substantial noninfringing uses? Unfortunately, instead of directly facing the consequentialist issues, the Court switched tactics, and, as Tim Wu argues, employed a 'bad actor' approach.[31]

Until the *Grokster* case, the dominant formula used to judge the legality of decentralized technologies was the formula just mentioned – whether

---

[29] It was this rationale that persuaded the U.S. Court of Appeals for the Ninth Circuit to give a judgment to *Grokster*. The U.S. Supreme Court reversed this, handing down a ruling that favored the copyright owners.

[30] Interestingly, the U.S. Supreme Court substituted for their lack of knowledge re individual infringements, a finding that the developers 'intended to induce' infringement in general. This is a deontological concept, arguably enlisted to serve the utilitarian end of increasing the amount of copyright enforcement.

[31] See generally Tim Wu (2005) (distinguishing 'bad actor' from 'welfarist' approaches). Wu criticizes the Court for taking this approach. My chapter's analysis of *Grokster* can be seen as a response to Wu, for I ask: Might the Court's use of a 'bad actor' approach be defended on philosophical grounds?

the technology is 'capable of substantial noninfringing uses'. This became known as the *Sony* formula, after the case where it was first enunciated.[32] If a technology was capable of substantial noninfringing uses, then under the *Sony* formula, the technology was (one thought) immune from liability and injunction. This was the formula that kept videocassette recorders free of copyright liability, even though people sometimes use them to infringe copyrights.[33]

How did the U.S. Supreme Court in *Grokster* handle the issue of secondary liability for technology? First, the Court refused to admit that anything of political significance could be lost if the technology were held liable. The Court paid only limited attention to noninfringing uses, and its tone in doing so was sometimes mocking: 'Users seeking Top 40 songs . . . or the latest release by Modest Mouse, are certain to be far more numerous than those seeking a free Decameron . . . '[34] Second – and this is the part of particular philosophical interest – the Court borrowed from the language of agent-relative morality. Instead of weighing the consequences of enjoining[35] the decentralized technology, the Court shifted to the language of 'intent'. It held that 'one who distributes a device *with the object of promoting its use* to infringe copyright . . . is liable for the resulting acts of infringement by third parties'.[36] Tim Wu has criticized the Court for having sought an 'easier way out'.[37]

OVERVIEW OF THE REMAINING ARGUMENT

In the beginning of the chapter, I emphasized the difficulty of the empirical and methodological questions a consequentialist would have to answer. Might the Court's shift to more deontological measures of morality such as

---

[32] *Sony Corp. of America v. Universal City Studios, Inc.*, 464 U.S. 417, 104 S. Ct. 774 (1984).

[33] It is not copyright infringement to use a VCR to make private copies of copyrighted works at home for purposes of time shifting; it can be copyright infringement to use a VCR to make copies of films for commercial purposes.

[34] *Grokster* at 125 S. Ct. 2774.

[35] The plaintiffs had sought damages and an injunction. *Grokster*, 125 S. Ct. 2764 at 2771. Although the U.S. Supreme Court's opinion did not address the issue of whether granting an injunctive remedy would be appropriate, the opinion is likely to lead to an injunction on remand.

[36] *Grokster* at 125 S. Ct. 2770 (emphasis added).

[37] Tim Wu (2005, p. 241) writes: 'Both sides warned of the terrible consequences of adjusting the *Sony* rule. The recording industry and some academics warned of chaos that might attend adopting an expanded *Sony* that declared *Grokster* legal. On the other side, the computer hardware, software, and electronics industries and others warned of the toil and trouble that would attend the destruction of their beloved *Sony* safe-harbor. Whatever the Court did with *Sony* it was sure, or so the amici seemed to suggest, would make life in America unlivable. Meanwhile there was a much easier way out. . . . The Court created a test designed to catch companies with a bad attitude'.

'intent'[38] constitute an improvement rather than an error in its copyright jurisprudence?[39] On the one hand, the closer the statutory legal duties track the duties that might be deontologically imposed, the more sense it would make for the U.S. Supreme Court to use a deontological approach when 'filling in the blanks' on matters, like secondary liability, that the copyright statute does not specifically address. On the other hand, the further the positive legal duties diverge from the deontological, the more the Court's apparent deontological approach would appear inconsistent with the statute the Court is interpreting. Therefore, I will look at two issues:

First, could a deontological approach impose moral duties on any copyists and their helpers?

Second, would these duties be coterminous with the legal duties that copyright statutes currently impose?

I will suggest that the first question (whether there can be any deontological duties not to copy) should be answered in the affirmative. I will employ as our vehicle an interpretation of John Locke's labor theory of property, a theory often viewed as deontological.[40] Under this theory, I will suggest, some copyist behaviors would be prima facie[41] immoral on deontological grounds.[42] These are acts of copying that occur despite the fact that the

---

[38] Intent also can have consequences. For example, someone with an intent to do X is more likely to accomplish X than someone who lacks the intent, and this, in turn, may affect the appropriate sanction. See Kenneth Simons (1992) and Wu (2005 pp. 249–251).

[39] Wu (2005, pp. 251–255) also notes the difficulty of the empirical questions, and raises interesting questions of institutional competence.

[40] See, for example, Kramer 2004, pp. 128–129. According to Kramer (p. 129), the deontological approach allows Locke 'to justify the specific links between persons and the products which they had shaped.'

[41] Some acts of intentional harming may be prima facie wrongful, but morally permissible on an all-things-considered basis. For example, twisting a child's arm might be justifiable if necessary to save lives. For another example, Anglo-American law provides a general liberty to inflict competitive harm, perhaps because an opposite rule would have deleterious consequences. This chapter does not need to face the question of whether consequences are ever capable of defeating a deontological duty.

[42] Locke's property theory has many strands, some of which are overtly utilitarian and others of which draw on notions we would today identify as deontological. See Simmons (1992, pp. 39–43) (noting affinities and differences between Locke and Kant). In this chapter, I articulate a deontological argument that appears capable of standing on its own, and that seems capable of generating prima-facie rights and duties that would make it wrongful to engage in some acts of nonconsensual or uncompensated copying. Seana Shiffrin has argued that Locke's general property arguments do not justify strong private rights of exclusive control over intellectual products. See Shiffrin (2001, pp. 141–143). She reads the text of the *Treatises* as 'begin[ning] with a common property presumption' that yields private property only 'when full and effective use of the property requires private appropriation' (2001, pp. 161–162). Because she sees most intellectual products as being fully usable without private rights of exclusion (2001, pp. 156–157), she would characterize those products as not being the 'sort' of things which are appropriable.

copyright claimant has left 'enough, and as good' in the common for all to use.[43] Although when the 'enough, and as good' proviso is unsatisfied an act of copying would be prima facie *moral* rather than immoral;[44] some copying would violate Lockean norms if the proviso is capable of being satisfied at least sometimes. Therefore, a deontological approach that is agent-relative and nonmaximizing[45] could impose moral duties on some copyists and, potentially, on their helpers.

As for the second question (consistency between a Lockean approach and what has been enacted in positive copyright legislation), it may appear at first glance that this question, too, can be resolved affirmatively. Because copyright law permits new artists to independently use the same public material that their predecessors used, the law's operation seems to leave 'enough, and as good' even after copyright is granted. However, I will argue that a rule that permits independent reuse of public domain material does *not* suffice to guarantee that 'enough, and as good' will be left. This is so even when the material copied would never have existed but for the efforts of the copyright claimant. Positive U.S. copyright law thus has the potential for markedly diverging from a Lockean pattern.

I then examine whether one can reformulate the 'enough, and as good' criterion into a matter of *intent*, and if so, whether that interpretation would bring copyright law in general, or the *Grokster* opinion in particular, into closer alignment with the Lockean approach. I conclude that a subset of the cases that satisfy the proviso can indeed be restated in terms of 'intent', but that this does not suffice to bring Locke and positive U.S. law into alignment.

Her reading is intriguing, and like mine results in the conclusion that violating copyright law is not equivalent to violating Lockean natural law. However, Shiffrin's argument works only against strong intellectual property rights (2001, p. 142), and the Court in *Grokster* could have premised its notion of wrongfulness on breach of a narrower natural duty, for example, to pay compensation.

Shiffrin's goal, like mine, is not to predict 'what John Locke, the person, would say' (2001, p. 141), but rather to explore what appears most valid and fundamental in his work. I see Locke's concern with equality as more fundamental than his concern with common ownership. Shiffrin (2001, p. 162) may in fact agree. I argue for an approach that implements Locke's concern with equality more directly than does Shiffrin's test for Lockean private property. See, *infra*, the section titled, 'Intent and the Lockean proviso.'

43 The condition that 'enough, and as good' be left is known as the Lockean proviso, and is discussed at some length below.

44 An example might be copying done to remedy an injury inflicted by the laborer's work or by her property claim.

45 It might legitimately be objected that Locke's labor theory also contains consequentialist elements. Yet for purposes of analyzing *Grokster*, two aspects of the typical deontological approach particularly interest us: rights and duties being linked to a particular person because of who he is or what he has done (a perspective that is agent-relative), and whether moral reasons for action are independent of whether the action will maximize a given consequence (a perspective that is nonmaximizing). As Locke's labor theory of property shares is both agent-relative and nonmaximizing, it fits the definition of deontological this chapter has stipulated.

Therefore, if the intentional acts on which the Court premises secondary liability do not necessarily amount to deontological wrongs, the Court needs to give another reason for abandoning consequential reasoning and taking refuge in an 'intent' test. That alternative justification it has not provided.

A DEONTOLOGICAL APPROACH TO COPYRIGHT

In examining the nonconsequentialist justifiability of copyright, let me briefly identify three of the many potential streams of analysis: what lawyers know as 'personhood' theories that are used by some commentators to link works to their creators; libertarian theories; and Lockean labor theory.

The legal commentators who link copyright to notions of personhood and Hegelian philosophy usually focus on the authorial person claiming copyright, emphasizing the integrity, autonomy, personality, and will that an author can express through controlling a work of authorship. Contrary implications could flow from this strand of analysis[46] by, for example, examining how the ability to use copyrighted material can affect the integrity, autonomy, personality, and will of audiences and follow-on creators. Although the very notion of authorship has been harshly criticized, this strand of argument is usually associated with strong property rights and moral rights in authors.

Another possible approach, sometimes linked with libertarianism, argues that people are not entitled to be paid for the 'fruits of their labor' except to the extent they have preexisting contracts with the people who consume those fruits. Under this view, a proper respect for the autonomy of each individual copier or user requires not imposing on that person an obligation to which the individual has not consented. Under such an approach, therefore, an inventor or writer who sells her invention or manuscript takes the risk that others will be able to copy it and sell in competition with her, unless those others have agreed with her not to do so. It is the responsibility of the author or inventor to find patrons or purchasers in advance, if she wishes to be paid for what she has produced. Under this kind of view, neither the downloaders of music, nor the technologies that they use, have violated any duty (except perhaps the prima facie duty to obey the law, which is a separate topic in itself) if they have not themselves made prior promises to refrain from copying.[47]

---

[46] Drahos suggests that Hegelian analysis does not support allowing 'a certain class of personality (authors, artists) . . . to make claims that other property-owning moral agents cannot' (1996, p. 80). He also argues that 'property in abstract objects increases the capacity of owners to place restrictions on the use of physical objects' (1996, p. 87), and that intellectual property rights can 'threaten the ethical life of individual communities' (1996, p. 91).

[47] For a counter-argument to this libertarian position, see Gordon (1989, pp. 1413–1436). For a libertarian attack on copyright that emphasizes the primacy of tangible over intangible property rights, see Palmer (2002).

The Hegelian and libertarian approaches lie outside our current scope. A primary issue for copyright today is how to allocate reward and control between creative generations. John Locke is the theorist who most explicitly addressed what rules should govern the relationships between an early appropriator who takes some of the common for himself and a later comer.

Many nonconsequentialist approaches would impose on the public some duties not to copy. Probably most observers have little problem with the argument that authors and inventors deserve some reward, and that, at least under some circumstances, users have some moral duty to provide reward, even if no contracts exist. As has often been observed, the larger problem is going from a moral claim to reward, to a moral claim to full property rights.

As Edwin Hettinger has argued, if a group of people are trying to lift an automobile, and another comes over to assist, should the last person get all the credit if it is his addition that makes it finally possible to lift the car?[48] Hettinger's analogy is imperfect, yet it has some 'fit'; as the last-comer built on the efforts of the other participants, all creative people build on what came before.

The usual term for the common heritage which all people are free to use is 'the public domain'. Consider how much each musician and other artist builds on his predecessors – on the people who invented the artistic genre the artist works in, the instruments the artist plays, the familiar patterns of chord changes that a new composer of popular music adapts to her own uses. Given all that, how can it be said that a musician or composer is morally entitled to 'own' the mixture of new and old which he calls his work of authorship? Might the public morally own most of what musicians and composers call their own?

The issue of 'how much credit' or reward is deserved is sharpened by examining the issue of whether natural rights and duties constrain individuals in how they use the common. Whether or not such constraints apply is usually stated in terms of whether *no one* owns the scientific and cultural heritage on which creative people build (which would be to characterize it as a 'negative' common), or whether *everyone* owns that heritage (a 'positive' common) (Drahos 1996, chapter 3; Thomson 1976, p. 664).[49] If we all own that heritage, then arguably we all should have some rights in what the heritage produces. If so, a private right of ownership that excludes other commoners would seem hard to justify, except in the unlikely event

---

[48] 'A person who relies on human intellectual history and makes a small modification to produce something of great value should no more receive what the market will bear than should the last person needed to lift a car receive full credit for lifting it' (Hettinger 1989, p. 38).

[49] But see Shiffrin (2001, p. 149), who suggests that the proviso 'could as easily have been posited from a no-ownership starting point – motivated by concerns of fairness about who should come to own the unowned'.

that the private claimant could obtain universal consent from all the other commoners.[50]

The most familiar theory to tackle a variant of this dilemma is John Locke's labor theory of property. He argued that under some circumstances, a person could justifiably take resources out of a common given to all mankind, and own the resources privately. The circumstances that make such an enclosure rightful are, inter alia, that the claimant has mixed the resources from the common with her own labor (for copyright, read 'labor' as 'creativity'), and that in claiming the piece of common for her own, she leaves 'enough, and as good' for others. Locke believed that the earth was originally owned by 'all in common' (a positive community)[51], and arguing for such co-ownership constituted part of his resistance to the divine right of kings. Yet, Locke's contemporaries believed that private ownership of land was justifiable, and Locke himself wished to believe that people in a state of nature who chose to enter civil government owned individualized private 'property' for whose stewardship they could hold government accountable. How could Locke square private ownership of land with a natural state where the whole earth was owned in common? His analytic solution is now known as the 'proviso' or 'sufficiency condition'.

The basic structure of his argument has two implicit stages. The first stage is centered on the laborer. Labor is mine and when I appropriate objects from the common I join my labor to them in a purposive way (Becker 1977, pp. 32–48). If you take the objects I have gathered you have also taken my labor because I have mixed my labor with the objects in question. '[N]o one ought to harm another in his Life, Health, Liberty, or Possessions' (Locke 1988, p. 271, bk. II, §6). To take my labor harms me and you should not harm me. You, therefore, have a duty to leave these objects alone. Therefore, I have a prima facie property in the objects. The second stage is centered on persons other than the laborer. Just as the laborer has a natural right not to be harmed, so do the other commoners. Therefore, when someone employs her labor to make the land or its fruits useful, 'mixing' her labor with the common, her private claim over the resulting mixture matures into a right only *provided that* she leaves 'enough, and as good' for the other commoners.[52]

---

[50] This was Filmer's argument in *Patriarcha*: that we know that the earth was *not* given to all men in common, but only to royalty, because initial co-ownership would be inconsistent with contemporary private property. If all persons owned the earth, private property could never exist because all the commoners would not consent to any one of them having private dominion. By contrast, vesting ownership in royalty eliminates the coordination problem.

[51] The Lockean common did not strictly follow the model of positive community as set out by Pufendorf. Rather, as Shiffrin observes, the Lockean common 'is available to nonaltering use by each and all' complemented with a 'right over exclusive use' that is 'jointly owned' (2001, p. 150).

[52] Locke argued against Filmer that unanimous consent was not required before one co-owner appropriated in circumstances where the complainer had 'as good' available. In

If the claimant's appropriation leaves 'enough, and as good', Locke reasons, then only the envious would object (and Locke cares nothing for objections of the envious).[53] If the claimant leaves 'enough, and as good', her appropriation 'does as good as take nothing at all' (Locke 1988, p. 291, §33).[54] The requirement that private property come into being only if the private appropriation leaves 'enough, and as good' for all the other commoners, is the proviso.

The proviso has additional functions within Locke's argument. For example, a principle that property results from mixing labor with the common could be absurdly overbroad, and the proviso that appropriations must leave behind 'enough, and as good' usefully limits the amount of property that can be claimed by an individual.

Thus, Robert Nozick famously asked 'if I own a can of tomato juice and spill it into the sea . . . do I thereby come to own the sea, or have I foolishly dissipated my tomato juice?' (Nozick 1974, p. 175). Once the proviso is added, Nozick's hypothetical is no longer so problematic. Artists like Christo are famous for their work in public spaces, stringing fences or wrapping areas of landscape. Suppose Christo hires tankers to stir tomato-colored dye into a bay, with the aim of changing the color of the water to complement the sunset one fine summer evening.[55] The artist would seem entitled to keep everyone else out of the colored area temporarily, to preserve his handiwork from being marred, provided that the world offers the other ocean users – boaters, swimmers, aestheticians, and water skiers – equally good and convenient areas of ocean for their use.

Some have argued that in the cases of copyright and patent the 'enough, and as good' proviso is easily satisfied.[56] This is facially plausible, given

such circumstances, the complainer was merely 'covetous' and 'quarrelsome' (Locke 1988, p. 291, §34).

[53] 'God gave the World. . . . To the use of the Industrious and Rational . . . not to the Fancy or Covetousness of the Quarrelsom and Contentious' (Locke 1988, p. 291, §34).

[54] It may be wondered, what happens if the laborer's appropriation would cause harm, but the stranger's copying would also cause harm? The structure of Locke's argument suggests the law of nature should create no property right in this case. In another setting, I defend this result on the ground that it is less important to prevent harms by individuals acting alone, than it is for the law of nature *itself* to assist in the doing of harm (Gordon 1993, p. 1561).

[55] For an analogous piece of art, see the photographs of 'Surrounded Islands' at http://www.christojeanneclaude.net/si.html.

[56] Interpretations of Locke's proviso vary widely. (See, for example, Fisher (2001) discussing the proviso in the context of intellectual property.) On one interpretation, for example, the proviso constrains only minimally; it permits privatization of the common whenever the results of the privatization make non-owners better off than they would be in a rude state of nature where no such privatization were permitted. Such an interpretation privileges the 'first to grab'. Another interpretation, put forward by Michael Otsuka, is more egalitarian: 'You may acquire previously unowned worldly resources if and only if you leave enough so that everyone else can acquire an equally advantageous share of unowned worldly resources' (Otsuka, 2003, p. 24).

that someone who makes a derivative work building on the public domain gains no rights in the underlying material.[57] Thus, for example, when Richie Valens made a rock version of the folk song, *La Bamba*, his copyright extended only to what he added; others could sing the public domain song without liability[58] and even obtain copyright in their own arrangement of the public domain song.[59] Similarly, obtaining a patent in a new method of turning wind into energy leaves the public unimpeded in its ability to use whatever the prior art taught about the construction of windmills. Copyright law even allows the newcomer freedom from liability if he produces something that duplicates the copyrighted work, provided the second artist came to the duplicate result independently.[60] Thus, copyright seems to leave 'enough, and as good' of the common heritage – in fact, it seems to leave the common heritage itself intact.

Similarly, many observers see what the creative person adds as a mere boon. For Locke, strangers in the absence of exigency or waste have 'no right' to 'the benefit of another's Pains' (Locke 1988, p. 291, §34). They only have rights to be protected from harm, and keeping them from a mere boon arguably causes no harm. Such a claim has been made about patent law: 'If the patented article is something which society without a patent system would not have secured at all – the inventor's monopoly hurts nobody . . . his gains consist in something which no one loses, even while he enjoys them' (Cheung 1986, p. 6).[61] In another connection, John Stuart Mill observed that no one ever 'loses' by being prohibited from 'sharing in what otherwise would not have existed at all' (Mill 1872, p. 142). But is this true?

---

[57] In the United States, this rule finds expression in 17 USC §103(b): 'The copyright in a compilation or derivative work extends only to the material contributed by the author of such work, as distinguished from the preexisting material employed in the work, and does not imply any exclusive right in the preexisting material'.

[58] Valens may have an effective monopoly on all rock versions of the song, however, because courts or juries might erroneously conclude as a factual matter that all other versions copied from Valens's hit. In American copyright law, even subconscious copying can give rise to liability. The possibility of fact-finding errors of this kind giving rise to an effective monopoly creates additional problems for the proviso.

[59] 17 USC §103.

[60] This is not necessarily true of patent. Many nations give patent owners the right to sue even independent creators; an inventor who is second-in-time, but has borrowed nothing from the inventor who preceded him, nevertheless is subject to injunction. In such cases, the second, independent inventor certainly seems to lack 'enough, and as good'. It requires some procrustean argument to suggest that the proviso is not violated, or for that matter, that the patent owner has any 'labor-based rights' that would justify his control over the independent inventor. See, for example, Becker (1993, p. 609): under the view he explores, 'authors who can show their intellectual independence from patented products [sh]ould be entitled to share the property rights in them'.

[61] Cheung goes on to note that contemporary economic scholarship recognizes that the patent system imposes significant social costs.

In making arguments about harm or loss, one must specify the baseline against which harm is measured. One baseline worth exploring is the level of welfare that the accused person had before the inventor/artist created and claimed ownership in her work.[62] By such a measure, it is *not* true that the creation of new inventions and works of authorship are necessarily harmless.

Arguments like this – that no one ever 'loses' by being prohibited from 'sharing in what otherwise would not have existed at all' (Mill 1872, p. 142) – overlook the way that creation of a new book or invention changes the social world, potentially impairing the value of the heritage, or causing other negative changes which only a freedom of copying can redress. Once an intellectual product influences the stream of culture and events, excluding the public from access to it can do harm. The same things may be in the common, but they may no longer be 'as good'. If a creative laborer *changes* the world, she should not be able to control what others can do to defend themselves from the change.

There is no way to avoid this harm by relying on the audience's foresight. How could we feasibly ask, 'Would you have wanted to be exposed to the work, knowing as you now do what it contains and that it comes with restraints on its reuse?' She could not answer without presupposing knowledge of the very sort she is supposedly deciding whether or not she wants to acquire.[63]

Moreover, we are ordinarily unable to choose what we will encounter, either in the realm of culture or of science. What looks like a boon can be (all things considered) a harm.

For example, assume that A takes substances from the common. From these, with great ingenuity, she manufactures an enzyme that greatly improves health. Because of its salutary properties, a decision is made to include the enzyme in the drinking water.

The benefits, however, come at the cost of a particular form of addiction: some people who drink the enzyme become unable to metabolize carbohydrates without continued intake of this elixir. To people so affected, much ordinary food becomes valueless for nourishment – it is useless unless eaten along with the enzyme. In such a case, the fact that the common continues to have an ample supply of both food and the elements from which the enzyme can be made is not sufficient to protect the public from harm. The addicted public also needs A's knowledge of how the enzyme is manufactured, for without it, they will starve in the midst of plenty. If, after the enzyme is put into the water supply, the inventor is given a right to prohibit others from

---

[62] The issue of what constitutes a proper comparison is notoriously controversial. See Simmons (1992, p. 294). In part, for reasons discussed in Gordon (1993, pp. 1570–1571), I examine whether an individual non-owner would have been better off never having been affected by a work, as compared to how he fares after being affected by (and barred from copying or adapting) a particular expressive work.

[63] This is closely related to the Arrow paradox.

using her manufacturing technique, addicted members of the community are worse off in their ability to use the common than they were before.[64]

Thus, the mere presence of abundant raw materials should not suffice to give A a right to exclude B and other strangers from the enzyme or from learning how it can be made. Giving A ownership of the enzyme or a patent over its method of manufacture would cause harm. Even if A's appropriation leaves 'as much' for others, it does not leave 'enough, and as good'. I would argue that mere quantitative identity is not enough.[65] This is essentially a reliance argument; having changed people's position, the inventor cannot then refuse them the tools they need for thriving under their new condition.

Authors no less than inventors are capable of changing the value of the common. Consider how the best-selling novel *Gone with the Wind* romanticized the practice of slave holding. Someone entranced by the novel's dramatic love story might find herself drawn into the narrator's assumptions about slavery; the reader's views of her own ancestors and of her nation's history (matters that lie in the common) might be negatively affected in a way that mere factual knowledge could not alone undo. To undo the novel's visceral effects, she might need to write or read a corrective that revisits the images or personages of the original. This is what author Alice Randall did in her novel, *The Wind Done Gone*: she wrote a book that took some of the *Gone with the Wind* characters and events, and recast them from an Afro-American perspective.

Sometimes the law must permit[66] re-use of authored work to avoid a historian or novelist permanently changing people's understanding of their heritage in ways that will devalue the common.[67] Current copyright law does not consistently permit such re-use. American law sometimes allows copyists

---

[64] Note that appealing to the public's ability to use the common (rather than its ownership of the common) is a controversial step.

[65] At least, this is how I interpret the proviso (1993, pp. 1562–1573). As John Simmons says, 'Neither the quantitative nor the qualitative aspects of the requirement [of leaving "enough, and as good"] wears its meaning on its face' (Simmons 1992, p. 295).

[66] Harms caused by expression raise institutional and free-speech issues beyond the scope of the instant paper. Nevertheless, the following distinction should be noted. The question is not whether the harms done by *Gone with the Wind* justify punishing its author or censoring the book. Rather, the question is whether the author of a harmful book should be given a property right that would affirmatively stop harmed parties from re-using the book to undo the injury done them. I argue that the proviso should be interpreted to stop a property right of the latter kind from arising.

[67] Said Alice Randall, 'My book is an antidote to what I perceive as the poison of the *Gone with the Wind* text' (*Alice Randall 'Speaking freely' transcript*). Randall's book was initially enjoined as a copyright infringement, and removed from bookstore shelves. Although the injunction was later lifted, the episode demonstrated a danger that copyright can pose. See *SunTrust Bank v. Houghton Mifflin Co.*, 136 F Supp 2d 1357 (ND Ga 2001) (enjoining production, display, distribution, advertising, sale, or offer for sale of *The Wind Done Gone*), rev'd, 268 F3d 1237 (11th Cir 2001) and 252 F3d 1165 (11th Cir 2001).

a privilege akin to self-defense under the doctrine of 'fair use',[68] but 'fair use' and related doctrines fall short of preserving the necessary liberty.[69] Therefore, it appears that American copyright law fails to track a Lockean approach.

INTENT AND THE LOCKEAN PROVISO

If the law of nature prohibits the doing of harm, we are entitled not to have our ability to use the common be made worse off[70] by the laborer's claim to property. This is an inherent right we would have as humans and not because of any particular act or effort on our part.[71] A Lockean copyright would arise under this schema *only* as to those persons whose exclusion from using the work would leave them no worse off (at least in regard to their ability to use the common)[72] than if the work never existed in the first place.[73] How do we identify those persons? How do we know who – if denied the liberty to copy, adapt, or otherwise make use of the creative laborer's output – would merely be restored to their status quo ante? It is only these persons who can be justifiably enjoined under the Lockean schema.

The key here may be the category so important in *Grokster*, namely, intent. Locke suggests that 'enough, and as good' is significant not only in itself, but, also because when 'enough, and as good' is present, we know something about the intent of persons complaining about the appropriation.

Locke writes:

He that had as good left for his Improvement, as was already taken up, needed not complain, ought not to meddle with what was already improved by another's Labour:

---

[68] '[A]n individual in rebutting a copyrighted work containing derogatory information about himself may copy such parts of the work as are necessary to permit understandable comment'. *Hustler Magazine Inc. v. Moral Majority Inc.*, 796 F.2d 1148, 1153 (9th Cir. 1986).

[69] See Gordon (1993).

[70] One can debate how broadly to interpret both the (primary) right against harm and the (derivative) proviso against harm. John Simmons, for example, suggests that some competition (and thus some harm) might be rightful under Locke's natural law, Simmons (1992, p. 71) As for the proviso, Simmons suggests that 'Locke is prohibiting appropriation that denies others an opportunity equal to one's own for self-preservation and self-government' (1992, p. 292).

[71] In Waldron's language, this would be a 'general right.' Waldron (1988, chapter 4) explores the distinction between 'special rights' that 'arise out of some special transaction or relationship' and 'general rights' that are not so limited, and which apply to everyone.

[72] It may be that the proviso should block the formation of private property when the private claim would cause harm of any kind, and not merely when it causes harm to the common. Such an approach would raise the question of whether the Lockean approach can be squared with the general liberty to compete because many intentional and even malicious harms are done in the course of socially desirable competitive activity.

[73] If my world has changed because of exposure to the work, if I have relied on or become affected by it, then denying me the ability to copy it freely may make me worse off than if the artist had never labored and the work had never come into existence. In the second situation, I would argue, the artist's claim to private ownership is (at best) incomplete.

If he did, *'tis plain he desired the benefit of another's Pains*, which he had no right to, and not the Ground which God had given him in common. (Locke 1988, p. 291, §34; emphasis added)

In this, Locke comes close to abandoning his props of mixing land, and labor, in favor of making a more general, quasi-Kantian point about ethics. The person who acts for the purpose of taking 'the benefit of another's Pains' (and no other purpose) we will call 'malicious'. The malicious person violates a deontological constraint when he does intentional harm. It may be that this constraint merely imposes a duty to avoid harm (e.g., by compensating) rather than a full duty to respect intellectual-property rights but that need not be fatal to the *Grokster* opinion if the Court was assuming that harm was done.[74]

The core of Kant's deontological view holds that it is wrong to treat another merely as a means rather than as an end in himself, 'to treat someone as if he existed for purposes he does not share' (Quinn 1992, p. 190 n.25). It denies the fundamental equality of persons so to prefer one's self over another. As Thomas Nagel notes:

The deontological constraint... expresses the direct appeal to the point of view of the agent from the point of view of the person on whom he is acting. It operates through that relation. The victim feels outrage when he is deliberately harmed... not simply because of the quantity of the harm but because of the assault on his value of having my actions guided by his evil. (Nagel 1986, p. 184)

Thus, let us examine copying by an artist/user who uses a preexisting work simply to save effort and expense; for this user, the more the other person has labored, the better. He is the person who merely desires the benefit of the other's 'Pains', and who will not be worse off if copyright is enforced against him. It is he who necessarily engages in the perversion of the personal depicted by Nagel.

Nagel gives this example of the 'sense of moral dislocation' that occurs when we aim intentionally at another's harm: An actor wants something whose acquisition will save lives, but can only be obtained by twisting a child's arm. 'If you twist the child's arm, your aim is to produce pain. So when the child cries, "Stop, it hurts!" his objection corresponds in perfect diametrical opposition to your intention. What he is pleading as your reason to stop is precisely your reason to go on' (Nagel 1986, p. 182).

---

74 Given the harm-based focus of Locke, one could argue that any *harmless* intentional copying is 'rightful' – even when such harmless copying is done by someone who seeks only to take advantage of 'another's Pains'. We need not reach this question. As my goal is to reconstruct the best argument the Court *could* have made for finding all infringement-inducers wrongful, I allow arguendo the assumption that harm was caused by the behavior at issue in *Grokster*.

Similarly, for the actor I call 'malicious', how does he react when he hears the laborer cry, 'Stop! I worked so hard on that!' His honest reply would be, 'To take advantage of your hard work is precisely why I seek it'.[75]

Copyright sweeps everybody into its reach. However, it is this first group, whom I call 'malicious' users, who stand as the target at copyright's conceptual core, if viewed deontologically.[76] These persons aim to take for their own use benefits toward which the author had labored, not to rectify a harm inflicted by the work, but simply because using the creation instrumentally facilitates the user's other ends. In Locke's words, the malicious person is the person who 'desired the benefit of another's Pains which he had no right to, and not the Ground' (Locke 1988, p. 291, §34) that was the common gift.

Preventing a malicious person from using the work for his own profit makes him no worse off than if the pre-existing work had never come to his notice. Excluding malicious users from the laborer's product still leaves them with 'enough, and as good' as the laborer herself possessed. Denying them use of a work or making them pay for it simply restores them to their status quo ante, which is the classic function of corrective justice. As to malicious users, then, the proviso is necessarily satisfied.

Beyond malicious users, there is a second group, defined by having a connection with the work itself. In the second group belongs the copying by any artist/user who has been affected by the prior work in some way other than a simple stimulated desire to better himself at the other's expense. Because they do not merely seek the 'benefit of another's Pains', the proviso might not be satisfied when suit is brought against members of this second group. From a Lockean perspective, such persons may be entitled to some freedom to borrow even when their use harms the original author.[77] To such a 'content-oriented user', the text is not just a commodity, an instrument, or a tool that can be exchanged with other tools. Such a user has an emotional reaction to the text that is nonfungible. The need to react to the text may involve use of the text; suppressing the need may violate Locke's proviso.[78]

---

[75] The analogy with Nagel's example is not perfect. The extent of the laborer's 'pains' will have only an inexact correlation with the value of the work produced. More importantly, the child's arm belongs to him more surely than the laborer's effort belongs to the laborer. The thesis I raise here is, therefore, overbroad unless one accepts with Locke some notion that the laborer's effort remains 'his' even after the labor is expended – or, alternatively, unless one accepts that the laborer's beneficial acts deserve some reward that the nonlaborer is morally obliged to honor.

[76] This and the following few paragraphs borrow language from my article (Gordon 2004), and at other points, the chapter borrows some language from another of my articles (Gordon 1993).

[77] I am speaking here of a Lockean approach. Liberties that might be justifiable under a Lockean approach might not be justified under other, for example, some consequentialist approaches.

[78] I do not contend that enforcing copyright will always suppress or distort the nonmalicious borrower's creative impulse. Some of the nonmalicious may be proper objects of Lockean

Do the copyright statutes of any nations limit the imposition of liability solely to cases where the proviso is satisfied? I know of no such provision. Do the copyright statutes of most nations limit liability to those copyists who are malicious? Again, the answer is 'no'.

Under the American rules that govern direct infringement, liability is imposed on virtually anyone who copies, regardless of motive. Even having a reasonable and good faith belief that one is copying lawfully will ordinarily give no defense to a civil suit. (Such a lack of intent to infringe might help in a prosecution for criminal copyright infringement,[79] but *Grokster* was a civil suit.) Therefore, copyright and the Lockean approach again seem to diverge.

But do copyright and the Lockean approach instead converge in the rare types of copyright liability (here, a form of secondary liability) that courts do premise on intent? *Grokster* after all is one such rare case.[80] The answer lies in comparing the kinds of intent the Court required in *Grokster* with the kind of intent that matters under the Lockean approach. For the Lockean approach, the question was whether the copyist was motivated by the desire to use another's labor as a substitute for his own, a desire to subordinate that other person to himself, to use the other merely as a means. For *Grokster*, the question was whether the defendant has 'distribute[d] a device with the object of promoting its use to infringe copyright'.[81] Are these intents necessarily equivalent?

LIABILITY FOR TECHNOLOGY

As discussed earlier, the U.S. Supreme Court in *Grokster* seems to have shifted ground from copyright's usual consequentialism to issues of intent. The Court seems to have switched from a consideration of agent-neutral principles, to an agent-relative emphasis. Presumably it is the defendant's intent to induce copyright infringement – a bad act – that makes the Court not care about the technology's potential for good consequences.[82]

Let us assume arguendo that a deontological constraint (of the kind that says, for example, 'do not murder') gives rise to a prima facie duty that can relieve us of any otherwise-applicable obligation to achieve the highest net

---

liability – namely, those who copy despite the fact that 'enough and as good' was left for them.

[79] United States v. Moran. 757 F. Supp. 1046, 1049 (D. Neb. 1991).

[80] Although copyright imposes 'strict liability' on copyists as part of the doctrine of 'direct' infringement, 'secondary' liability such as that which is at issue in *Grokster* is based on different rules.

[81] *Grokster*, 125 S. Ct. at 2780.

[82] Alternatively, the emphasis on 'intent' may really be an inquiry into defendant's 'lineage' (Wu 2005, p. 243), or may result from an assumption that 'inducement' 'suggests mass infringement' (Wu 2005, p. 250).

balance of good consequences over bad.[83] But what is an intent to induce copyright infringement? Is it an intent to commit an act that in itself violates a deontological constraint? If acting with an intent to induce infringement necessarily amounts to a deontological wrong, then, under our assumption, the Court was free (at least as a prima facie matter) to disregard consequences. However, if the act of inducement does not necessarily amount to a deontologic wrong, then the Court needs some other explanation (not yet supplied)[84] for employing an inquiry into 'intent' in lieu of undertaking a full consequentialist inquiry.

Let us look first at the intent involved in the underlying direct infringements, that is, the acts by file-traders from which the technology's secondary liability would be derived. Direct copyright infringement (unlike some forms of secondary liability) is premised on grounds independent of intent. Further, copyright infringement can be found even when the Lockean proviso is violated.[85] Thus, a file-trader may be legally liable despite the fact he lacks the kind of intent that in the Lockean approach would subject him to a duty, and despite the proviso being otherwise unsatisfied. Therefore, even if one could utilize some kind of doctrine of 'transferred intent' to attribute the direct infringers' motivations to the secondary party, it is not necessarily true that one or more of the direct infringers had the improper motivation. Some or even most file-traders *may* have had the kind of intent that the Lockean approach would condemn,[86] but this is neither something that the Court sought to demonstrate nor is it something that is logically entailed by the test for secondary liability that the Court used.

What about the intent of the secondary infringer himself? On the one hand, he is using others' 'property' for purposes of his own. On the other hand, as we have seen, what the positive law considers to be copyright 'property' is not always 'property' from a Lockean perspective. Therefore, again, it is difficult to be sure that, in a Lockean world, someone commits a deontological wrong when he facilitates copying.

---

[83] As mentioned earlier, this chapter does not need to reach the ultimate question of whether a deontological duty always carries the day despite consequences. Nevertheless, it is worth mentioning the classic literary example posing that question. In Dostoyevsky's *The Brothers Karamazov*, one brother poses roughly the following problem to another brother: 'Assume an evil deity credibly promises you that he will end all suffering experienced by all children. No more hungry children, or diseased children, or beaten children. But the evil deity specifies that he will grant this boon to the millions of future children only if you kill one innocent child. Would you do it?'

[84] I do not deny that precedent provided some support for the Court's rule, as did (by analogy) a provision in patent law. But existing precedent could also have supported alternative rules. The question is how the Court justified the path it took.

[85] See Gordon (1993).

[86] Although file-sharers have a personal connection to the work, having a personal connection does not always give rise to a liberty based on the proviso. See note 21, supra.

To sum up: when the proviso is violated, copying may be *rightful*. If so, then having the intent to induce such copying is not necessarily wrongful.

One might argue that the U.S. Supreme Court was acting not against the purportedly wrongful act of encouraging copying, but against the purportedly wrongful act of helping people to disobey the law. It is certainly possible to argue that we all have at least a prima facie moral obligation to obey the law. If so, might one defend the U.S. Supreme Court's *Grokster* decision on the ground that anyone who 'intentionally induces' lawbreaking is committing a deontological wrong? Conceivably. But to make such an argument would require explanations not ventured in the Court's opinion.[87]

In its prior decision, *Sony*, the Court had decided that, when a technology presented a mix of lawful and unlawful consequences, the 'capacity for substantial noninfringing uses' was sufficient to validate the technology's survival. In other words, the lawful consequences trumped the unlawful. In *Grokster*, the Court was asked to say more about what counted as this trump: how to define 'capacity' and 'substantiality', or to determine what balance between good and bad effects was necessary before copyright law should impose liability on a technology.[88] Instead of facing those questions, the Court reached for a trope.[89]

The Court essentially announced that, if a certain kind of intentional inducement is present, the trumping effect would switch to the unlawful effects: if 'intentional inducement' is present, then it is the lawful and beneficial effects that become irrelevant. That position would be controversial even if the Court's test for liability required proof that a defendant had committed a deontological wrong. But the Court's test seems to have no such component. So in the end, I agree with Tim Wu's criticism. One cannot escape the impression, reading the *Grokster* decision, that the language of intent was being used primarily to enable the Court to evade a difficult choice about what consequences should matter (Wu 2005).

CONCLUSION

Blocking an inquiry into consequences is a serious matter. Yet, in the *Grokster* case, the Court ducked difficult questions about consequences[90] and instead imposed liability on the ground that the defendant, Grokster, had 'intended' to facilitate copyright infringement.

[87] The Court does briefly exhibit some concern with the issue of lawbreaking: '[I]ndications are that the ease of copying songs or movies using software like Grokster's and Napster's is fostering disdain for copyright protection' (*Grokster*, 125 S. Ct. 2764 at p. 2775).

[88] See, generally, Wu (2005)

[89] Cf. Wu (2005).

[90] For example: What kind of effects should suffice for imposing secondary liability? How much good or bad did the Grokster technology facilitate? Of how much good or bad was it capable?

298 *Wendy J. Gordon*

The Court implicitly ruled that consequences didn't matter. Perhaps the Court believed that a concern with societal effects was trumped by a deontological concern with avoiding wrongful behavior.[91] Yet, the Court never really discussed why it thought the 'intentional' act of facilitating infringement was sufficiently evil to render the technology's potential benefits irrelevant. This chapter attempted to fill that gap, drawing on Lockean theory to identify a potentially applicable deontological wrong. The chapter concluded, however, that the Court's test for secondary liability does not depend on a defendant committing such a wrong.

The *Grokster* opinion is thus caught between two stools. It lurches from consequentialist considerations (e.g., where the Court says that making Grokster liable is the only 'practical' thing to do) to what sounds like non-consequentialist reasoning ('intent'), without at any point either pinning down the consequences at issue, or pinning down a deontological duty that would be violated by a defendant who induced copyright infringement. The opinion does justice to neither concern.

That the makers of a technology intentionally help someone else violate copyright law hardly seems like such an evil act that a lawmaking court should disregard the beneficial byproducts of the technology. Moreover, the Court's apparently deontological inquiry into 'intent' is engrafted onto a statute that was enacted pursuant to a consequentialist clause of the U.S. Constitution. After all, Congress is given power over copyright and patent 'To Promote the Progress of Science and the useful Arts'. By neither admitting or explaining why it was abandoning consequentialism, nor doing a full consequentialist analysis, the Court comes to a result whose basis is opaque. This chapter intends to help show how acknowledging the consequentialist/nonconsequentialist divide can help us reason more clearly.

References

Alice Randall 'Speaking freely' transcript. Recorded April 2, 2002, in Nashville, TN. http://www.firstamendmentcenter.org/about.aspx?id=12787

Becker, L. 1977. *Property rights: Philosophic foundations.* London: Routledge and Kegan Paul.

Becker, L. 1993. Deserving to own intellectual property. *Chicago-Kent Law Review, 68,* 609–629.

Broome, J. 1995. *Weighing Goods: Equality, Uncertainty and Time.* Oxford: Blackwell.

Bell, T. W. 1998. Fair use vs. fared use: The impact of automated rights management on copyright's fair use doctrine. *North Carolina Law Review, 76,* 557–619.

Calabresi, G. 1970. *The cost of accidents: A legal and economic analysis.* New Haven, CT: Yale University Press.

[91] We need not reach the question of whether deontological duties really should have such a trumping effect. The chapter addresses an issue that arises prior to that question, namely, the issue of whether people who 'induce copyright infringement' necessarily violate a deontological duty.

Cheung, S. N. S. 1986. Property rights and invention, in J. Palmer and R. O. Zerbe (Eds.), *Research in law and economics: The economics of patents and copyrights* (Vol. 8), Greenwich NJ: JAI Press, pp. 5–18.

Cohen, J., Loren, L. P., Okediji, R. G., and O'Rourke, M. A. 2002. *Copyright in a global information economy.* New York: Aspen Publishers.

Cohen, J. 2005. The place of the user in copyright law. *Fordham Law Review, 74,* 347–74.

Drahos, P. 1996. *A philosophy of intellectual property.* Dartmouth: Ashgate.

Fisher, W. 2001. Theories of intellectual property, in S. Munzer (Ed.), *New essays in the legal and political theory of property.* Cambridge, UK: Cambridge University Press.

Frankena, W. 1988. *Ethics* (2nd ed.). Englewood Cliffs, NJ: Prentice Hall.

Gordon, W. J. 1989. An inquiry into the merits of copyright: The challenges of consistency, consent and encouragement theory. *Stanford Law Review, 41,* 1343–1469.

Gordon, W. J. 1993. A property right in self-expression. *Yale Law Journal, 102,* 1533–1609.

Gordon, W. J. 2004. Render copyright unto Caesar: On taking incentives seriously. *University of Chicago Law Review, 71,* 75–92.

Hardy, T. 1996. *Property (and copyright) in Cyberspace,* University of Chicago Legal Forum, pp. 217–260.

Hettinger, E. C. 1989. Justifying intellectual property. *Philosophy and Public Affairs, 18,* 1, 31–52.

Kramer, M. H. 2004. *John Locke and the Origins of Private Property: Philosophical Explorations of Individualism, Community, and Equality.* Cambridge: Cambridge University Press.

Lange, D. 2003. Reimagining the public domain. *Law and Contemporary Problems, 66,* 463–483.

Lessig, L. 1999. *Code and other laws of cyberspace.* New York: Basic Books.

Litman, J. 1994. The exclusive right to read. *Cardozo Arts and Entertainment Law Journal, 29,* 13–54.

Litman, J. 2001. *Digital copyright.* Amherst, NY: Prometheus Books.

Litman, J. 2004. Sharing and stealing. *Hastings Communications and Entertainment Law Journal, 27,* 1–50.

Locke, J. 1988. *Two treatises of government.* Edited by Peter Laslett. Cambridge, UK: Cambridge University Press.

Lunney, G. 1996. Reexamining copyright's incentives-access paradigm. *Vanderbilt Law Review, 49,* 483–571.

Lunney, G. 2001. The death of copyright: digital technology, private copying, and the Digital Millennium Copyright Act. *Virginia Law Review, 87,* 813–920.

Michelman, F. 1967. Property, utility, and fairness: Comments on the ethical foundations of 'just compensation' law. *Harvard Law Review, 80,* 1165–1258.

Mill, J. S. 1872. *Principles of political economy.* Boston: Lee & Shepard.

Moor, J. 1985. What is computer ethics? in T. W. Bynum (Ed.), *Computers and ethics.* Oxford: Blackwell, pp. 266–275.

Nagel, T. 1986. *The view from nowhere.* New York: Oxford University Press.

Nozick, R. 1974. *Anarchy, state and utopia.* New York: Basic Books.

Otsuka, M. 2003. *Libertarianism without inequality.* Oxford: Oxford University Press.

Palmer, T. G. 2002. Are patents and copyrights morally justified? The philosophy of property rights and ideal objects, in A. Thierer and W. Crews (Eds.), *Copy fights: The future of intellectual property in the information age.* Washington DC: Cato Institute, pp. 43–93.

Portmore, D. W. 2001. can an act consequentialist theory be agent relative? *American Philosophical Quarterly, 38,* 363–377.

Quinn, W. S. 1992. Actions, intention, and consequences: the doctrine of double effect, in J. M. Fischer, and M. Ravizza, *Ethics: Problems and principles.* Fort Worth: Harcourt Brace Jovanovich, p. 179ff.

Shiffrin, S. V. 2001. Lockean arguments for private intellectual property, in S. R. Munzer, *New essays in the legal and political theory of property.* Cambridge, UK: Cambridge University Press.

Simmons, A. J. 1992. *The Lockean theory of rights.* Princeton: Princeton University Press.

Simons, K. 1992. Rethinking mental states. *Boston University Law Review, 72,* 463–554.

Stallman, R. 2002. *Free software, free society.* Boston: GNU Press

Thomson, J. J. 1976. Property acquisition. *Journal of Philosophy, 73,* 664–666.

Waldron, J. 1988. *The right to private property.* New York: Clarendon Press, Oxford University Press.

Wu, T. 2005. The copyright paradox. *Supreme Court Review, 2005,* 229–255.

15

Information Technology, Privacy, and the Protection of Personal Data

Jeroen van den Hoven

Information technology allows us to generate, store, and process huge quantities of data. Search engines, satellites, sensor networks, scientists, security agencies, marketers, and database managers are processing terabytes of data per day. A good part of these data are about persons – about their characteristics, their thoughts, their movements, behaviour, communications, and preferences – or they can be used to produce such data[1]. All countries and cultures in the present and past have constrained access to certain types of personal data in some way or the other (see Moore 1984). There are etiquettes, customs, artefacts, technologies, or laws, and combinations thereof, which prevent or proscribe against the use or dissemination of personal information. Walls, curtains, doors, veils, sealed envelopes, sunglasses, clothes, locked cabinets, privacy laws, secure databases, cryptographic keys, and passwords all serve the purpose of preventing individual persons to acquire and use information about other persons. The issues are often discussed in the context of a specific social sector or professional domain, such as health care, social or homeland security, search engines, marketing, or policing. More specifically the issues can be concerned with camera surveillance, the monitoring of Internet communications, the retention of Internet traffic data, the disclosure of passenger lists to security agencies, the availability of individual medical information in the public health system, the linking and matching of databases in social security to detect

---

[1] There is a widely accepted convention to distinguish between data (raw data), information (meaningful data), and knowledge. My main concern here is with data or the raw material that can be used and interpreted by a variety of methods and tools to serve many different purposes. This paper explores the moral foundations of data protection. In many cases, not much depends on whether we use 'data' instead of 'information'. It is important to realize though that, even when no meaning can be assigned to data (because there is too much data, and it is too difficult to interpret them), it does make sense to think about protecting them because they may start to make sense when new tools and techniques are applied to them, or when they are combined with other data.

fraud, and sifting and trawling through financial databases in order to find suspect transactions. In the near future, they may be about who has access to the scans and digital images of our brains or about who can track and trace tagged personal belongings, everyday objects, and consumer products.

Ethical issues concerning information about persons are typically cast in terms of *privacy*. Privacy is construed as a need, a right, a condition, or an aspect of human dignity. Sometimes it is construed as intrinsically valuable; sometimes it is construed as deriving its value from other sources, for example, from the fact that it is conducive to autonomy or freedom (see Shoeman 1984, Wagner DeCew 1997, Roessler 2005, Nissenbaum 2004, Solove 2002, Velleman 1996, and Nagel 1998). The largest part of privacy research is concerned with the moral justification of a right to privacy. There is little agreement about the most adequate moral justification[2], but there is consensus among privacy scholars about the fact that privacy is important and that privacy is vague, fuzzy, and hard to explicate or pin down (Wagner DeCew 1997).

In public debates about privacy at the beginning of the twenty-first century, there are roughly three positions. First, there is the view that we should stop worrying about privacy, because there is so much personal information available and everyone can know almost everything about everyone, if one would bother to make the effort.

Every credit card payment, Internet search, mobile telephone call, and every movement of a tagged object spawns data about its use and user (van den Hoven 2006). Our life worlds have turned into ambient intelligent environments (Aarts and Encarnacao 2006) which soak up, process, and disseminate personal data. There is so much information that the idea of constraining or controlling the flow in conformity with moral considerations, laws, and regulations is absurd (Safire 2005; Spinello 1997; Quittner 1997).

Second, there is the view that Western democracies cannot afford the high levels of individual privacy that they now attempt to provide. Even if it were technically feasible, high levels of privacy are undesirable[3]. Proponents of this view often also argue along utilitarian lines that modern societies involve large numbers of free moving individuals, exhibit high degrees of mobility, social and institutional complexity, and anonymity, which facilitate free-riding in the form of criminal behaviour, fraud, and tax evasion. In order to mitigate the adverse effects of anonymity and mobility, information about individuals should be made available to governments. It is assumed that groups and communities benefit significantly from knowledge about

---

[2] For a recent and comprehensive discussion of philosophical accounts, see Roessler (2005). Already, in 1986, Thomas Perry indicated that privacy was a battleground for different positions in applied ethics (Perry 1986).

[3] The most influential proponent of this idea seems to be communitarian thinker Amitai Etzioni (2005). For a short position paper, see Etzioni (1996): ' ... giving up some measure of privacy is exactly what the common good requires'.

their members. Third, another position is to argue that there are good moral reasons to protect individuals from Big Brother, data-greedy companies, and snooping fellow citizens. There are good moral reasons to justify a potent regime of individual rights which constrains access to information about individuals.

In discussions about privacy, those who represent the second view are mostly communitarians. Communitarians emphasize with respect to privacy that it offers a degree of anonymity that facilitates antisocial behaviour, whereas liberalists emphasize the importance of the individual's right to privacy. Michael Walzer has observed in this context that liberalism is, therefore, plagued by free-rider problems, 'by people who continue to enjoy the benefits of membership and identity although no longer participating in the activities that produce these benefits, whereas Communitarianism is the dream of a perfect free-riderlessness' (Walzer 1995). Or as Thomas Nagel has put it: 'Those of us who are not political communitarians want to leave each other some space...' (Nagel 1998, p. 20).

Ever since the debate about privacy was triggered by an article of Warren and Brandeis titled 'The Right to Privacy' at the end of the nineteenth century, the confusion and conceptual controversy concerning privacy has grown and one account of privacy after the other has been suggested (Warren and Brandeis 1890). I will not deal with the possible answers to the question as to what the best conceptual analysis of the term 'privacy' is because we can do without such an analysis and still articulate what bothers us about others having access to information about us that we did not volunteer. The analogy with contemporary epistemology may serve as a cautionary tale. The quest for the best analysis of knowledge has ended in a wild goose chase for necessary and sufficient conditions for the truth of 'John knows that p'. Several decades of philosophical research in epistemology have failed to yield a comprehensive and noncontroversial conclusion. In the case of knowledge, it is not problematic that all resources are used in theoretical epistemology, because there are not many hotly debated practical moral issues concerning knowledge.

Privacy research is different, however, in the sense that we are confronted by urgent and hard privacy problems in practice, and we need to justify and account for legal, practical, technical, and political decisions every day. Privacy issues are high on the political agenda and are hotly debated in software engineering and systems development, health care, e-government, criminal justice, law enforcement, marketing, and e-commerce. In the case of privacy, we need to repair our boat at sea and we cannot take it out of the stormy waters to study it for an indefinite period of time, with uncertain or highly controversial outcomes.

The central role given to the concept of *privacy* in our thinking about the moral issues concerning the protection of personal data obfuscates practical solutions to the everyday problems we encounter in law, public policy, and software engineering concerning them. It lands us in the middle of the controversy between liberal and communitarian political philosophies and the associated conceptions of the Self. Because this controversy cannot be easily decided in the favour of either point of view, I propose to address the central question of the moral problem underlying privacy issues head on: why should we protect personal data; what moral reasons do we have to protect personal data? I would like to construe this question on a par with questions, such as 'why should we protect nuclear reactors, medieval manuscripts, babies, and bird sanctuaries?' In each of these cases, we have good reasons to constrain access, think about visiting hours, stipulate how different persons or groups ought to behave in the vicinity of these entities, and how they may interact with them. In each of these examples, protection takes on a different form and has a different rationale. What would count as a good moral reason to protect personal data and what type of reasons would justify putting limits to the freedom of others to get access to them? This I will discuss in Section 2. First I will discuss our long-lasting interest in personal data.

1. WHY PERSONAL DATA WILL ALWAYS BE IN DEMAND

Personal data will always be in demand. We will continue to amass personal data in the future and questions concerning their protection are therefore unlikely to subside. First, I distinguish between reasons that governments and nongovernmental parties may have to gather information about individuals. Second, I distinguish between reasons for acquiring information about a person that are primarily directed at the interest of the data subject and reasons primarily concerned with the interests of others than the data subject. This gives us four types of reasons for data collection, which help us to understand the logic which drives the accumulation of personal data, now and in the future.

First, government agencies may want to have access to data about citizens to serve them better. In order to provide better services, they will have to know a good deal about them. Government agencies could alert individual citizens to the fact that they are entitled to benefits they did not know about. This type of proactive service delivery to citizens has become more common in recent years. In the Scandinavian countries, citizens seem to be at ease with the idea that the government thinks on their behalf about their welfare and citizens seem to be comfortable with fewer impediments for government to find out details about their individual lives.

Second, the same logic applies to commercial parties and companies. Commercial parties want to be able to serve their customers or clients better. The more they know about them, the better they can fine-tune their propositions to their preferences and needs. Attention of consumers is scarce and commercial proposals therefore need to raise the immediate interest of

potential customers. Many customers have no problems with alerts by businesses which draw their attention to bargains in the areas they are interested
in and many seem willing to volunteer personal information in exchange
for bargains.

Third, companies or commercial parties also have strictly prudential reasons to collect or accumulate personal data, both about their customers,
their partners in transactions and their employees. These reasons are not at
all concerned with the interests of the data subjects. Transactions between
private parties always present chances for exploitation. Other parties can
break their promises, break the contract, or buy without paying. In these
cases, adequate information about the partners one is dealing with, for
example, information about credit risks or commercial past performance
are thought to be extremely helpful in gauging the risks associated with
the transaction. Perhaps even more fundamental; in order to be able to
trust parties, re-identification of individual partners is a necessary condition for building up a reliable picture of someone's track record in interactions. In game theory and the study of iterated prisoners' dilemmas, the
(re)identification of players in consecutive rounds is simply assumed. In
the real world, however, (re)identification is often a practical problem.
Computer applications concerning the identity and relevant properties of
individuals are widely used to counter the problem of reliable identification
and authentication of persons in private interactions. Information technology holds up the promise that it can deal with the knowledge deficit we are
often confronted with in our dealings with strangers and people we know
very little about.

The deployment of information technology in the relation between
employer and employee may be accounted for in terms of the Principal–
Agent theory, according to which the Principal, for example, an employer,
always has the problem of making sure that the employee (the agent) is
doing what he or she ought to do, when he or she is out of sight. The Principal, therefore, has to make so-called agent cost and has to monitor the
agent and check what he or she is doing. This accounts for the incredible
explosion of workplace monitoring and surveillance by means of logging,
CCTV cameras, smart badges, and black boxes in cars.

Finally, government also has reasons to try and get information on citizens, which are not primarily and directly concerned with the individual
interests of individual citizens about whom information is collected, but are
primarily concerned with the public good. One of the central tasks of government is the production and maintenance of public goods. One of the
central problems of the management of public goods is managing the access
to public goods and more specifically the problem of excluding those who
are benefiting from the public good without contributing to the maintenance and reproduction of the public good. This category of individuals is
referred to as 'free riders'. The containment of free riders is a central task for

government. Free riders can thrive and exist only if they are anonymous.[4] If they can be identified government can affect their pay-off matrix and their self-interested calculation. Identifying information is thus very helpful to governments as managers of public goods.

These four types of 'logic of the situation' explain why a range of actors in the government and the market sector, will engage in massive computer-supported data collection, and will continue to do so for reasons both concerning the good of the data subject or the good of others than the data subject. They will always welcome and use new developments in information technology that may support their attempts to reach these goals.

What do people object to when they object to gathering personal data in these and other cases? We need to distinguish between different objects of concerns. When a man who enters an almost empty restaurant picks the table right next to me, there are several things I may object to. First, I may not at all be concerned with *my* personal data, but rather with *his* personal data. I may in other words not be concerned with what this person is learning about *me*, but rather with what I am learning about *him*. I just don't want to know the things that I am about to find out about him. A further concern may be the fact that my choice not to learn anything about anybody at that moment is preempted by his decision to sit next to me. I will hear what he orders, smell his aftershave, hear him turn the pages of his newspaper and hear his mobile phone conversation. A perceptual relation is imposed upon me, because he chose to move into my perceptual field without my consent. In that sense, the setting is turned into a source of personal data about the intruder. Data are stored in my brain, and I may forget about them immediately or may remember them later.

A second possible object of my discontentment in the restaurant may be that this person has manoeuvred himself into a position where he is now able to acquire data about *me*, which can be passed on – about what I was having for dinner that evening, what I was wearing, and so forth. He may decide to tell others, or, in secret, make video footage of me munching my garlic bread. Even if I would know that the merely onlooking person would not be recording or storing information in an external information carrier, or would not be able – as a result of a rare brain disease – to retain the data acquired beyond the specious present, I could still feel uncomfortable and awkward because the imposed perceptual relationship heightens my aware-ness of myself and forces an external – and not freely chosen – perspective upon me.

The ethics of data protection is first and foremost about the second and third type of grievance of the lonely diner. These grievances come under the heading of informational privacy or tort privacy and need to be distinguished

---

[4] De Jasay (1989) observes: '...it is not non-exclusion that makes retaliation impossible...,
but anonymity of the free-rider'.

from the first problem sketched above (the right 'to be left alone') and also from what has been termed 'decisional or constitutional privacy', that is, the right to decide without government interference – for example, the right to decide in which kinds of sexual behaviour to engage between consenting adults in the privacy of one's bedroom, or to decide to have an abortion or to use contraceptives. Sandel refers to the latter as the *new privacy* and to the former as the *old privacy* (Sandel 1989). In Sandel's classification, data protection is about the old privacy.

2. PERSONAL DATA

Personal data are and will remain a valuable asset, but what counts as personal data? If one wants to protect X, one needs to know what X is.

Before we start answering this question a couple of things need to be observed about personal data. First of all, personal data are multiple-realizable, that is, they may be stored in different places and in different media. They may be generated and acquired by different types of information processors, whether human or artificial and silicon-based, or a combination thereof. Second, data may be generated by means of a variety of methods, techniques, and artefacts. Individuals may be monitored by cameras, by persons using binoculars, by scanners which track RFID tagged items they carry around, a discussion may be overheard, or agencies may trawl and sift through databases. And, finally and importantly, data do not have a meaning separate from the context in which they are used.

So when is someone else acquiring and storing information *about* me? When is someone processing my personal data? Let's consider the following two claims C1: 'X is in restaurant A at time $t1$' and C2: 'Y is in Restaurant A at time $t1$'. Is C2 *about* X? C2 presents itself obviously as information about Y. When looked at in isolation 'Y is in the Restaurant at time $t1$' does not tell you anything about X, but when combined with C1, it does provide information about X which was not contained in C1. Good detective stories often present information to the reader which is seemingly irrelevant to the crime or to the biography of the protagonist, but later turns out to be, in an unexpected sense, *about* the murderer or his victim. As the story unfolds and the plot unravels, the insignificant piece of information is situated in a context where it suddenly picks out an individual. We suddenly see how the insignificant and seemingly irrelevant piece of information suddenly applies to the protagonist.

We are introduced to people and get to know people under certain descriptions and modes of presentation or 'guises' as H.-N. Castaneda has called them (Castaneda 1989). Some individuals present themselves in misleading ways or 'dis-guise' themselves. Personal data believed to be applicable to a person are often stored in different mental files because there were different representations or self-presentations of the person (let us call them m1 and m2), while there is no belief to the effect that m1 = m2. New beliefs about the person under mode of presentation m1 can thus not be added to the beliefs filed under m2[5].

The practical importance of identification may be illustrated by a discussion of attempts to uncover tax evaders[6]. The government registers all bank accounts in the owner's true name. Two names for the same account holder would ideally be codesignative. Tax fraud, however, is about having accounts under different names so that the noninterchangeability of the names blocks the tax office's access to the person holding accounts under different names.

1. The tax authorities know that taxpayer x has more than $1.000.000 in the bank
2. Taxpayer x also has an additional $500.000 in an account under the false name 'y'
3. Since x = y, the tax authorities know that y has more than $1.000.000 in the bank

By mere manipulation of symbols we have arrived at statement (3), which is clearly false.... Although 'x' and 'y' are both names for the same tax evader, they are not interchangeable because each name is associated with a different sense, with a different way in which the reference is given. (Ortiz Hill 1997, p. 117)

Being able to recognize and (re)identify people unambiguously and in a coordinated way is a very important feature of human life. Without the ability to know 'who is who', and without the ability to tell people apart and physically locate them and thereby to 'arrest' them, modern nation states cannot get off the ground and could not be sustained (see Caplan and Torpey 2001). The state's monopoly of violence and the exercise of legitimate power over individual citizens could not be effective if the state were unable to identify individuals in a straightforward referential sense, that is, in a way that allows for physical encounters, such as arrests and imprisonment.

'The man at the table next to me', 'a former colleague', 'the guy with the awful aftershave', 'John', 'John Smith', 'the guy who always takes the 9.45 train and gets off at central station', 'the owner of a blue Ford', 'the person who collected 200 Euro at the teller machine in the Centre of Amsterdam at 14:21:11 at August 1 2005', 'the person on the CCTV tape who put two orange boxes in the trunk of a blue Ford', 'the owner of a bank account 1234567', 'the person on Flight Q1 from Sydney to London on 2 October 2005 in seat 55c', 'the idiot with the baseball cap', 'the guy who dumped Alice' these descriptions could all be about different persons, but they could

---

[5] John Perry (2002) observes that 'What unifies files, and makes two beliefs about the same person relevant to each other, is not that they are about the same person, but that they contain the same notion or linked notion.'

[6] I have taken this example from Claire Ortiz Hill (1997, pp. 116–117).

also be about the same person (in which case the descriptions provide a lot of information about John Smith).

I could rapidly expand my knowledge of the persons who chose to sit next to me in the restaurant by making one or two identifications, for example, 'the person next to me is identical with the guy who dumped Alice' and 'the guy who dumped Alice owns a blue Ford'. Ruth Gavison's anecdote is instructive in this context:

Consider the famous anecdote about the priest who was asked, at a party, whether he had heard any exceptional stories during confessionals. 'In fact', the priest replied, 'my first confessor is a good example, since he confessed to murder'. A few minutes later, an elegant man joined the group, saw the priest, and greeted him warmly. When he asked how he knew the priest, the man replied: 'Why, I had the honour of being his first confessor'. (Gavison 1980)

Gavison presents this anecdote in the context of a discussion of the various problems associated with the clarification of the notion of privacy. It all starts with the requirement 'that for a loss of privacy to occur, the information must be 'about' the individual' (Gavison 1980). It is essential to the ethics, law, and technology of data protection to be able to articulate what counts as worthy of protection and what does not, in other words to be able to articulate and define what counts as personal data, and what does not. The legal definition is not of much help here. According to the very influential EU data- protection laws, personal data are characterized as follows: '"personal data" shall mean any information relating to an identified or identifiable natural person ("data subject"); an identifiable person is one who can be identified, directly or indirectly, in particular by reference to an identification number or to one or more factors specific to his physical, physiological, mental, economic, cultural or social identity' (European Parliament 1995). The priest initially did not provide personal data according to the standard legal definition of personal data.

There is a basic ambiguity here, however, that needs to be brought out because it is relevant to ethical discussions of the protection of personal data. Keith Donellan distinguished between *referential* use of descriptions and *attributive* use of descriptions[7]. 'The owner of a blue Ford living in postal code area 2345' could have more than one individual satisfying the description, and the user of these descriptions may not have a particular individual in mind; he just thinks about the owner of a blue Ford 'whoever he is'. 'The owner of a blue Ford', however, could also be used referentially, when we have a particular person in mind or in attendance. 'The man sipping his whisky' (pointing to the person at a party) is used referentially, and is *about* the person the speaker mistakenly thought was drinking whisky,

---

[7] First suggested in my 'Information Technology and Moral Philosophy' (PhD thesis, Erasmus University Rotterdam, 1995; see also Donellan 1966).

even when it turns out he is having apple juice instead of whisky, and there is, strictly speaking, no one over there sipping his whisky.

The important thing to note is that both attributively used and referentially used descriptions figure in epistemic and doxastic strategies to collect information on people and directly or indirectly help to expand our knowledge about them. Both represent *identity-relevant information*. One may open a mental or another type of file on a person under the label 'the murderer of Kennedy', in the same way crime investigators do, in the hope to find out more information about this person who ever he is, or turns out to be. These initially nondescript identifications may eventually lead to a physical encounter (i.e., arrest or interrogation) later. The history of a particular criminal investigation is at the same time the history of filling the file[8] with identity-relevant information.

The referential reading of 'personal data', 'identity' and 'identifiability' of the EU data-protection laws leads to an unduly narrow construal of moral constraints on the use of personal data. As a result, attributively used descriptions could go unprotected. This seems a major weakness of data-protection regimes, because we know that large amounts of data are used attributively in marketing and homeland security investigations, for example, and are the stepping stones to find out about people. One could have a file on an owner of a blue Ford, and add a long list of descriptions, all used attributively, but one piece of information added to the rich and anonymous file could suddenly make the data set uniquely referring.

It may well be the case that given the prominence and importance of identity management technology, RFID technology, profiling and data mining, and genetic profiling, we need to have a new look at the dominant referential interpretation of personal data. Instead of defining the object of protection in terms of referentially used descriptions, we need to define the object of protection in terms of the broader notion of 'identity relevant information' (van den Hoven and Manders, 2006).

3. MORAL REASONS FOR PROTECTING PERSONAL DATA

Having qualified the object of protection and, thereby, extended the scope of data protection, from referentially used personal data to both referentially and attributively used identity-relevant data, I will now discuss four types of moral reasons for engaging in data protection, that is, moral justifications

---

[8] The world of personal data contains objective representations, singular reference to persons by means of descriptions and proper names, passwords, personal identification numbers, and user names. We use descriptions when we are not presented or acquainted with persons, when there is no *de re* or perceptual thought. According to John Perry (2002) thinking of a person by name or description can be construed in terms of 'calling up a file on that individual'.

for constraining actions[9] regarding identity-relevant information. These moral reasons provide the grounds to have principles like those of the 1995 EU data-protection act and the Organisation for Economic Cooperation and Development (OECD) principles in place. These legal regimes give to individuals autonomy and the right to control their personal data.

3.1. Information-Based Harm

The first type of moral reason for thinking about constraining the flow of identity-relevant data is concerned with the prevention of harm. Information is a very useful thing for criminals and crooks to have. A random attack in the street on an anonymous individual does not require information, but a bank robbery requires a good deal of intelligence and information, planning, and foresight. Some harms could not have been inflicted (or at least not as easy) if certain information would not have been available. Let's refer to this type of harm as 'information-based harm'. Cybercriminals and malevolent hackers use databases and the Internet to get information on their victims in order to prepare and stage their crimes. One of the most pressing problems is 'identity theft' and identity fraud, which brings high risk of financial damages and emotional distress. One's bank account may get plundered and one's credit reports may be irreversibly tainted so as to exclude one from future financial benefits and services. Stalkers and rapists have used the Internet and online databases to track down their victims. They could not have done what they did without access to electronic resources and without accessing some of the details of their victim's lives.

In an information society, there is a new vulnerability to harm done on the basis of personal data – theft, identity fraud, or straightforward harm on the basis of identifying information. Constraining the freedom to access information of persons who could cause, threaten to cause, or are likely to cause information-based harm can be justified on the basis of Mill's Harm Principle. Protecting identifying information, instead of leaving it in the open, diminishes epistemic freedom of all to know, but also diminishes the likelihood that some will come to harm, analogous to the way in which restricting access to firearms diminishes both freedom and the likelihood that people will get shot in the street. In information societies, identity-relevant information resembles guns and ammunition. Preventing information-based harm clearly provides us with a strong moral reason to limit the access to personal data. Arguments against central databases with personal data of individual citizens in The Netherlands often makes reference to World War II when the Nazis occupied The Netherlands and found a well-organized population registration very conducive to their targeting and deportation of the Jews in Holland. It would be strange, however, to claim that the Nazis violated the

---

9 These actions include: generation, acquisition, processing, and dissemination.

privacy of the Jews. A better description seems to say that they used insufficiently protected personal data to take people out of their houses and send
them to the concentration camps. Access to personal information made
possible the most horrible of all harms. This is the first thing we want to
prevent, and we do it by effectively protecting identity-relevant information.

There is, of course, a broad range of harms to individuals that can be
inflicted on the basis of personal information. Someone's career may be
systematically corroded by the piecemeal release of selected information.
This may start to add up in the eyes of others, and lead to serious reputational
harm.

Another type of harm could be the harm that lies in classifying people in
such a way that their chances of getting some good are diminished. Being
classified as Muslim in many Western countries implies a reduced chance
of getting a job. Accumulative information-based harm would refer to the
releasing snippets of identity-relevant information at different occasions on
the basis of which others may eventually form a rich and comprehensive
picture of a person and inflict harm on him or her.

3.2. Informational Inequality

The second type of moral reason to justify constraints on our actions with
identity-relevant information is concerned with equality and fairness. More
and more people are keenly aware of the benefits the market for identity
information can provide them with. If a consumer buys coffee at the modern
shopping mall, information about that transaction is generated and added
to his file or profile. Many consumers now begin to realize that every time
they come to the counter to buy something, they can also *sell* something,
namely, the information about their purchase or transaction, the so-called
transactional data. Likewise, sharing information about ourselves on the
Web with Web sites, browsers, and autonomous agents may pay off in terms of
more and more adequate information (or discounts and convenience) later.
Many privacy concerns have therefore been and will continue to be resolved
in *quid pro quo* practices and private contracts about the use and secondary
use of personal data. But, although a market mechanism for trading personal
data seems to be kicking in on a global scale, not all individual consumers are
aware of their economic opportunities, and if they are, they are not always
in a position to trade their data or pursue their interests in a transparent
and fair market environment so as to get a fair price for them. The use
of RFID chips in consumer products in shops, the use of extensive cross-
domain consumer profiling combined with dynamic pricing may facilitate
price discrimination.

Consumers do not always know what the implications are of what they
are consenting to when they sign a contract for the use of identity-relevant
information. We simply cannot assume that the conditions of the developing

market for identity-relevant information guarantees fair transactions by independent standards. Constraints on the flow of personal data need to be put in place in order to guarantee equality of arms, transparency, and a fair market for identity-relevant information as a new commodity.

3.3. Informational Injustice

A third and very important moral reason to justify constraints on processing of identity-relevant information is concerned with justice in a sense which is associated with the work of Michael Walzer. Michael Walzer has objected to the simplicity of Rawls's conception of primary goods and universal rules of distributive justice by pointing out that 'there is no set of basic goods across all moral and material worlds, or they would have to be so abstract that they would be of little use in thinking about particular distributions' (Walzer 1983, p. 8). Goods have no natural meaning; their meaning is the result of sociocultural construction and interpretation. In order to determine what is a just distribution of the good, we have to determine what it means to those for whom it is a good. In the medical, the political, and the commercial sphere there are different goods (medical treatment, political office, money) which are allocated by means of different allocation criteria or distributive practices: medical treatment is allocated on the basis of need, political office on the basis democratic election, and money on the basis of free exchange. What ought to be prevented, and often is prevented as a matter of fact, is dominance of particular goods. Walzer calls a good *dominant* if the individuals that have it, because they have it, can command a wide range of other goods. A monopoly is a way of controlling certain social goods in order to exploit their dominance. In that case, advantages in one sphere can be converted as a matter of course into advantages in other spheres. This happens when money (commercial sphere) could buy you a vote (political sphere) and would give you preferential treatment in health care (medical), would get you a university degree (educational), and so forth. We resist the dominance of money – and other social goods for that matter (land, physical strength) – and we think that political arrangements allowing for it are unjust. No social good x should be distributed to men and women who possess some other good y merely because they possess y and without regard to the meaning of x.

What is especially offensive to our sense of justice is, first, the allocation of goods internal to sphere A on the basis of the distributive logic associated with sphere B, second, the transfer of goods across the boundaries of separate spheres and third, the dominance and tyranny of some goods over others. In order to prevent this, the 'art of separation' of spheres has to be practised and 'blocked exchanges' between them have to be put in place. If the art of separation is practised effectively and the autonomy of the spheres of justice is guaranteed then 'complex equality' is established. One's status in terms of the holdings and properties in one sphere is irrelevant – ceteris paribus – to the distribution of the goods internal to another sphere.

Walzer's analysis also applies to information. The meaning and value of information is local and allocation schemes and local practices that distribute access to information should accommodate local *meanings* and should, therefore, be associated with specific spheres.

Many people do not object to the use of their personal medical data for *medical* purposes, confined to the medical sphere, whether these are directly related to their own personal health affairs, to those of their family, perhaps even to their community or the world population at large, as long as they can be absolutely certain that the only use that is made of it is medical, that is, to cure people from diseases. They do object, however, to their medical data being used to classify them or disadvantage them socioeconomically, to discriminate against them in the workplace, refuse them commercial services, deny them social benefits, or turn them down for mortgages or political office.

They do not mind if their library search data are used to provide them with better *library* services, but they do mind if these data are used to criticize their tastes and character. They would also object to these informational cross-contaminations when they would benefit from them, as when the librarian would advise them a book on low-fat meals on the basis of knowledge of their medical record and cholesterol values, or when a doctor asks questions on the basis of the information that one has borrowed a book from the public library about AIDS.

We may thus distinguish a third moral reason to constrain actions regarding identity-relevant information: prevention of 'informational injustice', that is, disrespect for the boundaries of what we may refer to, following Michael Walzer, as 'spheres of justice' or 'spheres of access'. What is often seen as a violation of privacy is often more adequately construed as the morally inappropriate transfer of personal data across the boundaries of what we intuitively think of as separate 'spheres of justice' or 'spheres of access' (van den Hoven 1999; van den Hoven and Cushman 1996).

A couple of illustrations are in order. When government agencies, such as social security agencies, outsource part of their operations to commercial banks, the part of the bank that will take care of the public tasks needs to be separated from the commercial branches. Software protections are put in place, referred to as 'Chinese Walls', which separate the commercial from the public social security sphere. In this way, a Walzerian *blocked exchange* for personal data is implemented, and the *art of information sphere separation* is put into practice.

We have seen a similar normative logic of spheres being operative in constraining cookies to retrieve information across the boundaries of top level domains. We do not mind if the .com site we visit collects information about our search profile on that particular site. We may not even mind if .com sites exchange information. We probably would mind if .com sites used information from .org sites or .gov sites, or vice versa. The lessons learned from the so-called DoubleClick case[10], where clickstream data were collected by cookies working across sites in different top-level domains seem to confirm these Walzerian intuitions about blocked exchanges between spheres.

A Walzerian account along these lines also accommodates the idea, incorporated in many legal data-protection regimes in the world, of 'purpose specification and use limitation' which ensures that information is not used outside the area for which informed consent was given by the data subject. Helen Nissenbaum has introduced the term 'contextual integrity' to refer to these Walzerian type constraints (Nissenbaum 2004). According to Nissenbaum, the benchmark of privacy is contextual integrity. She distinguishes between norms of appropriateness and norms of flow or distribution. Contextual integrity is maintained when both types of norms are upheld, and it is violated when either of the norms is violated.

Nissenbaum does not provide an account of the nature of the context boundaries. A Theory of Sphere or Context Boundaries is crucial because boundaries are disputed, fuzzy, in flux and deemed important. Without such an account, the idea of separate spheres or contexts is practically empty. Wiegel, Lokhorst, and van den Hoven provide a reconstruction of the idea of a boundary between two spheres in terms of a list of deontic statements about which actions with data are (not) permitted or (not) obligatory (Wiegel, van den Hoven, and Lokhorst 2005; van den Hoven and Lokhorst 2002). Per case, or type of case, we need to draw the boundaries and argue for the deontic constraints that we want to impose. In the context of software engineering, this comes down to a specification of a fine-grained authorization matrix and role-based access management scheme. In the design of a hospital information system for example, difficult privacy issues may be resolved by deciding in which situation which professionals can do what to which types of information. Can the janitor print electronic patient records? No. Can the nurse change lab tests? No. Information maps are thus drawn up and 'privacy issues' are addressed in detail. Moral arguments about privacy are given a distributed treatment and, instead of discussing 'The Privacy Issue in Health Care' in abstracto, we address more tractable and more precise questions[11].

3.4. Moral Autonomy and Moral Identification

A fourth type of moral reason for constraining the flow of identity-relevant information could be referred to as *moral autonomy*, that is, the capacity to

---

[10] For case descriptions, see: http://www.epic.org/privacy/doubletrouble.

[11] Wiegel, van den Hoven, and Lokhorst introduce the idea of 'deontic isographs' – boundary lines, composed of lists of implementable deontic statements which apply equally and, therefore, connect positions in the information landscape to positions with equal deontic status, between which data may flow. See also Moor (2006).

shape our own moral biographies, to present ourselves as we think fit and appropriate, to reflect on our moral careers, and to evaluate and identify with our moral choices, without the critical gaze and interference of others and without a pressure to conform to the 'normal' or socially desired identities. We want to be able to present ourselves and be identified as the ones we identify with.

David Velleman, in his analysis of shame and privacy, draws attention to self-presentation as a constitutive feature of moral persons, namely their capacity and need for self-presentation. What it means to be a person is, according to Velleman, to be engaged in self-presentation. Persons 'have a fundamental interest in being recognized as a self-presenting creature' (Velleman 2001). Failures of privacy and the accompanying emotion of shame are not so much about disapprobation concerning what is revealed when others get access to information we did not volunteer, but are about disqualification of the person who failed to prevent the revelation. Teenagers are very open in their interactions and communications on the Web 2.0. Nudity and explicit material may sometimes leak out of their circle of chat friends. The content, it seems, is not what embarrasses them, but the fact that they failed to manage their public face, and that, as a result, their carefully cultivated identity was spoiled. Therefore, the realm of privacy, according to Velleman, is the central arena for threats to one's standing as a social agent.

A *moral* person is thus characteristically engaged in self-presentation, but, at the same time, she experiences the normative pressures which public opinion and moral judgements of others exert. When information about Bill becomes available, it facilitates the formation of beliefs and judgements about Bill. Beliefs and judgements about Bill, when he learns about them, when he suspects that they are made, or fears that they are made, may bring about a change in his view of himself. They may induce him to behave and feel differently than he would have done without them. This is what Berlin calls 'the most heteronomous condition imaginable'[12]. What others know about you can radically affect your view of yourself, although seeing yourself as others see you does not necessarily make your view of yourself more true or more adequate (Benn, 1988).

Stereotyping is an extreme case of casting people and preempting their choice to present themselves. Modern individuals who have cast aside the ideas of historical necessity, and who live in a highly volatile socioeconomic environment, confront a great diversity of audiences in different roles and settings, the rigging of one's moral identity by means of public opinion, beliefs, and judgements of others is felt as an obstacle to 'experiments in living', as Mill called them. The modern individual wants to be able to

---

[12] 'I cannot ignore the attitude of others with Byronic disdain, . . . for I am in my own eyes as others see me, I identify myself with the point of view of my milieu' (Berlin 1969).

determine himself morally or to undo his previous determinations on the basis of more profuse experiences in life or on the basis of additional factual information. Some have argued that privacy creates a time out from social morality, in order to engage in ever new experiments in living. Privacy covers purely self-regarding acts and, therefore, implies a right to nonjustification (Monteiro 2004). As Newton Garver aptly put it:

Contemporary freedom and choice go farther than Mill suspected – we all choose our identities, and make that choice from among a heterogeneous set of data, . . . we rarely choose our nationality, sex or religion, but we do choose to make these data part of our identity. (Garver 1990)

The conception of the person as being morally autonomous, as being the author and experimentator of his or her own moral career, provides a justification for constraining others in their attempts to engineer and directly or indirectly shape the subject's identity, either by stereotyping, or by the application of identity-management tools and techniques. Data-protection laws thus justifiably provide protection against the fixation of one's moral identity by others. They do so by requiring informed consent for the processing of identity-relevant information. If there are domains where for obvious reasons individuals in well-ordered societies cannot be allowed to write their own biographies from cover to cover, they at least should be allowed to write those parts that are amenable to it and individuals should be given an opportunity to authorize the parts that were, or had to be, written by others.

A further explanation for the importance of respect for moral autonomy may be provided along the following lines. Factual knowledge of another person is always *knowledge by description*. The person himself, however, does not only know the facts of his biography, but he is the only person who is *acquainted* with the associated thoughts, desires, emotions, and aspirations. However detailed and elaborate our files and profiles on a particular individual may be, we are never able to refer to the data subject as he himself is able to do. We may only approximate his knowledge and self-understanding[13].

Bernard Williams has pointed out that respecting a person involves 'identification' in a very special sense, which I refer to as 'moral identification'.

. . . in professional relations and the world of work, a man operates, and his activities come up for criticism, under a variety of professional or technical titles, such as 'miner or 'agricultural labourer' or 'junior executive'. The technical or professional attitude is that which regards the man solely under that title, the human approach that which regards him as a man who has that title (among others), willingly, unwillingly, through lack of alternatives, with pride, etc. . . . each man is owed an effort at

---

[13] Russell says, 'When we say anything about Bismarck, we should like, if we could, to make the judgement which Bismarck alone can make . . . In this we are necessarily defeated' (Russell 1978, p. 31).

identification: that he should not be regarded as the surface to which a certain label can be applied, but one should try to see the world (including the label) from his point of view. (Williams 1973)

Moral identification thus presupposes knowledge of the point of view of the data subject and a concern with what it is for a person to live that life. Persons have aspirations, higher-order evaluations, and attitudes, and they see the things they do in a certain light. Representation of this aspect of persons seems exactly what is missing when identity-relevant data are piled up in our databases and persons are represented in administrative procedures, are profiled or construed in statistical terms. Thomas Nagel observes that 'To really accept people as they are requires an understanding that there is much more to them than could possibly be integrated into a common social space' (Nagel 1998, p. 16).

The simple identifications made on the basis of our data fall short of accepting and respecting the individual person, because they will never match the identity as it is experienced by the data subject. It fails because it does not conceive of the other on his or her, own terms.

Because we feel we have inaccessible qualitative aspects of our own private mental states – that is, that we have hopes and purposes and there is something that it is like to have them which cannot be known from the outside – we insist on epistemic modesty on the part of others in their claims to know who we are and in their involvement in the management of our identities. Moreover, we see ourselves as our own moral projects, subject to moral development and capable of moral improvement, so the result of the management of our identities seems a premature fixation of what is an essentially dynamic project.

An outsider's understanding of a person needs to include, ideally, not only the objective representations, but also what he wants or hopes to be, his gratitude or pride or shame or remorse, and how the person interprets them. These conditions are conditions of the whole person. The very object of the outsider's interpretation ought to aim at representing and understanding the person's second-order as well as first-order attitudes, which is not only difficult, but impossible in principle.

... the apprehension of the mind of another person may thus only count as knowledge to the extent that it can approximate to this kind of awareness ... such an approximation can never be more than a very distant one. (Moran 2001, p. 154)

When a person is considered as 'one person among others', his attitude and self-directed reactive attitudes (his shame or shamelessness) expresses the kind of person he is. It is the sort of thing we take into account in determining how we feel about him. Moran argues that not doing so would be wrong because it would be failing to respect the 'total evidence' of the case. For responding to what he did with shame, pride, or gratitude constitutes a new fact about him, which is morally salient and provides part of the total evidence of who he is. Anything less would not only be wrong, but also epistemically irresponsible (Moran 2001, pp. 182–183).

Respect for privacy of persons can thus be seen to have a distinctly epistemic dimension. It expresses an acknowledgement that it is impossible to know other persons as they know and experience themselves. Even if we could get it right about persons at any given point in time, by exhibit of extraordinary empathy and attention, then it is highly questionable whether the data subject's experience of himself, as far as the *dynamics* of the moral person is concerned, can be captured and adequately represented. The person conceives of himself as dynamic and as trying to improve himself morally. The person cannot be identified, not even in the sense articulated by Bernard Williams, with something limited, definite, and unchanging. The person always sees itself as becoming, as something that perhaps even has to be *overcome*, not as a fixed reality, but as something in the making, something that has to be improved upon. As Gabriel Marcel puts it, the individual's motto is not *sum* (I am) but *sursum* (higher)[14].

CONCLUSION

I have argued that data about persons are very important and will remain important and much sought after in the future. I have argued that personal data need to be construed in a broad sense to include attributively used descriptions. I have provided four moral reasons for the protection of personal data. The first three reasons (concerning avoiding harm, preventing exploitation in markets for personal data, and preventing inequality and discrimination) can be shared by both liberals and communitarians; they both oppose inflicting harm, exploitation, and discrimination. The fourth reason, however, invokes the essentially contested liberal self. It is the liberal self that wants to decide what to think of itself and what to make of him or herself. And how others should identify him or her, preferably identify with what he himself identifies with. There is probably always over-determination of these moral reasons at stake, so that these reasons can be invoked simultaneously in the moral discussion about data protection.

This analysis opens up a space of potential agreement between parties that are usually deeply divided concerning 'privacy issues'. The analysis provides three central and weighty reasons to engage in the protection of personal information in the light of new technologies, which they can share. So, instead of arguing over necessary and sufficient conditions of 'privacy', we can actually think about designing smart schemes of justified and implementable deontic constraints on flows of personal data.

[14] This is also suggested by Isaiah Berlin: ' . . . what I may seek to avoid [is to be] insufficiently recognized, . . . a statistical unit without identifiable . . . purposes of my own.' (Berlin 1969).

References

Aarts, E., and Encarnacao, J. L. (Eds.). 2006. *True Visions. The Emergence of Ambient Intelligence.* Berlin/Heidelberg: Springer.

Bach, K. 1987. *Thought and Reference.* Oxford: Oxford University Press.

Benn, S. 1988. *A Theory of Freedom.* Cambridge, UK: Cambridge University Press, pp. 277, 288 (resp).

Berlin, I. 1969. *Four Essays on Liberty.* Oxford: Oxford University Press, p. 156, n. 1.

Caplan, J., and Torpey, J. C. (Eds.). 2001. *Documenting Individual Identity: The Development of State Practices in the Modern World.* Princeton: Princeton University Press.

Castaneda, H.-N. 1989. *Thinking, Language and Experience.* Minneapolis: University of Minnesota Press.

De Jasay, A. 1989. *Social Contract, Free Ride: A Study of the Public Goods.* Oxford: Clarendon Press.

Donellan, K. 1966. Reference and definite descriptions. *Philosophical Review, 75,* 281–304

Etzioni, A. 1996. Less privacy is good for us. *The Responsive Community, Summer,* 11–13. Available at www.gwu.edu/~ccps/etzioni/M28.pdf.

Etzioni, A. 2005. Limits of privacy, in A. I. Cohen and C. H. Wellman (Eds.), *Contemporary Debates in Applied Ethics.* Oxford: Blackwell, pp. 253–262.

European Parliament. 1995. *Directive 95/46/EC* on The protection of individuals with regard to the processing of personal data and the free movement of such data, adopted October 24 1195, *Official Journal, 281,* pp. 31–50, Brussels.

Garver, N. 1990. Why pluralism now? *Monist, 7,* 388–410.

Gavison, R. 1980. Privacy and the limits of law. *Yale Law Journal, 89,* 421–471. Reprinted in Schoeman, F. (Ed.). 1984. *Philosophical Dimensions of Privacy.* Cambridge, UK: Cambridge University Press, pp. 346–402.

Monteiro, N. P. 2004. No privacy, no poetry, no progress. Department of Political Science, University of Chicago, Political Theory Workshop, 18 October 2004. Available at www.pwt.uchicago.edu/monteiro002.pdf.

Moor, J. H. 2006. The nature, importance, and difficulty of machine ethics. *Machine Ethics, 21,* 4, 18–21.

Moore, B. 1984. *Privacy: Studies in Social and Cultural History.* New York: M. E. Sharpe.

Moran, R. 2001. *Authority and Estrangement. An Essay on Self-Knowledge.* Princeton: Princeton University Press.

Nagel, T. 1998. Concealment and exposure. *Philosophy and Public Affairs, 27,* 1, 3–30.

Nissenbaum, H. 2004. Privacy as contextual integrity. *Washington Law Review, 79,* 1, 119–158.

Ortiz Hill, C. 1997. *Rethinking Identity and Metaphysics, On the Foundations of Analytic Philosophy.* New Haven: Yale University Press.

Perry, J. 2002. *Identity, Personal Identity and the Self.* Indianapolis: Hackett Publishing Company, p. 195.

Perry, T. D. 1986. *Professional Philosophy. What it is and Why it Matters.* Dordrecht: D. Reidel Publishing Company.

Quittner, J. 1997. The death of privacy. *Time,* 25 August, p. 18.

Roessler, B. 2005. *The Value of Privacy.* Cambridge, UK: Polity Press.

Russell, B. 1978. *The Problems of Philosophy.* Oxford: Oxford University Press.

Safire, W. 2005. Goodbye to Privacy. *New York Times,* April 10.

Sandel, M. J. 1989. Moral argument and liberal toleration: Abortion and homosexuality. *California Law Review, 77*, 521–538.

Schoeman, F. (Ed.). 1984. *Philosophical Dimensions of Privacy*. Cambridge, UK: Cambridge University Press, pp. 346–402.

Solove, D. J. 2002. Conceptualizing privacy. *California Law Review, 90*, 4, 1087–1155.

Spinello, R. 1997. End of privacy. *America, 176*, January 4–11, 9–13.

van den Hoven, M. J. 1999. Privacy and the varieties of informational wrongdoing. *Australian Journal of Professional and Applied Ethics, 1*, 1, 30–44.

van den Hoven, M. J. 2006. Nanotechnology and privacy: the instructive case of RFID. *International Journal of Applied Philosophy, 20*, 2.

van den Hoven, J., and Cushman, R. 1996. Privacy, Health Care Data and Information Technology, Conference Report. *Journal of Information, Law, and Technology (JILT)*, 3. Available at http://www2.warwick.ac.uk/fac/soc/law/elj/jilt/1996-3/hoven/

van den Hoven, M. J., and Manders, M. 2006. Identiteitsmanagement en morele identificatie' (Identity management and moral identification). *ANTW, 98*, 2, 111–128.

Velleman, J. D. 1996. Self to self. *Philosophical Review, 105*, 1, 39–76.

Velleman, J. D. 2001. The genesis of shame. *Philosophy and Public Affairs, 30*, 27–52.

Wagner DeCew, J. 1997. *In Pursuit of Privacy: Law, Ethics, and the Limits of Technology*. Ithaca and London: Cornell Press.

Walzer, M. 1983. *Spheres of Justice*. Oxford: Blackwell.

Walzer, M. 1995. Critique of liberalism, in Amitai Etzioni (Ed.), *New Communitarian Thinking*. Richmond: University Press of Virginia, p. 63.

Warren, S., and Brandeis L. D. 1890. The right to privacy. *Harvard Law Review, 4*, 193–220.

Wiegel, V., van den Hoven, M. J., and Lokhorst, G. J. C. 2005. Privacy, deontic epistemic action logic and software agents: An executable approach to modeling moral constraints in complex informational relationships. *Ethics and Information Technology, 7*, 4, 251–264.

Williams, B. 1973. *Problems of the Self*. Cambridge, UK: Cambridge University Press.

16

Embodying Values in Technology

Theory and Practice[1]

Mary Flanagan, Daniel C. Howe, and Helen Nissenbaum

INTRODUCTION

The idea that values may be embodied in technical systems and devices (artifacts) has taken root in a variety of disciplinary approaches to the study of technology, society, and humanity (Winner 1986; Latour 1992; Hughes 2004; MacKenzie and Wajcman 1985). A pragmatic turn from this largely descriptive posture sets forth values as a design aspiration, exhorting designers and producers to include values, purposively, in the set of criteria by which the excellence of technologies is judged. If an ideal world is one in which technologies promote not only instrumental values such as functional efficiency, safety, reliability, and ease of use, but also the substantive social, moral, and political values to which societies and their peoples subscribe, then those who design systems have a responsibility to take these latter values as well as the former into consideration as they work. (See, for example, Friedman and Nissenbaum 1996, Mitcham 1995, and Nissenbaum 1998.) In technologically advanced, liberal democracies, this set of such values may include liberty, justice, enlightenment, privacy, security, friendship, comfort, trust, autonomy, and sustenance.[2]

[1] We would like to thank members of the RAPUNSEL team for their dedicated work on the project, especially the Co-PIs Perlin and Hollingshead. Our ideas benefited enormously from audience comments at the Workshop on New Directions in Understanding Ethics and Technology, University of Virginia (particularly Dean Neusma, who commented on our paper), colloquia in the Schools of Information Science at Bathurst and Wagga Wagga campuses of Charles Sturt University, and at CHI2005. RAPUNSEL is supported by NSF's Program Research on Gender in Science and Engineering, HRD-0332898. Values in Design research was supported by the Ford Foundation's Program in Knowledge, Creativity, and Freedom for the project, *Values in Technology Design: Democracy, Autonomy, and Justice*. We thank Maja Petric for providing excellent research assistance.
[2] Following the line of work inspired by Langdon Winner's assertion that technical artifacts 'have' politics, researchers studying social and philosophical dimensions of technology have

It is one thing to subscribe, generally, to these ideals, even to make a pragmatic commitment to them, but putting them into practice, which can be considered a form of political or moral activism, in the design of technical systems is not straightforward. Experienced designers will recall the not too distant past when interface, usability, and even safety were overlooked features of software system design. Although these have edged into the mainstream of research and practice, we are still at the shaky beginnings of thinking systematically about the practice of designing with values in mind. Even conscientious designers, by which we mean those who support the principle of integrating values into systems and devices, will not find it easy to apply standard design methodologies, honed for the purpose of meeting functional requirements, to the unfamiliar turf of values.[3]

At least two sets of factors contribute to the difficulty of taking values into consideration during design. One which strikes us as epistemological in origin stems from the need to incorporate diverse and frequently far-flung areas of knowledge and know-how into the design process that are not normally conceived as elements of the design toolkit. Design teams that commit to taking values seriously might even need to innovate in these unfamiliar terrains. The other set of factors stem from the scarcity of explicit guidelines, or methodologies, for reliably embodying values in software systems (and in technology, in general). We refer to these as practical. Accordingly, this paper is divided into two parts. In Part 1, we describe the epistemological challenges facing conscientious designers. In Part 2, we address the practical challenges by offering our own methodological framework for systematically bringing values into the process of design. We illustrate key elements of the methodology by applying it to RAPUNSEL, a research project aimed at designing and building a game environment for teaching girls to program computers (http://www.RAPUNSEL.org).

Because we view these epistemological and practical factors as two dimensions of a single phenomenon, with neither taking priority, the order in which we have chosen to discuss them is somewhat arbitrary. Readers with primarily pragmatic interests can skip ahead to Part 2, dipping back to Part 1 as needed. Those less concerned with process and method may skip ahead to the Conclusion after completing Part 1.

used a variety of terms to label and extend his ideas, such as the 'embeddedness' of values in technology, the value-ladenness of technology, and others (Winner 1986). We prefer values 'embodied' to evoke the systematic causal correspondence between gritty design features with specific social outcomes. The nature of this causal correspondence is complex and, although relevant to this project, it would require too great a detour from its central path.

[3] Nevertheless, there have been exemplary practical efforts to integrate values into design, such as: for privacy (Ackerman & Cranor 1999; Agre 1997a); universal usability (Shneiderman 2000); community (Druin 1999); social justice (Borning, Friedman, and Kahn 2004), and informed consent (Friedman, Howe, and Felten 2002).

PART 1: EPISTEMOLOGY

One reason the study of human and social dimensions of technology is so demanding is that the areas of knowledge and the methodologies it straddles are traditionally both far-flung and self-contained. This separation is reflected in the disciplinary organization of almost all universities where the study of technology itself, through the basic sciences and engineering, is typically segregated from the study of social science and humanities. When undertaking the practical task of developing technologies with attention to values, however, designers must engage simultaneously with these distinct areas of knowledge and their respective methodologies. For this task, their intellectual distinctiveness and historical separation is problematic.

Normally, designers of technical systems and devices hold some variables fixed as background assumptions[4], while they evaluate design alternatives in search of ones that most effectively achieve explicit functional ends. In designing an interface, for example, they might fix assumptions about the visual capacities of users to within a particular range and evaluate alternatives in relation to that fixed range. When values are included as ends, alongside typical functionalities, designers must grapple with an extended set of variables, but more importantly, variables that lie outside their usual fields of expertise. Specifically, this means that design and engineering projects must incorporate contextual knowledge about values and, where such knowledge is not readily available, designers will need to grapple directly with questions about the relevant values. Not only does this lie outside the usual boundaries of engineering expertise – whether theory or practice – but is attainable through modes of inquiry, such as systematic analysis of values, unfamiliar in the technical and scientific environments.

Achieving technical design that soundly incorporates values requires not only competence in the technical arts and sciences, but also a reflective understanding of the relevant values and how these values function in the lives of people and possibly groups affected by the systems in question. Within the academy, systematic reflection on values generally takes place in humanistic areas, such as moral and political philosophy, as well as in empirical and theoretical social sciences. For some of the purposes of technical design, what is readily drawn from these fields is sufficient, but for others, the puzzles raised by technologies push beyond standard boundaries. Both circumstances demand more comprehensive interactions among diverse areas of knowledge than is the norm; in the first instance calling for sufficient familiarity to locate relevant insights from prior work, in the second, requiring deliberate efforts to extend what is known in order to address the hard and sometimes novel questions technology raises. The metaphor of 'balls in play' captures the nature of these active interdependencies because

4 Some would say, they 'black box' these factors.

conscientious designers must juggle relevant dimensions of at least three modes of inquiry: First they must engage actively with scientific and technical results. Second, beyond these, they will need to absorb relevant philosophical reflections on values. And third, they must consider the results of empirical investigations of values in relation to individuals and their societies. With the metaphor of balls in play, we call to mind the need to maintain attention on all three dynamically evolving dimensions simultaneously, not only keeping an eye on each individually, but also on the ways they interact with, or move in relation to one another.

A. Technical Mode

In the technical mode, a designer or design team brings to bear state-of-the-art knowledge on design specifications that might realize given values within the context of an overarching design project. In a project to build a hospital's patient record system, for example, they may be charged with the task of building privacy protection into the system. Responding to this charge, they might conclude that privacy is best approximated by a system that places ultimate control of access to information in the hands of the information subject, believing that the right to privacy is the right to control information about oneself. With this in mind, they set about designing the system and identify the necessary mechanisms to achieve these specifications. In some cases, they may draw on existing state-of-the-art technology. Where nothing suitable can be found they may need to invent, to innovate, or to settle for a compromise. These iterative steps toward the design and development of a system will not be unfamiliar ones for systems designers; the key departure is the focus on embodying values in addition to conventional requirements of functionality and efficiency.

B. Philosophical Mode

Whereas the technical mode calls on designers and engineers to seek and invent mechanisms, the key demands of the philosophical mode are to address questions about the origin and scope of relevant values, their conceptual meaning, and the basis of their prescriptive force. Although the deep and contentious question about the nature of values, in general, is foundational to the other three, it cannot be addressed in the context of this work. Too little has been written about it within the domain of analytic philosophy. Here, we simply assert a commitment to a general construction of values as purposes, ends, or goals of human action and our intention to focus on those that are generally construed as social, moral, and political, including in this wide-ranging category abstract values such as freedom, autonomy, equality, justice, equality, democracy, and privacy, as well as more concrete ones such as friendship, safety, sociality, and comfort.

Questions about the origin and source of values are of particular interest to creators of technologies if they consider who might use or be affected by systems under construction. They may worry whether values in question are universal to all humans or pertinent only to local groupings only, whether nations, societies, cultures, religions, communities, or families. They may wonder how one best answers such questions, whether through philosophical analysis alone or through empirical methods of the social sciences. Although the most general forms of these questions lie outside the scope of this discussion, more concrete versions ought to be asked by engineers and designers as they settle the parameters of their systems and determine the people and groups likely to be affected by them. Although designers and developers of technology in the United States (and other technology-producing liberal democracies) may confidently assume the importance of constitutional values of free speech, association, and equality, due process, privacy, and property, or other values such individualism, autonomy, creativity, and liberation, they should, at least, give consideration to the value commitments of other countries where these technologies are likely to be distributed.

Here, too, the study of values in technologies pushes us to ask questions about origins and sources that are far from settled in the general study of moral and political values. In the absence of clear answers to these questions, recourse to a pragmatic middle ground seems reasonable. This means going along with the idea of a hierarchy of values in which a 'thin' set are taken as common to all humanity and thicker sets associated with groups and subgroups of varying sizes and compositions (e.g., Moor 1999). How this bears on the responsibilities of designers and engineers who are, increasingly, developing technologies for global use, is another question of great interest. On the issue whether values can be derived, analytically, or must be discovered, empirically, a middle ground sees virtue in both, drawing conceptual clarity and normative justification from theoretical works in moral and political philosophy, while supplementing these with knowledge about actual interpretations and value commitments of populations relevant to technologies under study.

In addition to these general questions about values that might be raised in relation to technical design and development, the conceptual investigation of particular values is of great importance for the consistency and soundness of a given project. In undertaking to promote values, such as autonomy, equity, privacy, or well-being through technical systems, the choices designers make in shaping these systems will be guided by their understandings of the value concepts. In the case of the electronic patient record system, for example, it is important that designers draw on a sound conceptual grasp of the value of privacy so that their specifications define a system that yields privacy, and not something else. Of the proposal, mentioned earlier, to embody privacy by granting ultimate control of access to the information subject (and only through permission by the subject to others) a critic might say that it does not properly model the right to privacy. The critic might support an alternative design that, by default, grants variable access to the different fields of information by members of a hospital staff according to their roles, status, and relationships to the patient. This alternative is implied by a conception of privacy not as control by subject but 'contextual integrity,' which is a measure of the extent to which a particular activity respects entrenched norms of information flows tied to historically contingent contexts (Nissenbaum 2004). These norms specify not only what information is appropriate to a given context, but also the principles according to which it may be transmitted from one agent to another. The point of this example is not to settle the question of which design is preferable but to show how different understandings of privacy – the first as control by subject, the second as contextual integrity – have clear material implications for the specific features of a design.

A sound grasp of value terms is one of the necessary links between values and specific design features. Because of this, a significant part of keeping the philosophical ball in play is to develop concrete analyses of value terms for application in the design context. In the case of technologies developed within industrialized liberal democracies, centuries-long traditions of secular philosophical and political thought is a good, if daunting, source of insight, particularly for some of the contested and difficult value concepts that may emerge. Failure to take these concepts seriously can lead to bungled interpretations in the specification of design features. Tradition, however, may not be sufficient because technology, a source of radical change in the social and material world, sometimes forces a reconsideration of value concepts. Information technology, for example, has stimulated such reconsideration of the meaning and value of privacy. Keeping the philosophical ball-in-play means remaining astute to these demands and, where necessary, generating an analysis at the appropriate level of concreteness, which may call for original philosophical research on the affected concepts. One hopes that, over time, a library of analyses would be developed in service of the technical design context. Ideally, this would relieve the burden on designers, allowing them to draw on concrete definitions of past work rather than having to grapple directly with abstract conceptions of key values.

Finally, the philosophical mode of inquiry contributes to the effort of embodying values in design by articulating the rationale behind, or the justification for, commitments to particular values in a given system. Here, too, traditional moral and political theories are a source of explanation for why and when certain values ought to be promoted. This is particularly important when conflicts among values result from specific design choices and background theories may guide sound resolutions, or reasonable trade-offs. With the electronic patient record system, for example, designers might need to draw on underlying theory to persuade hospital administrators not only that privacy is relevant, important, or necessary, but also that it should be protected even if the cost rises, or access is slowed, as a result.

C. Empirical Mode

Empirical investigation answers questions that are as important to the goal of embodying values in design as the philosophical and technical. Not only does is it complement philosophical inquiry into what values are relevant to a given project, but it is the primary means for addressing, systematically, the question whether a given attempt at embodying values is successful, that is, whether designers have achieved their intended goals.

As we noted earlier, philosophical inquiry provides only one route to determining the values that ought to be considered. Even if we allow for the existence of a basic set of universal human values, many projects will take into consideration a far larger set of values, which may be determined by the cultural, historical, national, ethnic, and religious affiliations of those affected by them. It may be even more crucial to attend to these commitments when designers face a choice among design alternatives that favor some values over others because these could result in significant biases in favor of some users over others. Moreover, despite the enormous attention philosophers, and others, have paid to the problem of resolving values (and rights) in conflict, it remains notoriously difficult (e.g., Richardson 1994). Where practice requires decision, even in the absence of philosophical resolution, a sound alternative is to turn to empirical investigation of relevant populations, ascertaining their commitments and preferences through such mechanisms as surveys, interviews, testing under controlled conditions, and observations in the field.

Another task for which empirical inquiry is essential is in ascertaining whether a particular design embodies intended values. In the case of the electronic patient records system, for example, designers might be satisfied with the efficacy and reliability of particular security mechanisms for providing variable access but be disappointed to find, upon studying usage patterns, that users find them too onerous, and most simply bypass them, leaving the records more vulnerable than ever. Through empirical inquiry, therefore, they discover that their attempts to promote privacy are thwarted by a design that does not achieve the intended results. Here, too, various empirical methods may be useful, including usability testing, field studies, surveys, interviews, and so on.

D. Balls in Play

It is not only that the systematic consideration of values in design relies on results from three modes of inquiry. The metaphor of balls in play adds to the picture the dynamic nature of their respective contributions. Within a single project, findings from one area shape what happens in the others, which, in turn, feed back into the first area. Because progress is iterative in this way, design team members cannot seek solutions in each of the areas independently of the others but must keep an eye on the other two even while focusing on one. In the toughest design projects, calling for innovation in all three modes, experts will need to coordinate their efforts, progressing iteratively through the various stages. In less demanding cases – probably more common – designers will be able to rely on what is already known in at least one or two of the modes. As an example of the latter, consider what is needed to build an information system that embodies distributive justice. Designers might, without too much trouble, settle the philosophical question by adopting as their concrete interpretation of the value in question, robust access to people with a diverse range of mental and physical capacities, that is, taking accessibility to all mentally able individuals as the embodiment of the value of fairness. From there, they still must struggle with the technical challenges of how to go about doing so, and, finally, through empirical testing of one sort or another, must evaluate whether their designs have succeeded. Over time, with sustained attention to the study of values in technology, we would expect a body of findings, experience, results, definitions, and so forth will gradually alleviate some of the epistemological burdens.

PART 2: PRACTICE

The practical challenge that conscientious designers face integrating values into diverse design projects, is due, in large part, to the sparseness of methodologies and is related to the newness of the endeavor. If we characterize what designers need to know, metaphorically, as the ingredients of a recipe, the challenge of practice is coming up with a method for reliably combining these ingredients into a dish. The aim of the rest of this paper is to sketch one such methodological framework for incorporating values during design, demonstrating its application on a research project in progress, RAPUNSEL, a multiplayer game environment to teach middle-school-aged girls to program in Java.

A. The Design Context

In putting forward a methodology for incorporating values in the design process, our goal is not to replace, in blanket fashion, well-established, general design methodologies (Norman and Draper 1986), or the iterative design methods specific to game design (Crawford 1982; Zimmerman 2003) but rather to supplement them.[5] Our stance places values among, or alongside, other criteria of excellence in technical design, such as functional efficiency, reliability, robustness, elegance, and safety, and, recently, usability, and our methodology will augment other approaches which target these criteria.

[5] We are grateful to Dean Neusma for suggesting we bridge our work with other more general design methodologies. Although this task is too great for this chapter, we acknowledge a need for further development along these lines.

Ideally, the reciprocal consideration of functional factors together with values will result in designs that are good from material as well as moral perspectives. Although, here, we focus on the goal of designing software systems that manifest important social values, our background assumption is that successful systems will also meet traditional design criteria. We do not undertake the job of integrating the relevant methodologies, but ideally such a hybrid approach will evolve.

The framework we have developed for incorporating values in software design owes a debt to other important, related efforts. Participatory Design, for example, developed in the Scandinavian context to address concerns over new technologies that have entered the workplace, has built a substantial body of theory as well as a record of application. Its central tenet is that democratic participation by workers in the design of workplace systems is essential, not only because it is likely to produce workplace technologies that enhance efficiency and quality of product but also as the skill and well-being of workers themselves. Value-Sensitive Design is another approach to incorporating values in design that gives systematic consideration to the interests of all stakeholders in relation to a system under consideration. It shares with the framework discussed below the crucial relevance of empirical, philosophical, and technical modes of inquiry to the sound inclusion of values in design (Friedman 1996). Finally, various aspects of our framework have been influenced by Reflective Practice, an approach advocated by practitioners as described by Schön (Schön 1983) and Critical Technical Practice advanced primarily by computer science practitioners in artificial intelligence (Agre 1997b; Dourish, Finlay, Sengers, and Wright 2004; Mateas 2000).

Design, in general, is one among many steps that determines the shape of the technologies that fill our world. Other key junctures are foundational discoveries in science and engineering, production, testing, marketing, distribution, and adoption, and more (Hughes 2004; MacKenzie and Wajcman 1985; Kline and Pinch 1996). These, in turn, rest on a variety of political, economic and social interventions too numerous to specify here. One such key intervention, which bears mentioning, is the law itself. In the case of privacy, for example, the designers might not be free to embody their preferred conception of privacy, but need to take into consideration the sometimes detailed guidance of legal doctrine or explicit regulation.[6] Law might also indirectly affect system design by causing designers to adopt defensive design strategies to avoid liability for illegal or harmful uses of their systems.[7]

---

[6] In the United States, for example, anyone involved in designing systems for health-related information must comply with the regulation governing the flow of health-related information emanating from Health Insurance Portability and Accountability Act of 1996 (HIPAA).

[7] The development of peer-to-peer file-sharing systems from ones like Napster, which are mediated through central servers, to systems like KaZaA, which are distributed, is an illustration of how legal action can shape design.

Moreover, the particular steps and particular components vary according to particulars of the technology in question, from huge sprawling utility systems (e.g., Hughes 2004) to stand-alone wordprocessing applications. Whether devices and systems embody a given set of values is a function of wide-ranging factors, processes, and contingencies, influenced by economic and commercial dimensions, driven by corporate and marketing decision making, consumer moods and preferences, and political, policy, and cultural contexts. Yet, as the juncture in the life-cycle of technologies when ideas, goals, and intentions find concrete interpretation in specifications and prototypes, and when developers see the possibilities as well as the limits of these ideas, design is also a critical juncture for envisioning the values which a system in question embodies. It is primarily for this juncture that our methodology has been constructed.

B. Case Study: RAPUNSEL

Our methodology for incorporating values in technology has been influenced and refined by the experience of two of the coauthors, Flanagan and Howe, in their work on RAPUNSEL, a large multidisciplinary collaboration aimed at designing and implementing an experimental game prototype to promote interest and competence in computer programming among girls of middle-school age, including girls from disadvantaged home environments (http://www.RAPUNSEL.org). This three-year project includes a variety of interlinked components: engineering, pedagogy, interface, graphics, networking, and more. These components map roughly to core expertise of three Principal Investigators (PIs): coding tasks primarily managed by the computer science team led by Ken Perlin (New York University); game design led by Mary Flanagan (Hunter College), a new media designer; and educational assessment led by Andrea Hollingshead (University of Illinois). In addition to the PIs, the research team includes graduate and undergraduate students in computer science, media studies, and other fields who contribute both in design and implementation areas. Further, teachers, parents, scholars, and game designers, experts from industry, and children have observed the process and contributed from their specialty interest areas on an ad hoc basis. A subset of this group, known as 'design partners,' are middle-school girls who advise the project team through formal and informal feedback about elements of the game (Druin 1999). The team works together in face-to-face meetings as well as through an online team WIKI, presenting prototypes, reviewing news and related research, and discussing issues of design, implementation, feedback, and assessment.

In the current iteration of the game, each player logs onto and is assigned a home environment that houses a central character. Players are supposed to 'teach' these characters to move, dance, and behave in a variety of ways by programming them in a simplified variant of the Java language. In one scenario, for example, tying mastery of Java with game performance, players must program characters to perform increasingly complex dance behaviors which, according to the game's narrative, increase the characters' degree of satisfaction across a range of metrics, such as being allowed by a fearsome bouncer into a club, or excelling in a dance competition. The motivation for this narrative is its potential to serve as an attractive pedagogical medium for the target audience.

At the time of writing, the design of the RAPUNSEL game was, for the most part, complete. Attention was focused on completing implementation (coding). Preliminary testing indicated that the game was well-liked by the target audience during large-scale testing in schools in the United States (primarily New Jersey, New York, and California). Further into the future, related research will be needed to investigate pedagogical outcomes and to evaluate general contributions to the research area, including the project's innovative approach to game design, appropriately 'scaffolded' learning outcomes, and the use of repeatable processes. The game itself will be distributed online.

RAPUNSEL is an ideal test case because it is saturated with values questions and commitments. The project's core hypothesis is that the marked absence of women in the field of technology development, particularly in computer programming, is due, at least in part, to the style in which basic scientific subjects are taught. (Unambiguous data on the dearth of women in science and technology is well documented as, for example, in Brunner 1997, Flanagan 2003, Inkpen 1995, and Von Prummer 1994). Accordingly, they proposed as an initial strategy that, for female adolescents, socially oriented environments might be more conducive to learning mathematics and science. As computer games, especially the online variety, are a significant pastime for the target audience, a high-quality, socially oriented game space in which programming is an essential skill for navigation, interaction, and advancement, emerged as a robust initial project goal (Kafai 1998). This activist agenda immediately placed RAPUNSEL in a politically charged context (AAUW 2000; Mubireek 2003).

As project collaborators hope to address the needs of players generally overlooked by software industry (and even academic) designers, they explore questions like: What are the kinds of social situations and game goals that can be effectively incorporated into a multiplayer game design specifically for girls? What kinds of values do these decisions bring to the design of software usually considered 'activist' by mainstream designers? In attempting to answer these questions, investigators found that in addition to what had been articulated (e.g., in the funding proposal) as primary project objectives, several other core goals emerged. These included authorship, collaboration, and creativity, altering status quo perceptions and biases concerning gender, and enacting new possibilities, overall, for game reward systems, which would apply to a variety of types of learners. These goals were understood, progressively, to instantiate higher-order values such as equity, autonomy, and liberation, and raised challenging questions about how to recognize and integrate values as they emerge in practice.

The team encountered other values-related questions when deciding how to situate their project in relation to currently popular computer games, which are generally competitive and contain problematic representations of gender and race (over-sexualized characters, dark monsters vs. white heroes), social and hierarchical markings (advanced players with wealth and power), and interaction styles (killing vs. protecting vs. collaborating). The multidisciplinary research team, in conversation with other design participants representing a diverse range of sectors and interests, generated much discussion over values. Furthermore, as a social system where users engage in frequent interactions and exchanges, RAPUNSEL naturally raises considerations about how software design leads to the engineering of social relations, including right and wrong behavior in the treatment of others. The RAPUNSEL project prototype is still evolving as a test bed for how to embody values in a complex, real-world system. Throughout the rest of the paper, we pair theoretical propositions with examples encountered in the midst of work on RAPUNSEL.

It is important to acknowledge that a design project like this, pursued within an academic context, does not address all factors that, for example, a commercial project would be obliged to address. Assured funding from a government granting agency and placement within a research setting invokes a different set of demands from game-design projects in the for-profit commercial marketplace facing uncertainties in funding and potential clientele as well as stiff competition. Our ambition, nevertheless, is not merely to succeed in this particular instance, or this particular (academic) environment, but to develop and articulate methodological principles that can usefully be applied to a variety of cases and segments of society.

Finally, although game design has formed the testbed for our idea, our intention is to draft a methodology that will extend beyond games into other areas of software design including algorithms, system architecture, code, protocols, and interface. Indeed, for reasons we discuss later, these aspects of software systems may well involve fewer complications than games.

CONSTITUTIVE ACTIVITIES

Three types of activities constitute the method we have developed for systematically incorporating values in the design process: discovery, translation, and verification. These activities are intended as supplements to and not substitutes for other design methods that may guide a given project. As with the three modes of inquiry discussed in Part 1, the constitutive activities should be understood not as steps that designers would follow in serial order, but as aspects, or dimensions, of a single undertaking feeding back into one another, iteratively.

C.1 Discovery

This goal of this activity is to 'discover' the values that are relevant to, inspire, or inform a given design project, resulting in a list of values, and bringing into focus what often is implicit in a design project. The specific list of values will vary radically from project to project but here, because our interest is not so much in the content of specific lists but primarily with methodology, we have thought about process; that is, the systematic steps conscientious designer might follow in order to 'discover' the list of values relevant to any given project. A promising heuristic that emerged in the context of RAPUN-SEL was to attempt to answer the question, 'what values?' by reflecting on likely sources of values in relation to the system in question. Building on experience of diverse sources of values, including individuals, institutions, societies, religions, cultures, practices, and traditions, we looked to possible counterparts in the RAPUNSEL design context. Although the four discussed below were robust in this context, we would not be surprised to find that not all possibilities have been covered.

a. Values in the Definition of a Project
Sometimes, values are expressed explicitly in the functional definition of a system, although this need not always be so. Whereas with toasters and word-processors, for example, we would not expect to find values mentioned in the descriptions of their primary functions, with RAPUNSEL, part of the project's purpose, articulated in the proposal document, was 'to address gender inequities' and meet the technology learning needs of a sector over-looked by the software industry by constructing 'a game environment to teach disadvantaged middle-school girls to program computers' (Flanagan, Hollingshead, and Perlin 2003). Thus, gender equity, considered as an instance of social equity is built into the functional definition of the project to be designed. Likewise, as we mentioned earlier, systems and devices may be built with the explicit purpose of 'preserving privacy' or 'enhancing security,' and so forth.

b. Values that Emerge in Specifying (Gritty) Instrumental Design Features
Design is almost always under-determined by explicit functional require-ments (e.g., Whitbeck 1996), leaving to designers and developers numer-ous open-ended alternatives as they proceed through the process, including some that implicate values. Such values, as they are encountered, we label 'collateral' because they are not present in the functional definition of a project, but crop up as a function of the variety of detailed alternatives designers confront and from which they must select.

REWARD SYSTEM. A game's reward system is a crucial mechanism for expressing the game's goals and values. In the RAPUNSEL game, designers opted for a reward system that would reinforce larger project goals of cooperation in emerging social behaviors (Inkpen 1995). In the initial iteration, the team designed a mechanism based upon caregiving or nurturing, which they understood to have been popular with the target audience in similarly structured games. Although it was clear that alternate reward mechanisms could as successfully teach players the relevant programming concepts and skills, designers preferred the version that would appeal to players' sense of social interaction and achieve higher-level project goals such as cooperation and fair representation. (Kafai 1995; Laurel 2001; Margolis and Fisher 2002; Muller and Kuhn 1993).

PLAYER POINT OF VIEW. Another collateral value emerged in RAPUNSEL when designers attempted to determine the player's point-of-view. When developing the initial specification, the two basic options were: (a) allow players to manipulate characters from a three-dimensional, top down, 'god's eye view'; or (b) generate a subjective perspective by allowing players to 'become' the characters as first person avatars and thus 'see' only what the character could see. Team members thought that the choice of one or the other could more strongly affect the way players understood themselves in relation to game characters, the game world, and, importantly, how they conceived their own agency. Specifying point of view according to the first option – allowing players to program the behavior of characters from a god's eye view – worried team members because it might encourage players to view the characters as a sort of 'slave race'. But in the second, if players were identified in the game not as 'god' but as their avatars, it appeared difficult to get 'into the brains of characters' in order to program their behaviors. This assessment was drawn from comparisons with other existing game models, which allow players to control their characters directly with a mouse and thus provide a seamless relationship between a player's wishes and their avatar's onscreen goals. Programming the character's actions through script, however, added distance between player and avatar in an unprecedented way.

c. Designers' Values

Generally unstudied and frequently unnoticed, the values of members of a design team, even those who have not had a say in top level decisions, often shape a project in significant ways as it moves through the design process. Beliefs and commitments, and ethnic, economic, and disciplinary training and education, may frame their perspectives, preferences, and design tendencies, resulting eventually in features that affect the values embodied in particular systems.

DIVERSITY. An example of a designer-introduced value in the context of RAPUNSEL was diversity, which emerged in prototypes exploring other, more technical, issues. Once discovered and discussed, it became clear that this value was of importance to several members of the team and was then included, explicitly, in the list of values. To RAPUNSEL team members, diversity meant not only expanding the general activity of programming across boundaries of age, gender, economy, and ethnicity, but also fostering a diverse range of approaches to learning. Understood in this way, diversity links to high-level conceptions of distributive justice, such as Michael Walzer's 'complex equality' which portrays a just world as one in which a variety of principles determine the allocation of social goods across a variety of autonomous spheres, respectively, so that people who may not excel in one sphere, may do so in another (Walzer 1994). Although gender equity, arguably a form of diversity, was expressed in the functional definition of the project at its inception, team members became interested in additional dimensions of diversity, such as learning styles and cognitive abilities. These dimensions motivated the construction of multiple game goals rather than just one, allowing players to earn rewards in a variety of ways. So far these include points for decorating characters and home-space environments in unique and creative ways, and for sharing code with other players. Another mechanism that, so far, has only been sketched, will enable voting by other players on saved dance routines; positive community evaluation will translate to points in the reward scheme. This, further, will cause the most popular routines to bubble to the top, rewarding players as well as serving to showcase what is possible in the game-world. Other modes of reward include the traditional one of moving to higher levels when a player has mastered a lower one and, for players preferring a competitive style, the option of player-versus-player dance competitions. The idea is that these multiple dimensions of reward strategies will increase the range of players able to enjoy and excel in the game.

d. User Values

Another obvious source of values are users, or potential users, of any given system. Having recognized the importance of this key population in determining the values to be embodied in a system, the challenge is how to go about discovering the values that are important to them in relation to a given system. In recent years, as user testing has become an increasingly important aspect of systems design, designers have struggled for ways to assess, accurately, their particular propensities and preferences. As discussed in Part 1, in relation to values in technology, it is important for designers to assess not only what dimensions people care about, but how they rank these dimensions in the event of conflicts that arise in specific instances. In developing an e-mail system, for example, designers might puzzle over whether to protect senders' anonymity, and how important such a feature is – the capacity to speak freely without fear of retribution – in comparison with the opposite – identifiability and the capacity to hold senders accountable for what they say. Although it is less important which option is preferred, it is essential to obtain accurate measurements on such dimensions, which

may often be unclear. Conducting assessments calls for subtle appreciation of wide-ranging factors that play into people's responses to technologies shaped not only by explicit systems of ethical commitments but also
by cultural meanings and past experiences with existing, salient products,
which may generate a set of expectations that carry over from one context
to another. Studies have shown, for example, that users have expectations
about where information will appear on subsequent screens, moving their
eyes, in anticipation, before the screen appears (Hornoff and Halverson
2003). Ideally, designers will apply a variety of methods to answering questions about users' values. Results from focus groups, for example, offer one
perspective on explicit value commitments, but the results are not always
consistent with the behavioral observations of usability testing (Eysenbach
and Kohler 2002).

For RAPUNSEL, the team found prototyping to be an essential component in discovering users' beliefs, preferences, and values. They devised
and used a variety of prototyping methods, ranging from focus groups
and one-on-one sessions with design partners, to Web-based surveys, paper-
prototyping, digital mock-ups, to more traditional approaches using test
modules implemented in the software. Noting the pleasure users derived
from building and dressing up characters and from manipulating them
in the game to engage in relationships with other characters via flirting,
dancing, and other social behaviors, RAPUNSEL designers inferred users'
valuation of creative self-expression, authorship, community, and collaboration. One unexpected finding was the attractiveness of subversion to some
users, which we have interpreted, here, as a dimension of autonomy. (It
turns out that playing games, such as *The Sims* 'against the grain', is a significant pastime for several design partners, as well as many other players of
that game.)

SUBVERSION. Although there is potential to use RAPUNSEL in
classroom-based programming curricula, it is primarily intended for more
informal, entertainment-oriented environments. To succeed in this arena
the game needs to compete for its potential user-base with popular computer game titles. As we noted earlier, regular meetings with design partner
groups revealed a fascination with playing against the rules and engaging
in morbid or macabre behavior. Designers labeled this set of themes, 'subversion.' Some of the girls who enjoyed playing popular games such as *The
Sims*, often did so in significantly different ways from those advertised, or normally expected. They found ways around programmed 'intentions' of the
system, spending more time, for example, decorating their virtual houses;
making clothing for, or even abusing, their characters than playing 'by the
book,' and striving to achieve goals set out in game instructions and marketing, such as earning a living or getting promoted at a job. The same
principle applied in the context of other games, such as *Grand Theft Auto:
Vice City*, in which some design partners expressed a preference for simply
driving around a virtual Miami rather than engaging in the primary game

narrative. In allowing for such flavors of alternate play, these complex game systems revealed subversion as an important emergent value. Following this theme through in testing with RAPUNSEL prototypes, 11-to13-year-old players often requested unusual abilities in relation to their characters, such as 'Can you make it run off and die?' We interpret this notion of subversion as a dimension of freedom, autonomy, and creativity through resistance to pigeonholing, unnecessary constraint, and a desire for a more active authorial voice in the game context.

SMART CODE EDITOR. A second case of user-introduced values affected development of the game's 'smart code editor' interface. Designers noted early on in discussions that design partners valued transparency (the openness and accessibility of a given system) and self-expression. One design partner, age 12, reflected the interests of many in the user group by asking, 'Could we design the setting . . . and like . . . design the characters ourselves?' To encourage and maintain such creative interest it was important to facilitate programming in a manner that was easily comprehensible and empowering. Without sacrificing traditional criteria for successful design along the way (efficiency, robustness, usability, etc.), designers worked on inscribing the value of transparency into the interface of the smart code editor, producing a tool that, via coding, gave players access to the majority of the system and allowed them to influence the entire game world.

BIOPHILIA. We refer to a third example of values discovered via interaction with users as 'biophilia,' the tendency for players to be attracted to and care about life-like characters and processes (Wilson 1986), as exhibited in several products popular with the demographic (e.g., Tamagotchi toys and *The Sims* characters). Although many of the design partners enjoyed engaging with human characters and found babies, birds, and other animals similarly compelling, they were less attracted to characters that were too abstract (geometric shapes, stick figures, etc.). When faced with simple characters made from geometric shapes, girls noted the characters appeared quick and agile, but less than intelligent: 'My character is a little . . . not smart . . . maybe it could learn to swim?'

C.2 Translation

Where discovery consists of the activity of identifying the values pertinent to a given design project, translation is the activity of embodying or expressing these values in system design. Translation is further divided into operationalization, which involves defining, or articulating values in concrete terms, and implementation, which involves specifying corresponding design features.

a. Operationalization
The values that are 'discovered' in the context of a given project may be of a variety of types and take a variety of forms. For values to be accessible

to the design context, particularly those that are abstractly conceived, they must be rendered in sufficiently specific and concrete terms. The activity of analyzing and defining value concepts, is what we call 'operationalization.' Although it relies predominantly on the philosophical mode of inquiry, discussed in Part 1 of this chapter, it may also draw on results from other modes, particularly the empirical. Of course, no matter how well value concepts are operationalized – that is, made concrete – the efforts of conscientious designers will be seriously undermined if the substantive nature of the value is incorrectly interpreted. With controversial values such as privacy, for example, clarity, good intentions, and technical competence can be misdirected if not coupled with an accurate, reflective understanding of the nature of privacy itself.

SOCIAL JUSTICE. As we suggested earlier, the persuasive force of gender equity, expressed in the functional definition of RAPUNSEL, is derived from the commitment of liberal democracies to social justice. In the context of RAPUNSEL, social justice has been operationalized as improved mastery of a high status skill, in the target population. Drawing a legitimate connection between the value and concrete mastery of a specific skill is part of the task of operationalization. The relevant narrative is mediated by a number of key philosophical and empirical propositions. One is the prominent role of information technologies in Western, technologically literate societies of the late twentieth and early twenty-first centuries. Another is the importance of proficiency in mathematics, science, and programming as a source of social and cultural status as well as access to high paying jobs and generally positive career trajectories. A vision of these linkages is clearly seen in Seymour Papert's assertion: '. . . programming is the most powerful medium of developing the sophisticated and rigorous thinking needed for mathematics, for grammar, for physics, for statistics, and all the 'hard' subjects. In short, I believe more than ever that programming should be a key part of the intellectual development of people growing up' (Papert 2005, p. 38; Papert 1993). At the same time, data shows, unequivocally, a radical decline of interest in these subjects in female adolescents and, later on, a dearth of women in associated careers (Brunner 1997; Catsambis 1994; Chaika 1995; Clewell 2002; Kirkup and Abbot 1997; Haller and Fossum 1998; Norman 1990; Pearl et al. 1990). Accordingly, an effort to contribute toward a reversal of this trend can be understood as a push toward greater equity in access to important social goods – in this instance social status and lucrative employment. The link between access to social goods and social justice has been amply drawn in many works of political philosophy, including well-known contemporary works John Rawls (1971) and Michael Walzer (1994). Finally, the growing body of empirical evidence showing overwhelming popularity of networked computer games and social learning environments, such as e-mail, chat, and online gaming environments (Chmielewski 2004; Grinter and Palen 2002) and the success of games used in science education projects (Gorriz and Medina 2000; Inkpen 1995) inspired the creation of the RAPUNSEL. As a medium for raising the appeal of math, science, and programming, RAPUNSEL is a tool for promoting social justice – admittedly in a modest way – by encouraging the development of highly marketable skills.

b. Implementation

The activity of implementation is aimed at transforming value concepts into corresponding design specifications. This occurs, as we noted earlier, in tandem with the general design activity of transforming ideas, intentions, and concepts into material form, in the case of programming, ultimately into lines of code. Designers working on embodying values in design are simultaneously attending to functional requirements and other constraints. With values, no less than with traditional functional goals, the art of good design involves embodying specified requirements successfully in a given system and may be evaluated by similar methods, such as reflective practice (Schön 1983). As with other constitutive activities, implementation is dynamically interconnected with the others and can affect and be affected by them in a reflexive manner.

COOPERATION THROUGH CODE SHARING. As we mentioned earlier, sharing and cooperation had emerged as important project values and needed to be cleverly implemented in the game. One of the ways designers sought to do so was through development of robust mechanisms for sharing program code among players, allowing several participants to work together to achieve goals. To promote core project goals of acquiring and improving programming skills, players were encouraged to write new code, but the system as designed to make it possible (and easy) for players to share snippets of code with others. After considering various implementation strategies the design team devised a system in which players could compose, accumulate, and transport code segments, through the various stages of the game, in virtual libraries of 'backpacks.' The backpack serves a similar function to mechanisms in traditional adventure and conflict-oriented games which allow players to gather weapons or armor in a type of 'inventory.' In addition, an instant message (IM-like) system, known to be attractive to girls (Grinter and Palen 2002), would facilitate inter-player communication, enabling one player to query another to learn what pieces of code they are carrying, at which point, the other might agree to share some or all of the code segments in their backpack.[8]

---

[8] On a technical level, the implementation of sharing and collaboration in the manner described grew complicated as designers considered how players might save and transport pieces of code in various stages of the game. For example, it was clear that code segments for users at different levels should be created and saved at the same level of granularity, both for conceptual clarity and ease of sharing. Yet, requiring the code to conform to a high-level abstraction, such as a Class or Interface, seemed potentially difficult to grasp, perhaps even discouraging sharing among less experienced players. Through several prototype iterations,

REWARD SYSTEM II. As we mentioned earlier, the reward system is an important medium for expressing values in a game. Although the mechanisms described above *enable* code-sharing, it is through RAPUNSEL's unique scoring system, which incrementally rewards players both for authoring original sequences or programs and for sharing them, that cooperation is motivated. The reward system monitors backpack exchanges to reward players accordingly. Each time a player's code is viewed by another player, the author receives a few points; when the code is actually borrowed and used by another player, the originator receives many more points, thus encouraging players to concoct the most interesting and inventive dance sequences and agreeing to share them. In summary, through the integration of transportable code with a reward system that encouraged sharing, we were able to implement collaboration in both the technical framework and the game mechanic in an organic fashion. An added appeal of this solution over others we considered was that it rewarded players with the accumulation of knowledge, as represented by code segments, rather than with material items, like weapons, clothing, or money, and thus reinforced other core project values, specifically sustainability and nonviolence. Such synergies occurred somewhat frequently in the project; a fact we attributed to our continued attention to ways in which various project elements, whether technical, functional, or values-oriented, might mutually reinforce each other.

SMART CODE EDITOR II. The first design iteration idea was a 'type-in' code editor window with 'smart' features (spelling/syntax checking, automatic code-completion, etc.) to assist users new to programming. The hypothesis was that compared with a more constrained interface, the freedom afforded by a type-in method would foster creativity and expressivity. Concurrently, designers wanted to avoid imposing unnecessary layers between code input and resulting character behavior, believing that any such 'disconnects' might have negative effects on the efficacy of the system, blurring users' ability to see the big picture as well as complicating users' mapping between input and feedback (Norman 1990). This hypothesis was

we addressed this issue by integrating code sharing directly into the smart code editor in conjunction with a 'name-code' command. This functionality allowed a player to highlight a section of code in their editor and save it as a Java method. When 'name-code' was invoked, the system analyzed the code chunk selected, added a method signature with appropriate arguments, and prompted the user for a memorable name. At this point, the player could view and/or test the new method and approve its inclusion in their backpack. It was a pleasant surprise when we later saw how this design choice also served an important pedagogical goal, namely that of teaching 'encapsulation.' Our initial belief, that encapsulation (the combination of smaller code chunks into a functionally coherent whole, reusable without reference to its constituent parts) was among our 'advanced topics' and perhaps available only to 'expert' players, was revisited and the concept's importance in the game increased. The iterative dialogue between functional, values-based, and technical concerns again lead designers in interesting new directions, yielding positive externalities well beyond the initial 'problem' considered.

supported by informal empirical data that suggested that students who had learned to program in various 'drag-and-drop' environments (such as *Director, Flash, Max/MSP*, etc.) found these interfaces placed an unnecessary distance between the user and the internal workings of the system; distance that created confusion and frustrated learning.

SUBVERSION II. To implement the 'value' of subversion, the RAPUNSEL game, which is designed in the style of a simulation, is built upon and infrastructure that allows for (and supports) unexpected scenarios and user interactions. Instead of attempting to imagine and map out responses to all possible game-states, the world is built to run in a consistent fashion with, or without, the usual set of user-initiated actions. In this way, the game supports subversive activity without anyone knowing ahead of time what form the subversion might take, providing the necessary robustness to withstand a wide range of unexpected outcomes. In other words, the basic idea is to build a robust (real-world, physical) model that runs whether or not human players are present, making the characters 'smart' enough to deal with unanticipated states by continuing to pursue their goals, without crashing or falling apart. The team also designed an 'underworld' and nasty characters called 'gobblers' to address user interest in subversion.

c. Values in Conflict: Resolving, Dissolving, and Trading Off
Throughout a project, there is potential for incompatibilities to arise in the context of a particular design element. A source of such conflict is when designers who have committed to values that have emerged during discovery, find it impossible to embody all of them within the system in question. Engineering is rife with such conflicts – whether to favor safety over cost, transparency over privacy, aesthetics over functionality, with many more appearing at layers of finer granularity. The case of software is not significantly different. An example that has been much discussed is the conflict between system security and ease-of-use (an aspect of autonomy or self-determination) where a system that has been designed with a high degree of technical security might require more than an acceptable degree of effort on the part of users. Resolving conflicts of values is by no means a challenge for engineering only, but remains one of the most intractable problems in the field of practical ethics as well as in law, moral philosophy, and politics. Although there have been numerous efforts to clarify some of these problems (for one of the most thoughtful, see Richardson, 1994), those familiar with the field will understand why attempting to offer any simple, across-the-board solutions falls far outside the scope of the paper. Instead, some observations drawn from our experience thinking specific conflicts through, in the context of RAPUNSEL, may be useful for purposes of values in design.

Our experience with RAPUNSEL pointed to two key strategies for dealing with conflicts. In one set of cases, when confronting a conflict of values, designers would discover that the problem was not the result of fundamental incompatibilities between values themselves but the outcome of conflicting material constraints that each of the values seemed to impose on the given system or device. This discovery steered designers to look for solutions in the design itself to see how malleable the material limits are, in some cases, requiring advances in skill or knowledge beyond the existing state-of-art. Cases in which designers are able to find solutions, through creative redesign, which allowed both values to be instantiated, we label 'dissolving conflict.' Where it is not possible to dissolve conflict completely (in some cases, one could alleviate but not solve) through redesign, the alternative is either to trade one value off against another (or others), per the strength of value commitments, or to seek a compromise among conflicting values.

PLAYER POINT OF VIEW II. Recall the conflict we mentioned earlier between designers' preference for a subjective point-of-view, out of concern that a 'god's-eye' point-of-view might encourage a view of game characters as a 'slave race,' and the clear preference expressed by most players for a third-person perspective. This conflict, between user-preferences and designer-values, proved to be one that could be 'dissolved' through the integration of a third value on the list, biophilia. As we discussed earlier, design partners had shown a keen preference for engagement with life-like agents and processes. By leveraging biophilia, specifically by implementing a handful of simple AI techniques that provided a degree of autonomous behavior to non-player characters, designers were able offer a god's-eye view that avoided slippage to a conception of characters as mere slaves.

SMART CODE EDITOR II. In our earlier discussion of the 'smart code editor,' a programming interface for creating code, we reported that team members initially preferred a type-in version, thinking would be less confusing and constraining than a graphical editor. But they discovered that most of the middle-school design partners disliked typing their own code. Reporting that typing felt more like work than play, they made clear that they did not appreciate its advantages; for example, the sense of empowerment designers had hypothesized. In preferring the ease-of-use and efficiency offered through the direct manipulation of objects, via mouse input, players' values conflicted with core project values of exploration, creativity, and empowerment. The resolution, in this case, was a trade-off: a tiered interface system that began with a context-sensitive, pull-down menu, transitioned to a hybrid of menu and typing, and finally offered the ability for typing directly in a smart editor window equipped with assistive features such as keyword-completion, syntax-checking, and real-time compilation.

CHARACTER REPRESENTATION. The appearance, attitudes, and actions of characters have significant expressive meaning. Typically, enemies in popular commercial games are depicted as dark 'others', whereas heroes tend to look muscular and are often Caucasian. Characters act or speak in ways that mark them culturally and socially, and these markings are likely to influence the way other images and situations are read (Taylor and Jakobsson 2003). In RAPUNSEL, designers found that translating equity into particular character representations was a task of considerable difficulty. They found that relatively small alterations in a character's looks or behaviors could ripple out to alter meanings in subtle and important ways. For example, whether characters (even represented as abstract shapes) would be viewed as male or female was of concern both to designers – who were keen to create proactive female, or at least gender-neutral, characters – and to users. At first, the team used simple animated geometric shapes as characters, but these were often perceived as 'male' by our design partners and, moreover, were uninteresting to them. When design partners were asked if they would like to care for one of these abstract characters, a 14 year old replied, 'No, they just aren't . . . cool enough'.

To investigate this trend, the team created an online character survey of user preferences for a variety for character representation styles. The results of this survey showed that design partners consistently preferred overtly sexualized female figures to animals or abstract shapes. For example, one user stated, 'I didn't like any of them, I just chose the ones that look normal'. The design partners linked their preferences to the existing commercial products they enjoyed. Overall, the favorite character, a hip-hop styled female from a popular girls' Web site, was regarded by one 11-year-old design partner as a 'cool girl . . . she's modern, art-time; she has attitude.' Facing the implications of these findings, several members of the team, nevertheless, wished to resist reinforcing the stereotypical images of women often found in popular games. This conflict is a complex one, pitting ideologically driven system designers, against potential users, as well as background societal norms.

Although these tensions have not, to this point, been resolved, trade-off and compromise is the most likely path. Designers will not concede to the overly sexualized figures preferred by design partners but may yet opt for gendered characters of a more 'sporty' type. Team members continue to study the issue, and a variety of alternatives, through both empirical and philosophical modes of inquiry.

C.3 Verification

In the activity of verification, designers assess to what extent they have successfully implemented target values in a given system. Verifying the inclusion of values is likely to draw on strategies and methods not unlike those applied to other design criteria like functional efficiency and usability. These may include internal testing among the design team, user testing in controlled environments, formal and informal interviews and surveys, the use of prototypes, traditional quality assurance measures such as automated and regression-oriented testing, and more. Verifying the inclusion of values, however, introduces additional layers of complexity as it is important to determine not only that a particular value has been successfully implemented in a specific component, but also that its implementation does not detract from other design goals. To further complicate matters, our grasp of what it means for a value to be implemented in a system (e.g., claiming that a system is 'privacy-preserving' or 'autonomy enhancing'), is not nearly as firm as our grasp of what it means (according to the state of the art) for a system to function properly or be 'usable.' This difficulty arises not only from the more controversial and less concrete nature of value concepts – compare autonomy to usability – but because the means by which values are embodied are often more diverse. This point will be taken up again in the chapter's conclusion where we discuss the difference between values expressed directly in a system's content, and those embodied through material constraints or affordances that systematically prevent or enable certain types of actions. Although values may be related to specific system features (this is a core assumption of our work), they may also emerge, indirectly, as a property of the system's interaction with the contextual setting in which it operates. A final complexity involves the fact that the impact of some values may be experienced immediately, while others may emerge only in the long term. Although significantly more could be said on this subject, it should be clear that within the active design phase of a project, verification is likely to produce only partial results. Despite this limitation, values verification activities are an essential part of the iterative feedback loop.

In RAPUNSEL, the design team has explored diverse modes of verification, sampling from the range of empirical, technical, and conceptual (or analytical) approaches mentioned above. Testing via prototypes (e.g., Glass 2000; Laurel 2001; Rettig 1994; Zimmerman 2003) was found to be particularly useful in sorting through the complexities of values-oriented trade-offs. An iterative approach to assessing design outcomes, based upon a combination of methods, has allowed the team to move quickly through design cycles, incorporating feedback from a wide range of collaborators and users into successive prototypes (Bødker and Grønbaek 1991; Eysenbach 2002; Shneiderman 2000). In addition, the team has employed agile programming methods to aid in implementing technical aspects of the systems with changing requirements (Freeman-Benson and Borning 2003). In the RAPUNSEL process, verification has been facilitated through regular meetings with design partners, educators, and industry advisers. As promising ideas emerge, designers have tried to map these onto functional, technical, and values-oriented frameworks. At the same time, designers have been careful not to overlook the importance of playability and sheer entertainment value in order to ensure the success of RAPUNSEL as a game. Balancing this range of goals has proven a formidable challenge – one which would only have been more difficult without regular cycles of verification integrated within the process.

PLAYER POINT-OF-VIEW III. Findings so far suggest that introducing 'free will' into characters, as described above, has had the intended effect. At times, for example, players have had trouble 'catching up' with their characters. One 12-year-old design partner noted that they appeared quick and agile; 'they move really fast!' Such agency was apparent to the player when characters enacted surprising behaviors and created interesting tensions as they temporarily 'resisted' player instructions in order to satisfy their own 'personal' goals, pursuing behaviors dictated by their personalities and body types. By programming selected aspects of autonomy into character behaviors, RAPUNSEL designers were able to establish a balance – on the one hand avoiding an overly controlling relationship, while on the other, still supporting the consistent capacity of players to program their characters.

CHARACTER REPRESENTATION II. As described above, although issues surrounding character design have yet to be resolved, the team has developed several methods for obtaining feedback and verifying potential solutions. The online survey of a wide-range of characters, including images from familiar Web sites ('Neopets,' 'WhatsHerFace.com,' etc.) as well as RAPUNSEL's own animal, human, and geometrically generated characters, has elicited much useful feedback. A configurable mini-game environment that allows users to toggle between a range of character types has also provided detailed feedback on users' preferences. Eventually these and other measures will be used to verify that characters selected for RAPUNSEL, as well as their modes of interaction, successfully embody project values while still engaging users. It is worth mentioning that developing and applying verification measures before a solution has been found, is analogous to 'test-driven development', a relatively new technique in software engineering that has emerged out of the agile programming community. Although a full discussion of this approach is beyond the scope of this paper, we note that it maps quite well to values-oriented methods (Freeman-Benson and Borning 2003).

SMART CODE EDITOR III. Recall the debate surrounding RAPUNSEL's 'smart code editor' in which conflicts arose between ease of use and efficiency, on the one hand, and important project values of creativity, empowerment, and transparency, on the other. As noted, the design team settled on an editor with a scaffolded interface designed to 'grow with users' as they acquired experience, affording increasing dimensions of freedom with each successive transition. Thus, typing becomes available to users only when situations arise which necessitate additional expressivity. Usability tests with design partners have borne out these predictions, motivating eager users to pursue increasingly daunting tasks and gain access to the more powerful tools. One 12 year old, for example, declared, 'I want to knock down buildings...and want to design what I want it to be like'.

SUMMARY OF METHODOLOGY

In Part 2, we outlined a systematic approach to embodying values in design constituted by three distinct activities: (1) Discovery, in which a list of those values relevant to a project are compiled; (2) Translation, in which values are operationalized and implemented in material design features corresponding to these values; and (3) Verification, in which implementations are tested using variety of methods in order to ascertain whether designers' intentions have been met. It is worth repeating that these activities are not necessarily pursued in any fixed order. Although discovery is likely to take place early on in a project, the process need not be completed until quite a bit later, or, in some cases, it may keep cropping up all the way through until a product is, literally, out the door. When discovery persists long into a project it is not simply because designers were not thorough or astute at the start but because, as a design evolves through iterating phases of translation and verification and features are added, deleted, and changed, new versions of the systems might very well bring to light new value choices. Likewise, with verification, although it might seem inherently to represent a capstone activity, it actually functions most effectively if performed continuously throughout a project in a dynamic feedback loop with translation and discovery. And, so on.

REFLECTIONS ON VALUES IN DESIGN

Specific features of the approach we have presented are likely to evolve with further testing and critical scrutiny. Challenges that drive closer to the heart of the enterprise, however, are those that question two of its fundamental premises: first, that technologies do, in fact, embody values, and second, possibly more controversial, that values may be embodied in technical systems by deliberate design. The first of these premises positions our work within an extended discussion in the philosophy and social study of technology, placing it at odds first and foremost with claims of technology's neutrality. The neutrality claim does not deny that technical artifacts have or have had significant effects on social and political aspects of life, nor does it deny that technologies have affected the preeminence of certain social, moral, and political values over others. It denies only that these consequences are a function of system characteristics. Rather, they are a function of the uses to which they are put. Technologies are mere tools of human intention; morality (good or evil) and politics inhere in people and not in their tools. In contrast, we have been convinced by those who have argued that some technical artifacts bear directly and systematically on the realization, or suppression, of particular configurations of social, ethical, and political values (e.g., Winner 1986; Hughes 2004; Latour 1992).

Even accepting that artifacts embody values in the sense of fine-grain, systematic, and causal determination of social and political outcomes, there is still room to question how, or by what means they do. Although we are not able, here, to discuss this question fully, we reflect on lessons learned during the process of crafting the methodology that seem worthy of further study and elaboration. In honing the methodology in the context of RAPUNSEL, an important dichotomy, not fully acknowledged in the paper's main narrative, came to light. This is the dichotomy between values we might say are *expressed* in the game and those that are, for want of a better term, *materially* embodied. The former – values expressed – emerged in relation to game content, bearing on choices of character representation, for example, and game plot (narrative). For designers, the 'sporty' and nongendered characters avoided identification with stereotypical, hypersexualized representations common in other games and popular media. In this way, RAPUNSEL resembles other creative works – of literature, film, television, and so forth – that may express and symbolically represent values. How this happens and what can be said about the systematic effects on readers, audience, and so forth and communities, is an issue of great contention and much studied in the related scholarly areas of literary interpretation, media studies, and so forth.

The latter – values materially embodied – emerged in relation to constraints and affordances on users' actions that the game generated through particular design elements. The 'peep-chat' feature, for example, facilitates effective communication among players and the code-backpack facilitates effective viewing and sharing transactions. These, in turn, afford cooperation and learning, two of the game's primary values. The reward system also imposes material constraints but its effects are mediated through the general culture of videogaming and specifically the ways winning or earning points affects the behavior of players. Although something like the bias against the blind embodied in graphical user interfaces (Friedman and Nissenbaum 1996) is more readily traced through physical causal connections, other types of causal pathways, which depend on assumptions about deterministic relations between phenomena and social outcomes, are allowable as grounds for arguing that some or other material design feature embodies some or other value. It is less important that in particular cases the precise nature and extent of a relationship is contended. What matters is the claim that systems correspond to certain values generally, or do so at the micro-level of specific system features, including some that may be hidden from plain sight. The latter, due to what James Moor labeled as 'invisibility,' is especially pertinent to computer software (see, for example, Moor 1999). The mechanisms that we have touched on above deserve to be studied more intensively than we have been able to here.

As we stated earlier, our analysis assumes more than that technical artifacts embody values; it assumes the possibility of embodying values in technical artifacts by deliberate design, something that is disputable from various perspectives. For one, those who adhere to the neutrality claim, mentioned above, will find this assumption a nonstarter. Another skeptical reaction is likely to come from social constructivists who might question whether the efforts of conscientious or, for that matter, manipulative designers could have any causal bearing on the promotion or suppression of particular values. It is not through material design features that artifacts embody values, they could argue, but through interpretations and meanings imposed upon them as a function of politics, history, and culture, not to mention a myriad of uncontrollable social contingencies (see, for example, Woolgar 1991, Pinch and Bijker 1987, and Pfaffenberger 1992). Because these meanings and interpretations are not a determinate product of material design, it is pointless for designers, or direct participants in the development and production of technical artifacts, to set about the task of embodying values. A third objection, more practical in nature, is generally skeptical about the power of designers to shape technology and its outcomes. The innumerable junctures through which any noteworthy technical project must pass, from conception to realization in a manufactured product, makes it difficult for even the best-intentioned and best-informed designers (among the many others with power to shape a system) directing critical decisions points, to determine ultimate outcomes. This general dilution of agency is further amplified by the notorious problem of unintended consequences often associated with new and emerging technologies.

We take these objections seriously, but, in holding to the 'obduracy' of technology (MacKenzie and Wajcman 1985), we are unconvinced by social constructivist approaches that deny all deterministic links between technology's material forms and social and political outcomes. Yet, these and other challenges underscore a need to go beyond naïve determinism and to tackle relevant social mediators. Material features of technical systems are important, but so are others, including the individual, social, historical, and political contexts within which they operate. Hardest to fathom among these contextual factors are, perhaps, those that function expressively in a communicative chain from author, artist, designer, and producer, to reader, audience, user, and so forth. The varied results of efforts by social scientists and worried social and political leaders to predict or forestall the influence of violent, sexually explicit, and bigoted content on beliefs and behaviors demonstrate how much more we need to learn. Yet, even in acknowledging these difficulties, there remains a point of irreconcilable difference between the critical views mentioned and our own. This is most strikingly manifest where each would locate the burden of responsibility for the nature – the harms and benefits – of technical artifacts. Their view places the designers in an instrumental role subservient to other factors that are systematically outside their control. Our view keeps designers determinedly in the picture. Obviously, anyone can be political; the question is whether it is in one's capacity as a designer that one is, or is not. We hold not only that designers are designers but that it is their duty as *good* designers to embrace this dimension of their work, even if they are not always able to prevail against the tide of countervailing forces.

References

Ackerman, M. S., and Cranor, L. 1999. Privacy critics: UI components to safeguard users' privacy. *Extended Abstracts of CHI*. New York: ACM Press, pp. 258–259.

Agre, P. E. 1997a. Introduction, in P. E. Agre and M. Rotenberg (Eds.), *Technology and privacy: The new landscape*. Cambridge, MA: MIT Press, pp. 1–28.

Agre, P. E. 1997b. Toward a critical technical practice: Lessons learned in trying to reform AI, in G. Bowker et al. (Eds.), *Bridging the great divide: Social science, technical systems, and cooperative work*. Hillsdale, NJ: Erlbaum.

American Association of University Women (AAUW). 2000. Tech-savvy: Educating girls in the new computer age. Available at http://www.aauw.org/research/girls_education/techsavvy.cfm.

Bødker, S., and Grønbæk, K. 1991. Design in action: From prototyping by demonstration to cooperative prototyping, in J. Greenbaum and M. Kyng (Eds.), *Design at work: Cooperative design of computer systems*. Hillsdale, NJ: Erlbaum, pp. 197–218.

Borning, A. Friedman, B., and Kahn, P. 2004. Designing for human values in an urban simulation system: Value sensitive design and participatory design. *Proceedings of Eighth Biennial Participatory Design Conference*, Toronto. Toronto: ACM Press, pp. 64–67.

Brunner, C. 1997. Opening technology to girls: The approach computer-using teachers take may make the difference. *Electronic Learning, 16*, 4, 55.

Catsambis, S. 1994. The path to math: Gender and racial-ethnic differences in mathematics participation from middle to high school. *Sociology of Education, 67*, 3, 199–215.

Chaika, M. 1995. Ethical considerations in gender-oriented entertainment technology. *Crossroads of the ACM, 2*, 2, 11–13. Available at http://www.acm.org/crossroads/xrds2-2/gender.html.

Chmielewski, D. C. 2004. Kids turning to instant messaging. Knight Ridder. Available at http://www.azcentral.com/families/articles/0225faminstantmessage.html.

Clewell, B. 2002. Breaking the barriers: The critical middle school years, in *The Jossey-Bass reader on gender in education*. San Francisco: Jossey-Bass, pp. 301–313.

Crawford, C. 1982. The art of computer game design. Available at http://www.vancouver.wsu.edu/fac/peabody/game-book/Coverpage.html.

Dourish, P., Finlay, J., Sengers, P., and Wright, P. 2004. Reflective HCI: Towards a critical technical practice. *Proceedings of CHI, Vienna*, pp. 1727–1728.

Druin, A. 1999. Cooperative inquiry: Developing new technologies for children with children. *Proceedings of CHI, Pittsburgh*, pp. 592–599.

Eysenbach, G., and Kohler, C. 2002. How do consumers search for and appraise health information on the World Wide Web? *British Medical Journal, 324*, 7337, p. 9.

Flanagan, M. 2003. Next level: Women's digital activism through gaming, in A. Morrison, G. Liestøl, and T. Rasmussen (Eds.), *Digital media revisited.* Cambridge, MA: MIT Press, pp. 359–388.

Flanagan, M., Hollingshead, A., and Perlin, K. 2003. HRD-0332898, Gender in Science and Engineering Program (GSE) of the National Science Foundation.

Freeman-Benson, B., and Borning, A. 2003. YP and urban simulation: Applying an agile programming methodology in a politically tempestuous domain. *Proceedings of the Agile Development Conference (ADC '03)*, p. 2.

Friedman, B. 1996. Value-sensitive design. *Interactions, 3,* 6, 17–23.

Friedman, B., Howe, D. C., and Felten, E. 2002. Informed consent in the Mozilla browser: Implementing value-sensitive design. *Proceedings of 35th Annual Hawaii International Conference on System Sciences, IEEE Computer Society, 8,* p. 247.

Friedman, B., and Nissenbaum, H. 1996. Bias in computer systems. *ACM Transactions on Information Systems, 14,* 3, 330–347.

Glass, R. L. 2000. *Facts and fallacies of software engineering.* Lebanon, PA: Addison-Wesley Professional.

Gorriz, C., and Medina, C. 2000. Engaging girls with computers through software games. *Communications of the ACM, 43,* 1, 42–49.

Grinter, R., and Palen, L. 2002. Instant messaging in teen life. *Proceedings of Conference on Computer Supported Cooperative Work.* New York: ACM Press, pp. 21–30.

Haller, S., and Fossum, T. 1998. Retaining women in CS with accessible role models. *Proceedings of the Twenty-ninth SIGCSE Technical Symposium on Computer Science Education.* Atlanta, GA: Association for Computing Machinery (ACM) Special Interest Group on Computer Science Education. Also published in *ACM SIGCSE Bulletin, 30,* 1, 73–76.

Hornof, A. J., and Halverson, T. 2003. Cognitive strategies and eye movements for searching hierarchical computer displays. *Proceedings of the ACM SIGCHI Conference on Human Factors in Computing Systems, Fort Lauderdale, FL,* April 5–10, pp. 249–256.

Hughes, T. 2004. *Human-built world: How to think about technology and culture.* Chicago: University of Chicago Press.

Inkpen, K., Booth, K. S., Klawe, M., and Upitis, R. 1995. Playing together beats playing apart, especially for girls. *Proceedings of Computer Supported Collaborative Learning.* Hillsdale, NJ: Lawrence Erlbaum Associates, pp. 177–181.

Kafai, Y. B. 1995. *Minds in play: Computer game design as a context for children's learning.* Hillsdale, NJ: Erlbaum.

Kafai, Y. B. 1998. Video game designs by girls and boys: Variability and consistency of gender differences, in J. Cassel and H. Jenkins (Eds.), *From Barbie to Mortal Kombat: Gender and computer games.* Cambridge, MA: MIT Press, pp. 90–114.

Kirkup, G., and Abbot, J. 1997. *The gender gap: A gender analysis of the 1996 computing access survey* (PLUM Paper 80). Milton Keynes, UK: Open University.

Kline, R., and Pinch, T. 1996. Users as agents of technological change: The social construction of the automobile in the rural United States. *Technology and Culture, 37,* 4, 763–795.

Latour, B. 1992. Where are the missing masses? The sociology of a few mundane artifacts, in W. Bijker and J. Law (Eds.), *Shaping technology/building society.* Cambridge, MA: MIT Press, pp. 225–258.

Laurel, B. 2001. *The Utopian entrepreneur.* Cambridge, MA: MIT Press.

MacKenzie, D., and Wajcman, J. 1985. *The social shaping of technology.* Milton Keynes, UK: Open University Press.

Margolis, J., and Fisher, A. 2002. Unlocking the clubhouse: The Carnegie Mellon experience. *ACM SIGCSE Bulletin, 34*, 2, 79–83.

Mateas, M. 2000. Expressive AI, in *Electronic Art and Animation Catalog, Art and Culture Papers, SigGraph 2000, New Orleans, LA.*

Mitcham, C. 1995. Ethics into design, in R. Buchanan and V. Margolis, (Eds.), *Discovering design.* Chicago: University of Chicago Press, pp. 173–179.

Moor, J. H. 1999. Just consequentialism and computing. *Ethics and Information Technology, 1,* 1, 65–69.

Mubireek, K. A. 2003. *Gender-oriented vs. gender-neutral computer games in education.* PhD dissertation, Educational Policy and Leadership, Ohio State University. Available at http://www.ohiolink.edu/etd/view.cgi?osu1056139090.

Muller, M. J., and Kuhn, S. 1993. *Communications of the ACM, 36,* 6. Special issue on participatory design.

Nissenbaum, H. 1998. Values in the design of computer systems. *Computers in Society, March,* 38–39.

Nissenbaum, H. 2004. Privacy as contextual integrity. *Washington Law Review, 79,* 1, 119–158.

Norman, D. 1990. *The design of everyday things.* New York: Currency/Doubleday.

Norman, D. A., and Draper, S. W. 1986. *User-centered system design: New perspectives on human-computer interaction.* Hillsdale, NJ: Erlbaum.

Papert, S. 1993. *The children's machine: Rethinking school in the age of the computer.* New York: Basic Books.

Papert, S. 2005. The challenges of IDC: What have we learned from our past? A conversation with Seymour Papert, Marvin Minsky, and Alan Kay *Communications of the ACM, 48,* 1, 35–38.

Pearl, A., Pollock, M., Riskin, E., Thomas, B., Wolf, E., and Wu, A. 1990. Becoming a computer scientist. *Communications of the ACM, 33,* 11, 47–57.

Pfaffenberger, B. 1992. Technological dramas. *Science, Technology, and Human Values, 17,* 3, 282–312.

Pinch, T. J., and Bijker, W. E. 1987. The social construction of facts and artifacts, or, How the sociology of science and the sociology of technology might benefit each other, in W. E. Bijker, T. J. Pinch, and T. P. Hughes (Eds.), *The social construction of technological systems.* Cambridge, MA: MIT Press, pp. 17–50.

Rawls, J. 1971. *A theory of justice.* Cambridge, MA: Belknap Press of Harvard University Press.

Rettig, M. 1994. Prototyping for tiny fingers. *Communications of the ACM, 37,* 4, 21–27.

Richardson, H. S. 1994. *Practical reasoning about final ends.* Cambridge, UK: Cambridge University Press.

Schön, D. 1983. *The reflective practitioner.* New York: Basic Books.

Shneiderman, B. 2000. Universal usability. *Communications of the ACM, 43,* 3, 84–91.

Taylor, T. L., and Jakobsson, M. 2003. The Sopranos Meets EverQuest: Socialization processes in massively multiuser games. Paper presented at the 5th International Digital Arts and Culture Conference, Melbourne, May 19–23. Available at http://hypertext.rmit.edu.au/dac/papers/Jakobsson.pdf.

Von Prummer, C. 1994. Women-friendly perspectives in distance education. *Open Learning, 9,* 1, 3–12.

Walzer, M. 1984. *Spheres of justice: A defense of pluralism and equality.* New York: Basic Books.

Whitbeck, C. 1996. Ethics as design: Doing justice to moral problems. *Hastings Center Report, 26,* 3, 9–16.

Wilson, E. O. 1986. *Biophilia.* Cambridge, MA: Harvard University Press.

Winner, L. 1986. Do artifacts have politics? in *The whale and the reactor: A search for limits in an age of high technology.* Chicago: University of Chicago Press, pp. 19–39.

Woolgar, S. 1991. The turn to technology in social studies of science. *Science, Technology, and Human Values, 16,* 1, 20–50.

Zimmerman, E. 2003. Play as research: the iterative design process. Game Lab. Available at http://www.gmlb.com/articles/iterativedesign.html.

17

Information Technology Research Ethics*

Dag Elgesem

INTRODUCTION

Are there moral reasons for restricting information technology research? Let me start the discussion of this question by way of three examples of cases where it has been argued that research in this area should be restricted for ethical reasons.

In his article, 'Why the future doesn't need us,' written in response to Kurzweil (1999) and published in *Wired*, renowned computer scientist Bill Joy warns of the dangers of both the intended and unintended consequences of research into the area of the combinations of genetics, nanotechnology, and robotics (GNR). There is a new kind of risk of accidents, Joy argues, because 'robots, engineered organisms and nanobots share a dangerous amplifying factor: They can self-replicate.' Therefore, accidents with these technologies 'can spawn whole new classes of accidents and abuses. Most dangerously, for the first time, these accidents and abuses are widely within the reach of individuals or small groups. . . . Thus we have the possibility not just of weapons of mass destruction but of knowledge-enabled mass destruction (KMD), this destructiveness hugely amplified by the power of self-replication' (Joy 1999, p. 3).[1]

Apart from the specific risks that this kind of research gives rise to, the other aspect of the problem with this research, Joy warns, is that a 'dream of robotics is that we will gradually replace ourselves with our robotic technology, achieving near immortality by downloading our consciousness.' The consequence of this, Joy speculates, could be that the existence of the human species is in danger: 'But if we are downloaded in our technology, what are the chances that we will thereafter be ourselves or even human? It seems to

* I am grateful to Claus Huitfeldt, Jeroen van den Hoven, and John Weckert for helpful comments.

[1] For an updated discussion of the potentially catastrophic risks posed by nanotechnology, see Posner (2005).

me far more likely that a robotic existence would not be like a human one in any sense that we understand, that the robots would in no sense would be our children, that on this path our humanity may well be lost' (Joy 1999, p. 3).

The conclusion Joy draws from this is that research in the GNR field should be undertaken with greater awareness of the dangers and, perhaps, restricted in some sense in order to avoid 'knowledge-enabled mass destruction' (Joy 1999, p. 12).

Yes, I know, knowledge is good, as is search for new truths. We have been seeking knowledge since ancient times. Aristotle opened his Metaphysics with the simple statement: 'All men by nature desire to know.' We have, as a bedrock value in our society, long agreed on the value of open access to information, and recognize the problems that arise with attempts to restrict access to and development of knowledge. In recent times, we have come to revere scientific knowledge.

But despite the strong historical precedents, if open access to and unlimited development of knowledge henceforth puts us all in clear danger of extinction, then common sense demands that we re-examine even these basic, long-held beliefs. (Joy 1999, p. 2)

Hence, Joy opens up the possibility that the proscription of certain types of research might be justified.

In my second example, David Parnas's famous refusal to contribute to the Strategic Defence Initiative (SDI) project represents a different kind of restriction on research. Parnas, an expert on aspects of the safety critical computer systems involved in the project, argued that it would be impossible to create a system that would meet the requirements. He was initially positive to the initiative because, if effective, he thought it would put an end to the destructive arms race. When he came to the conclusion that the shield would not be effective, however, he argued that the world would be less safe, not safer, as a result of the shield. An unsafe shield, Parnas argued, would rather stimulate the race. Parnas felt that his expertise in the field and his professional responsibility gave him the obligation to make his views public. He emphasised that, as a professional, he has a responsibility to do what is best for society, and to make sure that his work really makes a contribution to the solution of the problem. The leaders of the project, however, argued that he should rather focus on the extraordinary possibilities for his field of research that the project offered. Parnas decided not to work on the project. He argued that it was his professional responsibility to inform the public of his assessment of the merits of the project:

It is not necessary for computer scientists to take a political position; they need only be true to their professional responsibilities. If the public were aware of the technical facts, if they knew how unlikely it is that such a shield would be effective, public support would evaporate. We do not need to tell them not to build SDI. We only need to help them understand why it will never be an effective and trustworthy shield. (Parnas 1987/1990, p. 363)

In my third example, research is sometimes restricted because the risk to research subjects is unacceptably high or because their integrity would be violated by the research. The principle of informed consent is therefore central in research ethics, and also in the ethics of research on information technology. The principle is codified both in guidelines for research ethics and in law. According to the recent European Union directive (European Parliament 1995), for example, all collection of personal information, including research, should normally be based on the informed consent of the research subjects. With research on information technology, and in particular in Internet research, it is often a problem to determine in which cases consent is required because the boundary between the public and the private spheres is more problematic in online contexts. Some have argued that all communication on the Net that is in principle openly accessible should be considered to be public.[2] Others have argued that the situation is not as simple as that and that other factors, such as the sensitivity of the communication, should be taken into consideration. One representative of this line of argument is the researcher Amy Bruckman, who has formulated her own set of guidelines. The first part of these guidelines runs as follows:

1. You may freely quote and analyze online information without consent if:
   - It is officially, publicly archived.
   - No password is required for archive access.
   - No site policy prohibits it.
   - The topic is not highly sensitive.
2. For everything else not covered by 1, you typically need consent (Bruckman 2002, p. 1).

One argument for this more careful attitude is the fact that some people do make themselves vulnerable online and act as if the communication is more protected than it actually is. Researchers ought to take this into account, Bruckman suggests. Again, this is an example of restrictions on research that are partly enforced by law, partly by ethical guidelines approved by the research community, and partly by the ethical considerations of the individual researcher.

I will refer to these examples in the following section. Despite differences, the cases have several things in common. First, they are examples of areas where research on complex computing systems is thought to have the possibility for harm. Second, they are examples of reasons that have

---

[2] See NESH (2003, §4): 'Even though information communicated in an open forum is of a private character, a researcher will – as a first rule – freely be able to use that information for research purposes'.

been offered for limiting research. Third, the examples show various ways in which research is concerned with values. There are several values involved here: the concern for research subjects, professional responsibility, the welfare of the society, the value of knowledge, and human dignity. Fourth, the examples show that the research community involved in the production of knowledge of various aspects of complex computing systems cannot ignore these value questions and the consequences of their research.

I will neither go into a discussion of the details of the substantial issues raised by the examples, nor into a discussion either of the risks involved in nanocomputing or of the risks involved in the design of control of complex weapons systems. Furthermore, I will not go into a discussion of what kinds of Internet research projects require informed consent. Instead, I will use the example as a starting point for a more general discussion of the regulation of research and the problems that this issue raises.

Traditionally, the fact-value distinction has been used as an argument against the external regulation of science. From the premise that a clear distinction can be made between judgments about facts and values, and that scientists qua scientists only make judgments about facts and not values, it is argued that it is inappropriate to regulate research on the basis of values. Also, a distinction between basic research and applied research has been used to argue that pure science – that is, scientific activity that is primarily theoretically motivated – should not be restricted in any way. I will argue that both the fact-value distinction and the distinction between pure and applied science are problematic. But still I am skeptical of attempts to regulate research on the basis of content. I will argue for an analogue of Scanlon's 'Millian principle' of freedom of expression:

There are certain harms which, although they would not occur but for certain acts of expression, nonetheless cannot be taken as part of a justification for legal restrictions on these acts. Those harms are: (a) Harms to certain individuals which consist in these coming to have false beliefs as a result of those acts of expression; (b) harmful consequences of acts performed as a result of those acts of expression, where the connection between the acts of expression and the subsequent harmful acts consists merely in the fact that the act of expression led the agents to believe (or increased their tendency to believe) that those acts were worth doing. (Scanlon 1979/1995, pp. 158–159)

Similarly, I will argue that it is not acceptable to proscribe research for the reason that it can give knowledge with potentially harmful applications. My question will be, then: what are the morally acceptable reasons for proscribing research? I will argue that a number of reasons for restricting research are unacceptable and that research activity should only be forbidden in cases where identifiable individuals are harmed as a direct consequence of that activity. Hence, I think the third example of the protection of research subjects' right to consent, is the kind of situation where restrictions are justified, but that the first is an example of a situation where prohibitions are not justified. But even if there are strict limits to the legitimate restrictions on research, researchers have, of course, a number of *obligations* concerning how they undertake their research. With information technology research ethics, as with research ethics in general, it is, therefore, more fruitful to ask what obligations researchers have rather than what their rights are. It is not clear that researchers have any special rights qua researchers. However, as a result of their special knowledge, researchers are bound by a number of duties and obligations to the research community, to the public and to the society at large. But I will argue that these are obligations that must be enforced by the research community itself and not through legislation.

The constraints provided by the funding of the research is, however, a third kind of restriction on research that is different from both proscription through legislation and the ethical obligation of researchers to restrict research in the light of potentially harmful consequences. Because resources are scarce and some lines of research are more fruitful than others, there have to be mechanisms for the selection of the research that is considered to be most important and relevant. Science policy and questions of the prioritization of research should be the subject of public debate and subject to the control of democratic institutions. How this should be implemented raises a number of complex and controversial questions that are beyond the scope of this paper.[3]

SCIENCE AND VALUES

Max Weber (1949) argued that the scientist qua scientist does not make value judgments. In the early history of sociology, in which Weber was a pioneer, the sociologists were accused of having a political agenda with a leaning towards socialism. Weber protested against this and formulated his doctrine that science must be value-free as part of his resistance to political regulation of science. Weber did not, however, argue that values and politics had no role to play in shaping the role of science in society. He made a distinction between three different phases in the research process: (1) The choice of research topics; (2) The scientific activity of accepting and rejecting statements on the basis of evidence; and (3) The use of the scientific results. Weber argued that political and other social values were legitimate in the first and third phases, but should not play any role in the second. Science qua science could only legitimately concern itself with the investigation of ends in one of three ways, Weber argued.[4] First science could study the effectiveness of alternative means to a given end. Second, it could study unintended side effects of various policies. Third, science could undertake

---

3 For an interesting treatment, see Kitcher's discussion what he calls 'well-ordered science' in *Science, truth, and democracy* (Kitcher 2001).

4 See Proctor (1991, p. 136 ff.) and Raatikainen (2006).

analyses of the presuppositions of various political goals. Thus, the import of Weber's argument seems to be that, because science is value-free, political interference with the core of the scientific activity is inappropriate. Thus, politicians should not interfere with the scientific activity as such, but leave the objective search for better knowledge to the scientists, he argued.[5]

Weber's argument involves a distinction between the issues that are internal to science and those that are external to it. The internal, scientific activity should be value-free, in the sense that the scientists' acceptance or rejection of statements should not be influenced by values while values are legitimate in the decisions involved in the two other phases. Weber emphasises the political values, but, in addition, other norms and values are also involved in the external activity of science. For example, as Tranøy (1988) has emphasised, values are involved in the justification of the scientific activity to the rest of society.[6] Historically, there are two main traditions. The oldest tradition, which Tranøy calls the Platonic-Aristotelian tradition, emphasises the value of cognitive activity as an essential human activity that is valuable as such. The other tradition, which Tranøy calls 'Baconian,' justifies the scientific activity by appeal to 'knowledge as power' to control the environment and to develop technology that can be used to increase human welfare. Both strategies can be seen to involve value judgments, of course.

But it is clear that even the internal activity of research is governed by norms and values. At least there are methodological norms that define what good science is. Examples are norms of consistency and coherence, simplicity, intersubjectivity, and objectivity. In this sense, science is *essentially evaluative*, as Michael Scriven (1972/1994, p. 55) put it. But Weber should not have any problem with accepting that science is normative in this sense, because these are epistemic and not *ethical* norms. The question, then, is whether there are any genuinely ethical norms governing the scientific activity.

CUDOS

One interesting candidate are the norms identified by the sociologist Robert Merton (1973). He suggested a set of basic norms for scientific activity known under the acronym CUDOS: *communalism, universalism, disinterestedness,* and *organized skepticism.* The first norm of 'communalism' is that scientific knowledge should be publicly available to everybody in the scientific community and that there should be no hindrances to the flow of information among scientists. 'Universalism' is the norm that science should be free from prejudice in the sense that all contributions should be evaluated on their own merits, irrespective of the colour, background, social position, and so forth of the individual making the contribution. Third, the norm of

[5] Conversely, he argued that science could not replace politics, and he thus opposed scientism.
[6] See also Putnam (2002, chapter 2).

'disinterestedness' says that the scientific results shall not be modified, or in any way adapted, to fit any external interests like power, money, or ideology. 'Organized skepticism' means that science is committed to the norm that everything, in principle, can be questioned and that nothing should be accepted only because of tradition or authority. This last norm is closely related to that of 'originality,' which Merton later added to his list together with 'humility.' These norms are an important part of the normative structure of science and can be seen to be *constitutive* of science. This means that, even though the system clearly does not always live up to these ideals, an activity that was not committed to these norms could not be called science in the normal sense of the world.

The CUDOS norms are clearly ethical norms. But the question was whether they are norms that govern the acceptance or rejection of propositions in science. In some sense they are. However, they are primarily concerned with the social interaction in the search community, and only indirectly with the activity of doing science. The norms protect the scientific process itself from disturbance from irrelevant factors. Therefore, the CUDOS norms are not clear counter-examples to the claim that science is free of political and ethical values in Weber's sense. They do show, however, that this doctrine of value freedom has to be qualified in significant ways.

ETHICAL JUDGMENTS QUA SCIENTISTS

But there is an interesting line of argument to suggest that ethical values enter into even the acceptance and rejection of propositions. One of the central proponents of this position was Richard Rudner, who claims that scientists qua scientists make value judgments. He argued that a scientist who is doing research on some problem has to consider the field of application in his acceptance or rejection of claims. In his acceptance or rejection of claims, he has to take into consideration the consequences of errors. If the potential harm of his decision is great, he has to require greater certainty in order to accept a proposition:

... if the hypothesis under consideration were to the effect that a toxic ingredient of a drug was not present in lethal quantity, we would require a relative high degree of confirmation or confidence before accepting the hypothesis – for the consequences of a mistake here are exceedingly grave by our moral standards... *How sure we need to be before we accept a hypothesis will depend on how serious a mistake would be.* (Rudner 1953, p. 3; italics as in original)

It is from this argument that Rudner concludes that, if we accept that scientists qua scientists accept and reject hypotheses, we also have to accept that 'the scientist *qua* scientist makes value judgments' (Rudner 1953, p. 4).[7] We

---

7 A number of authors have argued for similar conclusions. A recent version is Shrader-Frechette's argument that scientist should minimize type-II errors in applied research (Shrader-Frechette 1994, chapter 6).

have already seen this kind of reasoning above, with Parnas's explanation of his refusal to contribute to the SDI-project. His argument was that the chances of a successful shield were low, and that the consequences of an imperfect shield would be very grave. Hence, he would not commit himself to the project of trying to develop the shield and, thereby, to contribute to the impression that it was a viable task.

I accept Rudner's general argument that scientists qua scientists make value judgments, with some qualifications. One question is whether it actually is true that scientists accept and reject hypotheses. This is controversial, but the discussion will not be pursued here.[8] But another issue is that Rudner's argument is most convincing in the context of applied research. It seems plausible to claim that a scientist, for example a meteorologist who considers whether it is true that the global warming is caused by human activity, should take the consequences of being mistaken into consideration. But it is not equally plausible to claim this with respect to the theoretical computer scientist who, for example, proves theorems in some algebraic system.

Still, the claim that value judgments are essentially involved in at least some parts of science seems plausible. But is it possible to distinguish between pure and applied research in the way suggested above? Philip Kitcher (2001) has argued that it is not. He has offered an argument against the fact-value distinction in science that is more general than Rudner's. Against those who believe there is a clear distinction between facts and values, the value-free search for truth and politics, he argues that in science there is never a search for truth as such. Rather, there is a search for *significant* truths – that is, a search for truths that are considered to be significant enough to be worth pursuing. There are, of course, millions of trivial truths that nobody is interested in. Hence, all kinds of research are embedded in practical projects undertaken by humans, Kitcher argues, and for this reason the search for these truths is not value-free but based on consideration of significance relative to some goals. Therefore, science is always part of a *practical* project and, consequently, the scientific activity should be evaluated normatively.

Kitcher argues against what he calls 'the myth of purity,' which is the idea that:

The sciences seek to establish truths about nature. How the resultant knowledge is used is a matter for moral, social, and political debate. But it is intrinsically valuable for us to gain knowledge. If the circumstances in which knowledge is applied are likely to generate harmful consequences, then that is a sign of defects in the social milieu that surrounds the sciences. (Kitcher 2001, p. 85)

---

[8] Richard Jeffrey (1956) claimed that this picture of scientific activity is misleading. What scientists actually do, he argued, is only to assign probabilities to propositions. He used this to argue against Rudner's position. But my argument does not depend essentially on the assumption that scientists accept and reject propositions, so I will not discuss this issue further.

But this clearly presupposes that it is possible to make a distinction between pure science and the application of science in, for example, technology. 'The most popular form of the myth [of purity] supposes there is a straight-forward distinction between pure and applied science, or between 'basic research' and technology' (Kitcher 2001, p. 86). But Kitcher argues that the distinction is not so clear. He first argues that the only way to formu-late the distinction must be in terms of the aims of the individual scientist. The claim of the myth of purity has to be something like this: 'The aim of science (pure science, basic science) is to find truth; the aim of tech-nology (applied research) is to solve practical problems' (Kitcher 2001, p. 87). But it is not possible to make a clear distinction in this way, Kitcher argues: 'The aim of science is not to discover any old truths but to discover significant truths.' If we look at the aims of most individual scientists, there is a mix of motivation rooted in epistemic and practical significance. It is, therefore, not possible to draw a clear distinction between basic research and applied technological research. Rather than a clear distinction between context free basic science and technology, there is a *continuum* where we can distinguish extreme cases. And Kitcher admits: 'Even though we can't find a sharp distinction between pure science and technology, we can still use a vague distinction that separates very clear cases' (Kitcher 2001, p. 88).

In my view, we should not give up the idea that there are differences between basic research that is primarily motivated by theoretical questions and research aimed at the solution of technological problems. Niiniluoto (1993) has argued convincingly that we should distinguish between research aimed at the characterization of phenomena ('descriptive science') and research that is aimed at providing the basis for the design of artefacts of different kinds. Descriptive science aims at the characterization of facts about the world, for example the formulation of causal relationships. In this way, descriptive science can provide explanations and, in some cases, even predictions of events. Design science, in contrast, is concerned with the formulation of *technical norms*[9] of the form: 'If you want A, and you believe you are in situation B, then you ought to do X' (Niiniluoto 1993, p. 12).

Large parts of computer science fall into this category. This kind of sci-ence aims at providing knowledge that will be helpful in the construction of artefacts and in the manipulation of the environment for some purpose. Note that the antecedent here (A) has to be something that can be influ-enced by human action.

It is clear that design science, to a larger extent than descriptive science, involves value judgments. First of all, the statements of design sciences will have more direct practical consequences that give the researcher a respon-sibility for taking the risks involved into consideration in the dissemination of the research, as Rudner pointed out. Furthermore, the practical norms

9 The term 'technical norm' Niiniluoto borrows from von Wright (1963).

formulated by the design sciences give rise to normative questions concerning the goal in the antecedent, the judgment of the current situation B, and the relationship between X, B, and A (Niiniluoto 1993, p. 16). The same kind of value questions do not arise in connection with descriptive science. But we can maintain that there is this difference and at the same time admit that there is no clear distinction to be made but, rather, a continuum of cases: some parts of science will be both descriptive and oriented towards applications. At one end of the extreme, we will have basic, descriptive research that is relatively value-free, and at the other end, we have technological development that is permeated with normative issues.

Where has this discussion of the role of ethical values in science brought us with respect to the question of the restriction of science? The argument against the regulation of science with which we started was that the scientific activity is value-free and that science, therefore, could not be restricted for moral reasons without going against the very nature of the scientific activity. But with the rejection of the fact-value distinction, this position can no longer be maintained. This is true in particular in the case of research on information technology, which to a large extent can be classified as design science.

REGULATION OF RESEARCH

But, even if this line of argument against the regulation of science fails, it does not follow that no argument against the restriction of science is sound. It seems clear from the discussion here that researchers at least have an obligation to take ethical concerns into consideration in their research. Hence, scientists should in some cases restrict their own research activity for moral reasons. But this kind of restriction should be sharply distinguished from the external prohibition of certain types of research. The next question to be asked, then, is whether there are morally acceptable reasons for *proscribing* research. Could the research into certain subjects be forbidden because it has the potential for harm?

I will argue that research should be proscribed only if the research activity itself has harmful consequences for individuals. This kind of situation is exemplified by the third case above, where research is restricted because of concern for the well-being and integrity of research subjects. Conversely, I will argue that we should not proscribe research because it is considered by some to be offensive. In particular, I think the arguments that have been put forward in support of a proscription of some forms of artificial intelligence research are not convincing.

Let me start by briefly considering one aspect of the criticism of artificial intelligence research that I think is misguided. This is the charge that the result of this research will be dehumanization. Joseph Weizenbaum (1976) argued that artificial intelligence research would be dehumanizing in two ways. First, there is a gulf between humans and machines because machines cannot have access to the same experiences that humans have and that are characteristic of human life. In particular, machines can never experience the emotions involved in personal relations among humans. For this reason, Weizenbaum argued, there are some contexts in which it would be a violation of human integrity to put machines in the place of humans because it would always involve a kind of deceit. His favourite example was psychotherapy. Weizenbaum argued that it would be essentially deceptive to replace the therapist with a machine because a machine could never understand the experiences that the patient talked about. It is clear that if the patient believes that the machine understands what he is talking about in the same sense as a human being would understand it, then he would be deceived. The problem is that it is hard to understand why it would be deceptive if the patient is fully aware of the limitations of the machine and accepts the interaction on the basis of adequate information. Hence, it is not clear that the use of artificial intelligence in such contexts is essentially dehumanizing.

But Weizenbaum also argued that the research itself was dehumanizing because he felt that the models of man in artificial intelligence in the seventies were simplistic and reductionistic. There can be little doubt that the models Weizenbaum discussed were simplistic. However, it is not so clear that the effect of their employment was dehumanizing. As Margaret Boden (1987) has pointed out, one thing that we learned from this research was that many tasks that humans consider essentially trivial and simple, are in fact extremely difficult to model in a machine. The so-called frame problem is a case in point. But this, Boden argues, rather makes us more aware of and impressed with the complexity of the human mind than before. However, this effect is the opposite of dehumanization.

Similar remarks could be made about Bill Joy's fear that the development of technological extensions of humans, that is, the development of cyborgs, is dehumanizing. He fears that the 'dream of robotics' will eventually come true and that 'we will gradually replace ourselves with our robotic technology, achieving near immortality by downloading our consciousness.' But a different perspective on this development is possible. Andy Clark (2003) has argued that we are natural-born cyborgs, and that the technological extensions of the human mind and body are really a further development of our humanity:

My claim, in contrast, is that various kinds of deep human-machine symbiosis really do expand and alter the shape of the psychological processes of who we are. The old technologies of pen and paper have deeply impacted the shape and form of biological reason in mature, literate brains. The presence of such technologies, and their modern and more responsive counterparts, does not merely act as a convenient wrap around for a fixed biological engine of reason. Nor does it merely free up neural resources. It provides instead an array of resources to which biological brains, as they learn and grow, will dovetail their own activities. The moral, for now, is simply that this process of fitting, tailoring, and factoring in leads to the creation of extended computational and mental organizations: reasoning and thinking systems distributed across brain, body, and world. And it is in the operation of these extended systems that much of our distinctive human intelligence inheres. (Clark 2003, pp. 32–33)

It is not possible here to go into the details of the cognitive science research that Clark uses to substantiate his idea that we are natural-born cyborgs. The point for our discussion, however, is that he gives a very clear and detailed defence of the idea that there is not a biological core, but that the technological extensions of our minds and brains could be seen as a deepening of our characteristically human way of functioning in the world. Hence, the criticism that these forms of artificial intelligence and robotics research are potentially dehumanizing could be questioned.

It is also instructive to look very briefly on the most recent case of a restriction of research – the temporary ban on the cloning of humans. Most countries in the world have issued legislation that in effect proscribes human cloning. There are, of course, a lot of religious and ideological reasons for being against cloning, but such reasons are controversial and do not have universal acceptance. There is, however, one kind of argument that is uncontroversial and, in fact, seems to be decisive. This argument is not that a result in the form of a human clone would be ethically problematic, that the identity of the person would be unclear, for example. The decisive argument for the ban on human cloning is that the development of the technique would involve unacceptable risks to the clones (Brock 1998). It would not be ethically acceptable to do all the experiments that would be necessary in order to make the technique reliable. The creation of Dolly was successful only after a great number of failed attempts which resulted in stillborn individuals or individuals born with severely damaged bodies. The development of the techniques necessary for the cloning of a human being would be much more difficult than the cloning of a sheep and would thus involve highly unethical experiments. This seems to be the strongest and most universally accepted reason for the temporary ban on cloning. It is important to note here that this is precisely a reason that arises from the concern for the risk to research subjects, that is, the concern that the research would come up against the fundamental rights of identifiable human subjects. There is no general acceptance of the idea that the cloning itself would be so bad that the necessary knowledge should not be developed, or that cloning as such would be an unacceptable practice. The point here is not to discuss the problem of human cloning, as such. The point is only that it seems difficult to find modern examples of cases of proscription of research that are not related to harm to concrete individuals. This should make us at least slightly worried by the idea of proscribing research in the area of artificial intelligence where the concerns are much less clear than with human cloning.

FREEDOM OF SPEECH AND FREEDOM OF RESEARCH

I have argued that, even though we should reject the fact-value distinction, it is still an open question whether the value-ladenness of science licenses the restriction of science through legislation. In the previous section I have argued that there are certain arguments that have been used to criticize artificial intelligence research that give few clear reasons to think that the restriction of this research is a good idea. Furthermore, I have suggested that in the most recent case of the proscription of research, namely, cloning, it is the unacceptable risk to potential clones in the development of the cloning technique that is the problem, and not the fact that some find the idea of a human clone repulsive. Both of these sets of considerations, even though they are inconclusive, should make us skeptical of the idea of the proscription of research on the basis of *content* – in contrast to regulation on the basis of a risk of potential harm to concrete individuals. Let me turn now to the more general question about the proscription of research.

The connection between the ideas of freedom of expression and freedom of research is central to the argument that follows. That there is a strong connection between the freedom of expression and the freedom of research can be seen by considering the justifications for the freedom of expression. Following Scanlon (1979/1995), we can distinguish arguments for freedom of speech that are oriented towards the protection of the interests of the speaker in convincing his or her audience from those arguments that are oriented towards the interests of the *audience* in being reliably informed. The speaker-oriented justifications emphasise the value of free speech to the speaker's personal development, her autonomy, and so forth. This is the most important justification for free speech in the private sphere, and does not seem to apply to the freedom of research. Historically the most important justifications for the freedom of expression, however, are audience-oriented. These are the classical justification of the freedom of speech, which argues that it promotes the search for truth in the 'marketplace of ideas' (Mill) and the development of democracy (Meiklejohn). These audience-oriented reasons are obviously also central to the justification of freedom of research.

With this as a background, let me turn to the discussion of reasons for restricting research. In a recent paper, John Weckert sheds interesting light on the question of the regulation of research. Weckert starts with a discussion of an argument made by biologist and Nobel laureate David Baltimore. Baltimore's position is that no external limitations should be put on *basic research*. His arguments are directed against attempts to regulate science on the basis of content: 'society can choose to have more science or less science, but choosing *which* science to have is not a feasible alternative' (Baltimore 1979, p. 43). Baltimore gives several arguments for this view. One of his arguments is that knowledge increases freedom: 'Science creates freedom by widening our range of understanding and therefore the possibilities from which we can choose' (Baltimore 1979, p. 42). The argument is that the dissemination of research into society increases freedom, and that the restriction of research would reduce this freedom. Weckert points out that with this argument Baltimore defends freedom of research as a kind of freedom of speech. However, Weckert thinks that this argument is not decisive, because, although freedom of expression 'is an important good, it is not the only one, and it can be in conflict with others. In general, we are restricted in the performance of actions that will, or are likely to harm others. Again, it is not clear why research should be treated differently' (Weckert 2003, p. 277). Now, Weckert has to have in mind here cases where it would be *morally justified* to restrict the freedom of expression. He does not, however, give any examples of the cases he has in mind.

But I think Weckert's objection to the argument from freedom of expression is plausible, given Baltimore's version of it. But I think a much stronger version of an argument for the freedom of research as a kind of freedom of expression can be given. Note that freedom of expression is a right to freedom from certain forms of interference. This takes the form of rules that sets limitations to the types of restrictions that can be put on your speech. It is important, now, to distinguish between *different types* of regulations of speech and to see that some are more problematic than others. Sunstein (2003) distinguishes between three kinds of regulations. First, there are restrictions on the basis of 'time, place, and manner.' These are limitations on speech that are made for reasons that have nothing to do with the content of the utterances. This kind of regulation is often not controversial. For example, it is not a violation of the right to freedom of speech that it is prohibited to paint graffiti on the walls of public buildings. Second, there are limitations that are based on content but that are neutral with respect to viewpoint. For example, some countries do not allow political commercials on television. This is a restriction on the freedom of speech based on content, that is, on the specification of a certain type of speech, but it applies equally to all viewpoints. This is a controversial form of regulation, of course, but not as problematic as the third kind, restrictions of speech that are *viewpoint specific*. An example of this would be a prohibition of racist utterances.

Consider, first, the limitation of speech on the basis of 'time, place, and manner.' These are limitations on speech that are not concerned with the content of the speech but are justified on practical grounds or in order to protect individual rights. In particular, your right to privacy sets limitations on my right to freedom of expression; my right to freedom of speech does not give me the right to give speeches in your living room against your will. Hence, this kind of limitation of freedom of speech is considered to be uncontroversial. By the same token, the restriction of *research* because it is a violation of the integrity of research subjects is often considered to be uncontroversial as well. One problem with Baltimore's general argument against the regulation of research, then, is that it would serve equally well as an argument against the restriction of research in order to protect research subjects. This seems to me to be an indication that the argument is too broad.

But the observation above also points to a problem with Weckert's argument. Weckert correctly points out that we are willing to limit freedom of speech in some cases. But this fact does not show that it would be justified to make restrictions in every case where the freedom of speech is in conflict with other interests. In particular, the fact that we are willing to limit research on the basis of considerations pertaining to the right to privacy of research subjects does not show that it also would be acceptable to restrict research on the basis of content. In order to make progress on the question of the justifiability of restricting research, we have to be more specific in the framing of the question. The question is, to repeat, whether it is justified to proscribe research for the reason that its content is *potentially* harmful or repulsive. It is difficult to give a convincing argument to show this.

REASONS FOR FREEDOM OF RESEARCH

I do not know of a decisive argument to show that restrictions of research on the basis of content are never justified. I have not encountered any uncontroversial examples of such regulations, however. Furthermore, I think there are strong reasons for being skeptical of the regulation of research on the basis of content. Historically, there have been examples of ideologically motivated regulations of science that had disastrous consequences. For example, in the Soviet Union in the Stalin area, the state endorsed as an official doctrine Lysenko's theory of the inheritance of acquired traits and rejected Darwinism, together with the theory of relativity and quantum mechanics. And in Germany, under the Nazi regime, there was a ban on 'Jewish science' and only 'Aryan science' was accepted. Indeed, it was on the background of excesses like these that Robert Merton formulated his CUDOS norms. These norms are constitutive of the scientific activity itself and cannot be violated without undermining the science itself. Hence, regulations that violate these norms will turn research into a different kind of activity.

But, even if these examples show that regulations of science on the basis of content can be extremely problematic, they fail to show that such regulations are never justified. What the examples show, I think, is that *viewpoint-based* restrictions could be a threat to science itself. It is still possible, I think, that *viewpoint-neutral* regulations could be justified in some cases. But I think that there are reasons to be skeptical even here. Compare, first, with the potential viewpoint-neutral restrictions on the freedom of speech. In Norway, for example, there is a prohibition against political commercials on television. The argument for this is that is a special type of speech that is by its very nature manipulative. Therefore, it can be subject to special regulations that would not be acceptable for other types of speech. In particular, it would be highly problematic to subject scientific information to such a restriction. Hence, it is difficult to find examples of content-based restrictions on freedom of expression that would indicate that similar limitations on research might be justified.

There are also general reasons to be skeptical of even viewpoint-neutral restrictions on the basis of the contents of research. First, there is the argument concerning the marketplace of ideas. Second, it can be argued that it goes against the point, from society's perspective, of supporting science in the first place. Consider the following analogy of Tim Scanlon's:

Suppose that one person, call him the monarch, who is longer on money than on the time or inclination to do research, decides that the best way for him to be well informed on certain subjects is to hire another person, call him the counselor, to spend his full time investigating these subjects and reporting his findings. Once the monarch has made his decision and as long as he does not revoke it – as long, that is, as he continues to justify his support of the counselor in a way just described – it is irrational for him to influence the report anything other than his own considered opinions on the matters he is hired to investigate. . . . What would be irrational in the sense I have in mind would be, for example, for the monarch to forbid his counselor to consider certain evidence even if he thought it relevant, or for him to decree that the counselor will be fired if his findings run contrary to the opinions of the monarch's senile father. (Scanlon 1975, pp. 238–239)

Scanlon suggests that it would be irrational to regulate in a similar way how science is done in a university, for example. Now, Scanlon uses this analogy to argue that there is a right to academic freedom. This question of the rights of the individual researchers I will put to one side for now. But I do think the analogy illustrates the importance of the idea of freedom in the conduct of research to the rationale of science as a social institution.

Note that on this image not every kind of content-based restriction of research would be irrational. It would not be irrational of those who pay for the research to require that scientists use their research time to work on certain types of problems because they are considered to be of more importance than other problems. This is, of course, a kind of content-based restriction on research. Research institutions regularly restrict the research activity in this way. But this is a very different kind of restriction from one where certain topics of research are *prohibited* on a general basis so that a research institution is forbidden to choose to research the subject (because the knowledge would be harmful). For example, when the Lighthill report argued in 1973 that AI research had not tackled the problem of combinatorial explosion and had provided too little by way of practical applications, the result was a decrease in funding of AI research in Britain. Indeed, from the point of view of the individual scientist in AI, this might not seem very different in practice from a prohibition. But there are important differences both in the nature and the justification of the restriction. With the content-based restrictions deemed to be irrational by Scanlon above, research is proscribed because its results are *unwelcome*. In the case of AI research, however, there was not a proscription of the search for certain types of knowledge. For example, there was no ban on privately funded AI research. The argument was, rather, that the research – in the opinion of the Lighthill report – had not given enough significant results. I am not arguing that the Lighthill report was correct, of course.[10] The point is that resources will always be limited, and that some research programmes are more fruitful than others. Hence, there has to be a selection of what are the important areas of research that should be prioritized. How this should be done in a democratic society is an important and controversial issue, but one that cannot be pursued here.[11]

POTENTIALLY HARMFUL RESULTS

Kitcher has argued that even in cases where the content of the research gives the researchers themselves a reason to limit the research, the *proscription* of research is not justified. Kitcher starts with Mill's defence of freedom of speech. He suggests that the ideal of human flourishing that is central to Mill's argument could be turned on its head. In at least some cases where research negatively affects the potential for individual flourishing and development, research should be restricted. He argues by way of an analysis of an example inspired by the discussion of the consequences of sociobiological research. He constructs a case of an objectively underprivileged group of people in a society, and where the following is true (Kitcher 2001, p. 102ff.).

- There is a prejudice in the society that the characteristic C of the people within the underprivileged group makes them unsuitable to a particular role R. This prejudice used to be held generally but is now held only by a minority.
- It is known that people will tend to believe in evidence that would seem to support the prejudice but that they will tend to ignore evidence that it is not true.
- If the prejudice is again widely accepted, then the quality of life of people in the underprivileged group will be adversely affected.
- It is known that people will overestimate the probabilities assigned to a confirmation of the hypothesis that the prejudice is true and underestimate the probabilities assigned to the negation of the hypothesis.
- It is very likely that the evidence obtained from research on the hypothesis will be indecisive.
- There is a strong bias in favour of the hypothesis, so people will consequently assign a probability close to 1.

[10] See McCarthy's criticism (McCarthy 1993).
[11] See Kitcher (2001) for an interesting treatment of this issue.

In such a case, Kitcher argues, the concern for the quality of life for the underprivileged group would be a reason strong enough to limit research into the question. A number of empirical assumptions are involved here, but I think a situation like this is not unrealistic and that it is plausible to claim, as Kitcher does, that in this case it would be justified to restrict the research in order to avoid the negative consequences. Furthermore, this would be a restriction of research on the basis of the content of research.

The point, now, is that the risk of negative consequences of the research would give the researcher a reason to restrict their research but it is not clear that it would also give a good reason for the government to put a ban on this research. 'Demanding a ban on inquiry under such conditions would be to take a further, illegitimate, step' (Kitcher 2001, p. 105). Kitcher's argument against a proscription is that an institutionalized ban on research in this area would only make the situation worse for the underprivileged group it was intended to protect, because an official ban would increase the suspicion that the prejudice is correct:

In a world where (for example) research into race differences in I.Q. is banned, the residues of belief in the inferiority of members of certain races are reinforced by the idea that official ideology has stepped in to conceal an uncomfortable truth. Prejudice can be buttressed as those who oppose the ban proclaim themselves to be gallant heirs to Galileo. When the Caucasian child asks why research into differences between racial groups is not allowed, a superficially plausible answer will be that everyone knows what the research would show and that people are unwilling to face the unpleasant truth. Proscribing the research has consequences of the same general kind as allowing it – except that they are probably worse. (Kitcher 2001, p. 105)

The argument here is developed with reference to one particular kind of example with a number of empirical assumptions indicated rather vaguely. But I do think Kitcher's discussion brings out the more general point that the proscription of research into certain areas of knowledge will easily be counter-productive.[12]

The discussion of Kitcher's example shows that it is important to be careful with the distinction between rights and obligations in this context. I have argued that the freedom of expression is an important part of the freedom of research. However, there are clear cases where the right to freedom of research is limited by the rights of others, for example, research subjects. The regulation of research on the basis of content is more problematic, however. But still, as Kitcher's example shows, researchers will have obligations to take the consequences of their research into consideration and sometimes to restrict their research. It is worth noting, however, that the protection of research is on the institutional level. It is, of course, not the individual researcher's right to freedom of research that makes the regulation of

---

[12] That it is often not practically *possible* to stop the research in this way is another matter.

research on the basis of content problematic but rather the consequences for the role of research in society.

THE OBLIGATIONS OF RESEARCHERS

A richer perspective on the ethics of the limitations of research opens up if we focus on the obligations of researchers rather on their rights. Following Onora O'Neill (1996), let us make some distinctions among obligations. First, there is the distinction between perfect and imperfect obligations. Perfect obligations are such that there are corresponding rights, that is, that there are specific recipients of the obligations. The obligation not to violate the integrity of research subjects is an example of a perfect obligation. On the other hand, the duty to do research and to follow the methodological norms of science is an example of an imperfect obligation because there is no corresponding right. The second distinction is between general and special obligations. This is the distinction between obligations every person has, in contrast to the obligations that come from a special role. A researcher's special obligations are the obligations he has in virtue of being a researcher, for example, the obligations that arise from the special knowledge he possesses.

In my view, researchers qua researchers have no special rights in the moral sense. The right to freedom of expression is a general right. The freedom of research, however, is most fruitfully seen, I think, as a freedom enjoyed by the research community rather than an individual right of each researcher. But, on the other hand, researchers certainly have a number of special *obligations*, that is, duties they have by virtue of being researchers. These obligations are the basis for significant moral restrictions on research.

As an example let me mention Shrader-Frechette (1994), who gives a recent account of research ethics as a system of obligations. She argues, as others have done with respect to other professions, that many of the obligations of researchers are rooted in the fact that they have a specialised knowledge and that the scientific community is trusted with a high degree of autonomy. By way of example, Shrader-Frechette points out that the researchers have an obligation to do research, because:

along with special knowledge, power, and benefits, come special responsibilities. Scientists' responsibilities for research in their respective fields arise largely because they are the only people qualified to perform it. Hence they have a responsibility because of their trustee status, their ability, their near monopoly over advances in certain areas, their training, and their knowledge. (Shrader-Frechette 1994, p. 25)

But researchers also have the duty not to do certain kinds of research, for example, research that causes unjustified risk, research that violates informed consent, or biased research. And, again, researchers have obligations to consider the social consequences of their research. We saw that

Parnas argued extensively from these kinds of obligations in his refusal to take part in the SDI project.

There is not space here to go into an extensive discussion of this system of obligations. The examples are just meant to indicate the rich structure of obligations that imposes restrictions on research. The point I want to emphasise is that it is with these obligations that we find the most extensive moral restrictions on the research process.

CONCLUSION

I have argued that an analogue of the principle of freedom of expression formulated by Scanlon applies to the freedom of research. The principle rejects certain reasons for restricting research as unacceptable. Although it is acceptable to proscribe research because of risk of harm to identifiable individuals caused by the research process, it is not acceptable to proscribe research on the basis of content, I have argued. In Scanlon's terms, harmful consequences of research are not acceptable grounds for proscribing research 'if the harmful consequences of acts performed as a result of those acts of expression, where the connection between the acts of expression and the subsequent harmful acts consists merely in the fact that the act of expression led the agents to believe (or increased their tendency to believe) that those acts were worth doing.' Still, as Kitcher's example shows, in a case where there are such indirect relations as Scanlon describes between the dissemination of the research and the harms to the vulnerable group, the researchers might very well have the obligation to restrict their research in the light of the possible harms.

If we apply this analysis to the three examples with which the chapter started, I would reject Joy's suggestion that the freedom of research should be limited in the light of the possible negative influence on the development of the conception of what it is to be human. However, the proscription of research that poses unjustified risks to research subjects, as exemplified by the third case, would be acceptable on this analysis. But at the same time, the discussion has stressed the important role that the special obligations of researchers have in the restriction of research.

References

Baltimore, D. 1979. Limiting science: A biologist's perspective, in G. Holton and R. S. Morison, (Eds), *Limits of scientific inquiry*. New York: Norton, pp. 37–45.

Boden, M. A. 1987. Artificial intelligence: Cannibal or missionary? *AI and Society, 1*, 1, 17–23.

Brock, D. W. 1998. Cloning human beings: An assessment of the ethical issues pro and con, in M. C. Nussbaum and C. R. Sunstein (Eds.), *Clones and clones: Facts and fantasies about human cloning*. New York: Norton, pp. 141–164.

Bruckman, A. 2002. *Ethical guidelines for research online.* Retrieved June 18, 2005 from http://www.cc.gatech.edu/~asb/ethics/.

Clark, A. 2003. *Natural-born cyborgs.* Oxford: Oxford University Press.

European Parliament. 1995. *Directive 95/46/EC* on The protection of individuals with regard to the processing of personal data and the free movement of such data, adopted October 24 1195, *Official Journal, 281*, pp. 31–50, Brussels.

Jeffrey, R. 1956. Valuation and acceptance of scientific hypotheses. *Philosophy of Science, 23*, 3, 237–246.

Joy, B. 1999. Why the future doesn't need us. *Wired, 8,* 4. Retrieved June 28, 2005 from http://www.wired.com/wired/archive/8.04/joy.html.

Kitcher, P. 2001. *Science, truth, and democracy.* Oxford: Oxford University Press.

Kurzweil, R. 1999. *The age of spiritual machines.* New York: Textere.

McCarthy, J. 1993. Review of *Artificial intelligence: A general survey.* Retrieved August 15, 2005 from http://www.formal.stanford.edu/jmc/reviews/lighthill/lighthill.html.

Merton, R. 1973. *The sociology of science.* Chicago: University of Chicago Press.

NESH. 2003. *Research ethics guidelines for Internet research.* National Committee for Research Ethics in the Social Sciences and the Humanities, Oslo.

Niiniluoto, I. 1993. The aim and structure of applied research. *Erkenntnis, 38,* 1–21.

O'Neill, O. 1996. *Towards justice and virtue.* Cambridge, UK: Cambridge University Press.

Parnas, D. L. 1987/1990. Professional responsibility to blow the whistle on SDI, in M. D. Ermann et al. (Eds.), *Computers, ethics, and society.* Oxford: Oxford University Press, pp. 359–371.

Posner, R. A. 2005. *Catastrophe, risk and response.* Oxford: Oxford University Press.

Proctor, R. N. 1991. *Value-free science?* Cambridge, MA: Harvard University Press.

Putnam, H. 2002. *The collapse of the act/value distinction.* Cambridge, MA: Harvard University Press.

Raatikainen, P. 2006. The scope and limits of value-freedom in science, in H. Koskinen, S. Pihlström, and R. Vilkko (Eds.), *Science – A Challenge to Philosophy? (Scandinavian University Studies in the Humanities and Social Sciences, Vol. 27).* Frankfurt am Main: Peter Lang.

Rudner, R. 1953. The scientist qua scientist makes value judgments. *Philosophy of Science, 20,* 1, 1–6.

Scanlon, T. 1975. Academic freedom and the control of research, in E. L. Pincoffs, (Ed.), *The concept of academic freedom.* Austin: University of Texas Press, pp. 237–254.

Scanlon, T. M. 1979/1995. Freedom of expression and categories of expression, in R. M. Stewart (Ed.), *Readings in social and political philosophy.* Oxford: Oxford University Press, pp. 152–170.

Scanlon, T. 1990. Content regulation revisited, in J. Lichtenberg (Ed.), *Democracy and mass media.* Cambridge, UK: Cambridge University Press, pp. 331–354.

Scriven, M. 1972/1994. The exact role of value judgments in science, in E. Erwin, S. Gendin, and L. Kleinman (Eds.), *Ethical issues in scientific research.* New York: Garland, pp. 51–64.

Shrader-Frechette, K. 1994. *Ethics of scientific research.* London: Rowman & Littlefield.

Sunstein, C. R. 2003. *Why societies need dissent.* Cambridge, MA: Harvard University Press.

Tranøy, K. E. 1988. *The moral import of science.* Søreidgrend: Sigma.

von Wright, H. 1963. *Norm and action.* London: Routledge & Kegan Paul.

Weber, M. 1949. *The methodology of the social sciences.* Translated by E. A. Shils and H. A. Finch. Glencoe, IL: Free Press.

Weckert, J. 2003. Lilliputian computer ethics, in J. H. Moor and T. W. Bynum (Eds.), *Cyberphilosophy.* Oxford: Blackwell, pp. 271–279.

Weizenbaum, J. 1976. *Computer power and human reason.* Harmondsworth: Penguin.

18

Distributive Justice and the Value of Information

A *(Broadly) Rawlsian Approach*

Jeroen van den Hoven and Emma Rooksby

INTRODUCTION

Distributive justice in contemporary information societies concerns, among other issues, the distribution of information, information services, and information infrastructures. There is currently much enthusiasm about the potential of new information and communication technologies (ICTs), and the immense information resources contained on the World Wide Web, to improve the lives of those who have access to them. But at the same time, there is mounting concern over the uneven distribution of the new information wealth, both within nations and internationally. Some even fear that we may be heading for a regime of local and global 'information-apartheid' (Ratan 1995; Wresch 1996; Loader 1998; Schiller 1996), in which the 'information-haves' are segregated from the 'information have-nots'.

A host of empirical research adds force to such concerns. According to a 2005 UNCTAD study (UNCTAD 2006) the digital divide in the first years of the twenty-first century between nations is still wide. A person in a high-income country is more than twenty-two times more likely to be an Internet user than one in a low-income nation. In a high-income country, Internet affordability relative to income is more than 150 times better than in a low-income nation. Even in lower-middle-income countries, the cost of twenty hours of inferior Internet service is nearly one-third the average monthly income. In high-income countries the cost of Internet service is affordable for most households, although the report claims that, even within these countries, considerable digital divides continue to exist between urban and rural areas, genders, age groups, and racial groups.

Among some of the more obvious inequalities within countries are: that information infrastructures tend to be developed in affluent areas first or exclusively; that information routes charge tolls that only the rich can afford to pay; that information providers and electronic publishers charge high prices for access to interesting and high-quality information; and that, even when access is provided at affordable cost, not all are equally trained or equipped to use the technology effectively. Inequalities also exist, in related forms, at the international level. Many developing countries, particularly in Africa, have very little information infrastructure, and the majority of citizens in most developing countries have neither the bandwidth nor the currency to afford the prices often charged for information provided from developed countries. Most agricultural, genetic, medical and pharmacological information, and accurate long-term weather forecast information is proprietary, so that it is very difficult for poor citizens of developing countries to benefit directly from the advance in scientific disciplines that are most useful to their development. Highly restrictive global and bilateral regulations on intellectual property (IP) in the field of ICTs, and ever more stringent copyright systems for information content, have made the ideal of an information society for all appear even more remote in the opening years of the twenty-first century than in the last decade of the previous century. Many citizens in developing countries also lack access to affordable training in the use of information technology, and some lack one essential prerequisite for making use of information, namely, literacy.

The majority of commentators agree that, notwithstanding their much-discussed equalizing and empowering potential, new information and communication technologies may also maintain, and even exacerbate, existing inequalities as they are grafted onto preexisting socioeconomic structures. As the vast and growing literature focusing on the 'digital divide' attests, many researchers are alive to the existence of different levels of access to ICTs within and across countries. To date, many hundreds of articles have presented empirical studies of levels of access to ICTs, particularly within developed countries. Much, too, has been written on the policy implications of inequalities in access to ICTs. However, almost no work has been done in developing normative analyses of such inequalities, in order to demonstrate what is morally problematic about them.[1] Yet, we would maintain, normative principles are necessary for the articulation of cogent criticism of the market forces and allocation practices that sustain or exacerbate existing social and economic inequalities, as well as to develop proposals for reform, both nationally and internationally.

In this chapter we take up the task of developing a normative analysis of inequalities in relation to information goods. Building upon a chapter in *Information Technology and Moral Philosophy* (van den Hoven 1995), we develop a Rawlsian conception of justice, which we use as a framework for thinking about the just distribution of information, and, more generally, about social inclusion in information societies. Employment of the Rawlsian framework enables us to argue for the importance of information for citizens of a polity, and to articulate principles governing the distribution of

---

[1] One exception of which we are aware is Drahos and Braithwaite (1996, pp. 171–198).

information within a polity. Consideration of some of the major objections that have been made to Rawls's theory of justice helps to fine-tune the principles, whether by suggesting modification the Rawlsian framework, or by showing how it can accommodate the objections in question.

INFORMATION AS A PRIMARY GOOD

Rawls's Conception of Primary Goods

John Rawls's theory of justice has been a major influence in normative political theory, moral philosophy and applied ethics since the publication of his groundbreaking *A Theory of Justice* in 1971. This work and the literature it has inspired now cover many issues relevant to the design of a just society, including, for instance, health care, education, social security, and tax law.

In *A Theory of Justice*, Rawls presents a political theory of justice, that is, a theory that does not presume or entail any particular substantive moral theory. The aim of the book is to determine the correct principles of justice to guide the design of the basic institutions of a society; more detailed articulation of the workings of these institutions is not included. Rawls arrived at two principles of justice, which have been somewhat refined over the years:

FIRST PRINCIPLE: Each person is to have an equal right to a fully adequate scheme of equal basic liberties compatible with a similar system of liberties for all [*the liberty principle*].

SECOND PRINCIPLE: Social and economic inequalities are to satisfy two conditions. First, they must be attached to offices and positions open to all under conditions of fair equality of opportunity [*the opportunity principle*]; and, second, they must be to the greatest benefit of the least advantaged members of society [*the difference principle*]. (Rawls 1982a, p. 5)

Satisfaction of the first, or liberty, principle is to take lexicographical priority over the second; that is to say, the equality of liberties and rights available to all under the first principle may not be sacrificed for an improved satisfaction, no matter how large, of the second principle. For example, a small inequality in the liberty of conscience cannot be justified by any reduction, no matter how great, in social or economic inequality.

These are the principles of justice that, according to Rawls, would be agreed upon in a hypothetical choice situation (which he calls the 'Original Position') by rational, risk-averse, and mutually disinterested parties, when asked to agree together on the moral principles that ought to guide the design of the basic structures of society. The parties are taken to decide behind a 'veil of ignorance', unaware of their social situation, needs, interests, or natural endowments; the veil of ignorance prevents them from tailoring the principles to suit themselves to the disadvantage of others. The parties *do* have a general understanding of what is good for them, irrespective of their particular social situation and needs, and regardless of their comprehensive theory of the good. They are all taken to value what Rawls calls the 'primary goods', namely those goods of which all can agree that all require them as conditions for their well-being. (A more detailed specification of primary goods is given below.)

The four categories of primary goods that Rawls employs in his system are basic rights and liberties, opportunities, income and wealth, and the social bases of self-respect (Rawls 1971, pp. 79, 386).[2] As might be expected, basic rights and liberties are distributed on the basis of the first, or liberty, principle; opportunities are distributed by the opportunity principle, and income and wealth and the social bases of self-respect, known collectively as the social primary goods, are distributed by the difference principle. (Social primary goods, or primary goods for short, are distinguished from natural goods, such as intelligence and strength, the distribution of which is a matter of luck.) The principles of distributive justice are taken by Rawls to apply to primary goods rather than to, say, income or utility.[3] As the two principles suggest, his theory of justice does not require strict equality in the distribution of all primary goods, but only in the distribution of basic rights and liberties.

Before proceeding further, a preliminary question should be addressed. Is there any in-principle impediment to adding new elements to Rawls's original list of primary goods? We believe not. In *A Theory of Justice*, at the point where Rawls gives a list of the primary goods, he emphasises the point that the list is broad and not intended to be definitive (Rawls 1971, pp. 54, 79). He takes the same care elsewhere; for example, in *Political Liberalism* he indicates that the list of primary goods given there might be extended, to include, for example, 'health', 'educated intelligence', and 'leisure' (Rawls 1993, p. 192, n. 9). It seems, therefore, quite possible that candidates – even important candidates – for the status of primary good are not on Rawls's list. And it is clear, moreover, that Rawls anticipates that the list of primary goods may fruitfully be extended, with the addition of further goods that satisfy the conditions for being primary. Our view, developed below, is that there are persuasive arguments for treating information, appropriately defined, as a primary good.

---

[2] Rawls revised his list of primary goods, providing a new list in his 'Social Unity and Primary Goods' (1982b, p. 163).

[3] Rawls's reasons for taking primary goods to be the equalisandum of his theory of justice have changed since the publication of *A Theory of Justice*, but his commitment to primary goods as equalisandum has not wavered. We do not have space to consider, in any detail, the flourishing debate concerning the most appropriate equalisandum for theories of justice, but do address below the criticisms directed at Rawls's choice of equalisandum by Amartya Sen.

Information and Rational Plans of Life

In this section we argue that information is a Rawlsian primary good, a good that is universally required by persons as a condition for their well-being. But 'information' is a notoriously slippery term, with a number of quite distinct uses. To forestall misunderstandings, we begin by clarifying the sense in which we are using the term.

For the purposes of this article, we distinguish two main uses of 'information'. First, the term is often used to refer to knowledge, specifically to knowledge recently communicated regarding some particular subject. Second, the term is used to refer to objects that are regarded as being informative, whether of human manufacture (such as smoke signals, books, and databases) or not (such as rain clouds or animal tracks).[4] The distinction is a significant one. When, for instance, decision theorists make assumptions of 'complete information', they are assuming that the parties concerned know all the relevant facts, not that they possess items such as texts that could inform them of these facts.

Now, presumably, it is information conceived of as knowledge that is of greater value to people; for what use is information to people unless they actually acquire knowledge from it? Physical objects (texts such as books, databases and Web sites, and natural signs such as rain clouds and other features of the world around us) are of instrumental value as a means to the acquisition of knowledge. But possession of informative objects, such as books or databases, is neither necessary nor sufficient for knowledge. (One can know the contents of a book by heart without owning a copy of it, and one can own a copy of a book without being able to understand its contents. And, quite obviously, one does not need to own the sky in order to learn about the weather.) Informative objects are, then, instrumentally important, at least in some circumstances, as a means to the acquisition of knowledge.

Despite its obvious value, we do not take information conceived of as knowledge to be the most appropriate candidate for Rawlsian primary goods status. Knowledge, like good character or happiness, is not amenable to distribution by any agency of individual, for its acquisition depends in large part on the effort of individual agents. Easier to distribute are those goods that are effective means to knowledge, namely informative objects, and more specifically representations of knowledge embedded in physical implementations (such as books, databases, and so on). Henceforth, then, we use the term 'information' to mean 'informative objects'.

We should clarify that the distribution of information, conceived of as informative objects, can be achieved by means other than bringing it about that a person *possesses* certain informative objects (for example, by being

---

[4] As Buckland (1991) notes, objects other than human-generated documents may also be classified as 'information-as-thing'; most objects in the world around us are to some degree informative.

given a book or a database), but also under other circumstances. Information, conceived of as informative objects, also counts as being distributed to a person if they have a level of *access* to an informative object such that that access would be sufficient to produce knowledge (in a person of average cognitive competence).[5] Access to information could be afforded by possession of, or access to, books or information and communication technologies such as computers, mobile phones, and so on.

In this chapter, therefore, we take access to information to be the most appropriate candidate for primary good status, where access to information is afforded either by possession of information-bearing objects, or by access to such objects sufficient to produce knowledge. Ensuring that individuals have access to information thus may involve distribution of information-bearing objects, or ensuring that individuals have ready access to such objects. (It does not require that the distribution in question be performed via information and communication technology in particular; the medium of distribution is of not of primary importance.)

Rawls's justification for taking primary goods to be the good distributed by his theory changes, subsequent to the publication of *A Theory of Justice*. As we hope to show, information qualifies as a primary good on either justification. The value and significance of access to information can be illustrated by showing its (often underestimated) role in persons' lives. In his later account of primary goods, which may be considered definitive, Rawls characterizes a primary good as something that is necessary for an autonomous person to plan a rational life and to make rational choices:

The main idea is that primary goods are singled out by asking which things are generally necessary as social conditions and all-purpose means to enable persons to pursue their determinate conceptions of the good and to develop and exercise their two moral powers. (Rawls 1993, p. 307)

The two moral powers of autonomous persons to which Rawls here refers are (1) a capacity for a sense of justice, that is, a capacity to be reasonable and (2) a capacity for a conception of the good (life), that is, a capacity to be rational. The second of the moral powers, which is modelled in the Original Position by the rationality of the parties, is defined as a capacity to form, revise, and rationally pursue a determinate conception of the good. According to Rawls, 'We are to suppose that each individual has a rational plan of life drawn up subject to the conditions that confront him' (Rawls

---

5 Certain further complexities are raised by this claim. Whether a particular level of access to an information-bearing object is sufficient to produce knowledge for a given individual will depend on the cognitive capacities of the individual; people with strong cognitive skills may not require such a high level of access (e.g., so long a period of access) as people with weaker cognitive skills. It will also depend on other factors, such as whether the information-bearing object is written in a language familiar to the individual, and whether it is encoded in an information retrieval system familiar to the individual.

1971, pp. 93, 408 ff). A rational plan is defined as a plan that, given the available alternatives, cannot be improved, or a plan that is preferable, all things considered. The rational plan for a person determines his good. Rawls here refers to Josiah Royce's idea that a person is a human life lived according to a plan (Rawls 1971, p. 408). Primary goods are those things necessary for devising and carrying out rational plans successfully: 'Primary goods are . . . characterized as what persons need in their status as free and equal citizens, and as normal and fully cooperating members of society over a complete life' (Rawls 1999, p. xiii). And information is necessary in just this sense; it is necessary for rational life planning, and for making rational choices in carrying out a plan.

The idea of forming, revising, and pursuing a rational plan subject to the conditions that confront one hardly makes sense without assuming that information relevant to the task is relatively easy to come by. New information about the world is the first thing you need if you want to make, evaluate, and revise rational plans about your life. One needs to know the conditions that confront one, and which alternatives are, or could be made, available. Indeed, the notions of rationality, planning, decision, choice, and information are intimately related; and the importance of information is widely recognized in the philosophical literature, for instance, in discussions of problems associated with practical rationality, both individual and collective.

Of course, as Rawls notes, an individual's decision might count as fully rational even if it were made on the basis of extremely limited information, so long as, in making the decision, the individual assesses the facts correctly, and makes no errors of reasoning (Rawls 1971, pp. 366–367). We might say that such a decision is *subjectively rational*, to contrast it with the objectively rational decision that she would have made had she had all the information relevant to making that decision. Many decisions made by humans fail to be objectively rational because complete information is rarely available. But, other things equal, individuals aim to make their decisions as close to objectively rational as is feasible, given constraints on their time and cognitive capacities. Accordingly, the more (relevant) information an individual can access in her planning, the closer her subjectively rational planning will be to the objectively rational plan.

Access to information is, then, valued for the fact that it may be instrumental in adding alternatives to one's choice set, or in ruling out alternatives as unavailable. And it is valued for informing one about things one might have wanted more, or less, had one known more about them. The value of access to information is also, in some situations, a function of the potential of information to help reduce the number of an agent's unconnected preferences.[6] I may have a preference for longevity and a preference for smoking

---

[6] This notion was introduced by Amartya Sen. For references and a discussion of the relation between choice and knowledge and information, see Dowding (1992).

over nonsmoking; but, unaware of any empirical connection between these premises, I am also unaware that they offer potentially conflicting guidance for how I should live my life. In these circumstances, relevant epidemiological or medical information about the serious health risks of smoking may help me to connect these two preferences and set them in a coherent preference ordering.

Access to information is also valued for the fact that it helps groups of people to coordinate their plans and actions; in so doing it makes available additional alternatives for action. An opportunity for a mutually beneficial exchange may be missed simply because neither party is aware of the opportunity, or because, although both parties are aware of the opportunity, each is unaware that the other is also aware. Miscoordinated action, in such cases, is brought about by miscoordinated knowledge (Thomsen 1992, p. 88ff). In summary, the second of Rawls's two moral powers, the capacity for a conception of the good life, requires, as a condition for its exercise, that agents can find information relevant to developing and revising their rational plans.

The first edition of *A Theory of Justice* lists three general characteristics of primary goods,[7] which together suggest that access to information qualifies as a primary good on Rawls's earlier justification of primary goods. The three characteristics are as follows:

It is rational for a person P to want a primary good A, whatever P wants;
It is rational for a person P to prefer more rather than less of A;
A has a use whatever P's rational plan of life. (Rawls 1971, pp. 92, 433)

Consider the first characteristic; we all want access to information, irrespective of our goals in life or how our life plans are designed. Information may be relevant to us in a wide variety of ways, by assisting us to articulate our needs in light of our life plan and *vice versa*; information may also be instrumental in revising our life plans, for instance, by connecting and forcing changes to previously unconnected preferences. It will often be difficult to predict just what information will be of use in particular situations; accordingly, although we may not actually want to use all of the information to which we have access (and we may positively prefer *not* to use some of it) we will still want access to it. Accordingly, it is plausible to claim that access to information is relevant to every conceivable rational plan of life.

The second feature of a primary good is that it is rational for a person to want more of it rather than less. Access to information would appear to possess this feature too. When given a choice, one always prefers to have greater access to information rather than less, given some non-zero probability that the information in question may be useful. Given the immense range of circumstances in which information of various kinds may be of use, the more information the better. Again, not all information is useful

---

[7] For textual evidence of these characterizations, see Sessions (1981, p. 321, n. 14–16).

in all circumstances, but all, or almost all, information will be useful in *some* circumstances; equally, it is difficult to rule out in advance the possibility that a certain piece of information might be of use at some point in the future. Accordingly, it is rational to prefer a situation in which one has greater access to information to a situation in which one has less. The third feature of a primary good also appears to apply to access to information: whatever one's rational plan of life, in order to think out, analyse, and evaluate it, access to (potentially relevant) information is necessary. Whatever the life plan, access to information will be relevant to its formulation, revision, and pursuit. We can, then, conclude that access to information has all three general characteristics of a Rawlsian primary good, as described in the first edition of *A Theory of Justice*. It thus seems reasonable to claim that access to information can be construed as a Rawlsian primary good.

Categories of Primary Goods

We have developed some preliminary arguments that access to information is a Rawlsian primary good. We have chosen access to information as the candidate for the status of primary good, on the grounds that information stands in a relationship to knowledge such that access to information, in ordinary circumstances, will be sufficient for knowledge regarding that information. Our next step will be to consider what kind of primary good access to information might be.

Rawls divides primary goods into four categories: basic rights and liberties (distributed by the liberty principle), opportunities (distributed by the opportunity principle), income and wealth (distributed by the difference principle), and the social bases of self-respect (which Rawls considers to be provided for when the liberty principle is satisfied) (Rawls 1971, pp. 544–546). We believe that access to information is best treated as a basic liberty, namely a liberty to access any information that might be of use in rational life planning. For, as Rawls notes, 'The basic liberties . . . are the background institutions necessary for the development and exercise of the capacity to decide upon and revise, and rationally to pursue, a conception of the good' (Rawls 1982b, p. 165). Access to information, as we noted above, is one of the goods necessary in this sense.

There will undoubtedly be some restrictions on what information is freely available within a society,[8] just as private property systems impose certain restrictions on freedom of movement. For instance, information liberties would be most unlikely to extend to access to other people's personal information, no matter how useful this might be in life planning, because such access might substantially infringe on certain other basic rights and freedoms of citizens, such as their freedom of conscience. But such restrictions

---

[8] Plausible examples of such constraints would be those imposed by considerations of personal privacy and by protection of intellectual property.

are quite consistent with the spirit of Rawls's liberty principle. This principle gives citizens 'an equal right to a fully adequate scheme of equal basic liberties', but does not insist that the extent of citizens' liberties should be as wide as possible. So, accordingly, limits may be imposed on the extent of some liberties as part of the fully adequate scheme, so as to ensure that the system of basic liberties as a whole is adequate. And even when such limits are imposed, so long as they are imposed on all citizens, no inequality is thereby permitted in the degree of information liberty afforded to different citizens for use in their rational life planning. An example in which equal liberties are not afforded would be, a national information infrastructure that reaches urban citizens but not rural citizens, thereby preventing rural citizens from accessing relevant information stored only online. Such an institution unjustly imposes inequalities in information liberties on rural citizens.

But the protection of access to information provided by the first principle is not the only way in which access to information should feature in a Rawlsian theory of justice. This point can be demonstrated by considering the institutions that affect the distribution of information in modern information societies. In postindustrial societies, much of the information that would be useful for agents' rational planning is accessible principally, or even exclusively, via information and communication technologies, and information networks such as the World Wide Web. This goes for a great deal of scientific, academic, and commercial information, but also includes what has been termed citizenship information (Steele 1998, p. 161). Citizenship information is information that is valuable to all individuals for facilitating their participation in the life of the state; much citizenship information is also important for making, revising, and implementing rational plans. Citizenship information includes detailed information on a vast array of subjects such as citizens' rights and responsibilities; jurisprudence; the quality of food and standards for its production; drugs; transport; the environment and pollution; housing; employment trends; health care standards and risks; national safety, crime rates; opportunities for political participation; educational opportunities; economic prospects; political processes and so on.

Now if, in a society, a substantial proportion of information relevant to citizens' life planning is only accessible via information media, then, in that society, a guarantee of equal liberty to seek information will not be sufficient in itself to ensure that all citizens have access to all relevant information. In such a society, access to (often expensive and complex) information media will also be necessary for citizens to access much of the information relevant to their rational life planning. To put the point in general terms, ensuring a just distribution of information requires not only a just distribution of information liberties for all citizens, but also mechanisms to ensure that people's opportunities to exercise their information liberties are roughly equal.

We propose that Rawls's theory of justice would therefore require some coverage of access to information at the level of the opportunity, as well as at the level of the liberty principle. People's opportunities to access information should, like their opportunities to attain an education, be roughly equal, and the institutions of society should be so arranged to provide this, for instance by regulating to ensure that access-cost differentials between urban and rural areas are not too great. (No additional principle would be required to cover the application of the difference principle, as the costs of accessing information can be treated analogously to other expenses associated with citizens' exercise of their basic rights and liberties.)

Within Rawls's framework we can, then, assert the following two claims:

(PG1) The freedom to acquire information relevant to rational life planning qualifies as a BASIC LIBERTY under the first principle of justice.

(PG2) Opportunities to acquire information are, like opportunities for education or health care, afforded under the opportunity principle.

A restriction will apply to PG1, so as to limit individuals' freedom to acquire personal information about other individuals. This restriction is analogous to restrictions on individuals' freedom of movement and freedom of speech (also basic liberties under Rawls's first principle), and, applied equally to all citizens, is plausibly part of a fully adequate package of basic rights and liberties.

We conclude that the information liberties specified in (PG1) are highly significant. The connection between information and the exercise of the higher-order moral powers could even be construed as internal, because Rawls systematically uses the phrase 'the *informed* exercise of the moral powers'. Further, it might be hoped that together PG1 and PG2 will ensure a relatively equal distribution of access to information within a society.

In this section, we have argued that access to information is a Rawlsian primary good, and that Rawls's principles of justice can and should be extended to cover this new primary good. But there are many critics of Rawls's theory of justice, and their criticisms of the Rawlsian framework may require modifications to our development of his theory. In an article of this length, we cannot hope to respond to all the major criticisms of Rawls's theory in anything like a comprehensive way. Our aim is, rather, to enumerate some of the most significant criticisms and considerations that must be taken into account in any further development of Rawls's theory of justice to include access to information among the primary goods.

TOWARDS COMPLEX EQUALITY: OBJECTIONS TO THE RAWLSIAN FRAMEWORK

Basic Socioeconomic Needs: Pogge's Critique

We have addressed the question of what sort of primary good information might be, concluding that it is a liberty, and that it falls under Rawls's first principle of justice. What the first principle covers: all citizens should be afforded equal information liberties; adequate formal and legal protection should be given to safeguard these liberties, for instance, ensuring that nobody is debarred by law or interference by others from exercising the liberty to seek and access information relevant to their life planning.[9]

Thomas Pogge has argued that Rawls's two principles of justice do not in fact guarantee a high degree of social equality, or even a decent standard of material well-being, to a state's most disadvantaged citizens, despite the protection that is given to the safeguarding of rights and liberties under the first principle (Pogge 1989, p. 127). As it stands, Rawls's system provides formal liberties to all, yet may still leave the most disadvantaged in such a miserable material state that they can gain little from their possession of those liberties.

Pogge's criticism runs as follows. Rawls claims that the first principle of justice has lexicographical priority over the opportunity principle and the difference principle. That is to say, the equality of liberties and rights available to all under the first principle may not be sacrificed for an improved satisfaction, no matter how large, of the second principle. But, as Pogge points out, this entails that any available resources should always be devoted to achieving (feasible) improvements of first-principle liberties rather than to improving the socioeconomic position of the worst-off members of society. And this means that the worst-off members may end up, socioeconomically speaking, very badly off indeed. They may, indeed, end up too cold, hungry, and desperate to make anything like the same use of their first-principle liberties as is possible for the more advantaged members of society (Pogge 1989, p. 126).

A version of this problem also occurs in relation to PG1 and PG2 developed above. If information is distributed by a (merely) formal information liberty, and the costs of access to the information media via which information is available are fairly high, then the least advantaged members of a society may lack substantive access to information. In other words, under Rawls's theory of justice, it is perfectly possible that, even in a just society, the least advantaged will have a legal right, protected and enforced, of access to information, but lack the financial means to exercise that right, or to exercise it fully and effectively.

Thomas Pogge has proposed a solution to the general form of this difficulty, which, we believe, also applies to the distribution of information. Pogge observes that, at many points in *A Theory of Justice*, Rawls treats the interplay between his two principles of justice as rather closer than lexicographical priority will permit:

Freedom as equal liberty is the same for all: the question of compensating for a lesser than equal liberty does not arise. But the worth of liberty is not the same for everyone. Some have greater authority and wealth, and therefore greater means to

[9] For a characterization of the effective protection of basic liberties, see Pogge (1989, p. 135).

achieve their aims. The lesser worth of liberty is, however, compensated for, since the capacity of the less fortunate members of society to achieve their aims would be even less were they not to accept the existing inequalities whenever the difference principle is satisfied . . . Taking the two principles together, the basic structure is to be arranged to maximize the worth to the least advantaged of the complete scheme of equal liberty shared by all. (Rawls 1971, pp. 204–205)

As Pogge notes, Rawls does not deviate from this view in later works:

The basic liberties are specified by institutional rights and duties that entitle citizens to do certain things, if they wish, and forbid others to interfere. The basic liberties are a framework of legally protected paths and opportunities. Of course, ignorance and poverty, and the lack of material means generally, prevent people from exercising their rights and from taking advantage of these openings. But rather than counting these and similar obstacles as restricting a person's liberty, we count them as affecting the worth of liberty, that is, the usefulness to persons of their liberties. Now in justice as fairness, this usefulness is specified in terms of an index of the primary goods regulated by the second principle of justice . . . The basic structure of society is arranged so that it maximizes the primary goods available to the least advantaged to make use of the equal basic liberties enjoyed by everyone. (Rawls 1982a, pp. 41–42)

Pogge interprets Rawls as follows:

I believe Rawls's general idea is to conceive worth of freedom (what ultimately matters) as a function of three components: the *public recognition* of certain basic freedoms (the public understanding that it is legitimate for me to travel along certain paths); their *protection* (the maintenance of these paths as secure highways); and the *means* at one's disposal (my ability to obtain food and boots, a car and gasoline, without which I could not travel on even the best and safest highway). Let us say that the first component determines *(formal) legal freedom*; that the first two components together determine *effective legal freedom* . . . ; and that all three components together determine *worth of freedom*. (Pogge 1989, p. 128)

The conclusion to be drawn is that the justice of the basic institutions depends, to a greater degree than lexicographical priority can permit, on the least advantaged individuals possessing a sufficient share of (material) *means*, without which they will not be afforded equal worth of freedom.

Pogge suggests that the excessive requirement of lexicographical priority can be moderated by a modification to the first principle of justice. This first principle should include a reference to the means to the equal worth of freedom for all citizens that, in *A Theory of Justice* and elsewhere, Rawls relegates to the difference principle. Pogge suggests that the first principle of justice be modified to include a requirement that the *standard basic socioeconomic needs* of all citizens be satisfied (Pogge 1989, p. 143). Basic social and economic needs are those needs entailed by the highest-order interests of citizens, and must be satisfied in order for those interests to be pursued.

Standard basic socioeconomic needs include the following: '... food and drink, clothing and shelter, as well as some interaction including education and care' (Pogge 1989, p. 144). What is required to meet some of the basic socioeconomic needs, such as education, will depend on the particular conditions prevailing in the society in question: 'Persons will be presumed to need access to *enough* of an education to be able to understand and participate in their society's political, legal, and economic systems and associational life' (Pogge 1989, p. 144). Now, applying this general solution to information, persons born into postindustrial societies will have substantial informational needs in order to plan their lives rationally, and to participate adequately in the common life of their societies, in which so much information necessary to participation is available primarily or exclusively online. They will also require education in the use of information media via which they access information. On the proposed modification of Rawls's first principle, it would be a requirement of justice that, in high-technology information societies, people are educated in the use of information technologies, and afforded access to information media sufficient for them to be able to participate in their society's common life. Such education would be a basic social need in information societies.

Pogge's solution to this critique of Rawls's decision to give lexicographical priority of the basic liberties has since been accepted by Rawls himself, and is embodied in modifications made to his theory of justice in *Political Liberalism*. Pogge's solution can also, we conclude, be harnessed in relation to the distribution of information goods. The solution is to include appropriate requirements for access to ICTs and education in their use in that section of the first principle in which standard basic socioeconomic needs for citizens in postindustrial information societies are enumerated.[10]

Choice-Sensitivity: Dworkin's Critique

Ronald Dworkin's resource-based account of distributive justice holds that Rawls's theory gets the redistributory process wrong. It applies its redistributory machinery even in cases where some people do not deserve to benefit from such redistribution, but it has no redistributory mechanisms for some cases in which they should be introduced (Dworkin 1981a, 1981b). A key feature of Dworkin's own theory is the notion that people's fortunes should be determined by their choices about how to live, rather than by brute circumstances. Dworkin accepts as just situations in which inequalities of income and wealth arise as a result of the different choices people have

---

[10] Of course, from a global perspective, the citizens of even relatively undeveloped countries stand to be further disadvantaged by the benefits accrued to the citizens of developed countries.

made about how to lead their lives (including their choices about their work, education, leisure, tastes, investments, and so on). But where inequalities of income and wealth result from differences in brute circumstances, then those inequalities are unjust because they are morally arbitrary. Morally arbitrary inequalities may arise as a result of unfortunate social circumstances, such as being born into a poor or very dysfunctional family. Equally, they may result from the unequal distribution of natural endowments, where some are born with many talents and others with few, some born able-bodied, and others with physical or mental handicaps. A just distributory system compensates those who suffer from unfortunate social circumstances or meagre natural endowments. As Dworkin put it in 2000, distribution should be 'endowment-insensitive' but 'ambition-sensitive' (Dworkin 2000).

The Rawlsian account of justice, Dworkin argues, leaves no room for choice sensitivity and gives no principled criteria for dealing with unequal natural endowments.[11] Dworkin's concerns about Rawls's theory as a whole, applied to the distribution of access to information, suggest two main criticisms. The first criticism, associated with the complaint of ambition-sensitivity, is that a Rawlsian approach to access to information pays insufficient attention to individuals' differing life choices, specifically choices regarding the degree to which they wish to use information and communication technologies. Perhaps a one-size-fits-all approach is simply not appropriate in the distribution of a good that is arguably more useful to information workers than to manual workers, and more interesting to those who wish to capitalize on available information-based opportunities than to those who wish to live a simple life unencumbered by technology.

The second criticism, associated with the complaint of endowment insensitivity, is that Rawls's theory, as we have applied it to information, may produce unjust outcomes. It may do so because the levels of access to information guaranteed by PG1 and PG2 will be less beneficial to those who are less well-endowed with the skills valuable for using and benefiting from new information and communication technologies. Even if, in line with PG1 and PG2 above, citizens have equal freedom to access information, and a roughly equal opportunity to gain access to information, those citizens who are naturally better-endowed with skills for using and manipulating information may extract far more welfare from PG1 and PG2 than those who are less adept. Surely this is not an acceptable outcome.

Dworkin's approach to equality is closer to Rawls's than many of his other critics, but, for all that, the Dworkin-inspired criticisms we have articulated demand a response, particularly the first. Distributions of access to information that assume similar levels of interest in technology may be less

---

[11] Dworkin's concerns have been echoed and developed by other resource egalitarians, including Gerald Cohen, Jan Narveson, and Thomas Pogge, who has focused on its endowment insensitivity rather than its ambition sensitivity.

problematic, because they provide a similar level of *access to technology* without assuming or requiring that individuals make the same kinds of *uses* of those technologies; but still, the costs associated with satisfying PG1 and PG2 may still seem unreasonable, given that some people have much more interest than others in using new information and communication technologies. Distributions of access to information that ignore real, but morally arbitrary, differences in people's aptitudes to acquire and use information are quite plausibly unjust. Further attention to Dworkin's theoretical position may help to refine a broadly Rawlsian approach to information justice to avoid this problem.

Functionalism: Sen's Critique

Amartya Sen has criticized the very idea of primary goods on the basis of its simplistic orientation towards outcomes. Sen remarks that equal shares of a good may, depending upon the *capabilities* of individuals, do radically different things for different persons: ' . . . a person may have more income and more nutritional intake than another person, but less freedom to live a well-nourished existence because of a higher basal metabolic rate, greater vulnerability to parasitic diseases, larger body size, or pregnancy' (Sen 1990, p. 114).

Applied to information, one could say that there are differences between persons regarding their possession of natural goods, specifically their cognitive ability to transform information into knowledge that helps them to devise and pursue their rational life plans. There are significant variations in people's information-processing capabilities, correlating roughly with variations in intelligence.[12] What value, Sen might ask, do information liberties have for someone with a substantial mental impairment, or for someone who is physically incapable of using a computer? It may be reasonable, as Sen suggests, to 'move away from a focus on goods as such to what goods *do* for human beings' (Sen 1990).

Sen's concerns are certainly salient in any consideration of the distribution of information goods. As we noted above, citizens are not equally endowed with the natural talents so important for making use of information goods, namely, cognitive abilities. Consequently, an equal distribution of information goods would probably not benefit all citizens equally. Rawls's theory of justice, which is only concerned with distribution of primary goods among normally functioning citizens, makes no allowances for the incapacitated or for those with significantly subnormal levels of natural talents.

---

[12] Their capability to actively seek information, to make it available, to make sense of it, and draw relevant conclusions on the basis of it, as Sen has argued. See Sen (1992, p. 148): 'A person less able or gifted in using primary goods to secure freedoms . . . is disadvantaged compared with another more favourably placed in that respect even if both have the same bundle of primary goods'.

Sen's criticism can be answered in part by observing that Rawls's theory of justice does not attempt to equalize outcomes for individuals. Rather, it aims to ensure that all citizens have a sufficient share of primary goods (including nonmaterial goods such as freedoms) to exercise the two highest-order moral powers (discussed above in 'Information and rational plans of life'). In the words of Norman Daniels, 'the primary goods are not defended on the grounds that they approximate a dimension of basic moral value (like positive freedom or capability). Rather, they are defended because of their connection to the limited political ideal of a free and equal citizen' (Daniels 1990).

But, as many commentators have observed, Rawls's theory of justice, which treats natural contingencies (such as gender, ethnicity, or disparities in cognitive power) as morally insignificant, but grants moral significance to social contingencies (such as class), may be extraordinarily severe on those whose natural condition (including cognitive abilities) already places them at a social disadvantage. Any attempt to extend Rawls's theory of justice to information goods should take Sen's concerns into account.

Positionality: Garfinkel's Critique

Alan Garfinkel and others have criticized Rawls' assumption that the contractors in the Original Position are nonenvious with respect to shares of social primary goods (Garfinkel 1981). According to Rawls the contractors are not interested in the levels of holdings of primary goods of others per se. Given a choice between distribution scheme A, where three individuals all get three units of primary goods, and distribution scheme B, where they get respectively 4, 5, and 10 units, the difference principle, given a Maximin Principle of rational choice, would not rule out scheme B, because, however the lottery turned out, anyone would be better off with the worst position under B.

Garfinkel, however, points to an important class of cases where this assumption of independence does not hold, because the level of holdings of some enables them to affect the well-being of others. Scheme B may be perfect for sandwiches, but it is not for levels of armament. And there are many other examples of goods with respect to which it is rational to be concerned with how much others have of it, and not only with how much of it one possesses oneself. It seems clear to us that this holds true for much of the information currently available via ICTs. More specifically, much, though not all, information would seem to be a *positional good*.[13] A positional good is one that a person values only on condition that others lack it (Hollis 1984). For instance, information relevant to competition in business, and

[13] For an excellent overview, see Bates (1988).

many other fields of endeavour, is positional; so is information about the availability of scarce resources. This can be summarized as:

(VP) Information I is positional only if the value of I for a particular person, or a particular group of persons, is increased by the fact that there are no other persons – or just a limited number of them – that have access to I.

Now, of course, much information is not positional in this way. There is some information that it is rational to value more, the more widely it is shared, such as information necessary to cooperative endeavours such as the maintenance of public health and sanitation. But the positionality of many kinds of information seems to point in the direction of more radical forms of egalitarianism than are allowed for on the basis of the difference principle.

The positionality of much information, and its tendency to become a good whose unequal distribution could easily be exploited, suggests that we may want information infrastructures that provide access to information that concern citizens as moral persons to be designed in such a way as to reduce the number of cases where access to information I is of value to a person P only because no one else or only a small number of other people have it. (Note that we are concerned here with access to citizenship information, rather than commercial information or information of other kinds.) There may even be a moral obligation incumbent upon governments to reduce the incidence of positionality regarding citizenship information, and perhaps even to prevent some unequal distributions of information that would be justifiable under the difference principle.

However, any attempt to reduce positionality in this way might run up against another of Rawls's requirements for his principles of justice: that of practicability. Unequal distributions of access to information that tolerate some degree of positionality may indeed be compatible with the difference principle. But, Rawls might respond, there is no easy way for a government, with limited means at its disposal and with little control over the rate of innovation in information technology, to avoid inequality in access to information. As in the case of education, a typical positional good, those with most wealth will generally be in a position to dedicate sufficient extra resources to access to information that they will gain whatever positional advantage there is to gain. As in the case of education, the positionality of much information, including citizenship information, poses a practical challenge to the Rawlsian theory of justice.

Pluralism: Walzer's Critique

Michael Walzer has also objected to Rawls's conception of primary goods as too simplistic, arguing that 'there is no set of basic goods across all moral and material worlds, or they would have to be so abstract that they would be of little use in thinking about particular distributions' (Walzer 1983, p. 8). According to Walzer, goods have no natural meaning; their meaning is the result of sociocultural construction and interpretation. In order to determine what is a just distribution of the good, we have to determine what it means to those for whom it is a good. Thus, for example, in the medical, the political, and commercial spheres, there are different goods (medical treatment, political office, money); these goods are allocated by means of different distributive practices: medical treatment on the basis of need, political office on the basis of desert, and money on the basis of free exchange.

What ought to be prevented (and often is in fact prevented) is the dominance of particular goods across multiple spheres. Walzer calls a good *dominant* if the individuals who have it can, just because they have it, command a wide range of other goods. A monopoly is a way of controlling certain social goods in order to exploit their dominance. In that case, advantages in one sphere can be converted as a matter of course into advantages in other spheres. This happens when, for instance, money (pertaining to the commercial sphere) could buy you a seat in Parliament (thus affording you advantage in the political sphere), preferential treatment in health care (medical sphere), a university degree (educational sphere), and so on. Generally, we resist the dominance of money (and other social goods, such as property or physical strength) and believe that political arrangements that allow for such dominance are unjust. Walzer thus holds the view that no social good φ should be distributed to someone who possesses some other good ψ merely because they possess ψ, and without regard to the meaning of φ.

What is especially offensive to our sense of justice, Walzer argues, is the allocation of goods internal to sphere A on the basis of the distributive logic or the allocation scheme associated with sphere B, second, the transfer of goods across the boundaries of separate spheres and third, the dominance and tyranny of some goods over others. In order to prevent this, the 'art of separation' of spheres must be practised, and certain types of exchanges between the spheres blocked. If the art of separation is effectively practised, and the autonomy of the spheres of justice is guaranteed, then complex equality is established.

Walzer's analysis might also be extended to include the good of information. The meaning and value of information is local, and allocative schemes and local practices that distribute access to information are also associated with specific spheres, such as the political, medical, and commercial spheres. As one of us has argued elsewhere, many of the privacy or data protection rules that prevent medical information to flow into the market sector, or criminal records being used in selecting patients can be accounted for in this way (van den Hoven 2000, pp. 5–6). The restriction on insider trading can be seen as blocking exchanges between the private or familial sphere and the market sphere of business information.

In fact, Rawls might dismiss the Walzerian critique, arguing that his own theory of justice is consistent with the main thrust of Walzer's argument, namely that the distribution of highly abstract social primary goods gives little concrete advice about the justice of particular distributions of goods. Walzer has misinterpreted Rawls's scheme as incomplete because he has failed to notice that the work of detailed articulation of distributions (which might include blocks on exchanges such as Walzer recommends) is left to the legislative phases of Rawls's scheme, and is, therefore, left aside in *A Theory of Justice*. Accordingly, we can conclude that a Walzerian analysis of spheres of justice, including information justice, might function as a complement to Rawls's scheme of justice, more specifically as an articulation of a set of plausible guidelines for particular distributions of goods. As such, Walzer's account of spheres of justice would seem to be a promising avenue in the articulation of concrete principles and guidelines for the just distribution of information.

CONCLUSIONS

In this chapter, we have begun the work of extending John Rawls's theory of justice to include information goods. We have presented an argument that information should be accepted as a primary good within Rawls's theory, and that its distribution, therefore, should be governed by that theory (or some suitable further development of it). We have considered the most likely objections to a Rawlsian approach to information justice, and suggested some ways of moving forward with these objections in mind. A fully-fledged theory of justice that takes adequate account of the new information goods that are rapidly evolving is still some way off, as is the extension of such a theory to the international level, at which information inequality, and other far graver inequalities, are presently extensive.

References

Bates, B. 1988. Information as an economic good: Sources of individual and social value, in V. Mosco and J. Wasco (Eds.), *The political economy of information*. Madison, WI: University of Wisconsin Press, pp. 76–94.

Buckland, M. 1991. Information as thing. *Journal of the American Society of Information Science*, *42*, 5, pp. 351–360.

Daniels, N. 1990. Equality of what: Welfare, resources, or capabilities? *Philosophy and Phenomenological Research*, *1*, suppl., 273–296.

Dowding, K. 1992. Choice: Its increase and its value. *British Journal of Political Science*, *22*, pp. 301–314.

Drahos, P., and Braithwaite, J. 1996, *A history of intellectual property*. Ashgate: Aldershot.

Dworkin, R. 1981a. What is equality? Part 1: Equality of resources. *Philosophy and Public Affairs, 10,* 185–246;

Dworkin, R. 1981b. What is equality? Part 2: Equality of welfare. *Philosophy and Public Affairs, 10,* 283–345.

Dworkin, R. 2000. *The sovereign virtue: The theory and practice of equality* Cambridge, MA: Harvard University Press.

Garfinkel, A. 1981. *Forms of explanation, rethinking the questions in social theory.* New Haven and London: Yale University Press.

Hollis, M. 1984. Positional goods. *Philosophy, 18,* suppl., 97–110.

Loader, B. (Ed.). 1998. *Cyberspace divide.* London: Routledge.

Pogge, T. 1989. *Realizing Rawls.* Ithaca and London: Cornell University Press.

Ratan, S. 1995. A new divide between haves and have-nots? *Time Special Issue: Welcome to Cyberspace,* Spring, pp. 17–18.

Rawls, J. 1971. *A theory of justice.* Oxford: Oxford University Press.

Rawls, J. 1982a. The basic liberties and their priority, in S. M. McMurrin (Ed.), *The Tanner Lectures on Human Value* 3. Salt Lake City: University of Utah Press, pp. 1–87.

Rawls, J. 1982b. Social unity and primary goods, in A. Sen and B. Williams (Eds.), *Utilitarianism and beyond.* Cambridge, UK: Cambridge University Press, pp. 159–185.

Rawls, J. 1993. *Political liberalism.* New York: Columbia University Press.

Rawls, J. 1999. *A theory of justice* (2nd ed.). Oxford: Oxford University Press.

Schiller, H. 1996. *Information inequality: The deepening social crisis in America.* London: Routledge.

Sen, A. 1990. Justice: Means versus freedom. *Philosophy and Public Affairs, 19,* 2, 111–121.

Sen, A. 1992. *Inequality reexamined.* Oxford: Clarendon Press.

Sessions, W. L. 1981. Rawls's concept and conception of primary good. *Social Theory and Practice, 7,* 3, 303–324.

Steele, J. Information and citizenship in Europe, in B. Loader (Ed.), *Cyberspace divide.* London: Routledge.

Thomsen, E. F. 1992. *Prices and knowledge: A market-process perspective.* London: Routledge.

United Nations Conference on Trade and Development (UNCTAD). 2006. *The Digital divide: ICT diffusion index* 2005. United Nations, New York. Retrieved 3 August 2006 from http://www.unctad.org/en/docs/iteipc20065_en.pdf.

van den Hoven, M. J. 1995. Equal access and social justice, in *Information technology and moral philosophy.* PhD thesis, Erasmus University, Rotterdam. (See also http://www.ccsr.cse.dmu.ac.uk/conferences/ethicomp/ethicomp95/abstracts.vandenHoven.html.)

van den Hoven, M. J. 2000. Privacy and health information: The need for a fine-grained account. *International Journal for Quality in Health Care, 12,* 1, 5–6.

Walzer, M. 1983. *Spheres of justice.* Oxford: Basil Blackwell.

Wresch, W. 1996. *Disconnected: Haves and have-nots in the Information Age.* New Brunswick, NJ: Rutgers University Press.

Select Bibliography

Becker, L. 1977. *Property rights: Philosophic foundations*. London: Routledge and Kegan Paul.

Bohman, J. 2004. Expanding dialogue: The public sphere, the Internet and transnational democracy, in J. Roberts and N. Crossley (Eds.), *After Habermas: Perspectives on the public sphere*. London: Blackwell, pp. 131–155.

Brennan, G., and Pettit, P. 2004. *The economy of esteem: An essay on civil and political society*. Oxford: Oxford University Press.

Bynum, T. W. 1999. The development of computer ethics as a philosophical field of study. *Australian Journal of Professional and Applied Ethics, 1*, 1–29.

Bynum, T. W. 2005. The impact of the 'Automatic Age' on our moral lives, in R. Cavalier (Ed.), *The Impact of the Internet on Our Moral Lives*, New York: State University of New York Press pp. 11–25.

Bynum, T. W., and Moor, J. H. (Eds.). 1998. *The digital phoenix: How computers are changing philosophy*. Oxford: Blackwell.

Clark, A. 2003. *Natural-born cyborgs*. Oxford: Oxford University Press.

Cocking, D., and Kennett, J. 1998. Friendship and the self. *Ethics, 108*, 3, 502–527.

Dahl, R. 1999. Can international organizations be democratic? A skeptic's view, in I. Shapiro and C. Hacker-Cordón (Eds.), *Democracy's edges*. New York: Cambridge University Press.

Dewey, J. 1988. The public and its problems, in *John Dewey: The later works, 1925–1927* (Vol. 2). Carbondale, IL: Southern Illinois University Press.

Drahos, P. 1996. *A philosophy of intellectual property*. Dartmouth: Ashgate.

Dreyfus, H. 2001. *On the Internet*. New York: Routledge.

Ess, C. 2002a. Cultures in collision: Philosophical lessons from computer-mediated communication, in J. H. Moor and T. W. Bynum (Eds), *CyberPhilosophy: The intersection of philosophy and computing*. Oxford: Blackwell, pp. 219–242.

Flanagan, O. 1991. *Varieties of moral personality*. Cambridge, MA: Harvard University Press.

Floridi, L. 1999. Information ethics: On the theoretical foundations of computer ethics, *Ethics and Information Technology, 1*, 1, 37–56.

Floridi, L. 2003. On the intrinsic value of information objects and the infosphere, *Ethics and Information Technology, 4*, 4, 287–304.

397

Frankfurt, H. 1988. Freedom of the will and the concept of a person, in *The importance of what we care about.* Cambridge, UK: Cambridge University Press, pp. 11–25.

Friedman, B. (Ed.). 1997. *Human values and the design of computer technology.* Cambridge, UK: Cambridge University Press.

Friedman, B. 1996. Value-sensitive design. *Interactions, 3*, 6, 17–23.

Friedman, B., Kahn, P. H., Jr., and Borning, A. 2006. Value sensitive design and information systems, in P. Zhang, and D. Galletta (Eds.), *Human-computer interaction in management information systems: Foundations.* New York: M. E. Sharpe.

Goldman, A. 1999. *Knowledge in a social world.* Oxford: Oxford University Press.

Goldman, A. 2004. The need for social epistemology, in B. Leiter (Ed.), *The future for philosophy.* Oxford: Oxford University Press, pp. 182–207.

Graham, G. 1999. *The Internet, a philosophical inquiry.* London: Routledge.

Gupta, B. 2002. *Ethical questions: East and West.* Lanham, MD: Rowman & Littlefield.

Habermas, J. 1981. *Theorie des Kommuikativen Handelns.* 2 vols. Suhrkamp, Frankfurt. Translated by T. McCarthy as *The theory of communicative action* and published by Beacon Press, Boston, 1984 (Vol. 1) and 1987 (Vol. 2).

Habermas, J. 1989. *The structural transformation of the public sphere.* Cambridge, MA: MIT Press.

Habermas, J. 1996. *Between facts and norms.* Cambridge, MA: MIT Press.

Hardin, R. 1992. The street-level epistemology of trust. *Politics and Society, 21*, 4, 505–529.

Hettinger, E. C. 1989. Justifying intellectual property. *Philosophy and Public Affairs, 18*, 1, 31–52.

Hinman, L. M. 1998. *Ethics: A pluralistic approach to moral theory.* Fort Worth: Harcourt Brace.

Holton, R. 1994. Deciding to trust, coming to believe. *Australasian Journal of Philosophy, 72*, 63–76.

Introna, L. D., and Nissenbaum, H. 2000. Shaping the Web: Why the Politics of Search Engines Matters. *The Information Society, 16*, 3, 169–185.

Johnson, D. G. 2001. *Computer ethics* (3rd ed.). Upper Saddle River, NJ: Prentice-Hall.

Joy, B. 1999. Why the future doesn't need us. *Wired, 8*, 4.

Kitcher, P. 2001. *Science, truth, and democracy.* Oxford: Oxford University Press.

Kuflik, A. 1999. Computers in control: Rational transfer of authority or irresponsible abdication of autonomy? *Ethics and Information Technology, 1*, 3, 173–184.

Kupfer, J. 1987. Privacy, autonomy, and self-concept. *American Philosophical Quarterly, 24*, 81–89.

Kymlicka, W. 1999. Citizenship in an era of globalization, in I. Shapiro and C. Hacker-Cordón (Eds.), *Democracy's edges.* New York: Cambridge University Press.

Lessig, L. 1999. *Code and other laws of Cyberspace.* New York: Basic Books.

Locke, J. 1988. *Two treatises of government.* Edited by Peter Laslett. Cambridge, UK: Cambridge University Press.

Miller, S. 2001. *Social action: A teleological account.* Cambridge, UK: Cambridge University Press.

Mitcham, C. 1995. Ethics into design, in R. Buchanan and V. Margolis (Eds.), *Discovering design.* Chicago: University of Chicago Press, pp. 173–179.

Moor, James H. 1985. What is computer ethics? in T. W. Bynum (Ed.), *Computers and Ethics.* Oxford: Blackwell, pp. 263–275. [Also published as the October 1985 special issue of *Metaphilosophy, 16*, 4.]

Moor, J. H., and Weckert, J. 2004. Nanoethics: Assessing the nanoscale from an ethical point of view, in D. Baird, A. Nordmann, and J. Schummer (Eds.), *Discovering the nanoscale*. Amsterdam: IOS Press, pp. 301–310.

Nagel, T. 1998. Concealment and exposure. *Philosophy and Public Affairs*, 27, 1, 3–30.

Naess, A. 1973. The shallow and the deep, long-range ecology movement. *Inquiry*, 16, 95–100.

Parfit, D. 1984. *Reasons and persons*. Oxford: Clarendon.

Pettit, P. 1995. The cunning of trust. *Philosophy and Public Affairs*, 24, 202–225.

Pitt, J. C. 2000. *Thinking about technology*. New York: Seven Bridges Press.

Pohl, K.-H. 2002. Chinese and Western values: Reflections on a cross-cultural dialogue on a universal ethics, in R. Elberfeld and G. Wohlfart (Eds.), *Komparative Ethik: das gute Leben zwischen den Kulturen*. München: Chora, pp. 213–232.

Posner, R. A. 2005. *Catastrophe, risk and response*. Oxford: Oxford University Press.

Rawls, J. 1999. *A theory of justice* (rev. ed.). Oxford: Oxford University Press.

Searle, J. 1984. *Minds, brains and science*. London: Pelican.

Shrader-Frechette, K. 1994. *Ethics of scientific research*. London: Rowman & Littlefield.

Sloman, A. 1978. *The Computer Revolution in Philosophy*. Atlantic Highlands, NJ: Humanities Press.

Stallman, R. 2002. *Free software, free society*. Boston: GNU Press.

Sunstein, C. R. 2006. *Infotopia: How many minds produce knowledge*. New York: Oxford University Press.

Tavani, H. 2004. *Ethics and technology: Ethical issues in an age of information and communication technology*. Danvers, MA: John Wiley and Sons.

Velleman, D. J. 2000. Well-being and time, in *The possibility of practical reason*. New York: Oxford University Press, pp. 56–84.

Walzer, M. 1984. *Spheres of justice: A defense of pluralism and equality*. New York: Basic Books.

Weizenbaum, Joseph. 1976. *Computer power and human reason: From judgement to calculation*. Harmondsworth, Middlesex: Penguin Books.

Wiener, N. 1948. *Cybernetics, or, Control and communication in the animal and the machine*. New York: Technology Press.

Wiener, N. 1950/1954. *The human use of human beings: Cybernetics and society*. New York: Houghton Mifflin. (Second revised edition published by Doubleday Anchor, 1954.)

Wiener, N. 1964. *God & Golem, Inc. – A Comment on Certain Points Where Cybernetics Impinges on Religion*. Cambridge MA: MIT Press.

Winner, L. 1986. Do artifacts have politics? in *The whale and the reactor: A search for limits in an age of high technology*. Chicago: University of Chicago Press, pp. 19–39.

Yu, J. Y. 2003. Virtue: Confucius and Aristotle, in X. Jiang (Ed.), *The examined life: The Chinese perspective*. Binghamton, NY: Global Publications, pp. 1–31.

Zatz, N. D. 1998. Sidewalks in Cyberspace: Making space for public forums in the electronic environment. *Harvard Journal of Law and Technology*, 12, 149.

Index

Index

Printed in Great Britain
by Amazon.co.uk, Ltd.,
Marston Gate.